Lecture Notes in Computer Science 10076

Commenced Publication in 1973
Founding and Former Series Editors:
Gerhard Goos, Juris Hartmanis, and Jan van Leeuwen

More information about this series at http://www.springer.com/series/7410

Claude Carlet · M. Anwar Hasan
Vishal Saraswat (Eds.)

Security, Privacy, and Applied Cryptography Engineering

6th International Conference, SPACE 2016
Hyderabad, India, December 14–18, 2016
Proceedings

 Springer

Editors
Claude Carlet
Universities of Paris 8 and Paris 13, LAGA
Paris
France

Vishal Saraswat
CRRao AIMSCS
Hyderabad
India

M. Anwar Hasan
University of Waterloo
Waterloo, ON
Canada

ISSN 0302-9743   ISSN 1611-3349 (electronic)
Lecture Notes in Computer Science
ISBN 978-3-319-49444-9   ISBN 978-3-319-49445-6 (eBook)
DOI 10.1007/978-3-319-49445-6

Library of Congress Control Number: 2016957643

LNCS Sublibrary: SL4 – Security and Cryptology

Preface

This volume contains the papers accepted for presentation at the 6th International Conference on Security, Privacy, and Applied Cryptography Engineering 2016 (SPACE 2016), held during December 14–18, 2016, at the C.R. Rao Advanced Institute of Mathematics, Statistics and Computer Science (AIMSCS), University of Hyderabad, India. This annual event is devoted to various aspects of security, privacy, applied cryptography, and cryptographic engineering. This is indeed a very challenging field, requiring expertise from diverse domains, ranging from mathematics to solid-state circuit design.

This year we received 54 submissions from about 20 countries, out of which, after an extensive review process, 16 papers were accepted for presentation at the conference, and one shorter paper was accepted for short presentation. The submissions were evaluated based on their significance, novelty, technical quality, and relevance to the SPACE conference. The submissions were reviewed in a double-blind mode by at least three members of the 35-member Program Committee (one more if at least one of the authors was member of the Program Committee). The Program Committee was aided by 36 additional reviewers. The Program Committee meetings were held electronically, with intensive discussions.

The program also included eight invited talks and four tutorials on several aspects of applied cryptology, delivered by world-renowned researchers: Lejla Batina, Shivam Bhasin, Swarup Bhunia, Craig Costello, Joan Daemen, Christian Grothoff, Debdeep Mukhopadhyay, Emmanuel Prouff, François-Xavier Standaert, and Ingrid Verbauwhede. We sincerely thank the invited speakers for accepting our invitations in spite of their busy schedules.

Like its previous editions, SPACE 2016 was organized in co-operation with the International Association for Cryptologic Research (IACR). We are thankful to AIMSCS for being the gracious host of SPACE 2016.

There is a long list of volunteers who invested their time and energy to put together the conference, and who deserve accolades for their efforts. We are grateful to all the members of the Program Committee and the additional reviewers for all their hard work in the evaluation of the submitted papers. We thank Cool Press Ltd., owner of the EasyChair conference management system, for allowing us to use it for SPACE 2016, which was a great help. We also sincerely thank our publisher Springer for agreeing to continue to publish the SPACE proceedings as a volume in the *Lecture Notes in Computer Science* (LNCS) series. We are further very grateful to the members of the local Organizing Committee, including Sahana Subbarao, for their assistance to Vishal Saraswat in ensuring the smooth organization of the conference. Special thanks to our general chairs, Arun Kumar, Arun Agarwal and Sitaram Chamarty, for their constant support and encouragement.

Last, but certainly not least, our sincere thanks go to all the authors who submitted papers to SPACE 2016, and to all the attendees. The conference was made possible by you, and the proceedings are dedicated to you. We sincerely hope you find the program proceedings stimulating and inspiring.

December 2016   Claude Carlet
                                                                M. Anwar Hasan
                                                                Vishal Saraswat

Organization

Chief Patron

V.K. Saraswat   NITI Aayog, India

Patron

Alok Joshi   NTRO, India

General Co-chairs

M. Arun Kumar   CRRao AIMSCS, India
Arun Agarwal   SCIS, University of Hyderabad, India
Sitaram Chamarty   Tata Consultancy Services, India

Program Co-chairs

Claude Carlet   Universities of Paris 8 and Paris 13, LAGA, France
M. Anwar Hasan   University of Waterloo, Canada
Vishal Saraswat   CRRao AIMSCS, India

Steering Committee

Debdeep Mukhopadhyay   IIT, Kharagpur, India
Veezhinathan Kamakoti   IIT, Madras, India
Sanjay Burman   CAIR-DRDO, India

Program Committee

Lejla Batina   Radboud University Nijmegen, The Netherlands
Guido Marco Bertoni   STMicroelectronics, Italy
Francesco Buccafurri   DIIES - Università Mediterranea di Reggio Calabria, Italy
Claude Carlet (Co-chair)   University of Paris 8 and LAGA, France
Rajat Subhra Chakraborty   IIT, Kharagpur, India
Pandu Rangan Chandrasekaran   IIT, Madras, India
Ashish Choudhury   IIIT, Bangalore, India
Giovanni Di Crescenzo   Applied Communication Sciences, USA
Sylvain Guilley   GET/ENST, CNRS/LTCI, France
Indivar Gupta   SAG, DRDO, India

M. Anwar Hasan (Co-chair)   University of Waterloo, Canada
Thomas Johansson   Lund University, Sweden
Marc Joye   NXP Semiconductors, USA
Subhamoy Maitra   Indian Statistical Institute, India
Keith Martin   Royal Holloway, University of London, UK
Mitsuru Matsui   Mitsubishi, Japan
Willi Meier   FHNW, Switzerland
Debdeep Mukhopadhyay   IIT, Kharagpur, India
Elisabeth Oswald   University of Bristol, UK
Gilles Piret   Oberthur Technologies, France
Emmanuel Prouff   SAFRAN Identity and Security, France
Matthieu Rivain   CryptoExperts, France
Bimal Roy   Indian Statistical Institute, Kolkata, India
Dipanwita Roy Chowdhury   IIT, Kharagpur, India
Rei Safavi-Naini   University of Calgary, Canada
Rajeev Anand Sahu   CRRao AIMSCS, Hyderabad, India
Somitra Sanadhya   IIT, Delhi, India
Vishal Saraswat (Co-chair) CRRao AIMSCS, Hyderabad, India
Palash Sarkar   Indian Statistical Institute, Kolkata, India
Kannan Srinathan   IIIT, Hyderabad, India
Sirisinahal Srinivasachary DRDO, India
François-Xavier Standaert   UCL Crypto Group, Belgium
Y.V. Subba Rao   University of Hyderabad, India
Venkaiah V. Ch   University of Hyderabad, India
Amr Youssuf   Concordia University, Canada

Additional Reviewers

Urbi Chatterjee   Philippe Loubet-Moundi   Stjepan Picek
Jean-Luc Danger   Houssem Maghrebi   Jeyavijayan Rajendran
Ashok Das   Marco Martinoli   Debapriya Basu Roy
Nicolas Debande   Pedro Maat Massolino   Durga Prasad Sahoo
Dhananjoy Dey   Filippo Melzani   Santanu Sarkar
Jacques Fournier   Prasanna Mishra   Ahmadou Séré
Mohona Ghosh   Surya Prakash Mishra   Takeshi Sugawara
Michael Hutter   Nicolas Morin   Ruggero Susella
Arpan Jati   Saibal Pal   Daisuke Suzuki
Anthony Journault   Kostas Papagiannopoulos   Toyohiro Tsurumaru
Sabyasachi Karat   Goutam Paul   Rei Uno
Ilya Kizhvatov   Thomas Peters   Srinivas Vivek

Organizing Institution

C.R. Rao Advanced Institute of Mathematics, Statistics and Computer Science (AIMSCS), Hyderabad, India

Organizing Chair

Vishal Saraswat   CRRao AIMSCS, Hyderabad, India

Abstracts of Tutorials

Side-Channel Attacks on PKC

Lejla Batina

Radboud University, Nijmegen, The Netherlands

Abstract. We give an introduction to physical attacks, in particular to passive attacks exploiting leakages of secret data from power consumption or EM emanations. Several issues such as leakage models, attack scenarios and countermeasures are outlined. We focus on public-key cryptosystems and their specifics with side-channel attacks and countermeasures. Recent attacks such as horizontal and online template attacks (OTA) are described and their experimental demonstrations on elliptic-curve cryptosystems are presented.

Sponge-Based Cryptography

Joan Daemen

STMicroelectronics, Diegem, Belgium
Radboud University, Nijmegen, The Netherlands

Abstract. Keccak, the winner of the SHA-3 competition, has at its core a permutation and uses this in a mode that is known as the sponge construction. Previous hash standards, from MD5 to SHA-2, all had at its core a block-cipher like primitive. Similarly, block ciphers have also been at the core of encryption, MAC computation and authenticated encryption schemes since the introduction of DES in the seventies. Recently, in the slipstream of Keccak, permutation-based alternatives have been proposed for all these cryptographic services. It turns out that they are at the same time more efficient and more elegant. In this tutorial we will give an introduction to unkeyed (sponge and SHA-3) and keyed (full-state keyed duplex and Keyak) permutation-based modes.

Elliptic Curve Cryptography
and Isogeny-Based Cryptography

Craig Costello

Microsoft Research, Redmond, WA, USA

Abstract. Elliptic curves have reigned supreme as a foundation for classical public-key cryptography due to the exponential hardness of the elliptic curve discrete logarithm problem (ECDLP). The gap between the hardness of the ECDLP and the subexponential hardness of problems like integer factorization and finite field discrete logarithms ultimately means that public-key cryptography based on elliptic curves is much faster and much more compact than its alternatives. The first half of this tutorial will give a gentle introduction to elliptic curve cryptography (ECC). All of the above classically difficult problems (including the ECDLP) become easy in the presence of a large-scale quantum computer. Thus, cryptographers are currently examining a range of new foundations that are believed to offer security against quantum adversaries. Interestingly, elliptic curves have also surfaced as a promising foundation in the post-quantum space, in particular in the realm of isogeny-based key exchange. The second half of this tutorial will give a gentle introduction to isogenies and their role in providing post-quantum primitives.

Abstracts of Keynotes

Secure Hardware and Hardware-Enabled Security

Swarup Bhunia

University of Florida, Gainesville, USA

Abstract. Security has emerged as a critical design parameter for modern electronic hardware that builds the foundation for exciting new applications from smart wearables to smart cities. However, recent discoveries and reports on numerous attacks on microchips violate the well-regarded concept of hardware trust anchors. It has prompted system designers to develop wide array of design-for-security and test/validation solutions to achieve high security assurance. At the same time, emerging security issues and countermeasures have led to interesting interplay between security, energy, reliability, and test. Hardware faults and parametric variations, on one hand, have created new barriers to establishing hardware integrity in ever-complex semiconductor supply chain. On the other hand, reliability issues – in particular, those induced by process variations and aging effects, create new opportunities in designing powerful security primitives to protect against supply chain security issues as well as to enable better functional security solutions. This talk will highlight the interaction of hardware security issues and protection mechanisms with hardware faults and reliability issues. It will present new frontiers in hardware security with the rapidly diversifying application space and their symbiosis as well as conflicts with test. The talk will also cover promising role of hardware in security of various consumables, including food, supplements, and medicine.

Practical Post-quantum Key Exchange from Supersingular Isogenies

Craig Costello

Microsoft Research, Redmond, WA, USA

Abstract. Academic groups, corporate bodies, and government agencies from all over the world are hastily examining a range of cryptographic primitives that are believed to remain secure in the presence of a large-scale quantum computer. Indeed, all of the currently standardized public-key cryptography will offer little or no security if such a computer is realized. In their Februrary 2016 report on post-quantum cryptography, NIST stated that "*It seems improbable that any of the currently known algorithms can serve as a drop-in replacement for what is in use today,*" citing one challenge as being that quantum resistant algorithms have larger key sizes than the algorithms they will replace. While this statement is certainly applicable to many of the lattice- and code-based schemes, Jao and De Feo's 2011 supersingular isogeny Diffie-Hellman (SIDH) proposal is one post-quantum candidate that could serve as a drop-in replacement to existing internet protocols. Not only are high-security SIDH public keys smaller than their lattice- and code-based counterparts, they are even smaller than some of the traditional (i.e., finite field) Diffie-Hellman public keys. Moreover, in contrast to the proposed lattice- and code-based schemes (which are all either KEMs or encryption protocols), SIDH affords the option of restoring the elegant symmetry of the original Diffie-Hellman protocol.

This talk will give a detailed overview of isogeny-based key exchange, and will present a full-fledged software implementation of SIDH that is designed to provide 128 bits of security against a quantum adversary. We will conclude by pointing out some important open problems and interesting research directions in the realm of isogeny-based cryptography.

This talk is based on recent work with Patrick Longa and Michael Naehrig [1], and in turn on the original paper(s) by De Feo, Jao and Plût [2]. The two tutorials preceding the talk will (1) give a gentle introduction to elliptic curve cryptography, and (2) give a gentle introduction to isogenies.

References

1. Costello, C., Longa, P., Naehrig, M.: Efficient algorithms for super-singular isogeny Diffie-Hellman. In: CRYPTO 2016, pp. 572–601 (2016)
2. De Feo, L., Jao, D., Plûut, J.: Towards quantum-resistant cryp-tosystems from supersingular elliptic curve isogenies. J. Math. Crypt. **8**(3), 209–247 (2014)

Contents

Hardware Security

Security

Post-quantum Cryptology

Leakage, Power and Fault Analysis

Deep Learning and Fault Based Attacks

Breaking Cryptographic Implementations Using Deep Learning Techniques

Houssem Maghrebi, Thibault Portigliatti, and Emmanuel Prouff[(✉)]

SAFRAN Identity and Security, 18, Chaussée Jules César, 95520 Osny, France
{houssem.maghrebi,thibault.portigliatti,emmanuel.prouff}@safrangroup.com

Abstract. Template attack is the most common and powerful profiled side channel attack. It relies on a realistic assumption regarding the noise of the device under attack: the probability density function of the data is a multivariate Gaussian distribution. To relax this assumption, a recent line of research has investigated new profiling approaches mainly by applying machine learning techniques. The obtained results are commensurate, and in some particular cases better, compared to template attack. In this work, we propose to continue this recent line of research by applying more sophisticated profiling techniques based on deep learning. Our experimental results confirm the overwhelming advantages of the resulting new attacks when targeting both unprotected and protected cryptographic implementations.

Keywords: Deep learning · Machine learning · Side channel attacks · Template attack · Unprotected AES implementation · Masked AES implementation

1 Introduction

Side Channel Attacks. Side Channel attacks (SCA) are nowadays well known and most designers of secure embedded systems are aware of them. They exploit information leaking from the physical implementations of cryptographic algorithms. Since, this leakage (*e.g.* the power consumption or the electromagnetic emanations) depends on the internally used secret key, the adversary may perform an efficient key-recovery attack to reveal these sensitive data. Since the first public reporting of these threats [30], a lot of effort has been devoted towards the research on side channel attacks and the development of corresponding countermeasures.

Amongst side channel attacks, two classes may be distinguished.

- The so-called *profiling SCA* are the most powerful kind of SCA and consist of two steps. First, the adversary procures a copy of the *target device* and uses it to characterize the dependency between the manipulated data and the device behavior. Secondly, he performs a key-recovery attack on the target

---

T. Portigliatti—Work done when the author was at SAFRAN Identity and Security.

© Springer International Publishing AG 2016
C. Carlet et al. (Eds.): SPACE 2016, LNCS 10076, pp. 3–26, 2016.
DOI: 10.1007/978-3-319-49445-6_1

device. The set of profiled attacks includes Template attacks [10] and Stochastic cryptanalyses (*aka* Linear Regression Analyses) [16,47,48].

- The set of so-called *non-profiling SCA* corresponds to a much weaker adversary who has only access to the physical leakage captured on the target device. To recover the secret key in use, he performs some statistical analyses to detect dependency between the leakage measurements and this sensitive variable. The set of non-profiled attacks includes Differential Power Analysis (DPA) [30], Correlation Power Analysis (CPA) [9] and Mutual Information Analysis (MIA) [20].

Side Channel Countermeasures. A deep look at the state-of-the-art shows that several countermeasures have been published to deal with side channel attacks. Amongst SCA countermeasures, two classes may be distinguished [36]:

- The set of so-called *masking countermeasures*: the core principle of masking is to ensure that every sensitive variable is randomly split into at least two shares so that the knowledge of a strict sub-part of the shares does not give information on the shared variable itself. Masking can be characterized by the number of random masks used per sensitive variable. So, it is possible to give a general definition for a dth-order masking scheme: every sensitive variable Z is randomly split into $d+1$ shares $M_0, \cdots, M_d$ in such a way that the relation $M_0 \perp \cdots \perp M_d = Z$ is satisfied for a group operation $\perp$ (*e.g.* the XOR operation used in the *Boolean masking*, denoted as $\oplus$) and no tuple of strictly less than $d+1$ shares depends on Z. In the literature, several provably secure higher-order masking schemes have been proposed (see for instance [13,19,44].).
- The set of so-called *hiding countermeasures*: the core idea is to render in making the activity of the physical implementation constant by either adding complementary logic to the existing logic [11] (in a hardware setting) or by using a *specific encoding* of the sensitive data [27,50] (in a software setting).

Machine Learning Based Attacks. A recent line of works has investigated new profiling attacks based on Machine Learning (ML) techniques to defeat both unprotected [5,23,28,32,34] and protected cryptographic implementations [21, 33]. These contributions focus mainly on two techniques: the Support Vector Machine (SVM) [14,57] and the Random Forest (RF) [45]. Practical results on several data-sets have demonstrated the ability of these attacks to perform successful key recoveries. Besides, authors in [23] have shown that the SVM-based attack outperforms the template attack when applied on highly noisy traces.

Mainly, ML-based attacks exploit the same discriminating criteria (*i.e.* the dependence between the sensitive data and some statistical moments of the leakage) as a template attack. Two major differences between these attacks exist. They are listed hereafter.

- The template attack approximates the data distribution by a multivariate Gaussian distribution (*aka Gaussian leakage assumption*) [10] whose parameters (*i.e.* the mean vector and the covariance matrix) are estimated during

the profiling phase. This implies that the statistical moments of the leakage distribution whose order is greater than 2 are not exploited which can make the attack sub-optimal and even ineffective in some contexts.
- The ML-based attacks make no assumption on the data distribution and build classifications directly from the raw data-set.

Despite the fact that Gaussian leakage is a fairly realistic assumption in side channel context [35,43], applying distribution-agnostic statistical techniques would appear to be a more rational approach.

Our Contribution. Over the past few years, there has been a resurgence of interest in using Deep Learning (DL) techniques which have been applied in several signal processing areas where they have produced interesting results [1,15]. Deep learning is a parallel branch of machine learning which relies on sets of algorithms that attempt to model high-level abstractions in data by using model architectures with multiple processing layers, composed of a sequence of scalar products and non-linear transformations called *activation functions* [51]. Several recent results have demonstrated that DL techniques have convincingly outperformed other existing machine learning approaches in image and automatic speech recognition.

In this work, we propose to apply DL techniques in side channel context. Actually, we highlight the ability of DL to build an accurate profiling leading to an efficient and successful side channel key recovery attack. Our experiments show that our proposed DL-based attacks are more efficient than the ML-based and template attacks when targeting either unprotected or masked cryptographic implementations.

Paper Outline. The paper is organized as follows. In Sects. 2 and 3, we provide an overview on machine learning and deep learning techniques. Then, in Sect. 4 we describe how to use deep learning techniques to perform a successful key recovery. This is followed in Sect. 5 by some practical attack experiments applied on unprotected and masked AES implementations. Finally, Sect. 6 draws general conclusions and opens some perspectives for future work.

2   Overview on Machine Learning Techniques

Machine learning techniques have been developed and used in order to build efficient pattern recognition and features extraction algorithms. Mainly, ML techniques are divided into three categories depending on the learning approach: *unsupervised*, *semi-supervised* and *supervised*. In this paper, we focus on supervised and unsupervised learning techniques.

- *Unsupervised learning* is mainly used when profiling information (*i.e.* training data-set) is not available. So, the purpose is to ensure an efficient data partitioning without any prior profiling or data modeling. Two classic examples of unsupervised learning techniques are *clustering* (*e.g.* K-means [17]) and *dimensionality reduction* (*e.g.* Principal Component Analysis (PCA)). These techniques have been widely used in side channel contexts to perform either successful key recovery [24,52] or some pre-processing of the physical leakage [4].
- *Supervised learning* refers to techniques that involve a training data-set[1] (*aka* labeled data-set) to build a model. Once the learning has been performed, a supervised learning algorithm is executed which returns, for a new incoming input, an output that is the most accurate one according to the previously learned model. Typical supervised learning techniques include neural networks [8], random forest [45] and support vector machines [14,57].

In the following sections we provide a survey of some supervised learning techniques and their applications in side channel analysis. All of them take as input a training data-set composed of vectors $X^{(i)} = (x_1, \ldots, x_n) \in \mathbb{R}^n$ and their corresponding labels $y_i \in \mathbb{R}$ (*e.g.* scores or values of the manipulated sensitive data). After the learning step, their goal is to associate a new vector X with the correct label y.

2.1   Perceptron

The perceptron is the simplest neural network model [8]. It is a linear classifier that uses a learning algorithm to tune its weights in order to minimize a so-called *loss function*[2] as described in Fig. 1. We detail hereafter how perceptron works to perform classification:

- first, an input vector $X = (x_1, \ldots, x_n) \in \mathbb{R}^n$ is presented as an entry to the perceptron.
- then, components of X are summed over the weights $w_i \in \mathbb{R}$ of the perceptron connections (*i.e.* $w_0 + \sum_{i=1}^{n} w_i x_i$, with w_0 being a bias[3]).
- finally, the output of the perceptron is computed by passing the previously computed sum to an *activation function*[4] denoted f.

---

[1] The training data-set is composed of pairs of some known (input, output).

[2] The loss (*aka* cost, error) function quantifies in a supervised learning problem the compatibility between a prediction and the ground truth label (output). The loss function is typically defined as the negative log-likelihood or the mean squared error.

[3] Introducing a value that is independent of the input shifts the boundary away from the origin.

[4] In the case of the perceptron, the activation function is commonly a Heaviside function. In more complex models (*e.g.* the multilayer perceptron that we will describe in the next section), this function can be chosen to be a sigmoid function (*tanh*).

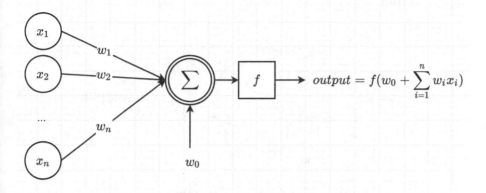

Fig. 1. Representation of a perceptron.

During the training phase, the perceptron weights, initialized at zeros or small random values, are learned and adjusted according to the profiling data-set $(X^{(i)}, y_i)$. By *e.g.* applying a *gardient descent* algorithm, the goal is to find/learn the optimal connecting weights moving the perceptron outputs as close as possible[5] to the correct labels/scores (*e.g.* to minimize the sum of squared differences between the labels y_i and the corresponding perceptron's output).

2.2 Multilayer Perceptron

A Multilayer Perceptron (MLP) is nothing more than a specific way to combine perceptrons[6] in order to build a classifier for more complex data-sets [8]. As shown in Fig. 2, the information is propagated from the left to the right and each units (perceptrons) of a layer is connected to every unit of the previous layer in this model. This is called a *fully connected network*. Each neuron belongs to a layer and the number of layers is a parameter which has to be carefully chosen by the user.

An MLP is made of three different types of layers:

- Input Layer: in the traditional model, this layer is only an intermediate between the input data and the rest of the network. Thus the output of the neurons belonging to this layer is simply the input vector itself.
- Hidden layer: this layer aims at introducing some non-linearity in the model so that the MLP will be able to fit a non-linear separable data-set. Indeed, if the data that have to be learned are linearly separable, there is no need for any hidden layer. Depending on the non-linearity and the complexity of the data model that has to be fit, the number of neurons on the hidden layer or even the number of these layers can be increased. However, one hidden layer is sufficient for a large number of natural problems.

---

[5] *E.g.* for the Euclidean distance.
[6] Perceptrons are also called "units", "nodes" or neurons in this model.

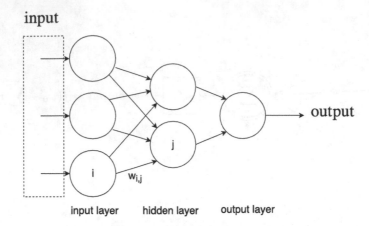

Fig. 2. Example of MLP, where each node is a perceptron as described in Sect. 2.1.

Regarding the number of neurons on the hidden layers, it has been demonstrated that using a huge number of neurons can lead to *over-fitting* if the model that has to be learned is close to a linear one [8]. It means that the algorithm is able to correctly learn weights leading to a perfect fit with the training data-set while these weights are not representative of the whole data. On the other hand, the opposite may happen: for a complex data-set, using too few neurons on the hidden layers may lead the gradient minimization approach to fail in returning an accurate solution.

– Output layer: this is the last layer of the network. The output of the nodes on this layer are directly mapped to classes that the user intends to predict.

Training a multilayer perceptron requires, for each layer, the learning of the weighting parameters minimizing the loss function. To do so, the so-called *back-propagation* [8] can be applied. It consists in computing the derivative of the loss function with respect to the weights, one layer after another, and then in modifying the corresponding weights by using the following formula:

$$w_{ij} = -\frac{\partial E}{\partial w_{i,j}} \ ,$$

where E is the loss function and $w_{i,j}$ denotes the weight of the connection between two neurons of indices (i, j).

In several recent works, MLP has been applied to perform successful side channel key recovery. For instance, in [21], authors have presented a neural network based side channel attack to break the masked AES implementation of the DPA contest V4 [55]. In fact, the authors of [21] assume that the adversary has access to the mask values during the profiling phase. Under this assumption, the proposed attack consists first in identifying the mask by applying a neural network mask recovery. Then, a second neural network based attack is performed to recover the secret key with a single trace. While the results of this work are quite interesting, the considered assumption is not always met in real world circumstances.

2.3 Decision Trees and Random Forest

A *decision tree* is a tool involving binary rules to classify data [45]. It is made of a root, several nodes and leaves. Each leaf is associated to a label corresponding to the target value to be recovered. Each node that is not a leaf can lead to two nodes (or leaves). First, the input is presented to the root. It is then forwarded to one of the possible branch starting from this node. The process is repeated until a leaf is reached. An illustration of this process for a 2-bit XOR operation is depicted in Fig. 3.

A random forest is composed of many decision trees, each one working with a different subset of the training data-set [45]. On the top of all of the trees, the global output is computed through a majority vote among these classification trees outputs. RFs have been successfully applied in SCA context to defeat

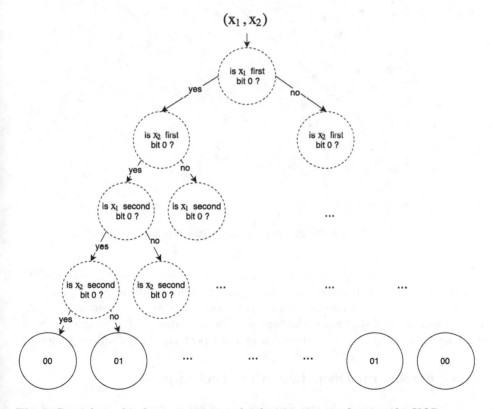

Fig. 3. Partial graphical representation of a decision tree performing the XOR operation between 2 bits variables x_1 and x_2. The leaves correspond to the XOR result.

cryptographic implementations [33,34]. In this paper, we will try to compare RF-based attack with deep learning ones in terms of key recovery effectiveness.

2.4 Support Vector Machine

A support vector machine [14,57] is a linear classifier that not only intends to find an hyper-plane to separate data classes but also intends to find the optimal one maximizing the margin between these classes as described in Fig. 4. To deal with non-linearly separable data-sets, it is possible for instance to use a *kernel function* for instance that maps these data into a feature space of higher dimensions in which the classes become linearly separable [49].

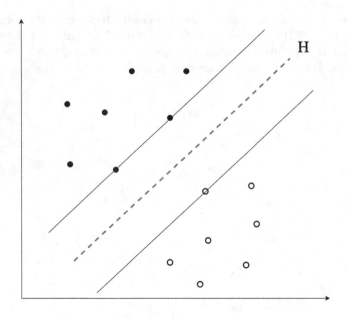

Fig. 4. Binary hyper-plane Classification.

In the side channel literature, several works have investigated the use of SVM towards performing successful attacks to break either unprotected [5,23,28,32, 34] or protected cryptographic implementations [33]. Actually, authors in [23] have demonstrated that when the Signal-to-Noise Ratio (SNR)[7] of the targeted data-set is very low, the SVM-based attack outperforms the template attack.

3   Overview on Deep Learning Techniques

For several reasons (mainly the *vanishing gradient problem* [25] and the lack of computational power), it was not possible to train many-layered neural networks

---

[7] The SNR is defined as the ratio of signal power to the noise power.

until a few years ago. Recent discoveries, taking full advantage of GPU for computations and using the *rectified linear unit function* ($f : x \mapsto max(0, x)$) as an activation function instead of the classical sigmoid ($g : x \mapsto \frac{1}{1+e^{-x}}$), made it possible to stack many layers allowing networks to learn more and more abstract representation of the training data-set [29]. This is known as deep learning techniques [1]. One major difference between deep learning and usual machine learning is that the latter ones are classifiers usually working from human-engineered features while the former ones learn the features directly from the raw data before making any classification [6]. In the following sections, some of the most widely used learning techniques are detailed.

3.1   Convolutional Neural Networks

A Convolutional Neural Network (CNN) is a specific kind of neural network built by stacking the following layers [31,40]:

- A convolutional layer: on this layer, during the forward computation phase, the input data are convoluted with some filters. The output of the convolution is commonly called a *feature map*. It shows where the features detected by the filter can be found on the input data. In Fig. 5, we provide an example of a convolutional layer where the input vector X is represented as a matrix (*i.e.* $X = (x_{i,j}) \in \mathbb{R}^{t \times t}$ where t is smallest square integer greater than the size n of X viewed as a vector) and padded with zeros around the border[8]. The output values can be expressed as $y_{i,j} = \sum\limits_{a=1}^{m} \sum\limits_{b=1}^{m} w_{a,b} x_{i+a,j+b}$, where $w_{a,b}$ denotes the weights of the filter viewed as an m-by-m matrix. During the backward computation, the filter weights are learned[9] by trying to minimize the overall loss.
- A Max Pooling layer: this is a sub-sampling layer. The feature map is divided into regions and the output of this layer is the concatenation of the maximum values of all these regions. Such layers can help reducing computation complexity and enhance the robustness of the model with respect to a translation of the input.
- A SoftMax layer: it is added on the top of the previous stacked layers. It converts scores from the previous layer to a probability distribution over the classes.

Learning the filters enables to extract high level features from the data. This step may therefore be used as a dimensionality reduction or a Points Of Interest (POI) selection technique (*e.g.* a PCA). Based on this remark, it would be interesting to assess the efficiency of the CNN internal features extraction function in selecting the most informative points to perform a successful key recovery attack.

---

[8] The goal is to control the size of the output.
[9] As for the MLP weights estimations, the filter parameters are learned using the back-propagation algorithm.

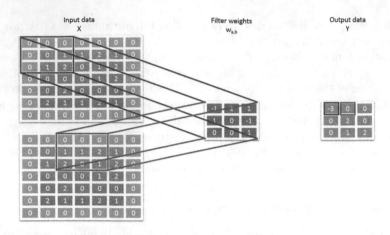

Fig. 5. An example of a convolutional layer where $n = 25$, $t = 5$ and $m = 3$.

3.2   Stacked Auto-Encoders

Stacked auto-encoders are artificial neural networks with many layers trained by following a very specific procedure [37]. This procedure consists in training each layer independently, using the output of the previous layer as input for the current one. Each layer is composed of an encoder and a decoder, both being a dense layer (*i.e.* fully connected layer)[10]. The role of the encoder is to generate higher level features from the inputs. Whereas, the decoder role is to reconstruct the inputs from the intermediate features learned by the encoder[11] as described in Fig. 6. A very uninteresting network would learn the identity function. To avoid such a behavior, a thumb rule could be that each layer has to be smaller than the previous one[12]. This way the network will be forced to learn a compressed representation of the input. Once the training is done, the decoder is removed, the newly generated encoder is stacked with the previously trained ones and the procedure can be repeated using the output of the newly trained layer.

On the top of the stacked auto-encoder layers, a SoftMax classifier is usually added to predict the class of the input using the high level extracted features of the last layer. Each of these layers (including the SoftMax layer) is trained sequentially. But once the last layer is trained, a global training using the well-known Back-propagation algorithm is performed. This technique is known as *fine tuning* [37].

---

[10] This is also known as a restricted Boltzmann machine [46].

[11] We refer the interested reader to another type of auto-encoder deep learning technique called *Denoising auto-encoder* [56,58]. This specific kind of auto-encoder aims at removing the noise when fed with a noisy input.

[12] This is not mandatory; some empirical results have shown that it might be better to sometimes have more neurons on the first hidden layer than on the output as a "pre-learning" step.

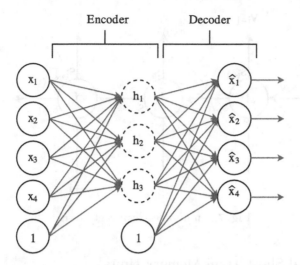

Fig. 6. *Learning an auto-encoder layer.* First, the input $X = (x_0, x_1, x_2, x_3, x_4) \in \mathbb{R}^5$ is encoded. Then, the obtained result $H = (h_0, h_1, h_2, h_3, h_4) \in \mathbb{R}^5$ is decoded using the second layer of the diagram to reconstruct the input $\widehat{X} = (\widehat{x}_0, \widehat{x}_1, \widehat{x}_2, \widehat{x}_3, \widehat{x}_4) \in \mathbb{R}^5$. The difference $(X - \widehat{X})$ is then computed and fed to the back-propagation algorithm to estimate the optimal weights minimizing the loss function.

Like CNN, auto-encoders are features extractors. Their role is to build high level features that are easier to use in a profiling task. This task is particularly meaningful in SCA where the features selection method is critical.

3.3 Recurrent Neural Networks

The Recurrent Neural Networks (RNN) [22] are dedicated to data for which the same information is spread over several time samples. Thus, instead of assuming that the components of the input vectors are mutually independent, each neuron will infer its output from both the current input and output of previous units. The RNN technique could be applied in the context of SCA since the leakage is spread actually over several time samples.

In Fig. 7, we explain how this time-dependency is used by the RNN during the profiling phase. Let n be the number of sample in our trace. For any i in $[1, n]$, the ith output s_i rewrites $s_i = f(U \cdot x_i + W \cdot s_{i-1})$, where (U, W) are the connecting weights that the RNN have to learn and f denotes the activation function. To get the ith output y_j, a SoftMax layer is added such that $y_j = \text{SoftMax}(V \cdot s_i)$ where V is a connecting weight. Unlike traditional deep learning techniques which use different weights at each layer, a RNN shares the same parameters (U, V, W) across all layers[13]. To adjust the network weights of the ith unit, two different back-propagation phases are processed: the classical one (to learn U) and a temporal one (to learn W which depends on $(i - 1)^{\text{th}}$ output).

---

[13] The purpose is to reduce the number of parameters to be learned.

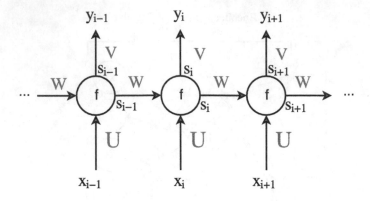

Fig. 7. An unrolled recurrent layer.

3.4   Long and Short Term Memory Units

The Long and Short Term Memory (LSTM) is based on the RNN [26]. It has been originally introduced to solve problems that had been reported when using RNN, mainly the vanishing or the exploding gradients [7]. It enables the network to deal with long time lags between relevant time-series of the processed dataset. To do so, a *cell state* (*aka* memory cell) is added inside each unit. It contains some statistical information (*e.g.* mean, variance) computed over a previously processed time-series of the data. This cell can either be written on or erased depending on the relevance of the stored information. The decision of writing on the cell or of clearing it is taken by a small neural network [26].

In side channel context, this feature is quite interesting when dealing with higher-order attacks where the adversary have to combine several delayed time samples in order to defeat masked implementations for instance.

In the rest of this paper, we will focus on LSTM rather than RNN for the reasons outlined above.

4   Towards New Profiling Methods

Several profiling approaches have been introduced in the literature. A common profiling side channel attack is the template attack proposed in [10] which is based on the Gaussian assumption[14]. It is known as the most powerful type of profiling in a SCA context when (1) the Gaussian assumption is verified and (2) the size of the leakage observations is small (typically smaller than 10.000).

When the Gaussian assumption is relaxed, several profiling based side channel attacks have been suggested including techniques based on machine learning. Actually, machine learning models make no assumption on the probability density function of the data. For example, random forest model builds a set of

---

[14] which is that the distribution of the leakage when the algorithm inputs are fixed is well estimated by a Gaussian Law.

decision trees that classifies the data-set based on a voting system [34] and SVM-based attack discriminates data-set using hyper-plane clustering [23]. Indeed, one of the main drawbacks of the template attacks is their high data complexity [12] as opposed to the ML-based attacks which are generally useful when dealing with very high-dimensional data [34].

In the following section, we describe the commonly used template attack before introducing our new profiling approaches based on deep learning techniques.

4.1   Template Attack

Template attacks have been introduced in 2002 by Chari *et al.* [10]. Since then, many works have been published proposing either some efficiency improvements (*e.g.* using Principal Component Analysis) [4,5,12] or to extend it to break protected implementations [41]. The seminal template attack consists first in using a set of profiling traces[15] and the corresponding intermediate results in order to estimate the probability density function (pdf) $f_z(L|Z = z)$ where Z and L are random variables respectively denoting the target intermediate result and the corresponding leakage during its processing by the device, and where z ranges over all the definition set of Z. Usually L is multivariate, say defined over $\mathbb{R}^d$ for some integer d (*e.g.* $d = 1.000$). Under the Gaussian assumption, this pdf is estimated by a multivariate normal law:

$$f_z(L|Z = z) \simeq \frac{1}{(2\pi)^d det(\Sigma_z)} exp\left(-\frac{1}{2}(L - \mu_z)^T \Sigma_z (L - \mu_z)\right) \ ,$$

where Σ_z denotes the $(d \times d)$-matrix of covariances of $(L|Z = z)$ and where the d-dimensional vector μ_z denotes its mean[16].

Next, during the attack phase, the adversary uses a new set of traces $(l_i)_{1 \leq i \leq n}$ for which the corresponding values z_i are unknown. From a key hypothesis k, he deduces predictions $\hat{z}_i$ on these values and computes the maximum likelihood approach $\prod_{j=1}^{n} f_{\hat{z}_j}(l_j|Z = \hat{z}_j)$. To minimize approximation errors, it is often more convenient in practice to process the log-likelihood.

4.2   Deep Learning in Side Channel Analysis Context

Like other machine learning techniques (*e.g.* SVM and RF), a deep learning technique builds a profiling model for each possible value z_i of the targeted sensitive variable Z during the training phase and, during the attack phase these models are involved to output the most likely key (*i.e.* label) k^* used during the acquisition of the attack traces set $(l_i)_{1 \leq i \leq n}$.

In side channel attack context, an adversary is rather interested in the computation of the probability of each possible value $\hat{z}_i$ deduced from a key hypothesis.

---

[15] This set of traces is typically acquired on an open copy of the targeted device.
[16] The couple (μ_z, Σ_z) represents the template of the value z.

Therefore, to recover the good key, the adversary computes the maximum or the log-maximum likelihood approach like for template attack ($\prod\limits_{j=1}^{n} P(l_j | Z = \hat{z}_j)$).

Indeed, our deep learning techniques only differs from the machine learning one in the method used to profile data. However, the attack phase remains the same for both kinds of attack.

5   Experimental Results

In the following section, we compare for different implementation sets the effectiveness and the efficiency of our proposed DL-based attacks with those of ML-based and template-based attacks. Mainly, we have targeted a hardware and a software implementation of an unprotected AES and a first-order masked AES implementation.

5.1   Experimental Setup

We detail hereafter our experimental setup.

Attacker Profile. Since we are dealing with profiled attacks, we assume an attacker who has full control of a training device during the profiling phase and is able to measure the power consumption during the execution of a cryptographic algorithm. Then during the attack phase, the adversary aims at recovering the unknown secret key, processed by the same device, by collecting a new set of power consumption traces. To guarantee a fair and realistic attack comparison, we stress the fact that the training and the attack data-sets must be different.

Targeted Operation. Regarding the targeted operation, we consider one or several AES SBox outputs during the first round: $Z = SBox[X \oplus k^*]$ where X and k^* respectively denote the plaintext and the secret key. We motivate our choice towards targeting this non-linear operation by the facts that it is a common target in side channel analysis and that it has a high level of confusion.

Training and Attack Phase Setup. For fair attack comparison, we have considered fixed size data-sets for the profiling and the attack: 1.000 power traces per sensitive value (*i.e.* $Z = z$) for the training phase and 20.000 power traces with a fixed key k^* for the attack phase.

Evaluation Metric. For the different targeted implementations, we have considered a fixed attack setup. In fact, each attack is conducted on 10 independent sets of 2.000 traces each (since we have a set of 20.000 power traces for the attack phase). Then, we have computed the averaged rank of the correct key among all key hypotheses (*aka* the *guessing entropy metric* [53]).

5.2   Unprotected AES Implementations

DPA Contest V2. Our first experiments were carried out on the DPA contest V2 data-set [54]. It is an FPGA-based unprotected AES implementation. Each trace contains 3.253 samples measuring the power consumption of an AES execution.

To break this hardware implementation, we have conducted 4 different DL-based attacks (AE, CNN, LSTM and MLP)[17]. For the MLP-based attack, we have considered two versions: for the first one, we have pre-processed traces by applying a PCA in order to extract the 16 most informative components (since we will target the 16 SBox outputs). For the second MLP-based attack, no dimensionality technique was applied. Our purpose here is to check if the commonly used PCA technique could enhance the efficiency of deep learning based attacks.

For the sake of completeness, we have performed the seminal template attack and the RF-based attack[18]. The evolution of the correct key rank according to the number of traces for each attack when targeting the first AES SBox is

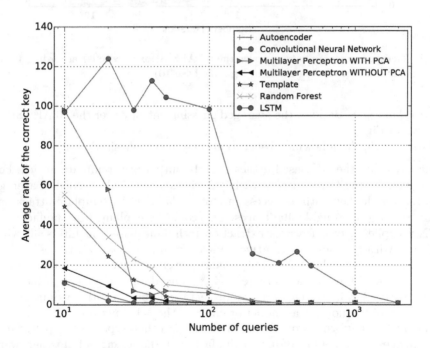

Fig. 8. Evolution of the correct key rank (y-axis) according to an increasing number of traces (x-axis in log scale base 10) for each attack when targeting the first AES SBox

---

[17] The parameters for each attack are detailed in Appendix A.

[18] In our attack experiments, we didn't reported the results of the SVM-based attack since it achieves a comparable results as those obtained for the RF-based attack. The same observations were highlighted in [33].

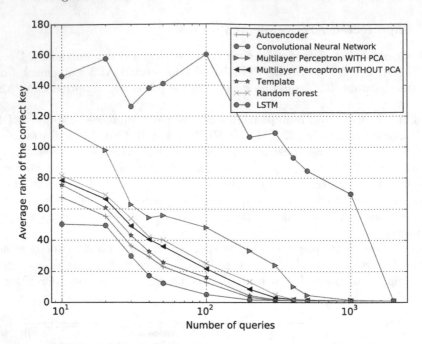

Fig. 9. Averaged guessing entropy over the 16 AES SBoxes (y-axis) according to an increasing number of traces (x-axis in log scale base 10).

described in Fig. 8. Besides, the averaged guessing entropy over the 16 AES SBox is shown in Fig. 9.

From Fig. 9, the following observations may be emphasized:

– the CNN and the AE-based attack slightly outperform template attack. For instance, for the CNN-based attack 200 traces are roughly needed in average to recover the key with a success rate of 100 %. For the template attack, an adversary needs roughly 400 traces. This could be explained by the fact that CNN applies a nice features extraction technique based on filters allowing dealing with the most informative samples form the processed traces.
– Prepossessing with PCA does not enhance the efficiency of MLP-based attack. In fact, the PCA is probably removing some data components which are informative for linear clustering representation, but negatively impact the accuracy of the non-linear model profiling of the MLP network.
– The LSTM performs worse compared to the other types of deep learning techniques. This could be due to the fact that the leakage of this hardware implementation is not time-dependent (*i.e.* the leakage is spread over few time samples).

Software Unprotected AES Implementation. For our second experiments, we have considered an unprotected AES implementation on the ChipWhisperer-Capture Rev2 board [39]. This board is a very compact side channel attack

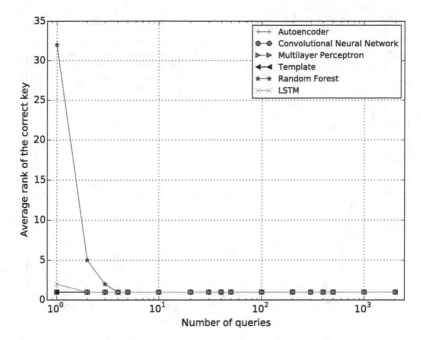

Fig. 10. Evolution of the correct key rank (y-axis) according to an increasing number of traces (x-axis in log scale base 10) for each attack when targeting the first AES SBox.

platform. It enables users to quickly and easily test their implementation against side channel attacks.

For the sake of comparison, we have performed the same attacks as these conducted on the DPA contest V2 implementation. In Figs. 10 and 11, we reported respectively the guessing entropy when targeting the first AES SBox and the averaged guessing entropy over the first four SBoxes for each attack and for an increasing attack traces set.

From Fig. 11, the following observations could be emphasized:

- Our proposed deep learning based attacks outperform both template and RF-based attack. For instance, for the AE-based attack 20 traces are roughly needed in average to recover the first four bytes of AES key with a success rate of 100 %. For the template attack and RF-based attack, an adversary needs respectively 100 and 80 traces.
- The performed attacks requires less than 100 traces to recover the first four bytes of the key. A natural explanation of this result could be that the SNR is very high on the ChipWhisperer side channel platform.
- The LSTM performs well compared to the results obtained on the DPA contest V2 data-set. This could be due to the facts that the leakage of a software implementation is very time-dependent and that the samples are less noisy.

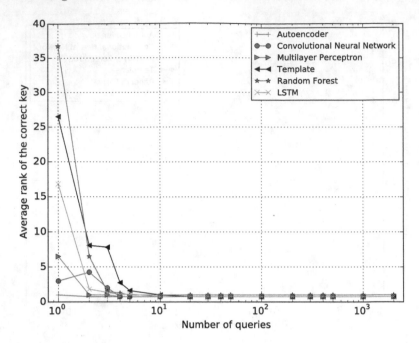

Fig. 11. Averaged guessing entropy over the first four AES SBoxes (y-axis) according to an increasing number of traces (x-axis in log scale base 10).

5.3   First-Order Masked AES Implementation

Our last experiments were carried out on a first-order masked AES implementation on the ChipWhisperer-Capture Rev2 board. The 16 SBoxes outputs are masked with the same mask. Our attacks were performed using the same leakage model as that used for the previously evaluated unprotected implementations (*i.e.* the training data were profiled with respect to the SBox output $S[X \oplus k]$). Unlike the recently published ML-based attacks to break masked implementations [21,33], we stress the fact that no prior profiling of the mask values was made during the training phase. The attack results when targeting the first SBox are shown in Fig. 12.

From Fig. 12, one can conclude that our deep learning based attacks perform well against masked implementation. In fact, 500 and 1000 traces are respectively needed for AE and CNN/MLP-based attacks to recover the key. Actually, the deep learning techniques apply some activation functions as described in Sect. 2.1. Those functions (*e.g.* a sigmoid) implicitly perform product combinations of the data samples which has as an effect the removal of the mask dependency[19] exactly like a second-order side channel attack [42].

For template attack and RF-based attack more traces are needed to reach a success rate of 100 %.

---

[19] The product combining function maps the leakages of the masked data $(Z \oplus M)$ and the mask (M) into a univariate sample depending on the sensitive data Z.

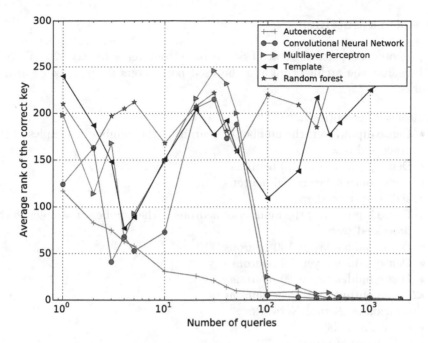

Fig. 12. Evolution of the correct key rank (y-axis) according to an increasing number of traces (x-axis in log scale base 10) for each attack when targeting the first AES SBox.

6   Conclusion and Perspectives

In this paper, to the best of our knowledge, we study for the first time the application of deep learning techniques in the context of side channel attacks. The deep learning techniques are based on some nice features suitable to perform successful key recovery. Mainly, they use different methods of features extraction (CNN and AE) and exploit time dependency of samples (RNN, LSTM). In order to evaluate the efficiency of our proposed attacks, we have compared them to the most commonly used template attack and machine learning attacks. The comparison between these attacks was conducted on three different data-sets by evaluating the number of traces required during the attack phase to achieve a unity guessing entropy with a fixed size of profiling data-set. Our practical results have shown the overwhelming advantage of our proposal in breaking both unprotected and protected AES implementations. Indeed, for the different targeted implementations, our attacks outperform the state-of-the-art profiling side channel attacks.

A future work may consist in targeting other types of protection (*e.g.* shuffling, combined masking and shuffling) with our proposed DL-based attacks. Moreover, our work opens avenues for further research of new deep learning techniques in order to better adapt them to challenge cryptographic implementations.

A   Attack Settings

Our proposed deep learning attacks are based on Keras library [2]. We provide hereafter the architecture and the used parameters for our deep learning networks.

- Multilayer Perceptron:
    - Dense input layer: the number of neurons = the number of samples in the processed trace
    - Dense hidden layer: 20 neurons
    - Dense output layer: 256 neurons
- Stacked Auto-Encoder:
    - Dense input layer: the number of neurons = the number of samples in the processed trace
    - Dense hidden layer: 100 neurons
    - Dense hidden layer: 50 neurons
    - Dense hidden layer: 20 neurons
    - Dense output layer: 256 neurons
- Convolutionnal Neural Network:
    - Convolution layer
        * Number of filters: 8
        * Filters length: 16
        * Activation function: Rectified Linear Unit
    - Dropout
    - Max pooling layer with a pooling size: 2
    - Convolution layer
        * Number of filters: 8
        * Filters length: 8
        * Activation function: $tanh(x)$
    - Dropout
    - Dense output layer: 256 neurons
- Long and Short Term Memory:
    - LSTM layer: 26 units
    - LSTM layer: 26 units
    - Dense output layer: 256 neurons
- Random Forest: For this machine learning based attack, we have used the *scikit-learn* python library [3].
    - Number of trees: 300

In several published works [23,28], authors have noticed the influence of the parameters chosen for SVM and RF networks on the attack results. When dealing with deep learning techniques we have observed the same effect. To find the optimal parameters setup for our practical attacks, a deeply analyzed method is detailed in the following section.

A.1 How to Choose the Optimal Parameters?

When dealing with *artificial neural networks*, several meta-parameters have to be tuned (*e.g.* number of layers, number of neurons on each layer, activation function, ...). One common technique to find the optimal parameters is to use *evolutionary algorithms* [18] and more precisely the so-called *genetic algorithm* [38].

At the beginning of the algorithm, a *population* (a set of *individuals* with different *genes*) is randomly initialized. In our case, an individual is a list of the parameters we want to estimate (*e.g.* number of layers, number of neurons on each layer, activation function, ...) and the genes are the corresponding values. Then, the performance of each individual is evaluated using what is called a *fitness function*. In our context, the fitness function is the guessing entropy outputted by the attack. Said, differently, for each set of parameters we perform the attack and we note the guessing entropy obtained. Only the individuals that achieve good guessing entropy scores are kept. Their genes are mutated and mixed to generate a better population. This process is repeated until a satisfying fitness is achieved (*i.e.* a guessing entropy equals one).

References

1. Deep learning website. http://deeplearning.net/tutorial/
2. Keras library. https://keras.io/
3. Scikit-learn library. http://scikit-learn.org/stable/
4. Archambeau, C., Peeters, E., Standaert, F.-X., Quisquater, J.-J.: Template attacks in principal subspaces. In: Goubin, L., Matsui, M. (eds.) CHES 2006. LNCS, vol. 4249, pp. 1–14. Springer, Heidelberg (2006). doi:10.1007/11894063_1
5. Bartkewitz, T., Lemke-Rust, K.: Efficient template attacks based on probabilistic multi-class support vector machines. In: Mangard, S. (ed.) CARDIS 2012. LNCS, vol. 7771, pp. 263–276. Springer, Heidelberg (2013). doi:10.1007/978-3-642-37288-9_18
6. Bengio, Y.: Learning deep architectures for ai. Found. Trends Mach. Learn. 2(1), 1–127 (2009)
7. Bengio, Y., Simard, P., Frasconi, P.: Learning long-term dependencies with gradient descent is difficult. Trans. Neur. Netw. 5(2), 157–166 (1994)
8. Bishop, C.M.: Neural Networks for Pattern Recognition. Oxford University Press Inc., New York (1995)
9. Brier, E., Clavier, C., Olivier, F.: Correlation power analysis with a leakage model. In: Joye, M., Quisquater, J.-J. (eds.) CHES 2004. LNCS, vol. 3156, pp. 16–29. Springer, Heidelberg (2004). doi:10.1007/978-3-540-28632-5_2
10. Chari, S., Rao, J.R., Rohatgi, P.: Template attacks. In: Kaliski, B.S., Koç, K., Paar, C. (eds.) CHES 2002. LNCS, vol. 2523, pp. 13–28. Springer, Heidelberg (2003). doi:10.1007/3-540-36400-5_3
11. Chen, Z., Zhou, Y.: Dual-rail random switching logic: a countermeasure to reduce side channel leakage. In: Goubin, L., Matsui, M. (eds.) CHES 2006. LNCS, vol. 4249, pp. 242–254. Springer, Heidelberg (2006). doi:10.1007/11894063_20
12. Choudary, O., Kuhn, M.G.: Efficient Template Attacks. Cryptology ePrint Archive, Report 2013/770 (2013). http://eprint.iacr.org/2013/770

13. Coron, J.-S.: Higher order masking of look-up tables. In: Nguyen, P.Q., Oswald, E. (eds.) EUROCRYPT 2014. LNCS, vol. 8441, pp. 441–458. Springer, Heidelberg (2014). doi:10.1007/978-3-642-55220-5_25

14. Cortes, C., Vapnik, V.: Support-vector networks. Mach. Learn. **20**(3), 273–297 (1995)

15. Deng, L., Yu, D.: Deep learning: methods and applications. Found. Trends Signal Process. **7**(3–4), 197–387 (2014)

16. Doget, J., Prouff, E., Rivain, M., Standaert, F.-X.: Univariate side channel attacks and leakage modeling. J. Cryptographic Eng. **1**(2), 123–144 (2011)

17. Duda, R.O., Hart, P.E., Stork, D.G.: Pattern Classification, 2nd edn. Wiley-Interscience (2000)

18. Eiben, A.E., Smith, J.E.: Introduction to Evolutionary Computing. Springer, Heidelberg (2003)

19. Genelle, L., Prouff, E., Quisquater, M.: Thwarting higher-order side channel analysis with additive and multiplicative maskings. In: Preneel, B., Takagi, T. (eds.) CHES 2011. LNCS, vol. 6917, pp. 240–255. Springer, Heidelberg (2011). doi:10.1007/978-3-642-23951-9_16

20. Gierlichs, B., Batina, L., Tuyls, P., Preneel, B.: Mutual information analysis. In: Oswald, E., Rohatgi, P. (eds.) CHES 2008. LNCS, vol. 5154, pp. 426–442. Springer, Heidelberg (2008). doi:10.1007/978-3-540-85053-3_27

21. Gilmore, R., Hanley, N., O'Neill, M.: Neural network based attack on a masked implementation of aes. In: 2015 IEEE International Symposium on Hardware Oriented Security and Trust (HOST), pp. 106–111, May 2015

22. Hermans, M., Schrauwen, B.: Training and analysing deep recurrent neural networks. In: Burges, C.J.C., Bottou, L., Welling, M., Ghahramani, Z., Weinberger, K.Q. (eds.) Advances in Neural Information Processing Systems 26, pp. 190–198. Curran Associates Inc. (2013)

23. Heuser, A., Zohner, M.: Intelligent machine homicide - breaking cryptographic devices using support vector machines. In: Schindler, W., Huss, S.A. (eds.) COSADE 2012. LNCS, vol. 7275, pp. 249–264. Springer, Heidelberg (2012). doi:10.1007/978-3-642-29912-4_18

24. Heyszl, J., Ibing, A., Mangard, S., Santis, F.D., Sigl, G.: Clustering Algorithms for Non-Profiled Single-Execution Attacks on Exponentiations. IACR Cryptology ePrint Archive 2013, 438 (2013)

25. Hochreiter, S.: The vanishing gradient problem during learning recurrent neural nets and problem solutions. Int. J. Uncertain. Fuzziness Knowl. Based Syst. **6**(2), 107–116 (1998)

26. Hochreiter, S., Schmidhuber, J.: Long short-term memory. Neural Comput. **9**(8), 1735–1780 (1997)

27. Hoogvorst, P., Danger, J.-L., Duc, G.: Software implementation of dual-rail representation. In: COSADE, Darmstadt, Germany, 24–25 February 2011

28. Hospodar, G., Gierlichs, B., De Mulder, E., Verbauwhede, I., Vandewalle, J.: Machine learning in side-channel analysis: a first study. J. Cryptographic Eng. **1**(4), 293–302 (2011)

29. Jarrett, K., Kavukcuoglu, K., Ranzato, M., LeCun, Y.: What is the best multistage architecture for object recognition? In: ICCV, pp. 2146–2153. IEEE (2009)

30. Kocher, P., Jaffe, J., Jun, B.: Differential power analysis. In: Wiener, M. (ed.) CRYPTO 1999. LNCS, vol. 1666, pp. 388–397. Springer, Heidelberg (1999). doi:10.1007/3-540-48405-1_25

31. LeCun, Y., Bengio, Y.: Convolutional networks for images, speech, and time series. In: Handbook of Brain Theory and Neural Networks, pp. 255–258. MIT Press, Cambridge (998)
32. Lerman, L., Bontempi, G., Markowitch, O.: Power analysis attack: an approach based on machine learning. Int. J. Appl. Cryptography **3**(2), 97–115 (2014)
33. Lerman, L., Medeiros, S.F., Bontempi, G., Markowitch, O.: A Machine Learning Approach Against a Masked AES. In: Francillon, A., Rohatgi, P. (eds.) CARDIS 2013. LNCS, vol. 8419, pp. 61–75. Springer, Heidelberg (2014). doi:10.1007/978-3-319-08302-5_5
34. Lerman, L., Poussier, R., Bontempi, G., Markowitch, O., Standaert, F.-X.: Template attacks vs. machine learning revisited (and the curse of dimensionality in side-channel analysis). In: Mangard, S., Poschmann, A.Y. (eds.) COSADE 2014. LNCS, vol. 9064, pp. 20–33. Springer, Heidelberg (2015). doi:10.1007/978-3-319-21476-4_2
35. Lomné, V., Prouff, E., Rivain, M., Roche, T., Thillard, A.: How to estimate the success rate of higher-order side-channel attacks, pp. 35–54. Heidelberg (2014)
36. Mangard, S., Oswald, E., Popp, T.: Power Analysis Attacks: Revealing the Secrets of Smart Cards. Springer, December 2006. ISBN 0-387-30857-1, http://www.dpabook.org/
37. Masci, J., Meier, U., Cireşan, D., Schmidhuber, J.: Stacked convolutional auto-encoders for hierarchical feature extraction. In: Honkela, T., Duch, W., Girolami, M., Kaski, S. (eds.) ICANN 2011. LNCS, vol. 6791, pp. 52–59. Springer, Heidelberg (2011). doi:10.1007/978-3-642-21735-7_7
38. Mitchell, M.: An Introduction to Genetic Algorithms. MIT Press, Cambridge (1998)
39. O'Flynn, C., Chen, Z.D.: Chipwhisperer: An open-source platform for hardware embedded security research. Cryptology ePrint Archive, Report 2014/204 (2014). http://eprint.iacr.org/2014/204
40. O'Shea, K., Nash, R.: An introduction to convolutional neural networks. CoRR, abs/1511.08458 (2015)
41. Oswald, E., Mangard, S.: Template attacks on masking—resistance is futile. In: Abe, M. (ed.) CT-RSA 2007. LNCS, vol. 4377, pp. 243–256. Springer, Heidelberg (2006). doi:10.1007/11967668_16
42. Prouff, E., Rivain, M., Bevan, R.: Statistical analysis of second order differential power analysis. IEEE Trans. Computers **58**(6), 799–811 (2009)
43. Rivain, M.: On the exact success rate of side channel analysis in the gaussian model. In: Avanzi, R.M., Keliher, L., Sica, F. (eds.) SAC 2008. LNCS, vol. 5381, pp. 165–183. Springer, Heidelberg (2009). doi:10.1007/978-3-642-04159-4_11
44. Rivain, M., Prouff, E.: Provably secure higher-order masking of AES. In: Mangard, S., Standaert, F.-X. (eds.) CHES 2010. LNCS, vol. 6225, pp. 413–427. Springer, Heidelberg (2010). doi:10.1007/978-3-642-15031-9_28
45. Rokach, L., Maimon, O.: Data Mining with Decision Trees: Theroy and Applications. World Scientific Publishing Co. Inc., River Edge (2008)
46. Salakhutdinov, R., Mnih, A., Hinton, G.: Restricted boltzmann machines for collaborative filtering. In: Proceedings of the 24th International Conference on Machine Learning, ICML 2007, pp. 791–798. ACM, New York (2007)
47. W. Schindler.: Advanced stochastic methods in side channel analysis on block ciphers in the presence of masking. J. Math. Cryptology **2**(3), 291–310 (2008). ISSN (Online) 1862–2984. ISSN (Print) 1862–2976. doi:10.1515/JMC.2008.013
48. Schindler, W., Lemke, K., Paar, C.: A Stochastic Model for Differential Side Channel Cryptanalysis. In: Rao, J.R., Sunar, B. (eds.) CHES 2005. LNCS, vol. 3659, pp. 30–46. Springer, Heidelberg (2005). doi:10.1007/11545262_3

49. Scholkopf, B., Smola, A.J.: Learning with Kernels: Support Vector Machines, Regularization, Optimization, and Beyond. MIT Press, Cambridge (2001)
50. Servant, V., Debande, N., Maghrebi, H., Bringer, J.: Study of a novel software constant weight implementation. In: Joye, M., Moradi, A. (eds.) CARDIS 2014. LNCS, vol. 8968, pp. 35–48. Springer, Heidelberg (2015). doi:10.1007/978-3-319-16763-3_3
51. Silva, T.C., Zhao, L.: Machine Learning in Complex Networks. Springer, Switzerland (2016)
52. Souissi, Y., Nassar, M., Guilley, S., Danger, J.-L., Flament, F.: First principal components analysis: a new side channel distinguisher. In: Rhee, K.-H., Nyang, D.H. (eds.) ICISC 2010. LNCS, vol. 6829, pp. 407–419. Springer, Heidelberg (2011). doi:10.1007/978-3-642-24209-0_27
53. Standaert, F.-X., Malkin, T.G., Yung, M.: A unified framework for the analysis of side-channel key recovery attacks. In: Joux, A. (ed.) EUROCRYPT 2009. LNCS, vol. 5479, pp. 443–461. Springer, Heidelberg (2009). doi:10.1007/978-3-642-01001-9_26
54. TELECOM ParisTech SEN research group. DPA Contest, 2nd edn. (2009–2010). http://www.DPAcontest.org/v2/
55. TELECOM ParisTech SEN research group. DPA Contest, 4th edn. (2013–2014). http://www.DPAcontest.org/v4/
56. Vincent, P., Larochelle, H., Bengio, Y., Manzagol, P.-A.: Extracting and composing robust features with denoising autoencoders. In: Proceedings of the 25th International Conference on Machine Learning, ICML 2008, pp. 1096–1103. ACM, New York (2008)
57. Weston, J., Watkins, C.: Multi-class support vector machines (1998)
58. Xie, J., Xu, L., Chen, E.: Image denoising and inpainting with deep neural networks. In: Pereira, F., Burges, C.J.C., Bottou, L., Weinberger, K.Q. (eds.) Advances in Neural Information Processing Systems 25, pp. 341–349. Curran Associates Inc. (2012)

Cheap and Cheerful: A Low-Cost Digital Sensor for Detecting Laser Fault Injection Attacks

Wei He[(✉)], Jakub Breier, and Shivam Bhasin

Temasek Laboratories, Physical Analysis and Cryptographic Engineering,
Nanyang Technological University, Singapore, Singapore
{he.wei,jbreier,sbhasin}@ntu.edu.sg

Abstract. Fault Injection Attacks (FIAs) have become a critical threat towards prevailing security embedded systems. FIA typically exploits the maliciously induced faults in security ICs for retrieving confidential internals. Since the faults are injected by disturbing circuit behaviors, FIA can possibly be detected in advance by integrating a sensitive sensor. In this paper, a full-digital detection logic against laser fault injection is proposed, which mainly consists of a high-frequency RO watchdog and a disturbance capture for sensing frequency ripples due to laser impact. Practical experiments on Virtex-5 FPGA show that the proposed sensor has fault detection rate of 100 % for both regional and single CLB injection, protecting critical registers of PRESENT-80 cipher, with superior power/spatial security margin compared to a prior PLL-based sensor, while maintaining extremely low cost in hardware. The proposed logic is further applied to protect complete cipher over larger fabric, and the fine-grained fault injection using pulse laser shows a detection rate of 94.20 %, and an alarm rate of 2.63 : 1 in this experiment. Owing to its simple digital architecture, this system can be easily applied into any security-critical ICs.

Keywords: Cryptography · Embedded system · Ring-oscillator · Semi-invasive attack · FPGA

1 Introduction

Hostile implementation circumstances in security applications demand the security-critical circuits to be integrated with a strong protection against various attack threats. In modern cryptography, confidential data is protected by utilizing strong algorithms. However, the real-world implementation of these algorithms in devices inevitably draws numerous vulnerabilities in their applications. Various attack methodologies on the physical layer have been proposed for breaking crypto algorithms or other security-critical applications. The two commonly known methodologies are leakage-based side-channel attacks (SCA [12]), and abnormality-based fault injection attacks [7]. In SCA, the leaked physical information (like power consumption, timing, etc.) is exploited for extracting the secrets [12]. On the other hand, FIA retrieves confidential information by

© Springer International Publishing AG 2016
C. Carlet et al. (Eds.): SPACE 2016, LNCS 10076, pp. 27–46, 2016.
DOI: 10.1007/978-3-319-49445-6_2

analyzing the faulty behavior or faulty outputs from the target when operated under hostile environment. FIA can be widely used for serving different purposes, the most common one being the secret key retrieval [4]. Besides, it can also be used for reverse engineering purpose to deduce the internal architecture of the attacked chip by analyzing its faulty behavior [16]. Moreover, FIA is also a promising method to break the defense of the system, for assisting other hardware-level attacks [1]. Owing to its wide potential in various attacks, fault injection attacks have evolved to be a critical security threat against all kinds of security ICs. It is also commonly tested by certification bodies when evaluating security-critical devices.

The fault injection can be conducted at two levels. First, faults can be globally injected by imposing disturbances into global variables, such as the clock system or power supply of the device under test (DUT) [2]. In this approach, noticeable disturbances are induced in clock or power lines, which are distributed through the global network and affect the critical logic points that are vulnerable in exposure of disturbance. Typically, it is the critical logic path which can easily suffer from setup-time violation by a ripple in clock or power. Another approach to conduct fault injection is to affect the local chip fabric relying on high-precision injection methodologies, as laser (laser fault injection - LFI) or electromagnetic (EM fault injection - EMFI). The faults are injected by making an impact on the signal propagation by external means like EM or directly upsetting stored data bits in memory cells by using strong laser. Since the disturbance can be strictly constrained to a specific chip region, and it is easy to tune the injection time from the equipment, LFI and EMFI are superior to global injections in terms of both precision and controllability. The disadvantage compared to global methods is a high cost of injection equipment.

Protection against fault attacks can be done either at information level or circuit level. Error detection and correction codes find wide applications in information based fault protection [11]. Other kinds of information redundancy, like duplication, can also be used for fault protection. The circuit modification for information redundancy has a finite and non-negligible cost. Moreover, it is a reactive protection, which acts when the fault has already been injected and potentially exploited [1]. The other family of protection is proactive in nature and based on environmental sensors [21]. It monitors environmental parameters and raises an alarm in hostile conditions. Such protections are better for LFI or EMFI techniques which inject faults by controllable injection using high-energy electromagnetic or laser pulses. In this paper, a low-cost and fully digital sensor system is presented for detecting a semi-invasive laser fault injection on-the-fly. This sensor relies on a strict timing violation, for detecting the slight signal oscillation alteration (phase shift) in a watchdog ring oscillator (RO) from laser fault injection.

Contribution: The merit of the proposed technique resides in (a) its superior detection sensitivity and protection coverage against semi-invasive disturbance; (b) the capability of detecting bi-directional frequency ripple (i.e., either acceleration or deceleration of sensitive signal); and (c) fully digital and cost-efficient architecture, which can be easily implemented into any digital/hybrid ICs and FPGAs, for high-security application.

Outline of this paper: The content of this paper is organized as follows: Sect. 2 recalls the technical backgrounds of laser-based fault attacks towards cryptographic primitives in hardware, and the prior countermeasures; In Sect. 3, the proposed low-cost digital sensor system against laser fault injection is elaborated; along with the FPGA implementation details. Sect. 4 describes a series of experimental evaluations in practical high-precision laser fault attacks, with a thorough comparison to a recently proposed PLL based sensor [10,13]. Finally, the work conclusions are drawn in Sect. 5.

2 Background

2.1 Fault Attacks on Cryptographic Primitives

Integrated circuits (IC) can be easily affected by environmental conditions they operate in. One of the first phenomena observed in this direction was a higher number of failures in satellite systems caused by cosmic rays [5]. A new area, testing reliability of IC has emerged since then - *failure analysis*. More then 20 years later, Boneh, DeMillo, and Lipton [7] have shown that such failures can be used for attacking cryptographic primitives implemented in integrated circuits, naming this area *fault injection attacks*.

Currently, fault attacks are among the most popular physical attacks on cryptographic implementations, together with side-channel attacks. There are various techniques allowing attackers to influence electronic devices, ranging from low-cost solutions, such as voltage or clock glitches, to expensive ones, such as laser fault injection or focused ion beam [3]. If the attacker can control the device in order to make a precise errors during computations, some confidential internals, particularly as crypto keys, can be easily revealed. For example, it was shown that the full AES key can be recovered by injecting just one fault in the penultimate round [15].

For testing our countermeasure, we have chosen the laser fault injection technique, which provides very good spatial and timing resolution and therefore can accurately measure the effectivity of the fault protection.

2.2 Laser Fault Injection

Optical fault injection attacks were presented by Skorobogatov and Anderson in 2002 [18]. In the paper, authors used a flashlight for inducing faults in a microcontroller. However, such technique is not very precise, therefore, laser fault injection has quickly become the most used optical fault attack technique.

In this approach, a laser source attached to a microscope is placed over the chip, so the laser beam can lead to charge transmission in signal paths, or the ionization effect on transistors. In general, one can decide whether to approach the chip from the frontside or the backside. For the *frontside injection,*

either green (532 nm) or red (808 nm) lasers are used because there is no need
to penetrate the silicon substrate. The advantage of this method is the direct
visibility of components of the chip. However, metallic layers can completely
nullify the effect of the beam. Especially modern ICs have several metal layers
and therefore, it makes it infeasible to use this method. In the *backside injection*,
one has to use at least near-infrared laser (1064 nm) because of the substrate. It is
advisable to mill down and polish the substrate in order to make the components
accessible and to achieve higher precision by avoiding the light refraction.

When it comes to effects on FPGAs, the resulted phenomena can cause a
direct bit upset in memory cells, either in the flip-flops, in block memories, or in
the configuration bits in reconfigurable circuit [17]. It can also affect the signal
propagation, by either increasing or decreasing the signal transmission, causing
timing violation in logic chain.

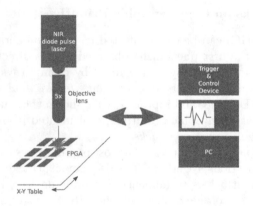

Fig. 1. Example of laser fault injection setup testbench.

An example of laser fault injection setup is depicted in Fig. 1. On the left
side, we can see the laser source, with the power usually ranging in several
Watts, attached to a magnifying objective lens (in our setup we use 5× magnification). There is also an X-Y table that is capable to precisely position the
device under test (FPGA in the picture). On the right side, there are acquisition,
communication and control devices. Normally, data is sent from the PC to the
DUT, which sends a trigger signal before processing the data. Trigger & Control
device captures this signal and sends a command to the laser source to perform
the injection. To get precise timing and laser diode current, it is advisable to use
a digital sampling oscilloscope.

2.3   Countermeasures

Numerous countermeasures against fault injection have been developed in prior
literatures, which basically drop within two scopes: First, the cipher itself is
fortified with capability of detecting data abnormality. In this approach, the

cipher primitive needs to be merged with the detection logic, as the concurrent error detection (CED) proposed by Karri et al. in [11]. In this method, parity bits are computed in advance to predict and compare with the parity of the output vector in each computation round. If they are equal, error check is passed, and otherwise, error/errors occurred in ciphering computation of this round. Another popular idea to detect the error is to simply duplicate the original cipher in parallel, and both are fed with the same plaintext. In the output side, the two outputs from the genuine and the duplicated rails are compared to see if any faults occurred in either rails. The pitfalls of these redundancy based detection can be summarized as follows:

1. **High-Cost:** The cost of these redundancy error check logics are resource consuming. This is because the detection needs to simulate the real data computation, or parity computation at each computation round, so as to be compared with real cipher outputs. Prior work reported roughly doubled hardware cost using these methods.
2. **Low-Detection Coverage:** Since these detection base on the data or parity comparison, a fatal problem arisen here is that not all the faults can be detected. For instance, parity comparison normally detect odd-number errors occurred inside the algorithm, and the duplication method cannot detect the faults that are simultaneously perturbated into the same logic points of the two rails.
3. **No Prediction Margin:** These detection logics can only detect the faults that have already been successfully injected into the cipher cores. In other words, the on-going injection campaign cannot be predicted in advance.

On contrary, sensor based countermeasures [13,21] are alternatively used for detecting the fault injection on-the-fly. In this approach, an independent logic can be used as the injection sensor, being implemented together with the protected cipher. The sensor should have a higher sensitivity against the disturbance induced by the injection equipment, which should have logic (`alarm`) signal responding to injection turbulence earlier than the accomplished cipher faults. More precisely, the injection disturbance should have more significant impacts on the sensor, by inducing specific alarm signal. Moreover, the detection coverage of fault types should also be sufficiently high.

2.4   Previous Works on Sensor Based Countermeasures

As a summary, all the injections discussed above can cause change on signal propagation. Therefore, if a logic can be sufficiently sensitive in detecting abnormal frequency change, the malicious injections can be detected.

There are several techniques that can be employed in FPGA in order to detect disturbances by a laser. In the following, we will explain the works proposed so far in this area.

Glitch Detector. Glitch detector is a timing-violation based sensor that was originally proposed for detecting any timing violation using power or clock global fault injections [8]. Later research mentions its partial effectiveness against EM fault injections [21]. This logic consists in detecting the violation of a guarding delay prior to any timing violation. The clock signal is used as a reference to be able to draw comparisons between the guarding delay and the clock period to a flip-flop, as illustrated in Fig. 2(a). The output of flip-flop serves as the alarm signal which stays in low voltage level in absence of disturbance. In case the external disturbance increases the signal delay in CK, the setup-time will be violated which triggers a high voltage level in alarm signal, as illustrated by the timing diagram in Fig. 2(b). The pitfalls of this logic are twofold. Firstly, the detector is suited for global disturbances. However, using a network of detectors can also detect local injections to some extent [21]. Secondly, the detector is designed against injection method which increases propagation delay, while remaining insensitive to techniques which can accelerate the signal propagation as shown in Fig. 2(c).

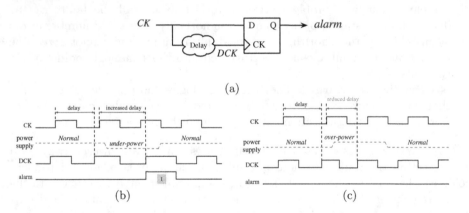

Fig. 2. (a) Topology of glitch detector; Timing diagram of disturbance detection by glitch detector under: (b) delayed signal propagation, and (c) accelerated signal propagation.

Ring-Oscillator with Frequency Counter. As a low-cost oscillation generator, digital Ring-Oscillator (RO) has been widely used in security applications, such as the unclonable crypto key generation [20]. RO is a closed loop chained an by odd number of inverters, as sketched in Fig. 3(a). The oscillation frequency of a RO is determined by the summed-up signal propagation time in this loop. Any anomaly or disturbance would normally impact the RO resulting in change of oscillation frequency and phase. As aforementioned, many fault injections can cause timing change in signal path, hence RO can be potentially used to detect the on-going injection campaign.

Basically, the oscillation distortion in either phase or frequency can be captured by a digital counter [9], and the size (bit-width) of the counter can be

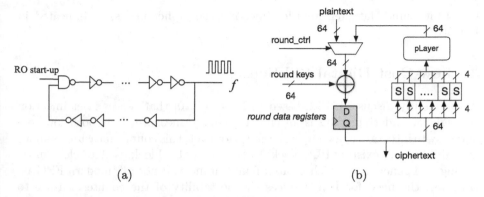

Fig. 3. (a) Inverter based digital ring-oscillator; (b) Round architecture of PRESENT-80 cipher.

determined by the used oscillation frequency and the time-window of the measurement. The drawbacks using frequency counter are clear. First, to enlarge the disturbance impact to a RO, the frequency of this RO should be high. Therefore, the required bit-width of the capture RO should be sufficiently big, in order to prevent any data overflow during the measurement in the time window. A smaller time window can reduce the size of the counter, however it risks the capture precision. In addition, the frequency measurement and comparison judgement by RO needs a significantly long time to be completed, hence the response to detected injection campaign cannot be immediate. And the large size of this logic is also vulnerable and easier to be affected by fault injections.

Ring-Oscillator with PLL. Phase-Locked-Loop (PLL) was originally used by Miura et al. in [13] for detecting the phase shift disturbance in RO by EMFI. In this proposal, the frequency of a RO is fed into the frequency input of a PLL, hence any disturbance in phase shift comparison (must have two frequencies, one is reference to check the change of phase/frequency distortion).

A technique, using digital RO for detecting frequency disturbance caused by laser, and a PLL, allowing detection of frequency changes in RO, was published in [10]. By using this technique, authors were able to detect faults caused by the laser with the detection rate more than 92 %.

Since the PLL is a scarce resource and not always available, we propose a fully-digital sensor which also allows us to achieve higher detection rates.

2.5 Lightweight PRESENT Cipher

To validate the effectiveness of the proposed countermeasure against LFIs, The *ISO/IEC* standardized PRESENT-80 block cipher [6] is selected as the protection target. This cipher is a classic substitution permutation network (SPN), which consists of 64-bit AddRoundKey, 16 4-bit S-box and 64 bit pLayers, to en-/decrypt 64-bit plaintext/ciphertext using 80- or 128-bit key. In this work, we target its 64-bit round data registers for injecting the cipher faults, as indicated in Fig. 3(b).

3   Low-Cost Digital LFI Sensor

As previously discussed, PLL-based LFI sensor [10] that senses laser injection through an underlying RO is an effective countermeasure. It is both low-cost and easy to integrate in a complex circuit. However, this countermeasure assumes availability of an existing PLL block. PLL is an analog block used for clock monitoring and generation which is often found in most, if not all, modern FPGAs. However, the need for PLL reduces the portability of the countermeasure to ASIC. Even if PLL are available in ASIC, being a scarce resource, it might not be viable to use it only for countermeasures due to area, power and cost consideration. To overcome this limitation, we propose a fully-digital low-cost LFI sensor. It precisely replaces the PLL with an all digital clock monitoring circuit while still keeping the watchdog RO. The fully digital nature of the sensor makes it versatile for different hardware platforms. The low-cost motivates the possibility of deploying several instances of the sensor if needed. As shown later, this all-digital sensor also shows a much higher detection rate than the original PLL-based solution. In the rest of the section, we discuss the design and features of the proposed sensor followed by its implementation details on FPGA platform. Being an all digital proposal, the cost in ASIC is also limited to only few gates.

3.1   Digital Fault Injection Detector

In this paper, we introduce a novel fault injection detector, as sketched in Fig. 4. This system consists of a multi-inverter RO serving as the frequency disturbance **Watchdog Sensor**, and a **Disturbance Capture** logic comprised of two flip-flops and a logic gate i.e. $(Q1\&\overline{Q2})$. The frequencies from two points $(f1.f2)$ on this RO loop are fetched to be sampled by two flip-flops $(FF1.FF2)$, being sampled by a derived frequency $(ck\text{-}delay)$. The two-bit vectors from the two flip-flops manifest whether abnormality occurred in the RO. The function of the entire detection system is detailed in Fig. 5.

In this work, the outputs of three consecutive inverters in **Watchdog Sensor** RO are used as the inputs for the **Disturbance Capture** part, named as $f1$, ck, $f2$ by signal propagation sequence. Given a stable electrical environment, the three signals will have the same frequency with fixed phase shift, and an opposite polarity to signal ck, w.r.t. $f1$ and $f2$. FF1 and FF2 are both triggered by the **falling edge** of ck, as seen in Fig. 5(a). In absence of signal delay from RO to flip-flops, the sampled values for FF1 and FF2 are respectively '1' and '0', as indicated by the blue dotted arrow lines in Fig. 5(a). **Noticeably**, the ripples in this RO will identically affect three frequencies, leading to no impact on the **Disturbance Capture** and thus giving false negatives.

In order to capture anomalies, a **delay factor** is intentionally inserted into the clock inputs of FF1 and FF2, which is used for introducing a propagation

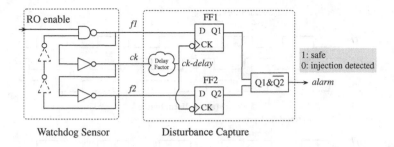

Fig. 4. Topology of the schemed fault injection sensor system.

delay of signal *ck* by several clock cycles. In the sequel, each flip-flop is actually clocked by the falling-edge of a delayed *ck* cycle or *ck-delay*, as highlighted by the red dotted arrow lines in Fig. 5(a). The significant merit here is that the ripple in RO only affects the *f1* and *f2* at the injection moment, without immediately affecting the sampling frequency (*ck-delay*) on Disturbance Capture. In this way, this system is able to capture bi-directional abnormalities in RO frequency ripples, as explained in the following subsection. The area report is given in Table 1. The delay can also be configured by appropriate routing only.

Table 1. Area report of the all-digital LFI sensor

Component	LUT	DFF
Watchdog sensor	3	0
Disturbance capture	1	2
Delay	1	0

3.2 Timing Violation Detection

In this part, we qualitatively analyse the proposed sensor against various timing impacts of laser injection to the RO.

Delayed Propagation. In case the signal propagation is delayed by the LFI, the frequency of RO can be reduced shortly, as indicated by Fig. 5(b). In this situation, the duty cycles of *f1* and *f2* are temporarily extended. As discussed before, both FF1 and FF2 are clocked by the delayed clock signal *ck-delay*, hence the sampling time in flip-flops at the injection moment is not impacted by the RO disturbance, which is very likely to result in the set-up time violation at *f2*. As can be seen in Fig. 5(a), the sampled value vector from FF1 and FF2 is '10' under normal operation. Hence, the sampled vector in presence of timing violation from delayed signal propagation is '11', as highlighted in Fig. 5(b).

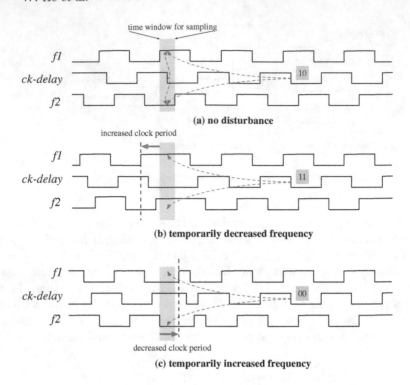

Fig. 5. Timing of low/high-frequency ripple detection. (Color figure online)

Accelerated Propagation. As aforementioned, the frequency can also be transiently increased by the LFI. In this way, the duty cycle of both *f1* and *f2* can be reduced when the injection affects the RO. Comparatively, the timing will be violated in FF1, rather than FF2, *cf.* preceding situation. As explained in Fig. 5(c), the sampled value vector from FF1 and FF2 becomes '00' from the normal '10'.

Complex Disturbances. It should be emphasized that the timing analyses of disturbance in RO frequency above only considers a single frequency cycle. In a real scenario, the disturbance can be more complex and prevail for several clock cycles to produce a prolonged impact. Hence the extended or shortened duty cycle in *f1* and *f2* can be longer and more complicated than those single-cycle ripples illustrated in Fig. 5(a) and (b). Nevertheless, these complex event can be seen as a combination of several delayed and accelerated event. The timing violation will still be captured as the proposed countermeasure latches the first alarm glitch appearing in each disturbance-period. It allows to alert the main system and launch the fault recovery mechanism. This would also cover the less frequent sampled value of '01'. Hence, the complexity in alarm pattern dropping inside the disturbance time window does not impede the disturbance detection.

Since alarm signal is computed from $Q1\&\overline{Q2}$, both abnormalities can result in an alarm value change from '1' to '0' for alerting the cipher to respond the on-going injection campaign immediately. Here, '&' represents logical AND.

3.3   Target FPGA and Digital-Sensor Implementation

As one of the major FPGA vendors, Xilinx provides a wide range of commercial FPGAs with different technologies. In our work, we tested our circuit on Virtex-5 FPGA which is one of the most popular SRAM based FPGAs on market in recent decade. The basic architecture includes a massive Configurable Logic Block (CLB) array, and numerous peripheral functional logic modules, as Block RAM, Digital Signal Processor (DSP), Digital Clock Manager (DCM), Phase Locked Loop (PLL), as well as rich routing resource channels. In Xilinx terminology, each CLB is comprised by two slices for deploying the implemented logic. Four Look-up-tables (LUTs) in each slice are the main logic resource for implementing the synthesized logic gates, and 4 flip-flops can be configured as registers or latches. A switch-box is deployed besides each CLB for providing rich interconnected resources between the CLB logic to external routing channels. In this work, we mainly target the 64-bit round data registers of PRESENT-80 cipher (see Fig. 3(b)), which are implemented inside the 4 flip-flops in each slice.

The implemented circuit in FPGA-editor view is shown in Fig. 6. To evaluate the detection capability of the proposed sensor system against the previously proposed PLL-based LFI sensor [10], we have deployed both of them on the target Virtex-5 FPGA with similar implementation scheme. Since each slice in Virtex-5 FPGA has 4 flip-flops, we implemented the 64-bit round data registers of PRESENT-80 cipher into 16 slices (8 CLBs) as a rectangle. The RO routing path is forced to cross the 4 corners, so as to encompass the protected data registers, as shown in Fig. 6. As shown in Fig. 6, the all-digital Disturbance Capture using the 3 inverter outputs from the RO are deployed outside the RO routings. In the second implementation, the Disturbance Capture is simply replaced by PLL (not shown) to restore the reference implementation of [10].

4   Experimental Evaluation

4.1   Experimental Setup

The device-under-test (DUT) is a Xilinx Virtex-5 (VLX50T) FPGA, manufactured by 65 nm technology with a flip-chip package. The mother FPGA board (Digilent *Genesys*) is fixed on a motorized 2-dimensional (X-Y) stepper stage, with 0.05 μm minimum step size. As the chip substrate may significantly absorb the energy carried by laser photons, we have mechanically milled down the substrate of this FPGA to roughly 130 μm, in order to have sufficient energy penetrated into the active logic (i.e., transistor) layer. Arduino Due board is programmed to bridge the controller GUI in computer and the cipher + countermeasure system implemented on FPGA. This setting allows

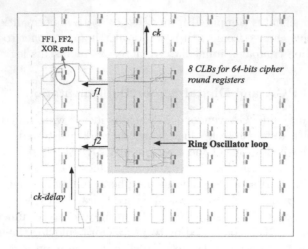

Fig. 6. FPGA implementation scheme of the proposed sensor system and the protected 64-bit round data registers of the PRESENT-80 cipher.

us to observe and record the real-time encryption outcome and the alarm signal, as well as the location coordinates for each injection of a LFI region scan. The setup is sketched in Fig. 7.

We used a diode pulse laser with 1064 nm wavelength. A 5× magnification reduced the spot size to 60×14 μm, but the effective size is roughly 10 % of this size, allowing us to do a very precise laser injection. Injection time can be varied in nanoseconds.

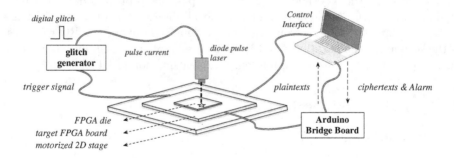

Fig. 7. Illustration of LFI experimental setup.

4.2   Timing Response

Figure 8 shows the timing of the critical signals of this system. `Injection Trigger` is provided by the cipher which denotes the start of the target computation round for a fault perturbation. `RO frequency` is a signal oscillation of

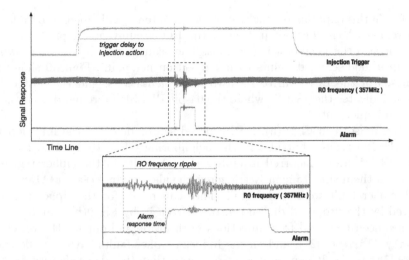

Fig. 8. Timing of signal response of a detected laser fault injection.

the watchdog RO. In this figure, we captured the signal from a tiny RO with 357 MHz frequency. `Alarm` flags the occurrence of timing violation induced by laser injection. The trigger delay is comprised by (i) the fixed signal delay (from trigger signal on chip glitch generator), and (ii) the adjustable delay time from glitch generator to activation of the diode pulse laser. In our setup, the first fixed delay portion is roughly 100 ns and the second delay is properly set to ensure the injection occurs roughly at the next clock edge. The pulse length of each injection is set randomly between 100 and 200 ns to guarantee the laser is sufficiently powerful to cause bit upsets in registers. The time period of RO ripple is determined by the laser pulse length of each injection. The response time from the frequency ripple appearance to the rising edge of set of the alarm signal is affected by prolonged signal propagation from *ck* to *ck-delay* (see Fig. 4).

4.3 Scanning Results

We have performed the LFI on two implementations on the DUT. The first one was a laser scan of regional CLB array, and the second was a fine-grained single CLB scan. We categorized the faults into three types: (a) `Only Alarm` (Case_(1)) represent the detected injection without cipher faults; (b) `Fault + Alarm` (Case_(2)) refer to the detected injections that induced cipher faults, and (c) `Only Fault` Case_(3) denote the injections that induced cipher faults without triggering the alarm. Scanning results are stated in the following subsections.

Regional Scan. In the first scenario, the implementation details of the cipher and the device architecture are supposed to be unknown to adversaries. For launching valid fault injection into the point-of-interest (POI), a coarse surface scan towards a big fabric region must be performed by adversaries for finding the POIs. In this experiment, the scan region is intentionally focused on a larger silicon region which does not just cover the RO circumvented cipher data registers, but also the neighbouring regions. The scan matrix is 300 × 300, which results in 90,000 scanned points with 1 injection per point. Figure 9 shows the comparison of the LFI scan of the two implementations, and the dotted line rectangle indicates the 8 CLBs where the 64-bit PRESENT round data registers have been implemented.

As can be seen in Fig. 9(a), a PLL-based sensor detected the injection not just in the RO region, but also in the neighboring CLBs (Only Alarm = 271). A few LFI injections incurred in cipher (Data) faults in the cipher registers, whilst all of them simultaneously triggered the alarm signal (Fault+Alarm = 3), i.e., no cipher fault went undetected. The scan result for the cipher registers protected by the proposed digital sensor is given in by Fig. 9(b). Similarly, the alarm has been triggered from injections both inside and outside the watchdog RO (Only Alarm = 5421), and all the induced cipher faults have been detected (Fault+Alarm = 8). It can be clearly observed that the alarm density for this scan is much higher (5421 vs 271), which implies that this digital sensor system is more sensitive to laser injection *cf.* PLL sensor.

If we only consider the cipher faults, the Detection Rate of the sensor can be computed by $detection\ rate = \frac{Case\_(2)}{Case\_(2)+Case\_(3)}$. According to our experimental results, the Detection Rates for both regional LFI scans are 100 %. Another metric that can be used for quantifying the countermeasure is the Alarm Rate, which gives the ratio between the triggered alarms and induced cipher faults. Alarm Rate is fair to be applied in a more realistic scenario, this is because the adversaries typically need to perform tedious scan over the chip for finding the exact location of POIs. Any triggered alarm (even without cipher faults) alerts the system to respond to the on-going LFIs, hence paralyzes the attackers. $Alarm\ rate = \frac{Case\_(1)+Case\_(2)}{Case\_(2)+Case\_(3)}$ is used to compute the ratio, which gives 91.33:1 for the PLL sensor, and 678.63:1 for the digital sensor in this experiment. In addition, for the digital sensor, the lowest laser power to induce the cipher faults is 75 % of its full strength, and the lowest power to trigger the alarm is 44 %, which further certifies that the sensor is more sensitive to the LFIs, which offers a power security margin of 31 %. The detailed comparison results are provided in the upper part of Table 2.

Single-CLB Scan. A more rigid scenario was also evaluated, which assumes that the adversary knows the details of the implementation and device architecture, particularly the accurate location of the CLB on chip where the security-sensitive round data registers were situated. This way, the adversary is able to directly focus on the CLB to launch a fine-grain fault injection campaign. In this attack, we target a single CLB which has 4 cipher registers implemented inside. Since the effective region of the laser beam is smaller than the CLB size, the scan is still necessary, but the chance to induce cipher faults in registers is much higher. Here, the scan matrix is reduced to 150 × 150, again with 1 injection per point. The experiment results are shown in Fig. 10. Similar to the region scan,

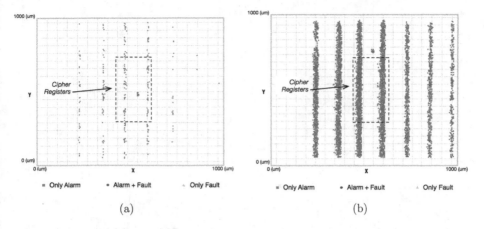

Fig. 9. Laser fault injection scan to regional silicon (a) PLL based LFI sensor; (b) the proposed digital LFI sensor.

injections to both implementation incurred cipher faults and alarm, as summarized in the lower part of Table 2. Results show that PLL sensor detected 284 injection without cipher faults, and 33 injections with cipher faults. Noticeably, 1 cipher fault went undetected. In comparison, 4461 injection without cipher faults have been detected using the proposed digital sensor, and all of the 99 cipher faults triggered the alarm. The result implies a higher sensitivity using this RO based digital sensor, *cf.* PLL sensor, under the assumption that the attack was performed by well-prepared adversaries. Similarly, for the digital sensor, the lowest power for triggering alarm (42 %) is lower than the minimum power inducing cipher fault (63 %), with a power security margin of 21 %.

While one cipher fault was missed by the PLL-based sensor (97.06 % detection rate), the digital sensor shows 100 % detection rate. The general **Alarm Rate** is noticeably higher than the PLL counterpart (46.06:1 vs 9.32:1), as seen in Table 2. As explained before, any triggered alarm (detected injection either with or without induced cipher faults) would prevent the attack in a more realistic scenario, so it is safe to conclude that this digital sensor is superior in defending the LFI attacks. At the same time, it has much lower area cost than a scarce PLL block.

4.4 Full Cipher Protection

In total, 24 CLBs are covered by this watchdog RO. However, previous experiments have shown that the injections to neighboring CLBs are also able to trigger the alarm (see Fig. 9), so this RO can actually cover a larger fabric region. In this experiment, we deployed 2 PRESENT-80 ciphers in parallel for filling up the logic resources in a big area of a clock region, as indicated by **PRESENT 1** and **PRESENT 2** in Fig. 11. The higher logic density helps to yield more valid cipher faults.

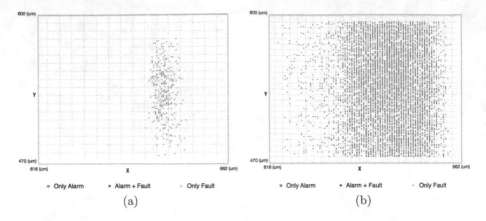

Fig. 10. Laser fault injection scan to a single CLB: (a) PLL based LFI sensor; (b) the proposed digital LFI sensor.

In this experiment, the LFI scan is launched towards the region of the two implemented ciphers, with the scan matrix of 300×300 with single injection per point. Similar to prior campaigns, the laser power level is set to random, between 40 % to 100 % of the full laser strength. Figure 12 gives the distributions of different fault types. Due to the lower injection density, the number of observed faults is less than the preceding experiments, while information can still be extracted. There were 69 injections resulting in cipher faults, and among those, 65 triggered the alarm (`Fault+Alarm` = 65), leaving only 4 undetected (`Only Fault` = 4). Besides, alarm has been triggered for 116 times without cipher faults (`Only Alarm` = 116). Thus, the `Detection Rate`, computed using the equations from Table 2, for this experiment is 94.20 %, and `Alarm Rate` is 2.63:1. This outcome demonstrates that the `Detection Rate` for protecting the whole cipher is still very high. Even with a reduced `Alarm Rate`, the chance to trigger the alarm is still 2.63 times of the chance to induce cipher faults for this densely implemented complete PRESENT-80 primitive. The faults marked as exceptional were faults observed on the I/O and power pads and not sensitive (unrelated to cipher) in nature.

4.5   Further Discussions

Timing Tuning of Delay Factor. As discussed in Sect. 3, a prolonged delay from *ck* to *ck-delay* must be ensured, in order to enforce the falling-edge of *ck-delay* dropping between the rising-edges of *f1* and *f2*, in absence of laser disturbance. This proper timing can be easily achieved by adjusting the propagation time of the routing. Two methods can be applied for this purpose: First, the third-party toolkit can be relied on to control the routing delay for Xilinx FPGAs, such as RapidSmith and Torc [14, 19]. Another, easier method, is to insert a transparent LUT between *ck* and *ck-delay*, configured as

Table 2. Experimental results comparison between the PLL based sensor and the presented digital sensor using LFIs.

		Only Alarm Case_(1)	Fault+Alarm Case_(2)	Only Fault Case_(3)	Scan Matrix	RO freq. (MHz)
PLL LFI Sensor (Region Scan)	No.	271	3	0	300×300	≈ 220
	min. Power	54 %	90 %	n/a		
	Detection	Successful		Failed		
	Detection rate	$\frac{Case\_(2)}{Case\_(2)+Case\_(3)} = 100\%$				
	Alarm rate	$\frac{Case\_(1)+Calse\_(2)}{Case\_(2)+Case\_(3)} = 91.33 : 1$				
Digital LFI Sensor (Region Scan)	No.	5421	8	0	300×300	≈ 206
	min. Power	44 %	75 %	n/a		
	Detection	Successful		Failed		
	Detection rate	$\frac{Case\_(2)}{Case\_(2)+Case\_(3)} = 100\%$				
	Alarm rate	$\frac{Case\_(1)+Calse\_(2)}{Case\_(2)+Case\_(3)} = 678.63 : 1$				
PLL LFI Sensor (CLB Scan)	No.	284	33	1	150×150	≈ 220
	min.Power	60 %	75 %	n/a		
	Detection	Successful		Failed		
	Detection rate	$\frac{Case\_(2)}{Case\_(2)+Case\_(3)} = 97.06\%$				
	Alarm rate	$\frac{Case\_(1)+Calse\_(2)}{Case\_(2)+Case\_(3)} = 9.32 : 1$				
Digital LFI Sensor (CLB Scan)	No.	4461	99	0	150×150	≈ 206
	min. Power	42 %	63 %	n/a		
	Detection	Successful		Failed		
	Detection rate	$\frac{Case\_(2)}{Case\_(2)+Case\_(3)} = 100\%$				
	Alarm rate	$\frac{Case\_(1)+Calse\_(2)}{Case\_(2)+Case\_(3)} = 46.06 : 1$				

''Route-Thrus'' property, where the LUT has no logic function, only serving as a route point. By relocating the location of this LUT, the delay can be adjusted.

Detection Capability Against Other Fault Injection Methods. In this paper, only laser based fault injection is discussed. However, the proposed logic is still promising to be used as a sensor against other fault perturbation techniques, such as EM based fault injection (EMFI). EMFI basically induces eddy current in circuit for causing signal errors, and the current direction relies on the direction of the pulse EM field, i.e., the position of the EM probe. If the current direction follows the signal propagation direction of the watchdog RO, RO frequency would be temporarily accelerated (high-frequency ripple), and otherwise, low-frequency ripple. Therefore, the bi-directional detection capability of the proposed digital sensor is specially useful to detect the EMFI. As well, glitches on power supply

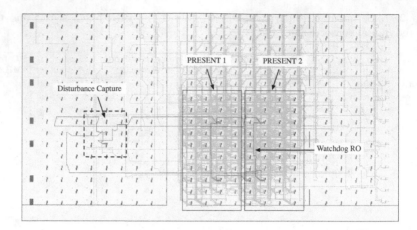

Fig. 11. Countermeasure configuration for protecting full PRESENT cipher.

would change the RO frequency, hence it should be also effective against global fault injection on power supply on the chip.

False Positives. One consideration for the proposed countermeasure is the unwanted false positives that may arise from neighbouring components or environmental variation. As shown in the results, the countermeasure can only be triggered when laser power is in medium to high ranges. Generating such high energy on board is not be obvious for a big range of devices. Moreover, environmental variations are gradual in nature and RO is inherently resistant to such changes. Thus the chances of false positives are quite low for the proposed countermeasure.

5   Conclusions

In this paper, a low-cost fully digital sensor for detecting the malicious laser fault injection in security-critical ICs is presented. This system consists of a multiple-inverter high-frequency RO for producing a stable frequency oscillation, and a disturbance capture logic for detecting the frequency ripple on this RO. In presence of any disturbance from an on-going laser injection, the frequency ripple on RO can be captured by timing violation in the two flip-flops, hence alerting the system with an alarm signal. The effectiveness of this system is validated on Xilinx 65 nm Virtex-5 FPGA. Experimental results on both round data registers and full PRESENT-80 cipher show that the proposed digital sensor has a high fault Detection Rate, as compare to PLL-based sensor, and being significantly superior in terms of alarm sensitivity (Alarm Rate) against laser injections. Since the timing violation can be bi-directionally detected by the two flip-flops, both low-frequency and high-frequency disturbances can be captured, which exceeds the prior glitch-detector countermeasure. Owing to its

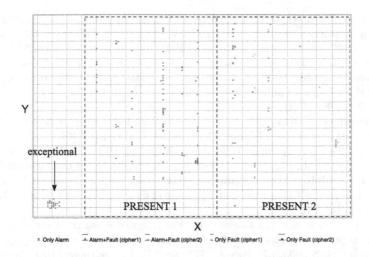

Y

exceptional

PRESENT 1   PRESENT 2

X

□ Only Alarm   ─▲─ Alarm+Fault (cipher1)   ─▲─ Alarm+Fault (cipher2)   ─ Only Fault (cipher1)   ─▲─ Only Fault (cipher2)

Fig. 12. LFI detection experiment on the two full PRESENT-80 ciphers.

pure digital and simple architecture, this system can be easily deployed into any digital/hybrid IC environments, particularly as Internet-of-Things (IoT) or embedded endpoints of Cyber-Physical System (CPS) with restricted power and hardware resources.

In the future work, we plan to validate its detection capability against EM and power/clock glitch injection. Moreover, it will be interesting to explore more precise laser setup and the physical limits of proposed countermeasure against laser spot size.

References

1. Amiel, F., Villegas, K., Feix, B., Marcel, L.: Passive and active combined attacks: combining fault attacks and side channel analysis. In: Workshop on Fault Diagnosis and Tolerance in Cryptography, FDTC 2007, pp. 92–102. IEEE (2007)
2. Bar-El, H., Choukri, H., Naccache, D., Tunstall, M., Whelan, C.: The sorcerer's apprentice guide to fault attacks. Proc. IEEE **94**(2), 370–382 (2006)
3. Barenghi, A., Breveglieri, L., Koren, I., Naccache, D.: Fault injection attacks on cryptographic devices: theory, practice, and countermeasures. Proc. IEEE **100**(11), 3056–3076 (2012)
4. Biham, E., Shamir, A.: Differential fault analysis of secret key cryptosystems. In: Kaliski, B.S. (ed.) CRYPTO 1997. LNCS, vol. 1294, pp. 513–525. Springer, Heidelberg (1997). doi:10.1007/BFb0052259
5. Binder, D., Smith, E.C., Holman, A.B.: Satellite anomalies from galactic cosmic rays. IEEE Trans. Nucl. Sci. **22**(6), 2675–2680 (1975)
6. Bogdanov, A., Knudsen, L.R., Leander, G., Paar, C., Poschmann, A., Robshaw, M.J.B., Seurin, Y., Vikkelsoe, C.: PRESENT: an ultra-lightweight block cipher. In: Paillier, P., Verbauwhede, I. (eds.) CHES 2007. LNCS, vol. 4727, pp. 450–466. Springer, Heidelberg (2007). doi:10.1007/978-3-540-74735-2_31

7. Boneh, D., DeMillo, R.A., Lipton, R.J.: On the importance of checking crypto-graphic protocols for faults. In: Fumy, W. (ed.) EUROCRYPT 1997. LNCS, vol. 1233, pp. 37–51. Springer, Heidelberg (1997). doi:10.1007/3-540-69053-0_4
8. Endo, S., Li, Y., Homma, N., Sakiyama, K., Ohta, K., Aoki, T.: An efficient coun-termeasure against fault sensitivity analysis using configurable delay blocks. In: 2012 Workshop on Fault Diagnosis and Tolerance in Cryptography (FDTC), pp. 95–102. IEEE (2012)
9. Hammouri, G., Akdemir, K., Sunar, B.: Novel PUF-based error detection methods in finite state machines. In: Lee, P.J., Cheon, J.H. (eds.) ICISC 2008. LNCS, vol. 5461, pp. 235–252. Springer, Heidelberg (2009). doi:10.1007/978-3-642-00730-9_15
10. He, W., Breier, J., Bhasin, S., Miura, N., Nagata, M.: Ring oscillator under laser: potential of pll based countermeasure against laser fault injection. In: International Workshop on Fault Diagnosis and Tolerance in Cryptography 2016, pp. 1–12. IEEE, August 2016
11. Karri, R., Kuznetsov, G., Goessel, M.: Parity-based concurrent error detection of substitution-permutation network block ciphers. In: Walter, C.D., Koç, Ç.K., Paar, C. (eds.) CHES 2003. LNCS, vol. 2779, pp. 113–124. Springer, Heidelberg (2003). doi:10.1007/978-3-540-45238-6_10
12. Kocher, P., Jaffe, J., Jun, B.: Differential power analysis. In: Wiener, M. (ed.) CRYPTO 1999. LNCS, vol. 1666, pp. 388–397. Springer, Heidelberg (1999). doi:10.1007/3-540-48405-1_25
13. Miura, N., Najm, Z., He, W., Bhasin, S., Ngo, X.T., Nagata, M., Danger, J.L.: Pll to the rescue: a novel em fault countermeasure. In: Proceedings of the 53rd Annual Design Automation Conference, p. 90. ACM (2016)
14. Moradi, A., Immler, V.: Early propagation and imbalanced routing, how to dimin-ish in FPGAs. In: Batina, L., Robshaw, M. (eds.) CHES 2014. LNCS, vol. 8731, pp. 598–615. Springer, Heidelberg (2014). doi:10.1007/978-3-662-44709-3_33
15. Saha, D., Mukhopadhyay, D., RoyChowdhury, D.: A diagonal fault attack on the advanced encryption standard. Cryptology ePrint Archive, Report 2009/581 (2009). http://eprint.iacr.org/2009/581
16. Pedro, M., Soos, M., Guilley, S.: FIRE: fault injection for reverse engineering. In: Ardagna, C.A., Zhou, J. (eds.) WISTP 2011. LNCS, vol. 6633, pp. 280–293. Springer, Heidelberg (2011). doi:10.1007/978-3-642-21040-2_20
17. Selmke, B., Brummer, S., Heyszl, J., Sigl, G.: Precise laser fault injections into 90 nm and 45 nm SRAM-cells. In: Homma, N., Medwed, M. (eds.) CARDIS 2015. LNCS, vol. 9514, pp. 193–205. Springer, Heidelberg (2016). doi:10.1007/978-3-319-31271-2_12
18. Skorobogatov, S.P., Anderson, R.J.: Optical fault induction attacks. In: Kaliski, B.S., Koç, K., Paar, C. (eds.) CHES 2002. LNCS, vol. 2523, pp. 2–12. Springer, Heidelberg (2003). doi:10.1007/3-540-36400-5_2
19. Steiner, N., Wood, A., Shojaei, H., Couch, J., Athanas, P., French, M.: Torc: towards an open-source tool flow. In: Proceedings of the 19th ACM/SIGDA Inter-national Symposium on Field Programmable Gate Arrays, pp. 41–44. ACM (2011)
20. Suh, G.E., Devadas, S.: Physical unclonable functions for device authentication and secret key generation. In: Proceedings of the 44th Annual Design Automation Conference, pp. 9–14. ACM (2007)
21. Zussa, L., Dehbaoui, A., Tobich, K., Dutertre, J.M., Maurine, P., Guillaume-Sage, L., Clediere, J., Tria, A.: Efficiency of a glitch detector against electromagnetic fault injection. In: Proceedings of the Conference on Design, Automation & Test in Europe, p. 203. European Design and Automation Association (2014)

Comprehensive Laser Sensitivity Profiling and Data Register Bit-Flips for Cryptographic Fault Attacks in 65 Nm FPGA

Wei He[1,4(✉)], Jakub Breier[1,4], Shivam Bhasin[1,4],
Dirmanto Jap[1,2], Hock Guan Ong[3,4], and Chee Lip Gan[3,4]

[1] Lab of Physical Analysis and Cryptographic Engineering,
Nanyang Technological University, Singapore, Singapore
[2] School of Physical and Mathematical Sciences,
Nanyang Technological University, Singapore, Singapore
djap@ntu.edu.sg
[3] School of Materials Science and Engineering,
Nanyang Technological University, Singapore, Singapore
[4] Temasek Laboratories, Nanyang Technological University, Singapore, Singapore
{he.wei,jbreier,sbhasin,hgong,clgan}@ntu.edu.sg

Abstract. FPGAs have emerged as a popular platform for security sensitive applications. As a practical attack methodology, laser based fault analyses have drawn much attention in the past years due to its superior accuracy in fault perturbation into security-critical Integrated Circuits (ICs). However, due to the insufficient device information, the practical injections work are not so efficient as expected. In this paper, we thoroughly analyze the laser fault injections to data flip-flops, instead of the widely studied configuration memory bits, of a modern nanoscale FPGA. A profiling campaign based on laser chip scan is performed on an exemplary 65 nm Virtex-5 FPGA, through the delayered silicon substrate, to identify the laser sensitivity distribution of the resource array and the fundamental logic cells. The sophisticated flip-flop bit flips are realized by launching fine-grained laser perturbations on an identified Configurable Logic Block (CLB) region. The profiled laser fault sensitivity map to FPGA resource significantly facilitate high-precision logic navigation and fault injection in practical cryptographic fault attacks. We show that the observed single- and multiple-bit faults are compatible with most proposed differential or algebraic fault analyses (DFA/AFA). Finally, further discussions on capability of reported fault models to bypass fault countermeasures like parity and dual-rail logic are also given.

Keywords: Cryptographic fault attack · Laser fault injection · Data bit-flip · FPGA

1 Introduction

Modern Field Programmable Gate Arrays (FPGAs) and programmable System on Chips (SoCs) come with interesting features like rich logic resource, real-time

© Springer International Publishing AG 2016
C. Carlet et al. (Eds.): SPACE 2016, LNCS 10076, pp. 47–65, 2016.
DOI: 10.1007/978-3-319-49445-6_3

reconfiguration, high-density memories, clock managers, environment sensors, etc. Owing to such features and low time-to-market, it enables deployment of FPGAs in many kinds of applications. FPGAs also find wide application in security-critical domains due to constantly evolving protection requirements like aerospace, defence etc. However, like other devices, FPGAs are also vulnerable to physical attacks, i.e., side-channel attacks [12], fault attacks [5] and probing [3].

Side-channel attacks (SCA) are passive and exploits unintentional physical leakages, while probing tries to read out sensitive values directly from the circuit [13]. Fault attacks stay in between SCA and Probing by operating the target device in a non-friendly environment and exploiting secrets from the faulty behaviors. The most common fault attack in context of cryptography is the differential fault analysis (DFA) [4] and the recently published algebraic fault analysis (AFA) [9]. For instance, in AES, DFA can extract the secret key by a single well-located fault [23]. This tampering or erroneous behavior can be accomplished in several ways, which are widely classified as global or local. Global fault injections are, in general, low-cost techniques which create disturbances on global parameters like voltage and clock system, etc. The resultant faults are more or less random in nature and the adversary might need repetitive injections to obtain exploitable faults. On the other hand, local injection techniques, like laser or electromagnetic injections, are more precise in terms of fault locations. This precision needs expensive equipments and more preparation efforts.

Laser fault injection (LFI) falls into optical fault injection methods. It is a semi-invasive perturbation technique, which requires decapsulation of the target device, followed by injection of high intensity laser. The injection can be theoretically performed at either frontside or backside of the target chip. However, because of the dense metal wires covering the active logic layer, it is highly challenging to realise successful fault perturbation from the frontside.

An alternative to laser method is the electromagnetic injection (EMI [17]) which uses a tiny EM probe with an intense transient pulse or a harmonic emission to (a) upset logic values in storage cells; (b) slow down the signal transmission to cause set-up time violation in flip-flops or faulty timing in internal clock generator [15]; (c) bias critical logic, e.g., key generation PUF [22]. However, the generated EM field is difficult to be restricted only to the Point-of-Interest (POI), so the accuracy of EMI is still comparatively lower than LFI.

In this paper, the LFI campaigns on a commercial 65 nm FPGA will be validated using pulse laser from its substrate (backside). A fault injection based laser sensitivity profiling of the exemplary FPGA is developed. We report successful data register bit flips in logic array using diode pulse laser with backside injection. We localize interesting logics within these blocks, and sketched the laser sensitivity regions, to demonstrate that the high-precision bit-flips in fundamental logic cells of nano-scale FPGA can be practical achieved using μm-level laser. The presented results and the derivatives certify the feasibility of realizing sophisticated bit-level fault injections to complex cryptographic algorithms on nano-scale FPGAs or programmable SoCs.

The rest of this paper is organized as follows. Sect. 2 discusses previous work and outlines our contributions. In Sect. 3, the related work about optical properties on silicon, chip preparation and configuration are presented. The profiling of laser sensitivity on chip and analysis methodologies are described in Sect. 4. Experimental results and further discussions are detailed in Sect. 5. Finally, conclusions are drawn in Sect. 6.

2   Related Work

Many techniques have been proposed in previous literatures for disturbing values processed and stored in ICs [1,6,8,10,18,19]. In general, results on microcontrollers show high degree of repeatability, mainly because of a stable clock and a possibility to predict the instruction order. Precision depends on the used CMOS technology and the size of the effective laser spot. Additionally to memory disturbances, it is also relatively easy to disturb instruction execution on these devices, leading to instruction skip or alteration faults. Previous papers about fault injection on FPGAs mostly aim at memory disturbances both on configuration memory of SRAM FPGAs and data Block RAM [7,16,21].

The fault injection into the configuration memory of SRAM FPGAs intrinsically incurs the alterations on logic functions or routings, and hence lead to permanent circuit malfunction until the device is reconfigured with a new bitstream. The faults are typically found and analyzed by *readback* the bitstream from device after each fault injection, to be compared with the unaffected *golden* sample [2,14], in order to figure out the affected tiles on the logic array. So the comparison efficiency is low and static, and furthermore the method is becoming challenging to apply to newer FPGAs with more obscured bitstream format.

In this work, we target the data bit flips in registers and perform the dynamic fault injection to a lightweight block cipher in a 65 nm commercial FPGA. Since the faults are inserted by flipping the data bit/bits, instead of the configuration faults in SRAM, the circuit function will not be disrupted. So it is more practical to be applied to real fault attack scenarios. The fault comparison is to analyze the faulty cipher outputs where the bitstream readback is not required, which makes the efficiency is much higher than bitstream comparison. In our work, we used a diode pulse laser with different lens fixed into a 2D (X-Y) motorized stage. The selected chip is encapsulated in a flip-chip package, hence a mechanical preprocess is conducted for thinning down the substrate for achieving better laser penetration.

Some previous works are summarized in Table 1 and compared with this work. The comparison is drawn in terms of platform (μC, FPGA, ASIC), technology node (Tech.), fault target (RAM, logic, flip-flop), chip position (front-side, backside), fault precision (bit, random), and purpose of fault injection.

Our Contributions: This work systematically presents the following improvements from the state-of-the-art. It:

Table 1. State of the art for laser fault injection.

Work	Platform	Tech	Target	Fault Model	Position	Purpose
Dutertre et al. [1,10,19]	μC	350 nm	SRAM	byte	Front	Attack
Courbon et al. [8]	ASIC	90 nm	FlipFlops	bit	Back	Attack
Breier et al. [6]	μC	350 nm	Register	bit	Back	Attack
Pouget et al. [16]	FPGA	150 nm	CLB/BRAM	random	Back	Reliability
Canivet et al. [7]	FPGA	150 nm	Logic	random	Back	Attack
Selmke et al. [21]	FPGA	90/45 nm	BRAM	bit	Back	Attack
This Work	**FPGA**	**65 nm**	**Flip-Flops**	**bit**	**Back**	**Attack**

- proposes a new methodology for laser sensitivity profiling of a nano-scale FPGA, ranging from the global resource array to the slice flip-flops. This method can be practically applied to a wider spectrum of FPGA devices.
- reports precise bit-flip faults exclusively to specific flip-flops in logic resource, instead of the configuration memory faults, inside the FPGAs.
- realises fault models in FPGA that are compatible with almost all proposed differential/algebraic fault analysis (DFA/AFA) on unprotected cryptographic primitives.
- discusses the possibilities of counteracting dual-rail or parity protected cryptographic primitives.

3   Chip Preparation and Device Configuration

For modern FPGAs, two packages styles are typically applied to encapsulate the naked dies. The first is the `bonded-wire` package (or frontside) in which the metal layer is placed up and the chip substrate is facing down to the PCB board. On the contrary, `flip-chip` package (or backside) places the substrate up and metal layers down. Due to the metal layer placed above the active logic layer, laser injection can hardly affect the logic cells (active transistor layer) below. In this work, we target to a 65 nm Virtex-5 FPGA (LX50T) with flip-chip package on Digilent's *Genesys* board. To allow effective laser impact to the internal logics, we have pre-processed the FPGA chip by thinning down the substrate layer using a mechanical solution.

3.1   Optical Property of Silicon

To understand laser effects in silicon we have to study its physical properties and the way how the energy traverse and affect the active logic layer. Schmid [20] provided a deep overview of optical absorption of Si:As and Si:B samples and addressed ionization process of pulsed lasers that produces electron-hole pairs. For linear absorption of semiconductor we can derive the linear transfer energy (LET), expressed in Eq. 1 as a function of the depth penetration z.

$$LET(z) = \frac{\alpha \lambda E_{e/h}}{\rho h c} E_{laser} e^{-\alpha x} \tag{1}$$

where $\alpha[cm^{-1}]$ is the absorption coefficient, $\lambda[nm]$ represents the wavelength of a pulse laser, the energy required to induce an electron-hole pair is denote as $E_{e/h}[eV]$, and $\rho[mg/cm^3]$ means the density of silicon, h, c and E_{laser} presents the Planc constant, the light velocity and the laser energy respectively.

Previous equation works for particles, however for laser we need to take a radial exposure into account. This is expressed in Eq. 2.

$$l(r, z) = l_0(z)e^{\frac{2r^2}{\omega(z)^2}} E_{laser}e^{-\alpha z} \tag{2}$$

where $\omega(z)^2$ expresses the radial properties of the laser as a function of the beam width, focalization point and refraction index.

Another important parameter to be identified is how deep we can reach the logic elements under the silicon surface. For this purpose we have to use absorption coefficient from Eq. 3.

$$\alpha = \frac{4\pi k}{\lambda} \tag{3}$$

where k is the extinction coefficient.

Values for absorption coefficients for silicon can be found in literatures. We plotted combined results from [11,24] in Fig. 1 for wavelengths that are mostly used for laser fault injections (530 nm – 1070 nm). It is seen that for green laser (532 nm), the absorption depth is $\approx 1.58\ \mu m$, for near infrared (NIR) laser (808 nm) it is $\approx 12.79\ \mu m$, and for NIR laser (1064 nm) it is $\approx 1100\ \mu m$. Accordingly, a conclusion can be drawn that for our case study, where the thickness of the thinned silicon substrate from the backside is $\approx 130\ \mu m$, it is necessary to use a laser with near infrared wavelengths or higher. Hence the diode pulse laser with 1064 nm wavelength is selected for our experiments.

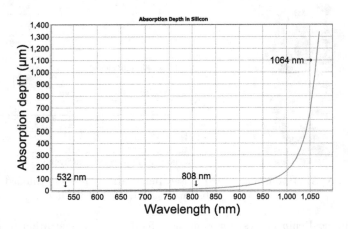

Fig. 1. Absorption depth in silicon for wavelengths from 530 nm to 1070 nm.

3.2   Backside Substrate Thinning of Virtex-5

We have employed a backside polishing technique, which involves the thinning down of the chip substrate layer. This process is typically useful in experiments where access from the back of a die is required for testing, such as laser probing, fault isolation and thermal imaging. A 1064 nm diode pulse laser is used to generate charges in the desired location in the silicon, with a thick silicon substrate, the amount of charges that are generated at the POIs in the active logic layer are rather limited because of the laser refraction and energy absorption. By thinning down the substrate, the amount of charges induced at the POIs can be significantly increased which makes flip-flop upsets possible. We performed backside polishing on our FPGA sample using *Ultra Tec ASAP-1* polishing machine (Fig. 2a). The heat-sink metal lid of the FPGA sample was removed to expose the backside substrate, and this substrate was mechanically reduced to ≈ 130 μm, removing ≈ 170 μm, as illustrated in Fig. 2b. The thinning process can be bypassed if the strength of laser source is high enough such that laser injection after absorption is enough for realizing event upsets. On the other hand, the silicon substrate can also be further thinned down to ≈ 50 μm to have, perhaps, very slight improvement in result, but the risk taken will be higher. As the silicon substrate is being thinned down, the integrity of the silicon structure will experience a bigger force. This will cause die warping and in some cases where the strain is too big, the sample will crack. Thus in our approach, we will want to achieve sample preparation able for testing with the least risk to be involved. Thinner silicon substrate is a much seek out goal in a lot of the backside sample preparation for other form of testing and/or with other wavelength of laser. However, in our experiment context, the advantage to have a much thinner substrate is being overshadowed by the risk of spoiling the onboard sample.

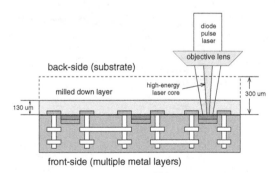

(a) Ultra Tec ASAP-1 polishing machine.

(b) Laser penetration through thinned silicon substrate to active transistor layer.

Fig. 2. Mechanical chip process for realizing effective laser penetration to transistor layer in FPGA.

3.3   Device Under Test and Configuration

The target Virtex 5 FPGA (LX50T) consists of 12 metal layers, manufactured in 65 nm technology in a 1136-pin flip-chip BGA package. The device provides 3,600 CLB (7,200 slices) deployed in 12 clock regions. Each slice contains 4 6-input look-up tables (LUTs) and 4 flip-flops. A number of BRAMs, digital clock mangers (DCMs), phase-locked loops (PLLs) and DSPs are located in columns of the logic resource array. A system monitor together with its temperature and power supply sensors are situated in the center of the die. Figure 3 (left) illustrates the basic architecture of the selected device. The CLB structure in Xilinx FPGA contains 2 slices, together with the route channel to a switch-box, as sketched in Fig. 3 (right).

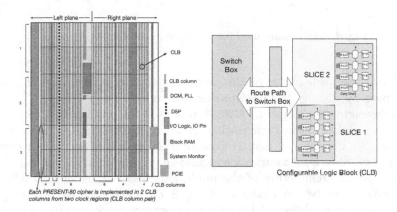

Fig. 3. Simplified view of the architecture of the target FPGA and CLB cell

The focal plane of the laser beam is critical for impacting the logic elements that are deployed under substrate. Due to the unrevealed bottom device information and the unknown dopant density in silicon that hinder the laser focalization, we have to empirically calibrate the focal plane to the active CLB layer relying on the number of generated faults, as an indicator, in a preliminary chip scan. As aforementioned, a diode pulse laser with a wavelength of 1064 nm was selected due to its superior penetration into silicon. The spot size of the chosen laser with a 5× lens is around $60 \times 14\ um^2$. The output power of the laser can be adjusted with an embedded attenuator with 1 % precision step from 0 to 100 % of its full power strength (10 Watt). The entire setup for performing fault injection experiments is depicted in Fig. 4.

Importantly, solid experiments prove that only the very center part of the claimed laser beam is powerful enough to trigger the faults (*'high-energy laser core'* illustrated in Fig. 2b), which is empirically tested to be roughly 1/10 of the claimed spot size ($\approx 60\ um^2$). This phenomenon is based on the nature of diode laser, and the *optical refraction* and *energy absorption* through the residual substrate ($\approx 100\ um$). We do not suggest a further substrate process since it

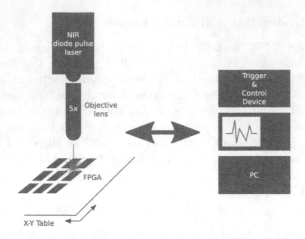

Fig. 4. Laser setup used for the experimental fault injection.

potentially causes side-effects on the electrical characteristics of FPGA, and also it risks physical damage to transistors or interconnects.

A lightweight block cipher PRESENT was used for profiling the logic array, which is a Substitution-Permutation Network (SPN) cipher with 64 bit block size, 80/128 bit key and 31 computation rounds. Each round contains AddRoundKey, Sbox Substitution and pLayer permutation. Figure 5 illustrates the round-based architecture of the implemented cipher. A single PRESENT can be tailored to be implemented in a CLB column pair. We define a CLB column pair as two adjacent CLB columns from two clock regions, as shown in Fig. 3 (left). We chose a CLB column pair as the cipher couldn't fit in a single CLB column. Moreover, the chosen CLB column must be vertically adjacent, as horizontally adjacent CLB columns would hinder establishment of column boundaries during the profiling.

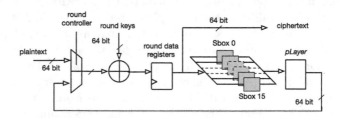

Fig. 5. Implemented PRESENT-80 cryptographic algorithm.

4   Laser Sensitivity Profiling

After preparing the device sample, we proceeded with identifying the laser sensitivity distribution of FPGA architecture by analyzing the unique faults from a number of ciphers implemented in parallel.

4.1   Global Array Scan

We applied a strategy by implementing a large number of PRESENT-80 cipher primitives into logic resource array, and each core is restricted into a specific CLB column pair by applying the placement constraints at the implementation stage. It is remarked that other algorithms or even a simply cascaded logic chain could be used for this purpose as well. We have chosen a cryptographic algorithm in our work owing to the following advantages:

- The PRESENT-80 occupies almost all the logic resources for each assigned CLB column pair, which provides a good coverage of resource occupation;
- The 32 encryption rounds provide a sufficiently big time window (32 clock cycles) to test the laser injection with varying glitch offsets;
- The exact logic points and affected timings could be simply determined by finding the collision round between the faulty ciphertext decryption and plaintext encryption;
- For the bit flips to the configuration memory of SRAM-FPGA, the faults change the basic circuit configuration, instead of the processed data, and it hence leads to permanent malfunction of the design [16]. Concretely, the malfunction stays for the following encryptions untill the FPGA is reconfigured with an uninfected bitstream. So, a practical algorithm (e.g., a cipher) used here shows if the faults are transient data bit upsets or permanent configuration bit flips in SRAM.

All the cores encrypt the same plaintext in parallel and all the output ciphertexts are compared in the output – a *tag* bit vector. The vector width is equal to the number of the implemented ciphers, and the value of each bit represents if the corresponding cipher is correct or faulty ('0': correct; '1': faulty). A fault in any of the PRESENT cores can be identified by the position of the exclusive tag bit. The scanning stage also records critical parameters, like scan coordinates, injection power and timing. Hence, each fault can be associated to a particular cipher and specific location on chip.

Since the peripheral logic (e.g., the output comparison) also occupies some resources, we have divided the complete die mapping into two parts: the left plane mapping and the right plane mapping. When the right part was scanned, peripheral logic was deployed to the left side, and vice versa, to avoid control interruption. Total 48 PRESENT cores are implemented in the right region and 42 in the left side, corresponding to the device architecture. The results are then merged to construct the fault map of the entire FPGA. Relying on the recorded coordinates of each fault, we provide the 2D plot in Fig. 6. The X and Y axis

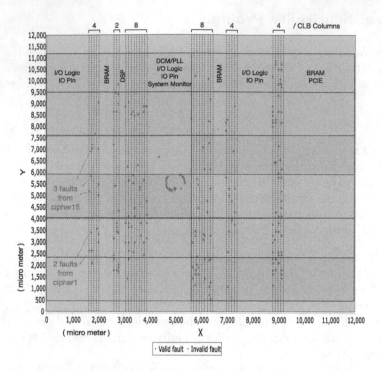

Fig. 6. Laser sensitivity properties of device under test (DUT), profilied by mapping tagged faults from implemented algorithm and scan coordinates. The plotted faults reveal the logic resource architecture of the exemplary FPGA.

are the dimensions of the thinned chip i.e., $12 \times 12 \ mm^2$. The blue dots represent the valid faults by laser injection (occurring in any single cipher). The red ones represent the unexpected (exceptional) invalid faults that simultaneously affected multiple ciphers. Based on this analysis, we could investigate the laser sensitivity on a specific CLB column.

CLB Column. According to our initial results, the faults from the same cipher come from the same rectangular region in Fig. 6. It also matches the user placement constraints. Since the coordinates base on the real dimensions of FPGA, not the virtual floor plan or FPGA editor view, Fig. 6 provides the exact scales of the on-chip instances. Comparing to the architectural view in Fig. 3, dimensions of other logic resources can be estimated. It is shown that the IO pad (IO Logic and IO Pin) and PCIE occupies significant die space, the width of BRAM and DSP are roughly equal to 4 and 2 CLB columns respectively. Besides, there are no faults from the extreme top and bottom (grey) regions. This indicates that the active logic array does not extend to the very edge of the die. Due to the insufficient information, we could not determine the boundaries on the left IO pad region and the right BRAM&PCIE region. Nevertheless, we have clearly identified and mapped the CLB columns to the physical dimensions of the chip. Based on this mapping, we further continue with a fine-grained scan within the CLB column to identify laser sensitivity for slices.

Impact of Substrate Thinning. To demonstrate the impact of thinning and polishing on laser fault injection, we repeated the experiments with another copy of the test board, where the FPGA substrate was not thinned down. Only the metal lid over the FPGA was removed. A global laser scan on the entire chip was repeated. The scan result has shown that faults only occur when conducting the laser injection to the center part of the chip, which exactly match the position and shape (ring shape) of the exceptional invalid faults in the center die, as shown in Fig. 6. The phenomenon demonstrates that only a specific center part of the chip without any substrate thinning is sensitive to the laser impacts. Noticeably, we are not able to trigger any events in the active CLB logic array where the ciphers are implemented, even with the maximum laser power. Thus substrate thinning enables exploitable transient fault injection with laser. The fault mechanism of center die will be discussed in Sect. 5. Please note that the coordinates in all the following figures are preserved with respect to Fig. 6.

4.2   Configurable Logic Block Column Scan

The laser fault tests with higher scan resolution are executed exclusively to a part of the CLB column where totally 10 CLBs (e.g., 20 slices) are occupied. We only implemented the round data registers of PRESENT-80 into the flip-flops of these CLBs. The scan matrix is 100×1400, so totally 140,000 positions will be evaluated by laser in this CLB column, and one injection is executed in each location. Note that either single-bit or multiple-bit fault from the 4 flip-flops of the each slice are tagged with the same color, which returns 20 different fault types to be observed, as plotted in Fig. 7. Hence the fault sensitivity distribution of the 10 CLBs can be distinctly identified, and the relative sensitivity positions of the 2 slices inside each CLB can also be established.

Figure 8 gives a closer view of the slice faults of CLB_6 from Fig. 7. Because the effective laser spot possibly impacts flip-flops from both slices in this CLB, the fault regions from the 2 slices show an overlapped region, as shown in Fig. 8. For most of the CLB regions, only the faults from the 2 slices of this CLB appear, but not symmetrically. This phenomenon is mainly due to the variant energy attenuations of laser beam through the residual but uneven substrate layer due to process variations. The thickness variation across the $12\,mm \times 12\,mm$ die is within $15\,\mu m$ and thus the substrate thinning is rather uniform.

Given the coordinates from both Figs. 7 and 8, the following important parameters can be estimated as follows:

- Distance between the neighbouring CLBs: $60\sim80\ \mu m$
- Width (X) of a CLB column: $7\sim15\ \mu m$;
- For this DUT, each clock region has 20 CLB rows, and regions are symmetrically divided by a global-clock routing channel. In Fig. 7, half of the

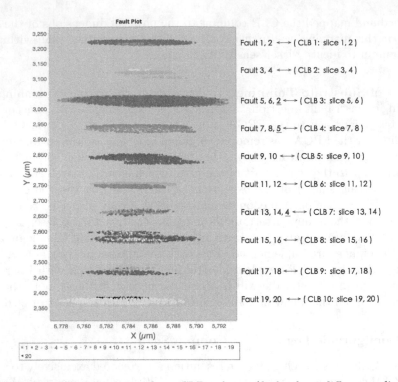

Fig. 7. 2D laser sensitivity map from CLB column (faults from difference slices are coloured differently).

clock region are measured, and the middle clock routing channel occupies around 700 μm. So the height (Y) of a CLB column in a clock region (e.g., the heigh of the clock region) in this Virtex-5 FPGA is estimated as: $(3250 - 2350) * 2 \ \mu m + 700 \ \mu m \approx 2500 \ \mu m$.

It should be noted these dimensions are the laser fault sensitivity regions, instead of the precise component sizes. However, they shows the critical scales that sensitive to the laser attacks, upon logic bits on devices. These parameters helps to efficiently navigate the laser to the POIs, for performing precise bit-level fault attacks against FPGA implemented ciphers. The estimated regions and dimensions are used in the following subsections.

Discussion of exceptional fault appearance: For some CLB regions, unexpected faults appeared. Note that *fault_2* (denoted as blue dot) is supposed to only appear in CLB_1. However it unexpectedly occurs when the laser targets to CLB_3 also. This phenomenon is mainly because the signal paths for register bit [4–7], that were deployed in slice_2, pass the routing channel close to CLB_3, and hence are affected by laser disturbance on CLB_3.

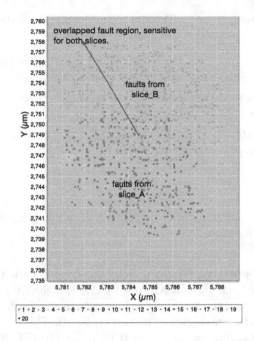

Fig. 8. Slice-exclusive faults for a single CLB.

4.3   Flip-Flop Scan

Recall the mapped device from Fig. 6, we could navigate the laser spot to a specific slice. Without loss of generality, we focus on a particular slice where 4 out of the total 64 round registers of PRESENT are deployed. In this slice registers storing bits 0, 1, 2 and 3 are respectively placed in its 4 flip-flops, and the 4 LUTs inside this slice are unused. In FPGA, LUT is actually a 6-input ROM by nature, and any bit upset in this memory changes the implemented Boolean function (potentially leads to computation errors) until FPGA is refreshed by new bitstream. So, no matter if the LUTs are used or not, it does not affect the registers implemented in this slice.

By scanning the interested single slice region: 6×13 μm^2, we obtained the following results. With the laser glitch length fixed to 282 ns and laser strength varying between 75 %–100 %, we have received 3918 faulty encryptions out of 10,000, with 1 injection for each position. In total, 6462 bits were flipped in the faulty ciphertexts, resulting to 3378 bit sets and 3084 bit resets. It shows that with the same laser settings, we can expect roughly the same number of bit sets and bit resets in flip-flops. If we focus on the flip-flops that were affected, most of the faults flipped flip-flop A, as can be seen in Table 2, following similar proportions of faults for the other three flip-flops. In Table 3 we can see numbers for different fault models we have obtained. More than one half of all the faults were 1-bit flips, following with $\approx 1/3$ 2-bit flips. 3- and 4-bit flips were less likely to occur, however still possible to obtain. Moreover, with high-precision scan,

Table 2. Percentages of faults for different registers (non-exclusive).

Register	% of faults
A	66.9
B	35.5
C	35.9
D	36.2

Table 3. Numbers of 1,2,3 and 4-bit flips from the total 3918 faults.

Fault model	# of faults
1-bit flip	2243
2-bit flip	947
3-bit flip	595
4-bit flip	135

we can find the POI affecting only one slice without having the laser injecting faults in neighbouring slices.

Flip-Flop Laser Sensitive Region. Four flip-flops (FF-A, FF-B, FF-C, FF-D) are placed inside each slice in Xilinx FPGAs, therefore each injection could cause multiple bit flips if the laser spot is bigger than the flip-flop scale. We show the faults when 2 adjacent registers flipped in Fig. 9. The red, blue, and green points represent 2-bit flips occurred on (FF-A, FF-B), (FF-B, FF-C), (FF-C, FF-D), respectively, being caused by single injection. It is clearly shown that different regions have slight offsets in X axis, and this offset is because the size of the effective laser beam covers two neighbouring registers in most. More specifically, $X1$ and $X2$ constitute middle lines of registers (C, D) and (A, B) in X axis ($X1 \approx 5782.4445 \ \mu m$, $X2 = 5781.9900 \ \mu m$). Due to the similarity of each register, $d/2 = (X2 - X1)/2 \approx 227 \ nm$ should be roughly equal with the fault sensitive region of a single register. It is stressed that register structure varies for devices manufactured with different technologies and devices, therefore this estimation is valid only for the tested Virtex-5 FPGA. However, the analysis solution is applicable to other FPGA devices.

As mentioned before, none of the faults were found in the configuration memory. Our laser equipement was operating at its maximum capability, we couldn't fiind advanced parameters to inject configuration faults. This could be due to different structure and/or layer placement for flip-flops and configuration memory.

5   Results and Discussions

In this section, we present more experiments to further analyze the fault topology and success probability. Next, we discuss the relevance of these fault models to fault attacks on cryptographic algorithms and fault countermeasures. Finally, we shed some light on the invalid faults found in the central region of the FPGA.

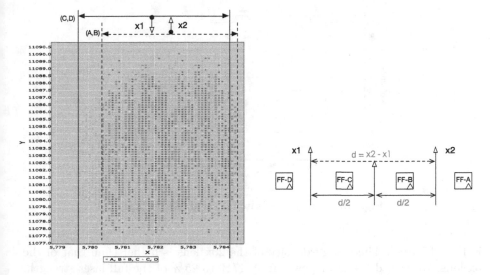

Fig. 9. Estimation of flip-flop laser sensitivity region basing on 2-bit faults from adjacent flip-flops.

5.1 Success Rate

Apart from different kind of faults, success rate is another important parameter. In this part we determine the manipulating power of the attacker for a given target. It is important to know which laser settings are the most efficient for producing bit flips or random byte faults, etc. The objective is to ascertain the minimum power required for fault injection with each fault model.

The experiment is conducted by injecting laser with varying power in the range 0 %–100 %. The injection campaign is performed on the POI of a slice region where 4-bit round data registers are implemented in the 4 flip-flops of this slice. 100 injections are performed per laser power, using PRESENT-80 encryption with random plaintext and fixed key. In Fig. 10, it can be observed that faults started appearing at 81 % laser power. With > 85 % laser power, over 90 % injections resulted in faults. The fault injection success is 100 %, when laser power is over 96 %. These faults included both bit-flips as well as random byte/nibble.

5.2 Discussion on Central Fault Region

A dense fault region appeared in the center of FPGA die. This region is not an active CLB region and no user logic is implemented in this area. The nature of injected faults in this region is also very different from the valid fault, i.e., several cores are faulted by single injection. Moreover, the faults started appearing at a much lower power (18 % as compared to 81 % for faults in CLB columns). To study this behavior, we have specially focused on this region with better scanning precision using a 20x laser lens. The size of the laser spot in this lens

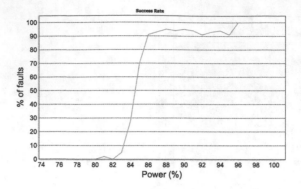

Fig. 10. Fault success rate for random byte flips.

is $15 \times 3.5 \ \mu m^2$. The energy density of the 20x lens is higher than that of the 5x lens. We varied the laser power from 17 % to 25 % of the full laser strength. Figure 11 gives the fault plot after the laser scan in this section. Points in different colours represent different laser strengths. Most faults are located in two regions, hereafter named "Region A" and "Region B" respectively. A very few number of faults are seen in some remote spots. A bitstream modification was never observed.

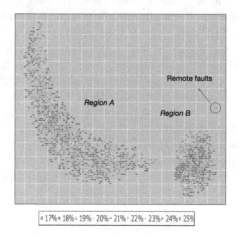

Fig. 11. Position and strength of faults in precise laser scan to the center of FPGA.

Due to the undisclosed transistor-level device information, clarifying the internal mechanism of the faults here is challenging. Even when the cipher and its peripheral logics are placed in far FPGA corner, the fault characteristic of central region remained unchanged. Also, multiple ciphers could be faulted by a single injection, when targeting this region. Thus, laser injection in this region causes

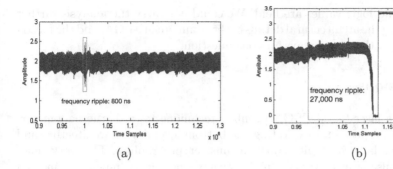

(a)   (b)

Fig. 12. RO response against laser injection targeting (a) CLB area; (b) `Region "A"`, respectively.

and propagates some global disturbance, which could affect multiple ciphers irrespective of the placement. Deeper analysis is conducted under two assumptions:

- The faults are triggered by the `global clock network`. Since the clock buffer that fans out the global clock is deployed in the die center, a fault on the buffer can spread to the whole chip. To validate, we removed the clock buffer and routed the clock system using the signal paths. However, the faults still persisted in the new experiment.
- The faults are triggered by the *system monitor*. System monitor is an environment sensor system (power supply, temperature etc.), deployed near the center of FPGA die. System monitor is activated by default and physically connected to the power network, that can possibly propagate the voltage disturbance induced by laser impact. However, fresh experiments after disabling the System Monitor, by connecting all its IO pins to GND on board, still reported similar faults in central region.

To continue our analysis, we implemented a ring oscillator (RO) in the CLB area, `far from the central region`, to conduct another test. The RO is composed of a single inverter (LUT) and routing wires, implemented in a CLB region to cover 9 CLBs through square routing, which results in a stable oscillation frequency of 230 MHz. We observed the signal oscillation of the RO from an oscilloscope, and the results are shown in Fig. 12. When the laser is shot in the CLB area, where the RO is deployed, we can see that laser injection disturbs the RO response for a short period of time with a oscillation ripple lasting around 800 ns, and then RO returns to the stable oscillation, as shown in Fig. 12 (a). On the other hand, when the laser is shot on either of `"Region A"` or `"B"`, the response of the RO is more noticeable. As shown in Fig. 12 (b), the RO stops to oscillate for a bigger period of time of roughly 27, 000 ns. From an oscillating state, the RO response is pulled down to zero and then the RO starts again to oscillate and lock itself. The phenomena can be described as a `soft` reset which occurs probably due to triggering of certain sensors or some impact on the power delivery network, which are not present in the documentation. We call it as soft reset because only the signals are disarmed but flip-flops and logic values are held. We could not carry the analysis further without knowing the architectural details of the commercial FPGA, and the reason for these faults at the center stays an open question.

6   Conclusions

In this paper, a laser based FPGA profiling technique towards the nanometer-level FPGAs is proposed for exploiting the bottom-level device architecture and realizing various bit-level fault attacks against cryptographies. The work relies on the diode pulse laser to trigger the bit events from algorithmic data, instead of the widely studied memory configuration bits of FPGAs, as to profile the device architecture and fundamental CLBs basing on the fault sensitivity distribution. Without loss of generality, a Xilinx 65 nm FPGA is selected as the DUT, and a series of laser scan campaigns from the thinned chip substrate lead to successful identification of critical architecture and internal component information. With further fine-grained scan on individual slice region both single- or multiple- data bit faults in flip-flops have been enabled, which are compatible with most differential and algebraic fault attack schemes proposed in previous literatures. The precisely induced bit faults can also compromise fault attack countermeasures like dual-rail logic and parity detection. Not restricted to the studied exemplary device, the proposed techniques could be applied to other FPGAs or programmable SoCs, to perform high-precision bit-level fault attacks against cryptographic primitives. To the best of our knowledge, this is the first work that thoroughly profiled the generic FPGA architecture and fundamental logic unit using laser based fault injection.

The following work will focus on the chip profiling and laser fault perturbation to FPGAs manufactured by 28 nm technology. The practical chip analysis and laser attack to an FPGA chip from a commercial security product will also be a part of further work.

References

1. Agoyan, M., Dutertre, J.M., Mirbaha, A.P., Naccache, D., Ribotta, A.L., Tria, A.: Single-bit DFA using multiple-byte laser fault injection. In: 2010 IEEE International Conference on HST, pp. 113–119 (2010)
2. Alderighi, M., Casini, F., d'Angelo, S., Mancini, M., Pastore, S., Sechi, G.R.: Evaluation of single event upset mitigation schemes for sram based FPGAs using the FLIPPER fault injection platform. In: 22nd IEEE International Symposium on Defect and Fault-Tolerance in VLSI Systems, DFT 2007, pp. 105–113. IEEE (2007)
3. Anderson, R.: Security engineering: A guide to building dependable distributed systems (2001)
4. Biham, E., Shamir, A.: Differential fault analysis of secret key cryptosystems. In: Kaliski, B.S. (ed.) CRYPTO 1997. LNCS, vol. 1294, pp. 513–525. Springer, Heidelberg (1997). doi:10.1007/BFb0052259
5. Boneh, D., DeMillo, R.A., Lipton, R.J.: On the importance of eliminating errors in cryptographic computations. J. Cryptology 14(2), 101–119 (2001)

6. Breier, J., Jap, D.: Testing feasibility of back-side laser fault injection on a micro-controller. In: Proceedings of the WESS 2015, pp. 5:1–5:6 (2015)
7. Canivet, G., Maistri, P., Leveugle, R., Cldire, J., Valette, F., Renaudin, M.: Glitch and laser fault attacks onto a secure AES implementation on a SRAM-based FPGA. J. Cryptology **24**(2), 247–268 (2011)
8. Courbon, F., Loubet-Moundi, P., Fournier, J.J.A., Tria, A.: Adjusting laser injections for fully controlled faults. In: Prouff, E. (ed.) COSADE 2014. LNCS, vol. 8622, pp. 229–242. Springer, Heidelberg (2014). doi:10.1007/978-3-319-10175-0_16
9. Courtois, N.T., Jackson, K., Ware, D.: Fault-algebraic attacks on inner rounds of des. In: e-Smart'10 Proceedings: The Future of Digital Security Technologies (2010)
10. Dutertre, J.M., Mirbaha, A.P., Naccache, D., Tria, A.: Reproducible single-byte laser fault injection. In: 2010 Conference on PRIME, pp. 1–4 (2010)
11. Green, M.A.: Self-consistent optical parameters of intrinsic silicon at 300 k including temperature coefficients. Solar Energy Mater. Solar Cells **92**(11), 1305–1310 (2008)
12. Kocher, P., Jaffe, J., Jun, B.: Differential power analysis. In: Wiener, M. (ed.) CRYPTO 1999. LNCS, vol. 1666, pp. 388–397. Springer, Heidelberg (1999). doi:10.1007/3-540-48405-1_25
13. Kömmerling, O., Kuhn, M.G.: Design principles for tamper-resistant smartcard processors. Smartcard **99**, 9–20 (1999)
14. Lima Kastensmidt, F., Tambara, L., Bobrovsky, D.V., Pechenkin, A.A., Nikiforov, A.Y.: Laser testing methodology for diagnosing diverse soft errors in a nanoscale sram-based fpga. Nucl. Sci. IEEE Trans. **61**(6), 3130–3137 (2014)
15. Maurine, P.: Techniques for em fault injection: equipments and experimental results. In: 2012 Workshop on Fault Diagnosis and Tolerance in Cryptography (FDTC), pp. 3–4. IEEE (2012)
16. Pouget, V., Douin, A., Lewis, D., Fouillat, P., Foucard, G., Peronnard, P., Maingot, V., Ferron, J., Anghel, L., Leveugle, R., Velazco, R.: Tools and methodology development for pulsed laser fault injection in SRAM-based FPGAs. In: 8th LATW 2007), p. Session 8. IEEE Computer Society, Cuzco, Peru (2007)
17. Quisquater, J.J., Samyde, D.: Eddy current for magnetic analysis with active sensor. In: Esmart 2002, Nice, France (2002)
18. Roscian, C., Dutertre, J.M., Tria, A.: Frontside laser fault injection on cryptosystems - Application to the AES' last round. In: 2013 IEEE International Symposium on HOST, pp. 119–124 (2013)
19. Roscian, C., Sarafianos, A., Dutertre, J.M., Tria, A.: Fault model analysis of laser-induced faults in SRAM memory cells. In: 2013 Workshop on FDTC, pp. 89–98 (2013)
20. Schmid, P.E.: Optical absorption in heavily doped silicon. Phys. Rev. B **23**, 5531–5536 (1981)
21. Selmke, B., Brummer, S., Heyszl, J., Sigl, G.: Precise laser fault injections into 90nm and 45nm SRAM-cells. In: CARDIS, pp. 1–13 (2015)
22. Trimberger, S.M., Moore, J.J.: Fpga security: Motivations, features, and applications. Proc. IEEE **102**(8), 1248–1265 (2014)
23. Tunstall, M., Mukhopadhyay, D., Ali, S.: Differential fault analysis of the advanced encryption standard using a single fault. In: Ardagna, C.A., Zhou, J. (eds.) WISTP 2011. LNCS, vol. 6633, pp. 224–233. Springer, Heidelberg (2011). doi:10.1007/978-3-642-21040-2_15
24. Wang, H., Liu, X., Zhang, Z.: Absorption coefficients of crystalline silicon at wavelengths from 500 nm to 1000 nm. Int. J. Thermophys. **34**(2), 213–225 (2013)

Fault Based Almost Universal Forgeries on CLOC and SILC

Debapriya Basu Roy[1(⊠)], Avik Chakraborti[2], Donghoon Chang[3],
S.V. Dilip Kumar[1], Debdeep Mukhopadhyay[1], and Mridul Nandi[2]

[1] Secured Embedded Architecture Laboratory (SEAL),
Department of Computer Science and Engineering,
Indian Institute of Technology Kharagpur, Kharagpur, India
{deb.basu.roy,debdeep}@cse.iitkgp.ernet.in, dilipkumar@iitkgp.ac.in
[2] Indian Statistical Institute, Kolkata, India
avikchkrbrti@gmail.com, mridul.nandi@gmail.com
[3] Indraprastha Institute of Information Technology, Delhi, India
pointchang@gmail.com

Abstract. CLOC and SILC are two blockcipher based authenticated encryption schemes, submitted to the CAESAR competition, that aim to use low area buffer and handle short input efficiently. The designers of the schemes claimed $\frac{n}{2}$-bit integrity security against nonce reusing adversaries, where n is the blockcipher state size in bits. In this paper, we present single fault-based almost universal forgeries on both CLOC and SILC with only one single bit fault at a fixed position of a specific blockcipher input. In the case of CLOC, the forgery can be done for almost any nonce, associated data and message triplet, except some nominal restrictions on associated data. In the case of SILC, the forgery can be done for almost any associated data and message, except some nominal restrictions on associated data along with a fixed nonce. Both the attacks on CLOC and SILC require several nonce-misusing encryption queries. This attack is independent of the underlying blockcipher and works on the encryption mode. In this paper, we also validate the proposed fault based forgery methodology by performing actual fault attacks by electromagnetic pulse injection which shows practicality of the proposed forgery procedure. Finally, we provide updated constructions, that can resist the fault attack on the mode assuming the underlying blockcipher is fault resistant. We would like to note that our attacks do not violate the designers' claims as our attacks require fault. However, it shows some vulnerability of the schemes when fault is feasible.

Keywords: Fault attack · Blockcipher · Authenticated encryption · CLOC · SILC

1 Introduction

An authenticated encryption scheme with associated data (AEAD) is a symmetric key cryptographic primitive that provides privacy of the plaintext, integrity of

© Springer International Publishing AG 2016
C. Carlet et al. (Eds.): SPACE 2016, LNCS 10076, pp. 66–86, 2016.
DOI: 10.1007/978-3-319-49445-6_4

the plaintext and the associated data. There exist several authenticated encryption schemes based on blockciphers or streamciphers. In 2002 Whiting et al. proposed a blockcipher based authenticated encryption scheme CCM [31] for use within the IEEE 802.11 standard for WLANs. It is later adopted as NIST standard [14]. Later Bellare et al. proposed EAX [5], Minematsu et al. proposed EAX+ [25] and Moise et al. proposed EAX' [26] to overcome some of the limitations of CCM.

CLOC [22] and SILC [21] are two of the candidates in the CAESAR [1] competition, a competition which attempts to standardize some efficient AEAD schemes. CLOC is an online authenticated encryption scheme which uses CFB blockcipher mode of operation with the underlying block ciphers AES-128 [11,12] and TWINE-80 [29]. CLOC aims to optimize the implementation overhead, precomputation complexity and memory requirements of CCM, EAX and EAX'. It has a unique feature of low overhead computation, which makes it efficient to handle short input and the only precomputation that CLOC does is the key scheduling. CLOC is considered to be a lightweight AEAD scheme useful for embedded devices. It is provably secure under the pseudorandomness property of the underlying blockciphers.

SILC aims to achieve a lightweight construction and built over CLOC. SILC is also an online authenticated encryption scheme and has been constructed using CFB mode with the underlying block cipher AES-128, PRESENT-80 [8] and LED-80 [15]. SILC has actually been constructed to optimize hardware implementation used for the CLOC. Thus, SILC is considered to be a lightweight AEAD scheme useful for hardware resource constrained devices. SILC is also provably secure under the pseudorandomness property of the underlying blockciphers.

Fault attacks on several cryptographic primitives are gaining lot of attentions. Introduction of smart cards, mobile devices and several other devices with cryptographic hardware require resistance against fault injections. The first fault based attacks on cryptographic devices has been introduced by Boneh et al. [9,10]. Later, this area of research has been expanded for both symmetric and asymmetric cryptography. Biham et al. in [6] has published a differential fault analysis (DFA) on DES. Later, many blockcipher and streamciphers have been successfully analyzed with fault attacks, such as on AES [13,27,30], LED [23,24], Trivium [18,19], RC4 [7,17], Grain [3,4], Mickey 2.0 [2]. Fault Attacks has also been proposed against SHA-1 compression function by Hemme et al. [16]. To the best of our knowledge, there is only one such fault attack on any authenticated encryption scheme. The attack has been proposed by Saha et al. [28] on a CAESAR candidate APE. The attack has been able to reduce the key search space for APE-80 by injecting two 5-bit diagonal faults.

Our Contribution. In this work, we have observed that both CLOC and SILC has the property of blockcipher input state separation for encryption and associated data processing phase. This separation is done by fixing the first bit of the blockcipher input state to 0 in the AD processing phase and 1 in the encryption phase. We briefly describe below how our attacks nullify this input separation effect for both CLOC and SILC.

Attack on CLOC: In the case of CLOC, the first bit of the first AD block is fixed to zero before the corresponding blockcipher call. The first bit of all the ciphertext blocks are fixed to one and then passed to the next blockcipher invocation. After the first bit of the first ciphertext block is fixed to 1, a fault is injected at the first bit of the block. The attack first uses this faulty input-output pair to simulate the AD processing phase to find a pair of colliding ADs and subsequently forge a valid ciphertext. If the fault is injected at the first bit then we can forge a valid ciphertext with only two nonce respecting encryption queries.

We next describe how we can use the above mentioned attack to make *almost universal forgery*. We clearly mention in the respective section what the term *almost* implies. In this case, we have to make several nonce respecting encryption queries and the number of queries depending on the number of associated data blocks. We show that fault based existential forgery on any authenticated encryption scheme is trivial, but this attack is purely nontrivial and interesting, since it is almost universal forgery.

Attack on SILC: In SILC, the nonce is padded with several zeroes in the prefix and the first bit of all the ciphertext blocks are first fixed to one and then send to the next blockcipher invocation. This attack tries to inject a fault in any one of such fixed ciphertext blocks such that the first bit of the block becomes zero. Note that, we can control all the bits by nonce reusing encryption queries or RUP decryption queries, except the first bit of the block. Thus, by adjusting the plaintext in the encryption queries or the ciphertext in the RUP queries we can find a fault injected input-output pair, where the input has the form of a nonce padded with zeroes in the prefix. The attack next finds a pair of colliding ADs and subsequently forge a valid ciphertext.

We next describe an *almost universal forgery* on SILC, which is almost same as that on CLOC, except the restriction on nonce.

Practical Validation of Fault Attack: We have validated our proposed fault based forgery attack on actual FPGA implementation. We have ported CLOC on a SPARTAN-6 FPGA (xc6slx75) and have enforced faults on the implementation to show that the proposed attack methodology is practically feasible, hence need to be addressed to maintain the security of CLOC and SILC.

Countermeasures Against Forgery: The attack mentioned above is based on the encryption modes and not on the underlying blockcipher. We propose three fault resistant encryption mode by updating only the message processing phase for both CLOC and SILC. Here, we assume that, the underlying blockcipher is **fault resistant**. We also briefly discuss the overheads of these constructions over CLOC and SILC in terms of hardware area and throughput.

2   Preliminaries

2.1   Description of CLOC

In this section we give a very brief description of CLOC and we follow the same notations and variable names as described in [22]. As described by the author, CLOC has several variants based on three parameters, the underlying block cipher E_k of length n bits, nonce length ℓ_N bits and tag length τ bits. CLOC has no secret message number and there are three additional requirements that $1 \le \ell_N \le n - 1$, $1 \le \tau \le n$ and $n \in \{64, 128\}$. We also assume that both $\ell_N/8$ and $\tau/8$ are integers.

(a) $Hash_k$ (b) Enc_k

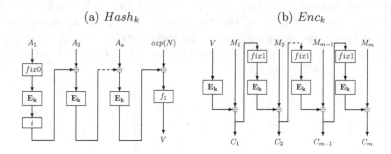

Fig. 1. $V \leftarrow Hash_k(N, A), |A| > 0$, $C \leftarrow Enc_k(V, M), |M| > 0$

Below, we describe the encryption circuit only, as the decryption circuit is not important to our attack. The encryption circuit runs $Hash_k$, Enc_k and the tag generation algorithm sequentially. It receives the nonce N, the associated data $A = (A_1, A_2, \cdots, A_a)$ and the message $M = (M_1, M_2, \cdots, M_m)$ and outputs the ciphertext $C = (C_1, C_2, \cdots, C_m)$ and the tag T, where m and a are the number of blocks in the message and the associated data respectively. We assume that A_a has full block length. As we can see from Fig. 1, the underlying key to block cipher E is k. First, N and A are processed by the algorithm $Hash_k$ to produce an intermediate value V. The Enc algorithm then gets V and M and uses the same block cipher E_k to produce the ciphertext $C = (C_1, C_2, \cdots, C_m) = Enc_k(V, M)$. The tag genration algorithm receives V and C to produce the final tag T. We intentionally omit the tag generation algorithm description as it is not important to our attack. $Hash_k$ and Enc_k are presented in Fig. 1.

We purposefully ignored the ozp, msb, h, g_1, g_2 and f_2 functions in [22], as they have no effect on attack and are not needed. We also assume that $i, f_1, fix0$ and $fix1$ are public reversible permutations. $fix0$ function with input x fix the first bit of x to 0 and $fix1$ function with input x fix the first bit of x to 1. i is the identity function.

Parameter Choice and Integrity Claims for CLOC. Recommended parameter sets and the corresponding integrity security claim in bits are proposed as follows.

- aes128n12clocv1: $E = AES\text{-}128$, $\ell_N = 96$, $\tau = 64$, 64-bit security.
- aes128n8clocv1: $E = AES\text{-}128$, $\ell_N = 64$, $\tau = 64$, 64-bit security.
- twine80n6clocv1: $E = TWINE\text{-}80$, $\ell_N = 48$, $\tau = 32$, 32-bit security.

2.2 Description of SILC

In this section we give a very brief description of SILC and we follow the same notations and variable names as described in [21]. As described by the author, SILC has several variants based on three parameters, the underlying block cipher E_k of length n, nonce length ℓ_N and tag length τ. SILC has no secret message number and there are three additional requirements that $1 \leq \ell_N \leq n - 1$, $1 \leq \tau \leq n$ and $n \in \{64, 128\}$. We assume that both $\ell_N/8$ and $\tau/8$ are integers.

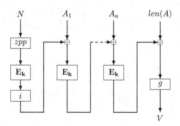

Fig. 2. $V \leftarrow Hash_k(N, A)$, $zpp(X) = 0^{n-(|X| \mod n)}||X$

Below, we describe both the encryption and the decryption circuit. The encryption circuit runs $Hash_k$, Enc_k and the tag generation algorithm sequentially. It receives the nonce N, the associated data $A = (A_1, A_2, \cdots, A_a)$ and the message $M = (M_1, M_2, \cdots, M_m)$ and outputs the ciphertext $C = (C_1, C_2, \cdots, C_m)$ and the tag T, where m and a are the number of blocks in the message and the associated data respectively. We assume that A_a has full block length. As we can see, from Figs. 2 and 3, the underlying key to block cipher E is k. First, N and A are processed by the algorithm $Hash_k$, using a block cipher E_k to produce an intermediate value V. The Enc algorithm then gets V and M and uses the same key k to produce the ciphertext $C = (C_1, C_2, \cdots, C_m) = Enc_k(V, M)$. The tag genration algorithm receives V and C to produce the final tag T. We intentionally omit the description for tag generation as it is not important to our attack.

The decryption circuit runs $Hash_k$ first and then Dec_k and tag generation algorithm parallely. It gets as input the nonce N, the associated data $A = (A_1, A_2, \cdots, A_a)$, the ciphertext $C = (C_1, C_2, \cdots, C_m)$ and the tag T. It first runs $Hash_k(A)$ to generate V. This V and C is passed through the

(a) Enc_k (b) Dec_k

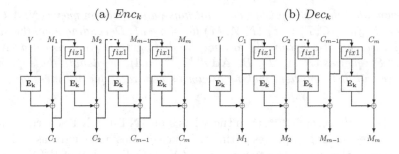

Fig. 3. $C \leftarrow Enc_k(V, M), |M| > 0, M \leftarrow Dec_k(V, C), |C| > 0$

Dec_k algorithm to compute M. The tag generation algorithm is run parallely to compute a tag T^*. If $T^* = T$ then the circuit outputs M, otherwise the input is rejected. $Hash_k$ and Enc_k are presented in Fig. 2 and Dec_k is presented in Fig. 3.

We purposefully ignored the *zap*, *msb* and *g* functions in [21] as they have no effect on our attack and are not needed. We also assume that $fix1$, g are public reversible permutations. *zpp* function is defined as $zpp(X) = X$, if $|X| = n$ and $zpp(X) = 0^{n-(|X| \mod n)}||X$, otherwise. $fix1$ is already defined in the description of CLOC.

Parameter Choice and Integrity Claims for SILC. Recommended parameter sets and the corresponding integrity security claim in bits are proposed as follows.

- aes128n12silcv1: $E = AES$-128, $\ell_N = 96$, $\tau = 64$, 64-bit security.
- aes128n8silcv1: $E = AES$-128, $\ell_N = 64$, $\tau = 64$, 64-bit security.
- present80n6silcv1: $E = PRESENT$-80, $\ell_N = 48$, $\tau = 32$, 32-bit security.
- led80n6silcv1: $E = LED$-80, $\ell_N = 48$, $\tau = 32$, 32-bit security.

2.3 Integrity Security Models

Let $x \in_R X$ denotes that x is sampled uniformly from some finite set X. Let, $\perp$ denotes a special symbol *reject*. We next define the integrity security notion, **INT-CTXT** or the unforgeability of an adversary with access to both encryption and verification oracle and can repeat nonce in the encryption queries multiple times. Let $\pi = (\mathcal{K}, \mathcal{E}, \mathcal{D}, \mathcal{V})$ be an authenticated encryption scheme, where $\mathcal{K}$ is the key generation algorithm, $\mathcal{E}$ is the encryption algorithm, $\mathcal{D}$ is decryption algorithm and $\mathcal{V}$ is the verification algorithm.

Definition 1. *The **INT-CTXT** advantage of a distinguisher D with respect to π, is defined as*

$$Adv_{\pi}^{int-ctxt}(D) = |Pr[K \in_R \mathcal{K} : D^{\mathcal{E}_K, \mathcal{V}_K} \neq \perp]|$$

We assume that the distinguisher does not make a verification query (N, A, C, T) if it ever obtained $(C, T) \leftarrow \mathcal{E}_K(N, A, M)$ for some M. Depending upon the attack scenario, we can also optionally restrict the distinguisher from repeating N for different $\mathcal{E}_k$ queries (N, A, M). By $\mathbf{Adv}_\pi^{int-ctxt}(\mathbf{q}, \mathbf{l})$, we denote the supremum taken over all distinguishers making q queries with total queried message length as l bits.

If $\mathbf{Adv}_\pi^{int-ctxt}(q, l) \leq 2^{-s}$, then the π has s bit **INT-CTXT** security against all adversaries making q queries with total queried message length as l bits.

Informally, the goal of D is to compute a (N, A, C, T) such that $\mathcal{V}_k(N, A, C, T) \neq \perp$. Here the output of the verification $\neq \perp$ implies that $\exists M$, such that $(C, T) = \mathcal{E}_k(N, A, M)$. If the adversary can generate a valid ciphertext and tag pair for any message, associated data and nonce then the adversary is said to make a *universally* forgery.

In the case of fault based forgery, D can inject faults in the intermediate encryption states during the encryption queries. This means, D can forcefully change the normal execution of the encryption process $\mathcal{E}_k$. In other words, he can simulate a new circuit $\mathcal{E}_k'$ (the encryption procedure after fault injection) from $\mathcal{E}_k$, by injecting the fault. In this case, D gets the extra power to change the circuit. The goal of D will be as the INT-CTXT security model described above.

3   Motivation

In this section, we provide the motivation behind this work. The fault based existential forgery does not posses much importance as the output from this attack does not provide much benefit to the attacker. Moreover, in the case of blockcipher based authenticated encryption schemes, where the master secret key is solely used inside the underlying blokcipher, the key recovery of the scheme implies the key recovery of the blockcipher. Thus it would be really relevant to achieve something more than existential forgery on the encryption mode using fault injection(s), assuming the underlying blockcipher is fault resistant.

For example, let us consider the scenario of a low resource embedded device(e.g., smart card) with an authenticated encryption algorithm embedded inside the chip for secure communications. If the attacker has access to the chip, he can inject a fault and forge with false information. However, injeting a fault may be costly and may take long time. In that case, existential forgery by injecting a fault may not be the goal of the attacker as he can forge only a single valid ciphertext and does not gain much advantage from this procedure. In this scenario, universal forgery or even multiple forgery could be more interesting and non trivial task.

However, doing existential forgery with a single fault could be possible on any of the authenticated encryption schemes. As pointed out by Iwata et al. [20] any authenticated encryption scheme can be existentially forged by the following procedure.

- Make a fault injected encryption query (N, A, M) and receive (C, T). The fault is injected at known bit positions N and A to result in N' and A' respectively.
- Make a valid forge with (N', A', C, T).

This attack can forge a valid ciphertext for any nonce, associated data and message triplet by injecting a fault. In a generic sense, if the adversary wants to forge k ciphertexts, he has to inject faults k times. However, this procedure is not efficient as fault injection is not cheap in itself and we have to insert k faults here. Thus, it will be a really interesting problem to see whether k $(k \gg 1)$ forgery can be done with one or a very few number of faults. Since, injecting one fault may be costly, making multiple forgeries with a very few number of faults could be an efficient fault based attack. In this work, we address this problem and shown that, in the case of CLOC and SILC, we can forge a valid ciphertext for almost all the nonce, associated data and message with only one single bit fault.

This attack is on the encryption mode and does not exploit the underlying blockcipher structure. Hence, it would also be really interesting to see, if there exists an encryption mode, that can resist similar attack strategies.

4 Fault Based Existential Forgery on CLOC

4.1 A Fault Based Forgery on CLOC with Nonce Respecting Encryption Queries

We first describe the fault model and next the forgery under this fault model.

Fault Model and Motivation of the Attack. Here, we assume that a fault e has been injected at the first bit position of the n-bit input state corresponding to the second block cipher call for processing the first ciphertext block in Enc_k. We next describe how we can forge a valid ciphertext assuming that a fault e has been injected at the first bit position of a specific n-bit input state.

Different Phases of the Forgery. The several phases of the forgery are described below.

- **Phase 1** : Construct a faulty input-output pair and 2 valid input output pairs corresponding to E_k by a single encryption query.
- **Phase 2** : Construct two colliding associated data (A, A'), that produces same V under the same nonce N.
- **Phase 3** : Construct (C^*, T^*) under N, A and a random message M^* by a single encryption query.
- **Phase 4** : Forge a valid ciphertext (N, A', C^*, T^*).

Phase 1: Construct a Faulty Input-Output Pair and 2 Valid Input Output Pairs Corresponding to E_k by a single encryption query. The attack first makes an encryption query with a random 4 block message $M = (M_1, M_2, M_3, M_4)$, a random nonce N^r and a random associated data A^r and receives a ciphertext tag pair $((C = C_1, C_2, C_3, C_4), T)$. We assume that the fault e is injected at the first bit of the n-bit input state $fix1(C_1)$ before the corresponding E_k call in Enc_k. We now construct two valid input-output pairs (X_1, Y_1) and (X_2, Y_2) corresponding to E_k, with $X_1 = fix1(C_2)$, $Y_1 = M_3 \oplus C_3$, $X_2 = fix1(C_3)$ and $Y_2 = M_4 \oplus C_4$. Note that, the first bit of $e(fix1(C_1))$ is 0 as the first bit of $fix1(C_1)$ is 1. Let us denote $e(fix1(C_1))$ by X and $E_k(X) = M_2 \oplus C_2$ by Y. This phase is described in Fig. 4.

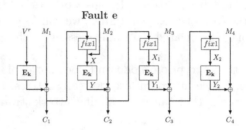

Fig. 4. Phase 1

Phase 2: Construct Two Colliding Associated Data. (A, A'), that produces same V under the same nonce N. We now construct two colliding associated data $A = (A_1, A_2, A_3)$ and $A' = (A_1, A'_2, A'_3)$, such that both of them produce the same V under the same nonce N. We set $A_1 = X$. As $A_1 = fix0(A_1)$, $E_k(A_1)$ is equal to Y. We now set $A_2 = Y \oplus X_1$ such that, input to the corresponding E_k call is X_1. As E_k outputs Y_1, set $A_3 = Y_1 \oplus X_2$ such that, input to the corresponding E_k call is X_2. Thus, $V = f_1(Y_2 \oplus ozp(N))$.

We construct A' by first setting $A'_2 = Y \oplus X_2$ such that, input to the corresponding E_k call is X_2. As E_k outputs Y_2, set $A'_3 = Y_2 \oplus X_2$ such that, input to the corresponding E_k call is X_2. Thus V gets the same value $f_1(Y_2 \oplus ozp(N))$. This phase is described in Fig. 5.

Phase 3: Construct. (C^*, T^*) under N, A and a random message M^* by a single encryption query. We now make an encryption query with N, A and a random message M^*. In response, we receive a valid ciphertext tag pair (C^*, T^*).

Phase 4: Forge a Ciphertext. (N, A', C^*, T^*). As both A and A' produces same V, the ciphertext tag pair produced for M^* with N and A' is (C^*, T^*). Thus we make a valid forgery (N, A', C^*, T^*).

(a) Compute A (b) Compute A'

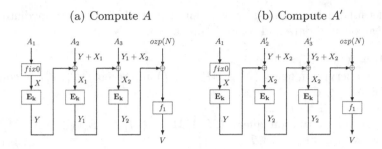

Fig. 5. Phase 2.

5   Fault Based Almost Universal Forgery on CLOC

The attack described in Sect. 4 first collects a set of input-output corresponding to E_k and then finds a colliding associated data pair and finally forge valid ciphertext-tag pair. In this section, we describe how this technique can be extended efficiently to almost universal forgery with some extra nonce-misusing encryption queries. Also, we first compute X and Y as described in Phase 1 in Sect. 4.1. We use this X and Y to describe the term *"almost universal forgeries"*

We first describe, what the term *"almost universal forgeries"* suggests in this scenario. This attack can create a valid forgery for almost all the $(N, A = (A_1, \cdots, A_a), M = (M_1, \cdots M_m))$ triplet for any a and m (a and m are bounded according to the specification). There is a nominal restriction on the choice of A. However, there is no restriction on the message M and the nonce N. We denote the intermediate inputs and outputs to and from the E_k for $A_2, \cdots, A_a$ are by $X_1, \cdots, X_{a-1}$ and $Y_1, \cdots, Y_{a-1}$ respectively. We also introduce I_1 and O_1 and they are described as follows.

$$I_1 = A_1 = X, O_1 = Y = E_k(I_1)$$
$$X_1 = A_2 \oplus i/h(O_1), Y_1 = E_k(X_1)$$

$$.$$
$$.$$

$$X_{a-1} = A_a \oplus Y_{a-2}, Y_{a-1} = E_k(X_{a-1})$$

In this attack we first make a fault injected encryption query to retrieve X and Y. The restriction on the associated data $A = (A_1, \cdots, A_a)$ can be viewed as A_1 is always equal to X, all the bits of $A_2, \cdots, A_a$ except the first bit can take any value and the first bit of $X_1, \cdots, X_{a-1}$ will be 1. This is a negligible restriction where all the A_is can take any of the 2^{127} values instead of 2^{128}. Here, we assume that all the A_is are full. The scenario is same for incomplete A_a, hence is omitted. We next describe the almost universal forgery for an arbitrary nonce, associated data and message triplet $(N, A = (A_1, \cdots, A_a), M = (M_1, \cdots, M_m))$, such that this triplet follows the "*almost*" restriction. Let the V be the intermediate value after the associated data and nonce is processed.

1. Set $A_1 = X$ and $X_1 = Y \oplus A_2$.
2. Make an encryption query $(N, A, M^r = M_1^r)$ and receive (C_1^r, T_1^r) to compute $E_k(V) = M_1^r \oplus C_1^r$.
3. Repeat for $i = 1$ to $a - 2$:
   - Make an encryption query $(N, A, M = (M_1' = E_k(V) \oplus X_i, M_2')$ and receive $(C' = (C_1', C_2'), T')$.
   - Compute $Y_i = M_2' \oplus C_2'$.
   - Compute $X_{i+1} = A_{i+2} \oplus X_i$.
4. Make an encryption query $(N, A, M = (M_1' = E_k(V) \oplus X_{a-1}, M_2')$ and receive $(C' = (C_1', C_2'), T')$.
5. Compute $Y_{a-1} = M_2' \oplus C_2'$.
6. Find a colliding associated data A' for A (colliding at V) following the Phase 2 in Sect. 4.1.
7. Make an encryption query (N, A', M) and receive (C, T).
8. Thus (C, T) is a valid forgery for (N, A, M).

6   Fault Based Existential Forgery on SILC

6.1   A Fault Based Forgery on SILC with Nonce Misusing Encryption Queries.

Fault Model and Motivation of the Attack. The fault model for this attack on SILC is similar to that for CLOC described in Sect. 4.1. This section describes how we can forge a valid ciphertext assuming that a fault e has been injected at the first bit position of the above mentioned n-bit input state. We denote the nonce length by ℓ_N and we define t by $t = n - \ell_N$, such that $zpp(N) = 0^t||N$.

(a) First Encryption Query   (b) Second Encryption Query

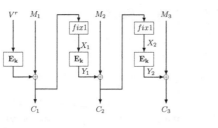
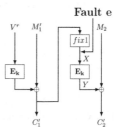

Fig. 6. First and the Second Encryption Query in Phase 1

Different Phases of the Forgery. The different phases are described below.

- **Phase 1** : Construct a faulty input-output pair and 2 valid input-output pairs corresponding to E_k by 2 encryption queries.
- **Phase 2** : Construct two colliding associated data (A, A'), that produces same V under the same nonce N.
- **Phase 3** : Construct (C^*, T^*) under N, A and a random message M^* by a single encryption query.
- **Phase 4** : Forge a valid ciphertext (N, A', C^*, T^*).

Phase 1: Construct a Faulty Input-Output Pair and 2 Valid Input Output Pairs Corresponding to E_k by 2 encryption queries. The attack first makes an encryption query with a random 3 block message $M = (M_1, M_2, M_3)$, a random nonce N^r and a random associated data A^r and receives a ciphertext tag pair $((C = C_1, C_2, C_3), T)$. The attack now construct two input-output pairs (X_1, Y_1) and (X_2, Y_2) corresponding to E_k, where $X_1 = fix1(C_1)$, $Y_1 = M_2 \oplus C_2$, $X_2 = fix1(C_2)$ and $Y_2 = M_3 \oplus C_3$. The attack now makes a two block encryption query $(N^r, A^r, M' = (M_1', M_2'))$ and receive $((C' = C_1', C_2'), T')$ where first t bits of M_1' adjusted in such a way such that first t bits of C_1' are 0. Note that, we inject a fault e at the first bit of $fix1(C_1')$ before the corresponding E_k call in Enc_k. As the first bit of $fix1(C_1')$ is one and next $t - 1$ bits of $fix1(C_1')$ are zero, first t bits of $e(fix1(C_1'))$ are zero. Let us denote $e(fix1(C_1'))$ by X and $E_k(X) = M_2 \oplus C_2'$ by Y. This phase is described in Fig. 6.

Phase 2: Construct Two Colliding Associated Data (A, A'), that produces same V under the same nonce N. The attack now construct two colliding associated associated data $A = (A_1, A_2)$ and $A' = (A_1', A_2')$, that produces same V under the same nonce with $zpp(N) = X$. We set $A_1 = Y \oplus X_1$, such that input to the corresponding E_k call is X_1. We set $A_2 = Y_1 \oplus X_2$, such that input to the corresponding E_k call is X_2. Thus, $V = g(Y_2 \oplus 2)$, with $len(A) = 2$.

We construct A' by setting $A_1' = Y \oplus X_2$, such that input to the corresponding E_k call is X_2. We set $A_2' = Y_2 \oplus X_2$, such that input to the corresponding E_k call is X_2. Thus, V will get the same value $g(Y_2 \oplus 2)$, as $len(A') = 2$. This phase is described in Fig. 7.

Phase 3 and **4** are the same as previous attack described in Sect. 4.1. The fault detection technique is also similar to that for the previous attack. We iterate this forging attempt n times and detect the fault if the forging attempt gets accepted by the decryption oracle.

6.2   Fault Based Almost Universal Forgery on SILC

The attack described in Sect. 6 is almost same as the attack on CLOC and it first collects a set of input-output corresponding to E_k and then finds a colliding associated data pair and finally forge and valid ciphertext-tag pair. In this

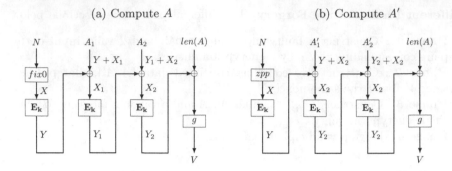

(a) Compute A (b) Compute A'

Fig. 7. Phase 2

section, we describe the *almost universal forgery* on SILC. We first compute X and Y and use them to describe the term *almost*.

The term *almost* is a nominal restriction on the possible value forgable (N, A, M) triplet. This attack can create a valid forgery for almost all the $(N, A = (A_1, \cdots, A_a), M = (M_1, \cdots M_m))$ triple for any a and m (a and m are bounded according to the specification). The nonce N is restricted in away, such that $zpp(N) = X$. There is a nominal restriction on the choice of A. However, there is no restriction on the message M. We denote the intermediate inputs and outputs to and from the E_k for $A_1, \cdots, A_a$ are by $X_1, \cdots, X_a$ and $Y_1, \cdots, Y_a$ respectively. The restriction is,

$$X_1 = zpp(N) = X, Y_1 = Y = E_k(X_1)$$
$$X_2 = A_1 \oplus (Y_1), Y_2 = E_k(X_2)$$

.

.

$$X_{a+1} = A_a \oplus Y_a, Y_{a+1} = E_k(X_{a+1})$$

In this attack we first make a fault injected encryption query to retrieve X and Y. The restriction on the associated data $A = (A_1, \cdots, A_a)$ can be viewed as $zpp(N)$ is always equal to X, all the bits of $A_1, \cdots, A_a$ except the first bit can take any value and the first bit of $X_2, \cdots X_{a+1}$ will be 1. This is a negligible restriction on A where all the A_is can take any of the 2^{127} values instead of 2^{128}. Here, we assume that all the A_is are full. The scenario is same for incomplete A_a, hence is omitted. However, the restriction on N is strict. We next describe the almost universal forgery for an arbitrary nonce, associated data and message triplet $(N, A = (A_1, \cdots, A_a), M = (M_1, \cdots, M_m))$, such that this triplet follows the *"almost"* restriction. Let the V be the intermediate value after the associated data and nonce is processed.

1. Set $zpp(N) = X$ and $X_1 = Y \oplus A_1$.
2. Make an encryption query $(N, A, M^r = M_1^r)$ and receive (C_1^r, T_1^r) to compute $E_k(V) = M_1^r \oplus C_1^r$.
3. Repeat for $i = 1$ to $a - 1$:
   - Make an encryption query $(N, A, M = (M_1' = E_k(V) \oplus X_i, M_2'))$ and receive $(C' = (C_1', C_2'), T')$.
   - Compute $Y_i = M_2' \oplus C_2'$.
   - Compute $X_{i+1} = A_{i+2} \oplus X_i$.
4. Make an encryption query $(N, A, M = (M_1' = E_k(V) \oplus X_a, M_2'))$ and receive $(C' = (C_1', C_2'), T')$.
5. Compute $Y_a = M_2' \oplus C_2'$.
6. Find a colliding associated data A' for A (colliding at V) following the Phase 2 in Sect. 6.1.
7. Make an encryption query (N, A', M) and receive (C, T).
8. Thus (C, T) is a valid forgery for (N, A, M).

7   Experimental Validation of Proposed Fault Based Forgery Attack

In the previous sections, we have depicted how fault injection in the *fix1* module of ENC_k operation will allow us to do successful forgeries on the CLOC and SILC. This section focusses on practical validation of the proposed fault based forgery attack.

For experimental validation, we have implemented CLOC in the SPARTAN-6 FPGA (xc6slx75) of SAKURA-G [37] board. The implementation requires 7776 LUTs and 5422 number of registers. The critical path of the design is 10.372 ns. It should be noted that from the operational point of view, *fix1* module does not involve any computation. It simply sets the *MSB* of the input register of E_k module. Instead of directly assigning logic one to the MSB, we have introduced some buffers in the path of this assignment. It should be noted that these buffers do not increase the critical path of the design and increase the area overhead of the design very slightly.

There are several ways by which one can inject fault into a device. Over-clocking [32], under-powering [33], laser shots [34], temperature increase [35] are few of them. In this experiment, we have used electromagnetic pulses as fault injector [36]. The fault attack set-up is shown in Fig. 8. For experimental valida-tion we have focussed only on the *fix1* module of CLOC. Hence we have ported the *fix1* module in the SPARTAN 6 FPGA (xc6slx75) of SAKURA G. This FPGA implementation triggers the connected *oscilloscope* for each execution of *fix1* module which in turn triggers the *delay generator* equipment. This allows us to choose a precise time moment at which we would like to inject fault. The *delay generator* equipment triggers the *RF generator* module which generates the electromagnetic pulses. Finally these electromagnetic pulses are amplified by a RF amplifier and are injected in to the FPGA by the electromagnetic probe.

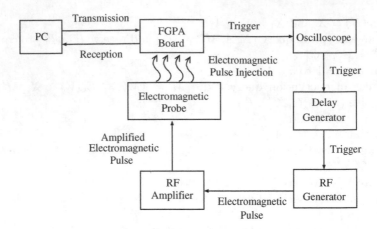

Fig. 8. Fault Attack Setup

Input and output of the *fix1* module, executing on the FPGA, are constantly monitored on PC to detect the occurrence of faults.

To execute the proposed forgery, we need to inject a stuck at zero fault at the *MSB* of the output of *fix1* module. In this case, the adversary has a very precise control over both fault location and fault nature which may be difficult to obtain without precise instruments like laser. However, here we show how an electromagnetic pulse base fault injection set-up can be utilized to induce a fault which can eventually corrupt the *MSB* as required in the proposed attack. More specifically, we are able to introduce a 32 bit left shift in the output of the *fix1* module. We have repeated our experiment multiple times and each time we have observed same fault pattern (32 bit left shift of the input). This deterministic nature of the fault pattern allows us to do the forgery by following steps:

1. We give a random message as input to the *fix1* module of ENC_k operation with only one constraint: 95th bit of should be set to zero. As the input is the previous ciphertext block, we can always query with a suitable message block in order to set the 95th bit of the ciphertext as zero.
2. Then we will inject fault on the *fix1* module which will left shift the *fix1* module output by 32 bits, making the 95th bit as *MSB*. Thus we have been able to input E_k operation with an input having its *MSB* set to zero. Also as the fault nature is deterministic, we know the output of *fix1* module which will allow us to construct the required associative data values to do the forgery. The main challenge was to query the blockcipher with an input having its *MSB* set to zero. Once we achieve that using the fault injection, the rest of the attack can be implemented as described in Sect. 4.
3. For SILC too, we can apply similar fault injection methodology with slight modification due to the *zpp* function. Let us assume that for one instance of SILC, *nonce* is of 120 bits. Then it needs to be padded with 8 bits of zero from the *MSB* side. Hence, for successful forgery we need to set the most significant byte of the *fix1* module to zero. This can be achieved by setting

from 95th to 88th bits of *fix1* input to zero. Thus when we inject fault, these bits will get shifted by 32 bits and will become the most significant byte which will allow us to do the forgery. This scheme can be extended for *nonce* of any length,

Thus, we have practically validated the fault based forgery attack in this section. In the next section, we will focus on the countermeasures where we provide two different constructions to prevent the proposed fault based forgery attack.

8   Preventing Fault Based Forgery on **CLOC** and **SILC**

In the previous sections, we had exploited the vulnerability of ENC_k and $HASH_k$ algorithms to produce a successful forgery attack on the $HASH_k$ implementation. The adversary in this case was able to obtain the input and output block of any E_k with the help of fault induction on the *fix1* module of encryption operation. This allows the adversary to query the $HASH_k$ implementation with specific choices of *associated data* which in turn produces a successful forgery. Structural modification of the $HASH_k$ algorithm doesn't improve the security of CLOC as long as the input-output pairs of E_k are available to the adversary. As the choice of associated data is at the liberty of the adversary, and *associated data* could always be chosen so as to produce desired input to the encryption block, and create duplicate *associated data* which would produce the same V value under identical *nonce* values.

8.1   Redesign of ENC_k algorithm

Since the root cause for the attack was the availability of input-output pairs to the adversary, in this section, we'll discuss upon the possible modification of ENC_k algorithm, which could prevent the fault attack. In order to make the input-output pairs of E_k unavailable, the output C_i is encrypted using another

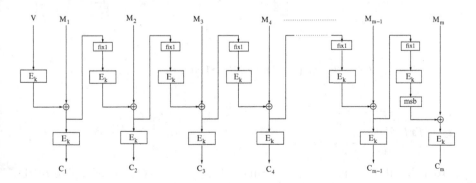

Fig. 9. $C \longleftarrow ENC_k(V, M)$ for $|M| \geq 1$

encryption block as shown in Fig. 9, where $i \in \{1, 2, ...n\}$. In this new algorithm, let $Y = (Y_1, Y_2....Y_n)$ be the outputs after the XOR operation of message $M = (M_1, M_2....M_n)$, $Y_1 = M_1 \oplus E_k(V)$ is not known to the adversary, so the consecutive $Y_i = M_i \oplus E_k(fix1(Y_{i-1}))$ remain unknown, where $i \in \{2, 3...n\}$. Hence we can predict neither the input nor the output of any E_k, and since *Phase 1* of the attack cannot be performed in modified Enc_k algorithm, the adversary will not be able to perform the attack on the cipher. Please also note that neither $HASH_k$ nor PRF_k algorithms are changed. This countermeasure can also be applied to SILC as its ENC_k operation is exactly similar to CLOC. The total number of blockcipher execution will be now $2n$ for encrypting n number of blocks and the timing overhead will be twice.

Cost Effective ENC_k algorithm. It is not necessary to prevent the adversary from knowing both the input as well as the output of any E_k, even if either the input or the output is known, the adversary would still be unable to attack the cryptosystem. To reduce the cost of the algorithm, alternate ciphertext blocks could be encrypted and still maintain protection against the attack as shown in Fig. 10. For any E_k, either the input or the output is known, but not both. The total number of blockcipher execution will be now $\frac{3n}{2}$ times for n number of blocks and timing complexity would be *1.5 times* that of the original ENC_k algorithm if the computation is performed with the existing implementation. But the timing could be made similar to the original ENC_k algorithm with twice the area of implementation which enables parallel computation.

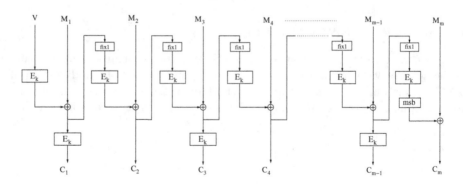

Fig. 10. $C \longleftarrow ENC_k(V, M)$ for $|M| \geq 1$ and m has an even value

$$I_1 = fix0(M_1 \oplus E_k(V)) \qquad O_1 = M_2 \oplus C_2$$
$$I_2 = fix1(C_2) \qquad O_2 = M_3 \oplus E_k^{-1}(C_3)$$
$$I_3 = fix1(M_3 \oplus E_k^{-1}(C[3])) \qquad O_3 = M_4 \oplus C_4$$

From the above equations, the values of O_1, I_2 and O_3 are available to the adversary but not I_1, O_2 and I_3, as the key is unknown, so are the values $E_k^{-1}(C_3)$ and $E_k(V)$.

8.2   Structural Modification of ENC_k algorithm

In this section, we introduce yet another possible modification to Enc_k algorithm which is more cost effective and faster in computation than redesigned algorithm discussed before. This algorithm exposes the output of any E_k but not the input, this has been achieved with the introduction of a secret parameter A, equal to $E_k(ozp(Nonce))$. As shown in Fig. 11, the output of E_k with input $fix1(C[i])$ is XORed with α^{i-1} *times* A, where α is a primitive element in $GF(2^{128})$. Except during the last encryption when A is multiplied with $(1 + \alpha)\alpha^{m-2}$, instead of α^{m-1}, m indicates the number of blocks of the message.

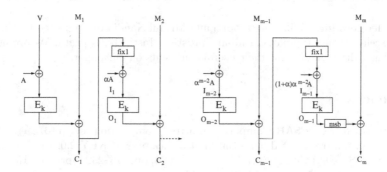

Fig. 11. $C \longleftarrow ENC_k(V, M)$ for $|M| \geq 1$

$$I_i = E_k(fix1(C_i) \oplus \alpha^i A) \qquad O_i = M_{i+1} \oplus C_{i+1}$$

We can see that the outputs of E_k are readily available to the adversary, but the inputs of E_k is not available to the adversary as it is now masked with secret parameter which depends upon A. As A is actually the encryption of *nonce*, it is unknown to the adversary. This rules out the attack proposed in this paper. The area and timing overhead of this scheme is due to the introduction of a field multiplication in $GF(2^{128})$ which can be implemented with very less area and timing requirement. The number of required E_k operations increases by one as now we also need to compute $A = E_k(ozp(N))$. Moreover we now need to store the value of A which requires additional storage.

To summarize, in this section we have provided two modified CLOC constructions to prevent previously discussed forgery attacks based on fault injection in the *fix1* module. An important observation is that the proposed attack works because the adversary has access to the both input and output of E_k in the encryption module. In the modified constructions, we have made sure that at any time an adversary will not have access to both input and output of E_k, which prevents the fault based forgery attack.

It should be also noted that ENC_k operation of both CLOC and SILC is similar. As we do not modify other operations $HASH_k$ and PRF, the countermeasures depicted in this section are equally applicable to both CLOC and SILC.

9   Conclusion

In this paper, we present fault based almost universal forgery on both CLOC and SILC with nonce misusing encryption queries and only one fault injected encryption query with a single fault at the *MSB* of a specific blockcipher input state. We first propose fault based existential forgeries on both the constructions. We next use these attacks to construct almost universal forgeries. All of the proposed forgery attacks requires fault injection at the output of the *fix1* module which we have practically validated by performing electromagnetic pulse based fault attack on *fix1* module. Finally, we propose three efficient constructions with small overheads to resist fault based forgeries on the encryption mode.

Acknowledgement. Avik Chakraborti and Mridul Nandi are supported by the Centre of Excellence in Cryptology, Indian Statistical Institute, Kolkata. We would also like to thank the reviewers for their useful comments on our paper.

References

1. — (no editor), CAESAR Competition. http://competitions.cr.yp.to/caesar.html
2. Banik, S., Maitra, S.: A differential fault attack on MICKEY 2.0. In: Bertoni, G., Coron, J.-S. (eds.) CHES 2013. LNCS, vol. 8086, pp. 215–232. Springer, Heidelberg (2013). doi:10.1007/978-3-642-40349-1_13
3. Banik, S., Maitra, S., Sarkar, S.: A differential fault attack on the grain family of stream ciphers. In: Prouff, E., Schaumont, P. (eds.) CHES 2012. LNCS, vol. 7428, pp. 122–139. Springer, Heidelberg (2012). doi:10.1007/978-3-642-33027-8_8
4. Banik, S., Maitra, S., Sarkar, S.: A differential fault attack on the grain family under reasonable assumptions. In: Galbraith, S., Nandi, M. (eds.) INDOCRYPT 2012. LNCS, vol. 7668, pp. 191–208. Springer, Heidelberg (2012). doi:10.1007/978-3-642-34931-7_12
5. Bellare, M., Rogaway, P., Wagner, D.: The EAX mode of operation. In: Roy, B., Meier, W. (eds.) FSE 2004. LNCS, vol. 3017, pp. 389–407. Springer, Heidelberg (2004). doi:10.1007/978-3-540-25937-4_25
6. Biham, E., Shamir, A.: Differential fault analysis of secret key cryptosystems. In: Kaliski, B.S. (ed.) CRYPTO 1997. LNCS, vol. 1294, pp. 513–525. Springer, Heidelberg (1997). doi:10.1007/BFb0052259
7. Biham, E., Granboulan, L., Nguyen, P.Q.: Impossible fault analysis of RC4 and differential fault analysis of RC4. In: Gilbert, H., Handschuh, H. (eds.) FSE 2005. LNCS, vol. 3557, pp. 359–367. Springer, Heidelberg (2005). doi:10.1007/11502760_24
8. Bogdanov, A., Knudsen, L.R., Leander, G., Paar, C., Poschmann, A., Robshaw, M.J.B., Seurin, Y., Vikkelsoe, C.: PRESENT: an ultra-lightweight block cipher. In: Paillier, P., Verbauwhede, I. (eds.) CHES 2007. LNCS, vol. 4727, pp. 450–466. Springer, Heidelberg (2007). doi:10.1007/978-3-540-74735-2_31
9. Boneh, D., DeMillo, R.A., Lipton, R.J.: On the importance of checking cryptographic protocols for faults. In: Fumy, W. (ed.) EUROCRYPT 1997. LNCS, vol. 1233, pp. 37–51. Springer, Heidelberg (1997). doi:10.1007/3-540-69053-0_4
10. Boneh, D., DeMillo, R.A., Lipton, R.J.: On the. Journal of Cryptography. **2001**, 101–119 (2001)

11. Daemen, J., Rijmen, V.: Rijndael for AES. In: AES Candidate Conference, pp. 343–348 (2000)
12. Daemen, J., Rijmen, V.: The design of Rijndael: AES - the advanced encryption standard. In: Information Security and Cryptography, Springer, Heidelberg (2002)
13. Dusart, P., Letourneux, G., Vivolo, O.: Differential fault analysis on A.E.S. In: Zhou, J., Yung, M., Han, Y. (eds.) ACNS 2003. LNCS, vol. 2846, pp. 293–306. Springer, Heidelberg (2003). doi:10.1007/978-3-540-45203-4_23
14. Dworkin, M.: Recommendation for Block Cipher Modes of Operation: The CCM Mode for Authentication and Confidentiality (2004). NIST Special, Publication, 800-38C (2004)
15. Guo, J., Peyrin, T., Poschmann, A., Robshaw, M.: The LED block cipher. In: Preneel, B., Takagi, T. (eds.) CHES 2011. LNCS, vol. 6917, pp. 326–341. Springer, Heidelberg (2011). doi:10.1007/978-3-642-23951-9_22
16. Hemme, L., Hoffman, L., Lee, C.: Differential Fault Analysis on the SHA1 Compression Function. In: FDTC 2011, pp. 54–62, 11 (2011)
17. Hoch, J.J., Shamir, A.: Fault analysis of stream ciphers. In: Joye, M., Quisquater, J.-J. (eds.) CHES 2004. LNCS, vol. 3156, pp. 240–253. Springer, Heidelberg (2004). doi:10.1007/978-3-540-28632-5_18
18. Hojsík, M., Rudolf, B.: Floating fault analysis of trivium. In: Chowdhury, D.R., Rijmen, V., Das, A. (eds.) INDOCRYPT 2008. LNCS, vol. 5365, pp. 239–250. Springer, Heidelberg (2008). doi:10.1007/978-3-540-89754-5_19
19. Hojsík, M., Rudolf, B.: Differential fault analysis of trivium. In: Nyberg, K. (ed.) FSE 2008. LNCS, vol. 5086, pp. 158–172. Springer, Heidelberg (2008). doi:10.1007/978-3-540-71039-4_10
20. Iwata, T., Minematsu, K., Guo, J., Morioka, S., Kobayashi, E.: Re: Fault Based Forgery on CLOC and SILC. https://groups.google.com/forum/#!topic/crypto-competitions/_qxORmqcSrY
21. Iwata, T., Minematsu, K., Guo, J., Morioka, S., Kobayashi, E.: SILC: SImple Lightweight CFB (2014). http://competitions.cr.yp.to/round1/silcv1.pdf
22. Iwata, T., Minematsu, K., Guo, J., Morioka, S., Kobayashi, E.: CLOC: Compact Low- Overhead CFB (2014). http://competitions.cr.yp.to/round1/clocv1.pdf
23. Jeong, K., Lee, C.: Differential fault analysis on block cipher LED-64. In: Park, J.J., Leung, V.C.M., Wang, C.-L., Shon, T. (eds.) Future Information Technology, Application, and Service. LNEE, vol. 164, pp. 747–755. Springer, Heidelberg (2012). doi:10.1007/978-94-007-4516-2_79
24. Jovanovic, P., Kreuzer, M., Polian, I.: A fault attack on the LED block cipher. In: Schindler, W., Huss, S.A. (eds.) COSADE 2012. LNCS, vol. 7275, pp. 120–134. Springer, Heidelberg (2012). doi:10.1007/978-3-642-29912-4_10
25. Minematsu, K., Lucks, S., Iwata, T.: Improved authenticity bound of EAX, and refinements. In: Susilo, W., Reyhanitabar, R. (eds.) ProvSec 2013. LNCS, vol. 8209, pp. 184–201. Springer, Heidelberg (2013). doi:10.1007/978-3-642-41227-1_11
26. Moise, A., Beroset, E., Phinney, T., Burns, M.: EAX0 Cipher Mode. NIST Submission, 2011: Technique against SPN Structures, with Application to the AES and KHAZAD(2011). http://csrc.nist.gov/groups/ST/toolkit/BCM/documents/proposedmodes/eax-prime/eax-prime-spec.pdf
27. Piret, G., Quisquater, J.-J.: A differential fault attack technique against SPN structures, with application to the AES and KHAZAD. In: Walter, C.D., Koç, Ç.K., Paar, C. (eds.) CHES 2003. LNCS, vol. 2779, pp. 77–88. Springer, Heidelberg (2003). doi:10.1007/978-3-540-45238-6_7

28. Saha, D., Kuila, S., Roy Chowdhury, D.: EscApe: diagonal fault analysis of APE. In: Meier, W., Mukhopadhyay, D. (eds.) INDOCRYPT 2014. LNCS, vol. 8885, pp. 197–216. Springer, Heidelberg (2014). doi:10.1007/978-3-319-13039-2_12

29. Suzaki, T., Minematsu, K., Morioka, S., Kobayashi, E.: *TWINE*: a lightweight block cipher for multiple platforms. In: Knudsen, L.R., Wu, H. (eds.) SAC 2012. LNCS, vol. 7707, pp. 339–354. Springer, Heidelberg (2013). doi:10.1007/978-3-642-35999-6_22

30. Tunstall, M., Mukhopadhyay, D., Ali, S.: Differential fault analysis of the advanced encryption standard using a single fault. In: Ardagna, C.A., Zhou, J. (eds.) WISTP 2011. LNCS, vol. 6633, pp. 224–233. Springer, Heidelberg (2011). doi:10.1007/978-3-642-21040-2_15

31. Whiting, D., Houeley, R., Ferguson, N.: Counter with CBC-MAC, Submission to NIST: (2002). http://csrc.nist.gov/groups/ST/toolkit/BCM/modesdevelopment.html

32. Agoyan, M., Dutertre, J.-M., Mirbaha, A.-P., Tria, A.: How to Flip a Bit?, On-Line Testing Symposium (IOLTS). In: 2010 IEEE 16th International, 2010 (2010)

33. Fournier, J.J.A., Moore, S., Li, H., Mullins, R., Taylor, G.: Security evaluation of asynchronous circuits. In: Walter, C.D., Koç, Ç.K., Paar, C. (eds.) CHES 2003. LNCS, vol. 2779, pp. 137–151. Springer, Heidelberg (2003). doi:10.1007/978-3-540-45238-6_12

34. Skorobogatov, S.P., Anderson, R.J.: Optical fault induction attacks. In: Kaliski, B.S., Koç, K., Paar, C. (eds.) CHES 2002. LNCS, vol. 2523, pp. 2–12. Springer, Heidelberg (2003). doi:10.1007/3-540-36400-5_2

35. Skorobogatov, S.: Local heating attacks on flash memory devices. In: IEEE International Workshop on Hardware-Oriented Security and Trust, 2009 (2009)

36. Dehbaoui, A., Dutertre, J.-M., Robisson, B., Tria, A.: Electromagnetic Transient Faults Injection on a Hardware and a Software Implementations of AES. Fault Diagnosis and Tolerance, 2012 (2012)

37. — (no editor). http://satoh.cs.uec.ac.jp/SAKURA/hardware/SAKURA-G_Spec_Ver1.0_English.pdf

Applied Cryptography

Implementing Complete Formulas on Weierstrass Curves in Hardware

Pedro Maat C. Massolino[✉], Joost Renes, and Lejla Batina

Radboud University, Nijmegen, The Netherlands
{p.massolino,j.renes,lejla}@cs.ru.nl

Abstract. This work revisits the recent complete addition formulas for prime order elliptic curves of Renes, Costello and Batina in light of parallelization. We introduce the first hardware implementation of the new formulas on an FPGA based on three arithmetic units performing Montgomery multiplication. Our results are competitive with current literature and show the potential of the new complete formulas in hardware design. Furthermore, we present algorithms to compute the formulas using anywhere between two and six processors, using the minimum number of field multiplications.

Keywords: Elliptic curve cryptography · FPGA · Weierstrass curves · Complete addition formulas

1 Introduction

The main operation in many cryptographic protocols based on elliptic curves is scalar multiplication, which is performed via repeated point addition and doubling. In early works formulas for the group operation used different sequences of instructions for addition and doubling [22,28]. This resulted in more optimized implementations, since doublings can be faster than general additions, but naïve implementations suffered from side-channel attacks [23]. Indeed, as all special cases have to be treated differently, it is not straightforward to come up with an efficient and side-channel secure implementation.

A class of elliptic curves which avoids these problems is the family of curves proposed by Bernstein and Lange, the so-called Edwards curves [8]. Arguably, the primary reason for their popularity is their "complete" addition law. That is, a single addition law which can be used for all inputs. The benefit of having a complete addition law is obvious for both simplicity and side-channel security. Namely, having only one set of formulas that works for all inputs simplifies the task of implementers and thwarts side-channel analysis and more refined attacks, e. g. safe-error attacks [38]. After the introduction of Edwards curves, more curves models have been shown to possess complete addition laws [6,7].

This work was supported in part by the Technology Foundation STW (project 13499 - TYPHOON & ASPASIA), from the Dutch government.

© Springer International Publishing AG 2016
C. Carlet et al. (Eds.): SPACE 2016, LNCS 10076, pp. 89–108, 2016.
DOI: 10.1007/978-3-319-49445-6_5

Moreover, (twisted) Edwards curves are being deployed in software, for example in the library NaCl [10]. In particular, software implementations typically rely on specific curves, e. g. on the Montgomery curves Curve25519 [5] by Bernstein or Curve448 [19] proposed by Hamburg.

Moving to a hardware scenario, using the nice properties of these specific curves is not as straightforward anymore. Hardware development is costly, and industry prefers IP cores as generic solutions for all possible clients. Moreover, backwards compatibility is a serious concern, and most current standards [12,15,29] regarding large prime fields contain prime order curves in short Weierstrass form. This prohibits using (twisted) Edwards, (twisted) Hessian and Montgomery curves. The desire for complete addition formulas for prime order curves in short Weierstrass form was recognized and Renes, Costello and Batina [31] proved this to be realistic. They present complete addition formulas with an efficiency loss of 34 %–44 % in software when compared to formulas based on Jacobian coordinates, depending on the size of the field.

As the authors mention, one can expect to have better performance in hardware, but they do not present results. In particular, when using Montgomery multiplication one can benefit from very efficient modular additions and subtractions (which appear a lot in their formulas), which changes the performance ratio derived in the original paper. Therefore, it is of interest to investigate the new complete formulas from a hardware point of view. In this paper we show that the hardware performance is competitive with the literature, building scalar multiplication on top of three parallel Montgomery multipliers. In more detail, we summarize our contributions as follows:

- we present the first hardware implementation based on the work of [26], working for every prime order curve over a prime field of up to 522 bits, and obtain competitive results;
- we present algorithms for various levels of parallelism for the new formulas to boost the performance.

Related Work. Mainly there are numerous works on curve-based hardware implementations. These are on various FPGA platforms, making a meaningful comparison very difficult. Güneysu and Paar [17] proposed a new speed-optimized architecture that makes intensive use of the DSP blocks in an FPGA platform. Guillermin [18] introduced a prime field ECC hardware architecture and implemented it on several Altera FPGA boards. The design is based on Residue Number System (RNS), facilitating carry-free arithmetic and parallelism. Yao et al. [37] followed the idea of using RNS to design a high-speed ECC co-processor for pairings. Sakiyama et al. [33] proposed a superscalar coprocessor that could deal with three different curve-based cryptosystems, all in characteristic 2 fields. Varchola et al. [35] designed a processor-like architecture, with instruction set and decoder, on top of which they implemented ECC. This approach has the benefit of having a portion written in software, which can be easily maintained and updated, while having special optimized instructions for the elliptic curve operations. The downside of this approach is that the resource costs are higher than a fully optimized processor. As was the case for Güneysu and Paar [17], their targets were standardized NIST prime curves P–224 and P–256. Consequently, each of their synthesized circuit would only work for one of the two primes. Pöpper et al. [30] follow the same approach as Varchola et al. [35], with some side-channel related improvements. The paper focuses on an analysis of each countermeasure and its effective cost. Roy et al. [32] followed the same path, but with more optimizations with respect to resources and only for curve NIST P–256. However, the number of Block RAMs necessary for the architecture is much larger than of Pöpper et al. [30] or Varchola et al. [35]. Fan et al. [16] created an architecture for special primes and curves, namely the standardized NIST P–192. The approach was to parallelize Montgomery multiplication and formulas for point addition and doubling on the curve. Vliegen et al. [36] attempted to reduce the resources with a small core aimed at 256-bit primes.

Organization. We start with preliminaries in Sect. 2, and briefly discuss parallelism for the complete formulas in Sect. 3. Finally we present our hardware implementation using three Montgomery multipliers in Sect. 4.

2 Preliminaries for Elliptic Curve Cryptography

Let $\mathbb{F}_q$ be a finite field of characteristic p, i.e. $q = p^n$ for some n, and assume that p is not two or three. For well-chosen $a, b \in \mathbb{F}_q$, an *elliptic curve* E over $\mathbb{F}_q$ is defined as the set of solutions (x, y) to the curve equation $E : y^2 = x^3 + ax + b$ with an additional point $\mathcal{O}$, called the *point at infinity*. The $\mathbb{F}_q$-rational points $E(\mathbb{F}_q)$ are all $(x, y) \in E$ such that $(x, y) \in \mathbb{F}_q^2$, together with $\mathcal{O}$. They form a group, with $\mathcal{O}$ as its identity element. From now on when we write E, we mean $E(\mathbb{F}_q)$. The *order* of E is the order of this group. To compute the group law on E one can use the chord and tangent process. To implement this, however, it is necessary to use at least one inversion. Since inversions are very costly, we choose a different point representation to avoid them.

Define an equivalence relation on $\mathbb{F}_q^3$ by letting $(x_0, x_1, x_2) \sim (y_0, y_1, y_2)$ if and only if there exists $\lambda \in \mathbb{F}_q^*$ such that $(x_0, x_1, x_2) = (\lambda y_0, \lambda y_1, \lambda y_2)$. Then the *projective plane* over $\mathbb{F}_q$, denoted $\mathbb{P}^2(\mathbb{F}_q)$, is defined by $\mathbb{F}_q^3 \setminus \{(0, 0, 0)\}$ modulo the equivalence relation $\sim$. We write $(x_0 : x_1 : x_2)$ to emphasize that the tuple belongs to $\mathbb{P}^2(\mathbb{F}_q)$ as opposed to $\mathbb{F}_q^3$. Now we can define $E(\mathbb{F}_q)$ to be the set of solutions $(X : Y : Z) \in \mathbb{P}^2(\mathbb{F}_q)$ to the curve equation $E : Y^2 = X^3 + aXZ^2 + bZ^3$. Note that we can easily map between the two representations by $(x, y) \mapsto (x : y : 1)$, $\mathcal{O} \mapsto (0 : 1 : 0)$, and $(X : Y : Z) \mapsto (X/Z, Y/Z)$ (for $Z \neq 0$), $(0 : 1 : 0) \mapsto \mathcal{O}$.

There are many ways to compute the group law on E, see [9]. These differ depending on the representation of the curve and the points. As mentioned in the introduction, we put emphasis on complete addition formulas for prime order elliptic curves. The work of Renes et al. [31] presents addition formulas for curves in short Weierstrass form embedded in the projective plane. They compute the sum of two points $P = (X_1 : Y_1 : Z_1)$ and $Q = (X_2 : Y_2 : Z_2)$ as $P + Q = (X_3 : Y_3 : Z_3)$, where

$$
\begin{aligned}
X_3 &= (X_1Y_2 + X_2Y_1)(Y_1Y_2 - a(X_1Z_2 + X_2Z_1) - 3bZ_1Z_2) \\
&\quad - (Y_1Z_2 + Y_2Z_1)(aX_1X_2 + 3b(X_1Z_2 + X_2Z_1) - a^2Z_1Z_2), \\
Y_3 &= (3X_1X_2 + aZ_1Z_2)(aX_1X_2 + 3b(X_1Z_2 + X_2Z_1) - a^2Z_1Z_2) \\
&\quad + (Y_1Y_2 + a(X_1Z_2 + X_2Z_1) + 3bZ_1Z_2)(Y_1Y_2 - a(X_1Z_2 + X_2Z_1) - 3bZ_1Z_2), \\
Z_3 &= (Y_1Z_2 + Y_2Z_1)(Y_1Y_2 + a(X_1Z_2 + X_2Z_1) + 3bZ_1Z_2) \\
&\quad + (X_1Y_2 + X_2Y_1)(3X_1X_2 + aZ_1Z_2).
\end{aligned}
\tag{1}
$$

Elliptic curve cryptography [22,28] commonly relies on the hard problem called the "Elliptic Curve Discrete Logarithm Problem (ECDLP)". This means that given two points P, Q on an elliptic curve, it is hard to find a scalar $k \in \mathbb{Z}$ such that $Q = kP$, if it exists. Therefore the main component of curve based cryptosystems is the scalar multiplication operation $(k, P) \mapsto kP$. Since in many cases k is a secret, this operation is very sensitive to attacks. In particular many side-channel attacks [4,23] and countermeasures [14] have been proposed. To ensure protection against simple power analysis (SPA) attacks it is important to use regular scalar multiplication algorithms, e.g. Montgomery ladder [20] or Double-And-Add-Always [14], executing both an addition and a doubling operation per scalar bit.

3 Parallelism

An important way to increase the efficiency of the implementation is to use multiple Montgomery multipliers in parallel. In this section we give a brief explanation for our choice of three multipliers.

The addition formulas on which our scalar multiplication is built are shown in Algorithm 1 of [31]. We choose to ignore additions and subtractions since we assume to be relying on a Montgomery multiplier for which the cost of field multiplications is far higher than that of field additions. The total (multiplicative) cost in the most general case is $12\mathbf{M} + 2\mathbf{m_a} + 3\mathbf{m_{3b}}$[1]. Because our processors do not distinguish full multiplications and multiplications by constants, we consider this cost simply as $17\mathbf{M}$. The authors of [31] introduce optimizations for mixed addition and doubling, but in our case this only saves a single multiplication (and some additions). Since this does not make up for the price we would have to pay for the implementation of a second algorithm, we only examine the most general case. In Table 1 we show the interdependencies of the multiplications.

---

[1] We denote by $\mathbf{M}, \mathbf{m_a}, \mathbf{m_{3b}}, \mathbf{a}$ the cost of a general multiplication, a multiplication by curve constant a, a multiplication by curve constant $3b$, and an addition respectively.

Table 1. Dependencies of multiplications inside the complete addition formulas

Stage	Result	Multiplication	Dependent on
0	ℓ_0	$X_1 \cdot X_2$	-
0	ℓ_1	$Y_1 \cdot Y_2$	-
0	ℓ_2	$Z_1 \cdot Z_2$	-
0	ℓ_3	$(X_1 + Y_1) \cdot (X_2 + Y_2)$	-
0	ℓ_4	$(X_1 + Z_1) \cdot (X_2 + Z_2)$	-
0	ℓ_5	$(Y_1 + Z_1) \cdot (Y_2 + Z_2)$	-
1	ℓ_6	$b_3 \cdot \ell_2$	ℓ_2
1	ℓ_7	$a \cdot \ell_2$	ℓ_2
1	ℓ_8	$a \cdot (\ell_4 - \ell_0 - \ell_2)$	ℓ_0, ℓ_2, ℓ_4
1	ℓ_9	$b_3 \cdot (\ell_4 - \ell_0 - \ell_2)$	ℓ_0, ℓ_2, ℓ_4
2	ℓ_{10}	$a \cdot (\ell_0 - \ell_7)$	ℓ_0, ℓ_7
2	ℓ_{11}	$(\ell_3 - \ell_0 - \ell_1) \cdot (\ell_1 - \ell_8 - \ell_6)$	$\ell_0, \ell_1, \ell_3, \ell_6, \ell_8$
2	ℓ_{13}	$(\ell_1 + \ell_8 + \ell_6) \cdot (\ell_1 - \ell_8 - \ell_6)$	ℓ_1, ℓ_6, ℓ_8
2	ℓ_{15}	$(\ell_5 - \ell_1 - \ell_2) \cdot (\ell_1 + \ell_8 + \ell_6)$	$\ell_1, \ell_2, \ell_5, \ell_6, \ell_8$
2	ℓ_{16}	$(\ell_3 - \ell_0 - \ell_1) \cdot (3\ell_0 + \ell_7)$	$\ell_0, \ell_1, \ell_3, \ell_7$
3	ℓ_{12}	$(\ell_5 - \ell_1 - \ell_2) \cdot (\ell_{10} + \ell_9)$	$\ell_1, \ell_2, \ell_5, \ell_9, \ell_{10}$
3	ℓ_{14}	$(3\ell_0 + \ell_7) \cdot (\ell_{10} + \ell_9)$	$\ell_0, \ell_7, \ell_9, \ell_{10}$

Table 2. Efficiency approximation of the number of Montgomery multipliers against the area used.

n	$Cost$	$Area \times Time$	$Algorithm$
1	$17M + 23a$	$17M + 23a$	1 in [31]
2	$9M_2 + 12a_2$	$18M + 24a$	1
3	$6M_3 + 8a_3$	$18M + 24a$	2
4	$5M_4 + 7a_4$	$20M + 28a$	3
5	$4M_5 + 6a_5$	$20M + 30a$	4
6	$3M_6 + 6a_6$	$18M + 36a$	5

This allows us to write down algorithms for implementations running n processors in parallel. Denote by M_n resp. a_n the cost of doing n multiplications resp. additions (or subtractions) in parallel. In Table 2 we present the costs for $1 \leq n \leq 6$. We make the simple approximations that $M_n = M$ and $a_n = a$. We note that this ignores some practical aspects. For example a larger number of Montgomery multipliers can result in scheduling overhead, which we do not take into account. All algorithms and their respective Magma [11] verification code can be found in Appendices B and C. For our implementation we have chosen for $n = 3$, i.e. three Montgomery multipliers. This number of multipliers achieves a great area-time trade-off, while obtaining a good speed-up compared to $n = 1$. Moreover, the aforementioned practical issues (e. g. scheduling) are not as complicated to deal with as for larger n.

4   Implementation of the Formulas with Three Processors

In this section we introduce a novel hardware implementation, parallelizing the new formulas using three Montgomery processors. We make use of the Montgomery processors which have been proposed by Massolino et al. [26] for Microsemi® IGLOO2® FPGAs, for which the architecture is shown in Fig. 1. We give a short description of the processor in Sect. 4.1, but for more details on its internals we refer to [26]. As a consequence of building on top of this processor, we target the same FPGA. However, it is straightforward to port to other FPGA's or even ASICs which have a Montgomery multiplier with the same interface and instructions.

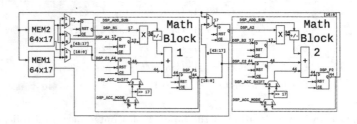

Fig. 1. Montgomery addition, subtraction and multiplication processor.

The elliptic curve scalar multiplication routine is constructed on top of the Montgomery processors. As mentioned before, to protect against simple power analysis attacks, we implement a regular scalar multiplication algorithm (i. e. Double-And-Add-Always [14]). The algorithm relies on three registers R_0, R_1 and R_2. The register R_0 contains the operand which is always doubled. The registers R_1 resp. R_2 contain the result of the addition when the exponent bit is zero resp. one. This algorithm should be applied carefully since it is prone to fault attacks [3]. From a very high level point of view the architecture consists of the three Montgomery multipliers and a single BRAM block, shown in Fig. 2. We note that this BRAM block is more than large enough to store the necessary temporary variables. So although Algorithm 2 tries to minimize the number of these, this is not necessary for our case. In the rest of this section we elaborate on the details of the implementation.

4.1   The Montgomery Processor

Massolino et al. [26] proposed two different Montgomery processors. Our scalar multiplication builds on top of "version 2", which has support for two internal multipliers and two memory blocks. It can perform three operations: Montgomery multiplication, addition without reduction and subtraction without reduction. To perform Montgomery multiplication, the processor employs the FIOS algorithm proposed by Koç et al. [21]. In short, FIOS computes the partial product and partial reduction inside the same iterative loop. This can be translated into a hardware architecture, see Fig. 1, with a unit for the partial product and another partial modular reduction. The circuit behaves like a three-stage pipeline: in the first stage operands are fed into the circuit, in the second they are computed and in the third they are stored into memory. The pipeline system is reused for the addition and subtraction operation in the multiplier, and values are added or subtracted directly. In case of subtraction the computation also adds a multiple of the prime modulus. Those operations can be done without applying reduction, because reduction will be applied later during a multiplication operation. However, there is a limit to the number of consecutive additions/subtractions with no reduction, on which we elaborate in Sect. 4.4.

4.2   Memory

The main RAM memory in Fig. 2 is subdivided in order to lower control logic resources and to facilitate the interface. The main memory operates as a true dual port memory of 1024 words of 17 bits. We create a separation in the memory, composing a *big word* of 32 words (i. e. 544 bits). This way we construct the memory as 32×32 big words. A big word can accommodate any temporary variable, input or output of our architecture. An exception is possibly the scalar of the point scalar multiplication. Although a single word would be large enough to contain 523-bit scalars (in the largest case of a 523-bit field), the scalar blinding technique can double the size of the scalar. Therefore, we use two words to store the scalar. By doing this, it will in the future be possible to execute scalar multiplication with a blinded scalar [13]. Lastly, there is a 17-bit shift register into which the scalar is loaded word by word.

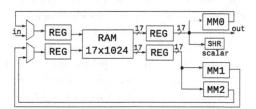

Fig. 2. Entire architecture with three Montgomery processors from [26], where MM = Montgomery processor, SHR = Shift register, REG = Register.

4.3   Control Logic

The formulas and control system are done through two state machines: a main one which controls everything, and one related to memory transfer.

The memory-transfer state machine was created with the purpose to reduce the number of states in the main machine. This was done by providing the operation of transfer between the main memory and the Montgomery processors memory. Therefore, the main machine can transfer values with just one state, and can reuse most of the transfer logic. This memory-transfer machine becomes responsible for various parts of the bus between main memories, processors and other counters. However, the main state machine still has to be able to control everything. Hence, the main state machine shares some components with the memory transfer machine, increasing control circuit costs.

The main state machine controls all the circuits that compose the entire cryptographic core. Given it controls the entire circuit, the machine also has the entire Table 2 scheduling implemented as states. The advantage of doing this through states is the possible optimization of the design and the entire control. However, the cost of maintenance is a lot higher than a small instruction set or microcode that can also implement the addition formulas or scalar multi-plication. Because the addition formulas are complete, it is possible to reduce the costs of performing both addition and doubling through only the addition formulas. This decreases the amount of states and therefore makes the final implementation a lot more compact. Hence, the implementation only iterates over the addition formulas, until the end of the computations.

4.4   Consecutive Additions

For the Montgomery processor to work in our architecture, part of the origi-nal design was changed. The authors of [26] did not need to reduce after each addition or subtraction, as they assumed that these operations would always be followed by Montgomery multiplications (and its corresponding reduction). However, they were not able to do multiple consecutive additions and subtrac-tions, as the Montgomery division value r was chosen to be only 4 bits larger than the prime. On the other hand, it is readily seen that in Algorithm 2 there are several consecutive additions and subtractions. One example of such addi-tions is t_9 in line 7, then latter on line 8 is added and stored on t_{10}, which on line 10 is added with a fourth value. To be able to execute these without having to reduce, we need a Montgomery division value at least 5 bits larger than the prime. As a consequence, the processor only works for primes up to 522 bits (as opposed to 523), which is still one bit more than the largest standardized prime curve [29].

Table 3. Scheduling for point addition $P \leftarrow P + Q$, where $P = (X_1 : Y_1 : Z_1)$ and $Q = (X_2 : Y_2 : Z_2)$. For doubling simply put $P = Q$.

Line # Algorithm 2	MM0	MM1	MM2
1	$t_0 \leftarrow X_1 \cdot X_2$	$t_1 \leftarrow Y_1 \cdot Y_2$	
			$t_2 \leftarrow Z_1 \cdot Z_2$
2	$t_3 \leftarrow X_1 + Y_1$	$t_4 \leftarrow X_2 + Y_2$	
			$t_5 \leftarrow Y_1 + Z_1$
3	$t_7 \leftarrow X_1 + Z_1$	$t_8 \leftarrow X_2 + Z_2$	
			$t_6 \leftarrow Y_2 + Z_2$
4	$t_9 \leftarrow t_3 \cdot t_4$	$t_{11} \leftarrow t_7 \cdot t_8$	
			$t_{10} \leftarrow t_5 \cdot t_6$
5	$t_4 \leftarrow t_1 + t_2$	$t_5 \leftarrow t_0 + t_2$	
			$t_3 \leftarrow t_0 + t_1$
6,7,8	$t_6 \leftarrow b_3 \cdot t_2$	$t_8 \leftarrow a \cdot t_2$	
			$t_2 \leftarrow t_9 - t_3$
			$t_3 \leftarrow t_{10} - t_4$
			$t_4 \leftarrow t_{11} - t_5$
			$t_9 \leftarrow t_0 + t_0$
			$t_{10} \leftarrow t_9 + t_0$
9	$t_5 \leftarrow b_3 \cdot t_4$	$t_{11} \leftarrow a \cdot t_4$	
			$t_7 \leftarrow t_0 - t_8$
			$t_9 \leftarrow a \cdot t_7$
10	$t_0 \leftarrow t_8 + t_{10}$	$t_4 \leftarrow t_{11} + t_6$	
			$t_7 \leftarrow t_5 + t_9$
11	$t_5 \leftarrow t_1 - t_4$	$t_6 \leftarrow t_1 + t_4$	
12	$t_4 \leftarrow t_0 \cdot t_7$	$t_1 \leftarrow t_5 \cdot t_6$	
			$t_8 \leftarrow t_3 \cdot t_7$
13	$t_{11} \leftarrow t_0 \cdot t_2$	$t_9 \leftarrow t_2 \cdot t_5$	
			$t_{10} \leftarrow t_3 \cdot t_6$
14	$Y_1 \leftarrow t_1 + t_4$	$X_1 \leftarrow t_9 - t_8$	
			$Z_1 \leftarrow t_{10} + t_{11}$

4.5   Scheduling

The architecture presented in Fig. 2 has one dual port memory, whereas it has three processors. This means that we can only load values to two processors at the same time. As a consequence the three processors do not run completely in parallel, but one of the three is unsynchronized. Table 3 showcases how operations are split into different processors. They are distributed with the goal of minimizing the number of loads and stores for each processor and to minimize MM2 being idle. The process begins by loading the necessary values into MM0 and MM1 and executing their respective operations. As soon as the operations in MM0 and MM1 are initialized, it loads the corresponding value into MM2 and executes the operation. As soon as MM0 and MM1 finish their operations, this process restarts. Since the operations executed in MM2 are not synchronized with those in MM0 and MM1, both of the operations in MM0 and MM1 should be independent of the output of MM2, and vice versa. Furthermore, since multiplications are at least ten times slower than additions for our processor choice [26], the additions and subtractions from lines seven and eight in Algorithm 2 can be done by the otherwise idle processor MM2 in stage six. This makes them basically free of cost.

4.6   Comparison

As our architecture supports primes from 116 to 522 bits, we can run benchmarks and do comparisons for multiple bitsizes. The results for different common prime sizes are shown in Table 5 in Appendix A. In this section we consider only the currently widely adopted 128-bit security level, presented in Table 4. Integer addition, subtraction and Montgomery modular multiplication results are the same as in Massolino et al. [26]. This is the first work implementing the new complete formulas for elliptic curves in short Weierstrass form [31], and leads to a scalar multiplication routine which takes about 14.21 ms for a 256-bit prime.

It is not straightforward to do a well-founded comparison between work in the literature. Table 4 contains different implementations of elliptic curve scalar multiplication, but they have different optimization goals. For example we top [35, 36] in terms of milliseconds per scalar multiplication, but they use less multipliers or run at a lower frequency. On the other hand [1, 17, 18, 25, 27, 34] outperform our architecture in terms of speed, but use a much larger number of embedded multipliers. Also, implementations only focusing on NIST curves are able to use the special prime shape, yielding a significant speed-up. Depending on the needs of a specific hardware designer, this specialization of curves might not always be desirable. As mentioned before, many parties in industry might prefer generic cores. Despite these remarks, we argue that the implementation is competitive with the literature, making a similar trade-off between size and speed. Thus the new formulas can be implemented with little to no penalties, while having the benefit of not having to deal with exceptions.

A   More complete results comparison

Table 4. Comparison of our results to the literature on hardware implementations for ECC. The speed results are for one scalar multiplication.

Work	Field	FPGA	Slice/ ALM	LUT	FF	Emb. Mult.	BRAM 64 × 18	BRAM 1 k × 18	Freq. (MHz)	Scalar Mult. Cycles	(ms)
For all prime fields and prime order short Weierstrass curves											
Our	256	IGLOO 2[4]	–	2828	1048	6	6	1	100	1421312	14.21
For NIST curves [29] only											
[35]	256	SmartFusion[4]	–	3690	3690	0	0	12	109	2103941	19.3
[35]	256	Virtex II Pro[4]	773	1546[a]	1546[a]	1	0	3	210	2103941	10.02
[35]	256	Virtex II Pro[4]	1158	2316[a]	2316[a]	4	0	3	210	949951	4.52
[30]	256	Virtex 5[6c]	1914	7656[a]	7656[a]	4	0	12	210	830000	3.95
[16]	192	Virtex II Pro[4]	3173	6346[a]	6346[a]	16	0	6	93	920700[b]	9.90
[32]	256	Spartan 6[6]	72	193	35	8	0	24	156.25	1906250[b]	12.2
[24]	256	Virtex 4[4]	7020	12435	3545	8	0	4	182	993174[b]	5.457
[1]	256	Virtex 6[6c]	11.2 k	32.9 k	89.6 k[a]	289	0	256	100	39922	0.40
[17]	256	Virtex 4[4]	1715	2589	2028	32	0	11	490	303450	0.619
For only Edwards or Twisted Edwards curves											
[2]	192	Spartan 3E [4]	4654	9308[a]	9308[a]	0	0	0	10	125430[b]	12.543
[34]	256	Zynq[6c]	1029	2783	3592	20	0	4	200	64770	0.324
For only specific field size, but works with any prime											
[36]	256	Virtex II Pro[4]	1832	3664[a]	3664[a]	2	0	9	108.2	3227993	29.83
[36]	256	Virtex II Pro[4]	2085	4170[a]	4170[a]	7	0	9	68.17	1074625	15.76
[18]	256	Stratix II[4]	9177	18354[a]	18354[a]	96	0	0	157.2	106896[b]	0.68
[27]	256	Virtex II Pro[4]	15755	31510[a]	31510[a]	256	0	0	39.46	151360	3.86
[25]	256	Virtex 4[4]	4655	5740	4876	37	0	11	250	109297	0.44

[a] Maximum possible value assumed from the number of slices. Virtex II Pro and Spartan 3E slice is 2 LUTs and FFs, Virtex 5 is 4 LUTs and FFs, finally Virtex 6 is 4 LUTs and 8 FFs. Stratix II ALM can be configured into 2 LUTs and FFs.
[b] Values estimated by multiplying time by frequency.
[4] [6] indicates LUT size.
[c] BRAMs of Virtex 5, 6 and Zynq are 1 k × 36, so they account as 2 independent 1 k × 18.

Table 5. Complete comparison and results from Table 4

Work	Field	FPGA	Slice/ ALM	LUT	FF	Emb. Mult.	BRAM 64×18	BRAM 1k×18	Freq. (MHz)	Scalar Mult. Cycles	Scalar Mult. (ms)
For all prime fields and prime order short Weierstrass curves											
Our	192	IGLOO 2[4]	–	2828	1048	6	6	1	100	728448	7.28
Our	224	IGLOO 2[4]	–	2828	1048	6	6	1	100	1036224	10.36
Our	256	IGLOO 2[4]	–	2828	1048	6	6	1	100	1421312	14.21
Our	320	IGLOO 2[4]	–	2828	1048	6	6	1	100	2498560	24.99
Our	384	IGLOO 2[4]	–	2828	1048	6	6	1	100	3744768	37.45
Our	512	IGLOO 2[4]	–	2828	1048	6	6	1	100	8187904	81.88
Our	521	IGLOO 2[4]	–	2828	1048	6	6	1	100	8331832	83.32
For NIST curves [29] only											
[35]	224	SmartFusion[4]	–	3690	3690	0	0	12	109	1722088	15.8
[35]	256	SmartFusion[4]	–	3690	3690	0	0	12	109	2103941	19.3
[35]	224	Virtex II Pro[4]	773	1546[a]	1546[a]	1	0	3	210	1722088	8.2
[35]	256	Virtex II Pro[4]	773	1546[a]	1546[a]	1	0	3	210	2103941	10.02
[35]	224	Virtex II Pro[4]	1158	2316[a]	2316[a]	4	0	3	210	765072	3.64
[35]	256	Virtex II Pro[4]	1158	2316[a]	2316[a]	4	0	3	210	949951	4.52
[30]	256	Virtex 5[6c]	1914	7656[a]	7656[a]	4	0	12	210	830000	3.95
[16]	192	Virtex II Pro[4]	3173	6346[a]	6346[a]	16	0	6	93	920700[b]	9.90
[32]	256	Spartan 6[6]	72	193	35	8	0	24	156.25	1906250[b]	12.2
[24]	192	Virtex 4[4]	7020	12435	3545	8	0	4	182	429702[b]	2.361
[24]	224	Virtex 4[4]	7020	12435	3545	8	0	4	182	666666[b]	3.663
[24]	256	Virtex 4[4]	7020	12435	3545	8	0	4	182	993174[b]	5.457
[24]	384	Virtex 4[4]	7020	12435	3545	8	0	4	182	2968420[b]	16.31
[24]	521	Virtex 4[4]	7020	12435	3545	8	0	4	182	7048860[b]	38.73
[1]	192	Virtex 6[6c]	11.2 k	32.9 k	89.6 k[a]	289	0	256	100	29948	0.30
[1]	224	Virtex 6[6c]	11.2 k	32.9 k	89.6 k[a]	289	0	256	100	34999	0.35
[1]	256	Virtex 6[6c]	11.2 k	32.9 k	89.6 k[a]	289	0	256	100	39922	0.40
[1]	384	Virtex 6[6c]	11.2 k	32.9 k	89.6 k[a]	289	0	256	100	11722	1.18
[1]	521	Virtex 6[6c]	11.2 k	32.9 k	89.6 k[a]	289	0	256	100	159959	1.60
[17]	224	Virtex 4[4]	1580	1825	1892	26	0	11	487	219878	0.451
[17]	256	Virtex 4[4]	1715	2589	2028	32	0	11	490	303450	0.619
For only Edwards or Twisted Edwards curves											
[2]	192	Spartan 3E [4]	4654	9308[a]	9308[a]	0	0	0	10	125430[b]	12.543
[34]	256	Zynq[6c]	1029	2783	3592	20	0	4	200	64770	0.324
For only specific field size, but works with any prime											
[36]	256	Virtex II Pro[4]	1832	3664[a]	3664[a]	2	0	9	108.2	3227993	29.83
[36]	256	Virtex II Pro[4]	2085	4170[a]	4170[a]	7	0	9	68.17	1074625	15.76
[18]	192	Stratix II[4]	6203	12406[a]	12406[a]	92	0	0	160.5	70620[b]	0.44
[18]	256	Stratix II[4]	9177	18354[a]	18354[a]	96	0	0	157.2	106896[b]	0.68
[18]	384	Stratix II[4]	12958	25916[a]	25916[a]	177	0	0	150.9	203715[b]	1.35
[18]	512	Stratix II[4]	17017	34034[a]	34034[a]	244	0	0	144.97	323283[b]	2.23
[27]	256	Virtex II Pro[4]	15755	31510[a]	31510[a]	256	0	0	39.46	151360	3.86
[25]	256	Virtex 4[4]	4655	5740	4876	37	0	11	250	109297	0.44

B   Algorithms

Algorithm 1. Parallelized complete addition formulas for a prime order elliptic curve in Weierstrass form, using *two* processors

---

Require: $P = (X_1 : Y_1 : Z_1)$, $Q = (X_2 : Y_2 : Z_2)$, $E\colon Y^2 Z = X^3 + aXZ^2 + bZ^3$
and $b_3 = 3 \cdot b$.

Ensure: $(X_3 : Y_3 : Z_3) = P + Q$.

1. $t_0 \leftarrow X_1 + Y_1$; $t_1 \leftarrow X_2 + Y_2$;
2. $t_2 \leftarrow Y_1 + Z_1$; $t_3 \leftarrow Y_2 + Z_2$;
3. $t_0 \leftarrow t_0 \cdot t_1$; (ℓ_3) $t_1 \leftarrow t_2 \cdot t_3$; (ℓ_5)
4. $t_4 \leftarrow X_1 \cdot X_2$; (ℓ_0) $t_6 \leftarrow Z_1 \cdot Z_2$; (ℓ_2)
5. $t_2 \leftarrow X_1 + Z_1$; $t_3 \leftarrow X_2 + Z_2$;
6. $t_0 \leftarrow t_0 - t_4$; $t_1 \leftarrow t_1 - t_6$;
7. $t_5 \leftarrow Y_1 \cdot Y_2$; (ℓ_1) $t_2 \leftarrow t_2 \cdot t_3$; (ℓ_4)
8. $t_7 \leftarrow a \cdot t_6$; (ℓ_7) $t_8 \leftarrow b_3 \cdot t_6$; (ℓ_8)
9. $t_9 \leftarrow t_4 - t_7$; $t_{10} \leftarrow t_4 + t_4$;
10. $t_{11} \leftarrow t_4 + t_7$; $t_2 \leftarrow t_2 - t_4$;
11. $t_0 \leftarrow t_0 - t_5$; $t_1 \leftarrow t_1 - t_5$;
12. $t_2 \leftarrow t_2 - t_6$; $t_{10} \leftarrow t_{10} + t_{11}$;
13. $t_9 \leftarrow a \cdot t_9$; (ℓ_{10}) $t_{11} \leftarrow b_3 \cdot t_2$; (ℓ_9)
14. $t_2 \leftarrow a \cdot t_2$; (ℓ_8)
15. $t_9 \leftarrow t_9 + t_{11}$; $t_8 \leftarrow t_2 + t_8$;
16. $t_6 \leftarrow t_5 - t_8$; $t_5 \leftarrow t_5 + t_8$;
17. $t_3 \leftarrow t_1 \cdot t_9$; (ℓ_{12}) $t_9 \leftarrow t_9 \cdot t_{10}$; (ℓ_{14})
18. $t_{10} \leftarrow t_0 \cdot t_{10}$; (ℓ_{16}) $t_0 \leftarrow t_0 \cdot t_6$; (ℓ_{11})
19. $t_6 \leftarrow t_5 \cdot t_6$; (ℓ_{13}) $t_1 \leftarrow t_1 \cdot t_5$; (ℓ_{15})
20. $X_3 \leftarrow t_0 - t_3$; $Y_9 \leftarrow t_6 + t_9$;
21. $Z_3 \leftarrow t_1 + t_{10}$;

Algorithm 2. Parallelized complete addition formulas for a prime order elliptic curve in Weierstrass form, using *three* processors

Require: $P = (X_1 : Y_1 : Z_1)$, $Q = (X_2 : Y_2 : Z_2)$, $E\colon Y^2 Z = X^3 + a X Z^2 + b Z^3$ and $b_3 = 3 \cdot b$.
Ensure: $(X_3 : Y_3 : Z_3) = P + Q$.

1. $t_0 \leftarrow X_1 \cdot X_2; (\ell_0)$	$t_1 \leftarrow Y_1 \cdot Y_2; (\ell_1)$	$t_2 \leftarrow Z_1 \cdot Z_2; (\ell_2)$
2. $t_3 \leftarrow X_1 + Y_1;$	$t_4 \leftarrow X_2 + Y_2;$	$t_5 \leftarrow Y_1 + Z_1;$
3. $t_6 \leftarrow Y_2 + Z_2;$	$t_7 \leftarrow X_1 + Z_1;$	$t_8 \leftarrow X_2 + Z_2;$
4. $t_9 \leftarrow t_3 \cdot t_4; (\ell_3)$	$t_{10} \leftarrow t_5 \cdot t_6; (\ell_5)$	$t_{11} \leftarrow t_7 \cdot t_8; (\ell_4)$
5. $t_3 \leftarrow t_0 + t_1;$	$t_4 \leftarrow t_1 + t_2;$	$t_5 \leftarrow t_0 + t_2;$
6. $t_6 \leftarrow b_3 \cdot t_2; (\ell_6)$	$t_8 \leftarrow a \cdot t_2; (\ell_7)$	
7. $t_2 \leftarrow t_9 - t_3;$	$t_9 \leftarrow t_0 + t_0;$	$t_3 \leftarrow t_{10} - t_4;$
8. $t_{10} \leftarrow t_9 + t_0;$	$t_4 \leftarrow t_{11} - t_5;$	$t_7 \leftarrow t_0 - t_8;$
9. $t_0 \leftarrow a \cdot t_4; (\ell_8)$	$t_5 \leftarrow b_3 \cdot t_4; (\ell_9)$	$t_9 \leftarrow a \cdot t_7; (\ell_{10})$
10. $t_4 \leftarrow t_0 + t_6;$	$t_7 \leftarrow t_5 + t_9;$	$t_0 \leftarrow t_8 + t_{10};$
11. $t_5 \leftarrow t_1 - t_4;$	$t_6 \leftarrow t_1 + t_4;$	
12. $t_1 \leftarrow t_5 \cdot t_6; (\ell_{13})$	$t_4 \leftarrow t_0 \cdot t_7; (\ell_{14})$	$t_8 \leftarrow t_3 \cdot t_7; (\ell_{12})$
13. $t_9 \leftarrow t_2 \cdot t_5; (\ell_{11})$	$t_{10} \leftarrow t_3 \cdot t_6; (\ell_{15})$	$t_{11} \leftarrow t_0 \cdot t_2; (\ell_{16})$
14. $X_3 \leftarrow t_9 - t_8;$	$Y_3 \leftarrow t_1 + t_4;$	$Z_3 \leftarrow t_{10} + t_{11};$

Algorithm 3. Parallelized complete addition formulas for a prime order elliptic curve in Weierstrass form, using *four* processors

Require: $P = (X_1 : Y_1 : Z_1)$, $Q = (X_2 : Y_2 : Z_2)$, $E\colon Y^2 Z = X^3 + a X Z^2 + b Z^3$ and $b_3 = 3 \cdot b$.
Ensure: $(X_3 : Y_3 : Z_3) = P + Q$.

1. $t_0 \leftarrow X_1 + Y_1;$	$t_1 \leftarrow X_2 + Y_2;$	$t_2 \leftarrow Y_1 + Z_1;$	$t_3 \leftarrow Y_2 + Z_2;$
2. $t_0 \leftarrow t_0 \cdot t_1; (\ell_3)$	$t_1 \leftarrow t_2 \cdot t_3; (\ell_5)$	$t_4 \leftarrow X_1 \cdot X_2; (\ell_0)$	$t_6 \leftarrow Z_1 \cdot Z_2; (\ell_2)$
3. $t_2 \leftarrow X_1 + Z_1;$	$t_3 \leftarrow X_2 + Z_2;$	$t_0 \leftarrow t_0 - t_4;$	$t_1 \leftarrow t_1 - t_6;$
4. $t_5 \leftarrow Y_1 \cdot Y_2; (\ell_1)$	$t_2 \leftarrow t_2 \cdot t_3; (\ell_4)$	$t_7 \leftarrow a \cdot t_6; (\ell_7)$	$t_8 \leftarrow b_3 \cdot t_6; (\ell_6)$
5. $t_9 \leftarrow t_4 - t_7;$	$t_{10} \leftarrow t_4 + t_4;$	$t_{11} \leftarrow t_4 + t_7;$	$t_2 \leftarrow t_2 - t_4;$
6. $t_0 \leftarrow t_0 - t_5;$	$t_1 \leftarrow t_1 - t_5;$	$t_2 \leftarrow t_2 - t_6;$	$t_{10} \leftarrow t_{10} + t_{11};$
7. $t_9 \leftarrow a \cdot t_9; (\ell_{10})$	$t_{11} \leftarrow b_3 \cdot t_2; (\ell_9)$	$t_2 \leftarrow a \cdot t_2; (\ell_8)$	
8. $t_9 \leftarrow t_9 + t_{11};$			
9. $t_3 \leftarrow t_1 \cdot t_9; (\ell_{12})$	$t_9 \leftarrow t_9 \cdot t_{10}; (\ell_{14})$	$t_{10} \leftarrow t_0 \cdot t_{10}; (\ell_{16})$	$t_8 \leftarrow t_2 + t_8;$
10. $t_6 \leftarrow t_5 - t_8;$	$t_5 \leftarrow t_5 + t_8;$		
11. $t_0 \leftarrow t_0 \cdot t_6; (\ell_{11})$	$t_6 \leftarrow t_5 \cdot t_6; (\ell_{13})$	$t_1 \leftarrow t_1 \cdot t_5; (\ell_{15})$	
12. $X_3 \leftarrow t_0 - t_3;$	$Y_3 \leftarrow t_6 + t_9;$	$Z_3 \leftarrow t_1 + t_{10};$	

Algorithm 4. Parallelized complete addition formulas for a prime order elliptic curve in Weierstrass form, using *five* processors

Require: $P = (X_1 : Y_1 : Z_1)$, $Q = (X_2 : Y_2 : Z_2)$, $E: Y^2 Z = X^3 + aXZ^2 + bZ^3$
and $b_3 = 3 \cdot b$.

Ensure: $(X_3 : Y_3 : Z_3) = P + Q$.

1. $t_5 \leftarrow X_1 + Y_1$; $t_6 \leftarrow X_2 + Y_2$; $t_7 \leftarrow X_1 + Z_1$;
   $t_8 \leftarrow X_2 + Z_2$; $t_9 \leftarrow Y_1 + Z_1$;

2. $t_0 \leftarrow X_1 \cdot X_2$; (ℓ_0) $t_1 \leftarrow Y_1 \cdot Y_2$; (ℓ_1) $t_2 \leftarrow Z_1 \cdot Z_2$; (ℓ_2)
   $t_3 \leftarrow t_5 \cdot t_6$; (ℓ_3) $t_4 \leftarrow t_7 \cdot t_8$; (ℓ_4)

3. $t_{10} \leftarrow Y_2 + Z_2$; $t_3 \leftarrow t_3 - t_0$; $t_4 \leftarrow t_4 - t_0$;
   $t_{11} \leftarrow t_0 + t_0$;

4. $t_3 \leftarrow t_3 - t_1$;

5. $t_5 \leftarrow t_9 \cdot t_{10}$; (ℓ_5) $t_4 \leftarrow t_4 - t_2$; $t_{11} \leftarrow t_{11} + t_0$;
   $t_8 \leftarrow a \cdot t_4$; (ℓ_8) $t_6 \leftarrow b_3 \cdot t_2$; (ℓ_6) $t_7 \leftarrow a \cdot t_2$; (ℓ_7)

6. $t_5 \leftarrow t_5 - t_1$; $t_9 \leftarrow b_3 \cdot t_4$; (ℓ_9)
   $t_{10} \leftarrow t_6 + t_8$; $t_{11} \leftarrow t_{11} + t_7$;

7. $t_0 \leftarrow a \cdot t_4$; (ℓ_{10}) $t_6 \leftarrow t_3 \cdot t_{11}$; (ℓ_{16})
                    $t_4 \leftarrow t_0 - t_7$;

8. $t_0 \leftarrow t_0 + t_9$; $t_7 \leftarrow t_1 - t_{10}$; $t_{10} \leftarrow t_1 + t_{10}$;
   $t_5 \leftarrow t_5 - t_2$;

9. $t_1 \leftarrow t_3 \cdot t_7$; (ℓ_{11}) $t_2 \leftarrow t_5 \cdot t_0$; (ℓ_{12}) $t_4 \leftarrow t_{10} \cdot t_7$; (ℓ_{13})
   $t_8 \leftarrow t_{11} \cdot t_0$; (ℓ_{14}) $t_9 \leftarrow t_5 \cdot t_{10}$; (ℓ_{15})

10. $X_3 \leftarrow t_1 - t_2$; $Y_3 \leftarrow t_4 + t_8$; $Z_3 \leftarrow t_9 + t_6$;

Algorithm 5. Parallelized complete addition formulas for a prime order elliptic curve in Weierstrass form, using *six* processors

Require: $P = (X_1 : Y_1 : Z_1)$, $Q = (X_2 : Y_2 : Z_2)$, $E: Y^2 Z = X^3 + aXZ^2 + bZ^3$,
$b_3 = 3 \cdot b$ and $a_2 = a^2$.

Ensure: $(X_3 : Y_3 : Z_3) = P + Q$.

1. $t_0 \leftarrow X_1 + Y_1$; $t_1 \leftarrow X_2 + Y_2$; $t_2 \leftarrow Y_1 + Z_1$;
   $t_3 \leftarrow Y_2 + Z_2$; $t_4 \leftarrow X_1 + Z_1$; $t_5 \leftarrow X_2 + Z_2$;

2. $t_0 \leftarrow t_0 \cdot t_1$; (n_3) $t_1 \leftarrow t_2 \cdot t_3$; (n_5) $t_2 \leftarrow t_4 \cdot t_5$; (n_4)
   $t_3 \leftarrow X_1 \cdot X_2$; (n_0) $t_4 \leftarrow Y_1 \cdot Y_2$; (n_1) $t_5 \leftarrow Z_1 \cdot Z_2$; (n_2)

3. $t_0 \leftarrow t_0 - t_3$; $t_1 \leftarrow t_1 - t_4$; $t_2 \leftarrow t_2 - t_5$;

4. $t_0 \leftarrow t_0 - t_4$; $t_1 \leftarrow t_1 - t_5$; $t_2 \leftarrow t_2 - t_3$;

5. $t_6 \leftarrow b_3 \cdot t_5$; (n_6) $t_7 \leftarrow a \cdot t_5$; (n_7) $t_8 \leftarrow a \cdot t_2$; (n_8)
   $t_9 \leftarrow b_3 \cdot t_2$; (n_9) $t_{10} \leftarrow a \cdot t_3$; (n_{10}) $t_{11} \leftarrow a_2 \cdot t_5$; (n_{11})

6. $t_6 \leftarrow t_6 + t_8$; $t_7 \leftarrow t_3 + t_7$; $t_8 \leftarrow t_3 + t_3$;
   $t_9 \leftarrow t_9 + t_{10}$;

7. $t_9 \leftarrow t_9 - t_{11}$; $t_8 \leftarrow t_8 + t_7$; $t_7 \leftarrow t_4 - t_6$;
   $t_6 \leftarrow t_4 + t_6$;

8. $t_3 \leftarrow t_0 \cdot t_7$; (n_{12}) $t_4 \leftarrow t_0 \cdot t_8$; (n_{17}) $t_5 \leftarrow t_1 \cdot t_9$; (n_{13})
   $t_8 \leftarrow t_8 \cdot t_9$; (n_{15}) $t_7 \leftarrow t_6 \cdot t_7$; (n_{14}) $t_6 \leftarrow t_1 \cdot t_6$; (n_{16})

9. $X_3 \leftarrow t_3 - t_5$; $Y_3 \leftarrow t_7 + t_8$; $Z_3 \leftarrow t_6 + t_4$;

C   Verification code

```
ADD_two:=function(X1,Y1,Z1,X2,Y2,Z2,E,a,b3)
    t0  := X1+Y1;     t1  := X2+Y2;
    t2  := Y1+Z1;     t3  := Y2+Z2;
    t0  := t0*t1;     t1  := t2*t3;
    t4  := X1*X2;     t6  := Z1*Z2;
    t2  := X1+Z1;     t3  := X2+Z2;
    t0  := t0-t4;     t1  := t1-t6;
    t5  := Y1*Y2;     t2  := t2*t3;
    t7  := a*t6;      t8  := b3*t6;
    t9  := t4-t7;     t10 := t4+t4;
    t11 := t4+t7;     t2  := t2-t4;
    t0  := t0-t5;     t1  := t1-t5;
    t2  := t2-t6;     t10 := t10+t11;
    t9  := a*t9;      t11 := b3*t2;
    t2  := a*t2;
    t9  := t9+t11;    t8  := t2+t8;
    t6  := t5-t8;     t5  := t5+t8;
    t3  := t1*t9;     t9  := t9*t10;
    t10 := t0*t10;    t0  := t0*t6;
    t6  := t5*t6;     t1  := t1*t5;
    X3  := t0-t3;     Y3  := t6+t9;
    Z3  := t1+t10;
    return E![X3,Y3,Z3];
end function;

ADD_three:=function(X1,Y1,Z1,X2,Y2,Z2,E,a,b3);
    t0  := X1*X2;     t1  := Y1*Y2;     t2  := Z1*Z2;
    t3  := X1+Y1;     t4  := X2+Y2;     t5  := Y1+Z1;
    t6  := Y2+Z2;     t7  := X1+Z1;     t8  := X2+Z2;
    t9  := t3*t4;     t10 := t5*t6;     t11 := t7*t8;
    t3  := t0+t1;     t4  := t1+t2;     t5  := t0+t2;
    t6  := b3*t2;     t8  := a*t2;
    t2  := t9-t3;     t9  := t0+t0;     t3  := t10-t4;
    t10 := t9+t0;     t4  := t11-t5;    t7  := t0-t8;
    t0  := a*t4;      t5  := b3*t4;     t9  := a*t7;
    t4  := t0+t6;     t7  := t5+t9;     t0  := t8+t10;
    t5  := t1-t4;     t6  := t1+t4;
    t1  := t5*t6;     t4  := t0*t7;     t8  := t3*t7;
    t9  := t2*t5;     t10 := t3*t6;     t11 := t0*t2;
    X3  := t9-t8;     Y3  := t1+t4;     Z3  := t10+t11;
    return E![X3,Y3,Z3];
end function;

ADD_four:=function(X1,Y1,Z1,X2,Y2,Z2,E,a,b3);
    t0  := X1+Y1;   t1  := X2+Y2;   t2  := Y1+Z1;   t3  := Y2+Z2;
    t0  := t0*t1;   t1  := t2*t3;   t4  := X1*X2;   t6  := Z1*Z2;
    t2  := X1+Z1;   t3  := X2+Z2;   t0  := t0-t4;   t1  := t1-t6;
```

```
    t5  := Y1*Y2;   t2  := t2*t3;   t7  := a*t6;;     t8  := b3*t6;
    t9  := t4-t7;   t10 := t4+t4;   t11 := t4+t7;     t2  := t2-t4;
    t0  := t0-t5;   t1  := t1-t5;   t2  := t2-t6;     t10 := t10+t11;
    t9  := a*t9;    t11 := b3*t2;   t2  := a*t2;
    t9  := t9+t11;
    t3  := t1*t9;   t9  := t9*t10;  t10 := t0*t10;  t8  := t2+t8;
    t6  := t5-t8;   t5  := t5+t8;
    t0  := t0*t6;   t6  := t5*t6;   t1  := t1*t5;
    X3  := t0-t3;   Y3  := t6+t9;   Z3  := t1+t10;
    return E![X3,Y3,Z3];
end function;

ADD_five:=function(X1,Y1,Z1,X2,Y2,Z2,E,a,b3);
    t5  := X1+Y1;    t6  := X2+Y2;    t7  := X1+Z1;
    t8  := X2+Z2;    t9  := Y1+Z1;                   // 1
    t0  := X1*X2;    t1  := Y1*Y2;    t2  := Z1*Z2;
    t3  := t5*t6;    t4  := t7*t8;                   // 2
    t10 := Y2+Z2;    t3  := t3-t0;    t4  := t4-t0;
    t11 := t0+t0;                                     // 3
    t3  := t3-t1;    t4  := t4-t2;    t11 := t11+t0;  // 4
    t5  := t9*t10;   t6  := b3*t2;    t7  := a*t2;
    t8  := a*t4;     t9  := b3*t4;                   // 5
    t5  := t5-t1;    t11 := t11+t7;   t4  := t0-t7;
    t10 := t6+t8;                                    // 6
    t0  := a*t4;     t6  := t3*t11;                  // 7
    t0  := t0+t9;    t7  := t1-t10;   t10 := t1+t10;
    t5  := t5-t2;                                    // 8
    t1  := t3*t7;    t2  := t5*t0;    t4  := t10*t7;
    t8  := t11*t0;   t9  := t5*t10;                  // 9
    X3  := t1-t2;    Y3  := t4+t8;    Z3  := t9+t6;  // 10
    return E![X3,Y3,Z3];
end function;

ADD_six:=function(X1,Y1,Z1,X2,Y2,Z2,E,a,b3)
    t0  := X1+Y1;    t1  := X2+Y2;    t2  := Y1+Z1;
    t3  := Y2+Z2;    t4  := X1+Z1;    t5  := X2+Z2;  // 1
    t0  := t0*t1;    t1  := t2*t3;    t2  := t4*t5;
    t3  := X1*X2;    t4  := Y1*Y2;    t5  := Z1*Z2;  // 2
    t0  := t0-t3;    t1  := t1-t4;    t2  := t2-t5;  // 3
    t0  := t0-t4;    t1  := t1-t5;    t2  := t2-t3;  // 4
    t6  := b3*t5;    t7  := a*t5;     t8  := a*t2;
    t9  := b3*t2;    t10 := a*t3;     t11 := a^2*t5; // 5
    t6  := t6+t8;    t7  := t3+t7;    t8  := t3+t3;
    t9  := t9+t10;                                   // 6
    t9  := t9-t11;   t8  := t8+t7;    t7  := t4-t6;
    t6  := t4+t6;                                    // 7
    t3  := t0*t7;    t4  := t0*t8;    t5  := t1*t9;
    t8  := t8*t9;    t7  := t6*t7;    t6  := t1*t6;  // 8
    X3  := t3-t5;    Y3  := t7+t8;    Z3  := t6+t4;  // 9
    return E![X3,Y3,Z3];
```

```
end function;

while(true) do
    repeat q:=RandomPrime(8); until q gt 3;
    Fq:=GF(q);
    repeat repeat a:=Random(Fq); b:=Random(Fq); until not (4*
        a^3+27*b^2 eq 0);
        E:=EllipticCurve([Fq|a,b]);
        b3 := 3*b;
    until IsOdd(#E);

    for P in Set(E) do
        for Q in Set(E) do
            repeat Z1 := Random(Fq); until Z1 ne 0;
            repeat Z2 := Random(Fq); until Z2 ne 0;
            X1 := P[1]*Z1;    Y1 := P[2]*Z1;   Z1 := P[3]*Z1;
            X2 := Q[1]*Z2;    Y2 := Q[2]*Z2;   Z2 := Q[3]*Z2;

            assert P+Q eq ADD_two(X1,Y1,Z1,X2,Y2,Z2,E,a,b3);
            assert P+Q eq ADD_three(X1,Y1,Z1,X2,Y2,Z2,E,a,b3);
            assert P+Q eq ADD_four(X1,Y1,Z1,X2,Y2,Z2,E,a,b3);
            assert P+Q eq ADD_five(X1,Y1,Z1,X2,Y2,Z2,E,a,b3);
            assert P+Q eq ADD_six(X1,Y1,Z1,X2,Y2,Z2,E,a,b3);
        end for;
    end for;
    print"Correct:", E;
end while;
```

References

1. Alrimeih, H., Rakhmatov, D.: Fast and flexible hardware support for ECC over multiple standard prime fields. IEEE Trans. Very Large Scale Integr. (VLSI) Syst. **22**(12), 2661–2674 (2014)
2. Baldwin, B., Moloney, R., Byrne, A., McGuire, G., Marnane, W.P.: A hardware analysis of twisted edwards curves for an elliptic curve cryptosystem. In: Becker, J., Woods, R., Athanas, P., Morgan, F. (eds.) ARC 2009. LNCS, vol. 5453, pp. 355–361. Springer, Heidelberg (2009). doi:10.1007/978-3-642-00641-8_41
3. Barenghi, A., Breveglieri, L., Koren, I., Naccache, D.: Fault injection attacks on cryptographic devices: theory, practice, and countermeasures. Proc. IEEE **100**(11), 3056–3076 (2012)
4. Batina, L., Chmielewski, L., Papachristodoulou, L., Schwabe, P., Tunstall, M.: Online template attacks. In: Meier, W., Mukhopadhyay, D. (eds.) INDOCRYPT 2014. LNCS, vol. 8885, pp. 21–36. Springer, Heidelberg (2014). doi:10.1007/978-3-319-13039-2_2
5. Bernstein, D.J.: Curve25519: new diffie-hellman speed records. In: Yung, M., Dodis, Y., Kiayias, A., Malkin, T. (eds.) PKC 2006. LNCS, vol. 3958, pp. 207–228. Springer, Heidelberg (2006). doi:10.1007/11745853_14
6. Bernstein, D.J., Birkner, P., Joye, M., Lange, T., Peters, C.: Twisted edwards curves. In: Vaudenay, S. (ed.) AFRICACRYPT 2008. LNCS, vol. 5023, pp. 389–405. Springer, Heidelberg (2008). doi:10.1007/978-3-540-68164-9_26

7. Bernstein, D.J., Chuengsatiansup, C., Kohel, D., Lange, T.: Twisted hessian curves. In: Lauter, K., Rodríguez-Henríquez, F. (eds.) LATINCRYPT 2015. LNCS, vol. 9230, pp. 269–294. Springer, Heidelberg (2015). doi:10.1007/978-3-319-22174-8_15

8. Bernstein, D.J., Lange, T.: Faster addition and doubling on elliptic curves. In: Kurosawa, K. (ed.) ASIACRYPT 2007. LNCS, vol. 4833, pp. 29–50. Springer, Heidelberg (2007). doi:10.1007/978-3-540-76900-2_3

9. Bernstein, D.J., Lange, T.: Explicit-Formulas Database. http://hyperelliptic.org/EFD/index.html. Accessed 21 Feb 2015

10. Bernstein, D.J., Lange, T., Schwabe, P.: The security impact of a new cryptographic library. In: Hevia, A., Neven, G. (eds.) LATINCRYPT 2012. LNCS, vol. 7533, pp. 159–176. Springer, Heidelberg (2012). doi:10.1007/978-3-642-33481-8_9

11. Bosma, W., Cannon, J.J., Playoust, C.: The Magma algebra system I: the user language. J. Symb. Comput. 24(3/4), 235–265 (1997)

12. Certicom Research. SEC 2: Recommended Elliptic Curve Domain Parameters, Version 2.0. Technical report, Certicom Research (2010)

13. Clavier, C., Joye, M.: Universal exponentiation algorithm a first step towards *Provable* SPA-Resistance. In: Koç, Ç.K., Naccache, D., Paar, C. (eds.) CHES 2001. LNCS, vol. 2162, pp. 300–308. Springer, Heidelberg (2001). doi:10.1007/3-540-44709-1_25

14. Coron, J.-S.: Resistance against differential power analysis for elliptic curve cryptosystems. In: Koç, Ç.K., Paar, C. (eds.) CHES 1999. LNCS, vol. 1717, pp. 292–302. Springer, Heidelberg (1999). doi:10.1007/3-540-48059-5_25

15. ECC Brainpool: ECC Brainpool standard curves and curve generation. Technical report, Brainpool (2005)

16. Fan, J., Sakiyama, K., Verbauwhede, I.: Elliptic curve cryptography on embedded multicore systems. Design Autom. Embedded Syst. 12(3), 231–242 (2008). doi:10.1007/s10617-008-9021-3

17. Güneysu, T., Paar, C.: Ultra high performance ECC over NIST primes on commercial FPGAs. In: Oswald, E., Rohatgi, P. (eds.) CHES 2008. LNCS, vol. 5154, pp. 62–78. Springer, Heidelberg (2008). doi:10.1007/978-3-540-85053-3_5

18. Guillermin, N.: A high speed coprocessor for elliptic curve scalar multiplications over $\mathbb{F}_p$. In: Mangard, S., Standaert, F.-X. (eds.) CHES 2010. LNCS, vol. 6225, pp. 48–64. Springer, Heidelberg (2010). doi:10.1007/978-3-642-15031-9_4

19. Hamburg, M.: Ed448-Goldilocks, a new elliptic curve. Cryptology ePrint Archive, Report 2015/625 (2015). http://eprint.iacr.org/2015/625.pdf

20. Joye, M., Yen, S.-M.: The montgomery powering ladder. In: Kaliski, B.S., Koç, K., Paar, C. (eds.) CHES 2002. LNCS, vol. 2523, pp. 291–302. Springer, Heidelberg (2003). doi:10.1007/3-540-36400-5_22

21. Koç, Ç.K., Acar, T., Kaliski, B.S.: Analyzing and comparing Montgomery multiplication algorithms. IEEE Micro 16(3), 26–33 (1996)

22. Koblitz, N.: Elliptic curve cryptosystems. Math. Comput. 48, 203–209 (1987)

23. Kocher, P., Jaffe, J., Jun, B.: Differential power analysis. In: Wiener, M. (ed.) CRYPTO 1999. LNCS, vol. 1666, pp. 388–397. Springer, Heidelberg (1999). doi:10.1007/3-540-48405-1_25

24. Loi, K.C.C., Ko, S.B.: Scalable elliptic curve cryptosystem FPGA processor for NIST prime curves. IEEE Trans. Very Large Scale Integration (VLSI) Syst. 23(11), 2753–2756 (2015)

25. Ma, Y., Liu, Z., Pan, W., Jing, J.: A high-speed elliptic curve cryptographic processor for generic curves over GF (p). In: Lange, T., Lauter, K., Lisoněk, P. (eds.) SAC 2013. LNCS, vol. 8282, pp. 421–437. Springer, Heidelberg (2014)

26. Massolino, P.M.C., Batina, L., Chaves, R., Mentens, N.: Low Power Montgomery Modular Multiplication on Reconfigurable Systems. Cryptology ePrint Archive, Report 2016/280 (2016). http://eprint.iacr.org/2016/280

27. McIvor, C., McLoone, M., McCanny, J.V.: Hardware elliptic curve cryptographic processor over GF(p). IEEE Trans. Circuits Syst. I Regul. Pap. **53**(9), 1946–1957 (2006)

28. Miller, V.S.: Use of elliptic curves in cryptography. In: Williams, H.C. (ed.) CRYPTO 1985. LNCS, vol. 218, pp. 417–426. Springer, Heidelberg (1986). doi:10. 1007/3-540-39799-X_31

29. National Institute for Standards and Technology. Federal information processing standards publication 186–4. digital signature standard. Technical report, NIST (2013)

30. Pöpper, C., Mischke, O., Güneysu, T.: MicroACP - a fast and secure reconfigurable asymmetric crypto-processor. In: Goehringer, D., Santambrogio, M.D., Cardoso, J.M.P., Bertels, K. (eds.) ARC 2014. LNCS, vol. 8405, pp. 240–247. Springer, Heidelberg (2014). doi:10.1007/978-3-319-05960-0_24

31. Renes, J., Costello, C., Batina, L.: Complete addition formulas for prime order elliptic curves. In: Fischlin, M., Coron, J.-S. (eds.) EUROCRYPT 2016. LNCS, vol. 9665, pp. 403–428. Springer, Heidelberg (2016). doi:10.1007/978-3-662-49890-3_16

32. Roy, D.B., Das, P., Mukhopadhyay, D.: ECC on your fingertips: a single instruction approach for lightweight ECC design in GF(p). In: Dunkelman, O., Keliher, L. (eds.) SAC 2015. LNCS, vol. 9566, pp. 161–177. Springer, Heidelberg (2015)

33. Sakiyama, K., Batina, L., Preneel, B., Verbauwhede, I.: Superscalar coprocessor for high-speed curve-based cryptography. In: Goubin, L., Matsui, M. (eds.) CHES 2006. LNCS, vol. 4249, pp. 415–429. Springer, Heidelberg (2006). doi:10.1007/ 11894063_33

34. Sasdrich, P., Güneysu, T.: Efficient elliptic-curve cryptography using curve25519 on reconfigurable devices. In: Goehringer, D., Santambrogio, M.D., Cardoso, J.M.P., Bertels, K. (eds.) ARC 2014. LNCS, vol. 8405, pp. 25–36. Springer, Heidelberg (2014). doi:10.1007/978-3-319-05960-0_3

35. Varchola, M., Guneysu, T., Mischke, O.: MicroECC: A lightweight reconfigurable elliptic curve crypto-processor. In: 2011 International Conference on Reconfigurable Computing and FPGAs (ReConFig), pp. 204–210, November 2011

36. Vliegen, J., Mentens, N., Genoe, J., Braeken, A., Kubera, S., Touhafi, A., Verbauwhede, I.: A compact FPGA-based architecture for elliptic curve cryptography over prime fields. In: 2010 21st IEEE International Conference on Application-specific Systems Architectures and Processors (ASAP), pp. 313–316, July 2010

37. Yao, G.X., Fan, J., Cheung, R.C.C., Verbauwhede, I.: Faster pairing coprocessor architecture. In: Abdalla, M., Lange, T. (eds.) Pairing 2012. LNCS, vol. 7708, pp. 160–176. Springer, Heidelberg (2013). doi:10.1007/978-3-642-36334-4_10

38. Yen, S., Joye, M.: Checking before output may not be enough against fault-based cryptanalysis. IEEE Trans. Comput. **49**(9), 967–970 (2000)

Partially Homomorphic Encryption Schemes
over Finite Fields

Jian Liu[1,2], Sihem Mesnager[3(✉)], and Lusheng Chen[4]

[1] School of Computer Software,
Tianjin University, Tianjin 300072, People's Republic of China
jianliu.nk@gmail.com
[2] CNRS, UMR 7539 LAGA, Paris, France
[3] Department of Mathematics, University of Paris VIII, University of Paris XIII,
CNRS, UMR 7539 LAGA and Telecom ParisTech, Paris, France
smesnager@univ-paris8.fr
[4] School of Mathematical Sciences, Nankai University,
Tianjin 300071, People's Republic of China
lschen@nankai.edu.cn

Abstract. Homomorphic encryption scheme enables computation in the encrypted domain, which is of great importance because of its wide and growing range of applications. The main issue with the known fully (or partially) homomorphic encryption schemes is the high computational complexity and large communication cost required for their execution. In this work, we study symmetric partially homomorphic encryption schemes over finite fields, establishing relationships between homomorphisms over finite fields with q-ary functions. Our proposed partially homomorphic encryption schemes have perfect secrecy and resist cipheronly attacks to some extent.

Keywords: Homomorphic encryption · q-ary functions · Perfect secrecy · Finite fields · Symmetric cryptography

1 Introduction

Homomorphic encryption schemes are cryptographic constructions which enable to securely perform operations on encrypted data without ever decrypting them. More precisely, a (group) homomorphic encryption scheme over a group $(G, *)$ satisfies that given two encryptions $c_1 = \mathrm{E}_k(m_1)$ and $c_2 = \mathrm{E}_k(m_2)$, where $m_1, m_2 \in G$ and k is the encryption key, one can efficiently compute $\mathrm{E}_k(m_1 * m_2)$ without decrypting c_1 and c_2. Homomorphic encryption schemes are widely used in many interesting applications, such as private information retrieval [6], electronic voting [2], multiparty computation [7], and cloud computing etc. Generally, fully homomorphic encryption schemes that support two operations over

This work is supported by the National Key Basic Research Program of China under Grant 2013CB834204.

C. Carlet et al. (Eds.): SPACE 2016, LNCS 10076, pp. 109–123, 2016.
DOI: 10.1007/978-3-319-49445-6_6

the underlying algebraic structure, i.e., addition and multiplication, will benefit more problems with different notions of security and cost.

The possibilities of homomorphic encryption were first explored by Rivest, Adleman, and Dertouzos in [20] shortly after the presentation of RSA, where homomorphic encryption was called "privacy homomorphism". Multiplicative homomorphic encryption scheme based on basic RSA [20] is an asymmetric encryption system, which is useful for many applications. ElGamal [9] is also a multiplicative homomorphic encryption scheme which is asymmetric. Some additive homomorphic encryption schemes exist, see e.g. [18,19]. The first candidate for fully homomorphic encryption scheme was presented by Gentry [10]. After that, a number of fully homomorphic encryption schemes were proposed [4,5,12,23]. The security of these homomorphic encryption schemes (including partially and fully homomorphic variants) relies on the hardness of some problems. The main limitation for such homomorphic encryption schemes in practice concerns computational cost and communication efficiency.

Homomorphic encryption schemes allow to securely delegate computation, which have important significance in many client-server applications (e.g. cloud computing). In a client-server framework, it is more preferable to select efficient symmetric encryption schemes which are computationally "light" (e.g. over finite fields or rings), since the clients have limited computation ability and want to make communication cost small. However, such homomorphic encryption schemes are not easy to design, and the known constructions cannot completely suffice the needs of practical applications. In [8], Domingo-Ferrer proposed a symmetric fully homomorphic encryption scheme over polynomial rings, but at each time we multiply the ciphertexts, the size of the ciphertexts grows. Domingo-Ferrer's scheme has been broken by using a small pool of known plaintexts (see e.g. [24]). Armknecht and Sadeghi [1] also construct a symmetric additive homomorphic encryption scheme based on Reed-Solomon code, which also allows few number of multiplications. However, Armknecht's scheme suffers from the weakness that at some point, the error may become large enough to cause incorrect decryption (see [11]). In [4], there is a symmetric fully homomorphic encryption scheme based on the ring learning with errors assumption. Recently, a typical framework combining a symmetric encryption scheme and an asymmetric homomorphic encryption scheme was introduced to reduce the time and memory complexity, see [17].

In this paper, we mainly consider symmetric partially homomorphic encryption schemes over finite fields, which are not based on hardness assumptions. In a previous work, it was proved by Boneh and Lipton [3] that under a number theoretic assumption, any fully homomorphic encryption scheme over a ring $\mathbb{Z}_n$ can be broken in sub-exponential time by cipher-only attacks. More explicitly, given any ciphertext, the cryptanalyst who knows nothing about the secret key can find the encrypted plaintext in sub-exponential time. Later, Maurer and Raub [16] extended Boneh et al.'s work to finite fields of small characteristic. Thus, fully homomorphic encryption schemes over finite fields or rings would be vulnerable to cipher-only attacks. We propose two symmetric partially homomorphic encryption schemes. After some security analyses, we show that the multiplicative homomorphic encryption scheme and the additive homomorphic encryption scheme can achieve perfect secrecy, i.e., given any ciphertext, the cryptanalyst who does not know the secret key can determine nothing about the encrypted plaintext. Furthermore, we claim that even the presented schemes are not in a one-time pad setting, they can resist against cipher-only attacks to some extent (if the size of the finite field is large enough). In addition, we get that over finite fields, non-zero multiplicative homomorphisms are equivalent to power functions, and non-zero additive homomorphisms are equivalent to non-constant homogeneous affine functions.

2   Preliminaries

Let $(G, *)$ and $(H, \cdot)$ be two groups. A mapping f of G into H is called a *homomorphism* if it preserves the operation of G, i.e., for all $x, y \in G$, we have $f(x * y) = f(x) \cdot f(y)$.

Let $\mathbb{F}_q$ be a finite field, where q is a power of a prime. A function $F : \mathbb{F}_q \to \mathbb{F}_q$ is called a *q-ary function*, which admits a unique univariate polynomial representation over $\mathbb{F}_q$:

$$F(x) = \sum_{i=0}^{q-1} \delta_i x^i, \qquad \delta_i \in \mathbb{F}_q, \tag{1}$$

where the multiple sum is calculated in finite field $\mathbb{F}_q$. The representation (1) of F can be obtained by the interpolation formula below

$$F(x) = \sum_{a \in \mathbb{F}_q} F(a) \left(1 - (x - a)^{q-1} \right).$$

In fact, denote by $\mathcal{P}$ and $\mathcal{Q}$ the set of all the polynomials in (1) and the set of all q-ary functions respectively. Then, define a mapping $L : \mathcal{P} \to \mathcal{Q}$, which maps any polynomial in $\mathcal{P}$ to the corresponding q-ary function. Because of the interpolation formula, we know that L is surjective. Since it is clear that $|\mathcal{P}| = |\mathcal{Q}| = q^q$, then L is bijective. A q-ary function F is called a *power function* if $F(x) = x^d$ for some $d \in \mathbb{Z}_q$, where $\mathbb{Z}_q$ is the residue class ring modulo q. Let $q = p^s$ for some positive integer s, where p is a prime. For $i \in \mathbb{Z}_q$, we use $\mathrm{wt}_p(i)$ to denote the sum of nonzero coefficients in the p-ary expansion $i = \sum_{k=0}^{s-1} i_k p^k$, i.e., $\mathrm{wt}_p(i) = \sum_{k=0}^{s-1} i_k$. Then, for a non-zero q-ary function $F(x) = \sum_{i=0}^{q-1} \delta_i x^i$, the *algebraic degree* of F is defined as $AD(F) = \max\{\mathrm{wt}_p(i) \mid \delta_i \neq 0, i \in \mathbb{Z}_q\}$. In this paper, if all the terms of F have the same algebraic degree, then F is called *homogeneous*. A function F is called *affine* if $AD(F) \leqslant 1$.

A function $G : \mathbb{F}_q \times \mathbb{F}_q \to \mathbb{F}_q$, where q is a power of a prime, can be represented as a bivariate polynomial over $\mathbb{F}_q$,

$$G(x, y) = \sum_{i,j \in \mathbb{Z}_q} \gamma_{i,j} x^i y^j, \qquad \gamma_{i,j} \in \mathbb{F}_q, \tag{2}$$

where the multiple sum is calculated in finite field $\mathbb{F}_q$. All such polynomials form a vector space over $\mathbb{F}_q$ which has dimension q^2 and $\{x^i y^j \mid i, j \in \mathbb{Z}_q\}$ as its basis. For $i, j \in \mathbb{Z}_q$, the *degree* of $x^i y^j$, denoted by $\deg(x^i y^j)$, equals $i + j$, where the addition is calculated in characteristic 0.

Let q be a power of a prime and n be a positive integer. The *trace function* from $\mathbb{F}_{q^n}$ to $\mathbb{F}_q$ is defined as

$$\mathrm{Tr}_1^n(x) = x + x^q + x^{q^2} + \cdots + x^{q^{n-1}}, \quad x \in \mathbb{F}_{q^n}.$$

The trace function $\mathrm{Tr}_1^n(\cdot)$ is a linear transformation from $\mathbb{F}_{q^n}$ onto $\mathbb{F}_q$, i.e., $\mathrm{Tr}_1^n(\cdot)$ is surjective, for any $a, b \in \mathbb{F}_{q^n}$, $\mathrm{Tr}_1^n(a+b) = \mathrm{Tr}_1^n(a) + \mathrm{Tr}_1^n(b)$, and for any $c \in \mathbb{F}_q$, any $a \in \mathbb{F}_{q^n}$, $\mathrm{Tr}_1^n(ca) = c\mathrm{Tr}_1^n(a)$.

We consider that in a cryptosystem, a particular key is used for one encryption, then *perfect secrecy* provides unconditional security.

Definition 1. *Let $\mathcal{P}$ and $\mathcal{C}$ be the plaintext space and the ciphertext space respectively. A cryptosystem has* perfect secrecy *if for any $m \in \mathcal{P}$ and any $c \in \mathcal{C}$,*

$$\Pr(\mathbf{m} = m \mid \mathbf{c} = c) = \Pr(\mathbf{m} = m).$$

3   Relationships Between Homomorphisms over Finite Fields with q-Ary Functions

In this section, we study q-ary functions which are homomorphisms over finite fields. These functions preserve the multiplication and addition operations respectively. The results in Theorems 1 and 2 are more or less known, but it is difficult to find explicit references in the books. For completeness, we provide their proofs in the Appendix.

Theorem 1. *A non-zero q-ary function F is a homomorphism preserving the multiplication operation if and only if F is a power function.*

Theorem 2. *A non-zero q-ary function F is a homomorphism preserving the addition operation if and only if F is a non-constant homogeneous affine function.*

Combining Theorem 1 with Theorem 2, one can obtain the following corollary immediately.

Corollary 1. *A non-zero q-ary function F is a homomorphism preserving both the multiplication and the addition operations if and only if $F(x) = x^{p^i}$ for some integer $i \geqslant 0$, where p is the characteristic of the finite field $\mathbb{F}_q$.*

Remark 1. It is well known that the only automorphisms of a finite field $\mathbb{F}_{p^s}$ are the Frobenius automorphisms $x \mapsto x^{p^i}$ for $i = 0, \ldots, s-1$, where p is a prime. In Corollary 1, we claim that the only non-zero homomorphisms of $\mathbb{F}_{p^s}$ into itself are Frobenius automorphisms.

Remark 2. Corollary 1 essentially states that any non-zero homomorphism of finite field $\mathbb{F}_q$ into itself is an automorphism. In fact, let F be a non-zero homomorphism of $\mathbb{F}_q$, then $\text{Ker}(F) = \{x \in \mathbb{F}_q \mid F(x) = 0\}$ is an ideal of $\mathbb{F}_q$, and thus $\text{Ker}(F) = \{0\}$ or $\text{Ker}(F) = \mathbb{F}_q$. Since F is non-zero, then $\text{Ker}(F) = \{0\}$, which implies that F is bijective. Hence, F is an automorphism.

4 Partially Homomorphic Encryption Schemes

In this section, we provide two partially homomorphic encryption schemes over finite fields and give the security analysis. These encryption schemes are symmetric.

4.1 A Multiplicative Homomorphic Encryption Scheme

Let $\mathbb{F}_q^* = \mathbb{F}_q \setminus \{0\}$ and $\mathbb{Z}_{q-1}^* = \{k \in \mathbb{Z}_{q-1} \mid \gcd(k, q-1) = 1\}$, where q is a power of a prime. For a positive integer n, let η be a primitive element of $\mathbb{F}_{q^n}$, then $\beta = \eta^{(q^n-1)/(q-1)}$ is a primitive element of $\mathbb{F}_q$. For integers a and b such that $a|b$, we use a/b or $\frac{a}{b}$ to denote division of a by b. For a ring R, if $a \in R$ is invertible, then we use a^{-1} to denote the inverse of a.

- *Key-Generation*
  Choose a positive integer d such that $d|(q^n - 1)/(q-1)$ and $\gcd(d, q-1) = 1$, and choose $l \in \mathbb{Z}_{q-1}^*$. The tuple (d, l) is the secret key.
- *Encryption*
  Let $\alpha = \eta^{(q^n-1)/d}$, which is a primitive d-th root of unity over $\mathbb{F}_q$. To encrypt a plaintext $m \in \mathbb{F}_q^*$, one randomly chooses $r \in \{0, 1, \ldots, d-1\}$ and computes the ciphertext as
  $$c = \gamma^{\log_\beta m} \alpha^r,$$
  where $\gamma = \eta^{l(q^n-1)/d(q-1)}$, the discrete logarithm $\log_\beta m = a$ if $\beta^a = m$.
- *Decryption*
  For $c \in \mathbb{F}_{q^n}^*$, one computes
  $$m' = c^{d \cdot l^{-1}},$$
  where l^{-1} is the inverse of l in $\mathbb{Z}_{q-1}^*$.

Remark 3. In the encryption phase, since $d|(q^n - 1)/(q-1)$ implies $d|(q^n - 1)$, then the splitting field of $x^d - 1$ over $\mathbb{F}_q$ is a subfield of $\mathbb{F}_{q^n}$. Thus, $\{x \in \mathbb{F}_{q^n} \mid x^d = 1\} = \{1, \alpha, \alpha^2, \ldots, \alpha^{d-1}\}$. We also assume that the discrete logarithm over $\mathbb{F}_q$ is easy to find (that is to say, the parameter q is much less than 2^{1880}, see Footnote 1 on the next page).

Theorem 3. *The multiplicative homomorphic encryption scheme described above is correct, and it is multiplicative homomorphic.*

Proof. To show the correctness, we have to prove that the decryption of an encrypted plaintext yields the same plaintext again. To decrypt a ciphertext $c = \gamma^{\log_\beta m} \alpha^r$, one computes

$$
\begin{aligned}
m' = c^{d \cdot l^{-1}} &= (\gamma^{\log_\beta m})^{d \cdot l^{-1}} (\alpha^r)^{d \cdot l^{-1}} \\
&= (\gamma^d)^{l^{-1} \cdot \log_\beta m} (\alpha^d)^{r \cdot l^{-1}} \\
&= \beta^{l \cdot l^{-1} \cdot \log_\beta m} \qquad\qquad (3) \\
&= m,
\end{aligned}
$$

where Eq. (3) is due to the facts that $\gamma^d = \beta^l$ and $\alpha^d = 1$.

The multiplicative homomorphic property is an immediate consequence of Theorem 1. More explicitly, let c_1 and c_2 be two encryptions of the plaintexts m_1 and m_2 respectively. Since the decryption function $F(x) = x^{d \cdot l^{-1}}$ is a power function, then F is a multiplicative homomorphism, i.e., decrypting $c_1 \cdot c_2$ yields $(c_1 \cdot c_2)^{d \cdot l^{-1}} = c_1^{d \cdot l^{-1}} \cdot c_2^{d \cdot l^{-1}} = m_1 \cdot m_2$. □

Security Analysis. In this paper, we only consider ciphertext-only attacks. We argue that the multiplicative homomorphic encryption scheme described above cannot be broken in general by ciphertext-only attacks if the parameter q satisfies some restrictions.

We first give some notations. Let n be an integer. For $i|n$, define

$$
\mathcal{O}_i(n) = \{il \mod n \mid l \in \mathbb{Z}_n^*\},
$$

where $\mathbb{Z}_n^* = \{k \in \mathbb{Z}_n \mid \gcd(k, n) = 1\}$. Clearly, if i and j are distinct factors of n, then $\mathcal{O}_i(n) \cap \mathcal{O}_j(n) = \emptyset$, and we have $\bigcup_{i|n} \mathcal{O}_i(n) = \mathbb{Z}_n$. Hence, the sets $\mathcal{O}_i(n)$, $i|n$, form a partition of $\mathbb{Z}_n$.

In the above multiplicative homomorphic encryption scheme, we know that $\alpha = \eta^{(q^n - 1)/d}$ is a primitive d-th root of unity over $\mathbb{F}_q$, and $\gamma = \eta^{l(q^n - 1)/d(q-1)}$, where $d|(q^n - 1)/(q - 1)$, $\gcd(d, q - 1) = 1$, $l \in \mathbb{Z}_{q-1}^*$, and η is a primitive element of $\mathbb{F}_{q^n}$. Suppose that the cryptanalyst gets c as a ciphertext. Then, there exists a plaintext $m \in \mathbb{F}_q^*$ and an integer $r \in \{0, 1, \ldots, d - 1\}$ such that $c = \gamma^{\log_\beta m} \alpha^r$, where $\beta = \eta^{(q^n - 1)/(q-1)}$. Hence, the cryptanalyst has

$$
c = \eta^{\frac{q^n - 1}{q - 1} \cdot \frac{1}{d}(l \log_\beta m + r(q-1))},
$$

and thus $x := \frac{1}{d}(l \log_\beta m + r(q-1))$ is known.[1] The cryptanalyst will try to guess m from x, but d, l, r are unknown to him. Let $d_0 := \gcd(l \log_\beta m + r(q - 1), d)$

---

[1] Note that here we do not need to make a requirement on q such that the *Discrete Logarithm* problem (DLP) in $\mathbb{F}_{q^n}^*$ is hard to solve. Indeed, it is suggested that q^n needs to be at least 2^{1880} to make known discrete logarithm algorithms infeasible [22, Chapter 6]. Nowadays DLP can be solved for some special fields (especially with small characteristic) of size larger than 1880 bits, e.g., discrete logarithm in $\mathbb{F}_{2^{6168}}$ is solved [14].

and $d_1 := \min\{d' \mid c^{d'(q-1)} = 1\} = d/d_0 \leqslant d$. From the cryptanalyst's point of view, he can compute d_1 and

$$c^{d_1} = \eta^{\frac{q^n-1}{q-1} \cdot \frac{1}{d_0}(l \log_\beta m + r(q-1))} = \beta^{\frac{1}{d_0}(l \log_\beta m + r(q-1))}$$

$$= \beta^{\frac{1}{d_0}(l' \log_\beta m' + r'(q-1))} \qquad (4)$$

where l', r' are the guessed parameters, $m' \in \mathbb{F}_q^*$ is the guessed plaintext, and d_0 is unknown to the cryptanalyst.

From the above discussion, we now prove the following lemma.

Lemma 1. *For $m, m' \in \mathbb{F}_q^*$, there exists $l' \in \mathbb{Z}_{q-1}^*$ such that (4) holds if and only if $\gcd(\log_\beta m, q - 1) = \gcd(\log_\beta m', q - 1)$, i.e., $\log_\beta m, \log_\beta m' \in \mathcal{O}_i(q - 1)$ for some $i \mid (q - 1)$.*

Proof. It is clear that (4) holds if and only if

$$\frac{1}{d_0}(l \log_\beta m + r(q-1)) \equiv \frac{1}{d_0}(l' \log_\beta m' + r'(q-1)) \pmod{q-1}. \qquad (5)$$

Since $\gcd(d, q-1) = 1$, which implies $\gcd(d_0, q-1) = 1$, and thus d_0 is invertible modulo $q - 1$. Hence, (5) holds if and only if $l \log_\beta m \equiv l' \log_\beta m' \pmod{q - 1}$. This is equivalent to saying that $\gcd(l \log_\beta m, q - 1) = \gcd(l' \log_\beta m', q - 1)$, or equivalently, $\gcd(\log_\beta m, q - 1) = \gcd(\log_\beta m', q - 1)$, because l and l' are in $\mathbb{Z}_{q-1}^*$. $\qquad\square$

Theorem 4. *In the above multiplicative homomorphic encryption scheme, if a cryptanalyst gets a ciphertext c and knows nothing about the secret key, then he can only find a factor i of $q - 1$ such that the encrypted plaintext m satisfies $\log_\beta m \in \mathcal{O}_i(q - 1)$. Moreover, for any m such that $\log_\beta m \in \mathcal{O}_i(q - 1)$, the conditional probability of m given c is*

$$\Pr(\mathbf{m} = m \mid \mathbf{c} = c) = \frac{1}{|\mathcal{O}_i(q - 1)|},$$

which implies that the cryptanalyst will succeed in guessing which plaintext was encrypted with probability $1/|\mathcal{O}_i(q - 1)|$.

Proof. From the discussion above, we know that given a ciphertext c, a cryptanalyst can compute $d_1 = \min\{d' \mid c^{d'(q-1)} = 1\}$ and

$$c^{d_1} = \beta^{\frac{1}{d_0}(l \log_\beta m + r(q-1))} = \beta^{e_c}, \qquad (6)$$

where $e_c := \frac{1}{d_0}(l \log_\beta m + r(q-1))$ is known but $d_0 = \gcd(l \log_\beta m + r(q-1), d)$, l, r, and m are unknown. Since $\gcd(d_0, q-1) = 1$, then $\log_\beta m \in \mathcal{O}_i(q-1)$ if and only if $\gcd(e_c, q - 1) = i$. Therefore, the cryptanalyst determines the factor i of $q - 1$ such that $\log_\beta m \in \mathcal{O}_i(q - 1)$. Thanks to Lemma 1, there exists $l' \in \mathbb{Z}_{q-1}^*$ such that (4) holds if and only if $\log_\beta m' \in \mathcal{O}_i(q - 1)$. Hence, the cryptanalyst cannot find the exact plaintext m.

Suppose that the encrypted plaintext m satisfies $\log_\beta m \in \mathcal{O}_i(q-1)$, where $i|(q-1)$. It is easy to see that for any $j \in \mathcal{O}_i(q-1)$, the number of $l \in \mathbb{Z}_{q-1}^*$ such that $lj \mod (q-1) = j$ is exactly $\phi(q-1)/|\mathcal{O}_i(q-1)|$, where ϕ is the Euler phi function. For a fixed d, let $\mathcal{C}$ be the ciphertext space. For any $c \in \mathcal{C}$, denote by e_c the exponent of c^{d_1} based on β defined in (6). Hence, for any $m \in \mathbb{F}_q^*$ and any $c \in \mathcal{C}$, since r is randomly chosen from $\{0, \ldots, d-1\}$, then one can obtain

$$\Pr(\mathbf{c} = c \mid \mathbf{m} = m) = \frac{\phi(q-1)}{|\mathcal{O}_i(q-1)|} \cdot \frac{1}{d \cdot \phi(q-1)} = \frac{1}{d \cdot |\mathcal{O}_i(q-1)|}$$

if $\log_\beta m \in \mathcal{O}_i(q-1)$ and $\gcd(e_c, q-1) = i$, and $\Pr(\mathbf{c} = c \mid \mathbf{m} = m) = 0$ otherwise. Since for any $m \in \mathbb{F}_q^*$, $\Pr(\mathbf{m} = m) = 1/(q-1)$, then for any c such that $\gcd(e_c, q-1) = i$,

$$\Pr(\mathbf{c} = c) = \sum_{m \in \mathbb{F}_q^*} \Pr(\mathbf{m} = m)\Pr(\mathbf{c} = c \mid \mathbf{m} = m)$$

$$= \sum_{\substack{m \in \mathbb{F}_q^* \\ \log_\beta m \in \mathcal{O}_i(q-1)}} \frac{1}{q-1} \cdot \frac{1}{d \cdot |\mathcal{O}_i(q-1)|} = \frac{1}{(q-1)d}.$$

By using Bayes' theorem, we have that for any $m \in \mathbb{F}_q^*$ and any $c \in \mathcal{C}$,

$$\Pr(\mathbf{m} = m \mid \mathbf{c} = c) = \frac{\Pr(\mathbf{c} = c \mid \mathbf{m} = m)\Pr(\mathbf{m} = m)}{\Pr(\mathbf{c} = c)}$$

$$= \begin{cases} \frac{1}{|\mathcal{O}_i(q-1)|}, & \text{if } \log_\beta m \in \mathcal{O}_i(q-1) \text{ and } \gcd(e_c, q-1) = i, \\ 0, & \text{otherwise.} \end{cases}$$

Therefore, the cryptanalyst will succeed in guessing the encrypted plaintext with probability $1/|\mathcal{O}_i(q-1)|$. $\square$

Corollary 2. *In the above multiplicative homomorphic encryption scheme, if the plaintext space is restricted to $\mathbb{F}_q^* \setminus \{1\}$, then for a cryptanalyst, by cipher-only attacks, the probability of success of guessing the plaintext from a known ciphertext is at most $1/\min_{i|(q-1), i<q-1} |\mathcal{O}_i(q-1)|$.*

Proof. From Theorem 4, it is known that for a plaintext m satisfying $\log_\beta m \in \mathcal{O}_i(q-1)$, where $i|(q-1)$, a cryptanalyst will succeed in guessing m from the corresponding ciphertext c with probability $1/|\mathcal{O}_i(q-1)|$. Note that the set $\{\mathcal{O}_i(q-1) \mid i|(q-1), i < q-1\}$ forms a partition of $\mathbb{Z}_{q-1} \setminus \{0\}$. Since the plaintext space is restricted to $\mathbb{F}_q^* \setminus \{1\}$, then for a cryptanalyst, the probability of success of guessing the plaintext m is at most $1/\min_{i|(q-1), i<q-1} |\mathcal{O}_i(q-1)|$. $\square$

Remark 4. If q is odd, then $\min_{i|(q-1), i<q-1} |\mathcal{O}_i(q-1)| = |\mathcal{O}_{(q-1)/2}(q-1)| = 1$. Thus, from Corollary 2, a cryptanalyst may succeed in guessing the plaintext from the ciphertext with probability 1. In fact, if $m = \beta^{(q-1)/2}$ is encrypted as c, where β is a primitive element of $\mathbb{F}_q$, then for a cryptanalyst, the probability of success of guessing m from c is 1. To increase the security of the system, we

Table 1. All numbers $9 \leqslant q \leqslant 3^{100}$ satisfying $q = 3^s$ and $(q-1)/2$ is a prime

q	$(q-1)/2$
3^3	13
3^7	1093
3^{13}	797161
3^{71}	3754733257489862401973357979128773

can choose odd q such that $(q-1)/2$ is a prime, and then restrict the plaintext space to $\mathbb{F}_q^* \setminus \{1, \beta^{(q-1)/2}\}$. In this case, it is easy to check that

$$\min_{i|(q-1), i<q-1, i\neq(q-1)/2} |\mathcal{O}_i(q-1)| = |\mathcal{O}_1(q-1)| = \phi(q-1) = (q-3)/2.$$

Hence, a cryptanalyst can succeed in guessing the plaintext with probability at most $2/(q-3)$. In Table 1, we list some examples of $q = 3^s$, where $2 \leqslant s \leqslant 100$, which satisfy $(q-1)/2$ is a prime.

Proposition 1. *Let the plaintext space be restricted to $\mathbb{F}_q^* \setminus \{1\}$. Then, the multiplicative homomorphic encryption scheme described above has perfect secrecy if and only if $q - 1$ is a Mersenne prime (see e.g. [21]), i.e., $q - 1 = 2^s - 1$ is a prime for some prime s.*

Proof. Sufficiency. Since $q-1$ is a prime, then $\mathbb{Z}_{q-1} \setminus \{0\} = \mathcal{O}_1(q-1)$. Let β be a primitive element of $\mathbb{F}_q$, then for any $m \in \mathbb{F}_q^* \setminus \{1\}$, we have $\log_\beta m \in \mathbb{Z}_{q-1} \setminus \{0\} = \mathcal{O}_1(q-1)$. According to Theorem 4, we have that for every $m \in \mathbb{F}_q^* \setminus \{1\}$ and every $c \in \mathcal{C}$, the conditional probability of m given a ciphertext c, is

$$\Pr(\mathbf{m} = m \mid \mathbf{c} = c) = \frac{1}{|\mathcal{O}_1(q-1)|} = \Pr(\mathbf{m} = m).$$

Therefore, from Definition 1, the multiplicative homomorphic encryption scheme has perfect secrecy.

Necessity. It is known that for every $m \in \mathbb{F}_q^* \setminus \{1\}$ and every $c \in \mathcal{C}$,

$$\Pr(\mathbf{m} = m \mid \mathbf{c} = c) = \Pr(\mathbf{m} = m) = \frac{1}{q-2}.$$

From Theorem 4, we have that $\Pr(\mathbf{m} = m \mid \mathbf{c} = c) = 1/|\mathcal{O}_i(q-1)|$ for some $i|(q-1)$. Therefore, for every integer i satisfying $i|(q-1)$ and $i < q-1$, we have $|\mathcal{O}_i(q-1)| = q-2$, which implies that $q-1$ is a prime. Note that q is a power of a prime. If q is odd, then $q-1$ is even which cannot be a prime. Hence, q is a power of 2 such that $q-1$ is a prime, i.e., $q-1$ is a Mersenne prime. $\square$

Remark 5. From Proposition 1, we know that to achieve perfect secrecy, the parameter q chosen in the multiplicative homomorphic encryption scheme should satisfy $q - 1$ is a Mersenne prime. In practice, it would be suitable to choose some prime power q such that $\min_{i \mid (q-1), i \notin A} |\mathcal{O}_i(q-1)|$ takes a high value, where $A \subseteq \{1, 2, \ldots, q-1\}$, and the plaintext space is restricted to $m \in \mathbb{F}_q^* \backslash \{\beta^i \mid i \in A\}$. See Remark 4 for example.

Remark 6. Note that in the multiplicative homomorphic encryption scheme with constraints in Proposition 1, we have proved that for only one encryption, the scheme has perfect secrecy. In fact, homomorphic encryption schemes cannot in a one-time pad setting, and a reuse of the secret key could lead to a break of the scheme. However, if the size of the finite field is chosen to be large enough, we can show that the proposed multiplicative homomorphic encryption scheme can resist cipher-only attacks to some extent. Suppose that the cryptanalyst gets a sequence of ciphertexts $c_1, \ldots, c_s$ encrypted by the secret key (d, l). Then, he can compute $\bar{d} = \max_{1 \leqslant i \leqslant s} \left\{ \min \left\{ d' \mid c_i^{d'(q-1)} = 1 \right\} \right\}$ and get the multiset $C = \{* \, c_1^{\bar{d}}, \ldots, c_s^{\bar{d}} \, *\}$. In the case $\bar{d} = d$, the cryptanalyst can only guess the encrypted plaintext sequence $m_1, \ldots, m_s$ correctly with probability $1/(q-2)$, since he knows nothing about the parameter l. Thus, when q is large enough (but much less than 2^{1880}, see Remark 3), the probability of success of guessing the correct plaintext sequence is still very small.

4.2   An Additive Homomorphic Encryption Scheme

Let q be a power of a prime and n be a positive integer, and $F(x) = \sum_{i=0}^{n-1} \delta_i x^{q^i} - \alpha$ be a q^n-ary affine function, where $\alpha \in \mathbb{F}_{q^n}$ and $\delta_i \in \mathbb{F}_{q^n}$, $i = 0, \ldots, n-1$. An element $\beta \in \mathbb{F}_{q^n}$ is a *root* of $F(x)$ if and only if $F(\beta) = \alpha$. For a q^n-ary affine function F, the determination of all the roots of F in $\mathbb{F}_{q^n}$ is an easy task (see e.g. [15, Chapter 3]).

- *Key-Generation*
  Choose $\alpha \in \mathbb{F}_{q^n}^*$ as the secret key. Define a q^n-ary function $F(x) = \mathrm{Tr}_1^n(\alpha x)$.
- *Encryption*
  To encrypt a plaintext $m \in \mathbb{F}_q$, one randomly chooses a root $c \in \mathbb{F}_{q^n}$ of the affine q-polynomial $F(x) - m$. Then, c is the ciphertext.
- *Decryption*
  For $c \in \mathbb{F}_{q^n}$, one computes $m' = F(c)$.

Theorem 5. *The additive homomorphic encryption scheme described above is correct, and it is additive homomorphic.*

Proof. The correctness of the scheme is obvious. The additive homomorphic property is an immediate consequence of the fact that the trace function is linear, i.e., decrypting $c_1 + c_2$ yields $F(c_1 + c_2) = \mathrm{Tr}_1^n(\alpha(c_1 + c_2)) = \mathrm{Tr}_1^n(\alpha c_1) + \mathrm{Tr}_1^n(\alpha c_2) = F(c_1) + F(c_2) = m_1 + m_2$. $\qquad\square$

Security Analysis. In this paper, we only consider ciphertext-only attacks. In the above additive homomorphic encryption scheme, if a ciphertext $c = 0$, then the encrypted plaintext m must be 0. Therefore, we always assume that $m = 0$ is encrypted as a nonzero element in $\mathbb{F}_{q^n}$.

Theorem 6. *The additive homomorphic encryption scheme described above has perfect secrecy.*

Proof. Let $\{\beta_1, \ldots, \beta_n\}$ be a basis of $\mathbb{F}_{q^n}$ over $\mathbb{F}_q$. For a ciphertext $c \in \mathbb{F}_{q^n}^*$, there must exist $j \in \{1, \ldots, n\}$ such that $\mathrm{Tr}_1^n(\beta_j c) \neq 0$. For any $m \in \mathbb{F}_q$ and any $a_i \in \mathbb{F}_q$, $i \in \{1, \ldots, n\} \setminus \{j\}$, define

$$a_j = \left(m - \sum_{i \in \{1, \ldots, n\} \setminus \{j\}} a_i \mathrm{Tr}_1^n(\beta_i c) \right) \left(\mathrm{Tr}_1^n(\beta_j c) \right)^{-1}.$$

Then, we have $\sum_{i=1}^n a_i \mathrm{Tr}_1^n(\beta_i c) = m$, i.e., $\mathrm{Tr}_1^n(\sum_{i=1}^n a_i \beta_i c) = m$. Define $\alpha = \sum_{i=1}^n a_i \beta_i$, then $\mathrm{Tr}_1^n(\alpha c) = m$. For $m \in \mathbb{F}_q^*$, there are q^{n-1} possible $\alpha \in \mathbb{F}_{q^n}^*$ such that $\mathrm{Tr}_1^n(\alpha c) = m$. If $m = 0$ and $a_i = 0$ for $i \in \{1, \ldots, n\} \setminus \{j\}$, then $a_j = 0$, which leads to $\alpha = 0$. So, for $m = 0$, there are only $q^{n-1} - 1$ possible $\alpha \in \mathbb{F}_{q^n}^*$ such that $\mathrm{Tr}_1^n(\alpha c) = m$. Note that we always assume that $m = 0$ is encrypted as a nonzero element in $\mathbb{F}_{q^n}$. Hence, for any $m \in \mathbb{F}_q$ and any $c \in \mathbb{F}_{q^n}^*$, since a root $c \in \mathbb{F}_{q^n}^*$ is randomly chosen from the solution space of dimension $n - 1$, then we have

$$\Pr(\mathbf{c} = c \mid \mathbf{m} = m) = \begin{cases} \frac{q^{n-1}}{q^n - 1} \cdot \frac{1}{q^{n-1}} = \frac{1}{q^n - 1}, & \text{if } m \in \mathbb{F}_q^*, \\ \frac{q^{n-1} - 1}{q^n - 1} \cdot \frac{1}{q^{n-1} - 1} = \frac{1}{q^n - 1}, & \text{if } m = 0. \end{cases}$$

Since for any $m \in \mathbb{F}_q$, $\Pr(\mathbf{m} = m) = 1/q$, then for any $c \in \mathbb{F}_{q^n}^*$,

$$\Pr(\mathbf{c} = c) = \sum_{m \in \mathbb{F}_q} \Pr(\mathbf{m} = m) \Pr(\mathbf{c} = c \mid \mathbf{m} = m) = \frac{1}{q^n - 1}.$$

By using Bayes' theorem, we have that for any $m \in \mathbb{F}_q$ and any $c \in \mathbb{F}_{q^n}^*$,

$$\Pr(\mathbf{m} = m \mid \mathbf{c} = c) = \frac{\Pr(\mathbf{c} = c \mid \mathbf{m} = m) \Pr(\mathbf{m} = m)}{\Pr(\mathbf{c} = c)} = \frac{1}{q} = \Pr(\mathbf{m} = m).$$

Therefore, from Definition 1, the additive homomorphic encryption scheme has perfect secrecy. □

Remark 7. In the additive homomorphic encryption scheme described above, we have proved that for only one encryption, the scheme has perfect secrecy. Similar to the discussion in Remark 6, we will show that if the size of the finite field is chosen to be large enough, the proposed additive homomorphic encryption scheme can resist cipher-only attacks to some extent. Suppose that the cryptanalyst gets a sequence of ciphertexts $c_1, \ldots, c_s$ encrypted by the secret key α. If $c_1, \ldots, c_s$ span a t-dimensional vector space over $\mathbb{F}_q$, then the cryptanalyst can only guess the encrypted plaintext sequence $m_1, \ldots, m_s$ correctly with probability $1/q^t$ if $t < n$, and $1/(q^n - 1)$ otherwise, since he knows nothing about the parameter α. Thus, when q is large enough, the probability of success of guessing the correct plaintext sequence is still very small.

5   Concluding Remarks

In this paper, we studied symmetric partially homomorphic encryption schemes over finite fields. We showed that non-zero multiplicative (or additive) homomorphisms over finite fields are equivalent to power functions (or non-constant homogeneous affine functions). We proposed two homomorphic encryption schemes with reasonable computation and communication costs, and discussed security of our schemes in terms of cipher-only attacks. Since our schemes are not based on hardness assumptions, semantic security (see [13]) is not considered here (this concept is mainly discussed under a given hardness assumption). In [3,16], it is proved that any fully homomorphic encryption scheme over finite fields (or rings) cannot resist against cipher-only attacks. As an extended work, we find two partially homomorphic encryption schemes which have perfect secrecy and can resist against cipher-only attacks to some extent.

Appendix: The Proofs of Theorems 1 and 2

The Proof of Theorem 1. The sufficiency is obvious since that for any $x, y \in \mathbb{F}_q$, we have $F(xy) = (xy)^d = x^d y^d = F(x)F(y)$. We prove the necessity below.

Since F is a homomorphism, we have $F(0) = F(0)^2$, which implies $F(0) = 1$ or 0. If $F(0) = 1$, then for any $x \in \mathbb{F}_q$, $F(x) = F(x)F(0) = F(0) = 1$. Define $0^0 = 1$, and thus $F(x) = x^0$ is a power function. In the following, we consider the case $F(0) = 0$.

From $F(1) = F(1)^2$, one can deduce $F(1) = 1$, since if $F(1) = 0$, then for any $x \in \mathbb{F}_q$, $F(x) = F(x)F(1) = 0$, which contradicts that F is non-zero. Let α be a primitive element of $\mathbb{F}_q$. Note that $F(\alpha) \neq 0$, since otherwise, we have $0 = F(\alpha^{q-2})F(\alpha) = F(\alpha^{q-1}) = F(1) = 1$, a contradiction. Thus, for any $i \in \mathbb{Z}_q$,

$$F(\alpha^i) = F(\alpha)^i = \alpha^{\log_\alpha F(\alpha)^i} = \alpha^{i \log_\alpha F(\alpha)}. \tag{7}$$

Combining $F(0) = 0$ with (7), we have that for any $x \in \mathbb{F}_q$,

$$F(x) = x^{\log_\alpha F(\alpha)}.$$

Therefore, F is a power function.

The Proof of Theorem 2. *Sufficiency.* Let $F(x) = \sum_{i=0}^{s-1} \delta_i x^{p^i}$, where $\delta_i \in \mathbb{F}_q$. Then, for any $x, y \in \mathbb{F}_q$,

$$F(x+y) = \sum_{i=0}^{s-1} \delta_i (x+y)^{p^i} = \sum_{i=0}^{s-1} \delta_i x^{p^i} + \sum_{i=0}^{s-1} \delta_i y^{p^i} = F(x) + F(y).$$

Necessity. Let $F(x) = \sum_{i=0}^{q-1} \delta_i x^i$, where $\delta_i \in \mathbb{F}_q$. Define a function from $\mathbb{F}_q \times \mathbb{F}_q$ to $\mathbb{F}_q$ as

$$\Delta(x, y) = F(x + y) - F(x) - F(y), \qquad (x, y) \in \mathbb{F}_q \times \mathbb{F}_q. \tag{8}$$

Since for any integer $k \geqslant 0$, $(x + y)^{p^k} = x^{p^k} + y^{p^k}$, then from (8), we have

$$\Delta(x, y) = \sum_{i \in I} \delta_i (x + y)^i - \sum_{i \in I} \delta_i x^i - \sum_{i \in I} \delta_i y^i, \tag{9}$$

where the set I satisfies for any $i \in I$, $\delta_i \neq 0$ and $\mathrm{wt}_p(i) \geqslant 2$. Suppose that $AD(F) = \max\{\mathrm{wt}_p(i) \mid \delta_i \neq 0, i \in \mathbb{Z}_q\} \geqslant 2$, then it follows that $I \neq \emptyset$. Let $j = \sum_{k=0}^{s-1} j_k p^k \in I$, then we have

$$\begin{aligned}
\delta_j (x + y)^j &= \delta_j (x + y)^{\sum_{k=0}^{s-1} j_k p^k} \\
&= \delta_j \prod_{k=0}^{s-1} \left(x^{p^k} + y^{p^k} \right)^{j_k} \\
&= \delta_j \prod_{k=0}^{s-1} \left(\sum_{l=0}^{j_k} \binom{j_k}{l} x^{l p^k} y^{(j_k - l) p^k} \right).
\end{aligned}$$

If there exists $k_0 \in \mathbb{Z}_s$ such that $2 \leqslant j_{k_0} \leqslant p - 1$, then since $p \nmid \binom{j_{k_0}}{l}$, there must exist a nonzero term with degree j in the expansion of $\delta_j (x + y)^j$, which can be divided by $x^{p^{k_0}} y^{p^{k_0}}$. Thus, combining (9) with the fact that $x^i y^j$, $i, j \in \mathbb{Z}_q$ are linearly independent over $\mathbb{F}_q$, we have that $\Delta(x, y)$ is a nonzero function. On the other hand, if there exist distinct $k_1, k_2 \in \mathbb{Z}_s$ such that $j_{k_1} = j_{k_2} = 1$, then there must exist a nonzero term with degree j in the expansion of $\delta_j (x + y)^j$, which can be divided by $x^{p^{k_1}} y^{p^{k_2}}$. Similarly, it follows that $\Delta(x, y)$ is a nonzero function. Hence, $F(x + y) \neq F(x) + F(y)$, a contradiction to that F is an additive homomorphism. Therefore, since $F(0) = F(0) + F(0)$, we have $AD(F) = 1$ with $F(0) = 0$.

References

1. Armknecht, F., Sadeghi, A.-R.: A new approach for algebraically homomorphic encryption. Cryptology ePrint Archive, Report 2008/422 (2008). https://eprint.iacr.org/2008/422
2. Benaloh, J.: Verifiable secret-ballot elections. Ph.D. thesis, Yale University, New Haven, USA (1987)
3. Boneh, J., Lipton, R.: Searching for elements in black-box fields and applications. In: Koblitz, N. (ed.) CRYPTO 1996. LNCS, vol. 1109, pp. 283–297. Springer, Heidelberg (1996)
4. Brakerski, Z., Vaikuntanathan, V.: Fully homomorphic encryption from ring-LWE and security for key dependent messages. In: Rogaway, P. (ed.) CRYPTO 2011. LNCS, vol. 6841, pp. 505–524. Springer, Heidelberg (2011). doi:10.1007/978-3-642-22792-9_29

5. Brakerski, Z.: Fully homomorphic encryption without modulus switching from classical GapSVP. In: Safavi-Naini, R., Canetti, R. (eds.) CRYPTO 2012. LNCS, vol. 7417, pp. 868–886. Springer, Heidelberg (2012). doi:10.1007/978-3-642-32009-5_50
6. Chor, B., Kushilevitz, E., Goldreich, O., Sudan, M.: Private information retrieval. J. ACM **45**(6), 965–981 (1998)
7. Cramer, R., Damgård, I., Nielsen, J.B.: Multiparty computation from threshold homomorphic encryption. In: Pfitzmann, B. (ed.) EUROCRYPT 2001. LNCS, vol. 2045, pp. 280–300. Springer, Heidelberg (2001). doi:10.1007/3-540-44987-6_18
8. Domingo-Ferrer, J.: A provably secure additive and multiplicative privacy homomorphism. In: Chan, A.H., Gligor, V. (eds.) ISC 2002. LNCS, vol. 2433, pp. 471–483. Springer, Heidelberg (2002). doi:10.1007/3-540-45811-5_37
9. ElGamal, T.: A public key cryptosystem and a signature scheme based on discrete logarithms. In: Blakley, G.R., Chaum, D. (eds.) CRYPTO 1984. LNCS, vol. 196, pp. 10–18. Springer, Heidelberg (1985). doi:10.1007/3-540-39568-7_2
10. Gentry, C.: Fully homomorphic encryption using ideal lattices. In: Proceedings of the 41st Annual ACM Symposium on Theory of Computing, STOC 2009, pp. 169–178. ACM (2009)
11. Gentry, C.: A fully homomorphic encryption scheme. Ph.D. thesis, Stanford University, California, USA (2009)
12. Gentry, C., Sahai, A., Waters, B.: Homomorphic encryption from learning with errors: conceptually-simpler, asymptotically-faster, attribute-based. In: Canetti, R., Garay, J.A. (eds.) CRYPTO 2013. LNCS, vol. 8042, pp. 75–92. Springer, Heidelberg (2013). doi:10.1007/978-3-642-40041-4_5
13. Goldwasser, S., Micali, S.: Probabilistic encryption and how to play mental poker keeping secret all partial information. In: Proceedings of the 14th Annual ACM Symposium on Theory of Computing, STOC 1982, pp. 365–377. ACM (1982)
14. Joux, A.: Discrete logarithm in $\mathbb{F}_{2^{6168}}$. Announcement to the Number Theory List (2013)
15. Lidl, R., Niederreiter, H.: Finite Fields. Encyclopedia of Mathematics and its Applications. Cambridge University Press, New York (1997)
16. Maurer, U., Raub, D.: Black-box extension fields and the inexistence of field-homomorphic one-way permutations. In: Kurosawa, K. (ed.) ASIACRYPT 2007. LNCS, vol. 4833, pp. 427–443. Springer, Heidelberg (2007). doi:10.1007/978-3-540-76900-2_26
17. Méaux, P., Journault, A., Standaert, F.-X., Carlet, C.: Towards stream ciphers for efficient FHE with low-noise ciphertexts. In: Fischlin, M., Coron, J.-S. (eds.) EUROCRYPT 2016. LNCS, vol. 9665, pp. 311–343. Springer, Heidelberg (2016). doi:10.1007/978-3-662-49890-3_13
18. Okamoto, T., Uchiyama, S.: A new public-key cryptosystem as secure as factoring. In: Nyberg, K. (ed.) EUROCRYPT 1998. LNCS, vol. 1403, pp. 308–318. Springer, Heidelberg (1998). doi:10.1007/BFb0054135
19. Paillier, P.: Public-key cryptosystems based on composite degree residuosity classes. In: Stern, J. (ed.) EUROCRYPT 1999. LNCS, vol. 1592, pp. 223–238. Springer, Heidelberg (1999). doi:10.1007/3-540-48910-X_16
20. Rivest, R., Adleman, L., Dertouzos, M.: On data banks and privacy homomorphisms. In: Foundations of Secure Computation, pp. 169–179. Academic Press, New York (1978)
21. Sloane, N.J.A.: A Handbook of Integer Sequences. Academic Press, New York (1973)
22. Stinson, D.R.: Cryptography: Theory and Practice, 3rd edn. CRC Press, Boca Raton (2006)

23. Dijk, M., Gentry, C., Halevi, S., Vaikuntanathan, V.: Fully homomorphic encryption over the integers. In: Gilbert, H. (ed.) EUROCRYPT 2010. LNCS, vol. 6110, pp. 24–43. Springer, Heidelberg (2010). doi:10.1007/978-3-642-13190-5_2
24. Wagner, D.: Cryptanalysis of an algebraic privacy homomorphism. In: Boyd, C., Mao, W. (eds.) ISC 2003. LNCS, vol. 2851, pp. 234–239. Springer, Heidelberg (2003). doi:10.1007/10958513_18

Light Weight Key Establishment Scheme for Wireless Sensor Networks

Payingat Jilna[✉] and P.P. Deepthi

National Institute of Technology, Calicut, India
jilnaprakash@yahoo.co.in

Abstract. This paper presents a light weight key establishment technique for wireless sensor networks. The proposed method is a hybrid of two popular key exchange protocols LEAP (Localised encryption and authentication protocol) and COKE (Crypto-less over the air key establishment) and addresses the weakness of both schemes. The security analysis shows that the system is secure against active adversaries and node compromise. Compared to COKE, the proposed scheme guarantees a secret key establishment and is energy efficient with a single MAC computation for secret key establishment.

Keywords: Key management · Resilience · Node addition attack · Wireless sensor network

1 Introduction

Wireless sensor networks (WSNs) are used in a wide range of applications including critical applications such as military surveillance and health care. Securing these networks against adversaries is a challenging issue due to the resource limitations of sensor nodes. The security of the sensor network depends on the secrecy of the symmetric key used for encryption and thereby on the security and reliability of key distribution protocols. The limited energy, communication bandwidth and computational capabilities of a wireless sensor node make the use of conventional key distribution schemes difficult.

Many light weight key management schemes specific to the resource constrained WSNs are available in the literature [1]. One approach is key pre-deployment in which secret keys are loaded in to the sensor nodes prior to deployment. The use of global key/network-wide key is one such scheme in which a single key is preloaded to all sensor nodes in the network. The scheme is efficient in the sense that no communication or computation is required to establish the key. But since the compromise of a single node will lead to the compromise of the whole network, the scheme lacks security. To overcome this security risk, in another scheme of the network-wide key, each node is preloaded with pair wise keys to communicate with every other node in the network. That is, in a network of n nodes, each node has to store (n-1) pair wise keys. The scheme is secure in the sense that when a node is compromised only the links established

© Springer International Publishing AG 2016
C. Carlet et al. (Eds.): SPACE 2016, LNCS 10076, pp. 124–137, 2016.
DOI: 10.1007/978-3-319-49445-6_7

by that node are compromised. But it is not scalable due to memory constraints of sensor nodes and cannot support node additions. A number of probabilistic key distribution schemes exist in which each node is loaded with a set of keys chosen randomly from a key pool. Once deployed, the nodes try to identify their neighbours and their shared secret keys. These schemes offer a performance in between the other two extremes in terms of security, scalability and storage with an added issue that it is not certain to establish a link between a pair of nodes.

The key derivation information pre-deployment is another approach in which the sensor nodes generate shared secret keys after deployment using the pre-loaded information. Sensor nodes are loaded with a secret master key and some mathematical functions which are used to compute the shared secrets. Though these schemes are efficient in terms of storage and computations, the whole network will be compromised if the nodes are compromised in the initialization phase.

The key management scheme in [2] make use of auxiliary nodes for key establishment. In addition to regular nodes, additional nodes called assisting nodes are deployed to help pair wise key set up between regular nodes. The scheme is storage efficient but the security depends on the number of assisting nodes involved in establishing a pair-wise secret key. The communication overhead and the computational cost increase with the increase in number of assisting nodes. In the group based key distribution [3] the nodes are deployed in groups and is expected that nodes in the same group will lie close to each other. The node ids and key pre-distribution instances are loaded into the sensor nodes such that each node can establish an in-group key and a cross-group key. Though security is improved in comparison with related works, the scheme is not scalable due to large storage requirements.

The key management schemes based on hard mathematical problems (modular arithmetic based key management, elliptic curve based key management etc.) [4,5] provide high resilience even if nodes are compromised in the initialization phase. In [6] the authors have presented an efficient key management technique based on elliptic curves (EC) for homogeneous static WSNs. The performance of this scheme is evaluated and it is established that this scheme outperforms most of the key management protocols available in the literature in terms of parameters such as communication overhead, storage requirement etc. Similarly an EC based certificateless key establishment scheme for heterogeneous dynamic WSNs is presented in [7]. The performance is evaluated in terms of computation time and energy consumption and demonstrates the trade off between energy consumption and security level. The complex computations associated with EC point multiplication may become too expensive to afford in sensor nodes with stringent energy constraints.

To increase the energy efficiency by reducing the computations, over-the-air key establishment protocols were introduced. The two methods adopted are (i) to extract secret keys from the received signal strength (RSS) [8] and (ii) to leverage channel anonymity for generating pair wise secret keys [9]. For the first method to be secure, the communicating channel must be highly dynamic in nature which is not guaranteed always. The key exchange protocols based on channel anonymity assume the adversary to be a passive eavesdropper and cannot retain security in the presence of active adversaries. This paper presents a hybrid of master key based and over-the-air key establishment protocols such that the proposed method is efficient in terms of energy consumption and is secure against active adversary and node compromise.

The rest of the paper is organised as follows. The related works are given in Sect. 2 and in Sect. 3 the proposed protocol is presented. In Sect. 4, the performance of the proposed scheme is evaluated and in Sect. 5 comparison with related works is done. In Sect. 6 some conclusions are drawn.

2   Related Works and Their Security Analysis

In this work we have considered a static homogeneous wireless sensor network with high security requirements and strict energy constraints. The adversary is modelled as an active adversary. The EC based approaches are not suitable because of the intensive mathematical computations involved in key establishment. The schemes based on deployment knowledge of the sensor nodes is also not considered due to strict energy constraints. Many other light weight schemes are ruled out because of lack of scalability and low security. The two widely accepted key establishment schemes with minimum computations is chosen and their pros and cons are analysed in this section.

2.1   LEAP+

LEAP+ introduced in [10] is widely accepted for key establishment in WSN due to reduced communication overhead and increased security compared to random key pre-distribution schemes. In LEAP+, each node is pre-loaded with an initial master key, node identity and a pseudo random function. Once deployed, each node derives its own master key as a function of initial master key and node identity. The node then broadcasts its identity as a hello message. On receiving this hello message, the neighbouring nodes send acknowledgement which consist of the node id and MAC for authentication. The shared secret key is generated as a function of private master key and node identity.

The security of LEAP+ depends on the secrecy of the initial master key which is erased after T_{min} time period where T_{min} is the lower bound on the time required to establish pair-wise secret key with the neighbouring nodes. The security of the protocol is based on the assumption that no nodes are compromised within this time period. But if T_{min} is kept very small, the probability that a pair-wise secret key is established between every neighbouring node pair becomes low. So, in order to ensure connectivity of the network T_{min} must be kept sufficiently large which also causes an increase in the probability that a node is compromised in the initialization phase. If the adversary gets the initial master key then the whole network will be compromised. Thus choice of T_{min} sets a trade-off between security and connectivity of the network.

It is also seen that LEAP+ is prone to jamming attacks [11]. Since the key establishment is done within the short time-out period T_{min}, the adversary can easily generate jamming signals for this small duration and prevent the pair-wise key establishment and thereby spoiling connectivity of the network.

In [12] a modified scheme with reduced performance overhead is introduced. The communication overhead and the number of computations required for pair-wise key set up are reduced so that T_{min} can be kept very small without compromising the connectivity. Though the probability that nodes are compromised in the initialization phase is less compared to LEAP+, the scheme is more prone to jamming attacks.

2.2   COKE

Crypto-less over-the-air key exchange protocol introduced in 2012 is a probabilistic protocol which allows two neighbouring nodes establish a shared secret without using cryptographic functions. This scheme takes advantage of the source in-distinguishability of anonymous channels to establish the shared secret. A brief description of the algorithm is given below.

Let A and B be the two neighbouring nodes trying to establish a shared secret. It is assumed that both A and B are able to estimate the minimum transmission power required for communicating with each other. Both nodes A and B randomly generate secret keys K_A and K_B each of length k bits. In each time slot, both nodes choose a random waiting time. In the ith time slot, if the waiting time of A(B) is elapsed and no packet is received then the node A(B) transmits the ith bit of $K_A(K_B)$. Node A(B) randomly decides to use its own ID or the ID of neighbouring node in the sender field. If the bit is transmitted by A then it is stored as such at both nodes and if it is transmitted by B, its complement is stored at each node. Thus after k time slots both nodes A and B will have a string of k bits K_s. The shared secret key is derived as $H(K_s)$ where H is a hash function.

In this scheme, the adversary is modelled as a globally eavesdropping adversary and is passive. It is assumed that the adversary has prior information about the location at which the nodes will be deployed and the attacker nodes are present at this location. Even though plain text bits are transmitted, the probability that the adversary identifies the exact source depends on the maximum transmitted power and the geographical location of the adversary. The authors have shown that the probability of secret bit transmission between nodes A and B is high if the adversary is located midway from A to B and reduces to zero with the decrease in this distance ratio. That is, if the adversary is positioned in close proximity of any of the nodes then the probability of secret bit transmission is zero. This is a major drawback of the COKE algorithm as the position of the adversary cannot be predicted or determined in real scenarios. The number of transmissions required to establish a shared secret key under various conditions is also well analysed in the paper. But the scheme is secure only against passive eavesdropping adversaries and is easily prone to node addition attacks as there is no authentication mechanism involved in key establishment. Any active adversary can easily guess a valid node id by eavesdropping the network and convince the neighbouring nodes that it is a part of the network even without compromising a node. The valid nodes will then set up shared secrets with these attacker nodes and be part of the network. Once these attacker nodes join as a part of the network, they can launch various insider attacks such as injecting false messages, spoofing, altering or replaying routing information, selective forwarding attack etc.

From the analysis above it can be seen that the COKE algorithm is energy efficient as it involves only a single hash computation; but it is not secure against active adversaries. In the LEAP+ protocol, compromising a single node in the initialisation phase causes the whole network to be compromised. To mitigate these attacks, a new energy efficient and secure key establishment protocol is proposed which combines the concepts of transitory master key approach and COKE algorithm in such a way that the proposed scheme is energy efficient, secure against active adversaries and defends jamming attacks.

3   Proposed Method for Key Establishment

In this section we present the proposed key exchange protocol which is designed as a hybrid of COKE and LEAP for increased security and efficiency. We assume the network to be static and the nodes to be unaware of their neighbours prior to deployment (Fig. 1).

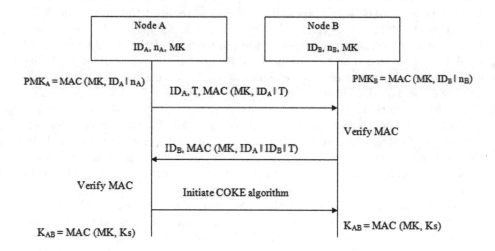

Fig. 1. Proposed method of key establishment

3.1   Adversary Model

The adversary is assumed to be active in contradiction to a passive adversary in COKE. The adversary can eavesdrop on all the communication between nodes, guess valid node ids and inject messages into the networks. It is assumed that the adversary has prior information of the location at which the nodes will be deployed especially, in military scenarios.

3.2 System Model

The wireless sensor network is considered to be homogeneous and static. Prior to deployment a node id and master key (MK) are loaded into each sensor node. In the beginning of each node addition phase, the node ids are generated by the base station using a random number generator and the base station broadcasts the valid node ids added.

Initialization Phase. In this phase, the sensor nodes discovers its neighbours through broadcast of hello messages and establishes the pair-wise secret keys. Once deployed each node, say node A, generates a private master key as $PMK_A = prf(MK, ID_A)$ in the initialisation phase where prf is a pseudo random function. This is to enable addition of new nodes as neighbours in the network after the initialisation phase, since MK is erased at the end of this phase. The node broadcasts a *hello* message which consists of its id, a time stamp (T) and an authentication code. The authentication code for node A is computed as $MAC(MK, ID_A \parallel T)$. The use of time stamp and authentication code prevents replay attack and Hello flood attack in sensor nodes as analysed in Sect. 4. Each of the neighbouring nodes, say node B, authenticates the sender and acknowledges with its id and authentication code ($MAC(MK, ID_A \parallel ID_B \parallel T)$). Node A now verifies these acknowledgement signals from various nodes and generates a table with entries as ids of neighbouring nodes. The COKE algorithm is then initiated and the pair-wise secret key is computed as $MAC(MK, K_s)$ where K_s is the shared secret key. Once the pair-wise secret key is established between every neighbouring node pair, the MK is erased. This is to ensure that once the network comes out of initialisation phase, capturing of a node won't allow the adversary to compute the shared secret keys of various links even when the probability of secret bit transmission is very low.

Working Phase. In this phase, the nodes perform the data processing functions and communicate using the shared secret keys established in the initialization phase. In many practical applications, to extend the life time of the sensor network, new nodes are added in to the network at various time intervals. At this stage, the existing nodes will be in their working phase and the newly deployed nodes in their initialization phase. The key establishment between a node in the working phase and a node in the initialization phase is explained below.

Each new node in the node addition phase is loaded with its id and the master key. These nodes broadcast their hello message and wait for the acknowledgement from the neighbouring nodes. Each of the neighbouring nodes in the working phase adds these new ids into its existing list of neighbouring nodes and broadcasts its id and $MAC(PMK_i, ID_i \parallel T)$. The nodes in the initialization phase compute the private master key of the neighbouring nodes PMK_i, using the received data. The base station now broadcasts the list of newly added valid node ids and each node verifies the new entries in its list. This will help to prevent node addition attack. Now the nodes initiate COKE algorithm and generate the pair-wise secret key as $MAC(PMK_i, K_s)$.

4   Performance Evaluation of the Proposed Scheme

The security, computation cost, storage requirement, connectivity and communication cost of the proposed key establishment scheme are analysed in this section.

4.1   Security Analysis

The security of a key management scheme can be quantified through its resilience and security against a variety of attacks in WSNs.

Resilience. Resilience is the probability that a link between uncompromised nodes is not compromised due to other compromised nodes in the network. When a node is compromised it is assumed that all the data in the node is available to the attacker. If a node is compromised in the working phase of the proposed scheme, the private master key PMK_i, node id and the pair-wise secret key $MAC(PMK_i, K_s)$ with the neighbouring nodes will be available to the attacker. But this data is not sufficient to compromise any other link in the network. The key in any link depends upon random data exchanged between the node pair through COKE algorithm. The difficulty of the attacker to identify the source of each transmitted bit and thereby collect the random bit stream exchanged is analysed in [9] and is shown to be very high. Even if a node is compromised in the initialization phase and the master key is available to the attacker, computation of the shared secret key requires knowledge of source of each bit transmitted. Since the COKE algorithm leverage channel anonymity and the probability that the source is identified is very low, the probability that an uncompromised link is compromised is very low. Thus the key establishment scheme offers high resilience even if the nodes are compromised in the initialization phase.

Hello Flood Attack. In a Hello flood attack, the adversary sends hello messages to the neighbouring nodes with high transmission power to convince the nodes that it is their nearest neighbour. The nodes may then start the key establishment process with the attacker nodes which unnecessarily drains their energy. In the proposed scheme, both hello message and acknowledgement message consist of authentication codes computed through stored master key. Further processing and initialisation of COKE algorithm is done only after verification of these codes. Thus the proposed scheme defends this attack because only authenticated hello messages are processed by the nodes and other hello messages are discarded. Though it involves an additional MAC computation at each node this cost is negligible in comparison with the transmission cost involved in executing the COKE algorithm. Hence the proposed algorithm resists Hello flood attack through authentication.

Node Cloning/Node Replication Attack. When a node is compromised, the attacker loads its own nodes with the compromised information, deploys them at arbitrary locations in the network and tries to establish pair-wise keys with the neighbouring nodes. This is known as node cloning or node replication attack. In case of EG [13] and other random key pre-distribution schemes where a single key is shared by more than one link, a few such cloned nodes are enough to bring down the entire network. In the proposed scheme, if a node is compromised in the working phase, the data available to the adversary are PMK_i, node ids and shared secret keys of neighbouring nodes. In this scheme, the probability that a pair-wise secret key is shared by more than one link is negligibly small. Establishment of pair-wise keys by the clone nodes demands the knowledge of the MK and verification of the node id by the neighbouring nodes. Even if the node is compromised in the initialization phase and the master key MK is available to the attacker, the probability that the clone node passes the verification is negligible as the node ids are generated randomly by the base station. Hence it is not possible for the clone nodes to establish pair-wise keys with valid nodes.

Node Addition Attack. In a node addition attack, the adversary introduces new nodes into the network by loading it with the correct master key. These nodes can easily be a part of the network and the adversary can launch various insider attacks and defeat the purpose of the sensor network. In the proposed scheme, the node ids are randomly generated by the base station and in each node addition phase, the base station broadcasts a list of valid node ids added in that phase. Before initiating the COKE algorithm and establishing secret key with the new neighbours, the nodes verify their neighbour's ids based on the broadcast message from the base station. This reduces the probability that a random guess of node id by the adversary is a valid one. Thus the proposed scheme is less prone to node addition attack.

4.2   Computational Cost

The pair-wise secret key generation in the proposed scheme involves the computation of a single MAC at each node. In addition to this, one more MAC computation is performed to increase the security against Hello flood attack in WSNs. Both nodes authenticate each other before initiating the COKE algorithm. This additional computation helps the nodes to discard hello messages from adversaries and prevent unwanted energy consumption by executing COKE algorithm with an adversary. The energy consumed by the MAC computation is negligible in comparison with the transmission cost.

4.3 Memory Requirement

Prior to deployment, the data loaded into the node memory are the master key and the node id. In the working phase, the master key is replaced with a private master key. In addition, the node ids and shared secret keys of neighbouring nodes are also stored. Considering a node id of length 2 bytes, number of neighbouring nodes as 40 and length of master key and MAC as 16 bytes, the memory required in the initialization phase and working phase are 18 bytes and 738 bytes respectively. This requirement is much less compared to 4 KB memory available in sensor nodes.

4.4 Communication Cost

The parameters that determine the communication cost of the proposed scheme are length of node id, length of MAC, length of time stamp and the number of bits transmitted in the COKE algorithm. In [9], the authors have shown that the number of transmissions required for a fixed number of secret bits varies with P_{sb} where P_{sb} is the secret bit communication probability. Assuming that both nodes A and B have equal probability of transmission

$$P_{sb} = 1/2(P(\phi_A) + P(\phi_B)) \tag{1}$$

where $P(\phi_i)$ is the probability that adversary does not correctly guess the source i. These probabilities depend on the maximum transmitted power and the position of the adversary in the network. In [9] authors have provided the relationship between the secret-bit transmission probability (P_{sb}) and the average number of expected transmissions to commit on shared secret key of a minimum required length. The random variable X_i which takes a value 1 when the ith transmitted bit is secret follows Bernoulli distribution with probability of success P_{sb}. Then, as per central limit theorem, the random variable X counting the number of bits securely transmitted out of a total K emissions given by $X = \sum_{i=1}^{K} X_i$ will have a normal distribution with mean (μ) and variance (σ^2) as given below.

$$\mu = K P_{sb} \tag{2}$$

$$\sigma^2 = K P_{sb}(1 - P_{sb}) \tag{3}$$

Then the number of secret bits transmitted lie within $8\sqrt{K P_{sb}(1 - P_{sb})}$ of $K P_{sb}$ with probability greater than $1 - \epsilon$ for $\epsilon = 2^{-48}$. The variation of number of secret bits transmitted with secret bit transmission probability (P_{sb}) is sketched in Fig. 2. From the simulation results given in [9] it can be seen that P_{sb} is approximately zero if the distance ratio is less than 0.6 and hence secret key establishment is not possible. In the proposed scheme, the pair-wise secret key is generated as a function of MK and shared bits K_s. Thus the scheme guarantees a secret key establishment through MK even if $P_{sb} = 0$. In the proposed scheme the number of bits transmitted by nodes A and B is fixed as 1000 so that, on an average 100 secret bits will be available even when $P_{sb} = 0.1$ as shown in Fig. 2.

The received 1000 bits are now given as input to the MAC function. The MAC function can be either a keyed hash function or a block cipher in cipher block chaining (CBC) mode of operation. In both cases, even a single bit change in the input can cause considerable change in the output due to the in-built properties of MAC function. So with an over the air transmission of 1000 bits, an adversary at a favourable position from the node, has to randomly guess the 100 secret bits transmitted and the stored MK to compute the shared secret key which is an infeasible task. Hence in the proposed algorithm, the number of bits transmitted is fixed as 1000. Thus, considering a node id of length 2 bytes, length of MAC = 16 bytes, length of time stamp = 2 bytes and the number of bits transmitted in the COKE algorithm as 1000, the communication over head of the proposed scheme is 163 bytes.

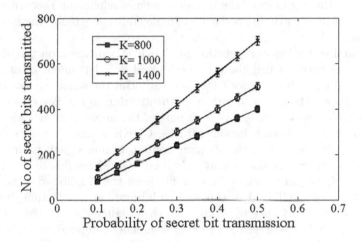

Fig. 2. Number of secret bits transmitted for different values of K

4.5 Connectivity

In the proposed scheme, after deployment, the nodes identify their neighbours and generate a table with entries as ids of neighbouring nodes. A pair wise secret key is established with every authenticated neighbour irrespective of the number of secret bits received through COKE algorithm. The presence of common master key in the initialization phase and private master key in the working phase ensures the connectivity of the network in both phases.

4.6 Structural Complexity

The computations involved in the proposed secret key establishment scheme are the execution of pseudo random function and MAC. In order to achieve reduced structural complexity, both these functions can be performed by time sharing a single hardware unit. AES is the best option as it can be used both as a pseudo random function and MAC in cipher block chaining mode.

5   Comparison with Related Works

In this section, the proposed method is compared with LEAP+ and COKE in terms of security, efficiency and scalability metrics that are used to evaluate the key management schemes in WSNs.

5.1   Security Metric

In this metric, the resilience of the key management scheme and security against various attacks such as Hello flood attack, node addition attack, sink hole attack etc. are analysed.

The shared secret key computation in COKE is dependent on the plain text bits exchanged between neighbouring nodes and is independent of other links thereby providing high resilience to the network. But the scheme is not resistant to node addition attack due to lack of authentication in the key establishment process. Attacker nodes can easily be a part of the network even without node compromise and can launch insider attacks. COKE is also prone to sink hole attack. In a sink hole attack, the attacker node transmits signals with increased power and convinces the nodes that it is their nearest neighbour. It then creates a sink hole by attracting all the traffic from the neighbouring nodes and dropping it. As the COKE algorithm can be initiated at any instant during the life time of the network, the adversary can easily launch a sink hole attack. In COKE, the probability of secret key establishment is dependent on the maximum transmitted power and the adversarial position that cannot be determined. Thus COKE algorithm does not guarantee a secure network. In the proposed scheme, the nodes identify their neighbours at the beginning of the initialization phase and authenticate each other prior to key establishment using a secret master key. Similarly in the working phase, the node ids of new neighbours are verified based on the broadcast signals from the base station. This prevents the adversary from being a part of the network and convincing the nodes as their nearest neighbour to launch sink hole attack.

The security of LEAP+ is dependent on the secrecy of the master key which is loaded into the sensor node prior to deployment. If this MK is compromised, the whole network is compromised as the shared secret keys in the entire network are computed based on this MK. Thus LEAP+ offers zero resilience if a node is compromised in the initialization phase. The proposed scheme provides security at two levels, one through the master key and other through the source indistinguishability of COKE algorithm. Hence a link can be compromised only if both the MK and the source of transmitted bits are known to the adversary and hence provides high resilience even if nodes are compromised in the initialization phase which is the major drawback of LEAP+.

5.2   Efficiency Metric

The factors considered in an efficiency metric are storage requirement, communication overhead, computational cost and connectivity.

Storage Requirement. Similar to the proposed scheme, the data loaded into a sensor node prior to deployment in LEAP+ are node id and the initial master key. In the working phase, the initial master key is replaced with private master key. In addition, each node stores the id and shared secret keys of neighbouring nodes. Establishment of pair-wise keys using COKE algorithm do not require any pre-loaded information other than node id. The shared secrets and node ids of neighbouring nodes are stored in the working phase.

Considering a node id of length 2 bytes, number of neighbouring nodes as 40 and length of master key as 16 bytes, memory required in the working phase is 738 bytes for the proposed scheme and LEAP+ while it is 722 bytes in COKE. This shows that the proposed scheme offers more security and reliability without compromising the storage efficiency.

Communication Overhead. The key establishment with authentication in LEAP+ involves the transmission of two node ids and two MACs where as COKE algorithm does not have a constant communication overhead. LEAP+ has a very low communication cost with an overhead of 36 bytes based on the network assumptions. The number of bits transmitted for key establishment in COKE depends on the probability of safe bit transmission which in turn is dependent on the maximum power transmitted and the adversary position. Based on these factors, the number of bits varies from 300 bits (38 bytes) to 1400 bits (175 bytes) [9]. In the proposed scheme, the number of bits transmitted is fixed as 1000 bits giving a communication overhead of 163 bytes. Thus the proposed scheme outperforms COKE where a secret key establishment is not guaranteed even after transmission of plain text bits.

Computational Cost. The computation of pair-wise secret key in the proposed scheme, LEAP+ and COKE involves the execution of a MAC /pseudo random function. To increase the security of the key establishment scheme, two additional MAC computations are performed in the proposed scheme and LEAP+.

Connectivity. The connectivity in LEAP+ depends on the time-out period T_{min} after which the master key is erased. If the time-out period is chosen very small to ensure the security of the network, the number of links a node can establish will be reduced. Thus T_{min} presents a trade-off between security and connectivity of the network. Moreover, an attacker can easily generate jamming signals for this small duration and prevent the nodes from secret key establishment thereby reducing the connectivity of the network. COKE is a probabilistic protocol in which secret key establishment depends on the geographical position of the adversary in the network and the transmitted power. In [9] the authors have shown that increased transmission power slightly increases the probability of secret key establishment at the cost of reduced energy efficiency. The proposed key establishment scheme is deterministic and the master key is erased only when key establishment with neighbouring nodes is complete so that connectivity of the network is ensured. As the key establishment consists of multiple transmissions, jamming attacks cannot affect the connectivity of the network. This shows that the proposed scheme is more efficient compared to LEAP+ and COKE.

5.3   Scalability Metric

The proposed scheme is scalable, does not depend on deployment knowledge and can support large networks without compromising security and efficiency. The other two schemes under consideration, LEAP+ and COKE, are also scalable.

The overall comparison results are given in Table 1.

Table 1. Overall comparison

	Proposed scheme	LEAP+	COKE
Storage (in bytes)	738	738	722
Communication overhead (in bytes)	163	36	175
Prob. of eavesdropping a link with nodes compromised in the working phase	0	0	0
Prob. of eavesdropping a link with nodes compromised in the initialization phase	0	1	0
Prob. of node addition attack	0	0	1
Scalability support	YES	YES	YES

6   Conclusion

An energy efficient, secure and deterministic key exchange protocol for resource constrained WSNs is presented in this paper. The concepts of transitory master key and crypto-less over-the-air key establishment methods are combined in this scheme. The security analysis shows that the proposed method offers enhanced security against a variety of attacks in WSNs and active adversaries without increasing the computational cost. Compared to the crypto-less over-the-air key establishment protocols, the proposed method is deterministic, and a pair-wise secret key is established even if the probability of secret bit transmission is very low. In comparison with LEAP+, the proposed scheme offers high resilience even if the node is compromised in the initialization phase and resists jamming attacks.

References

1. Simplício, M.A., Barreto, P.S., Margi, C.B., Carvalho, T.C.: A survey on key management mechanisms for distributed wireless sensor networks. Comput. Netw. **54**(15), 2591–2612 (2010)
2. Dong, Q., Liu, D.: Using auxiliary sensors for pairwise key establishment in WSN. In: Akyildiz, I.F., Sivakumar, R., Ekici, E., Oliveira, J.C., McNair, J. (eds.) NET-WORKING 2007. LNCS, vol. 4479, pp. 251–262. Springer, Heidelberg (2007). doi:10.1007/978-3-540-72606-7_22
3. Liu, D., Ning, P., Du, W.: Group-based key predistribution for wireless sensor networks. ACM Trans. Sens. Netw. (TOSN) **4**(2), 11 (2008)
4. Kotzanikolaou, P., Magkos, E., Vergados, D., Stefanidakis, M.: Secure and practical key establishment for distributed sensor networks. Secur. Commun. Netw. **2**(6), 595–610 (2009)
5. Du, D., Xiong, H., Wang, H.: An efficient key management scheme for wireless sensor networks. Int. J. Distrib. Sens. Netw. **8**(1), 406254 (2012)
6. Jilna, P., Pattathil, D.P.: A key management technique based on elliptic curves for static wireless sensor networks. Secur. Commun. Netw. **8**(18), 3726–3738 (2015)
7. Seo, S.-H., Won, J., Sultana, S., Bertino, E.: Effective key management in dynamic wireless sensor networks. IEEE Trans. Inf. Forensics Secur. **10**(2), 371–383 (2015)
8. Barsocchi, P., Oligeri, G., Soriente, C.: Shake: single hash key establishment for resource constrained devices. Ad Hoc Netw. **11**(1), 288–297 (2013)
9. Di Pietro, R., Oligeri, G.: Coke crypto-less over-the-air key establishment. IEEE Trans. Inf. Forensics Secur. **8**(1), 163–173 (2013)
10. Zhu, S., Setia, S., Jajodia, S.: Leap+: efficient security mechanisms for large-scale distributed sensor networks. ACM Trans. Sens. Netw. (TOSN) **2**(4), 500–528 (2006)
11. Blackshear, S., Verma, R.M.: R-leap+: randomizing leap+ key distribution to resist replay and jamming attacks. In: Proceedings of the 2010 ACM Symposium on Applied Computing, pp. 1985–1992. ACM (2010)
12. Kim, Y.H., Lee, H., Lee, D.H., Lim, J.: A key management scheme for large scale distributed sensor networks. In: Cuenca, P., Orozco-Barbosa, L. (eds.) PWC 2006. LNCS, vol. 4217, pp. 437–446. Springer, Heidelberg (2006). doi:10.1007/11872153_38
13. Eschenauer, L., Gligor, V.D.: A key-management scheme for distributed sensor networks. In: Proceedings of the 9th ACM Conference on Computer and Communications Security, pp. 41–47. ACM (2002)

A Scalable and Systolic Architectures of Montgomery Modular Multiplication for Public Key Cryptosystems Based on DSPs

Amine Mrabet[1,3,5]($\boxtimes$), Nadia El-Mrabet[2], Ronan Lashermes[7],
Jean-Baptiste Rigaud[2], Belgacem Bouallegue[6], Sihem Mesnager[1,4],
and Mohsen Machhout[3]

[1] University of Paris XIII, CNRS, UMR 7539 LAGA, Villetaneuse, France
amine_mrabet_eniso@yahoo.fr
[2] Ecole des Mines de St-Etienne, SAS-CMP, Gardanne, France
[3] University of Monastir EμE Lab, Monastir, Tunisia
[4] Tlcom ParisTech, Paris, France
[5] National Engineering School of Tunis, Tunis, Tunisia
[6] King Khalid University, Abha, Saudi Arabia
[7] LHS-PEC TAMIS INRIA-Rennes, Rennes, France

Abstract. The arithmetic in a finite field constitutes the core of Public Key Cryptography like RSA, ECC or pairing-based cryptography. This paper discusses an efficient hardware implementation of the Coarsely Integrated Operand Scanning method (CIOS) of Montgomery modular multiplication combined with an effective systolic architecture designed with a Two-dimensional array of Processing Elements. The systolic architecture increases the speed of calculation by combining the concepts of pipelining and the parallel processing into a single concept. We propose the CIOS method for the Montgomery multiplication using a systolic architecture. As far as we know this is the first implementation of such design. The proposed architectures are designed for Field Programmable Gate Array platforms. They targeted to reduce the number of clock cycles of the modular multiplication. The presented implementation results of the CIOS algorithms focuses on different security levels useful in cryptography. This architecture have been designed in order to use the flexible DSP48 on Xilinx FPGAs. Our architecture is scalable and depends only on the number and size of words. For instance, we provide results of implementation for 8, 16, 32 and 64 bit long words in 33, 66, 132 and 264 clock cycles. We highlight the fact that for a given number of word, the number of clock cycles is constant.

Keywords: Systolic hardware implementation · Modular multiplication · Montgomery algorithm · CIOS method · Systolic architecture · DSP48

© Springer International Publishing AG 2016
C. Carlet et al. (Eds.): SPACE 2016, LNCS 10076, pp. 138–156, 2016.
DOI: 10.1007/978-3-319-49445-6_8

1   Introduction

Since 1976, many Public Key Cryptosystems (PKC) have been proposed and all these cryptosystems based their security on the difficulty of some mathematical problem. The hardness of this underlying mathematical problem is essential for security. Elliptic Curve Cryptosystems which were proposed by Koblitz [12] and Miller [15], RSA [19] and the Pairing-Based Cryptography [10] are examples of PKCs. All these systems rely on an efficient finite field multiplication. As a consequence, the development of efficient architecture for modular multiplication has been a very popular subject of research. In 1985, Montgomery has presented a new method for modular multiplication [16]. It's one of the most suitable algorithm for performing modular multiplications in hardware and software implementations. The efficient implementation of the Montgomery modular multiplication in hardware was considered by many authors [3,6,9,17,18,20]. There are a variety of ways to perform the Montgomery multiplication, considering if multiplication and reduction are separated or integrated. The separated approach consists in first performing the product and then the Montgomery reduction. It was presented in 1996 by Koç and Tolga in [11]. This method is called the Separated Operand Scanning method (SOS). On the contrary, the integrated approach is characterized by an alternation between multiplication and reduction. Several integrated approaches are presented in [11]: the Coarsely Integrated Operand Scanning Method (CIOS), the Finely Integrated Operand Scanning Method (FIOS), the Finely Integrated Product Scanning Method (FIPS) and the Coarsely Integrated Hybrid Scanning Method (CIHS). According to Koç and Tolga in [11] the CIOS method is a scalable word-based method for Montgomery multiplication, and it is the most efficient algorithm that integrates the multiplication with reduction steps. A systolic array architecture [13,21] is one possibility for the implementation of the Montgomery algorithm in hardware [3,17,18,20]. These architectures offer Processing Elements (PE) array where each Processing Element performs arithmetic computation additions and multiplications. In accordance with the number of words used, the architecture can employ a variable number of PEs. The systolic architecture uses very simples Processing Elements. As a consequence, the systolic architecture decreases the needs for logic elements in hardware implementations. Our contribution in this work is to combine a systolic architecture, which is assumed to be the best choice for FPGA implementation, with the CIOS method of Montgomery modular multiplication. We optimize the number of clock cycles required to compute a n-bit Montgomery multiplication and we reduce the utilization of FPGA resources. We have implemented the modular multiplication in a fixed number of clock cycles. To the best of our knowledge, this is the first time that a hardware or a software multiplier of modular Montgomery multiplication, suitable for various security level, is performed in just 33 clock cycles. Furthermore, as far as we know, our work is the first one dealing with systolic architecture and CIOS method over large prime characteristic finite fields. This paper is organized as follows: Sect. 2 discusses related state-of-the-art works. Section 3 presents the Montgomery modular multiplication algorithm. The proposed architectures and results are presented in Sects. 4 and 5. Finally, the conclusion is presented in Sect. 6.

2   Brief State of the Art

In hardware design, the systolic architecture [13] is a pipelined network arrangement of Processing Elements (or cells). It is a specialized form of parallel design. Each cell compute the data which is coming as input and calculate data independently. In [21] the authors proposed a systolic design for FPGA implementation. Several works are devoted to the implementation of the Montgomery multiplication [2,3,6,8,9,11,16–18,20]. The first ones to our knowledge who proposed a systolic array are Iwamura, Matsumoto and Imai [8,9]. They presented a systolic architecture that can execute a modular exponentiation using Montgomery multiplications. In [20] Tenca and Koç introduced a pipelined Montgomery modular multiplication, which has the ability to work in any given operand precision and which is adjustable to any chip area. Harris et al. in [4] improve the result of [20] using a systolic architecture for the Montgomery multiplication. Siddika Berna Örs, Lejla Batina, Bart Preneel and Joos Vandewalle presented in [17] a modular exponentiation based on the modular Montgomery. In [18] Guilherme Perin, Daniel Gomes Mesquita and Jõao Baptista Martins proposed a comparison between two modular multiplication architectures: a systolic and a very high-radix multiplexed implementation. Their approach uses a radix-16 and radix-32 decomposition. Both implementations targeted a Virtex-4 and a Virtex-5 FPGA. (A radix-n word is a word of size n.) Their work is the latest and the most efficient describing the use of a systolic approach for the Montgomery multiplication. We briefly recall the definition of a systolic architecture before a summary of their work. A systolic architecture is a pipelined network arrangement of PEs called cells. It is a specialized form of parallel computing, where cells compute the data which is coming as input and store them independently. A systolic architecture is an array composed of matrix-like rows of cells. Each PE shares the information with its neighbours immediately after processing. Cell at each step takes input data from one or more neighbours. The systolic architecture proposed in the work [18] is composed of s Processing Elements distributed in a one-dimensional array. The number s is the number of words. At each iteration of the Montgomery Algorithm, the words are read from an external memory (BRAM) and passed to their architecture. To evaluate the number of clock cycles for a Montgomery multiplication in the systolic architecture, they have to consider the first s cycles to read the input operands from RAM memories. Furthermore the first iteration of algorithm also needs s clock cycles. Finally the remaining iterations of algorithm are performed in $4 \times s$ clock cycles. As a consequence, this architecture requires a $6 \times s (= s + s + 4 \times s)$ clock cycles. For the multiplexed architecture, the first steps are identical to thus of the systolic architecture $(2 \times s)$. The number of clock cycles required to remaining iterations of Montgomery Algorithm is $6 \times s$ clock cycles. In order to perform the multiplexed architecture the algorithm requires $8 \times s (= 2 \times s + 6 \times s)$ clock cycles.

3   Montgomery Multiplication

The Montgomery Multiplication Algorithm for large prime characteristic finite fields [16] is a method for performing modular multiplication without needing to divide by the modulus. In cryptography, the Montgomery Algorithm is the most used modular multiplication to perform the operation $a \times b \mod p$. The Montgomery multiplication transforms the division by p into several divisions by a power of 2, which consists only in shifts in hardware and software implementation. Furthermore, the Montgomery multiplication among large numbers can be constructed using a radix representation of the numbers. Let p be an odd prime number. Let $n = \lceil log_2(p) \rceil$ be the length of the binary decomposition of p. We choose the base of numeration to be $R = 2^n$, such that $p < R$. As p and R are coprime, we can define $p' = -p^{-1} \mod R$. The choice of R is motivated by the facts that $\gcd(R, p) = 1$ and reductions and divisions by R must be efficient. As R is a power of 2, divisions are right shifts and the modulo operation is a simple assignment of the first n-bit. Montgomery multiplication is performed with numbers represented in the Montgomery representation. The conversion from ordinary domain to Montgomery domaine detailed in Table 1. The map $M : a \in \mathbb{F}_p \rightarrow aR \in \mathbb{F}_p$ is a bijection and a field isomorphism of $\mathbb{F}_p$. For any element a of $\mathbb{F}_p$, the product $aR \in \mathbb{F}_p$ is called the Montgomery representation of a in basis R and it is denoted $M(a)$. We describe the Montgomery multiplication in Algorithm 1. The Montgomery multiplication computes $M(a) \times M(b)$ and gives as result $M(ab)$.

Algorithm 1. Montgomery Modular Multiplication

Input: p an odd prime, $n = \lceil log_2(p) \rceil$, $R = 2^n$, $p' = -p^{-1} mod\ R$, $M(a)$,
  $M(b) \in \mathbb{F}_p$
Output: $M(ab) \mod p$
1 $\gamma \leftarrow M(a) \times M(b)$
2 $\delta \leftarrow \gamma \times p' \mod R$
3 $T \leftarrow \frac{\gamma + \delta \times p}{R}$
4 **If** $T \geq p$ **then** $T \leftarrow T - p$
5 **return** T

Table 1. Conversion between montgomery and ordinary domains

Ordinary domain	$\Longleftrightarrow$	Montgomery domain
a	$\longleftrightarrow$	M(a)=a·R mod p
b	$\longleftrightarrow$	M(b)=b·R mod p
a·b	$\longleftrightarrow$	M(a·b)=a·b·R mod p

3.1   CIOS Method

The Coarsely Integrated Operand Scanning (CIOS) method presented in Algorithm 2, improves the Montgomery Algorithm by integrating the multiplication and reduction. More specifically, instead of computing the product $a \cdot b$, then reducing the result, this method allows an alternation between iterations of the outer loops for multiplication and reduction. The integers (p, a and b) are seen as lists of s words of size w. In order to perform this algorithm we need an array T of size only $s + 2$. The intermediate results are stored in T. The final result of the CIOS algorithm is composed by the $s + 1$ least significant words of this array. The alternation between multiplication and reduction is possible since the value

---

Algorithm 2. CIOS algorithm for Montgomery multiplication [11]

Input: $p < 2^K$, $p' = -p^{-1} mod\ 2^w$, w, s, $K = s \cdot w$:bit length, $R = 2^K$, $a, b < p$
Output: $a \cdot b \cdot R^{-1}$ mod p
1 $T \leftarrow Null$;
2 **for** $i \leftarrow 0$ *to* $s - 1$ **do**
3     $C \leftarrow 0$;
4   **for** $j \leftarrow 0$ *to* $s - 1$ **do**
5        $(C, S) \leftarrow T[j] + a[i] \cdot b[j] + C$
6        $T[j] \leftarrow S$
7     $(C, S) \leftarrow T[s] + C$
8     $T[s] \leftarrow S$
9     $T[s + 1] \leftarrow C$
10    $C \leftarrow 0$;
11    $m \leftarrow T[0] \cdot p'$ mod 2^w
12    $(C, S) \leftarrow T[0] + m \cdot p[0]$ **for** $j \leftarrow 1$ *to* $s - 1$ **do**
13       $(C, S) \leftarrow T[j] + m \cdot p[j] + C$
14       $T[j] \leftarrow S$
15    $(C, S) \leftarrow T[s] + C$
16    $T[s - 1] \leftarrow S$
17    $T[s] \leftarrow T[s + 1] + C$
18 **return** T;

---

of m (in line 11 of the Algorithm 2) in the ith iteration of the outer loop for reduction depends only on the value $T[j]$, which is computed by the ith iteration of the outer loop for the multiplication. In order to perform the multiplication, we have modified the CIOS algorithm of [11] and designed this method with a systolic architecture. Indeed, instead of using an array to store the intermediate result, we replace T by Input and Output signals for each Processing Element. As a consequence, our design uses fewer of multiplexers and then we have better results considering the number of slices.

4 Hardware Implementation

4.1 Block DSP in Xilinx FPGAs

Modern FPGA devices like Xilinx Virtex-4, Virtex-5 and Artix-7 as well as Altera Stratix FPGAs have been equipped with arithmetic hardcore extensions

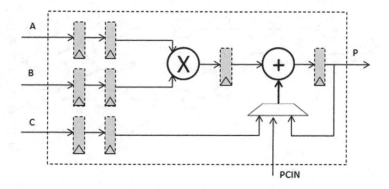

Fig. 1. Structure of DSP block in modern FPGA device.

to accelerate digital signal processing applications. These function DSP blocks can be used to build a more efficient implementation interms of performance and reduce at the same time the demand for areas. DSP blocks can be programmed to perform basic arithmetic functions, multiplication, addition and subtraction of unsigned integers. Figure 1 shows the generic DSP structure in advanced FPGAs. DSP can operate on external Input A,B and C as well as on feedback values from P or result PCIN.

4.2   Proposed Architecture

The idea of our design is to combine the CIOS method of Montgomery Modular multiplier presented in [11] with a two-dimensional systolic architecture in the model of [7,21]. As seen in Sect. 3.1, the CIOS method is an alternation between iterations of the loops for multiplication and reduction. The concept of the two-dimensional systolic architecture presented in Sect. 2 combines an identical Processing Elements with local connections, which take external inputs and handle them with a predetermined manner in a pipelined fashion. This new architecture is directly based on the arithmetic operations of the CIOS method of Montgomery Algorithm. The arithmetic is performed in a radix-w base (2^w). The input operands are processed in s words of w bits. We present many versions of this method. We illustrate our design for $s = 8$, $s = 16$, $s = 32$ and a $s = 64$ architectures, respectively denoted NW-8 (for Number of Words), NW-16, NW-32 and NW-64. Before the descriptions of the architectures NW-8 and NW-16, we begin with a generic description of our systolic architecture. Our proposed architectures for the implementation of the Montgomery modular multiplication is detailed in this section. We describe it in detail as well as the different Processing Element behaviours. In order to have less of states in our Final State Machine (FSM), we divided our Algorithm 2 of Montgomery on five kinds of PE noted:

- cells alpha denoted α;
- cells beta denoted β;
- cells gamma denoted γ;

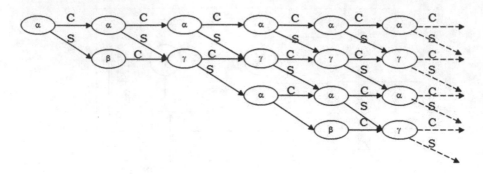

Fig. 2. Data dependency in general systolic architecture.

- cells alpha final denoted α_f;
- cells gamma final denoted γ_f.

Figure 2 presents the dependency of the different cells. Below we describe precisely each cells. The letters MSB stand for the Most Significant Bits and LSB for the Least Significant Bits. In our notation the letter C denote the MSB of the results and the letter S the LSB.

1. alpha : Presented by the lines 4 and 5 in the Algorithm 2 and detailed in Algorithm 3. The PEs alpha are scalable according to the NW in the design. We use this cell to perform the multiplication step. The input of the cell alpha are: S_In provided by the previous step, C_In provided by the previous step, $a[i]$: The words of the operand a, and $b[j]$: The words of the operand b. The output of the cell alpha are: S provided to the next step and C provided to the next step.

2. beta : Presented by the lines 9, 10 and 11 in the Algorithm 2 and detailed in Algorithm 4. The input of the cell beta are: S_In provided by the previous step, $p[0]$: The first word of the modulo p and p': predefined. The output of the cell beta are: m provided to the next step and C provided to the next step.

3. gamma : Presented by the lines 13 and 14 in the Algorithm 2 and detailed in Algorithm 5. The PEs gamma are scalable according to the NW in the design. We use this cell to perform the reduction step. The input of the cell gamma are: S_In provided by the previous step, C_In provided by the previous step, $p[j]$: The words of the modulo p and m provide by the cell beta. The output of the cell gamma are: S provided to the next step and C provided to the next step.

4. alpha_final : Presented by the lines lines 6, 7 and 8 in the Algorithm 2 and detailed in Algorithm 6. The input of the cell alpha_final are: S_In provided by the previous step and C_In provided by the previous step. The output of the cell alpha_final are: $S1$ provided to the next step and $S2$ provide to the next step.

5. gamma_final : Presented by the lines 15, 16 and 17 in the Algorithm 2 and detailed in Algorithm 7. The input of the cell gamma_final are: $S1\_In$ provided by the previous step, $S2\_In$ provided by the previous step and C_In provided by the previous step. The output of the cell gamma_final are: $S1$ provided to the next step and $S2$ provided to the next step.

Algorithm 3. Cell alpha

Input: $a[i]$, $b[j]$, C_In, S_In
Output: C, S
1 $tmp1 \leftarrow S\_In + C\_In$
2 $tmp2 \leftarrow a[i] \cdot b[j]$
3 $tmp2 \leftarrow tmp2 + tmp1$
4 $C \leftarrow$ MSB($tmp2$)
5 $S \leftarrow$ LSB($tmp2$)
6 **return** C, S;

Algorithm 4. Cell beta

Input: S_in, $p[0]$, $p' = -p^{-1} mod\ 2^w$
Output: C, m
1 $tmp1 \leftarrow S\_in \cdot p'$
2 $m \leftarrow LSB(tmp1)$
3 $tmp1 \leftarrow p[0] \cdot m$
4 $tmp1 \leftarrow S\_in + tmp1$
5 $C \leftarrow$ MSB($tmp1$)
6 **return** C, m;

Algorithm 5. Cell gamma

Input: $p[i]$, m, C_in, S_in
Output: C, S
1 $tmp1 \leftarrow S\_in + C\_in$
2 $tmp2 \leftarrow p[i] \cdot m$
3 $tmp2 \leftarrow tmp2 + tmp1$
4 $C \leftarrow$ MSB($tmp2$)
5 $S \leftarrow$ LSB($tmp2$)
6 **return** C, S;

This organization allows us to optimize the number of clock cycles. Each Processing Element in Fig. 10 is responsible for performing arithmetic operations. The different Processing Elements establish communication with the control block (FSM) as shown in Fig. 9 by receiving starts signals at each state of Montgomery Algorithm iteration. Each PE sends a done signal to the FSM at each end of the calculation. The final result is a concatenation of the last output of gamma and gamma_final PEs. The structure of all PEs have a combinational behaviour.

Algorithm 6. Cell alpha_final

Input: C_in, S_in
Output: $S1$, $S2$
1 $tmp1 \leftarrow S\_in + C\_in$
2 $S1 \leftarrow \text{LSB}(tmp1)$
3 $S2 \leftarrow \text{MSB}(tmp1)$
4 **return** C, S;

Algorithm 7. Cell gamma_final

Input: C_in, $S1\_in$, $S2\_in$
Output: $S1$, $S2$
1 $tmp1 \leftarrow S1\_in + C\_in$
2 $S1 \leftarrow \text{LSB}(tmp1)$
3 $S2 \leftarrow \text{MSB}(tmp1)$
4 $S2 \leftarrow S2\_in + S2$
5 **return** $S1$, $S2$;

4.3   Internals Architectures of Cells

In this section we will describe the internals architectures of PEs used in these designs. Our five cells are designed in order to use DSP(s) blocks.

Description of the Cell α. As illustrated in Fig. 4, the multiplication between $a[i]$ and $b[j]$ words returns a $2w$ bits result. This result is added thereafter to S_α_In. This latter is the least significant bits of the result of Processing Element gamma, which is provided through the output multiplexer. The last add is also added to C_α_In. The C_α_In is the most significant bits of the result of the previous Processing Element alpha, which is provided also through an output of a second multiplexer. The different inputs outputs of the PE alpha are presented in Fig. 9. The most significant bits of the result of alpha is propagated to the

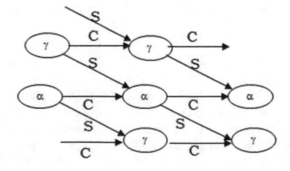

Fig. 3. PEs of Systolic Architecture in two-dimensional array.

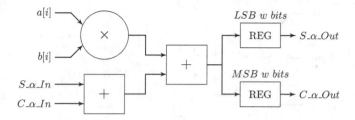

Fig. 4. Alpha Processing Element internal architecture.

multiplexer to fix the next PE of alpha. Whereas the least significant bits are propagated to an other multiplexer to fix the next PE of gamma. After each computation of the alpha PE a shift in the input b is triggered.

Description of the Cell β. According to our Algorithm 4 and as illustrated in Fig. 5, the zero index word of p ($p[0]$) and p' are provided to this beta Processing Element. The number p' corresponds the modular inverse of p modulo 2^w. The multiplication between p' and S_β_In returns a $2w$ bits result, where only the least significant bits of this multiplication is multiplied by the first word of p and returns a $2w$ bits result. Finally, this result is added to a w bits word S_β_In. Only the most significant bit part of this result is used in the next gamma PE. The different inputs/outputs of PE beta are presented in Fig. 9.

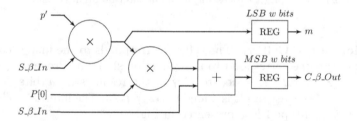

Fig. 5. Beta Processing Element internal architecture.

Description of the Cell γ. As illustrated in Fig. 6, the multiplication between m and $p[j]$ words returns a $2w$ bits result. This latter is added thereafter to S_γ_In. The number S_γ_In corresponds to the least significant bits of the result of Processing Element alpha, which is provided through an output multiplexer. This add is also added to C_γ_In, where C_γ_In is the most significant bits of the result of the previous Processing Element gamma. This PE gamma is provided also through an output of a second multiplexer. The different inputs/outputs of the gamma PE are shown in Fig. 9. The most significant bits of result are propagated to the multiplexer to fix the next PE of gamma. Whereas the least significant bits are propagated to an other multiplexer to fix the next PE of alpha.

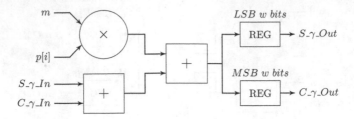

Fig. 6. Gamma Processing Element internal architecture.

Description of the Cell α_f. The cell α_f corresponds to the final α computed at the end of the line correspond to the multiplication step. In the PE alpha_final, the $S\_\alpha\_f\_In$ added to C_α_f returns a $2w$ bits result as presented in Fig. 7.

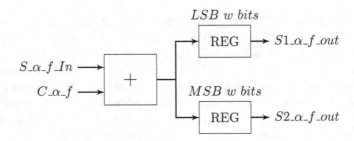

Fig. 7. Alpha_f Processing Element internal architecture.

Description of the Cell γ_f. The cell γ_f corresponds to the final γ computed at the end of the line correspond to the reduction step. For Processing Element gamma_final, $S1\_\gamma\_f\_In$ is added to C_γ_f, the result is a $2w$ bits. The least significant bits of the last result is added to $S2\_\gamma\_f\_In$. The internal architecture of the gamma_final type PE is presented in Fig. 8.

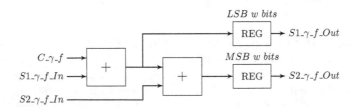

Fig. 8. Gamma_f Processing Element internal architecture.

In the remainder of this section we detail our design for a $s = 8$ and a $s = 16$ architectures, respectively denoted NW-8 and NW-16.

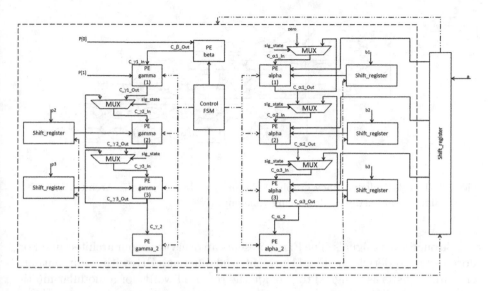

Fig. 9. Proposed Montgomery modular multiplication architecture.

4.4 Our Architectures

Firstly, we will start with the NW-8 architecture which contains 3 PEs of type alpha and 3 of type gamma. With this design we can compute a modular multiplication in 33 clock cycles. Secondly we will present the NW-16 architecture that is composed by 6 PEs of type alpha and 6 PEs of type gamma. And we can perform a modular multiplication with this architecture in 66 clock cycles. Similarly, in order to implement the NW-32 architecture and the NW-64 architecture we need every time to double the number of cells. We provide a comparison of our architectures at the end of this section.

NW-8 Architecture. In this architecture, the operands and the modulo are divided in 8 words as illustrated in Fig. 10. The NW-8 architecture is composed of 9 Processing Elements distributed in a two-dimensional array. Every Processing Elements are responsible for the calculus involving w bits words of the input operands. For example, for a 256 bits modular multiplication with NW-8, the operands are split in 8 words of 32 bits which results in a two-dimensional array of 9 Processing Elements. The 9 Processing Elements are divided in the following manner: 3 cells alpha, 1 cell alpha_final, 1 cell beta, 3 cells gamma, et 1 cell gamma_final.

Those choices were made in order to optimize the number of states in our FSM. As seen in Sect. 2 each PE in the N-dimensional array is connected to 2 N data In/Out paths for communicating with 2N PEs in the N-dimensional array. Since we are working with two-dimensional elements, each PE in our design is connected to 4 data paths, 2 Input and 2 Output as presented in Fig. 3.

In this architecture, the Processing Elements are designed with finite state machines (FSM). The control block communicates with the PEs and shift regis-

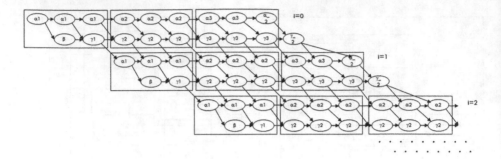

Fig. 10. The data dependency graph of the proposed new Systolic Architecture with a Two-dimensional array of Processing Elements (NW-8).

ters through starts signals. The Fig. 9 presents an overview of our architecture. For more technical details the Fig. 11 presents the differents PEs with input/output. The shift register is designed to provide the required words for a modular multiplication to the PEs. The Processing Element alpha requires words $a[i]$ and $b[j]$ of the operands a and b, on the other side the Processing Element gamma required a words of the operand p. Thus, these operands are defined in the package body. At the end of the Montgomery modular multiplication, the control block provides the multiplication result $a \cdot b \cdot R^{-1} \mod p$ through the outputs of the last gamma and gamma_final Processing Elements. To evaluate the number of clock cycles for a CIOS method of modular multiplication in NW-8, the first parameter is max{number of alpha, number of gamma} $= 3$, it means that our design can handle three iterations of i at the same time as illustrated in Fig. 10. Implying that our algorithm require to loop $s+3$ times. We can performing our design in 33 clock cycles since our design requires three states ($33 = 3 \times (s+3)$). The different results of this architecture in bit-length 256 are given in Table 2.

Table 2. Implementations of cells and MMM (NW-8).

Artix-7	DSP	Frequency (MHz)	Clock cycle
MMM (s = 8/K = 256)	31	105.275	33
Alpha	4	291.023	1
Gamma	4	291.023	1
Beta	4	388.350	1
Alpha_final	1	459.918	1
Gamma_final	2	442.811	1

NW-16 Architecture. In this architecture, the operands and the modulo are divided in 16 words. The NW-16 architecture is designed in the same way as the NW-8. This example illustrates the scalability of our design. The NW-16 architecture is composed of 15 Processing Elements distributed in a two-dimensional array, where every Processing Elements are responsible for the calculus involving w bits words of the input operands. The 15 Processing Elements are divided like this: 6 cells alpha, 1 cell alpha_final, 1 cell beta, 6 cells gamma et 1 cell gamma_final. We can remark that the number of PEs of type alpha and gamma are the double of the number for NW-8. As said previously, the number of other PE type (alpha_final, beta, gamma_final) remains unchanged whatever the number of words in the design. In order to evaluate the number of clock cycles of the NW-16 architecture, the first parameter is max{number of alpha, number of gamma} = 6, implying that our algorithm requires to loop $s + 6$ times. We can perform the multiplication with our design in 66 clock cycles since our design requires three states ($66 = 3 \times (s + 6)$). The different results of this architecture in bit-length 256 are given in Table 3.

Table 3. Implementations of cells and MMM (NW-16).

Artix-7	DSP	Frequency (MHz)	Clock cycle
MMM (s = 16/K = 256)	29	145.892	66
Alpha	2	379.341	1
Gamma	2	379.341	1
Beta	2	453.104	1
Alpha_final	1	459.918	1
Gamma_final	2	442.811	1

NW-32 Architecture. In this architecture, the operands and the modulo are divided in 32 words. The NW-32 architecture is composed of 27 Processing Elements distributed in a two-dimensional array, where every Processing Elements are responsible for the calculus involving w bits words of the input operands. The 27 Processing Elements are divided like this: 12 cells alpha, 1 cell alpha_final, 1 cell beta, 12 cells gamma et cell gamma_final. In order to evaluate the number of clock cycles of the NW-32 architecture, the first parameter as we have seen previously is max{number of alpha, number of gamma} = 12, implying that our algorithm require to loop $s + 12$ times. We can perform the multiplication with our design in 132 clock cycles since our design requires three states ($132 = 3 \times (s + 12)$).

NW-64 Architecture. In this architecture, the operands and the modulo are divided in 64 words. The NW-64 architecture is composed of 51 Processing Elements distributed in a two-dimensional array, where every Processing Elements are responsible for the calculus involving w bits words of the input operands. The 51 Processing Elements are divided like this: 24 cells alpha, 1 cell alpha_final, 1 cell beta, 24 cells gamma et 1 cell gamma_final. In order to evaluate the number of clock cycles of the NW-64 architecture, the first parameter is max{number of alpha, number of gamma} = 24, implying that our algorithm require to loop

$s + 24$ times. We can perform the multiplication with our design in 264 clock cycles since our design requires three states $(264 = 3 \times (s + 24))$.

Architectures Comparison. The Table 4 explains a comparison between the different architectures. Number of clock cycles for every architecture equal to 3 $\times$ (s+nb), such that nb=max{number of cells alpha, number of cells gamma}, implying that our algorithm require to loop $s + nb$ times. It is interesting to notice that all our architectures are scalable and targeting the different security levels useful in cryptography.

Table 4. Comparison of our architectures

CIOS	$s = 8$	$s = 16$	$s = 32$	$s = 64$
K = 256	32	16	8	4
K = 512	64	32	16	8
K = 1024	128	64	32	16
K = 2048	256	128	64	32
Clock cycles = 3 $\times$ (s+nb)	33	66	132	264
Number of cells	6 +3	12 +3	24 +3	48 +3

5 Results

The Table 5 summarizes the FPGA results postimplementation of the proposed versions of modular multiplication architectures. We present a results for the both architectures NW-8 and NW-16. The designs were described in hardware description languages (VHDL) and synthesized for Artix-7 and Virtex-5 Xilinx FPGAs. In order to check the correctness of the result, we compare the results given by the FPGA with the sage code. We present the different results after implementation of bit-length k which are given in Table 5. These circuits have the advantage of suitability to various applications with different bit lengths like RSA, ECC and pairings. As it is shown in Table 5, an interesting property of our design is the fact that the clock cycles are independent from the bit length. This property gives to our design the advantage of suitability to different security level. In order to implement the modular Montgomery multiplication for fixed security level, we must choose the most suitable architecture. The results presented in this work are compared with the previous work [4,5,17,18] in the Table 6. We could notice that our results are better then [18] considering every point of comparison i.e. the number of slice and the number of clock cycles. Considering the number of slices, we recall that [18] used an external memory to optimize the number of slices used by their algorithms. Considering the comparison with [17], our design requires less number of slices, and a better frequency and we really improve the number of clock cycles. Our design performed the Montgomery multiplication in 66 clock cycles for the 512 and 1024 bit length corresponding to AES-256 and

Table 5. Illustration of the scalabilty of our architecture.

Artix 7- Nexys 4						
	NW-8			NW-16		
	128	256	512	256	512	1024
Freq MHz	198	106	65	146	106	65
Cycles	33	33	33	66	66	66
Slice registers	487	870	1614	1123	2164	4208
Slice LUTs	355	809	2650	846	1789	5242
Slices	206	352	878	402	798	2072
DSP	19	31	87	29	57	161

Table 6. Comparaison of our work with state-of-art implementations.

Xilinx FPGAs														
	Our A7		Our V5		[18] V5		[17] VE		[5] VII	[4] VII	[14] V		[1] K7 and V5	
	512	1024	512	1024	512	1024	512	1024	1024	1024	512	1024	512 K7	512 V5
Freq MHz	106	65	97	65	95	130	95.229	95.620	116.4	119	72.1	79.2	176	123
Cycles	66	66	66	66	96	384	1540	3076	1088	1167	–	–	66	66
Speed μs	0.622	1.013	0680	1.015	1.010	2.953	16.031	32.021	9.34	9.80	–	–	0.374	0536
Slice Registers	2164	4208	3046	6072	3876	6642	–	–	–	–	–	–	5076	4960
Slice LUTs	1789	5242	1781	5824	–	–	2972	5706	9319	9271	3125	6243	8757	10877
BRAM	0	0	0	0	128	256	–	–	–	–	–	–	0	0

AES-512 security level, while [17] performed the multiplication in 1540 clock cycles for the AES-256 security level and 3076 for the AES-512 security level.

6   Conclusion

In this paper we have presented an efficient hardware implementation of the CIOS method of Montgomery multiplication Algorithm over large prime characteristic finite fields $\mathbb{F}_p$. We give the results of our design after routing and placement using a Artix-7 and Virtex-5 Xilinx FPGAs. Our systolic implementations is suitable for every implementation implying a modular multiplication, for example RSA, ECC and pairing-based cryptography. Our architectures and the designs were matched with features of the FPGAs. The NW-8 design presented a good performance considering *latency × area* efficiency. This architecture can run for all the bit length corresponding to classical security levels (128, 256, 512 or 1024 bits) in just 33 clock cycles. On the other hand the NW-16 perform the same bit length in 66 clock cycles, but improve in area compared to NW-8 work. Our systolic design using this method CIOS is scalable for other number of words.

A   Architecture

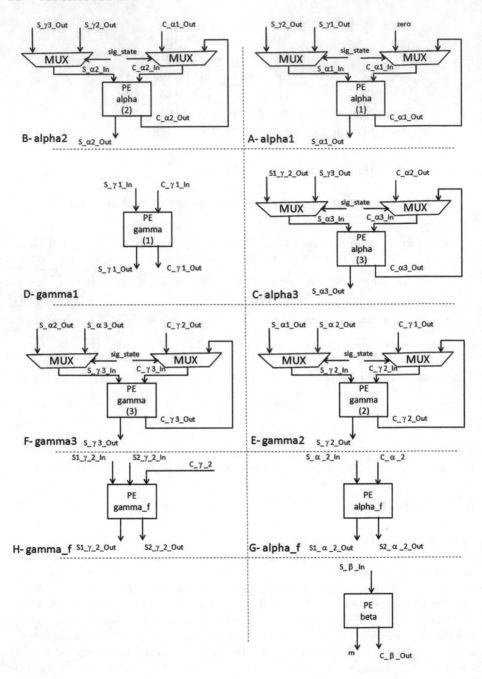

Fig. 11. All processing elements.

References

1. Bigou, K., Tisserand, A.: Single base modular multiplication for efficient hardware rns implementations of ecc. In: Conference on Cryptographic Hardware and Embedded Systems, pp. 123–140, September 2015
2. Junfeng, F., Sakiyama, K., Verbauwhede, I.: Montgomery modular multiplication algorithm on multi-core systems. In: 2007 IEEE Workshop on Signal Processing Systems, pp. 261–266, October 2007
3. Hariri, A., Reyhani-Masoleh, A.: Bit-serial and bit-parallel montgomery multiplication and squaring over gf. IEEE Trans. Comput. **58**(10), 1332–1345 (2009)
4. Harris, D., Krishnamurthy, R., Anders, M., Mathew, S., Hsu, S.: An improved unified scalable radix-2 montgomery multiplier. In: 17th IEEE Symposium on Computer Arithmetic, ARITH-17 2005, pp. 172–178, June 2005
5. Huang, M., Gaj, K., El-Ghazawi, T.: New hardware architectures for montgomery modular multiplication algorithm. IEEE Trans. Comput. **60**(7), 923–936 (2011)
6. Huang, M., Gaj, K., Kwon, S., El-Ghazawi, T.: An optimized hardware architecture for the montgomery multiplication algorithm. In: Cramer, R. (ed.) PKC 2008. LNCS, vol. 4939, pp. 214–228. Springer, Heidelberg (2008). doi:10.1007/978-3-540-78440-1_13
7. Lee, K.I.: Algorithm and VLSI architecture design for H.264/AVC Inter Frame Coding. Ph.D. thesis, National Cheng Kung University, Tainan, Taiwan (2007)
8. Iwamura, K., Matsumoto, T., Imai, H.: High-speed implementation methods for RSA scheme. In: Rueppel, R.A. (ed.) EUROCRYPT 1992. LNCS, vol. 658, pp. 221–238. Springer, Heidelberg (1993). doi:10.1007/3-540-47555-9_20
9. Iwamura, K., Matsumoto, T., Imai, H.: Systolic-arrays for modular exponentiation using montgomery method. In: Rueppel, R.A. (ed.) EUROCRYPT 1992. LNCS, vol. 658, pp. 477–481. Springer, Heidelberg (1993). doi:10.1007/3-540-47555-9_43
10. Joux, A.: A one round protocol for tripartite diffiehellman. J. Cryptology **17**(4): 263–276 (2004)
11. Ko, C.K., Acar, T., Jr. Kaliski, B.S.: Analyzing and comparing montgomery multiplication algorithms. IEEE Micro **16**(3), 26–33 (1996)
12. Koblitz, N.: Elliptic curve cryptosystems. Math. Comput. **48**(177), 203–209 (1987)
13. Kung, H.T.: Why systolic architectures? Computer **15**(1), 37–46 (1982)
14. Manochehri, K., Pourmozafari, S., Sadeghiyan, B.: Montgomery, rns for rsa hardware implementation. In: Computing and Informatics, vol. 29, pp. 849–880, December 201
15. Miller, V.S.: Use of elliptic curves in cryptography. In: Williams, H.C. (ed.) CRYPTO 1985. LNCS, vol. 218, pp. 417–426. Springer, Heidelberg (1986). doi:10.1007/3-540-39799-X_31
16. Montgomery, P.L.: Modular multiplication without trial division. Math. Comput. **44**(170), 519–521 (1985)
17. Ors, S.B., Batina, L., Preneel, B., Vandewalle, J.: Hardware implementation of a montgomery modular multiplier in a systolic array. In: Parallel and Distributed Processing Symposium, p. 8, April 2003
18. Perin, G., Mesquita, D.G., Martins, J.B.: Montgomery modular multiplication on reconfigurable hardware: systolic versus multiplexed implementation. Int. J. Reconfig. Comput. **2011**, 601–610 (2011)

19. Rivest, R.L., Shamir, A., Adleman, L.: A method for obtaining digital signatures and public-key cryptosystems. Commun. ACM **21**, 120–126 (1978)
20. Tenca, A.F., Koç, Ç.K.: A scalable architecture for montgomery nultiplication. In: Koç, Ç.K., Paar, C. (eds.) CHES 1999. LNCS, vol. 1717, pp. 94–108. Springer, Heidelberg (1999). doi:10.1007/3-540-48059-5_10
21. Vucha, M., Rajawat, A.: Design and fpga implementation of systolic array architecture for matrix multiplication. Int. J. Comput. Appl. **26**(3), 0975 s8887 (2011)

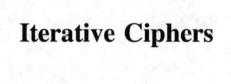

Iterative Ciphers

Spectral Characterization of Iterating Lossy Mappings

Joan Daemen[1,2(✉)]

[1] STMicroelectronics, Diegem, Belgium
[2] Radboud University, Nijmegen, Netherlands
joan@cs.ru.nl

Abstract. In this paper we study what happens to sets when we iteratively apply lossy (round) mappings to them. We describe the information loss as imbalances of parities of intermediate distributions and show that their evolution is governed by the correlation matrices of the mappings. At the macroscopic level we show that iterating lossy mappings results in an increase of a quantity we call *total imbalance*. We quantify the increase in total imbalance as a function of the number of iterations and of round mapping characteristics. At the microscopic level we show that the imbalance of a parity located in some round, dubbed *final*, is the sum of distinct terms. Each of these terms consists of the imbalance of a parity located at the output of a round, multiplied by the sum of the correlation contributions of all linear trails between that parity and the final parity. We illustrate our theory with experimental data. The developed theory can be applied whenever lossy mappings are repeatedly applied to a state. This is the case in many modes of block ciphers and permutations for, e.g., iterated hashing or self-synchronizing stream encryption. The main reason why we have developed it however, is for applying it to study the security implications of using non-uniform threshold schemes as countermeasure against differential power and electromagnetic analysis.

Keywords: Iterative lossy mappings · Correlation matrices · Non-uniformity

1 Introduction

Differential power analysis (DPA) is a class of statistical attacks allowing to extract the key out of cipher implementations exploiting dependence of the power consumption on the data being processed. As a countermeasure to be used in hardware implementations, so-called threshold schemes have been proposed [11,12]. These schemes are a special case of masking schemes, where the sensitive intermediate variables are represented by a number c of shares and the represented value, dubbed *native*, is the (bitwise) sum of those shares. A threshold scheme is designed such that any combinatorial circuit in the implementation takes as input at most $c - 1$ shares. If the sharing is uniform, i.e., if the missing

© Springer International Publishing AG 2016
C. Carlet et al. (Eds.): SPACE 2016, LNCS 10076, pp. 159–178, 2016.
DOI: 10.1007/978-3-319-49445-6_9

share is uniformly distributed, the power consumption of such a combinatorial circuit is independent of the native value for the same reason that the one-time pad is provably secure. From this it is easy to prove that a threshold scheme is provably secure against first-order DPA as long as the shares are uniform.

We have proposed to apply a 3-share threshold schemes to the KECCAK-f permutation [3] to be used for keyed modes of KECCAK or KECCAK-f itself [2]. However, the threshold sharing we proposed for the non-linear layer is not *uniform*. Concretely, our shared implementation of the non-linear step χ is not invertible and it seems no invertible 3-share threshold scheme exists for χ. This implies that if we start with a uniformly shared state, it is no longer uniform after an iteration. We have proposed different fixes for this problem [4]. In fact, the loss of uniformity can be compensated by some extra circuitry and injecting 4 random bits per round. However, some of us felt that this may be unnecessary. To better understand this, we thought it would be good to take a closer look at this loss of uniformity. The result of these investigations lead to some theory that is not specific for the threshold sharing setting and insights specific for threshold sharing. This paper reports on the former.

Although non-uniformity threshold schemes is the trigger for this work, it can be applied to other settings. For example Merkle-Damgård based or sponge-based hashing, self-synchronizing stream ciphers or ciphers with a non-invertible state-updating function. An example of the latter is the sponge function Gluon [1]. Gluon was already investigated in [14], that can be considered prior art to this work. As opposed to [14] that concentrates on macroscopic aspects, we start from the spectral domain and make extensive use of correlation matrices to derive macroscopic metrics for non-uniformity in a second stage.

1.1   Overview

Section 2 explains how distributions over $GF(2)^n$ can be fully characterized by the imbalances of their parities. The array of imbalances is called the imbalance spectrum and the link between the probability distribution and the imbalance spectrum is the Walsh-Hadamard transformation. We derive how to compute the spectrum of the product of independent distributions and of a projected distribution.

Section 3 recalls correlation matrices of Boolean mappings and linear trails in iterative mappings. It provides expressions for the occurrence of imbalances in (iterative) Boolean mappings and iterative mappings and their propagation through them. These expressions are the basis for the remainder of the paper.

Section 4 defines macroscopic non-uniformity metrics for distributions and mappings: the total imbalance (contribution) and collision probability. It shows that under independence assumptions, iteratively applying lossy mappings to a variable accumulates the imbalance contributions of the lossy mappings in the total imbalance of the variable.

In Sect. 5 we characterize the distributions, spectra and total imbalance that result when sampling $GF(2)^n$ both for the cases with and without replacement and the corresponding distributions of random mappings.

In Sect. 6 we show that for some classes of mappings, i.e., lossy round functions, it is easy to determine their so-called *collision profile* that fully determines their total imbalance. We illustrate this with an example.

Finally, in Sect. 7 we provide some experimental evidence that the independence assumptions of Sect. 4 are reasonable.

1.2 Conventions and Notation

We consider distributions over domains of type $GF(2)^n$, i.e., sets of n-bit vectors. We denote them by a capital, e.g., X. For a given n-bit value x, we denote $\Pr(X = x)$, the probability that $X = x$, by $X(x)$.

We use the Kronecker delta function with a slightly different notation than usual for clarity: $\delta(x = y)$. This function takes two arguments x and y and is 1 if $x = y$ and zero otherwise.

If x is an n-bit vector and y is an m-bit vector $x\|y$ denotes the $n + m$-bit vector with first n components those of x and m last components those of y.

For quantities a and b, we use $a \ggg b$ to indicate that a is much larger than b. When using addition and summation, the kind of addition (in $GF(2)^n$, in $\mathbb{R}$, . . .) performed is implicitly determined by the type of summands.

We use vectors and matrices and their products. The vectors are supposed to be column vectors and the transpose operation applied to a vector or matrix switches rows and columns. The transpose of vector v is denoted as v^T and the transpose of matrix M is denoted as M^T. We denote the $n \times n$ unity matrix by $\mathbf{I_n}$. The component of a vector v with index i is denoted as v_i and the element in a matrix M in row with index r and column with index c is denoted as $M_{r,c}$.

2 Distributions and Their (imbalance) Spectrum

In this section we show how distributions can be characterized in the spectral domain by means of imbalances in certain parities. Large imbalances can give rise to cryptanalytic or side-channel attacks.

2.1 Parities, Imbalances and Spectrum

Definition 1. *A distribution X over $GF(2)^n$ is uniform if $X(x) = 2^{-n}$ for all $x \in GF(2)^n$.*

We can describe distributions over $GF(2)^n$ with *imbalances* over *parities* that are defined by n-dimensional binary vectors called *masks*.

Definition 2. *The parity of a vector x defined by a mask v is the linear function $v^T x$ from $GF(2)^n$ to $GF(2)$ given by*

$$v^T x = \sum_i v_i x_i \,,$$

where the summation corresponds to the addition in $GF(2)$.

Definition 3. *The imbalance* $\widetilde{X}(v)$ *of a mask* v *for a distribution* X *is given by*

$$\widetilde{X}(v) = \sum_x X(x)(-1)^{v^\mathrm{T} x} . \tag{1}$$

Imbalances range between -1 (parity is always 1) and $+1$ (parity is always 0). If it is zero we say it is *balanced*.

Filling in $v = 0$ in Eq. (1) yields $\widetilde{X}(0) = 1$. Naturally, $\widetilde{X}(0)$ is the imbalance of the constant function zero and so equal to 1. This leads us to the following definition.

Definition 4. *The spectrum of a distribution with* $\widetilde{X}(0)$ *omitted is the* reduced spectrum *and denoted by* $\widehat{X}$.

Let $\mathcal{L}$ be a mapping from the space of binary vectors to the space of real-valued vector that transforms a binary vector of dimension n to a real-valued vector of dimension 2^n. $\mathcal{L}$ is defined by

$$\mathcal{L} : \mathrm{GF}(2)^n \to \mathbb{R}^{2^n} : a \mapsto \mathcal{L}(x) \Leftrightarrow \forall u \in \mathrm{GF}(2)^n : \mathcal{L}(x)_u = (-1)^{u^\mathrm{T} x} . \tag{2}$$

Since $\mathcal{L}(x \oplus y) = \mathcal{L}(x) \cdot \mathcal{L}(y)$, $\mathcal{L}$ is a group homomorphism from $\langle \mathrm{GF}(2)^n, + \rangle$ to $\langle (\mathbb{R} \backslash \{0\})^{2^n}, \cdot \rangle$, where ' $\cdot$ ' denotes the component-wise product.

$\mathcal{L}(x)$ contains the 2^n parities of an n-bit vector x. Equivalently, it contains the parities of the distribution X over $\mathrm{GF}(2)^n$ that has probability 1 in x and zero elsewhere: $\Pr(X = x) = \delta(x = a)$. We can express the spectrum of a distribution X in terms of $\mathcal{L}$:

$$\widetilde{X} = \sum_x X(x)\mathcal{L}(x) . \tag{3}$$

2.2   The Walsh-Hadamard Transform

From Eq. (1), it is clear that the vector $\widetilde{X}$ of values $\widetilde{X}(v)$ for all v can be obtained by applying the Walsh-Hadamard transform [8] to X. This transform is a linear transformation operating on a vector space $\mathbb{R}^{2^n}$ that can be modelled as multiplication by a square matrix W with 2^n rows and columns. The rows and columns are not indexed by integers but rather by n-bit binary vectors and the element in row v and column x is given by $(-1)^{v^\mathrm{T} x} = \mathcal{L}(x)_v$. So we have $\widetilde{X} = W \times X$. Clearly, $v^\mathrm{T} x = x^\mathrm{T} v$ so W is symmetric: $W^\mathrm{T} = W$.

We can define an inner product $\langle A, B \rangle$ with A and B vectors in $\mathbb{R}^{2^n}$. Assuming A and B are column arrays containing coordinates with respect to an orthonormal basis, this inner products is given by $\langle A, B \rangle = A^\mathrm{T} B = \sum_i A_i B_i$. Two vectors A and B are orthogonal if their inner product is zero.

A transformation $\mathcal{M}$ is said to be orthogonal if for all vectors A and B it holds that $\langle \mathcal{M}A, \mathcal{M}B \rangle = \langle A, B \rangle$. It is easy to see that this is the case if the columns of $\mathcal{M}$ form an orthonormal basis, i.e., if we denote two columns of $\mathcal{M}$ by M_i and M_j, we have $M_i{}^\mathrm{T} M_j = \delta(i = j)$. This can be expressed more compactly as $\mathcal{M}^\mathrm{T} \mathcal{M} = \mathbf{I}_{2^n}$.

The Walsh-Hadamard transform can be decomposed in an orthogonal transformation and an expansion by $2^{n/2}$. We have $\mathcal{W} = 2^{n/2}\check{\mathcal{W}}$ and $\check{\mathcal{W}}\check{\mathcal{W}}^{\mathrm{T}} = \mathbf{I}_{2^n}$. The inverse of $\mathcal{W}$ is therefore given by $\mathcal{W}^{-1} = 2^{-n}\mathcal{W}^{\mathrm{T}} = 2^{-n}\mathcal{W}$. It follows that we can reconstruct a distribution X from its spectrum $\widetilde{X}$ in the following way:

$$X(x) = 2^{-n} \sum_v \widetilde{X}(v)(-1)^{v^{\mathrm{T}}x} \,, \tag{4}$$

or equivalently

$$X = 2^{-n} \sum_v \widetilde{X}(v)\mathcal{L}(v) \,.$$

2.3   Product of Independent Distributions

Let X be a distribution of a 2^n-bit string x and Y a distribution of a 2^m bit string y, with X and Y independent and let z be the joint distribution of x and y. Then the distribution Z of z is given by:

$$Z(z = (x,y)) = X(x)Y(y) \,.$$

For the imbalances this implies the following:

$$\widetilde{Z}(v = (v_x, v_y)) = \widetilde{X}(v_x)\widetilde{Y}(v_y) \,.$$

This can be generalized to the concatenation of s string with independent distributions. Let $x = (x_{(0)}, x_{(1)}, \ldots, x_{(s-1)})$ and $v = (v_{(0)}, v_{(1)}, \ldots, v_{(s-1)})$. We have:

$$\widetilde{X}(v) = \prod_i \widetilde{X_{(i)}}(v_{(i)}) \,. \tag{5}$$

Note that in the product on the right hand side of Eq. (5), only factors with $v_{(i)} \neq 0$ can be different from 1. We call these *active* component masks. Moreover, for $\widetilde{X}(v)$ to be non-zero, all terms in the product on the right hand side shall be different from zero. In words, for $v^{\mathrm{T}}x$ to be imbalanced, all parities $v_{(i)}{}^{\mathrm{T}}x_{(i)}$ must be imbalanced. This implies that $\widetilde{X}(v) = 0$ as soon as there is a single parity $v_{(i)}{}^{\mathrm{T}}x_{(i)}$ that is balanced.

2.4   Projection of a Distribution

Consider now the distribution of a subset of the bits of a string x. We denote this by the term *projection*. We consider the projection reducing x to its first k bits denoted by $x_{(u)}$ and denote the last $n - k$ bits by $x_{(\overline{u})}$. We have

$$X_{(u)}(x_{(u)}) = \sum_{x_{(\overline{u})}} X(x_{(u)}||x_{(\overline{u})}) \,,$$

and for the spectrum:

$$\widetilde{X_{(u)}}(v_{(u)}) = \widetilde{X}(v_{(u)}||0) \,.$$

So the spectrum of the projection of X is just a truncation of the spectrum of X. This can be generalized by defining $x_{(u)} = Zx$ with Z a binary *projection matrix* with k rows and n columns:

$$X_{(u)}(x_{(u)}) = \sum_x \delta(x_{(u)} = Zx)X(x),$$

and for the spectrum:

$$\widetilde{X_{(u)}}(v_{(u)}) = \widetilde{X}(Z^T v_{(u)}). \tag{6}$$

It may be the case that for a non-uniform distribution X, the projection is uniform. This is in fact the case if the spectrum is zero for all masks v that can be formed as $Z^T v_{(u)}$. So global non-uniformity and local uniformity are not mutually exclusive.

3   Lossy Mappings and Their Impact on Local Imbalance

In this section we show how mappings from $GF(2)^n$ to $GF(2)^m$ transform the spectrum of variables.

3.1   Correlation Matrices and Linear Trails

The correlation between two Boolean functions with domain $GF(2)^n$ can be expressed by a *correlation coefficient* that ranges between -1 and 1:

Definition 5. *The correlation coefficient* $C(g(x), h(x))$ *associated with a pair of Boolean functions* $g(x)$ *and* $h(x)$ *is given by*

$$C(g(x), h(x)) = 2 \cdot \Pr(g(x) = h(x)) - 1,$$

or equivalently

$$C(g(x), h(x)) = \sum_x (-1)^{g(x)+h(x)}.$$

The structure of input-output correlations of a Boolean mapping $f(x)$ form an equivalent representation in the spectral domain. In particular, this contains the correlations between Boolean functions $u^T f(x)$ on the one hand and $v^T x$ on the other. This structure is the *correlation matrix*[5].

The correlation between an input mask v and an output mask u of a Boolean mapping is defined as:

$$C(u^T f(x), v^T x) = \sum_x (-1)^{u^T f(x)+v^T x}.$$

Definition 6 (*[5]*). *The correlation matrix* C^f *of an n-bit to m-bit mapping* f *is a* $2^n \times 2^m$ *matrix with element* $C^f_{u,w}$ *in row* u *and column* w *equal to* $C(u^T f(x), w^T x)$.

Row u of a correlation matrix can be interpreted as

$$(-1)^{u^\mathrm{T} f(x)} = \sum_w C^f_{u,w} (-1)^{w^\mathrm{T} x}.$$

This expresses an output parity with respect to the basis of input parities.

A correlation matrix C^f defines a linear map with domain $\mathbb{R}^{2^n}$ and range $\mathbb{R}^{2^m}$. Clearly, we have

$$\mathcal{L}(f(x)) = C^f \mathcal{L}(x).$$

In words, applying a Boolean function f to a Boolean vector x and multiplying the corresponding vector $\mathcal{L}(x)$ with the correlation matrix C^f are just different representations of the same operation. This is illustrated in Fig. 1.

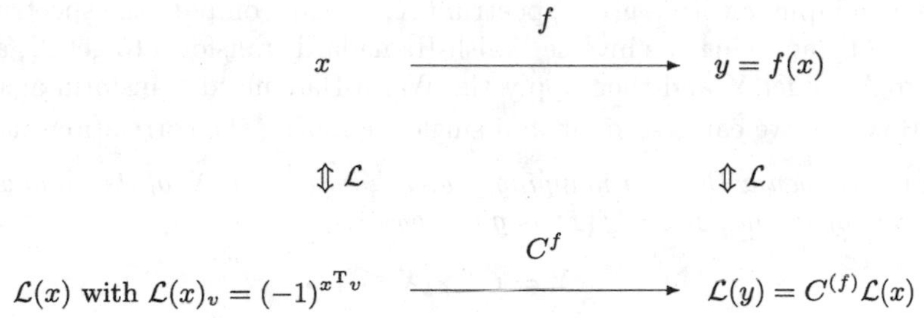

Fig. 1. The equivalence of a Boolean mapping and its correlation matrix.

Let F be a Boolean mapping that is the composition of a number of Boolean mappings f_i:

$$F = f_r \circ \ldots \circ f_2 \circ f_1.$$

We call the mappings f_i round mappings.

The correlation matrix of F is the product of the correlation matrices of the round mappings f_i. We have

$$C^F = C^{f_r} \times \ldots \times C^{f_2} \times C^{f_1}.$$

An r-round *linear trail* Q [5], denoted by

$$Q = (q_0, q_1, q_2, \ldots q_r),$$

consists of the chaining of r successive correlations of the type $C(q_i^\mathrm{T} f_i(x), q_{i-1}^\mathrm{T} x)$. To this linear trail corresponds a *correlation contribution coefficient* C_Q ranging between -1 and $+1$ defined as:

$$C_Q = \prod_i C^{f_i}_{q_i, q_{i-1}}.$$

From this we can derive following lemma.

Lemma 1 ([5]). *The correlation between $u^T F(x)$ and $w^T x$ is the sum of the correlation contribution coefficients of all r-round linear trails Q with initial selection vector w and terminal selection vector u.*

$$C(u^T F(x), w^T x) = \sum_{q_0 = w, q_r = u} C_Q.$$

3.2   Propagation of Imbalance Through a Mapping

Let f be a Boolean mapping from $\mathrm{GF}(2)^n$ to $\mathrm{GF}(2)^m$ and X is a distribution over $\mathrm{GF}(2)^n$, the domain of this mapping. Then the distribution Y of $y = f(x)$ is given by:

$$\Pr(Y = y) = \sum_x \delta(f(x) = y) \Pr(X = x). \tag{7}$$

Given an input x with a given spectrum $\widetilde{X}$, we can compute the spectrum $\widetilde{Y}$ of $y = f(x)$ by applying the inverse Walsh-Hamadard transform to get X, apply Eq. (7) to X to get Y and then apply the Walsh-Hadamard transform again to get $\widetilde{Y}$. However, we can also do it in a single step using the correlation matrix.

Lemma 2. *Given a Boolean mapping f and the spectrum $\widetilde{X}$ of its input x, the spectrum $\widetilde{Y}$ of its output $y = f(x)$ is given by*

$$\widetilde{Y} = C^f \times \widetilde{X}.$$

Proof. The spectrum of Y can be written as:

$$\widetilde{Y} = \sum_y \Pr(Y = y) \mathcal{L}(y).$$

For the probabilities of Y we have:

$$\Pr(Y = y) = \sum_x \Pr(X = x) \delta(y = f(x)).$$

Filling this in yields:

$$\widetilde{Y} = \sum_y \left(\sum_x \Pr(X = x) \delta(y = f(x)) \right) \mathcal{L}(y).$$

Re-ordering and re-grouping this gives:

$$\widetilde{Y} = \sum_x \Pr(X = x) \left(\sum_y \delta(y = f(x)) \mathcal{L}(y) \right)$$

$$= \sum_x \Pr(X = x) \mathcal{L}(f(x))$$

$$= \sum_x \Pr(X = x) C^f \mathcal{L}(x)$$

$$= C^f \sum_x \Pr(X = x) \mathcal{L}(x)$$

$$= C^f \widetilde{X}.$$

$\square$

In a correlation matrix, row 0 contains correlations where the output mask is all-zero. It immediately follows that in the correlation matrix of any mapping, all elements in row 0 are zero, except the element in column 0, that contains the correlation between two constant functions both equal to zero and is hence one. Column 0 contains correlations of output parities with input parities with zero input mask. An input x that is uniformly distributed has a spectrum that is all-zero for all non-zero masks and 1 in the zero mask. So column 0 contains the spectrum $\tilde{Y}$ of $y = f(x)$ given a uniformly distributed x.

Analogous to the reduced spectrum of a distribution, we can now define the reduced correlation matrix C^{*f} of a mapping f as C^f with row 0 and column 0 removed. This technique was also used by Jrmy Parriaux [13]. For an n-bit to m-bit mapping, C^{*f} has $2^m - 1$ rows and $2^n - 1$ columns. Moreover, we denote the first column of the correlation matrix, with the element in row 0 removed, by I^f and call it the *imbalance vector* of f. It is simply the reduced spectrum $\tilde{Y}$ of $y = f(x)$ with x uniformly distributed. Note that for a balanced mapping the imbalance vector I^f is all-zero. We have:

$$\begin{bmatrix} 1 \\ \hat{Y} \end{bmatrix} = \begin{bmatrix} 1 & 0 \\ I^f & C^{*(f)} \end{bmatrix} \times \begin{bmatrix} 1 \\ \hat{X} \end{bmatrix}.$$

We can now re-formulate Lemma 2 in terms of reduced spectra, correlation matrix and imbalance vector:

Lemma 3. *Given a Boolean mapping f and an input x with reduced spectrum $\hat{X}$, the reduced spectrum $\hat{Y}$ of $y = f(x)$ is given by*

$$\hat{Y} = I^f + C^{*f} \times \hat{X}.$$

In other words, the reduced spectrum of $y = f(x)$ consists of the sum of two terms. The first term is the imbalance vector of f and independent of x and the second term is the reduced spectrum of x multiplied by the reduced correlation matrix of f.

3.3   Propagation of Imbalance Through Iterative Mappings

Applying Lemma 3 to an iterative mapping $F = f_r \circ \ldots \circ f_2 \circ f_1$ yields following expression:

$$\hat{Y} = \sum_{1 \leq i \leq r} \left(\left(\prod_{i < j \leq r} C^{*f_j} \right) \times I^{f_i} \right) + \left(\prod_{1 \leq j \leq r} C^{*f_j} \right) \times \hat{X}. \tag{8}$$

When in Eq. (8) considering the imbalance of an individual mask in $\tilde{Y}$, we can express it using linear trails Q by applying Lemma 1 to the products of the round mapping correlation matrices:

$$\hat{Y}(u) = \sum_{1 \leq i \leq r} \sum_{w} \left(\sum_{\substack{Q \text{ with} \\ q_i = w, q_r = u}} C_Q \right) \times I^{f_i}[w] + \sum_{w} \left(\sum_{\substack{Q \text{ with} \\ q_0 = w, vq_r = u}} C_Q \right) \times \hat{X}(w). \tag{9}$$

So from Eq. (9) it follows that the imbalance of a mask u equals the sum of the products of the non-zero components $I^{f_i}[w]$ of the imbalance vectors of all previous rounds, each one multiplied by the sum of the correlation contributions of the linear trails from w to u. Note that the effect of the imbalance vector of the last round, $I^{f_r}[w]$ is immediate: $\widetilde{Y}(u) = I^{f_r}[u] + \text{other terms}$. The contribution of components of the imbalance vector of the penultimate round, $I^{f_{r-1}}[w]$ is diluted by the multiplication of correlations over f_{r-1}. In particular, a component $I^{f_{r-1}}[w]$ contributes $C_{u,w}^{f_{r-1}} I^{f_{r-1}}[w]$. Note that contributions can be constructive or destructive as the imbalances and correlations are signed. The contribution of components of earlier rounds becomes more and more diluted as the distance to the final round grows. They are multiplied by the correlation contribution of linear trails and typically cryptographic round functions are designed to not exhibit multiple-round linear trails with high correlation contribution. Equation (9) is useful when studying the possible loss of security due to non-uniformity of threshold scheme anti-DPA mechanisms [4].

4   Lossy Mappings and Their Impact on Macroscopic Imbalance

In this section we define macroscopic non-uniformity metrics for distributions and study their evolution through iterative mappings. We repeatedly apply transformations f_i from a fixed set of transformations with known imbalance contribution. This is similar to but different from studying the cycle structure of a single transformation f. In the latter case iteration leads to cycles while in the case of different transformations no such cycles appear.

4.1   Collision Probability and Total Imbalance

The *norm* of a vector A is defined as $\sqrt{\langle A, A \rangle}$. It turns out that a useful measure for the non-uniformity of a distribution X is the square of its norm, when seen as a vector, i.e., $\&X = \langle X, X \rangle$. This quantity coincides with the *collision probability* of X, defined as:

Definition 7. *The collision probability* $\mathrm{Pr}_{coll}(X)$ *of a distribution X is the probability that two elements independently chosen according to the distribution X are the same. It is given by:*

$$\Pr_{coll}(X) = \sum_x X(x)^2 = \&X \,.$$

The negative of the binary logarithm of the collision probability is the so-called *collision entropy* [15]. It can be shown that the collision entropy forms a lower bound for the more familiar Shannon entropy by Jensen's inequality [16].

As the Walsh-Hadamard transform is the composition of an orthogonal transformation and a scaling, we have $\&\widetilde{X} = 2^n \& X$, or equivalently:

$$\sum_v \widetilde{X}(v)^2 = 2^n \Pr_{coll}(X) \,. \tag{10}$$

In other words, the sum of the squared imbalances over all masks for a given distribution X is fully determined by its collision probability.

The squared norm of the reduced spectrum is the sum of the non-trivial squared imbalances and it plays a central role in our analysis.

Definition 8. *The total imbalance ϕ_X of a distribution X is the squared norm of its reduced spectrum:*

$$\phi_X = \&\widehat{X} = \sum_{u \neq 0} \widetilde{X}(u)^2.$$

Clearly, the total imbalance is fully determined by the collision probability through Eq. (10):

$$\phi_X = 2^n \Pr_{\text{coll}}(X) - 1. \tag{11}$$

The collision probability and total imbalance reach a minimum with a uniform distribution. A uniform distribution over $\text{GF}(2)^n$ has collision probability 2^{-n} and total imbalance 0. Uniformity of a distribution can be expressed alternatively as *having an all-zero reduced spectrum*.

The collision probability and total imbalance reach a maximum when the distribution is only non-zero for a single element in the domain. In that case the collision probability equals 1 and the total imbalance equals $2^n - 1$

For the collision probability of the product of independent distributions, it is trivial to prove following lemma.

Lemma 4. *The collision probability of a distribution that is the product of a number of independent distributions is the product of those of the component distributions*

$$\Pr_{\text{coll}}(X) = \prod_i \Pr_{\text{coll}}(X_{(i)}).$$

4.2 Collision Probability and Imbalance Contribution

We define the collision probability for a mapping f analogous to that of a distribution. It is the collision probability of the distribution Y of $y = f(x)$ if x has the uniform distribution.

Definition 9. *The collision probability $\Pr_{\text{coll}}(f)$ of a mapping f is the probability that $f(x) = f(x')$ holds for two randomly and uniformly chosen inputs x and x'.*

Similarly we can define the imbalance contribution in terms of its collision probability.

Definition 10. *The imbalance contribution ϕ_f of a mapping f is its collision probability multiplied by 2^m, minus 1:*

$$\phi_f = 2^m \Pr_{\text{coll}}(f) - 1.$$

Clearly, the imbalance contribution of a mapping f is simply the squared norm of its imbalance vector I^f.

We can now define *balancedness* of a mapping f.

Definition 11. *A mapping f is balanced if it transforms an input with a uniform distribution into an output with uniform distribution. Equivalently, a mapping is balanced if its imbalance contribution is zero, or equivalently, its imbalance vector is zero.*

Given two transformations f and g operating on domains $\mathrm{GF}(2)^m$ and $\mathrm{GF}(2)^k$ respectively, their Cartesian product $h = f \times g$ operates on $\mathrm{GF}(2)^{m+k}$ and is defined as $h(x, y) = (f(x), g(y))$. Transformation h simply consists of the parallel application of f and g.

The collision probability of $h = f \times g$ is simply the product of those of f and g.

Lemma 5. *If $h = f \times g$ then $\mathrm{Pr}_{coll}(h) = \mathrm{Pr}_{coll}(f)\,\mathrm{Pr}_{coll}(g)$.*

Proof. Consider $x = (x_{(f)}, x_{(g)})$ and $y = (y_{(f)}, y_{(g)})$. We have $h(x) = h(y)$ iff $f(x_{(f)}) = f(y_{(f)})$ and $g(x_{(g)}) = g(y_{(g)})$. It follows immediately that the probability of a collision in h is the product of the collision probabilities in f and g.   □

The following corollary is useful for computing the collision probability of S-box layers.

Corollary 1. *If h is the parallel application of a number of mappings f_i, then $\mathrm{Pr}_{coll}(h) = \prod_i \mathrm{Pr}_{coll}(f_i)$.*

For imbalance contributions this translates to:

$$\phi_f = \prod_i (\phi_{f_i} + 1) - 1 \,.$$

The properties of the serial composition of two transformations $h = g \circ f$ depends on the specific way f and g interact and in general not easy to determine exactly. In the special case that one of f and g is a permutation, the composed transformation simply inherits the collision probability and imbalance contribution of the other one.

4.3   Total Imbalance Evolution Through a Lossy Mapping

From Lemma 3, we see that the reduced spectrum after f consists of the sum of the imbalance vector I^f and the spectrum before f multiplied by the reduced correlation matrix of f. Making some independence assumptions allows us to say something about the expected total imbalance after f.

First, we quantify the effect of the multiplication with C^{*f} on the (squared) norm of a vector. It is well known that a permutation f has an orthogonal correlation matrix [5] and for that case multiplication by the correlation matrix, or its reduced version, does not impact the norm. The mappings we are interested in are not invertible and have some imbalance contribution. We now show that multiplication by C^{*f} tends to multiply the norm with $1 - \frac{\phi_f}{2^n - 1}$. We will denote this by c_f.

Lemma 6. *The expected value over the space of all possible input vectors X with $\&X = 1$ of $\&C^{*f} \times X$ is exactly $1 - \frac{\phi_f}{2^n - 1} = c_f$.*

Proof. For readability we will denote C^{*f} by C in this proof and use $E_{\text{condition}(X)}(f(X))$ to express the expected value of $f(X)$ chosen uniformly with only restriction that X satisfies the mentioned condition. Let $Y = C^{*f} \times X$. We have $\&Y = \&CX = (CX)^{\mathrm{T}}CX = X^{\mathrm{T}}C^{\mathrm{T}}CX$. Let UDV be the singular value decomposition of C[10]. Here U and V are orthonormal matrices and D a diagonal matrix with on the diagonal the singular values d_i of C. Then we have $\&Y = VX^{\mathrm{T}}D^{\mathrm{T}}U^{\mathrm{T}}UDVX = VX^{\mathrm{T}}D^2VX$ and hence $E_{\&X=1}(\&Y) = E_{\&X=1}(VX^{\mathrm{T}}D^2VX)$. If we denote VX by X', X' has the same norm as X as V is an orthonormal matrix. We now have (with x_i denoting the components of X':

$$E_{\&X'=1}(X'^{\mathrm{T}}D^2X') = E_{\sum_i x_i^2 = 1}(x_i^2 d_i^2) = \frac{\sum_i d_i^2}{2^n - 1}.$$

So c_f equals the average of the squared singular values of the reduced correlation matrix C^{*f}.

The sum of the squared singular values of a matrix equals the sum of squared elements of that matrix [10]. So $\sum_i d_i^2 = \sum_{u \neq 0, w \neq 0} C_{u,w}^2$. As the only non-zero element in the first row of any correlation matrix is the element in column zero, we have $\sum_i d_i^2 = \sum_{u,w} C_{u,w}^2 - \sum_u C_{u,0}^2$. Each row in a correlation matrix has norm 1, so this becomes $\sum_i D_i^2 = 2^n - 1 - \phi_f$. It follows that $c_f = 1 - \frac{\phi_f}{2^n - 1}$. $\square$

It follows that the term $C^{*f} \times \widehat{X}$ has an expected imbalance contribution $c_f \phi_X$. Second, we assume that I^f is independent of $C^{*f} \times \widehat{X}$. We think this is a reasonable assumption as they have different origins. In that case the squared norm of the sum of the two vectors is the sum of the squared norms of the vectors. We have:

$$\phi_Y \approx \phi_f + c_f \phi_X.$$

4.4   Total Imbalance Evolution in Iterative Mappings

If we make the same independence assumptions for Eq. (8) we obtain:

$$\phi_Y = \sum_{1 \leq i \leq r} \left(\left(\prod_{i < j \leq r} c_{f_j} \right) \times \phi_{f_i} \right) + \left(\prod_{1 \leq j \leq r} c_{f_j} \right) \times \phi_X. \tag{12}$$

In typical use cases we have $r \lll 2^n / \phi_{f_j}$ implying $r \lll (1 - c_{f_j})$ and hence $\prod_j c_{f_j} \approx 1$. This allows simplifying Eq. (12) to:

$$\phi_Y \approx \sum_{1 \leq i \leq r} \phi_{f_i} + \phi_X.$$

The expected total imbalance of Y is simply the sum of the imbalance contributions of the round mappings f_i plus the total imbalance of X. In other words, the total imbalance increases linearly with the number of rounds by simply accumulating their imbalance contributions. Similarly, the collision probability increases linearly and hence the collision entropy decreases logarithmically with the number of rounds.

Assuming all f_i have the same imbalance contribution ϕ_f, Eq. (12) simplifies to:

$$\phi_Y = \frac{1 - c_f{}^r}{1 - c_f}\phi_f + c_f{}^r\phi_X .$$

If the mappings f_i are not invertible we have $c_{f_i} < 1$ and for r going to infinity this expression becomes

$$\phi_Y = \frac{\phi_f}{1 - c_f} = 2^n - 1 .$$

This corresponds with Y having a peak distribution equal to 1 in a single value and zero elsewhere.

5   Sampling Noise and Random Mappings

In many applications one samples from a set. Even if the sampling is done according to a uniform distribution, the resulting sets will exhibit imbalance and have non-zero total imbalance (unless every element from the domain happens to be sampled exactly one time). In this section we characterize the distributions that result from random sampling of $GF(2)^n$, in a way similar to [6]. We consider two types of sampling: with and without replacement. It turns out that a random mapping can be modeled as a sampling. An injective random mapping corresponds to sampling without replacement and in absence of an injectivity requirement it corresponds to sampling with replacement.

5.1   Sampling with Replacement and Random Transformations

In sampling with replacement, we take z independent samples from $GF(2)^n$. Let U be the multi-set containing the z samples. It is well known that if $z \gg 1$, the number of times a given value x occurs in U, its *cardinality*, has a Poisson distribution with $\lambda = z2^{-n}$ [7]. Hence, the components of $X(x)$ are distributed according to a Poisson distribution scaled by a factor z^{-1}:

$$\Pr\left(X(x) = \frac{i}{z}\right) = \frac{z^i 2^{-ni}}{i!}e^{-z2^{-n}} .$$

We can compute the distribution of the imbalance of a non-zero parity v using the expression $\widetilde{X}(v) = z^{-1}\sum_{x \in U}(-1)^{v^{\mathrm{T}}x}$. The imbalance is given by $1 - 2p/z$ with p the number of elements x in U with parity 1 in v. Each element of U is independent and the probabilities of this parity being 1 or -1 are both

$1/2$. It follows that the number p has a binomial distribution with mean $z/2$ and variance $z/4$. So for non-zero v, $\widetilde{X}(v)$, has a distribution with mean 0 and variance z^{-1}. If $z \ggg 1$, this distribution has a normal shape.

The expected collision probability is $z^{-1} + (1 - z^{-1})2^{-n}$. The term z^{-1} is the probability of taking the same instance among the samples and the second term is the complement of that probability multiplied by the probability that two independent samples collide. Applying Eq. (11) yields an expected total imbalance equal to $(2^n - 1)z^{-1}$.

The set of images of a random mapping from $GF(2)^n$ to $GF(2)^m$ simply coincides with that of a random sample with replacement of 2^n elements out of 2^m and hence the expected collision probability is $2^{-n} + (1 - 2^{-n})2^{-m}$ and the expected imbalance contribution $(2^m - 1)2^{-n}$. For a random transformation we have $n = m$ and this becomes $2^{-n+1} - 2^{-2n}$ and $1 - 2^{-n}$ respectively. Remarkably, a random transformation has an imbalance contribution close to 1.

When applying Lemma 4 we see that parallel composition of mappings with an imbalance contribution lower than that of a random transformation may result in a mapping with imbalance contribution higher than that of a random transformation. For example, parallel application of d S-boxes with imbalance contribution 1 results in an S-box layer with imbalance contribution $2^d - 1$.

The effect of projection on total imbalance depends on the shape of the spectrum. Assuming that the imbalances have a (near) flat distribution, projection from n to k bits reduces the total imbalance by dividing it by a factor $(2^n - 1)/(2^k - 1) \approx 2^{n-k}$.

5.2 Sampling Without Replacement and Random Injective Mappings

In sampling without replacement, the sample set U contains z different elements from $GF(2)^n$, with $z \leq 2^n$. It follows that $X(x)$ has a two-valued distribution with value 0 in $2^n - z$ elements and z^{-1} in z elements. The collision probability equals $\Pr_{coll}(X) = z^{-1}$ and the total imbalance is $z^{-1}2^n - 1$. Note that if the size of the sample and the domain are equal, i.e. $z = 2^n$, we have a uniform distribution and the total imbalance becomes zero.

We can compute the distribution of the imbalance of a non-zero parity v using the expression $\widetilde{X}(v) = z^{-1}\sum_{x \in U}(-1)^{v^{\mathrm{T}}x}$. The imbalance is given by $1 - 2p/z$ with p the number of elements x in U with parity 1 in v. The number p has the probability distribution of p successes in z draws from a set of 2^n without replacement, where the total number of successes in the set is 2^{n-1}. This is given by the hypergeometric distribution [7]:

$$\Pr(p = i) = \frac{\binom{2^{n-1}}{i}\binom{2^{n-1}}{z-i}}{\binom{2^n}{z}}.$$

This distribution has mean $z/2$ and variance $(1 - z2^{-n})\frac{z}{4}$. It follows that for non-zero v, $\widetilde{X}(v)$ has a distribution with mean 0 and variance $(1 - z2^{-n})z^{-1}$. If $z \ggg 1$, this distribution has a normal shape.

The collision probability is equal to z^{-1}: one over the size of the sample. The total imbalance hence equals $z^{-1}2^n - 1$.

The collision probability of an injective mapping (implying $m \geq n$) coincides with that of a sample without replacement. The size of the sample is given by $z = 2^{-n}$, so we have $\text{Pr}_{\text{coll}}(f) = 2^{-n}$ and $\phi_f = 0$. An injective mapping with $n = m$ is a permutation and it has total imbalance 0 and collision probability 2^{-n}.

5.3   Summary of This Section

We summarize the results of this section in Table 1.

Table 1. Statistical characteristics of samples with size z.

	with replacement	without replacement
$X(x)$	scaled Poisson $\text{Pr}(X = \frac{i}{z}) = \frac{\lambda^i}{i!}e^{-\lambda}$ with $\lambda = \frac{z}{2^n}$	two-valued $\text{Pr}(X = 0) = 1 - \frac{z}{2^n}$ $\text{Pr}(X = \frac{1}{z}) = \frac{z}{2^n}$
$\widetilde{X}(v)$	very close to normal mean: 0 variance: z^{-1}	very close to normal mean: 0 variance: $(1 - z2^{-n})z^{-1}$
$\text{Pr}_{\text{coll}}(X)$	mean: $z^{-1} + (1 - z^{-1})2^{-n}$	equals z^{-1}
ϕ_X	mean: $z^{-1}(2^n - 1)$	equals $z^{-1}2^n - 1$
ϕ_X if $z = 2^n$	mean: $1 - 2^{-n}$	equals 0

6   Imbalance Contribution of Mappings with Known Collision Profile

In this section we deal with mappings where the non-uniformity can be quantitatively characterized by a so-called *collision profile*. It turns out that this fully determines the collision probability and imbalance contribution. We also provide some experimental evidence of the theoretically predicted evolution of the total imbalance.

6.1   Collision Profile and Implications

Definition 12. *The* collision partition *of a mapping f is the one defined by $f(x) = f(y)$. In other words, two elements x and y of the domain are in the same subset if and only if $f(x) = f(y)$. We call the subsets of the partition* collision sets *and a collision set with i elements an i-collision.*

Based on the collision partition of a transformation f we can define its collision profile.

Definition 13. *The collision profile of a transformation f is the list $(C_f[1], C_f[2], \ldots)$ where $C_f[i]$ denotes the number of i-collisions in f.*

Clearly, the total number of inputs in i-collisions is $iC_f[i]$ and so it follows that $\sum_i iC_f[i] = 2^n$.

The collision probability of a mapping f is determined by its collision profile.

Lemma 7. *The collision probability of an n-bit to m-bit mapping f with known collision profile is given by:*

$$\Pr_{coll}(f) = \frac{1}{2^{2n}} \sum_i i^2 C_f[i].$$

Proof. The probability equals the number of cases (x, y) leading to a collision divided by the total number of cases:

$$\Pr_{coll}(f) = \frac{1}{2^{2n}} \sum_{x,y} \delta(f(x) = f(y)).$$

In other words:

$$\Pr_{coll}(f) = \frac{1}{2^{2n}} \sum_{x,y} \delta(x \text{ and } y \text{ are in the same collision set}).$$

The number of colliding pairs (x, y) in an i-collision set is i^2, hence:

$$\Pr_{coll}(f) = \frac{1}{2^{2n}} \sum_i i^2 C_f[i].$$

$\square$

The value of the imbalance contribution follows from this:

Corollary 2. *The imbalance contribution of an n-bit to m-bit mapping f with known collision profile is given by:*

$$\phi_f = \frac{1}{2^{2n-m}} \sum_i i^2 C_f[i] - 1.$$

6.2 Example: A Round Function with Lossy S-Boxes

Assume we have a round function consisting of a lossy nonlinear S-box layer N and a linear layer L and we wish to determine its total imbalance. First, thanks to the invertibility of the linear layer, the total imbalance of the round function is the total imbalance of the lossy S-box layer. Second, for an S-box of reasonable width, it is easy to determine the collision profile and hence its collision probability. This allows determining the collision probability of the non-linear layer. Assume we have m identical S-boxes of width n. Then the collision probability of the nonlinear layer is $\mathrm{Pr}_{\mathrm{coll}}(N) = \mathrm{Pr}_{\mathrm{coll}}(S)^n$. Translated to total imbalances this gives: $\phi_N = 2^{nm}\mathrm{Pr}_{\mathrm{coll}}(S)^m - 1$.

Let now $\mathrm{Pr}_{\mathrm{coll}}(S)$ be 2^{-a}: the S-box reduces the set of 2^m inputs to a set with the same collision probability as a set of 2^a elements. Then we have $\phi_N = 2^{n(m-a)} - 1$ and $c_N = 1 - \frac{2^{n(m-a)}-1}{2^{nm}-1}$. If $n(m-a) \ggg 1$, we have these expressions simplify to $\phi_N \approx 2^{n(m-a)}$ and $c_N \approx 1 - 2^{-na}$. Assume we have a block cipher with a block size nm of 128 bits and a 4-bit S-box with $\mathrm{Pr}_{\mathrm{coll}}(S) = 2^{-3}$. Then we have $\phi_N \approx 2^{32}$ and $c_N \approx 1 - 2^{-96} \approx 1$. The total imbalance after r rounds is simply $2^{32}r$ implying a collision probability of $2^{-96}r$. This lower bounds the collision entropy, and hence also the Shannon entropy, to $96 - \log_2(r)$.

7   Experiments

We did a number of experiments to check the validity of our independence assumptions. More particularly, we randomly constructed transformations f with domains of size 2^e with e ranging from 22 to 27 and for each of them we tracked the total imbalance when applying randomized versions of f to it iteratively. We did this by tracking the image set as the number of rounds increases. We initialize the image set to the full domain and randomize the application of f by bitwise addition with a constant that is randomly generated for each i but equal for all elements in the image set.

Initially each element in the image set has probability 2^{-e} and the total imbalance is zero. If the first iteration of f maps w elements to some element, this element has probability $w2^{-e}$. In our experiments we keep track of these probabilities and compute from them the total imbalance.

We studied two types of pseudorandomly generated transformations. Those in the first category were generated without side conditions. Those in the second category satisfy specific collision profiles: only 2^{-f} of the images are possible and each image has 2^f pre-images. We composed these of a random permutation followed by a simple transformation satisfying the collision profile, followed by a (independently generated) random permutation. The random permutations were generated with the Fisher-Yates shuffle [9].

Figure 2 illustrates the outcome of our experiments. The continuous lines represent the values taken by simply multiplying the imbalance contribution of the transformations by the number of iterations for the random transformation (imbalance contribution 1) and the one that maps 64 values to a single one (imbalance contribution 63). The figure shows that the experimentally measured total imbalances follows these linear profiles quite closely.

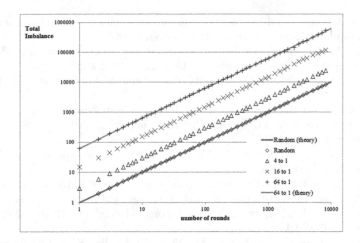

Fig. 2. Evolution of total imbalance for different transformations.

8 Conclusions and Acknowledgments

In this paper we have provided a formalism to describe non-uniformity in the spectral domain using imbalances. The occurrence and propagation of these imbalances can be described by correlation matrices and linear trails. We have introduced macroscopic metrics for non-uniformity in the form of total imbalance. When iteratively applying lossy mappings to a variable, its total imbalance increases linearly with the number of rounds and its entropy decreases logarithmically. The tools we provide in this paper are helpful when studying non-invertible cryptographic modes and primitives, including non-uniform threshold schemes.

Acknowledgements. I thank Gilles Van Assche, Guido Bertoni, Svetla Nikova, Ventzi Nikov and Begül Bilgin for useful comments.

References

1. Berger, T.P., D'Hayer, J., Marquet, K., Minier, M., Thomas, G.: The GLUON Family: a lightweight hash function family based on FCSRs. In: Mitrokotsa, A., Vaudenay, S. (eds.) AFRICACRYPT 2012. LNCS, vol. 7374, pp. 306–323. Springer, Heidelberg (2012). doi:10.1007/978-3-642-31410-0_19
2. Bertoni, G., Daemen, J., Peeters, M., Van Assche, G.: Building power analysis resistant implementations of Keccak. In: Second SHA-3 Candidate Conference, August 2010
3. Bertoni, G., Daemen, J., Peeters, M., Van Assche, G.: The Keccak reference. http://keccak.noekeon.org/, January 2011
4. Bilgin, B., Daemen, J., Nikov, V., Nikova, S., Rijmen, V., Assche, G.: Efficient and First-Order DPA resistant implementations of KECCAK. In: Francillon, A., Rohatgi, P. (eds.) CARDIS 2013. LNCS, vol. 8419, pp. 187–199. Springer, Heidelberg (2014). doi:10.1007/978-3-319-08302-5_13

5. Daemen, J.: Cipher and hash function design strategies based on linear and differential cryptanalysis, Ph.D. thesis, K.U.Leuven (1995)
6. Daemen, J., Rijmen, V.: Probability distributions of correlation and differentials in block ciphers. J. Math. Cryptology **1**(3), 221–242 (2007)
7. Feller, W.: Introduction to Probability Theory and its Applications, vol. 1. Wiley, New York (1968)
8. Golomb, S.: Shift Register Sequence. Holden-Day, San Francisco (1967)
9. Knuth, D.E.: The Art of Computer Programming, vol. 2, 3rd edn. Addison-Wesley Publishing, Boston (1998)
10. Lay, D., Lay, S., McDonald, J.: Linear Algebra and its Applications, 5th edn. Pearson, New York (2016)
11. Nikova, S., Rijmen, V., Schläffer, M.: Secure hardware implementation of nonlinear functions in the presence of glitches. In: Lee, P.J., Cheon, J.H. (eds.) ICISC 2008. LNCS, vol. 5461, pp. 218–234. Springer, Heidelberg (2009). doi:10.1007/978-3-642-00730-9_14
12. Bertoni, G., Daemen, J., Peeters, M., Van, G.: Assche.: Secure hardware implementation of nonlinear functions in the presence of glitches. J. Cryptology **24**(2), 292–321 (2011)
13. Parriaux, J., Guillot, P., Millerioux, G.: Towards a spectral approach for the design of self-synchronizing stream ciphers. Cryptography Commun. **3**(4), 259–274 (2011)
14. Perrin, L., Khovratovich, D.: Collision spectrum, entropy loss, T-sponges, and cryptanalysis of GLUON-64. In: Cid, C., Rechberger, C. (eds.) FSE 2014. LNCS, vol. 8540, pp. 82–103. Springer, Heidelberg (2015). doi:10.1007/978-3-662-46706-0_5
15. Rényi, A.: On measures of information and entropy. In: Proceedings of the Fourth Berkeley Symposium on Mathematics, pp. 547–561 (1960)
16. Weisstein, E.: Jensen's inequality from mathworld - a wolfram web resource. http://mathworld.wolfram.com/JensensInequality.html

Decomposed S-Boxes and DPA Attacks:
A Quantitative Case Study Using PRINCE

Ravikumar Selvam[✉], Dillibabu Shanmugam[✉], Suganya Annadurai[✉],
and Jothi Rangasamy[✉]

Society for Electronic Transactions and Security, Chennai, India
{ravikumar,dillibabu,asuganya,jothiram}@setsindia.net
http://www.setsindia.org/hardware.html

Abstract. Lightweight ciphers become indispensable and inevitable in the ubiquitous smart devices. However, the security of ciphers is often subverted by various types of attacks, especially, implementation attacks such as side-channel attacks. These attacks emphasise the necessity of providing efficient countermeasures. In this paper, our contribution is threefold: First, we propose a method to choose the efficient decomposition of S-box in terms of area. Then we slightly alter the widely used formula to improve the accuracy for weighted sum estimation of the shared S-Box and present the practical implementation of two level decomposition using PRINCE S-Box. Finally, we present the first quantitative study on the efficacy of Transparency Order (TO) of decomposed S-Boxes in thwarting a side-channel attack. For PRINCE S-Box we observe that TO-based decomposed implementation has better DPA resistivity than the naive implementation. To benchmark the DPA resistivity of TO(decomposed S-Box) implementation we arrive at an efficient threshold implementation of PRINCE, which itself merits to be an interesting contribution.

Keywords: Side-channel attack · Threshold implementation · Decomposition · Transparency Order

1 Introduction

Usage of smart electronic devices in our life is rapidly growing and almost unavoidable. Smart electronic devices are resource constrained having less memory, low power and limited computation capability. Since lightweight ciphers require only minimal resources, they are identified to provide compact solutions to achieve security goals to protect such devices. The theoretical proofs of security for cryptographic algorithms give us some confidence; but may not be sufficient to protect against real-world attacks.

As the smart devices are portable and easily accessible to the attacker, these devices are shown to be prone to implementation attacks in a rapid phase. Side-channel analysis attacks exploit the information leakage through physical medium to reveal the secret key of the device. In particular, Differential Power

© Springer International Publishing AG 2016
C. Carlet et al. (Eds.): SPACE 2016, LNCS 10076, pp. 179–193, 2016.
DOI: 10.1007/978-3-319-49445-6_10

Analysis (DPA) attack is considered as more effective form of side-channel attack that reveals the key with high probability [5]. These attacks brought the attention to develop effective and efficient countermeasures. One such countermeasure, which is widely studied and provably secure, is Threshold Implementation (TI) of block ciphers.

In TI, a non-linear component of block cipher is decomposed into secret shares and the method was first proposed by Nikova et al. [10,11]. The degree of S-Box, say d, decides the number of secret shares that must be greater than d. In TI the higher degree S-Box is decomposed into smaller degree S-Boxes so that the number of shares needed gets reduced, which in turn reduces the area requirement for TI. At the same time, the decomposed S-Boxes must satisfy the TI properties, such as correctness, non-completeness, and uniformity. Indeed not all decompositions need to satisfy the uniformity property, in such cases re-sharing is used to achieve it. However, non-uniform decomposition design is vulnerable to attack as shown in [1,18]. Efficient way of realising TI for lightweight cipher and a formula for estimating shared TI S-box were presented in [15]. Threshold Implementation of 4-bit S-Boxes is proposed in [6].

Leander et al. proposed sixteen optimal 4-bit S-Boxes [7] for lightweight block ciphers. It is stated that only eight out of sixteen are suitable for PRINCE in [2]. Then G_{13} (also represented as C_{231}) class of S-Box is taken for PRINCE implementation based on lexicographical order. S-Boxes are predominantly the point of interest for DPA, as bit flip occurs randomly in circuit. Theoretically the possible amount of information leakage has been studied by Prouff et al. [16] and quantified as a metric called Transparency Order (TO). Further, this metric is studied and explored in many papers [3,8,9,13,14]. TO is redefined in the paper [4]. In [14], it is found that G_{13} class of S-Box has high TO but it is vulnerable to power analysis attack. Subsequently, differential power analysis attack on PRINCE is demonstrated in [19]. It is stated in [13] that the small reduction in the TO will increase the trace requirement $2.5\,to\,3$ times for a successful DPA attack. However this prediction on TO is not explored with practical evaluation so far. In this paper, we analyse DPA resistance of a decomposed 4-bit S-Box using TO metrics.

Our contributions in this paper are as follows:

- We first observe the inaccuracy in the well-known and widely used formula proposed by Poschmann et al. in [15] for weighted sum estimation of shared function. In particular their formula leads to an incorrect result when used to compute the weighted sum for the shared implementation of a boolean function. We present a revised formula to produce accurate results in shared implementation.
- We then present an area-efficient TI of PRINCE block cipher before adopting for resource constrained devices. For this, we use two-level decomposition of PRINCE S-Box that falls in class G_{13}. The chosen decomposition, which satisfy all TI properties is taken and optimized further for implementation.
- We finally study the transparency order for S-Box decomposition and its influence in DPA attack. Our practical evaluations on PRINCE S-Box show that

the number of traces required for DPA attack on naive S-Box is increased significantly for the case of S-Box decomposition with lower transparency order. This implies that the TO-decomposed S-Box implementation is superior over the naive implementation. However benchmarking TO-decomposed S-Box implementation against TI implementation reveals that TI implementation should provide a much better security than any (even unrolled) unprotected implementation. Nevertheless, our experiments show that low transparency order implementation of decomposed S-Box may be considered as an intermediate countermeasure between the naive and TI implementations and the lesser TO means the better immunity against DPA attacks.

2   On Estimation Formula for Weighted Sum

To find the efficient decomposition, in terms of number of gate count (W_{sum}) for shared implementation, Poschmann et al. [15] proposed a formula to estimate a weighted sum of shared function. We observed that the proposed formula have an inconsistency in the result which differs from the actual gate count for the given shared function. This is illustrated below with a sample function (1). For simplicity, we have taken 1-bit inputs w, x, y, and z to compute F. We also define shares for the function F as f_1, f_2, and f_3.

$$F = 1 + x + y + w + xz \tag{1}$$
$$f_1 = 1 + x_2 + y_2 + w_2 + x_2z_2 + x_2z_3 + x_3z_2$$
$$f_2 = x_3 + y_3 + w_3 + x_3z_3 + x_3z_1 + x_1z_3$$
$$f_3 = x_1 + y_1 + w_1 + x_1z_1 + x_1z_2 + x_2z_1$$

Following [15], the XOR and AND gates are given the weightage of 2 and 1 GE respectively. With 16 XOR and 9 AND operations, the (manual) weighted sum calculation of the shared function results in 41 GE, whereas Poschmann et al. formula (2) outputs the estimated weighted sum as 47 GE. For fixing this inconsistency, we revise the formula (2) to (3).

$$W_{sum} = (2 \times C) + (6 \times L) + (27 \times Q) \tag{2}$$

$$W_{sum} = 2 \times ((3 \times C) - 2) + 6 \times (L + Q - 1) + 21 \times Q \tag{3}$$

where,
C is number of Constant
L is number of Linear Co-efficient
Q is number of Quadratic Co-efficient.

We calculated the weighted sum for the same function using our formula and obtained the result as 41 GE, which matches with the actual value of the shared function. The Table 1 presents the result obtained manually, using the revised formula and from formula (2). In the following sections, we use the revised formula to choose the efficient decomposition of S-box.

Table 1. Estimation of weighted sum

Function	Parameters			Weighted Sum		
	C	L	Q	Manual	Formula (2)	Revised formula
F = 1 + x + y + w + xz	1	3	1	41	47	41

3   Threshold Implementation of PRINCE S-Box

The PRINCE family proposed eight classes of S-Box for their design, in which the authors chose to use affine equivalent of eighth S-Box, as given in [2]. We studied the characteristics of that S-Box and its inverse using the TI Tool [12].

Table 2. S-Box and Inverse S-Box of PRINCE

x	0	1	2	3	4	5	6	7	8	9	A	B	C	D	E	F
$S(x)$	B	F	3	2	A	C	9	1	6	7	8	0	E	5	D	4
$S^{-1}(x)$	B	7	3	2	F	D	8	9	A	6	4	0	5	E	C	1

The S-Box of PRINCE is one of the eight golden S-Boxes proposed in [17], and it falls under the Class 231 with algebraic degree 3 and presented in Table 2. We have two choices for the implementation of TI: (a) to implement with 5 or 4 shares satisfying all the properties; (b) to implement the decomposed S-Box to reduce the number of required shares. In the first case, the implementation requires 5 or 4 times more area than the unprotected implementation. In the second case, if the S-Box is decomposed into lower degree functions, say quadratic functions, then the TI requires 3 shares to implement, which minimizes the required area. But the first level decomposition of PRINCE S-Box yields one cubic function and one quadratic function. This decomposition requires at least 4 shares that does not offer significant gain in the area requirement. Therefore to reduce the area requirement further, subsequent level of decomposition on cubic functions yields two quadratic functions as shown in Fig. 1. Finally, the PRINCE S-Box is decomposed into three quadratic functions.

Using TI tool [12], PRINCE S-Box in Table 2 is decomposed into 304 solutions in the first level of decomposition and 2576 solutions after the second level of decomposition. To construct a secure shared implementation, three TI properties are to be fulfilled [10]. We have taken first 644 solutions out of 2576 for our analysis. Though all 644 solutions satisfy, correctness and non-completeness properties; only 40 solutions satisfy uniformity properties of TI. The other solutions require either re-masking or virtual variable technique to make them satisfy the uniformity property. In decomposed S-Box, we analysed 644 solutions using our weighted sum formula which is given in (3). A solution that does not satisfy the uniformity property may also be area efficient after re-masking. To make

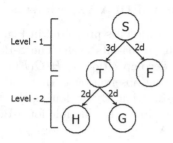

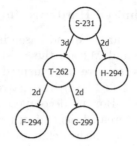

Fig. 1. Decomposition approach

Fig. 2. PRINCE S-Box decomposition

the process easy and efficient, we classify the solutions into two divisions. Solutions that satisfy the uniformity property and solutions that fail to satisfy the uniformity property of TI. Using (3), we calculated the weighted sum for all solutions of F, G and H functions. We identified the least weighted sum on both classifications separately and compared. The candidate of first category has the least weighted sum of 412 GE, which is quite lesser than the least weighted sum of 447 GE for the second category. Therefore, we chose the candidate with weighted sum 412 GE for hardware space efficient implementation of PRINCE S-Box whose classes are given in Fig. 2 and its shares are given in Appendix A.

Table 3. S-Box decomposition

x	0	1	2	3	4	5	6	7	8	9	A	B	C	D	E	F
$F(x)$	0	A	2	8	1	3	B	9	E	5	D	6	F	C	4	7
$G(x)$	E	4	0	A	2	8	C	6	9	7	5	B	D	3	1	F
$H(x)$	3	6	D	8	A	F	4	1	7	2	C	9	0	5	B	E

Table 4. Inverse S-Box decomposition

x	0	1	2	3	4	5	6	7	8	9	A	B	C	D	E	F
$F^{-1}(x)$	3	9	B	1	7	C	F	4	A	8	2	0	6	5	E	D
$G^{-1}(x)$	E	4	0	A	2	8	C	6	9	7	5	B	D	3	1	F
$H^{-1}(x)$	4	C	9	1	2	A	F	7	E	6	B	3	5	D	0	8

Similarly for Inverse S-Box, 2-level decomposition was performed and 644 solutions of quadratic functions were obtained. The solutions were divided into two divisions and the efficient implementation of Inverse S-Box was also obtained using the same procedure. The Inverse S-Box has the least weighted sum of 354 GE. The decomposed functions F, G and H for the S-box are presented in Table 3 and decomposed functions F^{-1}, G^{-1} and H^{-1} are presented in Table 4.

3.1   Optimised Hardware Implementation and DPA Experiments

The architecture of round based implementation with TI is presented in Fig. 3. Inputs M1 and M2 are the mask values, which are 64-bits each. The S-Box and its inverse were implemented with efficient decomposition as $H(G(F(x)))$ and $H^{-1}(G^{-1}(F^{-1}(x)))$ respectively. An interesting observation is that S-Box and Inverse S-Box are decomposed with same G-function. By exploiting this to improve the area efficiency further, we shared the G function module for S-Box and its Inverse which is elaborated in Appendix A.

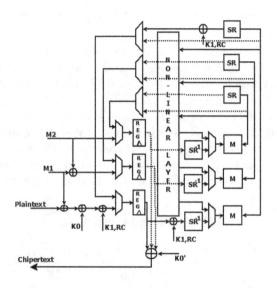

Fig. 3. Architecture of PRINCE with TI

To evaluate the security of protected implementation, we realised TI of PRINCE in SASEBO G board in which the target FPGA device is Xilinx Virtex2Pro. Power measurements were taken for 300,000 encryptions and Pearson's correlation coefficient analysis were performed for the attack. Figure 4 shows that the correct key (plotted in black) is hidden with the other key hypothesis that are plotted in grey. It is understood that TI is secure against DPA attack. In [19], the DPA attack was successful with 30,000 encryptions, whereas the protected implementation is secure up to 300,000 encryptions, which is 10 times more secure than the unprotected implementation. Due to resource limitations the protected implementation is tested up to 300,000 encryptions. However, TI is believed to provide more security as stated in [10].

4   Transparency Order and DPA Attacks

In general, TO is calculated for naive S-Box to measure the DPA resistivity of any cipher. In this paper, we analyse the influence of TO in decomposed S-Box.

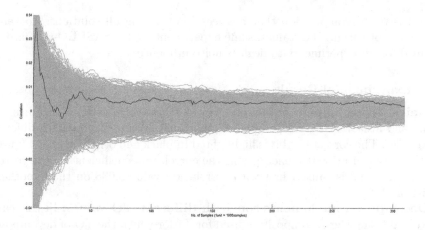

Fig. 4. Attack on Threshold Implementation

Our first observation is that TO of naive S-Box is not the same as the TO of decomposed S-Box. This observation motivates us to study the behaviour of TO value with respect to the DPA resistance of decomposed S-Box implementation. We use PRINCE for our case study.

The decomposition of PRINCE S-Box has many possible ways using cubic and quadratic functions. The first level decomposition, which comprises of a cubic and quadratic functions are analysed initially. We noted that the TO of the first level decomposed functions and naive S-Box has negligible difference and may not be suitable for the analysis. Therefore, we analysed the second level decomposition of PRINCE S-Box. The second level decomposition comprises of three quadratic functions and has 2576 (644 × 4) possible solutions. All solutions were taken for analysis and sorted the solutions based on least TO. We also estimated area requirement in terms of weighted sum as discussed in Sect. 2 for the chosen decomposition.

Table 5. Case 3 S-Box decomposition

x	0	1	2	3	4	5	6	7	8	9	A	B	C	D	E	F
$F(x)$	7	5	0	1	C	A	E	B	F	D	8	9	4	2	6	3
$G(x)$	7	4	5	6	E	9	C	B	8	3	A	1	D	2	F	0
$H(x)$	6	1	7	0	2	5	4	3	8	F	C	B	D	A	E	9

We performed DPA attack on three types of implementations: (1) Naive S-Box implementation as shown in Table 2 with the TO of 3.4; (2) decomposed implementation of quadratic functions F, G and H as shown in Table 3 with TO of 2.933, 3.2 and 3.46 respectively; and, (3) decomposed implementation of quadratic functions F, G and H as shown in Table 5 with TO of 2.933 each.

Case 3 is the decomposition that has least TO among all solutions. To verify the impact of varying TO values, same experiment setup (SASEBO-G board) is retained for all experiments to neglect noise influence.

4.1 Experimental Result

1. **Naive S-Box implementation:** Naive S-Box of PRINCE cipher has TO 3.4 and area 78 GE. We plot the correlation values at $2.021\,\mu s$ for different samples. The correct key bit is highlighted in black and others in grey. Figure 5 shows that after 30,000 encryptions the correlation coefficient for the correct key value 108 is ranked first with correlation value 0.038 on the hypothesis list of 2^{13}.

2. **Decomposed implementation with different TO values:** In this case, we had taken the decomposition used for TI for which the TO of decomposed functions are $(TO_{S_i}^F = 2.933, TO_{S_i}^G = 3.2, TO_{S_i}^H = 3.46)$ and the S-box area is measured as 72 GE. DPA attack on this implementation reveals secret key with 30,000 encryptions. In Fig. 6, the correct key value 108 (in decimal) is uniquely distinguishable which is having the correlation value of 0.03 at $2.032\,\mu s$. This decomposed function did not have any impact on the resistivity against DPA attack. The reason could be $TO_{S_i}^H = 3.46$, which is being the highest among three functions TO value. The higher TO of H function may have dominated the other functions. Subsequently, $TO_{S_i}^H = 3.4$ is same as $TO_{NS} = 3.4$. Therefore, the number of traces required to attack did not vary.

3. **Decomposed implementation with same TO values:** The least TO from the decomposed functions $(TO_{S_i}^F = TO_{S_i}^G = TO_{S_i}^H = 2.933)$ is taken for analysis and its area requirement is 87 GE. When DPA is explored for this decomposition, the cipher requires 2,50,000 traces to reveal 85 % of secret key. Figure 7 shows highest correlation value of 0.01 at $2.102\,\mu s$ for the key value 108. From this, we observe that the decomposed solution achieves eight times better security than the naive implementation in terms of DPA resistance. Hence, TO based decomposed implementation may be considered as an implementation strategy to resist DPA to certain extent.

We practically evaluate the impact of TO value on the DPA resistivity of S-Box, which has not been verified so far. From the experimental results we observe that TO-based decomposed implementation seems to provide a trade-off between naive and TI-based approaches. That is, TO-based decomposed implementation is superior to naive implementation but is inferior to TI-based approach. Experimentally we verified that there is an inverse relationship between TO value and the DPA resistance; that is, when the TO value increases, DPA resistance decreases.

4.2 Comparative Study of PRINCE S-Box Results for Constrained Device

Normally, constrained devices has low area, limited computational capability and low power consumption. Though a device has many limitations, it is expected to

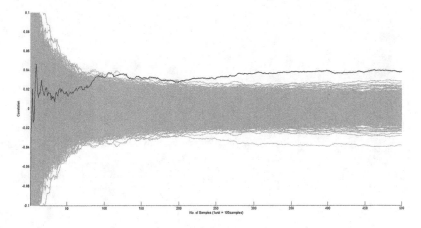

Fig. 5. Attack on naive S-Box

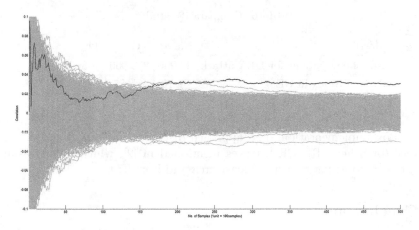

Fig. 6. Attack on decomposed S-Box with different TO values

match the security level offered by a conventional device, which may not be practically realisable. But, there are two choices for users depending on application requirement (Table 6).

- Select the specific parameter (in this case security)
- Parameter affordability (level of the security)

In this paper, security affordability is studied and its metrics are tabulated in Table 7. Three kinds of security affordability were discussed such as naive, decomposed S-Box (least TO) and decomposed TI (least area) of PRINCE. Even though decomposed TI has better security when compared to other implementations, it comes at the cost of area. Therefore, by far decomposed S-Box implementation achieves better trade-off, i.e. small increase in area, say about 10 GE in weighted sum, achieves eight times better security when compared to

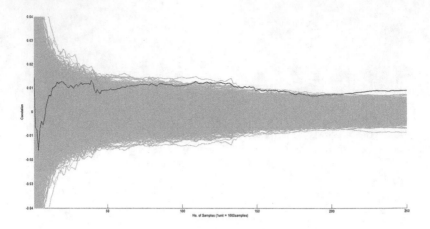

Fig. 7. Attack on decomposed S-Box with same TO values)

Table 6. Comparative study

Metrics	Naive	TO	TI
No. of encryptions for DPA attack	30,000	250,000	> 300,000
Area of S-box in GE	78	87	412

naive S-Box implementation. The approach discussed in Sects. 3 and 4 can be extended for other PRINCE S-Boxes mentioned in [2], which might result in efficient decomposition to achieve least area and least TO.

5   Conclusion

Protecting lightweight ciphers from side-channel attack is seen to be a mammoth task. In this paper, we observed and corrected the inaccuracy in the widely-accepted formula for estimating gate equivalents for shared implementation. Then we presented the first quantitative study on the efficacy of Transparency Order (TO) of decomposed functions of S-Boxes and its effectiveness in thwarting a specific side-channel attack, namely DPA. Using PRINCE S-Box we observed that TO-based S-Box decomposition may be considered as an intermediate countermeasure since TO-based decomposed implementation provides better DPA immunity than the naive implementation but not as strong as DPA immunity that can be achieved using the TI method. For this we arrived at an efficient threshold implementation (TI) for PRINCE block cipher using two-level decompositions, which itself is an interesting contribution.

Acknowledgments. This Research work was funded by Department of Atomic Energy (DAE), Govt. of India under the grant 12-R&D-IMS-5.01.0204. We would like to thank Prof. Svetla Nikova and anonymous reviewers for their useful comments.

A   TI Solution

This section elaborates the selection of efficient solution and its implementation approach.

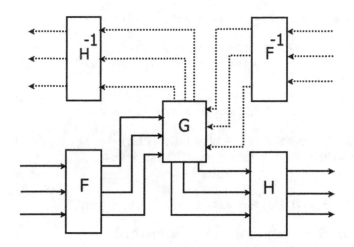

Fig. 8. Architecture of PRINCE non-linear function with TI

The Architecture of PRINCE non-linear function with the decomposition is depicted in Fig. 8. The weighted sum were calculated for 644 decomposed function and the value of the efficient function is given in Table 7. To implement the TI countermeasures on PRINCE non-linear function 766 GE were required.

Table 7. Weighted sum.

Functions	F	G	H	Total
S-Box	126	123	163	412
Inverse S-Box	F^{-1}	G	H^{-1}	354
	97	123	134	

We observed that the S-Box and Inverse S-Box has same $'G'$ function. This leads us to optimize the architecture by sharing the $'G'$ function between S-Box (F,G,H) and Inverse S-Box (F^{-1},G,H^{-1}). Hence the gate count is reduced to 643.

Listed below are the algebraic normal forms (ANFs) of the PRINCE S-Box decomposition with 3-shares for TI countermeasure.

F and H function

$F_1(w_2, x_2, y_2, z_2, w_3, x_3, y_3, z_3) = (f_{13}, f_{12}, f_{11}, f_{10})$
$f_{10} = x_2 + w_2 y_2 + w_2 y_3 + w_3 y_2 + w_2 z_2 + w_2 z_3 + w_3 z_2$
$f_{11} = z_2 + y_2 + w_2$
$f_{12} = w_2$
$f_{13} = z_2 + w_2 + x_2 z_2 + x_2 z_3 + x_3 z_2 + x_2 y_2 + x_2 y_3 + x_3 y_2$

$F_2(w_3, x_3, y_3, z_3, w_1, x_1, y_1, z_1) = (f_{23}, f_{22}, f_{21}, f_{20})$
$f_{20} = x_3 + w_3 y_3 + w_3 y_1 + w_1 y_3 + w_3 z_3 + w_3 z_1 + w_1 z_3$
$f_{21} = z_3 + y_3 + w_3$
$f_{22} = w_3$
$f_{23} = z_3 + w_3 + x_3 z_3 + x_3 z_1 + x_1 z_3 + x_3 y_3 + x_3 y_1 + x_1 y_3$

$F_3(w_1, x_1, y_1, z_1, w_2, x_2, y_2, z_2) = (f_{33}, f_{32}, f_{31}, f_{30})$
$f_{30} = x_1 + w_1 y_1 + w_1 y_2 + w_2 y_1 + w_1 z_1 + w_1 z_2 + w_2 z_1$
$f_{31} = z_1 + y_1 + w_1$
$f_{32} = w_1$
$f_{33} = z_1 + w_1 + x_1 z_1 + x_1 z_2 + x_2 z_1 + x_1 y_1 + x_1 y_2 + x_2 y_1$

$H_1(w_2, x_2, y_2, z_2, w_3, x_3, y_3, z_3) = (h_{13}, h_{12}, h_{11}, h_{10})$
$h_{10} = 1 + z_2 + x_2 + w_2 y_2 + w_2 y_3 + w_3 y_2$
$h_{11} = 1 + y_2 + w_2 x_2 + w_2 x_3 + w_3 x_2$
$h_{12} = z_2 + y_2 + w_2 + w_2 y_2 + w_2 y_3 + w_3 y_2 + w_2 x_2 + w_2 x_3 + w_3 x_2$
$h_{13} = y_2 + x_2 + w_2 x_2 + w_2 x_3 + w_3 x_2$

$H_2(w_3, x_3, y_3, z_3, w_1, x_1, y_1, z_1) = (h_{23}, h_{22}, h_{21}, h_{20})$
$h_{20} = z_3 + x_3 + w_3 y_3 + w_3 y_1 + w_1 y_3$
$h_{21} = y_3 + w_3 x_3 + w_3 x_1 + w_1 x_3$
$h_{22} = z_3 + y_3 + w_3 + w_3 y_3 + w_3 y_1 + w_1 y_3 + w_3 x_3 + w_3 x_1 + w_1 x_3$
$h_{23} = y_3 + x_3 + w_3 x_3 + w_3 x_1 + w_1 x_3$

$H_3(w_1, x_1, y_1, z_1, w_2, x_2, y_2, z_2) = (h_{33}, h_{32}, h_{31}, h_{30})$
$h_{30} = z_1 + x_1 + w_1 y_1 + w_1 y_2 + w_2 y_1$
$h_{31} = y_1 + w_1 x_1 + w_1 x_2 + w_2 x_1$
$h_{32} = z_1 + y_1 + w_1 + w_1 y_1 + w_1 y_2 + w_2 y_1 + w_1 x_1 + w_1 x_2 + w_2 x_1$
$h_{33} = y_1 + x_1 + w_1 x_1 + w_1 x_2 + w_2 x_1$

F^{-1} and H^{-1} function of inverse S-box:

$F_1^{-1}(w_2, x_2, y_2, z_2, w_3, x_3, y_3, z_3) = (f_{13}^{-1}, f_{12}^{-1} f_{11}^{-1}, f_{10}^{-1})$
$f_{10}^{-1} = 1 + w_2 + x_2 z_2 + x_2 z_3 + x_3 z_2$
$f_{11}^{-1} = 1 + z_2$
$f_{12}^{-1} = x_2$
$f_{13}^{-1} = z_2 + y_2 + w_2 + w_2 z_2 + w_2 z_3 + w_3 z_2 + w_2 x_2 + w_2 x_3 + w_3 x_2$

$F_2^{-1}(w_3, x_3, y_3, z_3, w_1, x_1, y_1, z_1) = (f_{23}^{-1}, f_{22}^{-1}, f_{21}^{-1}, f_{20}^{-1})$
$f_{20}^{-1} = w_3 + x_3 z_3 + x_3 z_1 + x_1 z_3$

$$f_{21}^{-1} = z_3$$
$$f_{22}^{-1} = x_3$$
$$f_{23}^{-1} = z_3 + y_3 + w_3 + w_3 z_3 + w_3 z_1 + w_1 z_3 + w_3 x_3 + w_3 x_1 + w_1 x_3$$

$$F_3^{-1}(w_1, x_1, y_1, z_1, w_2, x_2, y_2, z_2) = (f_{33}^{-1}, f_{32}^{-1}, f_{31}^{-1}, f_{30}^{-1})$$
$$f_{30}^{-1} = w_1 + x_1 z_1 + x_1 z_2 + x_2 z_1$$
$$f_{31}^{-1} = z_1$$
$$f_{32}^{-1} = x_1$$
$$f_{33}^{-1} = z_1 + y_1 + w_1 + w_1 z_1 + w_1 z_2 + w_2 z_1 + w_1 x_1 + w_1 x_2 + w_2 x_1$$

$$H_1^{-1}(w_2, x_2, y_2, z_2, w_3, x_3, y_3, z_3) = (h_{13}^{-1}, h_{12}^{-1}, h_{11}^{-1}, h_{10}^{-1})$$
$$h_{10}^{-1} = y_2 + w_2 x_2 + w_2 x_3 + w_3 x_2$$
$$h_{11}^{-1} = x_2 + w_2$$
$$h_{12}^{-1} = 1 + y_2 + x_2 + w_2 x_2 + w_2 x_3 + w_3 x_2$$
$$h_{13}^{-1} = z_2 + y_2 + w_2 + w_2 x_2 + w_2 x_3 + w_3 x_2 + w_2 y_2 + w_2 y_3 + w_3 y_2$$

$$H_2^{-1}(w_3, x_3, y_3, z_3, w_1, x_1, y_1, z_1) = (h_{23}^{-1}, h_{22}^{-1}, h_{21}^{-1}, h_{20}^{-1})$$
$$h_{20}^{-1} = y_3 + w_3 x_3 + w_3 x_1 + w_1 x_3$$
$$h_{21}^{-1} = x_3 + w_3$$
$$h_{22}^{-1} = y_3 + x_3 + w_3 x_3 + w_3 x_1 + w_1 x_3$$
$$h_{23}^{-1} = z_3 + y_3 + w_3 + w_3 x_3 + w_3 x_1 + w_1 x_3 + w_3 y_3 + w_3 y_1 + w_1 y_3$$

$$H_3^{-1}(w_1, x_1, y_1, z_1, w_2, x_2, y_2, z_2) = (h_{33}^{-1}, h_{32}^{-1}, h_{31}^{-1}, h_{30}^{-1})$$
$$h_{30}^{-1} = y_1 + w_1 x_1 + w_1 x_2 + w_2 x_1$$
$$h_{31}^{-1} = x_1 + w_1$$
$$h_{32}^{-1} = y_1 + x_1 + w_1 x_1 + w_1 x_2 + w_2 x_1$$
$$h_{33}^{-1} = z_1 + y_1 + w_1 + w_1 x_1 + w_1 x_2 + w_2 x_1 + w_1 y_1 + w_1 y_2 + w_2 y_1$$

Common G function of both S-box and inverse S-box:

$$G_1(w_2, x_2, y_2, z_2, w_3, x_3, y_3, z_3) = (g_{13}, g_{12}, g_{11}, g_{10})$$
$$g_{10} = w_2$$
$$g_{11} = 1 + z_2 + y_2 + w_2 + w_2 y_2 + w_2 y_3 + w_3 y_2$$
$$g_{12} = 1 + x_2 + y_2 + w_2 + w_2 z_2 + w_2 z_3 + w_3 z_2$$
$$g_{13} = 1 + z_2 + y_2 + x_2 + w_2 x_2 + w_2 x_3 + w_3 x_2$$

$$G_2(w_3, x_3, y_3, z_3, w_1, x_1, y_1, z_1) = (g_{23}, g_{22}, g_{21}, g_{20})$$
$$g_{20} = w_3$$
$$g_{21} = z_3 + y_3 + w_3 + w_3 y_3 + w_3 y_1 + w_1 y_3$$
$$g_{22} = x_3 + y_3 + w_3 + w_3 z_3 + w_3 z_1 + w_1 z_3$$
$$g_{23} = z_3 + y_3 + x_3 + w_3 x_3 + w_3 x_1 + w_1 x_3$$

$$G_3(w_1, x_1, y_1, z_1, w_2, x_2, y_2, z_2) = (g_{33}, g_{32}, g_{31}, g_{30})$$
$$g_{30} = w_1$$
$$g_{31} = z_1 + y_1 + w_1 + w_1 y_1 + w_1 y_2 + w_2 y_1$$
$$g_{32} = x_1 + y_1 + w_1 + w_1 z_1 + w_1 z_2 + w_2 z_1$$
$$g_{33} = z_1 + y_1 + x_1 + w_1 x_1 + w_1 x_2 + w_2 x_1$$

References

1. Bilgin, B.: Threshold Implementations: As Countermeasure Against Higher-Order Differential Power Analysis. Ph.D. thesis, KU Leuven and UTwente (2015). Pieter Hartel and Vincent Rijmen (promotors)
2. Borghoff, J., Canteaut, A., Güneysu, T., Kavun, E.B., Knezevic, M., Knudsen, L.R., Leander, G., Nikov, V., Paar, C., Rechberger, C., Rombouts, P., Thomsen, S.S., Yalçın, T.: PRINCE – a low-latency block cipher for pervasive computing applications. In: Wang, X., Sako, K. (eds.) ASIACRYPT 2012. LNCS, vol. 7658, pp. 208–225. Springer, Heidelberg (2012). doi:10.1007/978-3-642-34961-4_14
3. Carlet, C.: On highly nonlinear S-boxes and their inability to thwart DPA attacks. In: Maitra, S., Veni Madhavan, C.E., Venkatesan, R. (eds.) INDOCRYPT 2005. LNCS, vol. 3797, pp. 49–62. Springer, Heidelberg (2005). doi:10.1007/11596219_5
4. Chakraborty, K., Sarkar, S., Maitra, S., Mazumdar, B., Mukhopadhyay, D., Prouff, E.: Redefining the transparency order. In: WCC2015 - 9th International Workshop on Coding and Crypography 2015 (2015)
5. Kocher, P., Jaffe, J., Jun, B.: Differential power analysis. In: Wiener, M. (ed.) CRYPTO 1999. LNCS, vol. 1666, pp. 388–397. Springer, Heidelberg (1999). doi:10.1007/3-540-48405-1_25
6. Kutzner, S., Nguyen, P.H., Poschmann, A., Wang, H.: On 3-share threshold implementations for 4-bit S-boxes. In: Prouff, E. (ed.) COSADE 2013. LNCS, vol. 7864, pp. 99–113. Springer, Heidelberg (2013). doi:10.1007/978-3-642-40026-1_7
7. Leander, G., Poschmann, A.: On the classification of 4 bit S-boxes. In: Carlet, C., Sunar, B. (eds.) WAIFI 2007. LNCS, vol. 4547, pp. 159–176. Springer, Heidelberg (2007). doi:10.1007/978-3-540-73074-3_13
8. Mazumdar, B., Mukhopadhyay, D., Sengupta, I.: Constrained search for a class of good bijective S-boxes with improved DPA resistivity. IEEE Trans. Inf. Forensics Secur. 8(12), 2154–2163 (2013)
9. Mazumdar, B., Mukhopadhyay, D., Sengupta, I.: Design and implementation of rotation symmetric S-boxes with high nonlinearity and high DPA resilience. In: 2013 IEEE International Symposium on Hardware-Oriented Security and Trust, HOST 2013, pp. 87–92. IEEE Computer Society (2013)
10. Nikova, S., Rijmen, V., Schläffer, M.: Secure hardware implementation of nonlinear functions in the presence of glitches. In: Lee, P.J., Cheon, J.H. (eds.) ICISC 2008. LNCS, vol. 5461, pp. 218–234. Springer, Heidelberg (2009). doi:10.1007/978-3-642-00730-9_14
11. Nikova, S., Rechberger, C., Rijmen, V.: Threshold implementations against side-channel attacks and glitches. In: Ning, P., Qing, S., Li, N. (eds.) ICICS 2006. LNCS, vol. 4307, pp. 529–545. Springer, Heidelberg (2006). doi:10.1007/11935308_38
12. Petkova-Nikova, S.: TI Tools for the 3 x 3 and 4 x 4 S-boxes. http://homes.esat.kuleuven.be/~snikova/ti_tools.html. Accessed April 2016
13. Picek, S., Ege, B., Batina, L., Jakobovic, D., Chmielewski, L., Golub, M.: On using genetic algorithms for intrinsic side-channel resistance: the case of AES s-box. In: Knoop, J., Salapura, V., Koren, I., Pelosi, G. (eds.), Proceedings of the First Workshop on Cryptography and Security in Computing Systems (CS2@HiPEAC) 2014, pp. 13–18. ACM (2014)
14. Picek, S., Ege, B., Papagiannopoulos, K., Batina, L., Jakobovic, D.: Optimality and beyond: the case of 4 * 4 s-boxes. In: 2014 IEEE International Symposium on Hardware-Oriented Security and Trust, HOST 2014, pp. 80–83. IEEE Computer Society (2014)

15. Poschmann, A., Moradi, A., Khoo, K., Lim, C.-W., Wang, H., Ling, S.: Side-channel resistant crypto for less than 2,300 GE. J. Cryptology **24**(2), 322–345 (2010)
16. Prouff, E.: DPA attacks and S-boxes. In: Gilbert, H., Handschuh, H. (eds.) FSE 2005. LNCS, vol. 3557, pp. 424–441. Springer, Heidelberg (2005). doi:10.1007/11502760_29
17. Saarinen, M.-J.O.: Cryptographic analysis of all 4×4-bit S-boxes. In: Miri, A., Vaudenay, S. (eds.) SAC 2011. LNCS, vol. 7118, pp. 118–133. Springer, Heidelberg (2012). doi:10.1007/978-3-642-28496-0_7
18. Sasdrich, P., Moradi, A., Güneysu, T.: Affine equivalence and its application to tightening threshold implementations. Cryptology ePrint Archive, Report 2015/749 (2015). http://eprint.iacr.org/
19. Selvam, R., Shanmugam, D., Annadurai, S.: Vulnerability analysis of prince and rectangle using CPA. In: Proceedings of the 1st ACM Workshop on Cyber-Physical System Security, CPSS 2015, pp. 81–87. ACM (2015)

GAIN: Practical Key-Recovery Attacks on Round-reduced PAEQ

Dhiman Saha[(✉)], Sourya Kakarla, Srinath Mandava,
and Dipanwita Roy Chowdhury

Crypto Research Lab, Department of Computer Science and Engineering,
IIT Kharagpur, Kharagpur, India
{dhimans,skakarla,smandava,drc}@cse.iitkgp.ernet.in

Abstract. This work presents *practical* key-recovery attacks on round-reduced variants of CAESAR Round 2 candidate PAEQ by analyzing it in the light of guess-and-determine analysis. The attack developed here targets the mode of operation along with diffusion inside the AES based internal permutation AESQ. The first attack uses a *guess-and-invert* technique leading to a meet-in-the-middle attack that is able to recover the key for 6 out of the 20 rounds of paeq-64/80/128 with reduced key entropy of $1, 2^{16}$ and 2^{32} respectively. The second analysis extends the attack to 7 rounds using a *invert-and-guess* strategy which results in reduced key-space of $2^{24}, 2^{32}$ and 2^{40} for the same PAEQ variants. Finally, an 8-round attack is mounted using a *guess-invert-guess* strategy which works on any of the three variants with a complexity of 2^{48}. Moreover, unlike the CICO attack mounted by the designers which works with only AESQ, our 8-round attack additionally takes into account the mode of operation of PAEQ.

Keywords: Authenticated encryption · CAESAR competition · PAEQ · Guess and determine · AESQ · AES · Cryptanalysis

1 Introduction

Authenticated Encryption (AE) aims at *efficiently* unifying the cryptographic goals of privacy and integrity under a single crypto primitive. Since the introduction of the idea, there have been various attempts to address the challenge of designing efficient authenticated ciphers providing a reasonable security margin. However, the exposure of serious vulnerabilities [1,7] in OpenSSL and TLS highlighted the lack of proper understanding of the problem. Hence the need of well-studied innovative designs leading to possible standardization became imperative. This contributed to the initiation of the CAESAR [6] competition which is a new addition to a long standing tradition of public competitions of the cryptographic community. The competition assumes a rigorous approach in defining the requirements of an authenticated cipher and outlines a multi-year time-line for scrutinizing submissions to arrive at a final portfolio of AE schemes.

© Springer International Publishing AG 2016
C. Carlet et al. (Eds.): SPACE 2016, LNCS 10076, pp. 194–210, 2016.
DOI: 10.1007/978-3-319-49445-6_11

Presently, at the second Round, the competition witnessed 57 accepted submissions for Round 1 out of which 30 proposals have progressed to Round 2.

Among the Round 2 candidates of CAESAR is PAEQ which is an AES based parallelizable authenticated cipher designed by Biryukov and Khovratovich and introduced in ISC 2014 [4]. Internally, it instantiates a permutation called AESQ and uses a new mode of operation. The size of the permutation AESQ is 512 bits which is invariant across all PAEQ variants. In the submission document [2], the authors classify PAEQ in two sets: primary and secondary. The primary set constitutes paeq-64, paeq-80 and paeq-128 with key sizes of 64, 80 and 128 bits respectively. The secondary set includes variants with higher key-lengths and/or some additional features like quick tag update and nonce-misuse. As regards the cryptanalytic results on PAEQ, most of the analysis available is by the designers themselves. They provide a CICO (Constrained Input Constrained Output) attack on 8-rounds of AESQ with a complexity of 2^{32} where it is assumed that the last 384 bits of the input and output of AESQ are known. They also mount a rebound-attack to devise a 12-round distinguisher on AESQ with a complexity of 2^{256}. Among third party cryptanalysis, a new rebound attack has been mounted on AESQ in ACISP 2016 [3] while an internal differential fault-attack has been recently reported in CHES 2016 [9].

In this work, we exploit the mode of operation of PAEQ using a guess-and-determine strategy to perform a complete key recovery when the internal permutation is reduced from 20 rounds to 6, 7 and 8 rounds for paeq-64/80/128. Guess-and-determine techniques aim at guessing a part of the input/output to determine whole or part of the key leading to a reduced key-space. Complexity of these kind of attacks is generally directly determined by the complexity of guessing. This type of analysis has been successfully applied by Boura et al. [5] to CAESAR Round 2 candidate π-cipher [8]. There the authors exploited limited diffusion in a round-reduced version of the π-function to recover the key. In this work we also target the internal permutation AESQ reduced to 6, 7 and 8 rounds. First we show that by design most of the input to AESQ is known allowing an attacker to propagate the input state forward in the presence of the unknown key bytes. Secondly, we show that from the observable part of the output of AESQ an attacker can invert by guessing a part of the state independently without the knowledge of rest of the state. This helps to propagate the state backward assuming the remaining part to be unknown. Finally, we establish the condition for the forward and backward propagation to converge leading to a meet-in-the-middle scenario which is used to recover the key for 6-rounds of AESQ. The 6-round attack is used as a sub-routine to extend the strategy to 7-rounds and 8-rounds using some additional tweaks. The attacks presented in this work are referred to as GAIN to capture underlying theme of (G)UESS (A)ND (IN)VERT. Further, we show that the complexity of the entire attack can be reduced to the complexity of the guessing phase. Our results are summarized as below (Table 1):

The rest of the paper is organized as follows. Section 2 provides a brief description of PAEQ describing both the mode of operation PPAE and the internal permutation AESQ. Section 3 tries to formally capture the notion of partially

Table 1. Attack summary

PAEQ		GAIN complexities		
Variant	Security level	6-rounds	7-rounds	8-rounds
paeq-64	64-bit	1	2^{24}	2^{48}
paeq-80	80-bit	2^{16}	2^{32}	2^{48}
paeq-128	128-bit	2^{32}	2^{40}	2^{48}

specified state/sub-states and their behavior under AES round operations. The observations on PAEQ pertaining to the proposed attack are showcased in Sect. 4. The 6 round key-recovery of PAEQ is devised in Sect. 5 and the extensions to 7 and 8 rounds are done in Sects. 6 and 7 respectively. The complexity analysis is furnished in Sect. 8 while a discussion of the proposed attacks with respect to the CICO attack by the designers is given in Sect. 9. The concluding remarks are given in Sect. 10.

2   The Design of PAEQ

Parallelizable Authenticated Encryption based on Quadrupled AES or PAEQ was introduced by Biryukov and Khovratovich in ISC 2014 [4] and is also one of the Round 2 candidates in the on-going CAESAR competition for authenticated ciphers. It features a new generic mode of operation PPAE which stands for Parallelizable Permutation-based Authenticated Encryption. As the name suggests, PAEQ is AES based and has been designed to achieve a security level equal to the key-length. In order to arrive at a simplistic design the authors argued in favor of a permutation based construction. It is fully parallelizable and on-line and offers a security level up to 128 bits and higher (up to $w/3$, $w \leftarrow$ width of internal permutation). As mentioned earlier the different members of the PAEQ family are classified into two sets (p. 2, [2]) based on the security level and extra features. An interesting aspect of the PPAE mode of operation (denoted PPAE_f) is *the way the input to the internal permutation f is formatted*. This formatting plays a vital role in the attacks developed in this work. Next we touch upon PPAE_f and the internal permutation of PAEQ called AESQ.

2.1   PPAE Mode of Operation

PPAE_f (illustrated in Algorithm 1) can be instantiated with an n-bit permutation f. The inputs to the permutation are formatted as $(D_i||counter||N||K)$ for each plaintext block and $(D_i||counter||AD\text{-}block||K)$ for processing associated data (AD) where $D_i \rightarrow$ domain separator, $N \rightarrow$ nonce and $K \rightarrow$ key. The plaintext and AD are divided into blocks of size $n - k - 16$ and $n - 2k - 16$ respectively where k is the key-size. Incomplete last blocks are padded using the byte-length of the block and domain separators are changed accordingly. Plaintext processing and authentication calls f twice while AD data is authenticated using a single call. Partial authentication data from all branches are passed to a final call to f, the output of which is optionally truncated to get the tag. The entire operation is depicted in Fig. 1. An interested reader can refer to [2,4] for details.

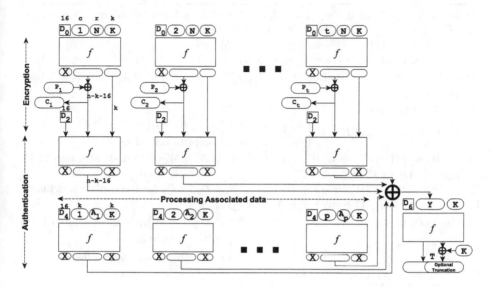

Fig. 1. Encryption & Authentication with PAEQ

2.2 The Internal Permutation: AESQ

Definition 1 (Word [9]). *Let $\mathbb{T} = \mathbb{F}[x]/(x^8 + x^4 + x^3 + x + 1)$ be the field $\mathbb{F}_{2^8}$ used in AES MixColumns operation. Then a **word** is defined as an element of $\mathbb{T}$.*

A **word** is just a **byte** redefined to account for the field arithmetic. In this work, we will come across *partially specified states/sub-states* where certain words might have unknown values. To capture this scenario, we use the symbol 'X' to represent unknown words. Thus, to be precise a **word** is an element of $\mathbb{T} \cup \{\,{}'X'\,\}$.

Definition 2 (Sub-state, State [9]). *The internal **state** of the AESQ permutation is defined as a 4-tuple of sub-states where each sub-state is a (4×4)-word matrix.*

A state is denoted by s, while each sub-state is represented by $s^m = [s^m_{i,j}]$ where $s^m_{i,j}$ are the elements of s^m and m denotes the **sub-state index** i.e., the relative position of the sub-state inside the state. We denote a column of $[s^m_{i,j}]$ as $s^m_{*,j}$ while a row is referred to as $s^m_{i,*}$.

$$s^m = [s^m_{i,j}], \text{ where } \begin{cases} s_{i,j} \in \mathbb{T} \cup \{\,'X'\,\} \\ 0 \leq i,j < 4; \quad m \in \{1,2,3,4\} \end{cases} \qquad s = (s^1, s^2, s^3, s^4)$$

Algorithm 1. $\text{PPAE}_f(P, N, K, A, n)[9]$

Input: $\begin{cases} P \to \text{Plaintext}, & N \to \text{Nonce}, \quad |N| = r, \quad K \to \text{Key}, \quad |K| = k \\ A \to \text{Associated Data}, & f \to \text{Internal permutation}, \quad n \to \text{Internal state size} \end{cases}$

Output: $C, T \to$ Ciphertext and Tag

1: $D_i = (k, (r + i) \mod 256)$, $i = 1, 2, \cdots, 6$ ▷ Generating 2-byte domain separators
2: $\{P_1, P_2, \cdots, P_t\} \leftarrow P$ $\quad |P_i| = (n - k - 16)$ bits
3: $\{A_1, A_2, \cdots, A_p\} \leftarrow A$ $\quad |A_i| = (n - 2k - 16)$ bits
4: **if** $(|P_t| < n - k - 16)$ **then** $P_t \leftarrow P_t||a||a\cdots||a$ $\quad \triangleright a = |P_t|/8$ and $|a| = 1$ byte
5: **if** $(|A_p| < n - 2k - 16)$ **then** $A_p \leftarrow A_p||b||b\cdots||b$ $\quad \triangleright b = |A_p|/8$ and $|b| = 1$ byte
6: $Y = 0$ $\quad \triangleright |Y| = n - k - 16$
7: **for** $i = 1$ to t **do**
8: $\quad V_i \leftarrow D_0||R_i||N||K$ $\quad \triangleright \begin{cases} R_i \to \text{Branch Index}, R_i = i, |R_i| = n - k - r - 16 \\ D_0 \to D_1 \text{ for incomplete last block} \end{cases}$
9: $\quad W_i \leftarrow f(V_i); \; C_i \leftarrow W_i[17\cdots(n-k)] \oplus P_i$ $\quad \triangleright W[i\cdots j]$ indicates part of W
   from i^{th} bit to j^{th} bit
10: $\quad X_i \leftarrow D_2||C_i||W_i[(n-k+1)\cdots n]$ $\quad \triangleright D_2 \to D_3$ for incomplete last block
11: $\quad Y_i \leftarrow (f(X_i))[17\cdots(n-k)]; \; Y \leftarrow Y \bigoplus Y_i$
12: **for** $i = 1$ to p **do** $\quad \triangleright$ Binding Associated Data
13: $\quad X_i' \leftarrow D_4||R_i||A_i||K$ $\quad \triangleright \begin{cases} R_i = i, \; |R_i| = k \\ D_4 \to D_5 \text{ for incomplete last block} \end{cases}$
14: $\quad Y_i' \leftarrow (f(X_i'))[17\cdots(n-k)]$
15: $\quad Y \leftarrow Y \bigoplus Y_i'$
16: $T \leftarrow f(D_6||Y||K) \oplus (0^{n-k}||K)$
17: $C = \{C_1, C_2, \cdots, C_t\}$ $\quad \triangleright$ Truncate C_t for incomplete last plaintext block

The AESQ permutation is a composition of 20 round functions with a Shuffle operation(denoted by $\mathscr{S}$, Ref. Table 2) after every 2 rounds. Each round-function is denoted by $\mathcal{R}_r$ where the index r denotes the rth round of AESQ. Every round applies on the internal state a composition of four bijective functions which are basically the standard AES round operations SubBytes, ShiftRows, MixColumns, AddRoundConstants applied individually on each sub-state. In the context, of a state we refer to these functions as QuadSubBytes, QuadShiftRows, QuadMixColumns, QuadAddRoundConstants and denote them as β_r, ρ_r, μ_r and α_r respectively. The reference to a sub-state is addressed by including the sub-state index in notation. For example, to refer to the MixColumns on the second sub-state in $\mathcal{R}_{17}$ we use μ_{17}^2. When considering a sub-state in $\mathcal{R}_r$ we refer to round function applied individually to the sub-state as $\mathcal{R}_r^m$ by including the sub-state index in the notation. This implies that for an internal state s the output of the rth round of AESQ is $\mathcal{R}_r(s) = \mathcal{R}_r^1(s^1)||\mathcal{R}_r^2(s^2)||\mathcal{R}_r^3(s^3)||\mathcal{R}_r^4(s^4)$.

$$\text{AESQ} = \mathscr{S} \circ \mathcal{R}_{20} \circ \mathcal{R}_{19} \circ \cdots \circ \mathscr{S} \circ \mathcal{R}_2 \circ \mathcal{R}_1$$
$$\mathcal{R}_r = \alpha_r \circ \mu_r \circ \rho_r \circ \beta_r; \quad \mathcal{R}_r^m = \alpha_r^m \circ \mu_r^m \circ \rho_r^m \circ \beta_r^m$$

Table 2. Column mapping under `Shuffle` ($\mathscr{S}$)

	s^1				s^2				s^3				s^4			
From	$s^1_{*,0}$	$s^1_{*,1}$	$s^1_{*,2}$	$s^1_{*,3}$	$s^2_{*,0}$	$s^2_{*,1}$	$s^2_{*,2}$	$s^2_{*,3}$	$s^3_{*,0}$	$s^3_{*,1}$	$s^3_{*,2}$	$s^3_{*,3}$	$s^4_{*,0}$	$s^4_{*,1}$	$s^4_{*,2}$	$s^4_{*,3}$
To	$s^1_{*,3}$	$s^4_{*,3}$	$s^3_{*,2}$	$s^2_{*,2}$	$s^1_{*,1}$	$s^4_{*,1}$	$s^3_{*,0}$	$s^2_{*,0}$	$s^1_{*,2}$	$s^4_{*,2}$	$s^3_{*,3}$	$s^2_{*,3}$	$s^1_{*,0}$	$s^4_{*,0}$	$s^3_{*,1}$	$s^2_{*,1}$

Round-reduced `AESQ` permutation is denoted by $\texttt{AESQ}^n$ where $n = 2k, 1 \leq k \leq 9$. Thus $\texttt{AESQ}^n = \mathscr{S} \circ \mathcal{R}_n \circ \mathcal{R}_{n-1} \circ \cdots \circ \mathscr{S} \circ \mathcal{R}_2 \circ \mathcal{R}_1$. Since n is even, it implies that we consider reductions in steps of two-rounds and $\texttt{AESQ}^n$ always ends in the $\mathscr{S}$ operation. Finally, the round constant for sub-state m in round r of `AESQ` is given by: $rc_r^m = ((r-1) * 4 + m)$. In α_r^m, rc_r^m is added to all words of row $s_{1,*}^m$.

3 Handling Partially Specified States/Sub-states

As mentioned earlier in this work we have to handle states or sub-states that may have multiple unknown values. To capture this notion formally we introduce the following definition.

Definition 3 (Byte-Entropy). *The Byte-Entropy of a state/sub-state, denoted by $\mathscr{E}$, is defined as the number of unknown bytes in the state/sub-state.*

$$\mathscr{E}(s^m) = \left|\{s_{i,j}^m = \text{`X'}, \forall i,j\}\right|; \qquad \mathscr{E}(s) = \sum_{\forall s^m \in s} \mathscr{E}(s^m)$$

Consequently, if a state/sub-state is completely specified, then its Byte-Entropy is zero. The definition can be analogously applied on individual columns in which case it would account for the number of unknown bytes in a column of a sub-state i.e., for the jth column of the mth sub-state, $\mathscr{E}(s_{*,j}^m) = \left|\{s_{i,j}^m = \text{`X'}, \forall i\}\right|$. We now define how the operations $\beta_r^m, \rho_r^m, \mu_r^m$ and α_r^m behave when the Byte-Entropy of a sub-state $s^m = [s_{i,j}^m]$ is $\mathscr{E}(s^m) > 0$.

- `SubBytes`: Under `SubBytes` unknowns remain unknown thereby preserving the Byte-Entropy of the sub-state: $\mathscr{E}(\beta_r^m(s^m)) = \mathscr{E}(s^m)$. Below SBOX denotes the AES Substitution box.

$$s_{i,j}^m \xrightarrow{\beta_r^m} \begin{cases} \text{X} & \text{if } s_{i,j}^m = \text{X} \\ \texttt{SBOX}(s_{i,j}^m) & \text{Otherwise} \end{cases}$$

- `ShiftRows`: ρ_r^m does not rely on values of s^m. Thus, the unknown values just shift their positions and we have $\mathscr{E}(\rho_r^m(s^m)) = \mathscr{E}(s^m)$.
- `MixColumns`: The situation changes with `MixColumns` since to apply μ_r^m one needs to know the entire input column. Hence, under μ_r^m the Byte-Entropy of a sub-state *may* increase: $\mathscr{E}(\mu_r^m(s^m)) \geq \mathscr{E}(s^m)$. Below M_μ denotes the `MixColumns` matrix.

$$s_{*,j}^m \xrightarrow{\mu_r^m} \begin{cases} M_\mu \times s_{*,j}^m & \text{if } \forall i, s_{i,j}^m \neq \text{X}; \\ \{\text{X}, \text{X}, \text{X}, \text{X}\}^T & \text{Otherwise}; \end{cases} \qquad \begin{aligned} \mathscr{E}(\mu_r^m(s_{*,j}^m)) &= \mathscr{E}(s_{*,j}^m) \\ \mathscr{E}(\mu_r^m(s_{*,j}^m)) &\geq \mathscr{E}(s_{*,j}^m) \end{aligned}$$

- AddRoundConstants: Here, again there is no effect on the Byte-Entropy i.e.,
$\mathscr{E}(\alpha_r^m(s^m)) = \mathscr{E}(s^m)$.

$$s_{i,j}^m \xrightarrow{\alpha_r^m} \begin{cases} s_{i,j}^m & \text{if } i \neq 1 \\ s_{i,j}^m \oplus rc_r^m & \text{if } s_{i,j}^m \neq \text{X} \\ \text{X} & \text{Otherwise} \end{cases}$$

Thus, we see that the only operation that affects the Byte-Entropy of a sub-state and thereby a state is MixColumns. It is evident that the inverse of these operations behave in the same way while dealing with partially specified states.

4   Some Observations on PAEQ

Observation 1 (Limited Key Diffusion). *For primary PAEQ variants, key diffusion is limited to the fourth sub-state after first two rounds of AESQ.*

Remark 1. This follows from the fact that for paeq-64/80/128 the key is absorbed in the fourth sub-state and the first two rounds only diffuse it inside the sub-state keeping the rest of the state independent of the key. This is depicted in Fig. 2. □

Observation 2 (The Three-Fourth Rule). *The Byte-Entropy of every column of every sub-state of the state after ρ_3 (i.e., before μ_3) is **one**, i.e., three-fourth of the state (each sub-state/column) is known to the attacker.*

$$\mathscr{E}(s_{*,j}^m) = 1, \quad \forall (m, j); \quad s \xleftarrow{\rho_3 \, \circ \, \beta_3 \, \circ \, AESQ^2} r$$

where, r is the input state of AESQ corresponding to any parallel branch during the encryption phase of PAEQ.

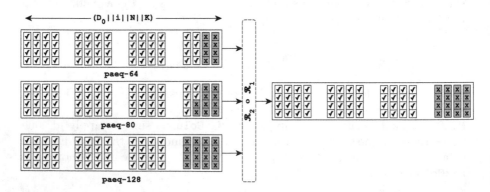

Fig. 2. Key Diffusion after first two rounds of AESQ. Unknown bytes before and after key diffusion are denoted by 'X'.

Remark 2. This property is an implication of Observation 1 and the fact that for any of `paeq-64/80/128` at least three-fourths of the input is always known to an attacker. One can recall that the input r to AESQ during the encryption phase is given by $r = (D_0||i||N||K)$ where, D_0 is the domain separator, i is the counter value for the particular parallel branch, N is the nonce while K forms the key. Here the only unknown is K and since $|K| \leq 128$ bits and $|(D_0||i||N||K)| = 512$ bits, so at least three-fourths of the input or three out of the four input sub-states are known. Now let us see how the Byte-Entropy changes:

- At input r: $\mathscr{E}(r^m) \begin{cases} = 0 & 1 \leq m \leq 3 \\ \leq 16 & m = 4. \end{cases}$
- After $\mathcal{R}_1$ and $\mathcal{R}_2$: The Byte-Entropy of the first three sub-states remains same since by Observation 1 they are independent of the fourth one.

$$q \xleftarrow{\mathcal{R}_2^m \circ \mathcal{R}_1^m} r; \qquad \mathscr{E}(q^m) = \begin{cases} 0 & 1 \leq m \leq 3 \\ 16 & m = 4. \end{cases}$$

- After $\mathscr{S}$: The $\mathscr{S}$ operation just permutes the known and unknown columns resulting in a state where each sub-state has one unknown column.

$$p \xleftarrow{\mathscr{S}} q; \qquad \mathscr{E}(p^m) = 4, \ \forall m; \qquad \mathscr{E}(p^m_{*,j}) = \begin{cases} 4 & \text{if } \mathscr{S}^{-1}(p^m_{*,j}) \in q^4; \\ 0 & \text{Otherwise;} \end{cases}$$

- After β_3 and ρ_3: As per Sect. 3, we know that β_3 and ρ_3 keep the Byte-Entropy unaltered. However, due to ρ_3, the unknown column of each sub-state is dispersed giving a state where every column has exactly one unknown byte.

$$s \xleftarrow{\rho_3 \circ \beta_3} q; \qquad \mathscr{E}(s^m) = 4, \ \forall m; \qquad \mathscr{E}(s^m_{*,j}) = 1, \ \forall (m,j)$$

At this point we stop as propagating forward leads to a completely unknown state. The entire forward propagation is illustrated in Fig. 3.   □

Observation 3 (One-Fourth Inversion). *If the attacker has knowledge of a single sub-state after $\mathcal{R}_n$, then he can invert and determine the partial state before α_{n-3} (or after μ_{n-3}) where exactly one byte is known in every column*[1].

$$\mathscr{E}(s^m_{*,j}) = 3, \quad \forall (m,j); \qquad s \xleftarrow{(\alpha_{n-3})^{-1} \circ \mathscr{S}^{-1} \circ (\mathcal{R}_{n-1})^{-1} \circ (\mathcal{R}_n)^{-1}} r$$

where, r is the state after $\mathcal{R}_n$ and $\exists k : \mathscr{E}(r^m) = 0$, if $m = k$.

Remark 3. A sub-state, if known at the end of of the nth round of AESQ, can be inverted two rounds without the knowledge of the entire state. After inversion the known sub-state diffuses in the remaining unknown state due to $\mathscr{S}^{-1}$. The resulting state has one known column in every sub-state. This partially specified

---

[1] It is understood that here $2|n$.

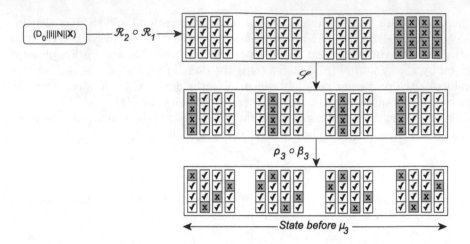

Fig. 3. Demonstration of Three-Fourth Rule applicable to `paeq-64/80/128`. Unknown bytes are shown as 'X'.

state can be inverted one more round followed by $(\alpha)^{-1}$ operation of the previous round. We can no longer *usefully* invert the state by applying $(\mu)^{-1}$ since now every column has only *one* known byte. The process of inverting a known sub-state to get a one-fourth partially specified state is captured by Algorithm 2 and also pictorially presented in Fig. 4.   □

Algorithm 2. ONEFOURTHINV(s^m, n)

Input: $\begin{cases} s^m \rightarrow \text{Input sub-state} \\ n \rightarrow \text{Round from which inversion starts } (2|n) \end{cases}$
Output: $t \rightarrow$ The partial state after μ_{n-3}

1: $s^m \leftarrow (\mathcal{R}_{n-1}^m)^{-1} \circ (\mathcal{R}_n^m)^{-1}(s^m)$
2: $t = (t^1, t^2, t^3, t^4) \leftarrow \mathbf{X}$ ▷ All unknown state
3: $t^m \leftarrow s^m$ ▷ Partial state with only sub-state m specified
4: $t \leftarrow \mathscr{S}^{-1}(t)$ ▷ One column of each sub-state known
5: $t \leftarrow (\alpha_{n-3})^{-1} \circ (\mathcal{R}_{n-2})^{-1}(t)$ ▷ Every column has exactly one *known* byte
6: **return** t

With these observations in place we now present a theorem which forms the basis of the key-recovery attack presented in this work.

Theorem 1 (Meet-in-the-middle). *For $n = 6$, the Three-fourth Rule and One-Fourth Inversion strategy converge at the input and output of μ_3 respectively which results in a unique solution for input of μ_3.*

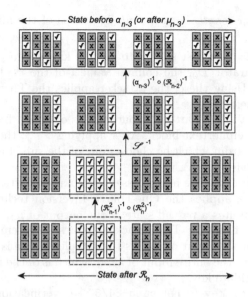

Fig. 4. Demonstration of One-Fourth Inversion (Observation 3) assuming that attacker has knowledge of sub-state 2 after $\mathcal{R}_n$ of AESQ.

Proof. The Three-fourth Rule always leads the attacker to a partial state before μ_3. As regards Observation 3, plugging the value of $n - 6$ shows that the attacker is able to reach a partial state after μ_3. So the convergence is apparent. Now to show that this leads to a unique solution for the unknown bytes of the input of μ_3 one has to just recall that the input and output of μ_3 are linearly related: $output = M_\mu \times input$. Now, for every input column we can form a linear equation using the known byte of the corresponding output column. Since these equations have only one[2] unknown, so solving all such equations gives unique solution for the input of μ_3.   □

In the next section we introduce the key-recovery attacks against PAEQ reduced to 6 and 7 rounds. We first illustrate the 6-round attack and then present the one-round extension.

5 Gain₆ : Key Recovery Attack on PAEQ⁶ = PPAE_{AESQ⁶}

Here we consider PAEQ with rounds of AESQ reduced to 6. As mentioned earlier AESQ⁶ is given as $AESQ^6 = \mathcal{S} \circ \mathcal{R}_6 \circ \mathcal{R}_5 \circ \cdots \circ \mathcal{S} \circ \mathcal{R}_2 \circ \mathcal{R}_1$. The attack requires a single plaintext/ciphertext block pair corresponding to *any*[3] parallel branch

---

[2] The unknown byte of the input column.

[3] Except the last branch when the last message block is incomplete. This is because for last incomplete block output is further truncated resulting in loss of information available to the attacker.

and is hence *message-length independent*. The steps of the attack are given as below:

- **Use AESQ^6 input**: The first step is to use the knowledge publicly available: the Domain separator D_0, the counter value i of the ith branch, the value of the nonce N. Using these, the attacker applies the Three-Fourth Rule to reach the state before μ_3.
- **Use AESQ^6 output**: The partial output state is obtained from the xor of the ith plaintext and ciphertext block. After applying $\mathscr{S}^{-1}$, the attacker reaches the output of $\mathcal{R}_6$ from which he chooses one of the sub-states with the least Byte-Entropy (Refer Fig. 5).
- **Guess and determine**: He now guesses the unknown bytes of the sub-state. For each guess he applies the One-Fourth Inversion technique (Ref. Algorithm 2) and computes a partial state at the output of μ_3.
- **Recover input of AESQ^6**: The attacker applies Theorem 1 to recover the unknown bytes at the input of μ_3. As the complete state is known, it can be inverted to retrieve the entire input of AESQ^6 which is of the form: $D_0||i||N||k$, k being the candidate key.
- **Verify candidate key k**: For paeq-64/80 key verification is equivalent to verifying the value of the nonce. This is because the a part of the nonce and the key together form the fourth sub-state of the input. This cannot be done for paeq-128 since the key forms the entire fourth sub-state. So for paeq-128 key verification is done by recomputing AESQ^6 and comparing with the values observed by the attacker from the xor of plaintext and ciphertext block. Algorithm 3 precisely states the verification procedure.

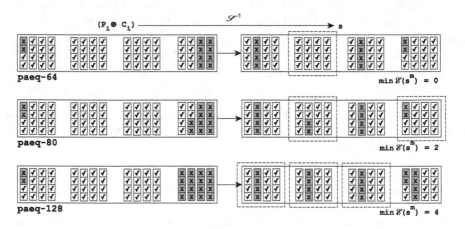

Fig. 5. Sub-state with minimum Byte-Entropy for AESQ^6.

The key verification concludes the key-recovery process. The complete attack on 6 rounds, referred to as GAIN$_6$ is given by Algorithm 4. In the next section we highlight how this attack can be extended one more round using an invert-guess-invert approach with re-uses the 6-round attack.

Algorithm 3. $\text{VERIFYKEY}(q, N_x, N, \Bbbk)$

$$\text{Input:} \begin{cases} q \to \text{Output state } (P_i \oplus C_i) \\ N_x \to \text{Computed Nonce} \quad N \to \text{Actual Nonce} \\ \Bbbk \to \text{Key candidate to be verified} \end{cases}$$

Output: TRUE/FALSE

1: **if** $(|\Bbbk| == 64) \,||\, (|\Bbbk| == 80)$ **then**
2:    **if** $N_x == N$ **then**
3:       **return** TRUE
4:    **else if** $(|\Bbbk| == 128)$ **then**
5:       **if** $(\text{AESQ}^6(D_0||i||N_x||\Bbbk) == q)$ **then**   ▷ Verify known values of q
6:          **return** TRUE
7: **return** FALSE

---

6 Gain_7 : Extending the attack to $\text{PAEQ}^7 = \text{PPAE}_{\text{AESQ}^7}$

Before we proceed with the attack, it is important to understand the way we visualize AESQ^7. This is because in Sect. 2.2 we mentioned that while considering round-reduced version of AESQ: AESQ^n, n is always even to ensure that AESQ^n always ends with the $\mathscr{S}$ operation. In order to meet this AESQ^7 is visualized as below:

$$\text{AESQ}^7 \equiv \text{AESQ}^8 - \mathcal{R}_8$$
$$= \mathscr{S} \circ \mathcal{R}_7 \circ \text{AESQ}^6$$

The attack on PAEQ^7 uses the attack on PAEQ^6 as a sub-routine. The attacker uses the observable output of AESQ^7 and inverts it up to the input of $\mathcal{R}_7$. This state can be directly used as an input to the PAEQ^6 key-recovery attack since it is equivalent to the output of AESQ^6. Consequently, the rest of the attack proceeds as before. The only difference inside the six round attack (Algorithm 4) is in Step 3 due to the following observation.

Observation 4. *The state* $\mathscr{S}^{-1} \circ (\mathcal{R}_7)^{-1} \circ \mathscr{S}^{-1}(P_i \oplus C_i)$ *has the property that every sub-state has the same Byte-Entropy.*

$$\mathscr{E}(s^m) = \mathscr{E}(s^n) \;\; \forall (s^m, s^n) \in s \;\; where \;\; s \xleftarrow{\;\mathscr{S}^{-1} \circ (\mathcal{R}_7)^{-1} \circ \mathscr{S}^{-1}\;} (P_i \oplus C_i)$$

Due to this, the attacker need not choose a sub-state with minimum Byte-Entropy and can instead choose any sub-state to start the guess and determine part without affecting the complexity of guessing. This extension to seven rounds is captured by Algorithm 5.

7 Gain_8 : A Guess-Invert-Guess attack on $\text{PAEQ}^8 = \text{PPAE}_{\text{AESQ}^{8\dagger}}$

As stated earlier, AESQ^n ends with the $\mathscr{S}$ operation. In the 8-round attack we deviate from this convention and drop the last shuffle. It is worth mentioning

---

Algorithm 4. $\text{GAIN}_6(q, i)$

Input: $\begin{cases} q = (q^1, q^2, q^3, q^4) \to P_i \oplus C_i & \text{(Output of 6 rounds as seen by attacker)} \\ i \to \text{Branch Index (Counter value)} \end{cases}$

Output: $k \to$ The Master Key

1: $v \xleftarrow[\text{Three-fourth Rule}]{\rho_3 \circ \beta_3 \circ \text{AESQ}^2} D_0||i||N||\mathbf{X}$ ▷ Columns of v have exactly one *unknown* byte

2: $s \leftarrow \mathscr{S}^{-1}(q)$

3: Choose $s^m \in \left\{ s^m : \min_{\forall s^m \in s} \mathscr{E}(s^m) \right\}$

4: **for** Each guess of $(s^m_{i,j} == \text{'X'}), \forall i, j$ **do**

5:     $t \leftarrow \text{ONEFOURTHINV}(s^m, 6)$ ▷ Columns of t have exactly one *known* byte

6:     $v \xleftarrow[\text{Theorem 1}]{\text{Solve } t = \mu_3(v)} (t, v)$ ▷ $\begin{cases} \text{Meet-in-the-middle step} \\ \text{Recovers unknown bytes of } v \end{cases}$

7:     $v \xleftarrow{(\text{AESQ}^2)^{-1} \circ (\beta_3)^{-1} \circ (\rho_3)^{-1}} v$ ▷ AESQ input state

8:     $v = (D_0||i||N_x||k)$

9:     **if** $\text{VERIFYKEY}(q, N_x, N, k) == \mathbf{TRUE}$ **then**

10:         **return** k

Algorithm 5. $\text{GAIN}_7(s, i)$

Input: $\begin{cases} q = (q^1, q^2, q^3, q^4) \to P_i \oplus C_i & \text{(Output of 7 rounds as seen by attacker)} \\ i \to \text{Branch Index (Counter value)} \end{cases}$

Output: $k \to$ The Master Key

1: $s = (\mathcal{R}_7)^{-1} \circ \mathscr{S}^{-1}(q)$ ▷ Inversion with partial state

2: $k \leftarrow \text{GAIN}_6(s, i)$

3: **return** k

---

that the CICO attack described by the designers of **PAEQ** also does the same thing while considering 8 rounds of **AESQ** permutation. This can be visualized as below:

$$\text{AESQ}^{8\dagger} \equiv \text{AESQ}^8 - \mathscr{S}$$
$$= \mathcal{R}_8 \circ \mathcal{R}_7 \circ \text{AESQ}^6$$

The 8-round attack is similar to the 7-round version with the only difference that it follows a guess-invert-guess approach. Here the attacker first guesses the first two bytes of the first substate of $(P_i \oplus C_i)$. It should be noted that this guess yields a state where the first three substates are completely known. He then inverts $\mathcal{R}_8$ and $\mathcal{R}_7$. The attack now be mapped to GAIN_6. Like the last section, we again have a uniform Byte-Entropy situation arising due to the following observation:

Observation 5. *For every guess of the first two bytes of the first substate of $P_i \oplus C_i$, all substates of the state $\mathscr{S}^{-1} \circ (\mathcal{R}_7)^{-1} \circ (\mathcal{R}_8)^{-1}(P_i \oplus C_i)$ have a Byte-*

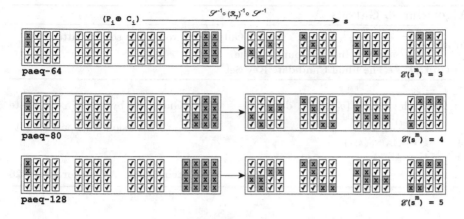

Fig. 6. Uniform Byte-Entropy at $\mathcal{R}_6$ output for AESQ[7].

Entropy = 4.

$$\mathcal{E}(s^m) = 4 \ \forall s^m \in s \ where \ s \xleftarrow{\mathscr{S}^{-1} \circ (\mathcal{R}_7)^{-1} \circ (\mathcal{R}_8)^{-1}} (P_i \oplus C_i)$$

This corresponding state configuration is depicted in Fig. 7. The uniform Byte-Entropy of 4 implies that the attacker can choose *any* substate to execute to continue with the guess-and-determine step of the 6-round attack and would in the process the would incur a complexity of 2^{32}. Since he has to repeat this for every guess of the first two bytes of $P_i \oplus C_i$, the final complexity of GAIN6 stands at $2^{16+32} = 2^{48}$. Algorithm 6 summarizes the idea of the attack. In the next section we present a overview of the complexity of the GAIN attacks.

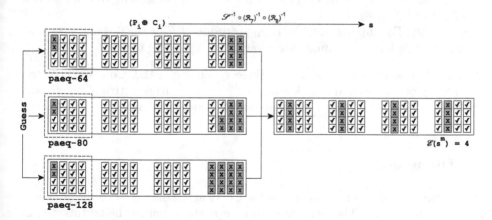

Fig. 7. Demonstration of uniform Byte-Entropy of 4 due to two byte guess of $P_i \oplus C_i$

Algorithm 6. $\text{GAIN}_8(s, i)$

Input: $\begin{cases} q = (q^1, q^2, q^3, q^4) \to P_i \oplus C_i & \text{(Output of 8 rounds as seen by attacker)} \\ i \to \text{Branch Index (Counter value)} \end{cases}$

Output: $\mathcal{K} \to$ The Final Candidate Key Set

1: $\mathcal{K} = \varnothing$

2: **for** Each guess of $(q_{0,0}^1, q_{1,0}^1)$ **do**   ▷ Guess two bytes of first substate

3:     $s \xleftarrow{(\mathcal{R}_7)^{-1} \circ (\mathcal{R}_8)^{-1}} q$ ▷ Inversion with partial state

4:     $k \leftarrow \text{GAIN}_6(s, i)$

5:     $\mathcal{K} \leftarrow \mathcal{K} \cup k$

6: **return** $\mathcal{K}$ ▷ $|\mathcal{K}| = 1$ for `paeq-64/80`, $|\mathcal{K}| > 1$ for `paeq-128`

---

8 Complexity Analysis

It suffices to study the complexity of the 6-round attack taking into account Observation 4 for the seven round version and Observation 5 for 8-round attack. As regards the attack on PAEQ^6 one can easily infer from Algorithm 4 that the complexity is governed by the loop (Step 4) pertaining to the guessing of the unknown bytes of the sub-state. Thus the complexity is given by 2^{8u}, where u is the minimum Byte-Entropy of a sub-state at the output of $\mathcal{R}_6$ i.e., $u = \min_{\forall s^m \in s} \mathscr{E}(s^m)$. However, as stated earlier, for GAIN_8, the 6-round attack needs to be repeated for every guess of the first two bytes of the first substate of the state observed by the attacker leading to a complexity of 2^{16+8u}.

- `paeq-64`: Interestingly, for `paeq-64`, $u = 0$ because the second sub-state is completely known. Thus we do not have to guess anything for GAIN_6. For, GAIN_7 $u = 3$ thereby increasing the complexity to 2^{24}.
- `paeq-80`: Here $u = 2$ for GAIN_6 and $u = 4$ for GAIN_7 leading to complexities of 2^{16} and 2^{32} respectively.
- `paeq-128`: For this variant, the complexity hits 2^{32} for the 6-round attack as $u = 4$ while for the 7-round extension it hits 2^{40} owing to $u = 5$.

As regards GAIN_8, $u = 4$ for all the three versions of PAEQ. Consequently, the complexity of the 8-round attack reaches $2^{16+32} = 2^{48}$ irrespective of the variant under consideration. Table 3 summarizes the complexity analysis of the GAIN attacks.

9 Discussion

It is worth comparing and contrasting the CICO attack mounted by the designers to the current work. The first thing to note is the primitive being targeted in each attack. While the CICO attack is based on the internal permutation AESQ, GAIN exploits properties of both AESQ and the PPAE mode of operation of PAEQ. Targeting only AESQ gives the designers higher degrees of freedom while choosing

Table 3. Complexities of GAIN.

GAIN	PAEQ	$u = \min\limits_{\forall s^m \in s} \mathscr{E}(s^m)$	$s^m : \mathscr{E}(s^m) = u$	Complexity $2^{8u} \leftarrow \text{GAIN}_{6/7}$ $2^{16+8u} \leftarrow \text{GAIN}_8$
GAIN$_6$ $s \xleftarrow{\mathscr{S}^{-1}} (P_i \oplus C_i)$	paeq-64	0	s^2	1
	paeq-80	2	s^2, s^3	2^{16}
	paeq-128	4	s^1, s^2, s^3	2^{32}
GAIN$_7$ $s \xleftarrow{\mathscr{S}^{-1} \circ (\mathcal{R}_7)^{-1} \circ \mathscr{S}^{-1}} (P_i \oplus C_i)$	paeq-64	3	s^1, s^2, s^3, s^4 Ref. Fig.6	2^{24}
	paeq-80	4		2^{32}
	paeq-128	5		2^{40}
GAIN$_8$ $s \xleftarrow{\mathscr{S}^{-1} \circ (\mathcal{R}_7)^{-1} \circ (\mathcal{R}_8)^{-1}} (P_i \oplus C_i)$ First Guess 2 Bytes (Ref. Algorithm 6)	paeq-64	4	s^1, s^2, s^3, s^4 Ref. Fig. 7	2^{48}
	paeq-80	4		2^{48}
	paeq-128	4		2^{48}

constrained-inputs and constrained-outputs since the input formatting and the output truncation are no longer a concern. Moreover, though the designers say that they consider a 8-round version of AESQ, they do not explicitly mention that they ignore the Shuffle operation after the 8th round. If the Shuffle is included, then the CICO attack with the claimed complexity of 2^{32} is not applicable anymore. In GAIN$_8$, we follow the same convention for 8-round AESQ as followed by the designers. However, we show an attack which is applicable to the entire scheme with 2^{16} times the overhead of the CICO attack.

10   Conclusion

This work deploys guess-and-determine analysis against variants of CAESAR Round 2 candidate PAEQ penetrating up to 8 out of the 20 rounds. A deterministic forward path is shown while a backward path is devised based on guessing the unknown bytes of the sub-state with least Byte-Entropy at the output of 6th round. The paths are shown to converge at input and output of the MixColumns of round 3. Solving linear system of equations leads to determination of the key bytes. The extension to seven rounds uses a simple tweak of inverting the seventh round and then applying the 6-round attack. The 8-round attack uses a similar approach but starts with an initial guess of two bytes. All attacks reported have practical complexities. For paeq-64/80/128, the key recovery complexity is respectively 1, 2^{16}, 2^{32} for GAIN_6 attack and 2^{24}, 2^{32}, 2^{40} for GAIN_7 attack while GAIN_8 can be mounted with a uniform complexity of 2^{48} for all the three variants.

References

1. Al Fardan, N.J., Paterson, K.G.: Lucky thirteen: breaking the TLS and DTLS record protocols. In: IEEE Symposium on Security and Privacy 2013, pp. 526–540. IEEE (2013)
2. Alex Biryukov, D.K.: PAEQ v1 (2014). http://competitions.cr.yp.to/round1/paeqv1.pdf
3. Bagheri, N., Mendel, F., Sasaki, Y.: Improved rebound attacks on AESQ: core permutation of CAESAR candidate PAEQ. In: Liu, J.K., Steinfeld, R. (eds.) ACISP 2016. LNCS, vol. 9723, pp. 301–316. Springer, Heidelberg (2016). doi:10.1007/978-3-319-40367-0_19
4. Biryukov, A., Khovratovich, D.: PAEQ: parallelizable permutation-based authenticated encryption. In: Chow, S.S.M., Camenisch, J., Hui, L.C.K., Yiu, S.M. (eds.) ISC 2014. LNCS, vol. 8783, pp. 72–89. Springer, Heidelberg (2014). doi:10.1007/978-3-319-13257-0_5
5. Boura, C., Chakraborti, A., Leurent, G., Paul, G., Saha, D., Soleimany, H., Suder, V.: Key recovery attack against 2.5-round π-cipher. In: Peyrin, T. (ed.) FSE 2016. LNCS, vol. 9783, pp. 535–553. Springer, Heidelberg (2016). doi:10.1007/978-3-662-52993-5_27
6. CAESAR: Competition for Authenticated Encryption: Security, Applicability, and Robustness (2014). http://competitions.cr.yp.to/caesar.html/
7. Duong, T., Rizzo, J.: Here Come The XOR Ninjas. White paper, Netifera (2011)
8. Gligoroski, D., Mihajloska, H., Samardjiska, S., Jacobsen, H., El-Hadedy, M., Jensen, R., Otte, D.: π-Cipher v2.0. Submission to the CAESAR Competition (2014). http://competitions.cr.yp.to/caesar-submissions.html/
9. Saha, D., Chowdhury, D.R.: EnCounter: on breaking the nonce barrier in differential fault analysis with a case-study on PAEQ. In: Gierlichs, B., Poschmann, A.Y. (eds.) CHES 2016. LNCS, vol. 9813, pp. 581–601. Springer, Heidelberg (2016). doi:10.1007/978-3-662-53140-2_28

Hardware Security

Predictive Aging of Reliability of Two Delay PUFs

Naghmeh Karimi[1]([⊠]), Jean-Luc Danger[2,3],
Florent Lozac'h[3], and Sylvain Guilley[2,3]

[1] ECE Department, Rutgers University, Piscataway, NJ 08854, USA
naghmeh.karimi@rutgers.edu
[2] LTCI, CNRS, Télécom ParisTech, Université Paris-Saclay, 75013 Paris, France
{jean-luc.danger,sylvain.guilley}@telecom-paristech.fr
[3] Secure-IC SAS, 35510 Cesson-Sévigné, France
{jean-luc.danger,florent.lozach,sylvain.guilley}@secure-ic.com

Abstract. To protect integrated circuits against IP piracy, Physically Unclonable Functions (PUFs) are deployed. PUFs provide a specific signature for each integrated circuit. However, environmental variations, (e.g., temperature change), power supply noise and more influential IC aging affect the functionally of PUFs. Thereby, it is important to evaluate aging effects as early as possible, preferentially at design time. In this paper we investigate the effect of aging on the stability of two delay PUFs: arbiter-PUFs and loop-PUFs and analyze the architectural impact of these PUFS on reliability decrease due to aging.

We observe that the reliability of the arbiter-PUF gets worse over time, whereas the reliability of the loop-PUF remains constant. We interpret this phenomenon by the asymmetric aging of the arbiter, because one half is active (hence aging fast) while the other is not (hence aging slow). Besides, we notice that the aging of the delay chain in the arbiter-PUF and in the loop-PUF has no impact on their reliability, since these PUFs operate differentially.

1 Introduction

With the advancement of VLSI technology, people are increasingly relying on electronic devices and in turn integrated circuits (ICs). Therefore, it is essential to assure the security of the sensitive tasks performed by such devices and to guarantee the security of information stored within these devices.

Having a unique identifier for each electronic chip offers many security benefits. If, for example, the chip is in a smartphone, the identifier can be used to associate the device with a specific service. The identifier can also be used to thwart overbuilding since it can be recorded at fabrication and can later be checked against a whitelist (in this way, overproduced or counterfeited chips can be detected). However, for the identifier to be trusted, it must meet some security properties: essentially, it must be *unique* and it must not be *tamperable*. Physically Unclonable Functions (PUFs) are known as technical solutions [1–3] as they can generate volatile secret keys for a system [4].

© Springer International Publishing AG 2016
C. Carlet et al. (Eds.): SPACE 2016, LNCS 10076, pp. 213–232, 2016.
DOI: 10.1007/978-3-319-49445-6_12

A PUF signature is used either via a Challenge-Response Pair (CRP) protocol for authentication, or to generate a private key or random variable in a ciphering operation. A PUF can avoid the use of digital memory to store a key imposed by the IC manufacturer or the user. Hence PUFs are well suited in low-cost devices such as the RFIDs or smartcards [5]. In practice, PUFs have different applications including cryptographic key generation, device authentication, Intellectual Property (IP) protection, etc.

Indeed, PUFs benefit from process variations which occur during the manufacturing of integrated circuits and thereby each PUF generates a unique signature extracted based on physical characteristics of the circuit elements. The unique behavior after fabrication stems from a *static randomness* due to technological dispersion. It is a well known source of mismatch in electronics circuits design and was characterized by Pelgrom [6] to follow a normal distribution.

The PUF responses are also subject to *dynamic randomness* due to measurement noise, which is detrimental to the reliability of the PUF measurement. For this reason, it is important in practice to increase the signal-to-noise ratio (SNR). In a so-called SRAM-PUF [7] which consists in one SRAM memory bit booting up at either value 0 or 1, it seems difficult to improve the SNR except by repeating measurements, which demands a power down between each measurement. In a delay-PUF [8], n elements are chained, and the total delay of the chain is measured. The SNR is then increased by a factor n as the signal power grows linearly with n. Because of this property, we focus in this paper on delay-PUFs, namely loop-PUF [5] and arbiter-PUF [2, Section 2.2].

PUFs can be deployed as identifiers of electronic chips if the responses (keys) generated by PUFs are reliable and do not change over time. However, similar to other ICs, PUFs are vulnerable to aging mechanisms that jeopardize their reliability over time. In practice, with the advancement of VLSI technology and moving towards nano technologies, run time degradation mechanisms such as Negative-Bias Temperature-Instability (NBTI), Hot-Carrier Injection (HCI), and gate Oxide Breakdown (OB) play a critical role in urging circuits malfunctions [9–13]. In these degradation mechanisms, so-called aging, electrical behavior of transistors eventually deviates from its original intended behavior. This deviation may degrade performance; and consequently, the chip suddenly fails to meet some of the required specifications [14,15].

In practice, NBTI is the main aging mechanism resulting in circuit malfunctions [16]. While NBTI happens continuously when the circuit is powered on, the HCI only happens provided the circuit has some activity: the more activity, the more HCI effect. In this paper, we investigate the effect of NBTI on the reliability of PUFs.

Problem Statement. Different schemes have been proposed in literature to improve the reliability of PUFs against aging effects. In particular, Error Correction Codes (ECCs) are employed in [17] to recover unwanted bit-flips (erroneous bits) in the output of PUFs. However, using ECC for error recovery is costly and its overhead is not negligible in case of multiple errors [4]. Software techniques have been proposed in [18] to combat the aging effects in PUFs. The proposed protocol-level solutions can either detect drifts in PUFs and update the affected challenge/response pairs or prevent such drifts by shortening the lifespan of challenge/response pairs [18].

Guajardo et al. investigated the robustness of SRAM-PUF against aging caused by a specific case of continuous writing of ones and zeros in SRAM cells [19]. Maes et al. also showed that SRAM-PUF aging can be inverted by programming them with the opposite value [20]. This reinforces the bias of the PUF, hence a rejuvenation. However, such technique does not apply to delay-PUFs.

In order to combat aging of ring oscillator PUFs (RO-PUFs), an aging resistant RO-PUF has been proposed in [4]. This ring oscillator stops oscillation when the PUF is not used. Such reconfiguration slows down the aging effects, but there is a need of custom design with the use of pass transistors. Maiti et al. conducted an accelerated aging to investigate the effect of aging on the functionality of RO-PUFs. They proposed a reconfigurable RO-PUF to mitigate aging effects [21]. As the RO-PUF consists in comparing two ROs among a set of identical ROs, the proposed anti-aging method is to choose the ROs which have the maximum frequency differences.

The RO-PUF has the specificity of having many ROs in parallel and the aging has a direct impact when two oscillators behave differently with aging. The contribution of this paper is to study the aging of simpler delay-PUF: the Loop-PUF which has a single delay chain, and the arbiter-PUF which uses two controllable delay chains.

Contributions. We notice that the reliability of the arbiter-PUF decreases with aging, whereas the reliability of the loop-PUF remains unchanged with aging. We manage to explain this discrepancy, by noting that the arbiter (seen as a hardware IP) becomes less reliable over time. The reason is the same as for SRAM-PUF aging: half of the PMOS transistors of the arbiter are conducting, while the other half are blocked. Regarding the delay chains, they age similarly: therefore, their timing difference is not impacted by aging. The loop-PUF does not use an arbiter, therefore its reliability is not affected by aging.

To support this interpretation, we use the fact that:

- Synopsys HSPICE MOSRA tool [22] can be used to simulate the aging effects in PUFs, and
- transient noise in the simulations can be used to simulate the reliability change over time of PUFs, in particular delay-PUFs.

The simulations are validated by real-world experiments on a 65 nm ASIC.

Outline. The remainder of this paper is organized as follows. Section 2 presents a preliminary background on aging mechanisms. Section 3 provides a description of the studied PUFs. The steps taken to evaluate the aging effects using Synopsys MOSRA tool are discussed in Sect. 4. Then, Sect. 5 presents the simulation results depicting the impact of aging on the reliability of PUFs. Confirmation of results on real silicon is presented in Sect. 6. Conclusions and perspectives are drawn in Sect. 7.

2   Aging Mechanisms

Digital circuits can be affected by various aging mechanisms including Negative Bias Temperature Instability (NBTI), Hot Carrier Injection (HCI), Time Dependent Dielectric Breakdown (TDDB), and Electro-Migration (EM) resulting in performance degradation and eventually design failure [23]. Among these aging mechanisms, the NBTI impact on PMOS transistors and the HCI impact on NMOS transistors are more prominent in the reliability of digital circuits. BTI, HCI, and TDDB aging all relate to gate oxides of transistors while EM happens in the interconnect metal lines.

NBTI occurs in a PMOS transistor when a negative voltage is applied to its gate. In this mechanism, positive interface traps are generated at the Si-SiO$_2$ interface. As a result, the threshold voltage increases and the PMOS transistor becomes slower and fails to meet timing constraints.

HCI occurs when hot carriers are injected into the gate dielectric during transistor switching and remain there. HCI is a function of switching activity and degrades the circuit by shifting the threshold voltage and the drain current of transistors under stress [4]. HCI mainly affects NMOS transistors.

TDDB relates to the creation of an electrical current conduction path through the gate oxide in the device. It degrades the isolation properties of gate dielectric, increasing the tunneling current across the transistor gate terminal. Ultimately, TDDB results in device breakdown [24].

High density currents result in EM aging. The currents create electron winds that cause metal atoms to migrate over time, gradually removing metal atoms from wires, thereby increasing interconnect resistance. EM eventually results in an open circuit, creating a permanent error [25].

As the PUF is used mainly to get an identifier or a response to a challenge for authentication, we can consider a rather low switching activity. Consequently we can assume less impact caused by HCI compared to NBTI. This is the reason why we mainly investigate the effect of NBTI on the reliability of PUFs, what follows discusses NBTI effects in more detail.

2.1   Background on NBTI Aging

NBTI is one of the leading factors in performance degradation of digital circuits. In practice, a PMOS transistor experiences two phases of NBTI depending on its bias condition. The first phase, i.e., the stress phase, occurs when the transistor is on, i.e., when a negative voltage (i.e. VGS < Vt, the threshold voltage Vt being negative for a PMOS) is applied to its gate. In the stress phase, positive interface traps are generated at the Si-SiO$_2$ interface. As a result, the magnitude of the threshold voltage Vt of the transistor is increased. In the second phase, i.e., recovery phase, a "positive" voltage (i.e. VGS > Vt) is applied to the gate of the transistor. In this phase, the threshold voltage drift induced by NBTI during the stress phase can partially "recover".

Threshold voltage drifts of a PMOS transistor under stress depend on the physical parameters of the transistor, supply voltage, temperature, and stress

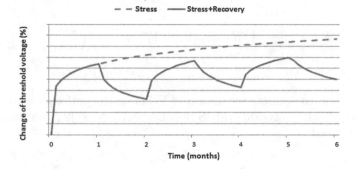

Fig. 1. Change in threshold voltage of a PMOS transistor over time.

time. Figure 1 shows the threshold voltage drift of a sample PMOS transistor that is continuously under stress for 6 months as well as a transistor that is under stress and recovery every other month. As shown, the NBTI effect is high in the first couple of months but the threshold voltage tends to saturate for long stress times. NBTI affect is exacerbated with thinner gate oxide and higher operating temperature [26,27].

Two prevalent theories, Reaction-Diffusion (R-D) and Trapping-Detrapping (T-D), have been proposed in literature to explain NBTI. The R-D model explains the NBTI phenomenon as the breaking and rebonding of hydrogen-silicon bonds at the silicon-gate dielectric interface of PMOS devices [28,29]. The T-D model considers a number of defect states with different energy levels, and capture and emission time constants. In the T-D model, the threshold voltage increases when a trap captures a charge carrier from the channel of a PMOS device [30].

Wang et al. presented an R-D model to evaluate the NBTI effects [31]. In this model, the change in threshold voltage of a PMOS transistor in stress and recovery modes at time t are evaluated by Eqs. (1) and (2), respectively.

$$\Delta V_{th} = \left(K_v (t - t_0)^{0.5} + \sqrt[2n]{\Delta V_{th0}} \right)^{2n} , \text{ and} \tag{1}$$

$$\Delta V_{th} = \Delta V_{th1} \left(1 - \frac{2\xi_1 t_e + \sqrt{\xi_2 C(t - t_1)}}{2t_{ox} + \sqrt{Ct}} \right), \tag{2}$$

where t_0 and t_1 denote the time at which the stress and recovery phases begin, t_e denotes the effective oxide thickness, and ξ_1 and ξ_2 are constants. Parameter n is the time exponent parameter, and for H_2 diffusion, it is $1/6$. K_v and C are computed by using Eqs. (3) and (4), where E_{ox} is the electrical field, T is the temperature, and E_a, K_1, T_0, and k are constants. As shown in Eq. (1), the magnitude of the threshold voltage of a PMOS transistor is increased during stress time.

$$K_v = \left(\frac{qt_{ox}}{\epsilon_{ox}}\right)^3 K_1{}^2 C_{ox}(V_{gs} - V_{th})\sqrt{C} \exp\left(\frac{2E_{ox}}{E_{01}}\right) \quad (3)$$

$$\text{where } C = \exp(-E_a/kT)/T_0. \quad (4)$$

In this paper, to evaluate the impact of NBTI on the performance of a circuit under stress, HSPICE MOSRA (MOS Reliability Analysis) [22] that uses an R-D model is deployed.

3   Loop-PUF and Arbiter-PUF

3.1   Loop-PUF

The *loop-PUF* structure [5] consists of a single delay chain which is looped to form a ring oscillator by means of an inverter. The delay can be obtained with high accuracy as many oscillations (N) are measured.

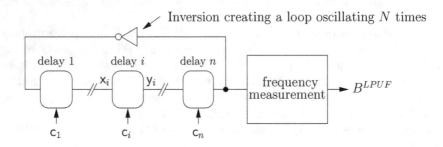

Fig. 2. Loop-PUF structure.

Figure 2 illustrates the Loop-PUF structure composed of n delay elements and Fig. 3 illustrates the detail of one delay element in the chain of n elements. For each $i = 1, 2, \ldots, n$ element, i can have two delays (theoretically equal at blueprint level), chosen according to one challenge bit $c_i \in \{0, 1\}$.

Let $d(c_i)$ be the corresponding delay. As time is an extensive physical quantity, we have

$$d(c_i) = \begin{cases} d_i^{T_1} + d_i^{B_2} = d_i^{TB} & \text{if } c_i = 0, \\ d_i^{B_1} + d_i^{T_2} = d_i^{BT} & \text{if } c_i = 1. \end{cases}$$

The delays d_i^{TB} and d_i^{BT} are modeled as i.i.d. normal random variables selected at fabrication [6]. Actually, variation at fabrication can be explained by many factors, amongst which random dopant fluctuation [32].

The n elements are chained by connecting y_i to x_{i+1}, for $i = 1, \ldots, n - 1$. The principle of the loop-PUF is to measure the difference Δ_C^{LPUF} of cumulative

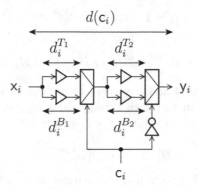

Fig. 3. Delay element i in a Loop-PUF. The output y_i is equal to the input x_i, but occurs after a delay $d(c_i)$.

delays $d(c) = \sum_{i=1}^{n} d(c_i)$ for a challenge $c = (c_1, \ldots, c_n)$ and its complementary value $\neg c = (\neg c_1, \ldots, \neg c_n)$:

$$\Delta_c^{\text{LPUF}} = \text{sign}(\lfloor N \sum_{i=1}^{n} d(c_i) \rfloor - \lfloor N \sum_{i=1}^{n} d(\neg c_i) \rfloor), \tag{5}$$

where N is the number of loops and the $\lfloor \cdot \rfloor$ symbol expresses the quantization of the number of loops. Thus, the LPUF computes response bits based on a mode of operation, given in Protocol 1.

Protocol 1. Protocol to get one bit out of an LPUF using challenge c.

input : Challenge c
output: Response B_c

1 Set challenge c
2 Measure $d_1 \leftarrow \lfloor N \sum_{i=1}^{n} d(c_i) \rfloor$
3 Set challenge $-c$
4 Measure $d_2 \leftarrow \lfloor N \sum_{i=1}^{n} d(\neg c_i) \rfloor$
5 **return** $B_c = \text{sign}(d_1 - d_2)$

The N oscillations contribute to diminish the noise impact. For simplification we can consider a single loop ($N = 1$) and a perfect quantization. Thus:

$$\Delta_c^{\text{LPUF}} = \sum_{i=1}^{n} d(c_i) - d(\neg c_i) = \sum_{i=1}^{n} (-1)^{c_i} (d_i^{TB} - d_i^{BT}) \tag{6}$$

$$= \sum_{i=1}^{n} (-1)^{c_i} \Delta_i, \tag{7}$$

where we have used that $\neg c_i = 1 - c_i$. Since d_i^{TB} and d_i^{BT} are i.i.d. normal, the random variables

$$\Delta_i = d_i^{TB} - d_i^{BT} \qquad (i = 1, 2, \ldots, n) \tag{8}$$

are themselves i.i.d. normal and have zero mean. Each Δ_i represents the delay difference from x_i to y_i in the path through first top/second bottom and first bottom/second top buffers. One bit of the identifier is the *sign* of the cumulative delay difference $\Delta(c)$:

$$B_c^{LPUF} = \text{sign}(\Delta_c^{LPUF}). \tag{9}$$

The overall loop-PUF function is summarized in Fig. 4. A unique identification number can be obtained by querying the PUF for M different challenges c.

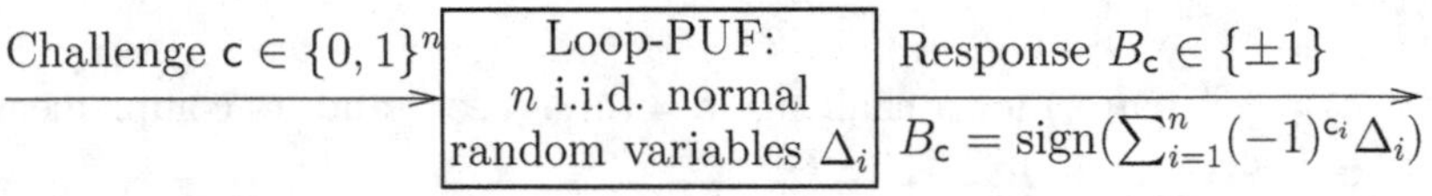

Challenge $c \in \{0, 1\}^n$ → | Loop-PUF: n i.i.d. normal random variables Δ_i | Response $B_c \in \{\pm 1\}$ → $B_c = \text{sign}(\sum_{i=1}^n (-1)^{c_i} \Delta_i)$

Fig. 4. Operation of a loop-PUF.

3.2   Arbiter-PUF

The arbiter-PUF (APUF) is an architecture [2, Section 2.2] with a pair of delay chains, so as to obtain one challenge bit per challenge, in one single query. Figure 5 represents the architecture of the Arbiter-PUF. The race of a signal along the top path and the bottom path is grabbed by the arbiter.

The PUF element thus consists in the duplication of the paths: the $x_i \rightarrow y_i$ path of Fig. 3 is turned into two parallel paths $(x_i, x_i' \rightarrow y_i, y_i')$. This is depicted in Fig. 6a.

We have

$$d(c) = \sum_{i=1}^n c_i d_i^T + \neg c_i d_i^B$$

$$d'(c) = \sum_{i=1}^n c_i d_i^{T'} + \neg c_i d_i^{B'},$$

and the APUF measures the fastest of the two cumulative paths. Therefore,

$$B_c^{APUF} = \text{sign}(\Delta_c^{APUF}), \qquad \text{where} \tag{10}$$

$$\Delta_c^{APUF} = d(c) - d'(c) = \sum_{i=1}^n c_i(d_i^T - d_i^{T'}) + (1 - c_i)(c_i d_i^B - c_i d_i^{B'}). \tag{11}$$

However, contrary to the case of the loop-PUF, this equation does not simplify as in (7).

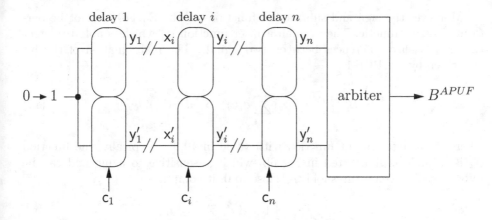

Fig. 5. Arbiter-PUF.

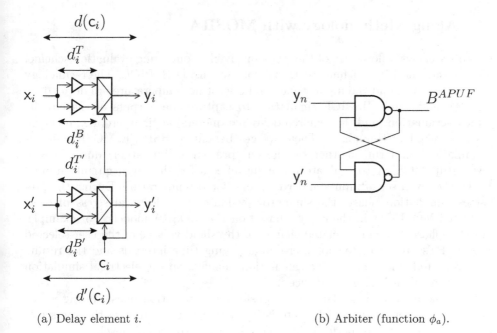

(a) Delay element i.

(b) Arbiter (function ϕ_a).

Fig. 6. Arbiter-PUF element examples.a

Indeed, we have that the expected value of Δ is not zero. The reason is that the delays in either input of the multiplexer are not the same. That is, let us denote $\mathbb{E}(d_i^T) = \mathbb{E}(d_i^{T'}) = \mathbb{E}(d^T)$, and $\mathbb{E}(d_i^B) = \mathbb{E}(d_i^{B'}) = \mathbb{E}(d^B)$. We have $\mathbb{E}(d^T) \neq \mathbb{E}(d^B)$. Thus,

$$\mathbb{E}(\Delta_{\mathrm{C}}^{\mathrm{APUF}}) = \sum_{i=1}^{n}(-1)^{c_i}\left(\mathbb{E}(d^B) - \mathbb{E}(d^T)\right) \neq 0.$$

Moreover the sign and subtraction functions of the Eq. (10) cannot be performed by arithmetic. They use an arbiter function ϕ_a which is able to detect the slight delay differences between two signals. The real equation of the bit generated by a APUF is:

$$B_C^{APUF} = \phi_a(\sum_{i=1}^{n} d(C_i), \sum_{i=1}^{n} d(\neg C_i)), \tag{12}$$

where ϕ_a is a two input function with value in $\{0, 1\}$. Typically, the function ϕ_a is a latch as illustrated in Fig. 6b, which is sensitive to aging and can be unbalanced. Given a threshold th_a close to 0, it computes:

$$\phi_a(d_1, d_2) = \begin{cases} 1 & \text{if } d_1 - d_2 \geq th_a, \\ 0 & \text{otherwise .} \end{cases}$$

4   Aging Methodology with MOSRA

Figure 7 shows a flowchart of the steps involved in our aging evaluation scheme. The circuit netlist is defined at transistor level using HSPICE. The technology library is given and the input values and operating temperature are decided.

We first run a HSPICE simulation to capture the outputs of the circuit-under-evaluation (and the required delay parameters) at time zero, i.e., no aging is considered in this phase. Then, we get benefit of HSPICE MOSRA in our simulations and run another simulation (pre-stress simulation) during which we setup MOSRA to evaluate the aging effects for the given circuit running with the given set of inputs under the considered temperature. During the pre-stress simulation phase, the simulator evaluates the electrical stress of user-selected MOSFETs in the circuit, based on the MOSRA models. For example, in this phase, the aging-related change of threshold voltage of the user-selected MOSFETs are evaluated for user-defined aging time intervals and the results are reported. In practice, The calculation depends on the electrical simulation conditions of each targeted device [22].

As the next step, we launch the post-stress simulation phase during which the degradation of device characteristics that was computed in the pre-stress phase is translated to performance degradation at the circuit level.

5   Impact of Aging on the Reliability of PUFs

5.1   Experimental Setup

In this section, we provide the details of the simulation setup used to evaluate the effect of aging on our targeted PUFs.

We first implemented our PUFs in a transistor level using a 45-nm technology extracted from the open-source NANGATE library [33]. We then used Synopsys

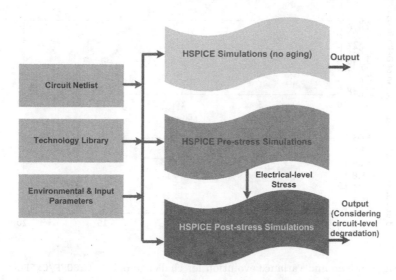

Fig. 7. Flowchart for applying HSPICE MOSRA to evaluate aging effects.

HSPICE for the transistor-level simulations and employed the HSPICE built-in MOSRA Level 1 model to capture NBTI effects in MOSFETs [22].

We ran Monte Carlo (MC) simulations for 8192 instances of loop-PUF and arbiter-PUF each including one PUF element. We then extracted the NBTI effects to extrapolate the effect of aging on 512 loop-PUFs and arbiter-PUFs each including 16 delay elements using our in-house tool. Simulations were carried out using the following process-variation parameters for a Gaussian distribution: transistor gate length L: $3\sigma = 10\%$; threshold voltage V_{TH}: $3\sigma = 30\%$, and gate-oxide thickness t_{OX}: $3\sigma = 3\%$.

Using HSPICE MOSRA, the effect of aging was evaluated for 20 months of PUF operation in time steps of one month. The operating temperature was considered as 45°C.

5.2   Experimental Results of the Loop-PUF Aging

The Loop-PUF aging has been simulated by considering 512 delay chains of 16 elements taken from the 8192 instances of one element. To be able to evaluate the effect of aging in the functionality of Loop-PUFs in different cases, we cut the closed loop of the Loop -PUF at point A in Fig. 2 and injected periodic pulses to the delay chain at point A. In order to measure the oscillation period of the loop-PUF which is now in an open loop, it is necessary to consider the delays from both rising-edge and falling edge from the SPICE simulation with the challenge bit then its complementary. The following delay is thus obtained:

$$\Delta_{\mathsf{C}}^{\mathrm{LPUF}} = \sum_{i=1}^{n} d(\mathsf{c}_i) - d(\neg \mathsf{c}_i). \tag{13}$$

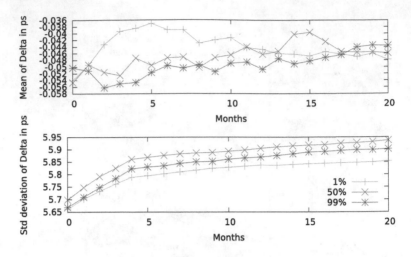

Fig. 8. Mean and variance evolution for challenge pair = 0x00FF/0xFF00.

As three extreme case, we considered that the duty cycle of the pulse can be either, 1 %, 50 % or 99 %. A duty cycle of X% means that the pulse is at level'0' X% of the time. Note that when a PMOS transistor gets a pulse at level'1' in its gate input, the NBTI impact is mitigated. Thereby, different PMOS transistors in a Loop-PUF may behave differently regarding the value of X. The simulation is performed during the equivalence of 20 months of aging at 45°C and 1.2 V instead of 1.0 V. The chosen challenges are selected amongst those given the maximum PUF entropy. The study in [34] has shown that the best challenges correspond to Hadamard codes, the way to construct them is explained in [35]. For the 16-element delay-PUF, there are 32 Hadamard codewords, giving 16 pairs of complementary challenges necessary for the Loop-PUF.

The results in terms of evolution of mean and standard deviation during 20 months for 3 challenge pairs are given in Figs. 8, 9, and 10.

These results provide many pieces of information:

1. The mean is not always a monotonous function, thus there is no direct relation between the aging and the mean. This can be explained by the independence of the delay elements. Hence when a delay element has a delay increase with aging, the other one decreases. All in one, there is not a unique tendency. As a straightforward consequence, a positively (resp. negatively) biased delay element remains positively (resp. negatively) biased over time.
2. The standard deviation is always increasing with aging. This behavior is intuitively that of the standard deviation of a random walk.
3. The aging impact is stronger at the beginning of the circuit life. This is a specificity of NBTI (recall Fig. 1).
4. The duty cycle of the pulse has a small impact on aging. The standard deviation slope is slightly smaller when the duty cycle is 1 % (than when it is 50 % or 99 %). The offset at time 0 of the standard deviation is not relevant, only

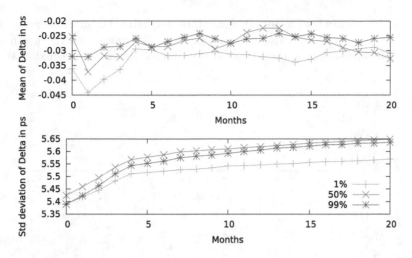

Fig. 9. Mean and variance evolution for challenge pair = 0x33CC/0xCC33.

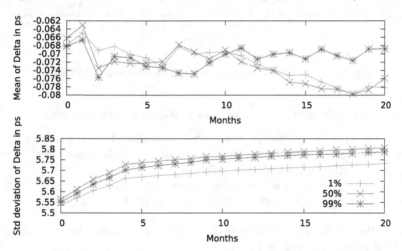

Fig. 10. Mean and variance evolution for challenge pair = 0x6996/0x9669.

the slope matters. The difference between the duty cycle value is not very significant. This means that the anti-NBTI aging strategy to force the PMOS to be most of the time "off" is not so efficient.

5. The challenges do not impact the observed behavior w.r.t. aging.

5.3 Experimental Results of the Arbiter-PUF Aging

The aging on the arbiter-PUF can be studied on separate parts which are the parallel delay chains and the arbiter.

Results of the delay chain part. The delay chain corresponds to Eq. (11) where the two paths are configured with complementary challenges. The delay chains have been configured with 16 elements, thus requiring 16-bit challenges. The results are very similar to the Loop-PUF. Figure 11 represents the mean and standard deviation among the 512 arbiter-PUFs for the challenge=0x5A5A.

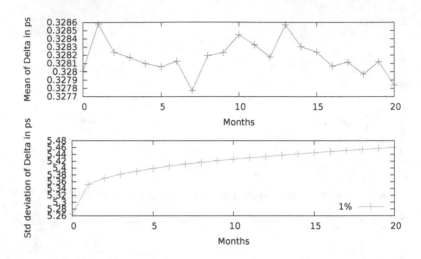

Fig. 11. Mean and variance evolution for challenge = 0x5A5A.

The same conclusions as the LPUF can be drawn from these results:

1. The mean is not always a monotonous function, thus there is no direct relation between the aging and the mean. Thus, if one chain is faster than the other initially, it will remain so despite aging.
2. The standard deviation is always increasing with aging.
3. The aging impact is stronger at the beginning of the circuit life.

Results of the arbiter part. The test design of arbiter uses a latch composed of two NAND gates as shown in Fig. 12.

The aging impact is assessed by counting the number of bit flips in the APUF response. Figure 13 illustrates the results obtained with 16384 APUF of one element.

It clearly shows that the number of bit flips increases with aging significantly as 1% of bit flips occurred after one year at 45°C. In order to make sure that these bit flips do not come from the delay chain, the bottom figure of Fig. 13 represents the dependence between the bit flip and the Δ value. It is expressed in probability to get a bit flip vs the sign of Δ. As it remains around 0.5, it indicates the delay chain has no noticeable impact.

5.4   Discussion

The fact that the arbiter reliability decreases over time can be accounted by the fact the steady state of the latch is asymmetrical. For example, if the arbiter

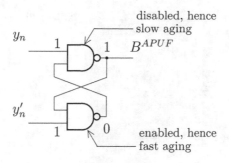

Fig. 12. Latch with two NAND gates.

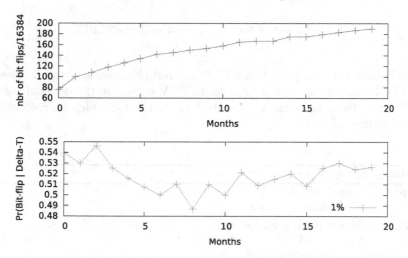

Fig. 13. Bit flips at the arbiter output.

evaluates to 0, then the logic states in the arbiter are represented in Fig. 12. One can see that one NAND gate is active, while the other one is not. This "asymmetric" state is similar to that of an SRAM memory point in the SRAM-PUF. Therefore, the reliability of the latch arbiter of Fig. 12 is decreasing over time.

Now, in a delay chain (recall Figs. 3 and 6a), each element ages independently. But, as the final measurement is a difference, the aging has no impact on the reliability.

6 Aging Acceleration on Real Silicon

6.1 Aging Acceleration Setup

An ASIC with 49 LPUF has been implemented in 65 nm technology. Figure 14 shows the layout with a 7 × 7 LPUF matrix which makes up the largest part in the upper right-hand corner of the layout.

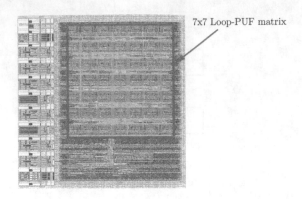

7x7 Loop-PUF matrix

Fig. 14. Layout of the test chip embedding 49 LPUFs.

The circuit has been placed on a PCB and put in a laboratory oven adjusted at 85°C. The power supply has been set to 2.0 V instead of the nominal voltage of 1.2 V. The test procedure is described in Protocol 2 which corresponds to cycles of 24 h.

Protocol 2. Aging acceleration Protocol.

Input: Non aged device
Output: Aged device

1 **STEP 1: Stress during 23 hours** ....
2 $V_{dd} \leftarrow 2.0$ V, $T°C \leftarrow 85°C$
3 Challenge $C_i \leftarrow$ 0x00000000FFFFFFFF
4 Always measure PUF_i, for $i \in \{0, \ldots, 7\}$
5 Measure PUF_j every 1/8 time, for $j \in \{8, \ldots, 15\}$
6 Measure PUF_k every 1/64 time, for $k \in \{16, \ldots, 31\}$
7 **STEP 2: Evaluation during 1 hour** ....
8 $V_{dd} \leftarrow 1.2$ V, $T°C \leftarrow 20°C$
9 Measurement of the 49 LPUFs with the Hadamard Challenges
10 Go to **STEP 1**

In this protocol the devices are placed in a high temperature, high voltage environment which should accelerate the NBTI and HCI effects [36, Section 5.3]. The first 8 PUFs PUF_0 to PUF_7 are always measured, whereas PUF_8 to PUF_{15} are measured 1/8 of the time, and PUF_{16} to PUF_{31} are measured 1/64 of the time. PUF_{32} to PUF_{48} are never measured. This differences in switching activity (X%) allows us to test the switching activity impact on the aging. Every 24 h and during one hour, the device is back in its typical environment and all the challenges are used to measure the PUF values.

The results in Fig. 15 represent the evolution of the mean delay $N \sum_{i=1}^{n} d(c_i)$, not the differential delay, for the challenge 0x00000000FFFFFFFF. This delay is measured when the device is back in its typical condition (**STEP 2** of the protocol).

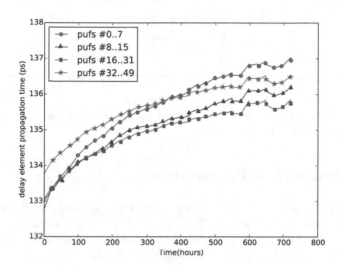

Fig. 15. Evolution of the mean delay with aging. Recall that switching rate X for $PUF_{[0,7]}$ is 100 %, for $PUF_{[8,15]}$ is 12.5 %, for $PUF_{[16,31]}$ is 1.6 %, and for $PUF_{[32,49]}$ is 0 %.

This figure brings a lot of information concerning the impact of aging:

1. The mean delay is always increasing with age.
2. Every 24 h, we can notice a small recovery phenomenon, as expected for NBTI.
3. The slopes satisfy $PUF_{[7:0]} > PUF_{[15:8]} > PUF_{[31:16]} > PUF_{[48:32]}$. This highlights the importance of the switching activity on the aging, as also observed in simulations (Figs. 8, 9, and 10) when X increases.

Now, considering the differential delay $\text{sign}(\lfloor N \sum_{i=1}^{n} d(c_i) \rfloor - \lfloor N \sum_{i=1}^{n} d(\neg c_i) \rfloor)$, we obtain the results shown in Fig. 16 (*left*). These results represent the mean of the differential delay for one delay element. As the evolution is very small we can notice the strong impact of the noise.

As it was observed for the simulation of the delay chain, the evolution of the differential delay is not monotonous. Hence we can conclude that the aging has a slight and non monotonous impact on the delay chain of the Loop-PUF. The evolution of the standard deviation is illustrated in Fig. 16 (*right*). The results are very noisy as the differential delay is very small. However it is possible to observe that the standard deviation is always increasing with a greater increase during the first hours. This confirms the simulation results.

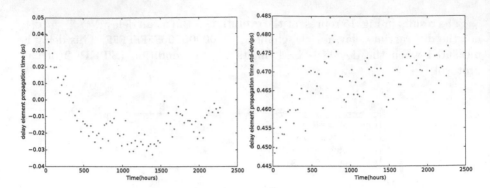

Fig. 16. Evolution of the mean (*left*) and of the standard deviation (*right*) of the differential delay with aging.

7   Conclusions and Perspectives

In this paper the aging on delay-PUFs has been evaluated by simulation and aging acceleration on a real silicon. Two types of PUF taking advantage of a delay chain have been considered: the Loop-PUF and the arbiter-PUF. It has been shown that the aging has a very small impact on delay chains as each element ages independently. However the memory point as the latch of the arbiter is much more sensitive to aging, due to the asymmetry of its dual structure. Hence the aging of element is different from the aging of its dual element, and the difference is always increasing. This also highlights the interest of using simple delay-PUFs as the Loop-PUF, to avoid the imbalance of the arbiter or SRAM memory points. It has also been noticed with the experiments on a real device that the NBTI impact is dominant and that the HCI is significant only with a high switching rate.

More generally, from a user perspective, it makes sense for low-power applications to switch off completely the PUF as the aging is mainly due to having it on. This does not apply for Loop-PUF which is naturally resilient against aging. A solution to counter the aging for arbiter-PUF would be to complement its state (as the SRAM anti-aging proposed in Maes et al. [20]) or use an arbiter based on RS latch based on NOR and forces the output at '0' to mitigate the NBTI impact.

References

1. Gassend, B., Clarke, D., van Dijk, M., Devadas, S.: Controlled physical random functions. In: Computer Security Applications Conference, pp. 149–160 (2002)
2. Suh, G.E., Devadas, S.: Physical unclonable functions for device authentication and secret key generation. In: Design Automation Conference (DAC), pp. 9–14 (2007)

3. Guajardo, J., Kumar, S.S., Schrijen, G.-J., Tuyls, P.: FPGA intrinsic PUFs and their use for IP protection. In: Paillier, P., Verbauwhede, I. (eds.) CHES 2007. LNCS, vol. 4727, pp. 63–80. Springer, Heidelberg (2007). doi:10.1007/978-3-540-74735-2_5
4. Rahman, M.T., Forte, D., Fahrny, J., Tehranipoor, M.: ARO-PUF: An aging-resistant ring oscillator PUF design. In: Design, Automation Test in Europe Conference (DATE), pp. 1–6 (2014)
5. Cherif, Z., Danger, J., Guilley, S., Bossuet, L.: An easy-to-design PUF based on a single oscillator: the loop PUF. In: Digital System Design (DSD), pp. 156–162 (2012)
6. Pelgrom, M.J., Duinmaijer, A.C., Welbers, A.P.: Matching properties of MOS transistors. IEEE J. Solid State Circ. **24**(5), 1433–1439 (1989)
7. Holcomb, D.E., Burleson, W.P., Fu, K.: Power-up SRAM state as an identifying fingerprint and source of true random numbers. IEEE Trans. Comput. **58**(9), 1198–1210 (2009)
8. Morozov, S., Maiti, A., Schaumont, P.: An analysis of delay based puf implementations on FPGA. In: Sirisuk, P., Morgan, F., El-Ghazawi, T., Amano, H. (eds.) ARC 2010. LNCS, vol. 5992, pp. 382–387. Springer, Heidelberg (2010). doi:10.1007/978-3-642-12133-3_37
9. Kufluoglu, H., Alam, M.A.: A generalized reaction-diffusion model with explicit H-H2 dynamics for Negative-Bias Temperature-Instability (NBTI) degradation. IEEE Trans. Electron Devices **54**(5), 1101–1107 (2007)
10. Lu, Y., Shang, L., Zhou, H., Zhu, H., Yang, F., Zeng, X.: Statistical reliability analysis under process variation and aging effects. In: Design Automation Conference (DAC), pp. 514–519, July 2009
11. Chakravarthi, S., Krishnan, A., Reddy, V., Machala, C.F., Krishnan, S.: A comprehensive framework for predictive modeling of negative bias temperature instability. In: Reliability Physics Symposium, pp. 273–282 (2004)
12. Saha, D., Varghese, D., Mahapatra, S.: Role of anode hole injection and valence band hole tunneling on interface trap generation during hot carrier injection stress. IEEE Electron Device Lett. **27**(7), 585–587 (2006)
13. Rodriguez, R., Stathis, J., Linder, B.: Modeling and experimental verification of the effect of gate oxide breakdown on CMOS inverters. In: IEEE Int'l Reliability Physics Symposium, pp. 11–16 (2003)
14. Sinanoglu, O., Karimi, N., Rajendran, J., Karri, R., Jin, Y., Huang, K., Makris, Y.: Reconciling the IC test and security dichotomy. In: European Test Symposium (ETS), pp. 1–6 (2013)
15. Khan, S., Haron, N.Z., Hamdioui, S., Catthoor, F.: NBTI monitoring and design for reliability in nanoscale circuits. In: Int'l Symposium on Defect and Fault Tolerance in VLSI and Nanotechnology Systems (DFT), pp. 68–76 (2011)
16. Yuan, J.-S., Yeh, W.-K., Chen, S., Hsu, C.-W.: NBTI reliability on high-k metal-gate SiGe transistor and circuit performances. Microelectron. Reliab. **51**(5), 914–918 (2011)
17. Yu, M., Devadas, S.: Secure and robust error correction for physical unclonable functions. Des. Test of Comput. **27**(1), 48–65 (2010)
18. Kirkpatrick, M.S., Bertino, E.: Software techniques to combat drift in PUF-based authentication systems. In: Workshop on Secure Component and System Identification (SECSI), p. 9 (2010)
19. Guajardo, J., Kumar, S.S., Schrijen, G.-J., Tuyls, P.: FPGA intrinsic PUFs and their use for IP protection. In: Paillier, P., Verbauwhede, I. (eds.) CHES 2007. LNCS, vol. 4727, pp. 63–80. Springer, Heidelberg (2007). doi:10.1007/978-3-540-74735-2_5

20. Maes, R., van der Leest, V.: Countering the effects of silicon aging on SRAM PUFs. In: Hardware-Oriented Security and Trust (HOST), pp. 148–153 (2014)

21. Maiti, A., Schaumont, P.: The impact of aging on a physical unclonable function. IEEE Trans. Very Large Scale Integr. Syst. **22**(9), 1854–1864 (2014)

22. Synopsys. HSPICE User Guide: Basic Simulation and Analysis (2016)

23. Kim, K.K.: On-chip delay degradation measurement for aging compensation. Indian J. Sci. Technol. **8**(8), 777–782 (2015)

24. Nunes, C., Butzen, P.F., Reis, A.I., Ribas, R.P.: BTI, HCI and TDDB aging impact in flip-flops. Microelectron. Reliab. **53**(9–11), 1355–1359 (2013)

25. Mizan, E.: Efficient fault tolerance for pipelined structures and its application to superscalar and dataflow machines. Ph.D. thesis, Electrical and Computer Engineering Department, University of Texas At Austin (2008)

26. Alam, M.A., Kufluoglu, H., Varghese, D., Mahapatra, S.: A comprehensive model for PMOS NBTI degradation: Recent progress. Microelectron. Reliab. **47**(6), 853–862 (2007)

27. Mahapatra, S., Saha, D., Varghese, D., Kumar, P.: On the generation and recovery of interface traps in MOSFETs subjected to NBTI, FN, and HCI stress. IEEE Trans. Electron Devices **53**(7), 1583–1592 (2006)

28. Schroder, D.K.: Negative bias temperature instability: What do we understand? Microelectron. Reliab. **47**(6), 841–852 (2007)

29. Cha, S., Chen, C.-C., Liu, T., Milor, L.S.: Extraction of threshold voltage degradation modeling due to negative bias temperature instability in circuits with I/O measurements. In: VLSI Test Symposium (VTS), pp. 1–6 (2014)

30. Sutaria, K.B., Velamala, J.B., Ramkumar, A., Cao, Y.: Compact modeling of BTI for circuit reliability analysis. In: Reis, R., Cao, Y., Wirth, G. (eds.) Circuit Design for Reliability, pp. 93–119. Springer, Heidelberg (2015). doi:10.1007/978-1-4614-4078-9_6

31. Wang, W., Yang, S., Bhardwaj, S., Vrudhula, S., Liu, F., Cao, Y.: The impact of NBTI effect on combinational circuit: modeling, simulation, and analysis. IEEE Trans. Very Large Scale Integr. Syst. **18**(2), 173–183 (2010)

32. Ye, Y., Liu, F., Chen, M., Nassif, S., Cao, Y.: Statistical modeling and simulation of threshold variation under random dopant fluctuations and line-edge roughness. IEEE Trans. VLSI Syst. **19**(6), 987–996 (2011)

33. Nangate 45nm Open Cell Library. http://www.nangate.com. Accessed 1 May, 2016

34. Rioul, O., Solé, P., Guilley, S., Danger, J.-L.: On the Entropy of Physically Unclonable Functions. In: IEEE Int'l Symposium on Information Theory (ISIT), Barcelona, Spain, July 2016

35. Hedayat, A.S., Wallis, W.D.: Hadamard matrices, their applications. Ann. Statist. **6**(6), 1184–1238 (1978). http://dx.doi.org/10.1214/aos/1176344370

36. JEDEC. JEP122G : Failure mechanisms and models for semiconductor devices. http://www.jedec.org/standards-documents/docs/jep-122e. October 2011

Towards Securing Low-Power Digital Circuits with Ultra-Low-Voltage Vdd Randomizers

Dina Kamel[✉], Guerric de Streel, Santos Merino Del Pozo, Kashif Nawaz, François-Xavier Standaert, Denis Flandre, and David Bol

ICTEAM/ELEN, Université catholique de Louvain, Louvain-la-neuve, Belgium
dina.kamel@uclouvain.be

Abstract. With the exploding number of connected objects and sensitive applications, security against side-channel attacks becomes critical in low-cost and low-power IoT applications. For this purpose, established mathematical countermeasures such as masking and shuffling always require a minimum amount of noise in the adversary's measurements, that may not be guaranteed by default because of good measurement setups and powerful signal processing. In this paper, we propose to improve the protection of sensitive digital circuits by operating them at a random ultra-low voltage (ULV) supplied by a V_{dd} randomizer. As the V_{dd} randomization modulates the switching current, it results in a multiplicative noise on both the current consumption amplitude and its time dependence. As ULV operation increases the sensitivity of the current on the supply voltage, it magnifies the generated noise while reducing the side-channel information signal thanks to the switching current reduction. As a proof-of-concept, we prototyped a simple V_{dd} randomizer based on a low-quiescent-current linear regulator with a digitally-controlled resistive feedback divider on which we apply a 4-bit random number stream. Using an information theoretic metric, the measurement results obtained in 65 nm low-power CMOS confirm that such randomizers can significantly improve the security of cryptographic implementations against standard side-channel attacks in case of low physical noise in the attacks' setups, hence enabling the use of mathematical countermeasures.

1 Introduction

With the increasing current trend of deploying billions of wireless Internet-of-Things (IoT) nodes, privacy and security concerns are raised [25]. However, due to strong power and area constraints, deploying cryptography for IoT systems is extremely challenging. Moreover, guaranteeing the physical security of these highly resource constrained applications against side-channel attacks is even more challenging. In a side-channel attack, the adversary exploits a physical signal (e.g. the supply current or electromagnetic field) to identify the secret key. Therefore, existing hardware countermeasures generally aim at reducing the side-channel signal-to-noise-ratio (SNR) [9] by decreasing the signal (e.g. [12,21,22]) or increasing the noise (e.g. [26]).

© Springer International Publishing AG 2016
C. Carlet et al. (Eds.): SPACE 2016, LNCS 10076, pp. 233–248, 2016.
DOI: 10.1007/978-3-319-49445-6_13

Following, the reduction of the SNR can be combined with mathematical countermeasures such as masking [18] and shuffling [24]. Nevertheless, for such mathematical countermeasures against side-channel attacks to be effective, it is strictly necessary that the original signal is hidden by a sufficient physical noise, i.e. that the original SNR is sufficiently small. Intuitively, this is because mathematical countermeasures can only amplify the impact of the physical noise (and therefore fall short if there is nothing to amplify). The usual approach for this purpose, that embeds sources of additive noise (algorithmic noise) in circuits [8], has an approximate cost that is linear with the noise level i.e. doubling the circuit size roughly doubles the noise variance, but also doubles the power consumption. A complementary approach would be to reduce the side-channel signal amplitude, for example by equalizing the power consumed with the design of custom logic gates (e.g. dual-rail pre-charged logic [21]). However, the power/area is approximately doubled and the design complexity is relatively high, which renders them unsuitable for resource-constrained applications. Other approaches to reduce the side-channel signal are the use of on-chip decoupling capacitors (current filtering) [12] and current equalization through switched capacitors [22].

This state-of-the-art raises new challenges regarding the design of advanced solutions that can be combined with mathematical countermeasures to increase the security regardless of the adversary's capabilities while keeping the cost and performance overheads limited. Therefore, we propose an ULV multiplicative source of noise in the form of a V_{dd} randomizer that embeds adequate noise due to the supply randomizataion in case the physical noise in the attack setup is insufficient, and at the same time reduces the side-channel signal due to its ULV operation ($< 0.55\,\mathrm{V}$). Our investigations show that this solution can be conveniently combined with mathematical countermeasures thanks to its low area ($1.8\times$) and low current consumption ($1.6\times$) overheads, and leads to a security improvement by a factor of 20 in case of low physical noise. Our results are based on real measurements of a fabricated chip using 65 nm low-power CMOS technology.

The rest of the paper is organized as follows. The related work and alternative approaches are discussed in Sect. 2, together with our contributions. We describe the V_{dd} randomizer implementation and the test setup in Sect. 3. We introduce our methodology for security evaluations in Sect. 4. This methodology is applied in Sect. 5, which details the security analysis of our side-channel signal reduction approach, and the embedding of the V_{dd} randomizer as a source of multiplicative noise. Finally, the design overheads are discussed in Sect. 6.

2   Related-Work and Contributions

2.1   Related Work

Countermeasures based on chip voltage regulation (VR) are currently gaining attention as they tend to pack the complexity into the regulator, which is a block present in almost all modern ICs, therefore reducing the power/energy and area overheads. In this trend, we see two directions. One is to de-correlate the current traces (at the supply of the voltage regulator) from the load current (drawn by the crypto engine), thus reducing the side-channel signal amplitude. A lot of research focused on switched-capacitor VR (e.g. [20]) or switched-inductor VR (e.g. [7]). In [20], the authors describe a bi-channel power structure voltage regulator composed of a linear converter supplying the slowly varying part of the load current and a switched-capacitor converter clocked by a random digital signal. They also use a low dropout (LDO) regulation subsystem to further enhance the de-correlation of the external current traces from the load current. Their design occupies an area of $0.8\,\mathrm{mm}^2$ using a $0.18\,\mu\mathrm{m}$ CMOS technology. However, their security evaluation only relies on visible inspection of the current traces to show the effectiveness of the hiding performed by the system, which makes it difficult to assess in front of advanced side-channel attacks. Also, the authors do not use a real circuit load in their power/energy and area efficiency evaluations, which prevents quantifying the cost of the system relative to such loads. In [7], the authors use switched-inductors to de-correlate the observed current from the load current traces. But both security and performance evaluations are limited for similar reasons. Low-dropout (LDO) regulators are also investigated in [16] to attenuate the high frequency variations of the load current by reducing the LDO bandwidth. Here the authors mounted a correlation power analysis (CPA) attack against a protected AES engine which shows an $800\times$ improvement in terms of the measurement to disclosure (MTD) metric (compared to an unprotected one) with $1.4\,\%$ area and $5\,\%$ power overheads. Yet, a possible shortcoming of their analysis is that the results they provided are based on simulation results without physical noise.

The second direction depends on creating multiple randomized observed current traces, thus introducing another source of noise (e.g. using multiphase switched-capacitor VR [26] or through random voltage scaling [1]). In [26], the authors propose to scramble the observed current by turning on and off the individual interleaved stages in a pseudo-random fashion. However, they do not provide the power/energy or area costs of their proposal and their security evaluation is uniquely based on power trace entropy, without indicating the amount of physical noise present in their evaluation system. The random voltage scaling technique proposed in [1] could lower the correlation coefficient by $10\times$ when applied to the complete AES. Their approach aimed at FPGA designs and the authors suggested to alter the supply voltage once every 200 encryption rounds since in their settings, a successful DPA attack can be mounted against an AES engine after 2500 rounds and they need a changing supply rate much less than that.

So overall, and while these previous solutions are intuitively appealing and technically innovative, a more formal/comparative treatment of their pros and cons is still missing. As detailed next, this paper aims to make one step in this direction, by investigating the security of a current randomizer based on advanced side-channel security metrics together with its performance results in a comprehensive manner. Furthermore, since we believe the impact of such

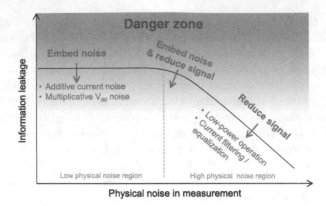

Fig. 1. Hardware countermeasures against side-channel analysis.

countermeasures are highly dependent on the actual level of physical noise found in the measurements, we propose to highlight trends in this respect, by considering noise as a parameter of our evaluations.

2.2 Contributions

First, we summarize the impact of these different countermeasures based on our understanding of their relevance in different physical noise regions as represented in Fig. 1. Generally, the side-channel information extracted from a circuit (precisely defined next) remains unchanged for low physical noise levels, and starts to decrease when increasing the physical noise. The gradient grey along the y-axis indicates the reduction of side-channel information as the color lightens. Therefore, the dark grey region is considered dangerous, since it corresponds to the case where mathematical countermeasures are ineffective. As clear from the figure, this typically happens in the low physical noise region. Fig. 1 also highlights the two main solutions for this purpose, namely embedding noise and reducing the side-channel signal. At the extreme, for extremely low physical noises, it is clear that the noise embedding approach is necessary. Similarly, in the large physical noise region, it is usually the signal reduction that brings the best benefits (since, e.g. additional additive noise could be small in front of the existing physical noise). Of course, most existing embedded devices fall inbetween these extremes and in this case, both approaches can be relevant. In the following, we pick up on this SNR reduction problem and investigate a new area- and power-efficient technique to generate hard-to-exploit noise that enables mathematical types of countermeasures. More precisely, our main contributions are threefold:

- We propose an ULV V_{dd} randomizer that modulates the switching current of a cryptographic implementation resulting in a multiplicative noise source. The V_{dd} randomizer employs an LDO regulator operating with sufficiently short transition times between V_{dd} levels in order to prevent an adversary from easily profiling the V_{dd}'s at which each operation is performed. In addition, we propose to combine this V_{dd} randomization with an operation of the circuit-to-protect at ultra-low voltage (ULV) which reduces the side-channel signal amplitude. Both techniques help reduce the information leakage of the circuit-to-protect in low and high physical noise regions.

- We provide a security assessment of the proposed technique using an information theoretic metric described in [14,17] based on template attacks [3]. This allows us to demonstrate the effectiveness of the technique across the whole range of physical noise. In addition, the information theoretic metric we used is proven to be directly proportional to the success rate of a maximum likelihood adversary [5], thus justifying its use in this context.
- We show that our solution can be conveniently combined with mathematical countermeasures thanks to its low area ($\sim 1.8\times$) and low current consumption ($< 1.6\times$) overheads in addition to the security improvement by a factor of 20 in case of low physical noise against a standard template adversary doing Gaussian profiling. Our results are based on real measurements of a fabricated chip using 65 nm low-power CMOS technology.

Eventually, we conclude by discussing the limitations of our randomizer against adversaries able to access the V_{dd} levels during profiling. We highlight that increasing the number of V_{dd} levels (limited to 16 in our work) would be necessary to prevent such worst-case attacks, which we leave as an interesting scope for further research.

3 Vdd Randomizer Design

3.1 Circuit Implementation

Intuitively, randomizing the supply voltage of the circuit to protect modulates the switching current or I_{on} in a multiplicative fashion. When the gates are switching at nominal V_{dd} the transistors mostly operate in saturation regime:

$$I_{on} \sim (V_{dd} - V_t)^\alpha. \tag{1}$$

where V_t is the transistor threshold voltage and α is a factor between 1 and 2 [15]. When the transistors operate in the subthreshold regime:

$$I_{on} \sim 10(V_{dd}/S). \tag{2}$$

where S is the subthreshold swing between 60 and 100 mV/decade [2]. At the supply voltage operating range of the V_{dd} randomizer in 65 nm LP CMOS, the transistors are in the near-threshold regime, which results in an I_{on} dependence on V_{dd} between Eqs. 1 and 2. Therefore, adding voltage noise on the supply voltage results in a multiplicative noise on the dynamic supply current as I_{on} is modulated with a dependence between linear-to-quadratic in saturation regime and exponential in subthreshold regime.

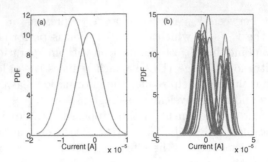

Fig. 2. Probability density functions of two (S-box) computations, for a prototype circuit operating under (a) a fixed supply (0.5 V) and (b) sixteen randomized supplies (from 0.45 V to 0.55 V).

Now, the main goal of a multiplicative noise source is to avoid the simple Gaussian leakage functions of unprotected implementations that easily allow distinguishing different events (e.g. S-box computations) happening in a target chip, as represented in Fig. 2(a)[1]. Instead, the V_{dd} randomizer turns the simple Gaussian leakage into a Gaussian mixture where every mode of the distribution represents one possible supply voltage, as represented in Fig. 2(b), thus increasing the overlap between these two events.

In this work, we use a simple V_{dd} randomizer to evaluate the security of the proposed approach. Its architecture is based on a conventional linear regulator with an error amplifier driving a power stage and a digitally-controlled 4-bit feedback resistive divider on which we apply a 4-bit random number stream generated off chip[2], as shown in Fig. 3. The error amplifier is a folded cascode amplifier and the power stage is an NMOS device with body connected to source [4]. The amplifier and its bias dissipates only 280 nA, whereas the feedback resistor network consumes about 1 μA, allowing the V_{dd} randomizer to limit the power overhead compared to the protected circuit. The feedback resistive divider is designed to provide a supply voltage to the digital circuit to protect ranging from 0.45 V to 0.55 V. This voltage range is carefully chosen in order to reduce the side-channel signal amplitude while operating the digital circuits at a maximum frequency of 1 MHz, suitable for low-speed IoT applications, and at the same time provide sufficient variations in the current traces as can be seen in Fig. 2. Current state of the art design of IoT sensor nodes uses ULV operation to minimize the energy consumption, e.g. in [19]. Therefore our analysis focuses only on the ULV region of operation which ranges from 0.45 V to 0.55 V in this case.

---

[1] The sign of the current is not preserved due to the clock coupling on the printed circuit board (PCB).

[2] We considered an off-chip implementation of the 4-bit random number stream generation as a proof of concept for demonstration purpose only. Of course, a full implementation of the V_{dd} randomizer would consider designing the random number stream on-chip to deny the adversary access.

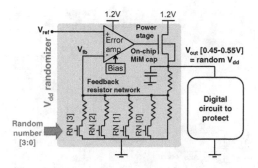

Fig. 3. Circuit architecture.

Notably, the randomness in the output voltage should come from the random number stream and not from the impact of the load current, which is correlated to the computation and might therefore leak side-channel information. Stability and load regulation can thus not be compromised in the Vdd randomizer, just as in conventional voltage regulators. In order to ensure stability over a wide range of loading currents, a current-mode capacitance multiplication in the bias of the error amplifier is used for pole splitting and an on-chip filtering MiM capacitor is added on the supply voltage output. As a result, stability is ensured for load currents up to 0.5 mA without an off-chip capacitor.

The slew rate of the randomizer is determined by the sizing of the power stage, and is in a direct trade-off with the area through the sizing of the stabilization capacitances. The slew rate specification is that the regulator has to render a transition time comparable with the clock period used in the digital circuit. This ensures sufficiently short transition times between V_{dd} levels in order to prevent an adversary from easily profiling the V_{dd}'s at which each operation is performed. In [1], which aimed at FPGA designs, the supply voltage is modified at a rate of one change per 200 encryptions. While this may be sufficient to improve security against certain types of Differential Power Analyses (DPA) attacks, it is still insufficient against advanced adversaries exploiting multiple samples/intermediate computations per encryption [10,23]. Therefore we target a slew rate of 10^5 V/s allowing the voltage to ramp from 0.45 V to 0.55 V in 1 μs compatible with the 1 MHz clock frequency.

3.2 Performance Benchmark and Test Setup

In order to characterize the V_{dd} randomizer, we designed a test chip implementing an 8-bit AES S-box as benchmark for the circuit to protect[3]. The input signal

---

[3] In our test chip we only implemented the 8-bit AES S-box instead of the whole AES as a proof of concept. Of course when used with the full AES, the V_{dd} randomizer should be able to drive the whole AES circuit. The results we later provide in Sect. 6 are for the measured V_{dd} randomizer with the AES S-box and also an estimation in case the randomizer operates with the full AES.

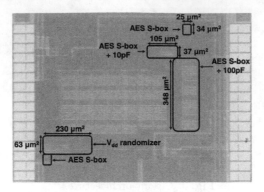

Fig. 4. Die microphotograph of the ultra-low-voltage V_{dd} randomizer and other structures of the AES S-box with decoupling capacitors.

has 256 possible values whose transitions are chosen between 0 and an arbitrary input.[4] In order to hide the impact of the supply voltage transients on the captured traces, the random number stream is clocked synchronously with the S-box input signal, i.e. the V_{dd} randomizer is synchronized with the operation of the circuit to protect. The V_{dd} randomizer was manufactured in 65 nm LP CMOS, and its area is $0.0145 \, \text{mm}^2$, as represented in Fig. 4. Our dies also contain several versions of an unprotected S-box with various levels of decoupling capacitances for comparison. All input signals were generated externally using a National instrument PXI 6552 waveform generator. The clock frequency of all circuits under test is 1 MHz. Current traces for security analysis were captured with a differential probe over a resistor with a 2 GS/s oscilloscope.

4   Methodology

4.1   Evaluation Settings

Capital letters are assigned to random variables, while lower case letters refer to samples of these random variables. The leakage function in case the implementation uses a fixed supply voltage has two input arguments: the discrete random variable X, which denotes the value of the processed data under investigation, and the continuous random variable N, which represents the physical noise in the measurements. When the V_{dd} randomizer is used, we also consider the discrete random variable V, which denotes the supply voltage. The leakage function variable denoted by $L(\,,\,)$ contains either random variable arguments or fixed arguments. We denote the tth time sample in a leakage trace as $L_t(\,,\,)$. We consider

---

[4] We only considered 256 input transitions for the S-box in order to limit the time of our measurement campaigns. Since our security evaluation will essentially reflect the improved overlap of Gaussian mixture models such as in Fig. 2, this should not impact our comparisons between fixed and randomized power supplies. Yet, a more expensive profiling of 256^2 transitions should admittedly allow adversaries to extract slightly more information from their traces.

two types of traces in our analysis. First, the real measurements with actual physical noise are denoted as $L_t^1(X, N) = L_t^{meas}(X, N)$. Second, "hybrid" traces, in which the average measurement traces $\overline{L_t^{meas}}(X) = \hat{\mathbf{E}}_n L(X, n)$ (where $\hat{\mathbf{E}}$ denotes the sample mean operator) are combined with simulated Gaussian noise. The leakage function in this context is denoted as $L_t^2(X, N) = \overline{L_t^{meas}}(X) + N$. These hybrid traces allow us to quantify the impact of a change of physical noise level in our different experiments.

4.2 Information Theoretic Metric

We evaluate the leakage information of the traces with the information theoretic metric described in [17] and refined in [14]. Namely, the Perceived Information (PI) corresponds to the amount of information that can be exploited by a side-channel adversary given a certain leakage model:

$$\hat{PI}(X; L) = H[X] - \sum_{x \in X} \Pr[x] \sum_{l \in L} \Pr_{chip}[l|x] \cdot \log_2 \left(\hat{\Pr}_{model}[x|l] \right).$$

In case the true (unknown) leakage distribution of an implementation (denoted as $\Pr_{chip}[l|x]$) and the adversary's leakage model estimate (given by $\hat{\Pr}_{model}[x|l]$) are identical (e.g. in a simulated environment), then a perfect evaluation is achieved. That is, the PI is equivalent to the standard definition of mutual information and it captures the worst-case information leakages. By contrast, if these distributions deviate (because of practical limitations which lead to bad profiling, or because there exists significant inter-chip variability, or because the adversary's model is simplified), then the PI is the best available estimate of the implementation's leakage. Compared to the previous analyses in [1], using such an information theoretic metric allows our conclusions to be closer to those of a worst-case security evaluation. Indeed, such a PI metric is directly proportional to the success rate of a maximum likelihood adversary (as proven in [5]).[5]

Note that the PI can be viewed as a generalization of the SNR metric discussed in introduction [5]. It is even proportional to the SNR in case of Gaussian leakages. We next use the PI (rather than the SNR) as evaluation metric since it can capture other types of leakage distributions, in particular the Gaussian mixtures that are relevant in our experiments.

4.3 Information Extraction Tools

In order to evaluate the previous information theoretic metric, one essentially requires a good model, aka estimation of the leakage probability function. For this purpose, our strategy will follow the one already established, e.g. in [13, 14], and consider a univariate setting as a starting point. That is, models will be built

---

[5] If positive, otherwise it indicates that the model exploited by the adversary does not guarantees successful key recoveries.

exhaustively for all the time samples of our leakage traces, and the PI value for the most informative time sample will be kept.[6] Concretely, building models for the fixed supply voltage case can directly exploit the Gaussian template attacks described in [3]. That is, in this case we start by building 256 templates of the form:

$$\hat{\Pr}_{model}[l|x] = \mathcal{N}(l|\mu_{x,N}, \sigma^2_{x,N}).$$ (3)

$\Pr_{model}[x|l]$ is then obtained by applying Bayes' rule. Eventually, the PI metric is directly estimated according to its equation, by sampling the true distribution $\Pr_{chip}[l|x]$ (i.e. by measuring the chip) and estimating the conditional probabilities of the 256 x values based on these measurements.

By contrast, the procedure can be slightly more involved in the case of randomized power supplies. We will consider two types of adversaries for this purpose: a standard one and powerful one. In the first case, the adversary is assumed incapable of identifying the 16 V_{dd} values during profiling. Therefore, the power supply randomizations are (wrongly) considered as a part of the measurement physical noise when building the templates and estimating the PI. In practice, such a setting would typically correspond to a context where the random numbers are unknown during profiling. As a result, the profiling phase exactly corresponds to the previous Gaussian templates building, but with $\sigma'^2_{x,N}$ made of a truly physical part $\sigma^2_{x,N_{meas}}$ to which we add a randomization part $\sigma^2_{x,N_{Vdd}}$. We call this scenario *Gaussian profiling*.

Next, the more powerful adversary is assumed capable of identifying the 16 random supply voltages during profiling. In this case we build 256×16 templates corresponding to the 256 S-box inputs and the 16 supply voltages:

$$\hat{\Pr}_{model}[x|l,v] = \mathcal{N}(l|\mu_{x,v,N}, \sigma^2_{x,v,N}).$$ (4)

Quite naturally, the random numbers selecting V_{dd} remain unknown during the PI estimation phase:

$$\hat{\text{PI}}(X;L) = \text{H}[X] - \sum_{x \in X} \Pr[x] \sum_{v \in V} \Pr[v]$$
$$\cdot \sum_{l \in L} \Pr_{chip}[l|x,v] \cdot \log_2(\hat{\Pr}_{model}[x|l]),$$

where the conditional probability of the events x given the leakages l is computed by summing over all possible v's, namely: $\Pr_{model}[x|l] = \sum_{v \in V} \Pr_{model}[x|l,v]$. In the following, we call this scenario *Gaussian mixture profiling*.

Note that the more powerful adversary could additionally target the leakage of the 4-bit random values controlling the randomizer. This is an interesting scope for further research. Yet, as the following results already show that our

---

[6] Extending this analysis towards multivariate attacks, possibly including a dimensionality reduction phase, is an interesting scope for further research. As for Footnote 1, it should not impact our comparisons between fixed and randomized supplies, but allow more efficient attacks.

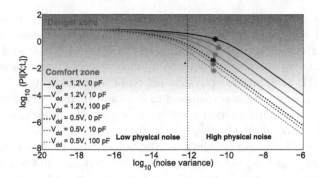

Fig. 5. Perceived information of the AES S-box with different decoupling capacitor values at a supply voltage of 1.2 V (solid lines) and 0.5 V (dashed lines). Curves correspond to the hybrid case with simulated Gaussian noise. The stars indicate the actual physical noise measured on chip.

instance of randomizer is not sufficient to prevent such powerful adversaries without this additional leakage, results in this direction will not affect our conclusions.

5 Security Analysis

5.1 ULV Operation and Decoupling Capacitors

In our analysis, the AES S-box is first operated at two different constant supply voltages: the nominal 1.2 V and a ULV (near-threshold) supply which is 0.5V. In each case, the impact of adding different values of on-chip decoupling capacitors is explored as well. Figure 5 exploits both the actual measured traces ($L_t^1(.)$) denoted by the stars and the hybrid traces ($L_t^2(.)$) explained in Sect. 4.1. It demonstrates how the reduction of the supply voltage and the addition of on-chip decoupling capacitors are effective in case the physical noise in the attack setup is high enough. Both techniques reduce the side-channel signal. This is clearly seen as the stars' horizontal positions in Fig. 5 remain nearly the same (corresponding to physical noise in the attack setup), whereas their vertical positions (corresponding to the perceived information) decreases while operating at ULV or using on-chip decoupling capacitors. However, if the physical noise can be reduced (e.g. thanks to a better measurement setup, or signal processing) as in the left part of the figure, neither lowering the supply voltage, nor using on-chip decoupling capacitors can help to escape the danger zone.

5.2 Vdd Randomizer

In Fig. 6 we compare the security of the V_{dd} randomizer implementation to the unprotected S-box at 0.5 V (without decoupling capacitors) again exploiting both the actual measured traces ($L_t^1(.)$) denoted by the stars and the hybrid traces

$(L_t^2(.))$ explained in Sect. 4.1. Furthermore, we have considered different settings for the actual measured traces to explore various physical noise values. The bandwidth of the oscilloscope was configured to full (600 MHz) and to 20 MHz in addition to using the singular spectrum analysis (SSA) post-processing tool introduced in [11] to reduce the physical noise in the attack setup[7]. First we consider Gaussian profiling that correspond to a standard adversary who (wrongly) considers the power supply randomizations as a part of the measurement physical noise. In the low physical noise region, the perceived information of the V_{dd} randomizer, using Gaussian profiling, is 20× better than the unprotected S-box at 0.5 V, thus approaching the comfort zone. Note that once in the comfort zone, typically corresponding to a PI below 0.1, a factor 20 for the PI reduction implies a multiplication of the attack's data complexity by the same factor in case of unprotected devices, and a factor 20^d if masking with d shares is exploited [5]. Meanwhile, the security of the V_{dd} randomizer is bounded by the unprotected S-box at 0.5 V in the high physical noise region which naturally lies in the comfort zone. This is expected as the physical noise dominates in this region. Consequently, these results prove the importance of combining the V_{dd} randomization technique with the ultra-low voltage operation to sustain sufficient security for the whole physical-noise range.

We insist that the concrete noise level of our experiments is in general less relevant than the trends indicated by our PI curves. In particular, since we target a combinatorial circuit, the SNR of these measurements is lower than what would be expected for sequential circuits and complete systems. Besides, it is interesting to see that the physical noise in the attack setup can be reduced by lowering the bandwidth of the oscilloscope to 20 MHz (acting as a low-pass filter) and by employing the SSA tool as shown by the symbols in Fig. 6. In general, the goal of the V_{dd} randomizer is indeed to mitigate the risk of a strong physical noise reduction.

On the other hand, if the Gaussian mixtures are considered, where the adversary is assumed capable of accurately identifying the 16 random supply voltages used, then there is obviously no security gain compared to the unprotected S-box at $0.5\,V$ in the low physical noise region. This is expected, since for the V_{dd} randomizer to be effective in this context, we need a noise such that the modes of the distributions in Fig. 2 start to overlap. In this respect, it is important to stress that this observation does not invalidate the interest of the randomizer. First, and very concretely, such a powerful profiling may be difficult to be performed by practical adversaries, since the internal randomness of the randomizer is not supposed to leave the chip. Yet, it is an interesting conceptual challenge to prevent even those adversaries (and their possible extension towards non-parametric pdf estimation techniques that would not require the knowledge of the masks during profiling, at the cost of higher sampling requirements). Second, and more importantly, V_{dd} randomizers can in principle enforce the modes of their Gaussian mixtures to be arbitrarily close, by increasing the range of

---

[7] SSA can be viewed as a type of filtering. Details are not necessary for the understanding of our results.

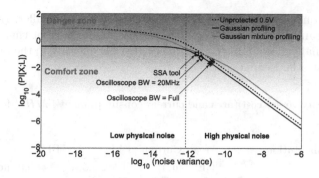

Fig. 6. Perceived information of the unprotected AES S-box at 0.5 V and the one with variable supply voltages using the Gaussian profiling and the perfect profiling scenarios. The symbols indicate the actual physical noise on chip with different settings.

the power supplies. Hence, our results show that our simple V_{dd} randomizer is already a good solution to prevent most state-of-the-art side-channel attacks, and that their generalization towards a wider range of V_{dd} levels to face even more powerful adversaries is an interesting research track. Note that by "most state-of-the-art attacks" we mean in particular all the CPA-like attacks that were used to assess the security of the solutions mentioned in Sect. 2.

More technically, it is worth mentioning that in the Gaussian mixture profiling we notice the "waved" shape of the information theoretic curve for the intermediate noise levels that is typical from masking [18]. It indicates that several moments of the statistical distribution are actually exploited for such noise levels. Besides, for the worst-case Gaussian mixture profiling, the V_{dd} randomizer actually leaks (slightly) more information than the unprotected chip running at 0.5 V in the high noise region. This is explained by the fact that the randomized supplies also lead to computations at (more informative) higher supplies in this case.

6   Cost Comparison

Table 1 summarizes the costs of the techniques in this paper. First, reducing the supply voltage of the unprotected S-box from 1.2 V to 0.5 V decreases both the current consumption and the PI at actual measured physical noise by 2.3× and 34×, respectively (for the standard side-channel adversary doing Gaussian profiling). Next, when the V_{dd} randomizer is used with the S-box, we gain a factor of 20 in PI at low physical noise for a similar increase of 17× in area, while maintaining the security gain of nearly 50× at the actual measured physical noise. This is more or less what additive noise would cost. But quite naturally, the performance gains are significantly amplified if the V_{dd} randomizer was used for a full AES design, since we could then amortize its cost (e.g. the area is expected to increase only by a factor of 1.8 compared to the unprotected AES reported in [6], still leading to the same security gain 20× at low physical noise).

The current consumption overheads in this case are even smaller: the full AES with the V_{dd} randomizer would consume $< 1.6\times$ higher current than the unprotected one. Finally, decoupling capacitances are only effective in the high physical noise region at a large area cost.

Table 1. Security versus cost (area and current consumption at $1\,MHz$) for a standard adversary.

Implementation	Area	Current	PI	PI
	[GE]	[μA]	@ low noise	@ actual noise
S-box (1.2 V)	220	0.74	8	1
S-box (0.5 V)	220	0.32	8	0.029
Full AES[a]	4,721	2.12	8	NA
S-box + V_{dd} rand	3,753	1.64	0.36	0.019
Full AES + V_{dd} rand	8,255	3.48	0.36	NA
S-box + 10 pF (0.5 V)	1,011	0.32	8	0.021
S-box + 100 pF (0.5 V)	6,849	0.32	8	0.007

[a] The power consumption of the unprotected full AES reported in [6] is at 0.4 V (890 kHz).

7   Conclusions

Noise is always assumed as the basic ingredient to prevent side-channel attacks. Confirming previous works in this direction, this paper shows that designing secure and efficient noise engines is not a trivial task, and certainly deserves more attention. In particular, while trying to hide the side-channel signal in a sufficient amount of physical noise with signal reduction techniques (as done with decaps in this paper) or mathematical countermeasures is well understood, how to generate hard-to-exploit noise in the low physical noise region is very challenging, especially in front of powerful adversaries able to perform Gaussian mixture profiling.

As a first step towards the better understanding of these issues, we analyzed the security improvements offered by a V_{dd} randomizer prototype to supply the digital circuits to protect at ULV. It shows good results against standard DPA adversaries usually considered in the literature (and evaluation laboratories), at a low die area cost. This confirms that randomizing the supplies can be used to make sure that the (possibly small) physical noise in an adversary's attack setup creates confusion when trying to distinguish cryptographic computations. Mathematical countermeasures such as masking can then be used to amplify this confusion.

But interestingly, our results also show that the impact of such randomizers may be limited in front of powerful adversaries able to profile the leakage distributions with full access to the chip's randomness (which is not advisable from a design point-of-view, but is interesting to reflect worst-case security levels). Our discussion (in Sect. 5.2) suggests that preventing such powerful adversaries is conceptually feasible, e.g. with supplies covering a wider range of V_{dd} levels, with a more granular randomization. So, our results raise new research challenges. Namely, how to design efficient noise engines that guarantee low information leakage (in the comfort zone) across the whole range of physical noise and against adversaries exploiting non-Gaussian profiling methods (either Gaussian mixtures, as in this paper, or non-parametric ones).

Acknowledgements. This work has been funded in parts by the ARC Project NANOSEC. François-Xavier Standaert is a research associate of the Belgian Fund for Scientific Research.

References

1. Baddam, K., Zwolinski, M.: Evaluation of dynamic voltage and frequency scaling as a differential power analysis countermeasure. In: VLSI Design, pp. 854–862. IEEE (2007)
2. Bol, D., Ambroise, R., Flandre, D., Legat, J.-D.: Interests and limitations of technology scaling for subthreshold logic. IEEE Trans. VLSI Syst. **17**(10), 1508–1519 (2009)
3. Chari, S., Rao, J.R., Rohatgi, P.: Template attacks. In: Kaliski, B.S., Koç, K., Paar, C. (eds.) CHES 2002. LNCS, vol. 2523, pp. 13–28. Springer, Heidelberg (2003). doi:10.1007/3-540-36400-5_3
4. de Streel, G., De Vos, J., Flandre, D., Bol, D.: A 65 nm 1 V to 0.5 V linear regulator with ultra low quiescent current for mixed-signal ULV SoCs. In: FTFC, pp. 1–4. IEEE (2014)
5. Duc, A., Faust, S., Standaert, F.-X.: Making masking security proofs concrete. In: Oswald, E., Fischlin, M. (eds.) EUROCRYPT 2015. LNCS, vol. 9056, pp. 401–429. Springer, Heidelberg (2015). doi:10.1007/978-3-662-46800-5_16
6. Hocquet, C., Kamel, D., Regazzoni, F., Legat, J.-D., Flandre, D., Bol, D., Standaert, F.-X.: Harvesting the potential of nano-CMOS for lightweight cryptography: an ultra-low-voltage 65 nm AES coprocessor for passive RFID tags. J. Cryptographic Eng. **1**(1), 79–86 (2011)
7. Kar, M., Lie, D., Wolf, M., De, V., Mukhopadhyay, S.: Impact of inductive integrated voltage regulator on the power attack vulnerability of encryption engines: a simulation study. In: CICC, pp. 1–4. IEEE (2014)
8. Mangard, S.: Hardware Countermeasures against DPA – a statistical analysis of their effectiveness. In: Okamoto, T. (ed.) CT-RSA 2004. LNCS, vol. 2964, pp. 222–235. Springer, Heidelberg (2004). doi:10.1007/978-3-540-24660-2_18
9. Mangard, S., Oswald, E., Popp, T.: Power Analysis Attacks: Revealing the Secrets of Smart Cards. Advances in Information Security. Springer, Secaucus (2007)
10. Mather, L., Oswald, E., Whitnall, C.: Multi-target DPA Attacks: pushing DPA beyond the limits of a desktop computer. In: Sarkar, P., Iwata, T. (eds.) ASIACRYPT 2014. LNCS, vol. 8873, pp. 243–261. Springer, Heidelberg (2014). doi:10.1007/978-3-662-45611-8_13

11. Merino Del Pozo, S., Standaert, F.-X.: Blind source separation from single measurements using singular spectrum analysis. In: Güneysu, T., Handschuh, H. (eds.) CHES 2015. LNCS, vol. 9293, pp. 42–59. Springer, Heidelberg (2015). doi:10.1007/978-3-662-48324-4_3

12. Nakai, T., Shiozaki, M., Kubota, T., Fujino, T.: Evaluation of on-chip decoupling capacitors effect on AES cryptographic circuit. In: SASIMI (2013)

13. Renauld, M., Kamel, D., Standaert, F.-X., Flandre, D.: Information theoretic and security analysis of a 65-nanometer DDSLL AES S-Box. In: CHES, pp. 223–239 (2011)

14. Renauld, M., Standaert, F.-X., Veyrat-Charvillon, N., Kamel, D., Flandre, D.: A formal study of power variability issues and side-channel attacks for nanoscale devices. In: Paterson, K.G. (ed.) EUROCRYPT 2011. LNCS, vol. 6632, pp. 109–128. Springer, Heidelberg (2011). doi:10.1007/978-3-642-20465-4_8

15. Sakurai, T., Newton, A.R.: Alpha-power law MOSFET model and its applications to CMOS inverter delay and other formulas. IEEE J. Solid-State Circuits 25(2), 584–594 (1990)

16. Singh, A., Kar, M., Ko, J. H., Mukhopadhyay, S.: Exploring power attack protection of resource constrained encryption engines using integrated low-drop-out regulators. In: ISLPED, pp. 134–139. IEEE/ACM (2015)

17. Standaert, F.-X., Malkin, T.G., Yung, M.: A unified framework for the analysis of side-channel key recovery attacks. In: Joux, A. (ed.) EUROCRYPT 2009. LNCS, vol. 5479, pp. 443–461. Springer, Heidelberg (2009). doi:10.1007/978-3-642-01001-9_26

18. Standaert, F.-X., Veyrat-Charvillon, N., Oswald, E., Gierlichs, B., Medwed, M., Kasper, M., Mangard, S.: The World Is Not Enough: another look on second-order DPA. In: Abe, M. (ed.) ASIACRYPT 2010. LNCS, vol. 6477, pp. 112–129. Springer, Heidelberg (2010). doi:10.1007/978-3-642-17373-8_7

19. Takamiya, M.: Energy efficient design and energy harvesting for energy autonomous systems. In: VLSI Design, Automation and Test, VLSI-DAT 2015, Hsinchu, Taiwan, 27–29 April 2015, pp. 1–3 (2015)

20. Telandro, V., Kussener, E., Malherbe, A., Barthelemy, H.: On-chip voltage regulator protecting against power analysis attacks. In: MWSCAS, pp. 507–511 (2006)

21. Tiri, K., Verbauwhede, I.: Securing encryption algorithms against DPA at the logic level: next generation smart card technology. In: Walter, C.D., Koç, Ç.K., Paar, C. (eds.) CHES 2003. LNCS, vol. 2779, pp. 125–136. Springer, Heidelberg (2003). doi:10.1007/978-3-540-45238-6_11

22. Tokunaga, C., Blaauw, D.: Secure AES engine with a local switched-capacitor current equalizer, In: ISSCC, pp. 64–65. IEEE (2009)

23. Veyrat-Charvillon, N., Gérard, B., Standaert, F.-X.: Soft analytical side-channel attacks. In: Sarkar, P., Iwata, T. (eds.) ASIACRYPT 2014. LNCS, vol. 8873, pp. 282–296. Springer, Heidelberg (2014). doi:10.1007/978-3-662-45611-8_15

24. Veyrat-Charvillon, N., Medwed, M., Kerckhof, S., Standaert, F.-X.: Shuffling against Side-Channel Attacks: a comprehensive study with cautionary note. In: Wang, X., Sako, K. (eds.) ASIACRYPT 2012. LNCS, vol. 7658, pp. 740–757. Springer, Heidelberg (2012). doi:10.1007/978-3-642-34961-4_44

25. Xu, T., Wendt, J. B., Potkonjak, M.: Security of IoT systems: design challenges and opportunities. In: ICCAD, pp. 417–423. IEEE/ACM (2014)

26. Weize, Y., Uzun, O.A., Köse, S.: Leveraging on-chip voltage regulators as a countermeasure against side-channel attacks. In: DAC, pp. 115:1–115:6. ACM/EDAC/IEEE (2015)

Security

Enabling Secure Web Payments with GNU Taler

Jeffrey Burdges, Florian Dold, Christian Grothoff$^{(\boxtimes)}$, and Marcello Stanisci

Inria Rennes - Bretagne Atlantique, Rennes, France
{jeffrey.burdges,florian.dold,
christian.grothoff,marcello.stanisci}@inria.fr

Abstract. GNU Taler is a new electronic online payment system which provides privacy for customers and accountability for merchants. It uses an exchange service to issue digital coins using blind signatures, and is thus not subject to the performance issues that plague Byzantine fault-tolerant consensus-based solutions.

The focus of this paper is addressing the challenges payment systems face in the context of the Web. We discuss how to address Web-specific challenges, such as handling bookmarks and sharing of links, as well as supporting users that have disabled JavaScript. Web payment systems must also navigate various constraints imposed by modern Web browser security architecture, such as same-origin policies and the separation between browser extensions and Web pages. While our analysis focuses on how Taler operates within the security infrastructure provided by the modern Web, the results partially generalize to other payment systems.

We also include the perspective of merchants, as existing systems have often struggled with securing payment information at the merchant's side. Here, challenges include avoiding database transactions for customers that do not actually go through with the purchase, as well as cleanly separating security-critical functions of the payment system from the rest of the Web service.

1 Introduction

The Internet needs a secure, usable and privacy-preserving micropayment system, which is not backed by a "crypto currency". Payment systems involving state-issued currencies have been used for centuries to facilitate transactions, and the involvement of the state has been critical as state institutions can dampen fluctuations in the value of the currency [9]. Controlling money supply is critical to ensure stable prices that facilitate trade [34] instead of speculation [19].

Internet transactions, such as sending an e-mail or reading a Web site, tend to be of smaller commercial value than traditional transactions involving the exchange of physical goods. Consequently, if we want to associate payments with these types of transactions, we face the challenge of reducing the mental and technical overheads of existing payment systems. For example, executing a 3-D Secure [22] payment process takes too long, is way too complex, and way too expensive to be used for payment for typical Web articles.

C. Carlet et al. (Eds.): SPACE 2016, LNCS 10076, pp. 251–270, 2016.
DOI: 10.1007/978-3-319-49445-6_14

Addressing this problem is urgent: ad-blocking technology is eroding advertising as a substitute for micropayments [31], and the Big Data business model in which citizens pay with their private information [11] in combination with the deep state hastens our society's regression towards post-democracy [30].

The focus of this paper is GNU Taler, a new free software payment system designed to meet certain key ethical considerations from a social liberalism perspective. In Taler, the paying customer remains anonymous while the merchant is easily identified and thus taxable. Here, *anonymous* simply means that the payment process does not require any personal information from the customer, and that different transactions by the same customer are unlinkable. Naturally, the specifics of the transaction—such as delivery of goods to a shipping address, or the use of non-anonymous IP-based communication—may still leak information about the customer's identity. *Taxable* means that for any transaction the state can easily obtain the necessary information about the identity of the merchant and the respective contract in order to levy income, sales, or value-added taxes. Taler uses blind signatures [5] to create digital coins and a new *refresh* protocol [8] to allow giving change and refunds while maintaining unlinkability.

This paper will not consider the details of Taler's cryptographic protocols.[1] The basic cryptography behind blind-signature based payment systems has been known for over 25 years [6]. However, it was not until 2015 that the W3C started the payments working group [35] to explore requirements for deploying payment systems that are more secure and easy to use for the Web. Our work describes how a modern payment system using blind signatures could practically be integrated with the modern Web to improve usability, security, and privacy. This includes the challenge of hiding the cryptography from the users, integrating with modern browsers, integrating with Web shops, providing proper cryptographic proofs for all operations, and handling network failures. We explain our design using terms from existing *mental models* that users have from widespread payment systems.

Key contributions of this paper are:

- A description of different payment systems using common terminology, which allows us to analytically compare these systems.
- An introduction to the Taler payment system from the perspective of users and merchants, with a focus on how to achieve secure payments in a way that is intuitive and has adequate fail-safes.
- Detailed considerations for how to adapt Taler to Web payments and the intricacies of securing payments within the constraints of modern browsers.
- A publicly available free software reference implementation of the presented architecture.

2   Existing Payment Workflows

Before we look at the payment workflow for Taler, we sketch the workflow of existing payment systems. This establishes a common terminology which we will use to compare different payment processes.

---

[1] Details of the protocol are documented at https://api.taler.net/.

2.1 Credit and Debit Cards

Credit and debit card payments operate by the customer providing their credentials to the merchant. Many different authentication and authorization schemes are in use in various combinations. Secure systems typically combine multiple forms of authentication including secret information, such as personal identification numbers (PINs), transaction numbers (TANs) [1] or credit card verification (CCV) codes, and physical security devices such cards with an EMV chip [2], TAN generators, or the customer's mobile phone [10]. A typical modern Web payment process involves: (1.) the merchant offering a secure communication channel using TLS based on the X.509 public key infrastructure;[2] (2.) selecting a *payment method*; (3.) entering the credit card details like the owner's name, card number, expiration time, CCV code, and billing address; and (4.) (optionally) authorizing the transaction via mobile TAN, or by authenticating against the customer's bank. Due to the complexity of this, the data entry is often performed on a Web site that is operated by a third-party payment processor and *not* the merchant or the customer's bank.

Given this process, there is an inherent risk of information leakage of customers' credentials. *Fraud detection* systems attempt to detect misuse of stolen credentials, and payment system providers handle disputes between customers and merchants. As a result, Web payment processes may finish with (5.) the payment being rejected for a variety of reasons, such as false positives in fraud detection or the merchant not accepting the particular card issuer.

Traditionally, merchants bear most of the financial risk, and a key "feature" of the 3DS process compared to traditional card payments is to shift dispute *liability* to the issuer of the card—who may then try to shift it to the customer [22, Sect. 2.4]. Even in cases where the issuer or the merchant remain legally first in line for liabilities, there are still risks customers incur from the card dispute procedures, such as neither them nor the payment processor noticing fraudulent transactions, or them noticing fraudulent transactions past the *deadline* until which their bank would reimburse them. The customer also typically only has a merchant-generated comment and the amount paid in his credit card statement as a proof for the transaction. Thus, the use of credit cards online does not generate any cryptographically *verifiable* electronic receipts for the customer, which theoretically enables malicious merchants to later change the terms of the contract.

Beyond these primary issues, customers face secondary risks of identity theft from the personal details exposed by the authentication procedures. In this case, even if the financial damages are ultimately covered by the bank, the customer always has to deal with the procedure of *notifying* the bank in the first place. As a result, customers must remain wary about using their cards, which limits their online shopping [27, p. 50].

---

[2] Given numerous TLS protocol and implementation flaws as well as X.509 key management incidents in recent years [15], one cannot generally assume that the security provided by TLS is adequate under all circumstances.

2.2   Bitcoin

Bitcoin operates by recording all transactions in a pseudonymous public *ledger*. A Bitcoin account is identified by its public key, and the owner must know the corresponding private key to authorize the transfer of Bitcoins from the account to other accounts. The information in the global public ledger allows everybody to compute the balances in all accounts and to see all transactions. Transactions are denominated in a new currency labeled BTC, whose valuation depends upon *speculation*, as there is no authority that could act to stabilize exchange rates or force anyone to accept BTC as *legal tender* to settle obligations. Adding transactions to the global public ledger involves broadcasting the transaction data, peers verifying and appending it to the public ledger, and some peer in the network solving a moderately hard computational proof-of-work puzzle, which is called *mining*.

The mining process is incentivised by a combination of transaction fees and mining rewards [23]. The latter process also provides primitive accumulation [25] for BTC. Conversion to BTC from other currencies and vice versa incurs substantial fees [4]. There is now an extreme diversity of Bitcoin-related payment technologies, but usability improvements are usually achieved by adding a trusted third party, and there have been many incidents where such parties then embezzled funds from their customers [33].

The classical Bitcoin payment workflow consisted of entering payment details into a peer-to-peer application. The user would access their Bitcoin *wallet* and instruct it to transfer a particular amount from one of his accounts to the account of the merchant. He could possibly include additional metadata to be associated with the transfer to be embedded into the global public ledger. The wallet application would then transmit the request to the Bitcoin peer-to-peer overlay network. The use of an external payment application makes payments significantly less browser-friendly than ordinary card payments. This has led to the development of browser-based wallets.[3]

Bitcoin payments are only confirmed when they appear in the public ledger, which is updated at an average frequency of once every 10 min. Even then, it is possible that a fork in the so-called block chain may void durability of the transaction; as a result, it is recommended to wait for 6 blocks (on average one hour) before considering a transaction committed [23]. In cases where merchants are unable to accommodate this delay, they incur significant fraud risks.

Bitcoin is considered to be secure against an adversary who cannot control around a fifth of the Bitcoin miner's computational resources [3,12,14]. As a result, the network must expend considerable computational resources to keep this value high. According to [20], a single Bitcoin transaction uses roughly enough electricity to power 1.57 American households for a day. These costs are largely hidden by speculation in BTC, but that speculation itself contributes to BTC's valuation being volatile [16].

Bitcoin's pseudononymity applies equally to both customers and merchants, which makes Bitcoin amenable to tax evasion, money laundering, sales of

---

[3] https://github.com/frozeman/bitcoin-browser-wallet.

contraband, and especially extorion [24]. As a result, anonymity tools like mixnets do not enjoy widespread support in the Bitcoin community where many participants seek to make the currency appear more legitimate. While Bitcoin's transactions are difficult to track, there are several examples of Bitcoin's pseudononymity being broken by investigators [26]. This has resulted in the development of new protocols with better privacy protections.

Zerocoin [21] is such an extension of Bitcoin: It affords protection against linkability of transactions, but at non-trivial additional computational costs even for spending coins. This currently makes using Zerocoin unattractive for payments, especially with mobile devices.

Bitcoin also faces serious scalability limitations, with the classic implementation being limited to at most 7 transactions per second globally on average.[4] There are a variety of efforts to confront Bitcoin's scaling problems with off-blockchain techniques, like side-chains. Amongst these, the blind off-chain lightweight transactions (BOLT) proposal [13] provides anonymity by routing off-blockchain transfers through bank-like intermediaries. Although interesting, there are numerous seemingly fragile aspects of the BOLT protocol, including aborts deanonymizing customers, intermediaries risking unlimited losses, and theft if a party fails to post a refute message in a timely fashion.

2.3 Walled Garden Payment Systems

Walled garden payment systems offer ease of use by processing payments using a trusted payment service provider. Here, the customer authenticates to the trusted service, and instructs the payment provider to execute a transaction on his behalf. In these payment systems, the provider basically acts like a bank with accounts carrying balances for the various users. In contrast to traditional banking systems, both customers and merchants are forced to have an account with the same provider. Each user must take the effort to establish his identity with a service provider to create an account. Merchants and customers obtain the best interoperability in return for their account creation efforts if they start with the biggest providers. As a result, there are a few dominating walled garden providers, with AliPay, ApplePay, GooglePay, SamsungPay and PayPal being the current *oligopoly*. In this paper, we will use PayPal as a representative example for our discussion of these payment systems.

As with card payment systems, these oligopolies are politically dangerous [29], and the lack of *competition* can result in excessive profit taking that may require political solutions [17] to the resulting *market failure*. The use of non-standard *proprietary* interfaces to the payment processing service of these providers serves to reinforce the customer *lock-in*.

3   Taler

Taler is a free software cryptographic payment system. It has an open protocol specification, which couples cash-like anonymity for customers with low

---

[4] http://hackingdistributed.com/2016/08/04/byzcoin/.

transaction costs, signed digital receipts, and accurate income information to facilitate taxation and anti-corruption efforts.

Taler achieves anonymity for buyers using *blind signatures* [5]. Since their discovery thirty years ago, cryptographers have viewed blind signatures as the optimal cryptographic primitive for privacy-preserving consumer-level transaction systems. However, previous transaction systems based on blind signatures have failed to see widespread adoption. This paper details strategies for hiding the complexity of the cryptography from users and integrating smoothly with the Web, thereby providing crucial steps to bridge the gap between good cryptography and real-world deployment.

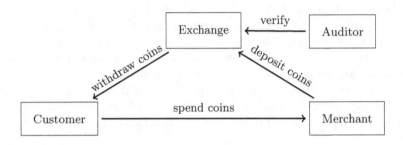

Fig. 1. Taler system overview.

There are four key roles in the Taler system (Fig. 1):

- *Customers* use a digital wallet to withdraw, hold, and spend coins. Wallets manage the customer's accounts at the exchange, and keep receipts in a transaction history. Wallets can be realized as browser extensions, mobile Apps or even in custom hardware. If a user's digital wallet is compromised, the current balance may be lost, just as with an ordinary wallet containing cash. A wallet includes a list of trusted auditors, and will warn users against using an exchange that is not certified by a trusted auditor.
- *Exchanges*, which are run by financial service providers, enable customers to withdraw anonymous digital coins, and merchants to deposit digital coins, in exchange for bank money. Coins are signed by the exchange using a blind signature scheme [5]. Thus, only an exchange can issue new coins, but coins cannot be traced back to the customer who withdrew them. Furthermore, exchanges learn the amounts withdrawn by customers and deposited by merchants, but they do not learn the relationship between customers and merchants. Exchanges perform online detection of double spending, thus providing merchants instant feedback —including digital proofs—in case of misbehaving customers.
- *Merchants* provide goods or services in exchange for coins held by customers' wallets. Merchants deposit these coins at the exchange used by the customer in return for a bank wire transfer of their value. While the exchange is determined by the customer, the merchant's contract specifies the currency, a list

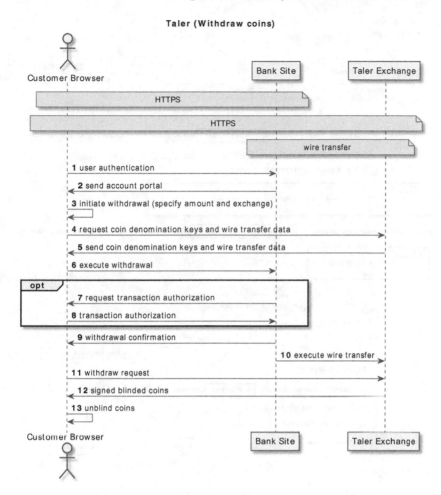

Fig. 2. Withdrawing coins with Taler.

of accepted auditors, and the maximum exchange deposit fee the merchant is willing to pay. Merchants consist of a *frontend*, which interacts with the customer's wallet, and a *backend*, which interacts with the exchange. Typical frontends include Web shops and point-of-sale systems.

– *Auditors* verify that exchanges operate correctly to limit the risk that customers and merchants incur by using a particular exchange. Auditors are typically operated by or on behalf of financial regulatory authorities. Depending on local legislation, auditors may mandate that exchanges have enough financial reserves before authorizing them to create a given volume of signed digital coins to provide a buffer against potential risks due to operational failures (such as data loss or theft of private keys) of the exchange. Auditors certify exchanges that they audit using digital signatures. The respective signing keys of the auditors are distributed to customer and merchants.

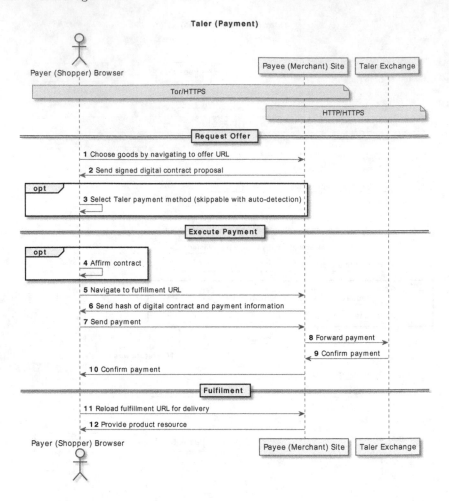

Fig. 3. Payment processing with Taler.

The specific protocol between wallet and merchant depends on the setting. For a traditional store, a near field communication (NFC) protocol might be used between a point-of-sale system and a mobile application. In this paper, we focus on Web payments for an online shop and explain how the actors in the Taler system interact by way of a typical payment.

Initially, the customer installs the Taler wallet extension for their browser. This only needs to be done once per browser. Naturally, this step may become superfluous if Taler is integrated tightly with browsers in the future. Regardless, installing the extension involves only one or two clicks to confirm the operation. Restarting the browser is not required.

3.1   Withdrawing Coins

As with cash, the customer must first withdraw digital coins (Fig. 2). For this, the customer must first visit the bank's online portal. Here, the bank will typically require some form of authentication; the specific method used depends on the bank.

The next step depends on the level of Taler support offered by the bank:

- If the bank does not offer integration with Taler, the customer needs to use the menu of the wallet to create a *reserve*. The wallet will ask which amount in which *currency* (e.g. EUR or USD) the customer wants to withdraw, and allow the customer to select an exchange. Given this information, the wallet will instruct the customer to transfer the respective amount to the account of the exchange. The customer will have to enter a 54-character reserve key, which includes 256 bits of entropy and an 8-bit checksum into the transfer subject. Naturally, the above is exactly the kind of interaction we would like to avoid for usability reasons.
- Otherwise, if the bank fully supports Taler, the customer has a form in the online banking portal in which they can specify an amount to withdraw. The bank then triggers an interaction with the wallet to allow the customer to select an exchange. Afterwards, the wallet instructs the bank about the details of the wire transfer. The bank asks the customer to authorize the transfer, and finally confirms to the wallet that the transfer has been successfully initiated.

In either case, the wallet can then withdraw the coins from the exchange, and does so in the background without further interaction with the customer.

In principle, the exchange can be directly operated by the bank, in which case the step where the customer selects an exchange could be skipped by default. However, we generally assume that the exchange is a separate entity, as this yields the largest anonymity set for customers, and may help create a competitive market.

3.2   Spending Coins

At a later point in time, the customer can spend their coins by visiting a merchant that accepts digital coins in the respective currency issued by the respective exchange (Fig. 3). Merchants are generally configured to either accept a specific exchange, or to accept all the exchanges audited by a particular auditor. Merchants can also set a ceiling for the maximum amount of transaction fees they are willing to cover. Usually these details do not matter for the customer, as we expect most merchants to accept most exchange providers accredited by the auditors that wallets include by default. Similarly, we expect exchanges to operate with transaction fees acceptable to most merchants to avoid giving customers a reason to switch to another exchange. If transaction fees are higher than what is covered by the merchant, the customer may choose to cover them.

As with traditional Web transactions, customers first select which items they wish to buy. This can involve building a traditional shopping cart, or simply

```
HTTP/1.1  402  Payment  Required
Content-Type:  text/html;  charset=UTF-8
X-Taler-Contract-Url:  https://shop/generate-contract/42

<!DOCTYPE html>
<html>
<!-- fallback for browsers without the Taler extension -->
You  do  not  have  Taler  installed.  Other  payment  options  are  ...
</html>
```

Fig. 4. Sample HTTP response to prompt the wallet to show an offer.

clicking on a particular link for the respective article. Once the articles have been selected, the Web shop directs the user to the *offer* URL, where the payment details are negotiated. The process usually starts by allowing the user to select a *payment method* from a set of methods supported by the Web shop. Taler also allows the Web shop to detect the presence of a Taler wallet, so that the selection of alternative payment methods can be skipped if a Taler wallet is installed.

Offer. The offer URL of the Web shop can then initiate payments by sending a *contract proposal* to the wallet, either via the HTTP status code 402 Payment Required (Fig. 4). The wallet then presents the contract to the user. The format of the contract is in an extensible JSON-based format defined by Taler and not HTML, as the rendering of the contract is done by the wallet to ensure correct visual representation of the terms and prices. In case that transaction fees need to be covered by the customer, these are shown together with the rest of the proposed contract.

The Taler wallet operates from a securely isolated *background* context on the client side. The user interface that displays the contract and allows the user to confirm the payment is displayed by this background context. By running in the background context, the wallet can perform the cryptographic operations protected from the main process of the Web site. In particular, this architecture is secure against a merchant that generates a page that looks like the wallet's payment page, as such a page would still not have access to the private keys of the coins that are exclusive to the background context.

If the customer approves the contract by clicking the "Confirm Payment" button on the payment page, their wallet signs the contract with enough coins to cover the contract's cost, stores all of the information in its local database, and redirects the browser to the *fulfillment* URL provided by the merchant in the contract.

Fulfillment. The fulfillment URL uniquely identifies a purchase by some customer, while the offer URL identifies a generic offer that is not specific to a customer. The purchase identified by a fulfillment URL may have been completed or still be in progress. The information contained in the fulfillment URL must allow the merchant to restore the full contract (including a unique transaction identifier) that was associated with the purchase, either directly from the URL or indirectly from an identifier in a database. Efficiently reconstructing the contract entirely from the URL instead of using costly database transactions can be important, as costly disk operations for incomplete purchases make merchants more susceptible to denial-of-service attacks from adversaries pretending to be customers.

```
HTTP/1.1 402 Payment Required
Content-Type: text/html; charset=UTF-8
X-Taler-Contract-Hash: 2BAH2AT4GSG5JRM2W4YWTSYGY66EK4X8C...
X-Taler-Pay-Url: https://shop/pay
X-Taler-Offer-Url: https://shop/article/42

<!DOCTYPE html>
<html>
<!-- fallback for browsers without the Taler extension -->
You do not have Taler installed. Other payment options are ...
</html>
```

Fig. 5. Sample HTTP response when the user agent navigates to a fulfillment URL without the session state that indicates they have paid for the resource. Note that unlike in Listing 4, the response references a contract that typically is already known to the wallet via its hash code.

When a customer has completed a purchase, navigating to the fulfillment URL in a browser will show the resource associated with the purchase. This resource can be a digital good such as a news article, or simply a confirmation for products that are delivered by other means.

When a customer has not yet completed a purchase (this is always the case when a customer visits the fulfillment URL for the first time), or when the Web shop cannot confirm that this visitor has paid for the contract, for example because the session state was lost,[5] the Web store responds by (again) triggering a payment process (either via JavaScript or using 402 Payment Required, see Fig. 5). However, unlike the response from the offer URL, the 402 response from the fulfillment page includes the headers X-Taler-Contract-Hash, X-Taler-Pay-Url and X-Taler-Offer-Url.

If the contract hash matches a payment which the user already previously approved, the wallet reacts to this by injecting the logic to transmit the payment to the *pay* URL of the Web shop into the page. Then the wallet inspects the response as it may contain error reports about a failed payment which the wallet has to handle. By submitting the payment this way, we also ensure that this intermediate request does not require JavaScript and still does not interfer with

---

[5] This can happen when privacy conscious users delete their cookies. Also, some user agents (such as the TOR browser) do not support persistent (non-session) cookies.

navigation. Once the Web shop confirms the payment, the wallet causes the fulfillment URL to be reloaded.

If the contract hash does not match a payment which the user already approved, for example because the user obtained the link from another user, the wallet navigates to the offer URL included in the header.

Discussion. Various failure modes are considered in this design:

- If the payment fails on the network, the request is typically retried. How often the client retries automatically before informing the user of the network issue is up to the merchant. If the network failure persists and is between the customer and the merchant, the wallet will try to recover control over the coins at the exchange by effectively spending the coins first using Taler's refresh protocol. In this case, later deposits by the merchant will simply fail. If the merchant already succeeded with the payment before the network failure, the customer can either retry the operation via the transaction history kept by the wallet, or demand a refund (see below). Handling these errors does not require the customer to give up his privacy.
- If the payment fails due to the exchange claiming that the request was invalid, the diagnostics created by the exchange are passed to the wallet for inspection. The wallet then decides whether the exchange was correct, and can then inform the user about a fraudulent or buggy exchange. At this time, it allows the user to export the relevant cryptographic data to be used in court. If the exchange's proofs were correct and coins were double-spent, the wallet informs the user that its database must have been out-of-date (e.g. because it was restored from backup), updates the database and allows the user to retry the transaction.

While our design requires a few extra roundtrips, it has the following key advantages:

- It works in the confines of the WebExtensions API.
- It supports restoring session state for bookmarked Web resources even after the session state is lost by the user agent.
- Sending deep links to fullfilment or offer pages to other users has the expected behavior of asking the other user to pay for the resource.
- Asynchronously transmitting coins from injected JavaScript costs one roundtrip, but does not interfer with navigation and allows proper error handling.
- The different pages of the merchant have clear delineations: the shopping pages conclude by making an offer, and the fulfillment page begins with processing an accepted contract. It is thus possible for these pages to be managed by separate parties. The control of the fulfillment page over the transmission of the payment data minimizes the need for exceptions to handle cross-origin resource sharing [18].
- The architecture supports security-conscious users that may have disabled JavaScript, as it is not necessary to execute JavaScript originating from Web pages to execute the payment process.

3.3   Giving Change and Refunds

An important cryptographic difference between Taler and previous transaction systems based on blind signing is that Taler is able to provide unlinkable change and refunds. From the user's point of view, obtaining change is automatic and handled by the wallet, i.e., if the user has a single coin worth €5 and wants to spend €2, the wallet may request three €1 coins in change. Critically, the change giving process is completely hidden from the user. In fact, our graphical user interface does not offer a way to inspect the denominations of the various coins in the wallet, it only shows the total amount available in each denomination. Expanding the views to show details may show the exchange providers and fee structure, but not the cryptographic coins. Consequently, the major cryptographic advances of Taler are invisible to the user.

Taler's refresh protocol [8] also allows merchants to give refunds to customers. To refund a purchase, the merchant obtains a signed refund permission from the exchange, which the customer's wallet processes to obtain new, unlinkable coins as refund. This process allows the customer to say anonymous when receiving refunds.

Taler's refresh protocol ensures unlinkability for both change and refunds, thereby assuring that the user has key conveniences of other payment systems while maintaining the security standard of an anonymous payment system.

3.4   Deployment Considerations for Merchants

Payment system security is not only a concern for customers, but also for merchants. For consumers, existing schemes may be inconvenient and not provide privacy, but remembering to protect a physical token (e.g. the card) and to guard a secret (e.g. the PIN) is relatively straightforward. In contrast, merchants are expected to securely handle sensitive customer payment data on networked computing devices. However, securing computer systems—and especially payment systems that represent substantial value—is a hard challenge, as evidenced by large-scale break-ins with millions of consumer card records being illicitly copied [28].

Taler simplifies the deployment of a secure payment system for merchants. The high-level cryptographic design provides the first major advantage, as merchants never receive sensitive payment-related customer information. Thus, they do not have to be subjected to costly audits or certified hardware, as is commonly the case for processing card payments [36]. In fact, the exchange does not need to have a formal business relationship with the merchant at all. According to our design, the exchange's contract with the state regulator or auditor and the customers ought to state that it must honor all (legal and valid) deposits it receives. Hence, a merchant supplying a valid deposit request should be able to enforce this in court without a prior direct business agreement with the exchange. This dramatically simplifies setting up a shop to the point that the respective software only needs to be provided with the merchant's wire transfer routing information to become operational.

The payment process requires a few cryptographic operations on the side of the merchant, such as signing a contract and verifying the customer's and the exchange's signatures. The merchant also needs to store transaction data, in particular so that the store can match sales with incoming wire transfers from the exchange. We simplify this for merchants by providing a generic payment processing *backend* for the Web shops.

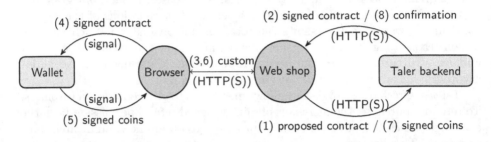

Fig. 6. Both the customer's client and the merchant's server execute sensitive cryptographic operations in a secured background/backend that is protected against direct access. Interactions with the Taler exchange from the wallet background to withdraw coins and the Taler backend to deposit coins are not shown. Existing system security mechanisms are used to isolate the cryptographic components (boxes) from the complex rendering logic (circles), hence the communication is restricted to JavaScript signals or HTTP(S), respectively.

Figure 6 shows how the secure payment components interact with the existing Web shop logic. First, the Web shop frontend is responsible for constructing the shopping cart. For this, the shop frontend generates the customary Web shop pages, which are transmitted to the customer's browser. Once the order has been constructed, the shop frontend provides a *proposed contract* in JSON format to the payment backend, which signs it and returns it to the frontend. The frontend then transfers the signed contract over the network, and passes it to the wallet (sample code for this is shown in Fig. 4).

Instead of adding any cryptographic logic to the merchant frontend, the Taler merchant backend allows the implementor to delegate coin handling to the payment backend, which validates the coins, deposits them at the exchange, and finally validates and persists the receipt from the exchange. The merchant backend then communicates the result of the transaction to the frontend, which is then responsible for executing the business logic to fulfill the order. As a result of this setup (Fig. 6), the cryptographic details of the Taler protocol do not have to be re-implemented by each merchant. Instead, existing Web shops implemented in a multitude of programming languages can add support for Taler by: **(0)** detecting in the browser that Taler is available; **(1)** upon request, generating a contract in JSON based on the shopping cart; **(2)** allowing the backend to sign the contract before sending it to the client; **(7)** passing coins received in payment for a contract to the backend; and, **(8)** executing fulfillment business logic if the backend confirms the validity of the payment.

To setup a Taler backend, the merchant only needs to configure the wire transfer routing details, such as the merchant's IBAN number, as well as a list of acceptable auditors and limits for transaction fees. Ideally, the merchant might also want to obtain a certificate for the public key generated by the backend for improved authentication. Otherwise, the customer's authentication of the Web shop simply continues to rely upon HTTPS/X.509.

4 Discussion

We will now discuss how customer's may experience relevant operational risks and failure modes of Taler, and relate them to failure modes in existing systems.

4.1 Security Risks

In Taler, customers incur the risk of wallet loss or theft. We believe customers can manage this risk effectively because they manage similar risks of losing cash in a physical wallet. Unlike physical wallets, Taler's wallet could be backed up to secure against loss of a device. We note that managing the risk does not imply that customers will never suffer from such a loss. We expect that customers will limit the balance they carry in their digital wallet. Ideally, the loss should be acceptable given that the customer gains the insight that their computer was compromised.

Taler's contracts provide a degree of protection for customers, because they are signed by the merchant and retained by the wallet. While they mirror the paper receipts that customers receive in physical stores, Taler's cryptographically signed contracts ought to carry more weight in courts than typical paper receipts. Customers can choose to discard the receipts, for example to avoid leaking their shopping history in case their computer is compromised.

Point-of-sale systems providing printed receipts have been compromised in the past by merchants to embezzle sales taxes. [32] With Taler, the merchant still generates a receipt for the customer, however, the record for the tax authorities ultimately is anchored with the exchange's wire transfer to the merchant. Using the subject of the wire transfer, the state can trace the payments and request the merchant provide cryptographically matching contracts. Thus, this type of tax fraud is no longer possible, which is why we call Taler *taxable*. The mere threat of the state sometimes tracing transactions and contracts back to the merchant also makes Taler unsuitable for illegal activities.

The exchange operator is obviously crucial for risk management in Taler, as the exchange operator holds the customer's funds in a reserve in escrow until the respective deposit request arrives[6] To ensure that the exchange operator does not

---

[6] As previously said, this *deposit request* is aimed to exchange *coins* for bank money, and it is made by a merchant after successfully receiving coins from a wallet during the payment process.

embezzle these funds, Taler expects exchange operators to be regularly audited by an independent auditor[7]. The auditor can then verify that the incoming and outgoing transactions, and the current balance of the exchange matches the logs with the cryptographically secured transaction records.

4.2   Failure Modes

There are several failure modes which a customer using a Taler wallet may encounter:

- As Taler supports multiple exchanges, there is a chance that a merchant might not support any exchange where the customer withdrew coins from. We mitigate this problem by allowing merchants to support all exchanges audited by a particular auditor. We believe this a reasonable approach, because auditors and merchants must operate with a particular legal and financial framework anyways. We note that a similar failure mode exists with credit cards where not all merchants accept all issuers, which is often the case internationally.
- Restoring the Taler wallet state from previous backups, or copying the wallet state to a new machine may cause honest users to attempt to double spend coins, as the wallet does not know when coins are spent between backup and recovery. In this case, the exchange provides cryptographic proof to the wallet that the coins were previously spent so the wallet can verify that the exchange and the merchant are behaving honestly.
- There could be insufficient funds in the Taler wallet when making a payment. Usually the wallet can trivially check this before beginning a transaction, but when double-spending is detected this may also happen after the wallet already initiated the payment. This would usually only happen if the wallet is unaware of a backup operation voiding its internal invariant of knowing which coins have already been spent. If a payment fails in-flight due to insufficient funds, the wallet can use Taler's refresh protocol to obtain a refund for those coins that were not actually double-spent, and then explain to the user that the balance was inaccurate due to inconsistencies, and insufficient for payment. For the user, this failure mode appears equivalent to an insufficient balance or credit line when paying with debit or credit cards.

In the future, we plan to make it easy for users to backup and synchronize wallets to reduce the probability of the later two failure modes. A key issue in this context is that these processes will need to be designed carefully to avoid leaking information that might allow adversaries to link purchases via side channels opened up by the synchronization protocol.

4.3   Comparison

The different payment systems discussed make use of different security technologies, which has an impact on their usability and the assurances they can

---

[7] Auditors are typically run by financial regulatory bodies of states.

provide. Except for Bitcoin, all payment systems described involve an authentication step. With Taler, the authentication itself is straightforward, as the customer is at the time visiting the Web portal of the bank, and the authentication is with the bank (Fig. 2). With PayPal, the shop redirects the customer to the PayPal portal after the user selects PayPal as the payment method. The customer then provides the proof of payment to the merchant. Again, this is reasonably natural. The 3DS workflow has to deal with a multitude of banks and their different implementations, and not just a single provider. Hence, the interactions are more complicated as the merchant needs to additionally perform a lookup in the card scheme directory and verify availability of the bank.

A key difference between Taler and 3DS or PayPal is that in Taler, authentication is done ahead of time. After authenticating once to withdraw digital coins, the customer can perform many micropayments without having to re-authenticate. While this simplifies the process of the individual purchase, it shifts the mental overhead to an earlier time, and thus requires some planning, especially given that the digital wallet is likely to only contain a small fraction of the customer's available funds. As a result, Taler improves usability if the customer withdraws funds once to then perform many micropayments, while Taler is likely less usable if for each transaction the customer first visits the bank to withdraw funds. This is *deliberate*, as Taler can only achieve reasonable privacy for customers if they keep a balance in their wallet, as this is necessary to break the association between withdrawal and deposit.

Bitcoin's payment process resembles that of Taler in one interesting point, namely that the wallet is given details about the contract the user enters. However, in contrast to Taler, Bitcoin wallets are expected to fetch the "invoice" from the merchant. In Taler, the browser can provide the proposed contract directly to the wallet. In PayPal and 3DS, the user is left without a cryptographically secured receipt.

Card-based payments (including 3DS) and PayPal also extensively rely on TLS for security. The customer is expected to verify that their connections to the various Web sites are properly authenticated using X.509, and to know that it is fine to provide their bank account credentials to the legitimate www.verifiedbyvisa.com.[8] However, relying on users understanding their browser's indications of the security context is inherently problematic. Taler addresses this challenge by ensuring that digital coins are only accessible from wallet-generated pages. As such there is no risk of Web pages mimicking the look of the respective page, as they would still not obtain access to the digital coins.

Once the payment process nears its completion, merchants need to have some assurance that the contract is valid. In Taler, merchants obtain a non-repudiable confirmation of the payment. With 3DS and PayPal, the confirmation may be disputed later (e.g. in case of fraud), or accounts may be frozen arbitrarily [7]. Payments in cash require the merchant to assume the risk of receiving counterfeit money. Furthermore, with cash merchants have the cost of maintaining change

---

[8] The search query "verifiedbyvisa.com legit" is so common that, when we entered "verifiedbyvisa" into a search engine, it was the suggested auto-completion.

and depositing the money earned. The most extreme case for lack of assurances upon "completion" is Bitcoin, where there is no time until a payment can be said to be definitively confirmed, leaving merchants in a bit of a tricky situation.

Finally, attempts to address the scalability hudles of Bitcoin using side-chains or schemes like BOLT introduce semi-centralized intermediaries, not wholey unlike Taler's use of exchanges. Compared to BOLT, we would expect a Taler exchange operating in BTC to offer stronger security to all parties and stronger anonymity to customers, as well as being vastly cheaper to operate.

5   Conclusions

Customers and merchants should be able to easily adapt their existing mental models and technical infrastructure to Taler. In contrast, Bitcoin's payment models fail to match common expectations be it in terms of performance, durability, security, or privacy. Minimizing the need to authenticate to pay fundamentally improves security and usability.

We expect that electronic wallets that automatically collect digitally signed receipts for transactions will become commonplace. By providing a free software wallet, Taler gives the user full control over the usage of their transaction history, as opposed to giving control to big data corporations.

We encourage readers to try our prototype for Taler at
https://demo.taler.net/.

Acknowledgements. This work benefits from the financial support of the Brittany Region (ARED 9178) and a grant from the Renewable Freedom Foundation. We thank Bruno Haible for his financial support enabling us to participate with the W3c payment working group. We thank the W3C payment working group for insightful discussions about Web payments. We thank Krista Grothoff and Neal Walfield for comments on an earlier draft of the paper. We thank Gabor Toth for his help with the implementation.

References

1. Chiptan/cardtan: What you see is what you sign (2016). http://www.kobil.com/solutions/identity-access-card-readers/chiptan/
2. EMVCO (2016). http://www.emvco.com/
3. Bahack, L.: Theoretical Bitcoin attacks with less than half of the computational power (draft). IACR Cryptology ePrint Archive 2013, 868 (2013). http://eprint.iacr.org/2013/868
4. Beigel, O.: What Bitcoin exchanges won't tell you about fees (2015). https://www.cryptocoinsnews.com/what-bitcoin-exchanges-wont-tell-you-about-fees/. Accessed 10 Feb 2016
5. Chaum, D.: Blind signatures for untraceable payments. In: Chaum, D., Rivest, R.L., Sherman, A.T. (eds.) Advances in cryptology, pp. 199–203. Springer, New York (1983)

6. Chaum, D., Fiat, A., Naor, M.: Untraceable electronic cash. In: Goldwasser, S. (ed.) CRYPTO 1988. LNCS, vol. 403, pp. 319–327. Springer, Heidelberg (1990). doi:10.1007/0-387-34799-2_25
7. Constine, J.: After the Regretsy and Diaspora account freezes, we've lost confidence in PayPal, December 2011. http://techcrunch.com/2011/12/06/paypal-account-freeze/
8. Dold, F., Totakura, S.H., Müller, B., Burdges, J., Grothoff, C.: Taler: taxable anonymous libre electronic reserves
9. Dominguez, K.M.: Does central bank intervention increase the volatility of foreign exchange rates? Working Paper 4532, National Bureau of Economic Research, November 1993. http://www.nber.org/papers/w4532
10. Dunn, J.E.: Eurograbber SMS trojan steals 36 million from online banks, December 2012. http://www.techworld.com/news/security/eurograbber-sms-trojan-steals-36-million-from-online-banks-3415014/
11. Ehrenberg, B.: How much is your personal data worth? April 2014. http://www.theguardian.com/news/datablog/2014/apr/22/how-much-is-personal-data-worth
12. Eyal, I., Sirer, E.G.: Majority is not enough: bitcoin mining is vulnerable. CoRR abs/1311.0243 (2013). http://arxiv.org/abs/1311.0243
13. Green, M., Miers, I.: Bolt: anonymous payment channels for decentralized currencies. Cryptology ePrint Archive, Report 2016/701 (2016). http://eprint.iacr.org/2016/701
14. Heilman, E., Kendler, A., Zohar, A., Goldberg, S.: Eclipse attacks on Bitcoin's peer-to-peer network. In: Proceedings of the 24th USENIX Conference on Security Symposium, SEC 2015, pp. 129–144. USENIX Association, Berkeley, CA, USA (2015). http://dl.acm.org/citation.cfm?id=2831143.2831152
15. Holz, R.: Empirical analysis of Public Key Infrastructures and investigation of improvements. Ph.D. thesis, TU Munich (2014)
16. Jeffries, A.: Why don't economists like Bitcoin? (2013). http://www.theverge.com/2013/12/31/5260534/krugman-bitcoin-evil-economists. Accessed 28 Feb 2016
17. Jones, R.: Cap on card fees could lead to lower prices for consumers, July 2015. http://www.theguardian.com/money/2015/jul/27/cap-on-card-fees-retailers
18. van Kersteren, A.: Cross-origin resource sharing, January 2014. http://www.w3.org/TR/cors/
19. Lewis, N.: Bitcoin is a junk currency, but it lays the foundation for better money (2013). http://www.forbes.com/sites/nathanlewis/2013/05/09/bitcoin-is-a-junk-currency-but-it-lays-the-foundation-for-better-money/. Accessed 28 Feb 2016
20. Malmo, C.: Bitcoin is unsustainable (2015). https://www.cryptocoinsnews.com/what-bitcoin-exchanges-wont-tell-you-about-fees/. Accessed 10 Feb 2016
21. Miers, I., Garman, C., Green, M., Rubin, A.D.: Zerocoin: Anonymous distributed e-cash from Bitcoin. In: IEEE Symposium on Security and Privacy (SP), pp. 397–411. IEEE (2013)
22. Murdoch, S.J., Anderson, R.: Verified by Visa and MasterCard SecureCode: or, how not to design authentication. In: Sion, R. (ed.) FC 2010. LNCS, vol. 6052, pp. 336–342. Springer, Heidelberg (2010). doi:10.1007/978-3-642-14577-3_27. https://www.cl.cam.ac.uk/~rja14/Papers/fc10vbvsecurecode.pdf
23. Nakamoto, S.: Bitcoin: a peer-to-peer electronic cash system (2008)
24. NYA International: Cyber extortion risk report 2015, October 2015. http://www.nyainternational.com/sites/default/files/nya-publications/151027_Cyber_Extortion_Risk_Report_2015_0.pdf
25. Perlman, M.: The Invention of Capitalism: Classical Political Economy and the Secret History of Primitive Accumulation. Duke University Press Books (2000)

26. Reid, F., Harrigan, M.: An analysis of anonymity in the bitcoin system. In: Altshuler, Y., Elovici, Y., Cremers, A.B., Aharony, N., Pentland, A. (eds.) Security and Privacy in Social Networks. Springer, New York (2013). http://arxiv.org/abs/1107.4524

27. IBI research: Digitalisierung der gesellschaft 2014 – aktuelle einschätzungen und trends (2014). http://www.ecommerce-leitfaden.de/digitalisierung-der-gesellschaft-2014.html

28. Riley, M., Elgin, B., Lawrence, D., Matlack, C.: Missed alarms and 40 million stolen credit card numbers: how target blew it, March 2013. http://www.bloomberg.com/bw/articles/2014-03-13/target-missed-alarms-in-epic-hack-of-credit-card-data

29. Rundle, G.: The humble credit card is now a political tool, October 2011. http://www.crikey.com.au/2011/10/25/rundle-humble-credit-card-now-a-political-tool-just-ask-wikileaks/

30. Stallman, R.: How much surveillance can democracy withstand? WIRED (2013)

31. Sweney, M.: City AM becomes first UK newspaper to ban ad blocker users, October 2015. http://www.theguardian.com/media/2015/oct/20/city-am-ban-ad-blocker-users

32. Szent-Ivanyi, T.: Wie firmen ihre kassen manipulieren, August 2015. http://www.fr-online.de/wirtschaft/steuerhinterziehung-wie-firmen-ihre-kassen-manipulieren-,1472780,31535960.html

33. Trautman, L.J.: Virtual currencies: Bitcoin & what now after Liberty Reserve, Silk Road, and Mt. Gox? Richmond J. Law Technol. **20**(4) (2014)

34. Volckart, O.: Early beginnings of the quantity theory of money and their context in polish and prussian monetary policies, c. 1520–1550. Economic Hist. Rev. **50**(3), 430–449 (1997). http://www.jstor.org/stable/2599810

35. W3c: Web payments payment flows, February 2016. https://github.com/w3c/webpayments/tree/gh-pages/PaymentFlows

36. Wright, S.: PCI DSS A Practical Guide to Implementing and Maintaining Compliance. 3rd edn. It Governance Ltd. (2011)

Malware Characterization Using
Windows API Call Sequences

Sanchit Gupta[1], Harshit Sharma[2(✉)], and Sarvjeet Kaur[1(✉)]

[1] Scientific Analysis Group, DRDO, Delhi, India
{sanchitgupta, sarvjeet}@sag.drdo.in
[2] NIIT University, Neemrana, India
harshit.sharma@st.niituniversity.in

Abstract. In this research we have used Windows API (Win-API) call sequences to capture the behaviour of malicious applications. Detours library by Microsoft has been used to hook the Win-APIs call sequences. To have a higher level of abstraction, related Win-APIs have been mapped to a single category. A total set of 534 important Win-APIs have been hooked and mapped to 26 categories (A...Z). Behaviour of any malicious application is captured through sequence of these 26 categories of APIs. In our study, five classes of malware have been analyzed: Worm, Trojan-Downloader, Trojan-Spy, Trojan-Dropper and Backdoor. 400 samples for each of these classes have been taken for experimentation. So a total of 2000 samples were taken as training set and their API call sequences were analyzed. For testing, 120 samples were taken for each class. Fuzzy hashing algorithm ssdeep was applied to generate fuzzy hash based signature. These signatures were matched to quantify the API call sequence homologies between test samples and training samples. Encouraging results have been obtained in classification of these samples to the above mentioned 5 categories. Further, N-gram analysis has also been done to extract different API call sequence patterns specific to each of the 5 categories of malware.

Keywords: Win-API · API hooking · Malware · Fuzzy hashing

1 Introduction

In today's world everyone is connected and uses internet for most of the things. This not only creates dependency on the internet but also increases possibility of exploitation via it. Besides computers, smartphones are also a great source of connectivity. Managing ever-evolving malware related to these devices is critical for proper functioning and security. Despite the use of anti-virus software, new malware and their variants are spreading continuously. Worms, Backdoors and Trojans are growing at tremendous rate thus affecting the secrecy, integrity and functionality of the systems. Thus the researchers and anti-malware vendors are always working in the area of developing new solutions to counter the effect of malware.

Various approaches like Static analysis and Dynamic analysis have been proposed for activities related to malware analysis. In Static analysis the binary code is analyzed without executing it, whereas in Dynamic analysis the code is executed and its behavior

© Springer International Publishing AG 2016
C. Carlet et al. (Eds.): SPACE 2016, LNCS 10076, pp. 271–280, 2016.
DOI: 10.1007/978-3-319-49445-6_15

is monitored. The advantage in dynamic analysis is that it even works for sophisticated obfuscated binaries where static analysis is quite challenging and time-consuming. However static features like Opcode n-gram, Byte code n-gram have been used as features for Malware detection systems [1–4].

New malware can easily evade traditional hash-based signature detection by just introducing slight modification in the code or applying obfuscation techniques. But signatures based on dynamic analysis provide better detection rate as they capture the behaviour of the malware which remains unaltered even after obfuscation. Further to categorize the malware in different classes, behaviour specific to particular class needs to be identified.

The main advantage in dynamic analysis is that the run-time behavior of the executable is difficult to obfuscate. Also, the dynamic malware analysis can be easily automated enabling analysis at large scale possible. But the disadvantage of dynamic analysis is that it captures only one execution trace of the whole program. Also the program must be run in secure run-time environment to evade the danger of getting infection while doing analysis. Both of these limitations can be addressed by using good test vectors for maximum code coverage and setting safe virtual environment. Egele et al. [5] given an extensive survey of dynamic malware analysis techniques. We have used dynamic analysis technique to analyze different class samples, where-in API call sequences are extracted by running the samples.

Using API-calls for dynamic malware analysis is not a new concept as many techniques have been proposed in the literature. Santos et al. [6] proposes a malware detector based upon frequency of occurrence of operational code and API-calls. Ye et al. [7] proposed malware detection system based on interpretable string analysis and uses SVM with bagging for classification purpose. Zolkipli and Jantan [8] presented malware behavior identification using run time analysis and resource monitoring and malware classification using artificial intelligence technique. Islam et al. [9] used static parameters namely string information, function length frequency and dynamic parameters namely API function name and function parameters to classify between malware and clean files. Gandotra et al. [10] gave extensive survey of various researches related to malware classification. Ranveer and Hirai [11] categorized various features used in the malware detection systems. They have compared features of static, dynamic and hybrid type. Youngjoon et al. [12] used API call sequences as features and they claimed to get accuracy of 0.998 in classification between benign and malware samples. They have used DNA sequence alignment algorithm for detection of malware samples.

Above mentioned research mainly is in the area of classification between malware and benign samples. Nothing much has been done in regard of sub-classification between various families of malwares. Park et al. [13] classified various variants of worms based on system call graph matching. They used maximal common subgraph as a feature to find similarities in worms. But their model is not able to provide higher classification accuracy. Nari et al. [14] presented a framework for malware classification into their respective families based on only the network behaviour. They have used network flow and their dependencies to build behavioral profile. Families considered for classification were variants of trojans, backdoors and worms. Their framework would not classify malwares with no network signatures.

In our study, five classes of malware have been analyzed: Worm, Trojan-Downloader, Trojan-Spy, Trojan-Dropper and Backdoor. We took the main classes of windows malware and observed their behaviors related to files, registry, network, services etc. by observing total 534 API calls related to each category. The main contribution in this paper is developing a technique for malware classification and further extracting signatures for all these five classes based on API call sequences.

2 Methodology

2.1 Overall Malware Classification and Characterization Framework

The Proposed Malware Characterization Framework is mainly using Win-API hooking technique for API call sequence extraction and Fuzzy Hashing technique for signature generation, matching and classification. To carry out this we have downloaded malware samples from available internet resources [15–17]. Further this malware dataset is tagged as per Kaspersky's Antivirus classification through free VirusTotal [18] scanning engine. In this work we have selected five classes of malware: Worm, Backdoor, Trojan-Downloader, Trojan-Dropper and Trojan-Spy. The reason for selecting these five classes is that we were able to get sufficient number of tagged samples for these categories. Modules for API hooking and DLL injection were implemented in C language to extract the Win-API call sequences. In all a set of 534 Win-APIs were hooked. All the samples were run and their API call sequence was observed. Repeated consecutive API calls were removed while generating signatures to remove redundancies.

To have higher level of abstraction, we bundled similar API-calls in one category. In all 26 such categories (A...Z) were created and all the API calls were replaced with the corresponding category. Fuzzy Hashing algorithm ssdeep [19] has been applied to the categorized API call sequences to get the fuzzy hash signature of each malware sample. Thus, a Fuzzy hash signature repository has been created for all the samples of different classes. For a given test sample, we use the same procedure to extract its fuzzy hash signature. Further we apply fuzzy hash signature matching algorithm [19] between the given test sample and all the samples in the signature repository. These matched values were averaged for each of the five classes and the sample is classified to the highest matched class. The schematic diagram of Malware Classification framework is shown in Fig. 1. Implementation details regarding all the above-mentioned steps are given in the Sects. 2.2, 2.3, 2.4 and 2.5.

2.2 Malware Dataset Preparation and Extraction of Win-API Calls

Malware samples were downloaded from internet [15–17]. These samples were not tagged, meaning no class specific information was available. But for training purpose we required tagged malware samples. To address this issue, we have used the online scanning services provided by Virustotal [18]. In particular, Kaspersky Anti-Virus engine classification was used to tag malware samples to appropriate classes.

For experimentation, we selected 400 samples for each class of malware: Worm, Backdoor, Trojan-Downloader, Trojan-Dropper and Trojan-Spy. We ran all these 2000

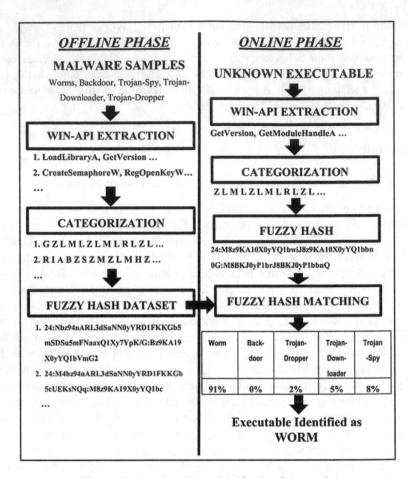

Fig. 1. Proposed malware classification framework.

samples in virtual machine and extracted their Win-API call sequences. A C-program was written for API hooking which uses Detours [20] library to extract the significant 534 Win-API calls. The Win-API call sequences were extracted by running every sample for 30 s in the Virtual environment on Windows-XP. Consecutive same API calls were clubbed together to remove redundant information from API call sequences.

2.3 Categorization of Win-API Calls

We have categorized the total set of 534 Win-API calls into 26 Categories based upon the function these APIs are performing. These categories are developed by us and are shown in Table 1. This categorization has been done to club all the APIs used to achieve a higher level functionality into a single category. For example Win-API calls like Send, Recv, WSARecv and Connect are related to socket communication and hence are placed in Socket Communication category.

Table 1. Categorization of Win-API calls.

Category	Code	No. of API	Some examples
Input/output Create	A	14	CreatefileA, CreatePipe, CreateNamedPipeA
Input/output Open	B	10	OpenFile, OpenFileMappingA
Input/output Write	C	25	WriteFile, WriteConsoleW, WriteFileEx
Input/output Find	D	13	FindFirstFileA, FindNextFileW
Input/output Read	E	18	ReadFile, ReadFileEx, ReadConsoleA
Input/output Access	F	19	SetFileAttributesW, SetConsoleMode
Loading Library	G	7	LoadLibraryExW, FreeLibrary
Registry Read	H	15	RegOpenKeyExW, RegQueryValueA
Registry Write	I	13	RegSetValueA, RegSetValueW
COM/OLE/DDE	J	154	OleCreate, OleLoad, CoBuildVersion
Process Create	K	10	CreateProcessA, ShellExecute, WinExec
Process Read	L	33	GetCurrentThreadId, ReadProcessMemory
Process Write	M	10	WriteProcessMemory, VirtualAllocEx
Process Change	N	12	SetThreadContext, SetProcessAffinityMask
Process Exit	O	3	TerminateProcess, ExitProcess
Hooking	P	5	SetWindowsHookA, CallNextHookEx
Anti-debugging	Q	4	IsDebuggerPresent, OutputDebugStringA
Synchronization	R	13	CreateMutexA, CreateSemaphoreW
Device Control	S	6	DeviceIoControl, GetDriveTypeW
Socket Comm.	T	70	Send, Recv, WSARecv, Connect
Network Information	U	17	Gethostbyname, InternetGetConnectedState
Internet Open/Read	V	13	InternetOpenUrlA, InternetReadFile
Internet Write	W	2	InternetWriteFile, TransactNamedPipe
Win-Service Create	X	2	CreateServiceW, CreateServiceA
Win-Service Other	Y	11	StartServiceW, ChangeServiceConfigA
System Information	Z	35	GetSystemDirectoryW, GetSystemTime
Total APIs		**534**	

2.4   Creating Fuzzy Hash Signatures

We have applied ssdeep [19] program to compute Context Triggered Piecewise Hash (CTPH), also called fuzzy hash, on the categorized API call sequences. The concept of fuzzy hashing has been used as it has the capability to compare two different samples and determine the level of similarity between them. Instead of generating a single hash for a file, piecewise hashing generates many hashes for a file based on different sections of the file. CTPH algorithm uses the rolling hash to determine the start and stop of each segment. CTPH Signature generation algorithm combines these section hashes in a particular way to generate the fuzzy hash of the file. Also, two inputs with sequence of identical bytes in between them can be identified using CTPH matching algorithm [19].

Table 2. Sample fuzzy hash signatures of worms.

Malware	API call sequence	Fuzzy hash
Worm 1	ZLMLZLMLRLZLZLSJLQBRLGSGSLZLDGZ LRZJLSJSLHLHGQGLGZBGZGZLZLZLML MLMHZGMLZLZAFWMWMWMF...	24:Nbz94nARL3dSaNN0yYRD1FKKGb 5mSDSu5mFNaaxQ1Xy7YpK/G:Bz9K A19X0yYQ1bVmG
Worm 2	ZLMLZLMLRLZLZLSJLQLZBRLSLSLDGZL RZJLSJSLHLHGQGLGZBGZGZLZLZLMLM LMHZGMLZLZAFWMLMLMZF...	24:M4hz94nARL3dSaNN0yYRD1FKKG b5cUEKsNQq:M8z9KA19X0yYQ1bc
Worm 3	SLZLGLZLZLQBRLTLHLHZSHMLZIRLZCA CSLSMGLSJSLHLHGQGLGZBGZGZLZLZL MLMLMHZGMLZLZAFLMLMLMZ...	24:lM2dV94nAsVPrr9WK0JPOEUf9uu SHS0uYC35AAW5AAtwYQ4l3qNb2X: NP9KAMPr6JPOE8935AAW5AAtwIlcc

We have selected this technique because CTPH can match inputs that have homologies and these sequences may be different in both content and length. As length of extracted Win-API sequences for each sample is different, fuzzy hashing technique suits us the most. These hashes constitute the signature repository. For our analysis, we have developed a repository of 2000 fuzzy hash signatures, 400 for each class. Table 2 shows API call sequences and their fuzzy hash signatures for few samples of class: Worm.

2.5   Matching Fuzzy Hash Signatures

Ssdeep [19] matching algorithm calculates the matching between fuzzy hashes of two different samples. This score is based on the edit distance algorithm: Damerau Levenshtein Distance between two strings. This matching function counts the minimum number of operations needed to transform one string into another. Allowed operations during string matching are insertions, deletions, transpositions of two adjacent characters and substitutions of a single character. After matching a comparison score is generated between 0 and 100. We have used this matching score as malware classification criteria.

3   Classification Results and Analysis

Our framework presently contains 2000 fuzzy hash signatures, 400 of each class. The ssdeep tool also has a fuzzy hash signature matching module which gives a matching score between 0 (totally different) and 100 (exactly same). For testing purpose, we took 120 samples for each category making a total of 600 samples. These samples were taken from different sources than the training samples. The test samples were run and their API call sequences were observed. Fuzzy hashes were calculated for all the samples. Fuzzy hash matching score was calculated between the test sample and all the samples of the training set. So average matching score is calculated for each class of test data. Table 3 gives the consolidated results for all the classes. It was observed that maximum matching is obtained between test samples and training samples of the same class.

Table 3. Average matching score (0–100) of fuzzy hashes between different classes of test samples and training samples.

Test samples (# 120)	Dataset of 2000 signatures (400*5)				
	Worm	Backdoor	Trojan-Dropper	Trojan-Downloader	Trojan-Spy
Worm	**25.28**	5.42	3.16	7.6	1.74
Backdoor	5.42	**22.14**	1.31	5.3	3.5
Trojan-Dropper	3.16	1.31	**24.77**	5.45	10.55
Trojan-Downloader	7.6	5.3	5.45	**27.73**	7.01
Trojan-Spy	1.74	3.5	10.55	7.01	**26.63**

These results gave us the confidence that fuzzy hashing can be used to classify the samples in different classes. So each of the 120 test samples were individually classified to the class based on maximum average matching score. Figure 2 gives the details of the classification results for 120 test samples of each of the five categories. Since there is no classification system available in literature for the above mentioned categories, so we have given comparison of our system with malware vs benign classifiers [11, 12], which are much simpler. For this we have divided our 5-class problem into five 2-class problems, namely: Worm vs rest, Backdoor vs rest, Trojan-Dropper vs rest, Trojan-Downloader vs rest and Trojan-Spy vs rest.

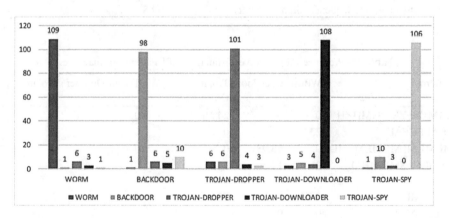

Fig. 2. Classification results of 600 (120 * 5) test samples.

Table 4 gives the classification accuracy and FPR for these five 2-class problems, and Table 5 gives the accuracy & FPR for 2 class classifier problems (Malware vs Benign) [11, 12].

Also this model is able to classify more generic classes as compared to only worm classification in [13] and it capture signatures of almost all possible activities of malware as compared to only network activity presented in [14].

These classification results indicate that there exist class specific signatures for every class which can be extracted manually by thorough inspection. Thus malware

Table 4. Performance of our framework.

Classification problem	Classification accuracy (%)	FPR
Worm vs rest	96.33	0.022
Backdoor vs rest	92.67	0.045
Trojan-Dropper vs rest	93.66	0.039
Trojan-Downloader vs rest	96	0.025
Trojan-Spy vs rest	95.33	0.029

Table 5. Performance of malware detection models given in [11, 12].

Malware detection model based on feature (Malware vs Benign)	Classification accuracy (%)	FPR
Opcode n-gram + Byte code n-gram [1]	95	0.06
Opcode n-gram [2]	99	0.03
Opcode n-gram [3]	92	0.03
Byte Code n-gram + Opcode n-gram [4]	96	0.01
Opcode n-gram + API [6]	96.22	0.07
API + String + function length frequency [5]	97.05	0.055
Portable Executable Header + Strings [7]	93.7	0.15
System Call [21]	96.8	0.04
API Call with DNA sequence alignment [12]	99.8	–

Table 6. Presence (%) of some distinctive API Patterns in malware.

Pattern	Worm	Backdoor	Trojan Downloader	Trojan-Dropper	Trojan-Spy
EBMZRFZRMHMHZH	0	0	**24.16**	0	0
LFAFECEAE	**23**	0	0	0	0
MLMLMLMLMLMLHD	0	**58.95**	0	0	0
GLGLGLSMHMHMHM	0	**12.3**	0	0	0
ZDGLMH	3.75	0	**25.83**	0	2.5
LSLZXMXL	0	0	0	0	**33.33**
FLHZSRGLMLPLPLPL	0	2.1	0	0	**32.51**
LPLP LMLZJL	**26.67**	0	0	0	0
FZRFM JRIHLFIM	0.83	0	0	**21.97**	1.25

class specific signatures in terms of patterns were extracted. Table 6 gives few of the distinctive patterns extracted for each category. The table also shows the presence of these patterns in the other classes.

4 Conclusion

API call sequence and Fuzzy hashing based classification gives good results to classify different kind of malware. Five different type of malware were studied: Worm, Backdoor, Trojan-Downloader, Trojan-Dropper and Trojan-Spy. The results indicate that Fuzzy hash matching is able to successfully capture the homologies in the behavior of the malware samples. The results also indicate that class specific patterns can be created for these classes of Malware.

5 Future Work

The proposed malware classification system will be extended to other malware classes. Fuzzy hash based matching scheme can be replaced with more sophisticated text pattern matching techniques. Number of samples in each category will be increased for more accuracy. We propose to integrate all the activities into a single automated system which will check all running programs for malicious behaviour. At present API hooking has been done at User level which will be extended to Kernel level, if possible. A similar approach will be used to capture behaviour of applications based on other Operating systems like Linux, Android etc.

References

1. Shafiq, M.Z., Tabish, S.M., Mirza, F., Farroq, M.: Pe-Miner: mining structural information to detect malicious executable in real time. In: 12th International Symposium on Recent Advances in Intrusion Detection (2009)
2. Moskovitch, R., Feher, C., Tzachar, N., Berger, E., Gitelman, M., Dolev, S., Elovici, Y.: Unknown malcode detection using OPCODE representation. In: Ortiz-Arroyo, D., Larsen, H.L., Zeng, D.D., Hicks, D., Wagner, G. (eds.) EuroIsI 2008. LNCS, vol. 5376, pp. 204–215. Springer, Heidelberg (2008). doi:10.1007/978-3-540-89900-6_21
3. Moskovitch, R., et al: Unknown malcode detection via text categorization and the imbalance problem. In: IEEE International Conference on Intelligence and Security Informatics, pp. 156–161 (2008)
4. Santos, I., et al.: Opcode sequences as representation of executables for data-mining based unknown malware detection. Inf. Sci. **231**, 64–82 (2013)
5. Egele, M., Scholte, T., Kirda, E., Kruegel, C.: A survey on automated dynamic malware analysis techniques and tools. ACM Comput. Surv. **44**(2), 1–42 (2012)
6. Santos, I., et al.: OPEM: a static-dynamic approach for machine-learning-based malware detection. In: International Conference CISIS12-ICEUTE12, vol. 189, pp. 271–280 (2013)
7. Ye, Y., et al.: SBMDS: an interpretable string based malware detection system using SVM ensemble with bagging. J. Comput. Virol. **5**(4), 283–293 (2009)
8. Zolkipli, M.F., Jantan, A.: Approach for malware behavior identification and classification. In: 3rd International Conference on Computer Research and Development, Shanghai, pp. 191–194 (2011)
9. Islam, M.R., Tian, R., Batten, L., Versteeg, S.: Classification of malware based on integrated static and dynamic features. J. Netw. Comput. Appl. **36**, 646–656 (2013)

10. Gandotra, E., Bansal, D., Sofat, S.: Malware analysis and classification: a survey. J. Inf. Secur. **5**, 56–64 (2014)
11. Ranveer, S., Hiray, S.: Comparative analysis of feature extraction methods of malware detection. Int. J. Comput. Appl. **120**(5), 1–7 (2015)
12. Youngjoon, K., Eunjin, K., HuyKang, K.: A novel approach to detect malware based on API call sequence analysis. Int. J. Distrib. Sens. Netw., Article no. 4 (2015)
13. Park, Y., Reeves, D., Mulukutla, V., Sundaravel, B.: Fast malware classification by automated behavioural graph matching. In: Sixth Annual Workshop on Cyber Security and Information Intelligence Research (2010)
14. Nari, S., Ghorbani, A.A.: Automated malware classification based on network behavior. In: International Conference on Computing, Networking and Communications (ICNC) (2013)
15. VxVault. http://www.vxvault.net
16. Vxheaven. http://www.vxheaven.org
17. VirusSign. http://www.virussign.com
18. VirusTotal. https://www.virustotal.com
19. Kornblum, J.: Identifying almost identical files using context triggered piecewise hashing. Digit. Invest. J. **3**, 91–97 (2006)
20. Hunt, G., Brubacher, D.: Detours: binary interception of Win32 functions. In: 3rd Conference on USENIX Windows NT Symposium, pp. 135–143 (1999)
21. Firdausi, I., et al.: Analysis of machine learning techniques used in behavior-based malware detection. In: Second International Conference on Advances in Computing, Control and Telecommunication Technologies (ACT), pp. 201–203. IEEE (2010)

VMI Based Automated Real-Time Malware Detector for Virtualized Cloud Environment

M.A. Ajay Kumara[(✉)] and C.D. Jaidhar

Department of Information Technology,
National Institute of Technology Karnataka, Surathkal, India
{ajayit13f01,jaidharcd}@nitk.edu.in

Abstract. The Virtual Machine Introspection (VMI) has evolved as a promising future security solution to performs an indirect investigation of the untrustworthy Guest Virtual Machine (GVM) in real-time by operating at the hypervisor in a virtualized cloud environment. The existing VMI techniques are not intelligent enough to read precisely the manipulated semantic information on their reconstructed high-level semantic view of the live GVM. In this paper, a VMI-based Automated-Internal-External (A-IntExt) system is presented that seamlessly introspects the untrustworthy Windows GVM internal semantic view (i.e. Processes) to detect the hidden, dead, and malicious processes. Further, it checks the detected, hidden as well as running processes (not hidden) as benign or malicious. The prime component of the A-IntExt is the Intelligent Cross-View Analyzer ($ICVA$), which is responsible for detecting hidden-state information from internally and externally gathered state information of the Monitored Virtual Machine (M_{ed-VM}). The A-IntExt is designed, implemented, and evaluated by using publicly available malware and Windows real-world rootkits to measure detection proficiency as well as execution speed. The experimental results demonstrate that A-IntExt is effective in detecting malicious and hidden-state information rapidly with maximum performance overhead of 7.2 %.

Keywords: Virtual Machine Introspection · Hypervisor · Malware · Semantic gap · Cross-view analysis · Rootkits

1 Introduction

The virtualization platform is becoming an attractive target for an adversary due to easy access of Virtual Machines (VMs) through the cloud service provider [1]. The proliferation of sophisticated rootkit or malware could alter the normal behavior of the legitimate GOS by altering the critical kernel data structures [2–4]. The traditional in-host antimalware defense solution is not only inadequate to thwart advanced malware, but it can also be easily removed by sophisticated rootkits or malware. For example, the malicious logic employed by the Agobot variant rootkit is powerful enough to bypass 105 antimalware defensive processes on the victims machine [5]. To detect the stealthy and elusive malware, the VMI

© Springer International Publishing AG 2016
C. Carlet et al. (Eds.): SPACE 2016, LNCS 10076, pp. 281–300, 2016.
DOI: 10.1007/978-3-319-49445-6_16

[6] has emerged as a tamper-resistant and Out-of-the-Box practical solution to enforce transparently the security assurance on the run state of the GVM [5,7,8].

The VMI is able to gather the run-state information of the M_{ed-VM} without the consent or knowledge of the one being monitored, while functioning at the hypervisor or the Virtual Machine Monitor (VMM). However, obtaining meaningful GVM state information such as process list, module list, system calls details, network connections, etc., from the viewable raw bytes of the GVM memory is a challenging task for the VMI and referred to as the semantic gap [9,10]. To tackle this problem, several approaches have evolved over the last few years by considering different constraints of the GOS [11,12]. However, the current challenges of VMI are: (1) It must have higher scalability features to introspect the rich semantic view of the live state of the GVM. To achieve this, it requires tremendous manual effort to build kernel data structure knowledge of large volumes of GOS [13], (2) The VMI solution requires frequent rewriting of the introspection program due to the dynamic and frequent upgrading of the kernel version, and (3) The VMI must be built with a robust introspection technique that would help to reduce the performance overhead and make the VMI automated with little human effort.

On the other hand, many modern families of malware leverages stealth rootkits functionality to conceals itself, and to evade detection system to tamper other critical kernel data structure such as files, directories, sockets, etc. of the GOS [14,15]. The best way of detecting it is by identifying the hidden running processes. This process is the key source of information for any introspection program to spot the existence of the malware. A prior attempt, the VMM-based Lycosid [16] is aimed at detecting and identifying only the hidden processes (HP) of the M_{ed-VM} at the VMM level. However, the current generation of evasive malware may create new malicious processes (not hidden) or attach itself to the existing legitimate running processes. In such cases, Lycosid is inadequate to detect such a malicious malware process. It does not identify the name or binary of the process and it is also inefficient in checking the detected hidden details are malicious or benign. Moreover, the process visible from the hypervisor may be noisy, most likely incorrect, and may lead to a false positive. Another approach, named the Linebacker [17], also uses the cross view analysis to investigate the rootkit running on the GVM. The efficiency of the Linebacker has been demonstrated on the VMware vSphere-based GVM. However, only the Windows GVMs were considered for evaluation.

The significant challenges in detecting the malicious and dead processes, particularly in a virtualized environment are:

- The number of running processes may significantly differ from time-to-time, even if there are no hidden processes at the moment of introspection (while checking inside the VM and viewed from the VMM). This is due to the fact that the number of processes available in the system is not constant and changes too frequently. This is due to the dynamic nature of the process creation. In such cases, it is highly dubious to rely on the introspected data.

– Estimating accurately the number of dead processes and precisely identifying the malicious processes (not hidden) in a timely manner on the run state of M_{ed-VM} is a challenging task.

In this work, the VMI-based A-IntExt system for a virtualized environment is presented. It mainly detects the hidden, dead and malicious processes that are invoked by rootkits or malware by leveraging Intelligent Cross-View Analysis for Process ($ICVA_p$) algorithm between the externally (VMM-level) captured run-state information and the internally (In-VM level) acquired execution-state information of the M_{ed-VM}. Further, it checks detected, hidden as well as running processes (not hidden) as benign or malicious.

The pertinent contributions of the present work are as follows:

1. We have designed, implemented, and evaluated a consistent and real-time A-IntExt system that periodically scrutinizes the state of the M_{ed-VM} to detect hidden, dead, and malicious processes by leveraging an open-source VMI[1] tool, while functioning at the hypervisor.
2. Our novel A-IntExt accurately detects malicious and hidden-state information on the externally reconstructed high-level semantic view of the M_{ed-VM}, and internally gathers state information of the same M_{ed-VM} by adopting its prime $ICVA_p$ algorithm. Further, it checks detected hidden as well as running processes (not-hidden) as benign or malicious by cross-checking with both local malware database and public malware scanner.
3. A mathematical model of the $ICVA_p$ algorithm has been designed, practically implemented, and implanted into the A-IntExt that detects and classifies suspicious activities of the M_{ed-VM}.
4. The other focus of the A-IntExt is to address the time synchronization problem associated with the internally and externally captured $GVMs'$ state information, which impacts on the hidden-state information detection. This issue is tackled by using the Time Interval Threshold (TIT).
5. The robustness of the A-IntExt was evaluated using publicly available Windows rootkits. In addition, malware was also employed in the experimental work to make the evaluation comprehensive. The A-IntExt correctly detected all of the hidden and malicious state information.

The rest of the paper is organized as fallows: Sect. 2 provides background and related work. Section 3 provides detailed overview of proposed A-IntExt system. Section 4 discusses memory state reconstruction. Section 5 presents experiment and results analysis. The performance overhead of A-IntExt described in Sect. 6. Finally discussion and conclusion addressed in Sects. 7 and 8 respectively.

2   Background and Related Work

To address the semantic gap impediment of the VMI, an attempt was made by Virtuno [9] that creates an introspection program automatically to extract

---

[1] http://libvmi.com/.

meaningful semantic information using the dynamic slicing algorithm based on the low-level data source of the M_{ed-VM}. The main limitation of this technique is not being fully automated and requires minimal human effort. VMST [11] significantly eliminated the limitation of Virtuoso, by enabling an automatic generation of a secure introspection tool with a number of new features and capabilities. The Virtuoso and VMST paid more attention to bridging the semantic gap, but were unable to satisfy the usefulness and practicality of the VMI. Moreover, these techniques have a high overhead. The system call redirection approach [18] proposed to meet the real-world needs of the VMI by significantly improving the practical usefulness of the VMI, and encouraged one inspection program to inspect the different versions of the GVM. The VMI-based open source tools called Xen Access [7] or LibVMI, VMI-PL [19], Vprobe [25], and HYPERSHELL [20] seamlessly address the semantic gap problem by extracting semantic low-level artifacts of the GVM from the hypervisor specific to the memory state introspection.

Hidden process detection: Antfarm [21] is a VMM based approach incorporated at the VMM to track implicitly and exploit the GOS activities. However, it is insufficient in detecting malicious processes, which are invoked for kernel code alteration. Lycosid [16] extends Antfarm as a VMM-based approach for hidden processes detection and identification, based on implicitly obtained process information from the GOS. Moreover, implicitly obtained information within the hypervisor can be noisy. The authors employed a statistical inference and hypothesis technique to address this challenge. Another out-of-VM hypervisor-based approach, namely, process out-grafting [8] focuses on analyzing the individual process of running all of the VMs processes to identify and detect the suspected process in an on-demand way. Patagonix [22] a hypervisor-based system that detects and identifies stealthily executing binaries regardless of the state of the OS kernel. To achieve this it uses knowledge of the hardware architecture.

The Ghostbuster [23], VM watcher [11] and Lycoside [16] commonly uses cross-view analysis technique to detect and identify of any discrepancy between the trusted view and the untrusted view of the M_{ed-VM}. However, comparison of the semantic data is manually achieved in most of these prior work. The main limitation of the VMI-based cross-view comparison is related to the time synchronization problem associated with the internal and external view acquired. In our work, this issue is addressed using TIT. The $ICVA_p$ is intelligent enough to distinguish between hidden, genuine, and dead processes.

3   Overview of the VMI Based Automated Internal-External System

The goal of the VMI-based A-IntExt system is to enable the inspection tool in a trusted Monitoring Virtual Machine (M_{ing-VM}) to investigate the hidden and malicious run state of the untrusted M_{ed-VM}. The overall architectural design

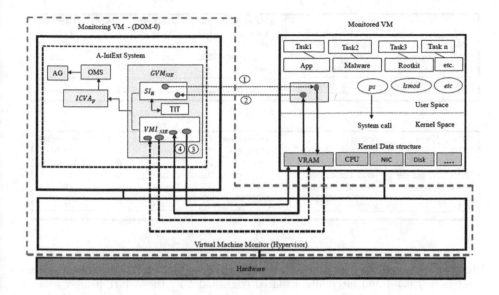

Fig. 1. The proposed VMI based A-IntExt system

of the A-IntExt is shown in Fig. 1. The prime idea is to introduce a hypervisor protected, automated, and independent system to introspect the volatile RAM pages of the M_{ed-VM} from the M_{ing-VM}, and then to identify the hidden execution state by performing an intelligent cross-comparison operation on the internally and externally captured state information. The A-IntExt achieves this goal by using the $ICVA$, which is an integral component. The major components of the A-IntExt are the Guest Virtual Machine State Information Extractor (GVM_{SIE}), $ICVA$, Online Malware Scanner(OMS) and Alert Generator(AG).

3.1 Guest Virtual Machine State Information Extractor

The prime function of the GVM_{SIE} is to extricate the run-state information of the M_{ed-VM}. Its components are: (1) State Information Requester (SI_R), and (2) VMI-based State Information Extractor (VMI_{SIE}). The GVM_{SIE} initiates the process of investigation by signaling the SI_R to send a state-information request to the M_{ed-VM} for currently running processes details. The SI_R makes use of the communication channel established between the M_{ing-VM} and M_{ed-VM} to send a request and to receive a reply. Upon receiving the state-information request (step 1), the M_{ed-VM} acquires the requested data locally, and then sends the results to SI_R after completion of the extraction operation. After receiving the internally gathered state information as a reply from M_{ed-VM} (step 2), the next task of the SI_R is to verify whether a reply arrived within TIT. If the time gap between the state-information request to state-information reply lies within TIT, then GVM_{SIE} immediately acquires the currently running processes of the M_{ed-VM} from the hypervisor to capture the current

PID	Name	Address		Process name	PID	Session name	Session #	Mem usage
[620]	chrome.exe	(struct addr:85be2020)		chrome.exe	620	Console	0	101,876 K
[2664]	alg.exe	(struct addr:85cd1020)		alg.exe	2664	Console	0	3,452 K
[2564]	chrome.exe	(struct addr:85bb5020)		chrome.exe	2564	Console	0	101,876 K
[3308]	svchost.exe	(struct addr:85e19020)		svchost.exe	3308	Console	0	4,708 K
[2992]	hxdef073.exe	(struct addr:85eed7b8)						

(a)

PID	Name	Address		Process name	PID	Session name	Session #	Mem usage
[1150]	cmd.exe	(struct addr:85589580)		chrome.exe	1150	Console	0	14,876 K
[2698]	conhost.exe	(struct addr:85cd5898)		conhost.exe	2698	Console	0	34,752 K
[2564]	chrome.exe	(struct addr:85bb5020)		chrome.exe	2564	Console	0	101,876 K
[2589]	csrss.exe	(struct addr:85e19623)		csrss.exe	2589	Console	0	58,808 K
[3355]	Kelihos_dec.exe	(struct addr:85eed7b8)		Kelihos_dec.exe	3355	Console	0	8,5858 K

(b)

Fig. 2. Hidden processes (a) dubious processes (b) details of M_{ed-VM} externally introspected (left side) and internally acquired (right side) by the A-IntExt after rootkit injection on Windows GVM

execution state by directly introspecting the RAM pages of the one being monitored (steps 3 and 4). The SI_R rejects the state-information reply and sends a fresh request whenever the time interval between the state-information request and state-information reply falls outside the TIT.

Figure 2 shows the processes of the M_{ed-VM} captured internally and externally after malware and the rootkit injection, it includes hidden, Dubious processes (DPs[2]) information. This is achieved by the well-built isolation property of the hypervisor guarantees that the state information captured from the M_{ing-VM} is accurate. The procedure followed by the VMI_{SIE} to reconstruct the M_{ed-VM} memory is described in Sect. 4. The GVM_{SIE} sends the gathered state information to the $ICVA_p$ for further analysis.

3.2 Time Interval Threshold

TIT is utilized in the GVM_{SIE} to address the time synchronization problem between the internal and external state-information captures. TIT is the time interval between the state-information request sent to M_{ed-VM} and state-information reply received by the SI_R. Figure 3 demonstrates the TIT used by the GVM_{SIE}. Let T_1 be the date and time at which the state-information request is sent to the M_{ed-VM}, and T_2 be the date and time at which the reply is received by the SI_R from the M_{ed-VM}. Upon receiving the state information, the SI_R

---

[2] Dubious Processes (DPs) are current state of executable processes it includes both benign and malicious processes (not hidden) on the M_{ing-VM}. Existing hypervisor-based VMI systems are not intelligent enough to detect and identify actual malicious processes that are running or attached to a benign one.

checks the time interval between T_2 and T_1; $T_2 - T_1 > \Delta T$, then the GVM_{SIE} rejects the received state information and resends the state information request, where, ΔT denotes the predefined threshold time. If, $T_2 - T_1 \leq \Delta T$, then, the GVM_{SIE} immediately acquires the execution state of the M_{ed-VM} from the hypervisor.

Assume that the processes $P_1, P_2, P_3 ...., P_N$ are currently being run at M_{ed-VM} and their details are extracted internally during the time interval between T_1 and T_1''. If any process expires or dies after T_1'' and before T_2, such process details do not show up in the state information caught externally by the M_{ing-VM}. As a result, a disparity emerges between the internally and externally captured state information of the M_{ed-VM}.

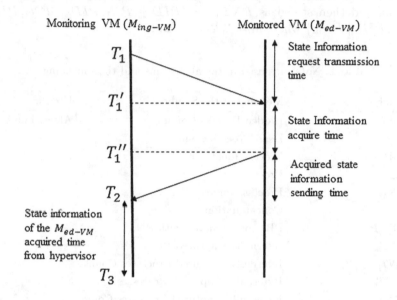

Fig. 3. Time interval threshold used by A-IntExt

The process details appear in the internally captured state information and are absent in the externally captured state information treated as dead processes. In contrast, if a new process P_{N+1} is created between T_1'' and T_3, such process details appear only in the externally captured state information and not in the internally captured state information. As a result, process P_{N+1} is recognized as a hidden process, even though process P_{N+1} is unconcealed. To tackle this issue, first, A-IntExt extracts the entire executable file of the corresponding process, and then, investigates to detect whether any malignant substance is present or not.

3.3   Intelligent Cross-View Analyser

The $ICVA$ is an integral component of the A-IntExt and its prime function is to recognize hidden and dead processes of the untrusted M_{ed-VM}, by performing an intelligent cross-examination between the internally and externally acquired execution-state information using $ICVA_P$ algorithm. A-IntExt ascertains the existence of hidden processes by examining Eq. (4); similarly, dead process presence is identified by checking Eq. (6). Further, A-IntExt classifies the introspected processes as hidden and DPs to ascertain whether the detected hidden process and DPs of M_{ed-VM} are benign or malicious by performing a cross-examination with the public OMS, as discussed in Sect. 3.4.

Model for Intelligent Cross-View Analyzer for Processes. The notations used in this section and in Algorithm 1 are depicted in Table 1. The process details captured from the hypervisor (externally) undergo the preprocessing operation, and then stored as $EXT_{ps} = \{PID \parallel PN_1, PID \parallel PN_2, PID \parallel PN_3....., PID \parallel PN_m\}$ where m = 1, 2, 3,..., and

Table 1. Notations used in the algorithms and their meaning

Symbol	Meaning of the Symbol	Used in
HPC	Hidden Process Count	Algorithms1
DPC	Dead Process Count	
PID	Process Identifier	
PS	Process	
PN	Process Name	
$\parallel$	Concatenation	
PID$\parallel$PN	PID concatenated with PN	
INT_{ps}	Internally Captured Processes	
INT_{psc}	Internally Captured Processes Count	
EXT_{ps}	Externally Captured Processes	
EXT_{psc}	Externally Captured Processes Count	
$EXT_{ps}(PID \parallel PN_m)$	m^{th} PID$\parallel$PN of EXT_{ps}	
$INT_{ps}(PID \parallel PN_n)$	n^{th} PID$\parallel$PN of INT_{ps}	

$PID \parallel PN_m$ represent the mth process. The internally captured process details after the preprocess operation are represented as $INT_{ps} = \{PID \parallel PN_1, PID \parallel PN_2, PID \parallel PN_3....., PID \parallel PN_n\}$ where n = 1, 2, 3,..., and $PID \parallel PN_n$ represent the nth process. The $ICVA_p$ performs the preprocessing operation to remove unimportant state information and sort the elements of both the EXT_{ps} and INT_{ps} in ascending order, based on the PID.

The total number of EXT_{ps} processes is symbolized as EXT_{psc}

$$EXT_{psc} = \sum_{j=1}^{m} PID \parallel PN_j \tag{1}$$

Algorithm 1. Intelligent Cross View Analyzer for Process ($ICVA_P$)

Input

1: Processes details captured externally from hypervisor stored as EXT_{ps}.
2: Process details captured and sent by the monitored virtual machine (Internally) stored as INT_{ps}.

Output

1: Hidden and dead processes details
2: Hidden Process Count (HPC) and Dead Processes Count (DPC)

1: Pre-process the EXT_{ps} and INT_{ps} such that their elements are in sorted order based on PID
2: Assign $HPC=0$, $DPC=0$, $p=EXT_{psc}$, $q=INT_{psc}$, $n=1$, m=1
3: **for all** m such that $1 \leq m \leq p$ **do**
4:    **if** $n > q$ **then**
5:       Break
6:    **else**
7:       compare $EXT_{ps}(PID \parallel PN_m)$ with $INT_{ps}(PID \parallel PN_n)$
8:       **if** $EXT_{ps}(PID \parallel PN_m) == INT_{ps}(PID \parallel PN_n)$ **then**
9:          $m=m+1$; $n=n+1$; goto step 4;
10:       **else**
11:          **if** $EXT_{ps}(PID \parallel PN_m) < INT_{ps}(PID \parallel PN_n)$ **then**
12:             store $EXT_{ps}(PID \parallel PN_m)$ as hidden process into HP.txt
13:             $m=m+1$; $HPC = HPC + 1$; goto step 4
14:          **else**
15:             **if** $EXT_{ps}(PID \parallel PN_m) > INT_{ps}(PID \parallel PN_n)$ **then**
16:                store $INT_{ps}(PID \parallel PN_n)$ as dead process into DP.txt
17:                $DPC = DPC + 1$; $n=n+1$; goto step 4
18:             **end if**
19:          **end if**
20:       **end if**
21:    **end if**
22: **end for**
23: **if** $m < p$ $\&\&n > q$ **then**
24:    Store $EXT_{ps}(PID \parallel PN_m),...,EXT_{ps}(PID \parallel PN_p)$ as hidden processes into HP.txt
25:    $HPC = HPC + (p\text{-}m)$.
26: **end if**
27: **if** $m > p$ $\&\&n < q$ **then**
28:    Store $INT_{ps}(PID \parallel PN_n),..., INT_{ps}(PID \parallel PN_q)$ as dead processes into DP.txt.
29:    $DPC=DPC + (q\text{-}n)$
30: **end if**

The total number of INT_{ps} processes is represented as INT_{psc}

$$INT_{psc} = \sum_{j=1}^{n} PID \parallel PN_j \qquad (2)$$

Any inconsistency between EXT_{psc} and INT_{psc} i.e. $EXT_{psc} \neq INT_{psc}$ indicates an abnormal state of the M_{ed-VM}. Algorithm 1 depicts the procedure followed by the $ICVA_P$ to perform the cross-examination between the EXT_{ps} and INT_{ps}. At the end of the scrutiny, $ICVA_P$ provides Hidden Process Count (HPC) and Dead Process Count (DPC), hidden and dead processes.

$$ICVA_P(EXT_{ps}, INT_{ps}) \rightarrow HPC, DPC, hidden, deadprocess \qquad (3)$$

To ascertain the hidden and dead processes, the $ICVA_P$ compares the $EXT_{ps}(PID \parallel PN_m)$ with $INT_{ps}(PID \parallel PN_m)$, where $(PID \parallel PN_m)$ is the mth PID and PN. It treats the examined processes as dubious when they are equal. If they are unequal, it checks further to determine whether $EXT_{ps}(PID \parallel PN_m)$ is greater than $INT_{ps}(PID \parallel PN_m)$; if the condition is satisfied, then the $ICVA_P$ declares the $INT_{ps}(PID \parallel PN_m)$ as a dead process. It continues the comparison operation $EXT_{ps}(PID \parallel PN_m)$ with $INT_{ps}(PID \parallel PN_j)$, where j = m + 1, m + 2,..., until it finds that $EXT_{ps}(PID \parallel PN_m)$ is equal to $INT_{ps}(PID \parallel PN_j)$, and then declares the processes from $INT_{ps} = \{PID \parallel PN_m, ..., PID \parallel PN_{j-1}\}$ as dead processes when the condition $EXT_{ps}(PID \parallel PN_m) == INT_{ps}(PID \parallel PN_j)$ is satisfied. If $EXT_{ps}(PID \parallel PN_m)$ is less than $INT_{ps}(PID \parallel PN_m)$, then the $ICVA_p$ declares the $EXT_{ps}(PID \parallel PN_m)$ as a hidden process. The comparison operation between the externally and internally captured state information is continued until all of the elements are examined.

Case 1: $HPC > 0$ indicates that some processes are hidden at the M_{ed-VM}. Equation (4) is an indication of malware infection.

$$((EXT_{psc} \neq INT_{psc}) \&\& (HPC > 0)) \qquad (4)$$

Case 2: HPC = 0 denotes that the processes viewed externally are the same as the processes viewed internally. The state of the M_{ed-VM} is dubious state when Eq. 5 is satisfied.

$$((EXT_{psc} == Int_{psc}) \&\& (HPC == 0)) \qquad (5)$$

Case 3: The dead process count indicates that the number of processes captured externally is smaller than the number of processes captured internally. This is due to the dynamic nature of the create and destroy of processes. To overcome this situation, A-IntExt first captures the state information of the M_{ed-VM} internally, followed by externally within the TIT.

$$(EXT_{psc} < INT_{psc}) \qquad (6)$$

3.4   Online Malware Scanner

The OMS is another key component of the A-IntExt and it performs two key functions. First, from the hypervisor it extracts the complete binary of the hidden process (executable file) that is reported by the $ICVA_P$. The OMS accomplishes this by utilizing *procdump* plugin of an open source tool[3] on the acquired memory dump of M_{ed-VMs}. For each executable file, it computes three distinct hash digests, such as Message Digest (MD5), Secure Hash Algorithm-1 (SHA-1), and Secure Hash Algorithm-256 (SHA-256). Further, these computed hash digests were checked with Local Malware Database (LMD[4]) to identify any types of hash digests were matched with stored hash digests of known malware types, if not it sends the computed hash digests to powerful public free OMSs and gets an examination report to ascertain whether the extracted executable file is benign or malignant. Similarly, OMS also extracts other processes executable files that are not classified as hidden processes by the $ICVA_P$ that are currently being running in the M_{ed-VM}. These processes are named as dubious processes. Like shrouded processes, the OMS additionally registers hash digest for non-concealed processes and sends them to OMS to identify whether the non-concealed process executable file is malevolent or benign. The procedure involved in determining whether the detected hidden and running dubious (not-hidden) processes are benign or malicious is shown in Fig. 4. The accurate identification and detection of hidden processes leads to A-IntExt generating an alert.

4 Windows VM Memory State Reconstruction

The Intel VT-X and AMD-V virtualization architectures provide hardware-assisted Extended Page Table (EPT) and nested page table to facilitate the address translation more efficiently by leveraging the EPT mechanism [26], the A-IntExt is able to read the guest virtual address from the raw memory contents of the GVM. However, due to the dynamic nature and consistent upgrading of the kernel version, reconstructing the semantic view of the virtual machine is a challenging task for the VMI technology. To reconstruct the memory state of the M_{ed-VM}, the A-IntExt prototype leverages an open-source VMI tool that uses the *xc_map_foreign_range()* function provided in the Xen Control Library (libxc) to understand and reconstruct volatile memory artifacts of the M_{ed-VM} without the consent of the M_{ed-VM}. Later, the same function accesses the RAM memory artifacts, and finally, converts the page frame number to the memory frame number.

Translation of the virtual machine memory address into the corresponding physical address in the host machine is needed to reconstruct the semantic view of the M_{ed-VM}. To reconstruct the memory state information for a commodity operating system (e.g., Windows), the VMI techniques require an in-depth knowledge of the GVM kernel data structures. Static data entries of the kernel symbol table are crucial for the kernel and boot-up procedures. Memory-state reconstruction is the initial step in extracting meaningful high-level information (*ps, lsmod*, etc.) from low-level artifacts of the live GVM. This is achieved in

---

[3] http://www.volatilityfoundation.org/.

[4] LMD consists of 107520 MD5,SHA-1, and SHA-256 hash digest for all previously identified well-known families of malware which was obtained by using https://virusshare.com/ malware repository.

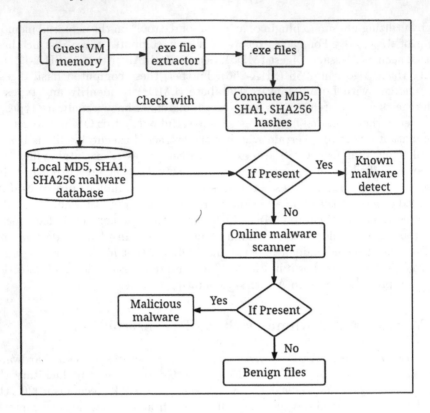

Fig. 4. Online malware scanner

the A-IntExt system by leveraging the VMI technology, while functioning at M_{ing-VM} of the hypervisor with the kernel symbol table of the corresponding GVM.

In the Windows system, each process associated with a data structure is called an *EPROCESS*. Each *EPROCESS* has many data fields and one Forward Link *(FLINK)* pointer and one Backward Link (*BLINK*) pointer. The *FLINK* contains the address of the next *EPROCESS* and *BLINK* stores the address of the previous *EPROCESS*. The first field of the *EPROCESS* is a process control block, which is a structure of type Kernel Process (*KPROCESS*). The *KPROCESS* is used to provide data related to scheduling and time accounting. Other data fields of the *EPROCESS* are PID, Parent PID (PPID), exit status, etc. [24]. The field position of the PID and the PPID in the *EPROCESS* structure may differ from one operating system version to another version, and the series of *FLINK* and *BLINK* systematizes the *EPROCESS* data structures in a circular doubly linked list. A Windows symbol, such as the *PsActiveProcessHead*, points to the doubly linked list. Traversing the *EPROCESS* doubly linked list from the beginning to the end provides all of the running process details.

5 Experimental Results and Evaluation

5.1 Experimental Setup

Experiments were conducted on the host system, which possessed the following specifications: Intel(R) core(TM) i7-3770 CPU@3.40 GHz, 8 GB RAM, and Ubuntu 14.04 (Trusty Tahr) 64-bit operating system. The popular open-source Xen 4.4 bare metal hypervisor was utilized to establish a virtualized environment. To introspect the run state of the live M_{ed-VM}, Windows XP-SP3 32 bit GVM created as DOMU-1 under the Xen hypervisor. The GVM was managed by the trusted VM (DOM-0 i.e. management unit) of the Xen hypervisor. The A-IntExt was installed on the DOM-0 VM, and it leveraged the popular VMI tool, namely, the LibVMI version 0.10.1 to introspect low-level artifacts of the GVMs. The LibVMI traps the hardware events and accesses the vCPU registers, while functioning at the hypervisor.

5.2 Implementation

The implementation of A-IntExt is at three levels: (i) it acts as a VMI system by leveraging a prominent VMI tool to introspect and acquire the GVM running state information without human intervention, (ii) the $ICVA_P$ algorithm is implemented as Proof of Concept (PoC) and induced into the A-IntExt, wherein the $ICVA_P$ detects hidden, dead and dubious processes. In addition, a program was developed that establishes a communication channel between the A-IntExt and the M_{ed-VM}, which also facilitates the transfer of state information by the M_{ed-VM} to the IS_R. (iii) The A-IntExt comprises another major component named OMS (see Sect. 3.4). It is used to identify whether the detected hidden and classified DPs are benign or malicious by auxiliary verification with LMD and large online free public malware scanners[5] while addressing the malicious processes (not hidden) detection challenges as discussed in Sect. 1.

5.3 Windows Malware and Windows Rootkits

To convert the benign Windows GVM into a malicious one and to perform malicious activities on the GVM, two stages of experiments were performed using a combination of both malware and publically available Windows rootkits. In the first stage, the evasive malware variant called Kelihos was directly collected from malware repository[6] to generate bulk malicious processes. In the second stage of the experiment, five publicly available real-world Windows rootkits that have the ability to hide the processes were used.

Experiment 1: Kelihos is a Windows malware also known as Hlux. Once it starts to execute, it generates a number of child processes, and then exits from the main process to conceal its existence. It launches a set of processes in a span

---

[5] https://www.virustotal.com/.
[6] http://openmalware.org/.

of a short interval, which influences the process count. The main function of the generated child process is to monitor user activities, and then report it to the Command and Control Server (C&C) to be joined into a botnet. The Kelihos malware was used to breed a number of processes, and at the same time, the Hacker defender rootkit was used to hide the process. This test was done to demonstrate the detection accuracy of the A-IntExt under a dynamic process creation environment. The A-IntExt extracts the manipulated semantic kernel data structure details related to the process by walking through the *EPROCESS* data structure and its associated *PsActiveProcessHead* symbol (see Sect. 4).

Table 2. Detection and classification of hidden, dead and DPs by the A-IntExt for windows GVM

Exp	PS used	PS visible at GVM	PS Introspected by A-IntExt	No. of PS classified by A-IntExt			Time in (Sec)
				HPC	DPC	DPs	
Test-1	25	20	25	5	0	20	0.22
Test-2	50	45	50	5	0	45	0.41
Test-3	75	70	74	5	1	69	0.63
Test-4	100	95	99	5	1	94	0.82
Test-5	125	120	123	5	2	118	1.03

The $ICVA_p$ is a subcomponent of the A-IntExt and its task is to identify hidden, dead and dubious processes by performing a comparison operation on the internally and externally captured state information of the M_{ed-VM}. The performance evaluation tests for both the $ICVA_p$ and the A-IntExt were conducted separately. To measure the execution speed of the $ICVA_P$ in detecting the hidden and dead processes, experiments were performed with different numbers of processes, i.e., 25, 50, 75, 100, and 125. The execution speed denotes the amount of time the $ICVA_P$ takes to derive a conclusion as to whether the process is hidden, dead or dubious processes. The last columns of Table 2 depicts the average detection time of the $ICVA_P$ for different numbers of processes on the Windows GVM. One can observe that the detection time of the $ICVA_P$ for 125 processes is less than 1.03 s.

Table 3. Identifying an actual malicious process from detected hidden processes by OMS of A-IntExt on Windows GVM.

Exp	No. of HP	Computed MD5 hash for classified HP	Checked as	PS name	D R
1	5	55cc1769cef44910bd91b7b73dee1f6c	Malicious	hxdef073.exe	37/53
		be046bab4a23f8db568535aaea565f87	NF	procdump.exe	0/53
		6cf0acd321c93eb978c4908deb79b7fb	NF	chrome.exe	0/53
		bf4177e1ee0290c97dbc796e37d9dc75	NF	iexplore.exe	0/53
		d068da81e1ab27dc330af91bffd36e6b	NF	firefox.exe	0/53

Table 4. Identifying an actual malicious processes from detected and classified DPs by OMS of A-IntExt on Windows GVM.

Exp	No.of DPs	Scanned result		Malicous PS reported with MD5 hash	Name	D R
		Benign	Malware			
1	20	18	2	0bf067750c7406cf3373525dd09c293c	EFMTnkT7m.exe	–
				5fcfe2ca8f6b8d93bda9b7933763002a	kelihos dec.exe	37/55

Twenty-five processes were considered in the first test; each test was performed five times to derive the average detection time. Prior to the evaluation, five processes were hidden at the M_{ed-VM} and all of them were correctly detected by the A-IntExt, including the hidden, dead, and DPs, as shown in Table 2. Further, A-IntExt precisely address the malicious process detection challenges (see Sect. 1) by leveraging its OMS component. As part of the experimental observations, Test-1 of Table 2 describes the 25 processes externally introspected by A-IntExt, which includes five hidden processes and twenty DPs that are classified by the $ICVA_P$; these hidden and DPs are propagated by the malware. In our experiment-1, we used kelihos malware to generate malicious processes (not hidden) and perform spiteful activity on M_{ed-VM}. At the same time, we used hacker defender rootkit to hide some processes. During introspection of the untrustworthy M_{ed-VM}, A-IntExt precisely classified the infection activity of the malware processes as hidden and DPs. Table 3 describes that from the five detected hidden processes, one process (*hxdef073.exe*) is correctly identified as malicious with Detection Rate(DR) of 37/53 based on the computed hash, and the other four processes such as the *procdump.exe*, *chrome.exe*, *iexplorer.exe*, and *firefox.exe*, which were actually hidden by the hacker defender rootkit, are reported as benign by the OMS. Similarly, Table 4 represents the 20 DPs that were classified by A-IntExt further, those processes were checked with both LMD and OMS based on the computed hashes. The time taken to compute MD5,SHA-1,SHA-256 hashes and cross-check with LMD are depicted in Fig. 5. As a result, one process (*EFMTnkT7m.exe*) is identified as malicious by locally checking with LMD (without forwarding to virustotal) and other advanced malware process (*kelihos_dec.exe*) identified as malicous checking with OMS as shown in Fig. 6, and the rest were recognized as benign or Nothing Found (NF).

Table 5. List and functionality of Windows rootkit

Rootkit name	User mode/Kernel mode	Target object	Hide PS	Detected by A-IntExt
Fu Rootkit	Kernel mode	EPPROCESS	Yes	Yes
HE4Hook	Kernel Mode	EPPROCESS	Yes	Yes
Vanquish(0.2.1)	User mode	IAT,DLL	Yes	Yes
Hacker Defender	User mode	IAT,DLL	Yes	Yes
AFX Rootkit	User mode	IAT,DLL	Yes	Yes

IAT: Interrupt Address Table, DLL: Dynamic Link Library

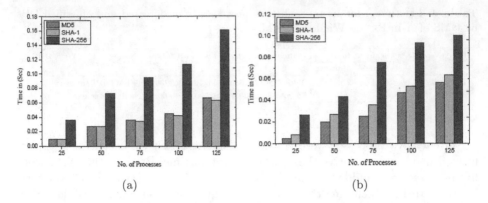

Fig. 5. The average time taken by OMS to compute MD5,SHA-1, and SHA-256 hashes for different processes (5a). Time taken by OMS to detect malware by cross-checking with LMD based on it's computed hashes (5b).

Experiment 2: In the second stage of the experiment, five publicly available Windows rootkits were used as shown in Table 5. The third and fourth columns of Table 5 represent target object and complete functionality of the rootkit, respectively. However, in this stage of the experiment, the detection capability of the A-IntExt was limited to only the processes. For example, the *FU rootkit* leverages the direct kernel object manipulation technique to hide a list of active processes by directly unlinking the doubly linked list *EPROCESS* data structure. It contains the *fu.exe* executable file and the *msdirectx.sys* system file. The function of hiding the kernel driver module files is achieved by the *msdirectx.sys*, whereas the *fu.exe* file is used to configure and command the driver. The *FU rootkit* is capable of achieving privilege escalation of the running processes and can also alter the DLL semantic object of the kernel data structure by rewriting the kernel memory. The *HE4Hook* is a kernel-mode rootkit and the user-mode rootkits are *Vanquish*, *Hacker defender*, and *AFX Rootkit*. These rootkits have the potential to hide the running processes on the Windows system. The fifth column of Table 5 represents the detection of hidden processes performed by the A-IntExt.

6   Performance Overhead

A series of tests were conducted using Windows system benchmark tools to determine the performance impact of the A-IntExt. The benchmark tests were executed on the Windows GVM in two different scenarios to evaluate the performance impact of the A-IntExt. In the first scenario, the A-IntExt was disabled (not functioning), and in the second scenario the A-IntExt was enabled (running). PCMark05, an industry standard benchmark, was executed on the Windows GVM to quantify the performance impact of the A-IntExt. Tests such as the CPU, Memory, and HDD of the PCMark05 suite were considered. These

```
OMS scan results for MD5 hash:
-------------------------------------------------------------------------------
MD5 value: 5fcfe2ca8f6b8d93bda9b7933763002a
Online Malware Scanner (OMS)   scan date: 2016-07-02 06:34:51
VirusTotal engine detections: 37/55
Link to VirusTotal report:
https://www.virustotal.com/en/file/9d48503fa42f4184873fbc796a2fb64ad61eb9fcb7a1647a4830aceaf9911
d22/analysis/
-------------------------------------------------------------------------------
OMS scan results for SHA-1 hash:
-------------------------------------------------------------------------------
SHA-1 value: 581c0425386c44b6056b66dbe36d50aefd4ca724
Online Malware Scanner (OMS)   scan date: 2016-07-02 06:34:51
VirusTotal engine detections: 37/55
Link to VirusTotal report:
https://www.virustotal.com/en/file/9d48503fa42f4184873fbc796a2fb64ad61eb9fcb7a1647a4830aceaf9911
d22/analysis/
-------------------------------------------------------------------------------
OMS scan results for SHA-256 hash:
-------------------------------------------------------------------------------
SHA-256 value: 9d48503fa42f4184873fbc796a2fb64ad61eb9fcb7a1647a4830aceaf9911d22
Online Malware Scanner (OMS)   scan date: 2016-07-02 06:34:51
VirusTotal engine detections: 37/55
Link to VirusTotal report:
https://www.virustotal.com/en/file/9d48503fa42f4184873fbc796a2fb64ad61eb9fcb7a1647a4830aceaf9911
d22/analysis/
-------------------------------------------------------------------------------
```

Fig. 6. OMS results for *kelihos_dec.exe* malware

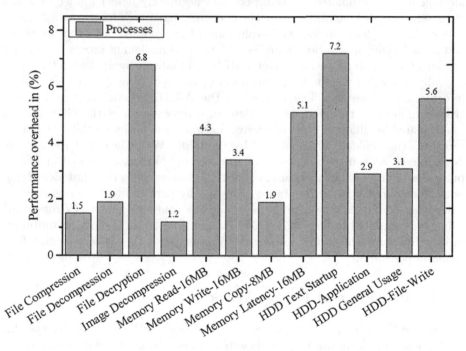

Fig. 7. Performance impact of A-IntExt on PCMark05 in detecting hidden and malicious state information of M_{ed-VM} for Windows GVM

tests were executed separately five time on the GVM. Finally, the results were considered on an average five-time execution of each test.

During hidden, dead and DPs process detection, tests such as File Decryption, HDD-Text Startup, and HDD-File-Write induced maximum performance overheads of 6.8 %, 7.2 %, and 5.6 %, respectively, other tests performance overheads observed is less than 5.5 %. These were noticed while the A-IntExt performed process introspection traces on the executed malware and rootkits. Figure 7 represents the overall performance of the A-IntExt in detecting hidden, dead and dubious processes detection.

The main reason for the performance loss is due to direct introspection and the semantic view reconstruction operation performed by the A-IntExt. As the $ICVA_P$ achieve the job offline, there is no performance overhead.

7   Discussion

The existing VMI techniques facilitate reconstructing a few semantic views of the M_{ed-VM} by directly intercepting the RAM contents of the live M_{ed-VM} by overcoming the semantic gap problem. However, these techniques are yet to be intelligent and automated to introspect and accurately detect hidden or malicious semantic state information on their reconstructed high-level semantic view. The design, implementation, and evolution of the proposed A-IntExt are signified as an intelligent solution to precisely detect the malignant processes running on the M_{ed-VM}. It acts as a perfect VMI-based malware symptoms detector by logically analyzing the malicious infection of the operating systems key source information (processes). The $ICVA_p$ of the A-IntExt judiciously performs a cross-examination to detect the hidden-state information of the GOS that is manipulated by different types of evasive malware or stealthy rootkits. Malicious processes (not-hidden) are identified by the OMS. We believe that the current development of A-IntExt is proficient in detecting hidden, dead, and malicious processes of any kind of malware or rootkit. However, detecting and identifying both known and unknown malware processes by performing cross-examination with both LMD and powerful online malicious content scanners (Viroustotal) using it's computed hashes (MD5, SHA-1, and SHA-256). The major limitation in identifying malicious processes by the Viroustotal is that it accepts only four requests per minute.

8   Conclusion and Future Work

In this work, we designed, implemented, and evaluated the A-IntExt system, which detects hidden, dead and malicious processes by performing an intelligent cross-view analysis on the internally and externally captured run-state information of the M_{ed-VM}. The A-IntExt abstracts the semantic view (processes) of the live Windows GVM externally (VMM-level). It uses an established communication channel between the M_{ing-VM} and M_{ed-VM} to receive internally captured run-state information (at-VM-level), further proficiently detecting hidden and malignant state information of the M_{ed-VM} that could be manipulated by sophisticated malware or real-world rootkits. The A-IntExt is intelligent enough to address the challenges that lie in detecting malicious (not-hidden) processes of the run state of the M_{ed-VM} using its OMS component. Publicly available evasive malware, real-world Windows rootkits were used to perform a series of experiments to accurately measure the hidden-state and malicious detection capability of the A-IntExt. The experimental results showed the accuracy of A-IntExt in detecting stealthy processes with a maximum performance overhead of 7.2 %.

As future work, we plan to enhance the detection capability of the A-IntExt to detect unknown malware which are not recognized by OMS of A-IntExt, by incorporating machine learning algorithms so that detection capability A-IntExt can be evaluated against most commonly emerging advanced persistent threats, elusive malware and rootkit.

References

1. Pearce, M., Zeadally, S., Hunt, R.: Virtualization: Issues, security threats, and solutions. ACM Comput. Surv. (CSUR) **45**(2), 17 (2013)
2. Barford, P., Yegneswaran, V.: An inside look at botnets. Malware Detection. Springer, New York (2007)
3. Lanzi, A., Sharif, M.I., Lee, W.: K-Tracer: a system for extracting kernel malware behavior. In: NDSS (2009)
4. Prakash, A., et al.: Manipulating semantic values in kernel data structures: attack assessments and implications. In: 2013 43rd Annual IEEE/IFIP International Conference on Dependable Systems and Networks (DSN). IEEE (2013)
5. Jiang, X., Wang, X., Dongyan, X.: Stealthy malware detection through vmm-based out-of-the-box semantic view reconstruction. In: Proceedings of the 14th ACM Conference on Computer and Communications Security. ACM (2007)
6. Garfinkel, T., Rosenblum, M.: A virtual machine introspection based architecture for intrusion detection. In: NDSS. vol. 3 (2003)
7. Payne, B.D., Martim, D.D.A., Lee, W.: Secure and flexible monitoring of virtual machines. In: Twenty-Third Annual Computer Security Applications Conference, ACSAC 2007. IEEE (2007)
8. Srinivasan, D., et al.: Process out-grafting: an efficient out-of-VM approach for fine-grained process execution monitoring. In: Proceedings of the 18th ACM Conference on Computer and Communications Security. ACM (2011)
9. Dolan-Gavitt, B., et al.: Virtuoso: narrowing the semantic gap in virtual machine introspection. In: 2011 IEEE Symposium on Security and Privacy. IEEE (2011)
10. Jain, B., et al.: SoK: introspections on trust and the semantic gap. In: 2014 IEEE Symposium on Security and Privacy. IEEE (2014)
11. Fu, Y., Lin, Z.: Bridging the semantic gap in virtual machine introspection via online kernel data redirection. ACM Trans. Inf. Syst. Secur. (TISSEC) **16**(2), 7 (2013)
12. Saberi, A., Yangchun, F., Lin, Z.: HYBRID-BRIDGE: Efficiently bridging the semantic gap in virtual machine introspection via decoupled execution and training memoization. In: Proceedings of the 21st Annual Network and Distributed System Security Symposium (NDSS-2014) (2014)
13. Bauman, E., Ayoade, G., Lin, Z.: A Survey on Hypervisor-Based Monitoring: approaches, applications, and evolutions. ACM Comput. Surv. (CSUR) **48**(1), 10 (2015)

14. Goudey, H.: Threat Report: Rootkits. https://www.microsoft.com/en-in/download/details.aspx?id=34797
15. Xuan, C., Copeland, J., Beyah, R.: Toward revealing kernel malware behavior in virtual execution environments. In: Kirda, E., Jha, S., Balzarotti, D. (eds.) RAID 2009. LNCS, vol. 5758, pp. 304–325. Springer, Heidelberg (2009). doi:10.1007/978-3-642-04342-0_16
16. Jones, S.T., Arpaci-Dusseau, A.C., Arpaci-Dusseau, R.H.: VMM-based hidden process detection and identification using Lycosid. In: Proceedings of the fourth ACM SIGPLAN/SIGOPS International Conference on Virtual Execution Environments. ACM (2008)
17. Richer, T.J., Neale, G., Osborne, G.: On the effectiveness of virtualisation assisted view comparison for rootkit detection. In: Proceedings of the 13th Australasian Information Security Conference (AISC 2015), vol. 27, p. 30 (2015)
18. Wu, R., et al.: System call redirection: A practical approach to meeting real-world virtual machine introspection needs. In: 2014 44th Annual IEEE/IFIP International Conference on Dependable Systems and Networks. IEEE (2014)
19. Westphal, F., et al.: VMI-PL: a monitoring language for virtual platforms using virtual machine introspection. Digital Invest. **11**, S85–S94 (2014)
20. Fu, Y., Zeng, J., Lin, Z.: HYPERSHELL: a practical hypervisor layer guest OS shell for automated in-VM management. In: 2014 USENIX Annual Technical Conference (USENIX ATC 2014) (2014)
21. Jones, S.T., Arpaci-Dusseau, A.C., Arpaci-Dusseau, R.H.: Antfarm: tracking processes in a virtual machine environment. In: USENIX Annual Technical Conference, General Track (2006)
22. Litty, L., Andres Lagar-Cavilla, H., Lie, D.: Hypervisor support for identifying covertly executing binaries. In: USENIX Security Symposium (2008)
23. Wang, Y.-M., et al.: Detecting stealth software with strider ghostbuster. 2005 International Conference on Dependable Systems and Networks (DSN 2005). IEEE (2005)
24. Lamps, J., Palmer, I., Sprabery, R.: WinWizard: expanding Xen with a LibVMI intrusion detection tool. In: 2014 IEEE 7th International Conference on Cloud Computing. IEEE (2014)
25. Vmware, 2011. Vmware, inc. vprobes programming reference. http://www.vmware.com/pdf/ws8_f4_vprobes_reference.pdf
26. Aneja, A.: Xen hypervisor case study-designing embedded virtualized Intel architecture platforms. Intel, March 2011. https://www.intel.in/content/dam/www/public/us/en/documents/white-papers/ia-embedded-virtualized-hypervisor-paper.pdf

Post-quantum Cryptology

Solving Binary $\mathcal{MQ}$ with Grover's Algorithm

Peter Schwabe and Bas Westerbaan[(✉)]

Digital Security Group, Radboud University, Nijmegen, The Netherlands
peter@cryptojedi.org, bas@westerbaan.name

Abstract. The problem of solving a system of quadratic equations in multiple variables—known as multivariate-quadratic or $\mathcal{MQ}$ problem—is the underlying hard problem of various cryptosystems. For efficiency reasons, a common instantiation is to consider quadratic equations over $\mathbb{F}_2$. The current state of the art in solving the $\mathcal{MQ}$ problem over $\mathbb{F}_2$ for sizes commonly used in cryptosystems is enumeration, which runs in time $\Theta(2^n)$ for a system of n variables. Grover's algorithm running on a large quantum computer is expected to reduce the time to $\Theta(2^{n/2})$. As a building block, Grover's algorithm requires an "oracle", which is used to evaluate the quadratic equations at a superposition of all possible inputs. In this paper, we describe two different quantum circuits that provide this oracle functionality. As a corollary, we show that even a relatively small quantum computer with as little as 92 logical qubits is sufficient to break $\mathcal{MQ}$ instances that have been proposed for 80-bit pre-quantum security.

Keywords: Grover's algorithm · Multivariate quadratics · Quantum resource estimates

1 Introduction

The effects of large quantum computers on the world of modern cryptography are often summarized roughly as follows: *"All factoring-based and discrete-log based cryptosystems are broken in polynomial time by Shor's algorithm* [Sho94,Sho97]*"* and *"symmetric crypto is affected by Grover's algorithm* [Gro96]*, but we just have to double the key size"*. A more detailed look also reveals applications of Grover's algorithm in various asymmetric schemes (as in this paper); an even more detailed look considers the question what exactly "large quantum computer" means, i.e., how many logical qubits and how much time is required to implement Shor's and Grover's algorithm. In the following, when we say "time" we always refer to the cumulative number of gates that need to be executed.

This work has been supported by the European Commission through the ICT program under contract ICT-645622 (PQCRYPTO); by the European Research Council under grant 320571 (QCLS) and by the Netherlands Organisation for Scientific Research (NWO) through Veni 2013 project 13114. Permanent ID of this document: 40eb0e1841618b99ae343ffa073d6c1e. Date: 2016-09-01.

© Springer International Publishing AG 2016
C. Carlet et al. (Eds.): SPACE 2016, LNCS 10076, pp. 303–322, 2016.
DOI: 10.1007/978-3-319-49445-6_17

This is obviously very different from the number of gates that might be physically implemented. For example, implementing a loop of length 100 around a certain circuit increases the number of executed gates (i.e., the time) by a factor of 100, but does not increase the number of physical gates (except maybe for the loop counter).

Recently, multiple papers have taken this more detailed approach of analyzing the cost of quantum attacks against cryptographic primitives. For example, in [GLRS16], Grassl, Langenberg, Roetteler, and Steinwandt describe how to attack AES-128 with Grover's algorithm using a quantum computer with 2953 logical qubits in time about 2^{87}. We note that with the results of [GLRS16] it would also be possible to perform this computation on a quantum computer with only 984 qubits, however, then increasing time by a factor of 3. In [AMG+16], Amy, Di Matteo, Gheorghiu, Mosca, Parent and Schanck describe how to compute SHA-2 preimages with Grover's algorithm on a quantum computer with 2402 logical qubits in time about 2^{148} and how to compute SHA-3 preimages using 3200 qubits in time about 2^{154}. For Shor's algorithm the common estimate is that one needs approximately $2n$ qubits to factor an n-bit number[1]. Breaking RSA-1024 thus needs a quantum computer with at least 2048 logical qubits.

These results seem to suggest that quantum computers only affect cryptography once they can be scaled to at least about one thousand qubits. In this paper we show that *much smaller* quantum computers can be used to break cryptographic schemes. Ironically, the schemes we are targeting are "post-quantum" schemes, i.e., schemes that have been proposed to replace factoring-based systems like RSA and discrete-log based systems like DSA to resist attacks by quantum computers. Specifically, we describe how to use Grover's algorithm to solve multivariate systems of equations over $\mathbb{F}_2$. This problem is known as the $\mathcal{MQ}$ problem and it is in general NP-complete [GJ79]. It is the underlying hard problem of various signature schemes like HFEv$^-$ [PCG01, PCY+15] and (variants of) Unbalanced Oil-and-Vinegar (UOV) [KPG99, DS05], and the identification scheme proposed in [SSH11].

It is long known that Grover's algorithm provides a square-root speedup in enumeration attacks against this problem. What is new in this paper are two implementations together with a detailed analysis of the cost of this attack in terms of the number of required qubits and time (in the number of gates). These numbers for Grover's algorithm are largely determined by the number of qubits and time required in an oracle that evaluates the target function. In the case of $\mathcal{MQ}$, evaluating the target function means evaluating the system of quadratic equations at a superposition of all possible inputs. In this paper we describe two such oracles for systems of quadratic equations over $\mathbb{F}_2$. The first oracle is easy to describe and for $m-1$ quadratic equations in $n-1$ variables it only needs $m+n+2$ qubits and at most $2m(n^2+2n)+1$ gates executed. The second oracle is more sophisticated and requires only $3+n+\lceil \log_2 m \rceil$ qubits, but approximately double the number of gates executed of the first oracle.

---

[1] The problem of factoring a number N is reduced to finding the order of an element x modulo N, which requires a bit more than $2\log_2 N$ qubits [NC10, §5.3.1].

As a consequence, we show that the "80-bit secure" parameters (84 equations in 80 variables) used, for example, in the identification scheme described in [SSH11] can be broken on a quantum computer with only 168 logical qubits in time about 2^{60} or on a quantum computer with only 92 logical qubits in time about 2^{61}.

Organization of this paper. Section 2 gives a very brief introduction to quantum computing to establish notation and to give the basic background required to follow the remainder of the paper. Section 3 collects the quantum gates we need in our oracles. Section 4 describes in detail our first Grover oracle for the $\mathcal{MQ}$ problem over binary fields with a careful analysis of the complexity. Section 5 continues with a description of the more complex second oracle which requires fewer qubits. Finally, in Sect. 6, we briefly sketch how to optimize for circuit depth instead of number of qubits. In Appendix A we provide quipper code to generate the oracles and Python code to generate the first oracle. We place this code into the public domain.

2   Preliminaries

In this section we will first give a concise definition of the problem we solve in this paper. Then we introduce the bare essentials of quantum computing to apply Grover's algorithm. For a proper introduction, see [NC10].

2.1   Problem Definition

Problem 1. A system of quadratic equations over $\mathbb{F}_2$ is given by a "cube" $(\lambda_{ij}^{(k)})_{i,j,k}$ over $\mathbb{F}_2$ and a vector $(v_1, \ldots, v_m) \in \mathbb{F}_2^m$. The goal is to find $(x_1, \ldots, x_n) \in \mathbb{F}_2^n$ such that

$$\sum_{1 \le i,j \le n} \lambda_{ij}^{(1)} x_i x_j = v_1 \quad \ldots \quad \sum_{1 \le i,j \le n} \lambda_{ij}^{(m)} x_i x_j = v_m.$$

Note that the system also contains linear terms as $x_i^2 = x_i$.

For sizes of this problem commonly used in cryptography, the best classical algorithm known is (Gray-code) enumeration [BCC+14]. Specifically, [YCC04, Sect. 2.2] estimates that asymptotically faster algorithms take over only for systems with about $n = 200$ variables. On a quantum computer, however, one can use Grover's algorithm [Gro96, BHT98]. To apply Grover's algorithm, we need to provide a suitable *oracle*: a quantum circuit that checks whether a vector (x_i) is a solution for a given system $(\lambda_{ij}^{(k)})$, (v_k). Every Boolean circuit can be translated into an equivalent quantum circuit, however, naïve translations typically require a vast amount of ancillary registers.

For notational convenience, we will solve the following equivalent problem.

Problem 2. A system of quadratic equations over $\mathbb{F}_2$ in **convenient form** is given by a 'cube' $(\lambda_{ij}^{(k)})_{i,j,k}$ in $\mathbb{F}_2$ where $\lambda_{ij}^{(k)} = 0$ whenever $i > j$. The goal is to find $x_1, \ldots, x_n \in \mathbb{F}_2$ such that

$$\sum_{1 \le i \le j \le n} \lambda_{ij}^{(1)} x_i x_j = 1 \quad \ldots \quad \sum_{1 \le i \le j \le n} \lambda_{ij}^{(m)} x_i x_j = 1.$$

Clearly every system in convenient form is also a regular system. Now we describe how to turn any system $(\lambda_{i,j}^{(k)})$, (v_k) of m equations in n variables into an equivalent system $(\lambda'^{(k)}_{i,j})$ of $m + 1$ equations in $n + 1$ variables that is in convenient form. For $1 \le i, j \le n + 1$ and $1 \le k \le m$ define

$$\lambda'^{(k)}_{i,j} := \begin{cases} \lambda_{i,j}^{(k)} & i = j \le n \\ \lambda_{i,j}^{(k)} + \lambda_{j,i}^{(k)} & i < j \le n \\ 1 + v_k & i = j = n+1 \\ 0 & \text{otherwise} \end{cases} \qquad \lambda'^{(m+1)}_{i,j} := \begin{cases} 1 & i = j = n+1 \\ 0 & \text{otherwise.} \end{cases}$$

The new equation forces $x_{n+1} = 1$ and so the new terms $\lambda'^{(k)}_{n+1,n+1} = 1 + v_k$ compensate for having a constant term 1.

The first oracle we construct, will use at most $n + m + 2$ qubit-registers and $O(mn^2)$ time for a system of m quadratic equations in convenient form with n variables. Our second oracle will only use $n + 3$ qubit-registers, but require approximately double the amount of time.

To conveniently describe our circuit later on, define

$$y_i^{(k)} = \sum_{1 \le j \le n} \lambda_{ij}^{(k)} x_j \qquad E^{(k)} = \sum_{1 \le i \le n} x_i y_i^{(k)}.$$

Then (x_i) is a solution if and only if $E^{(k)} = 1$ for every $1 \le k \le m$.

Example 1. As a running example throughout the paper, we will use the following small system:

$$x_1(1 + x_2 + x_3) + x_2 x_3 = 1$$
$$x_2(1 + x_3) = 1$$

Before we continue with a step-by-step definition of the circuit for the first oracle, we will review with the basics of quantum computing and in particular Grover's algorithm.

2.2   Quantum Computing

We start with finite classical computing and describe finite quantum computing later in a similar fashion. Write $\underline{n}$ for the set of natural numbers less than n. Clearly $\underline{2^n}$ is the set of possible states of an n-bit unsigned integer. Classically every function from $f \colon \underline{2^n} \to \underline{2^m}$ is computable. However, some are easy to compute and others are practically infeasible. One measure of complexity is the size of the smallest Boolean circuit containing just NAND-gates that computes f.

Later we will see that it is not easy for a quantum computer to efficiently compute any classical function f, because every quantum gate must be invertible. For every classical simple reversible gate, however, there exists a counterpart quantum gate. In the construction of our oracles we will only use (the quantum counterparts of) classical reversible gates.

The state of a quantum computer with n qubits is a tuple $(a_0, \ldots, a_{2^n-1})$ of 2^n complex numbers with $|a_0|^2 + \cdots + |a_{2^n-1}|^2 = 1$. It is convenient to write subscripts of a in binary, e.g. $a_{1\ldots 1} := a_{2^n-1}$. If one opens up the quantum computer and looks at the qubits, one will find that they *collapse* into some classical state of just n bits in a non-deterministic fashion. The chance to find all qubits in the classical state 0 is $|a_{0\ldots 0}|^2$. Similarly $|a_{b_1\ldots b_n}|^2$ is the chance to find the first qubit as the classical bit b_1, the second qubit as the classical bit b_2 and so on.

It is customary to define $|b_1 \ldots b_n\rangle$ to be the state which is zero everywhere except for on the $b_1 \ldots b_n^{\text{th}}$ place. For example $|0\ldots 0\rangle = (1, 0, \ldots, 0)$, $|1\ldots 1\rangle = (0, \ldots, 0, 1)$ and $\frac{|00\rangle + |11\rangle}{\sqrt{2}} = (\frac{1}{\sqrt{2}}, 0, 0, \frac{1}{\sqrt{2}})$. This last state is interesting: if one measures the first qubit to be 0 (resp. 1), one is sure that the second qubit must be 0 (resp. 1) as well. The two qubits are said to be *entangled*.

Every unitary complex $2^n \times 2^n$ matrix U preserves length and thus will send a state a to a new state Ua. Every operation a quantum computer can perform (except for measurement) will be of this form. Conversely, every unitary (matrix) is realizable by a universal quantum computer.

However, just like in the classical case, not every unitary is efficient to compute. It is not yet clear what the primitive operations of the first practical quantum computer will be and thus what would be the appropriate basic gates of this quantum computer — or whether gate-count itself would be the most apt measure of complexity. For instance, some gates (the Toffoli gates) in the gate set we will use are more costly to make fault tolerant with the current quantum error correcting codes than the others. For now we will make do.

If $f\colon \underline{2}^n \rightarrow \underline{2}^n$ is a reversible map, there is a unitary U_f fixed by $U_f |b_1 \ldots b_n\rangle = |f(b_1 \ldots b_n)\rangle$. In this way a reversible function corresponds to a quantum program.

2.3   Applying Grover's Algorithm

Problem 3. Let $f\colon \underline{2}^n \rightarrow \underline{2}$ be a function which is valued 0 everywhere except on one place. The problem is to find, given a Boolean circuit for f, the place where f is valued 1.

Classically one cannot do better in general than to try every possible input. On average one will have to execute f for 2^{n-1} times. With a quantum computer this problem can be solved with high probability by executing the quantum analogue of f just $2^{\frac{1}{2}n}$ times using just n qubits. This is done using Grover's algorithm. Actually, Grover's algorithm (with the quantum counting extension [BHT98]) solves the more general problem where f has arbitrarily many places where it is valued 1 and one is interested in any preimage of 1. In this paper, however, we only need the simpler version.

Clearly f is not reversible. How can we then feed it to a quantum computer where every operation should be invertible? One way is to define a new classical reversible function $R_f\colon \underline{2^{n+1}} \to \underline{2^{n+1}}$ by

$$R_f(b_1 \ldots b_n y) = \begin{cases} b_1 \ldots b_n y & f(b_1 \ldots b_n) = 0, \\ b_1 \ldots b_n \overline{y} & f(b_1 \ldots b_n) = 1. \end{cases}$$

Here overline denotes negation. For Grover's algorithm it is sufficient to provide a quantum circuit, the *oracle*, which is the quantum analogue of R_f. We claimed Grover only needs n qubits. This is true, however in practice the oracle might not be efficient to compute with just n qubits. Often the oracle itself requires some ancillary qubits, say m, as scratch space to be efficient. In that case Grover uses a total of $n + m$ qubits.

The gist of Grover's algorithm. To understand the remainder of this paper, it is not required to know how Grover's algorithm works (if the reader accepts that the core part are evaluations of the oracle). However, for completeness, we provide a brief summary of Grover's algorithm.

Let $f\colon \underline{2^n} \to \underline{2}$ be any function for which we want to find a $w \in \underline{2^n}$ with $f(w) = 1$. Write a, g, b respectively for the standard uniform superposition of all basisvectors, the basisvectors marked 1 by f, and the basisvectors marked 0 by f. Concretely, with $N = 2^n$ and $M = |f^{-1}(1)|$:

$$a = \sum_{w \in \underline{2^n}} \frac{1}{\sqrt{N}} |w\rangle \qquad g = \sum_{\substack{w \in \underline{2^n} \\ f(w)=1}} \frac{1}{\sqrt{M}} |w\rangle \qquad b = \sum_{\substack{w \in \underline{2^n} \\ f(w)=0}} \frac{1}{\sqrt{N-M}} |w\rangle$$

If we can put the quantum computer in state g, then a measurement will give a bitstring w with $f(w) = 1$ as desired. It is easy to see that a is actually a linear combination of b and g: $a = \frac{\sqrt{M}}{\sqrt{N}} g + \frac{\sqrt{N-M}}{\sqrt{N}} b$. As b and g are orthogonal, we can visualize a as a point on a grid with axes g and b. Let O be the unitary with $O|w\rangle = |w\rangle$ if $f(w) = 0$ and $O|w\rangle = -|w\rangle$ if $f(w) = 1$. It is not hard to construct O from the oracle discussed above (the quantum analogue of R_f). In our picture, O is simply a reflection over the b axis. Note how an arbitrary v on the grid is reflected to Ov. Let R denote the unitary that reflects over a. By adding some angles in the picture and a moments thought, one can see the action of RO is a counter-clockwise rotation in our grid by twice the angle a has with b. If M is known, this angle is straight-forward to compute. Grover's algorithm is to prepare the quantum computer in state a and then to execute as many times the unitary RO until the state of the computer

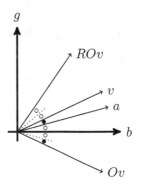

is close to g. Measuring the bits will then give a bitstring w with $f(w) = 1$ with high probability. The number of times that RO has to be executed can be shown [NC10, Eq. 6.17] to be at most $\lceil \frac{\pi}{4} \sqrt{N/M} \rceil$.

3   A Collection of Quantum Gates

In this section we collect the quantum gates that we will use for the oracles presented in Sects. 4 and 5. All quantum gates we will use are the quantum counterparts of reversible classical gates.

Gate 1. *We will use a **CNOT gate** (controlled not — also called the Feynman gate) to compute XOR. CNOT is usually drawn as shown below on the left. As unitary it is defined on the computational basis by* $\text{CNOT} \, |x\rangle \, |y\rangle = |x\rangle \, |x+y\rangle$. *It corresponds to the classical reversible Boolean function on the right.*

$$|x\rangle \longrightarrow \bullet \longrightarrow |x'\rangle \equiv |x\rangle$$
$$|y\rangle \longrightarrow \oplus \longrightarrow |y'\rangle \equiv |x+y\rangle$$

x	y	x'	y'
0	0	0	0
0	1	0	1
1	0	1	1
1	1	1	0

Gate 2. *To compute AND, we will use the **Toffoli gate** T. It's drawn below on the left. As unitary it is defined by* $T \, |x\rangle \, |y\rangle \, |z\rangle = |x\rangle \, |y\rangle \, |z+xy\rangle$ *(on the computation basis). It corresponds to the classical invertible Boolean function on the right.*

$$|x\rangle \longrightarrow \bullet \longrightarrow |x'\rangle \equiv |x\rangle$$
$$|y\rangle \longrightarrow \bullet \longrightarrow |y'\rangle \equiv |y\rangle$$
$$|z\rangle \longrightarrow \oplus \longrightarrow |z'\rangle \equiv |z+xy\rangle$$

x	y	z	x'	y'	z'
0	0	0	0	0	0
0	0	1	0	0	1
0	1	0	0	1	0
0	1	1	0	1	1
1	0	0	1	0	0
1	0	1	1	0	1
1	1	0	1	1	1
1	1	1	1	1	0

Gate 3. *To compute NOT, we use the **X-gate**, usually depicted by*

$$|x\rangle \longrightarrow \boxed{X} \longrightarrow |\bar{x}\rangle$$

As unitary it is defined by $X \, |x\rangle = |\bar{x}\rangle = |1+x\rangle$ *(on the computational basis).*

Gate 4. *To compute the AND of multiple bits, we will use the* n-**qubit Toffoli gate** (T_n). *It is a controlled not-gate with* $n-1$ *control-bits. That is: its action as a unitary on the computational basis is*

$$T_n \, |x_1\rangle \cdots |x_n\rangle = |x_1\rangle \cdots |x_{n-1}\rangle \, |x_n + (x_1 \cdots \cdots x_{n-1})\rangle.$$

Note that $T_1 = X$, $T_2 = $ CNOT *and* $T_3 = T$. *The n-qubit Toffoli gate is drawn similarly to the regular Toffoli gate. For instance, this is the 4-qubit Toffoli gate:*

$$
\begin{aligned}
|x\rangle &\longrightarrow |x\rangle \\
|y\rangle &\longrightarrow |y\rangle \\
|z\rangle &\longrightarrow |z\rangle \\
|w\rangle &\longrightarrow |w + xyz\rangle
\end{aligned}
$$

Gate 5. *For the second oracle we want to swap bits, which is done with the 2-qubit **swap-gate** S. It's drawn below on the left*[2] *As a unitary it is defined by $S|x\rangle|y\rangle = |y\rangle|x\rangle$ (on the computational basis). It corresponds to the classical invertible Boolean function on the right.*

$$
\begin{aligned}
|x\rangle &\longrightarrow |x'\rangle \equiv |y\rangle \\
|y\rangle &\longrightarrow |y'\rangle \equiv |x\rangle
\end{aligned}
$$

x	y	x'	y'
0	0	0	0
0	1	1	0
1	0	0	1
1	1	1	1

It is expected that the X, SWAP and CNOT gates will be cheap to execute and error correct on a quantum computer, whereas (n-qubit) Toffoli gates will be expensive. This is why papers often list gate-counts separately for 'easy' and 'hard' gates.

4   The First Grover Oracle for $\mathcal{MQ}$ over $\mathbb{F}_2$

Our circuit U_λ to check whether $(x_i)_i$ is a solution (of a system of m quadratic equations in n variables in convenient form), will use $n + m + 2$ registers. It will act as follows, where $r = |1\rangle$ if $(x_i)_i$ is a solution and $|0\rangle$ else.

$$
\begin{aligned}
|x_1\rangle &\quad\longrightarrow\quad |x_1\rangle \\
&\;\;\vdots \\
|x_n\rangle &\quad\longrightarrow\quad |x_n\rangle \\
t \equiv |0\rangle &\quad\longrightarrow\quad |0\rangle \\
e_1 \equiv |0\rangle &\quad\boxed{U_\lambda}\quad |0\rangle \\
&\;\;\vdots \\
e_m \equiv |0\rangle &\quad\longrightarrow\quad |0\rangle \\
y \equiv |0\rangle &\quad\longrightarrow\quad r
\end{aligned}
$$

The first n registers are the input and should be initialized with $x_1, \ldots, x_n$. The circuit will not change them – not even temporarily. The next register will be an ancillary register labelled t. It is intended to be initialized to $|0\rangle$. The

---

[2] Note that a SWAP gate can be written with CNOTs: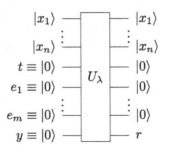

next m registers we will label e_1, ..., e_m and should all be initialized to $|0\rangle$. The final register is an output register labelled y.

We will construct our circuit U_λ step by step. Note that $1 + z = \bar{z}$. Thus, with at most $n - 1$ CNOT gates and possibly an X-gate, we can put $y_1^{(1)}$ into t. In our example (see Sect. 2):

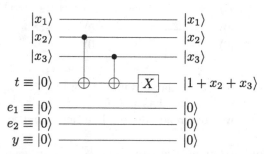

$$\begin{aligned}
|x_1\rangle &\longrightarrow |x_1\rangle \\
|x_2\rangle &\longrightarrow |x_2\rangle \\
|x_3\rangle &\longrightarrow |x_3\rangle \\
t \equiv |0\rangle &\longrightarrow |1 + x_2 + x_3\rangle \\
e_1 \equiv |0\rangle &\longrightarrow |0\rangle \\
e_2 \equiv |0\rangle &\longrightarrow |0\rangle \\
y \equiv |0\rangle &\longrightarrow |0\rangle
\end{aligned}$$

Using one Toffoli gate, we put $x_1 y_1^{(1)}$ into e_1. In our example:

$$\begin{aligned}
|x_1\rangle &\longrightarrow |x_1\rangle \\
|x_2\rangle &\longrightarrow |x_2\rangle \\
|x_3\rangle &\longrightarrow |x_3\rangle \\
|1 + x_2 + x_3\rangle &\longrightarrow |1 + x_2 + x_3\rangle \\
|0\rangle &\longrightarrow |x_1(1 + x_2 + x_3)\rangle \\
|0\rangle &\longrightarrow |0\rangle \\
|0\rangle &\longrightarrow |0\rangle
\end{aligned}$$

Then, by applying the inverse circuit used to put $y_1^{(1)}$ into t, we can return t to $|0\rangle$. As all the gates we use are self-inverse, the inverse circuit is simply the horizontal mirror-image. In our example:

$$\begin{aligned}
|x_1\rangle &\longrightarrow |x_1\rangle \\
|x_2\rangle &\longrightarrow |x_2\rangle \\
|x_3\rangle &\longrightarrow |x_3\rangle \\
|1 + x_2 + x_3\rangle &\longrightarrow |0\rangle \\
|x_1(1 + x_2 + x_3)\rangle &\longrightarrow |x_1(1 + x_2 + x_3)\rangle \\
|0\rangle &\longrightarrow |0\rangle
\end{aligned}$$

Using a similar circuit with at most $2n - 4$ CNOT-gates, two X-gate and a Toffoli-gate, we can add $y_2^{(1)}$ to e_1, leaving the remaining registers untouched. In our example $y_2^{(1)} = x_2 x_3$, hence we obtain the following:

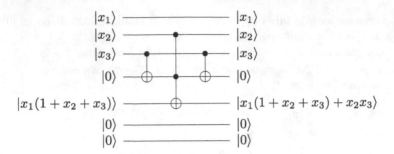

We continue with $n - 2$ similar circuits, to add $y_2^{(1)}$, ..., $y_n^{(1)}$ to e_1. Our complete circuit up to this point, has put $E^{(1)}$ into e_1 with at most $n^2 + 2n$ gates. (In our example we are already done.) The remaining registers are as they were.

With $m - 1$ similar circuits we can store $E^{(k)}$ into e_k for the other k. In total we will have used at most $m(n^2 + 2n)$ gates. In our example the remainder will be:

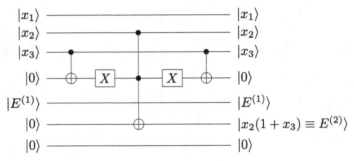

Next, compute $E^{(1)} \cdot E^{(2)} \cdots \cdot E^{(m)}$ and store it in y using an m-qubit Toffoli gate.

The circuit for our example is shown on the right. Finally, we reverse the computation of $E^{(1)}$, ..., $E^{(m)}$ to reset all but the output register to their initial state. We have used at most $2m(n^2 + 2n) + 1$ gates.

One might object to counting the n-qubit Toffoli gate with the same weight as the other gates. Indeed, classically one cannot even compute arbitrarily large reversible circuits if one is restricted to m-register gates and no temporary storage [Tof80, Thm. 5.2]. However, without ancillary qubits and just with CNOTs and one-qubit gates, one can create an n-qubit Toffoli gate. If one allows one ancillary qubit, one only needs $O(n)$ many $\leq$ 2-qubit gates to construct a n-qubit Tofolli gate [MD03]. The gates used in this construction are, however, expensive to error correct with current codes. For the next oracle, we will implicitly construct a 2^n-qubit Toffoli gate from an n-qubit Toffoli gate with n ancillary qubits.

Python and Quipper code to generate the oracle presented in this section are given in Appendix A.

5   The Second Grover Oracle for $\mathcal{MQ}$ over $\mathbb{F}_2$

In this section we will describe a second, more complex oracle, which requires fewer qubits, but approximately twice the number of gates. As for the first oracle, we give Quipper code to generate this second oracle in Appendix A.

In our first oracle we reserved for every equation a qubit register which stores whether that equation is satisfied. At the end the oracle checks whether every equation is satisfied by checking whether every of the corresponding registers is set to $|1\rangle$. Instead, for our second oracle we will only count the number of equations that are satisfied. Instead of m separate registers, we will only need $\lceil \log_2 m \rceil$ registers which act as a counter. Instead of storing $E^{(k)}$ into a separate register, the oracle will do a controlled increment on the counter. At the end the oracle will check whether the value in the counter is m. This can be done with suitably placed X-gates and a multi-qubit Toffoli.

Note that as the value of $E^{(k)}$ is not kept around anymore, it needs to be computed and uncomputed a second time compared to the first oracle to uncompute the counter qubits. This is the reason the second oracle requires approximately double the number of gates.

We still have to describe the increment circuit for the counter register. Using the standard binary encoding for the counter and the obvious increment is not a good a choice: the incrementation is hard to implement efficiently without using ancillary registers. We can do better by not adhering to the standard binary encoding.

For instance consider the 3-qubit circuit on the right. This circuit has two (classical) cycles: it will send $|000\rangle$ directly to $|000\rangle$ and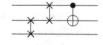

$$|111\rangle \mapsto |101\rangle \mapsto |100\rangle \mapsto |010\rangle \mapsto |001\rangle \mapsto |110\rangle \mapsto |011\rangle \mapsto |111\rangle.$$

This simple 3-qubit circuit can thus be used as a counter up to 7. For instance, to count 5 equations with this circuit one initializes the counter register to $|100\rangle$, applies the circuit for each valid equation and checks in the end whether the counter register is set to $|111\rangle$.

Now we will show how to construct a similar simple circuit for any number of qubits. For this construction we will need to think of the state $|v_1 \ldots v_n\rangle$ as the polynomial $v_n x^{n-1} + \cdots + v_2 x + v_1$ over $\mathbb{F}_2$. For instance $|1101\rangle$ corresponds to $1 + x^2 + x^3$. The circuit above corresponds to multiplying by x in the field $\mathbb{F}_2[x]/(x^3 + x + 1)$. Indeed: the ladder of swap gates at the start of the circuit is a rotation down and would correspond to multiplying by x in the ring $\mathbb{F}_2[x]/(x^3+1)$. The cNOT at the end of the circuit is responsible for the missing x term. The fact that the circuit cycles over all (7) invertible elements of the field is by definition equivalent to the fact that x^3+x+1 is a primitive polynomial.

So, to construct a counter on c-qubits, one picks a primitive polynomial $p(x)$ over $\mathbb{F}_2$ of degree c (eg. from [Wat62]) and builds the corresponding circuit. For instance, $x^5+x^4+x^3+x^2+1$ is a primitive polynomial and corresponds to the circuit on the right.

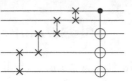

The following table lists the maximum number of each gate used in the second oracle compared to the first for a system of 85 equations in 81 variables.

	qubits	X	CNOT	Toffoli	and
First oracle	168	27,540	1,101,600	13,770	one 85-Toffoli
Second oracle	91	55,080	2,206,260	27,710	one 7-Toffoli

To find a solution to this example system, the oracle will be executed $\sim 2^{40}$ times interleaved with reflections, which yields a total of $\sim 2^{61}$ executed gates when using the second oracle.

6   Circuit Depth

If gates act on separate qubits, they might be executed in parallel. For this reason the depth of a circuit is often considered instead of the total number of gates executed. For our first two oracles we choose to optimize for qubit count instead of circuit depth. We will briefly sketch how to decrease the circuit depth by allowing for more qubit registers.

If one changes the first oracle to use a separate t register for each equation, the value of each equation can be computed practically in parallel and the circuit depth is reduced from $O(n^2 m)$ to $O(n^2+m)$ using a total of $n+2m+1$ registers.

There is still room for another trade-off: the terms $y_i^{(k)}$ for a single equation are not computed in parallel. If one uses a separate register for each $y_i^{(k)}$, one could reduce the circuit depth to $O(n+m)$ using a total of n^2+m registers.

7   Conclusion

We have shown step-by-step how to construct oracles for Grover's algorithm to solve binary $\mathcal{MQ}$, implement these in a quantum programming language, and estimate the resources it will use. As a corollary we find that some proposed choice of parameters for some "post-quantum" schemes seem practical to break on a quantum computer with less than a hundred logical qubits.

We finish with a table that shows the upper bound of resources required to solve a system with 84 equations in 80 variables with a single solution. (This is the hard problem underlying the identification scheme described in [SSH11] for "80-bits security".) We reiterate that the number of gates mentioned is the cumulative number of times that kind is executed.

	first oracle	second oracle
qubits	168	90
X gates	33,831,077,551,338,276	67,464,312,543,896,796
CNOT gates	1,345,329,399,702,340,800	2,690,658,799,404,681,600
Toffoli gates	16,816,617,496,279,260	33,840,847,554,240,980
7-qubit Toffoli gates	0	2,442,500,725,676
80-qubit Toffoli gates	1,221,250,362,838	1,221,250,362,838
85-qubit Toffoli gates	2,442,500,725,676	0
Hadamard gates	200,285,059,505,513	200,285,059,505,513
Controlled-Z gates	1,221,250,362,838	1,221,250,362,838
Total number of gates	1,430,025,554,865,881,938	2,861,116,040,048,158,450

Acknowledgments. The authors are grateful to Gauillaume Allais and Peter Selinger for their helpful suggestions. In particular, it was Peter Selinger's suggestion to construct a counter from a primitive polynomial.

A   Example code

The following is Python code that generates the first oracle circuit, which we described informally in Sect. 4.

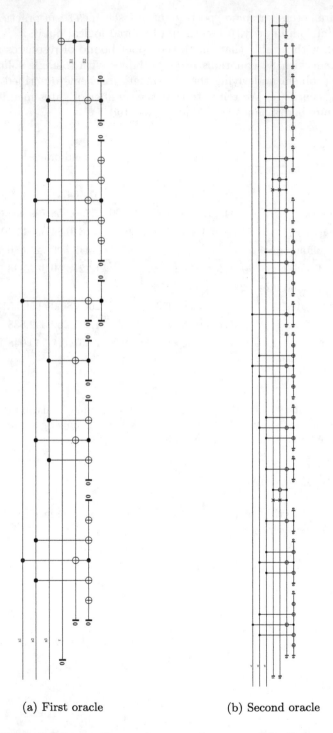

(a) First oracle   (b) Second oracle

Fig. 1. Oracles for the running example generated by Quipper

```
def create_circuit(n, m, sqe):
    """ Creates Circuit for Grover oracle that solves the system of
        quadratic equations sqe over F_2 in standard form

            n: number of variables x_i in sqe
            m: number of equations in sqe
            sqe[k][i][j]: true if x_ix_j occurs in the k-th equation. """
    # First, create helper circuit that puts E^(k) into e_k
    E_circuit = Circuit()
    for k in range(1, m+1):
        for i in range(1, n+1):
            if not any(sqe[k-1][i-1]): continue
            # Another helper circuit, that XORs y_i^(k) into t
            y_circuit = Circuit()
            for j in range(i+1, n+1):
                if sqe[k-1][i-1][j-1]:
                    y_circuit.CNOT('x'+str(j), 't')
            if sqe[k-1][i-1][i-1]:
                y_circuit.X('t')

            # XOR the value (x_i AND  y_i^(k)) into e_k
            # and clear t afterwards
            E_circuit.extend(y_circuit)  # first put y_i^(k) into t
            E_circuit.toffoli('x'+str(i), 't', 'e'+str(k))
            E_circuit.extend(y_circuit.inverse())  # uncompute t

    # Now, assemble the whole circuit
    circuit = Circuit()
    circuit.extend(E_circuit)  # put E^(k) into e_k
    # put result into y
    circuit.add('toffoli{0}'.format(m),
                    ['e{0}'.format(i) for i in range(1,m+1)] + ['y'])
    circuit.extend(E_circuit.inverse())  # uncompute e_k
    return circuit
```

To turn this into a useful commandline util that converts a system of quadratic equations into a quantum circuit in Nielsen and Chuang's QASM [Chu05] format, we need a few more lines of code.[3] One invokes the completed script as follows.

```
python mqgrover.py 3 2 111010000110
```

The second oracle is more complex and easier to synthesize in a special purpose language. The following is an implementation of the first and second oracle in the quipper programming language [GLR+13b, GLR+13a, Sel], which is based on Haskell.

---

[3] https://github.com/bwesterb/mqgrover.

```
module MQGrover (oracle1, oracle2) where

import Quipper
import Data.Bits
import Data.List
import Control.Monad
import Control.Applicative


--
-- First oracle
--


-- Compute y_i^(k) from the coefficients lambda_ii^(k), ..., lambda_in^(k)
       -- and the assignment x_1, ..., x_n.
       compute_y :: [Bool] -> [Qubit] -> Circ (Qubit)
       compute_y cs xs = withM (qinit False) $ \t ->
         unless (null cs) $ do
           when (head cs) $ qnot_at t
           zipWithM_ (\c x ->  when c (qnot_at t 'controlled' x)) (tail cs) (tail xs)

       -- Computes E^(k) from the "triangle" lambda^(k)_ij (1 <= j <= n)
       -- and the assignment x_1, ..., x_n.
       compute_e :: [Qubit] -> [[Bool]] -> Circ (Qubit)
       compute_e xs css =
         withM (qinit False) $ \e ->
           forM_ (zip css (init $ tails xs))  $ \(cs, xs') ->
             with_computed (compute_y cs xs') $ \t ->
               qnot_at e 'controlled' (t, head xs')

       -- The first (straight-forward) oracle.  Computes whether the
       -- assignment x_1, ..., x_n satisfies the given system of equations.
       oracle1 :: [[[Bool]]] -> [Qubit] -> Circ (Qubit)
       oracle1 csss xs =
         withM (qinit False) $ \r -> do
           label (r:xs) ("r":["x" ++ (show i) | i <- [1..length xs]])
           es <- mapM (compute_e xs) csss
           label es ["E" ++ (show i) | i <- [1..length es]]
           qnot_at r 'controlled' es


       --
       -- Second oracle that uses only n + ceil(log_2 m) + 3 registers, but requires
       -- more gates.
       --

       oracle2 :: [[[Bool]]] -> [Qubit] -> Circ (Qubit)
       oracle2 csss xs = do
         ctr <- init_counter $ length csss
         label xs ["x" ++ (show i) | i <- [1..length xs]]
         forM_ csss $ \css ->
           with_computed (compute_e xs css) $ controlled $ inc_counter ctr
         check_counter ctr


       --
       -- Helpers for the second oracle.
       --


       -- Rotates qubits around one turn
       qrotate :: [Qubit] -> Circ()
```

```
qrotate qs = zipWithM_ swap qs' $ tail qs' where qs' = reverse qs

-- Turns polynomial into corresponding circuit
apply_polynomial :: [Bool] -> [Qubit] -> Circ()
apply_polynomial cs qs = do
  qrotate qs
  zipWithM_ (\c q -> do
        when c $ qnot_at q 'controlled' head qs) (init $ tail cs) (tail qs)
  return ()

-- Returns number of bits in the binary expansion of a given integer
bits_required :: Int -> Int
bits_required 0 = 0
bits_required n = 1 + bits_required (n 'shiftR' 1)

type QCounter = (Int, [Qubit])
bound :: QCounter -> Int
bound (n, qs) = n
qbits :: QCounter -> [Qubit]
qbits (n, qs) = qs

-- Creates a new counter to count up to the given integer.
init_counter :: Int -> Circ(QCounter)
init_counter n = do
  qs <- qinit $ iterate (class_inc_counter zero_poly) (replicate nbits True)
                !! (2^nbits - n)
  return (n, qs)
    where
      nbits = bits_required n
      zero_poly = prim_poly nbits
      class_inc_counter :: [Bool] -> [Bool] -> [Bool]
      class_inc_counter zero_poly (False:cs) = cs ++ [False]
      class_inc_counter zero_poly (True:cs)
        = zipWith xor (cs ++ [False]) (tail zero_poly)

-- Increment the counter by one.
inc_counter :: QCounter -> Circ ()
inc_counter (n,qs) = prim_poly (bits_required n) 'apply_polynomial' qs

-- Check whether the counter has reached the desired value
check_counter :: QCounter -> Circ (Qubit)
check_counter qc = withM (qinit False) $ \t -> qnot_at t 'controlled' qbits qc

-- Returns a primitive polynomial over F_2 of given degree
prim_poly :: Int -> [Bool]
```

```
prim_poly n = map ('elem' 0:n:(watson_prim_polies!!n)) [0..n]

-- Contains for each n <= 32  a primitive polynomial of order n modulo F_2.
-- The number are the non-trivial powers of x that occur: for instance
-- the list [4,3,2] at index 8 represents the primitive polynomial
--        x^8 + x^4 + x^3 + x^2 + 1.
-- List taken from E. J. Watson, 1961.
watson_prim_polies = [
  [], [], [1], [1], [1], [2], [1], [1], [4, 3, 2], [4], [3], [2], [6,
  4, 1], [4, 3, 1], [5, 3, 1], [1], [5, 3, 2], [3], [5, 2, 1], [5,
  2, 1], [3], [2], [1], [5], [4, 3, 1], [3], [6, 2, 1], [5, 2, 1],
  [3], [2], [6, 4, 1], [3], [7, 5, 3, 2]]

withM :: Monad m =>  m a -> (a -> m ()) -> m a
withM f g = do
  t <- f
  g t
  return t
```

The gate counts mentioned in the conclusion were generated by the build-in `GateCount` functionality of Quipper, which was invoked (for the first oracle) with the following code.

```
print_simple GateCount $ grover (oracle1 sqe) 81 1
```

The variable `sqe` is set to the system of 85 equations in 81 variables where every coefficient is 1 as it requires most gates executed in our construction. We use the following implementation of Grover's algorithm.

```
module Grover (grover) where

import Quipper

import Control.Monad

-- |Reflects (in place) over the standard uniform superposition of qubits.
-- This is used as the second part of the Grover iteration.
reflect_over_a :: [Qubit] -> Circ ()
reflect_over_a qs = do
  with_basis_change (forM_ qs hadamard_at) $ do
    with_basis_change (forM_ qs qnot_at) $ do
      with_basis_change (hadamard_at $ head qs) $ do
        qnot_at (head qs) 'controlled' tail qs

-- |Grover's algorithm.  'oracle' is a circuit that should map exactly
-- 'm' 'n'-qubit-words to |1> and the others to |0>.  'grover' returns
-- a circuit that creates a superposition over all 'n'-qubit words that
```

```
-- are mapped to |1> by the oracle.
grover :: ([Qubit] -> Circ (Qubit)) -> Int -> Int -> Circ ()
grover oracle n m = do
  -- Create a standard uniform superposition over all qubits.
  qs <- qinit $ replicate n False
  forM_ qs hadamard_at
  iterations qs
  return ()
    where
      n_iters = floor $ pi / 4 / asin(sqrt((fromIntegral m) / (2^n)))
      iterations :: [Qubit] -> Circ ([Qubit])
      iterations = nbox "grover-iteration" n_iters $ \qs -> do
        -- First, the adapted oracle. The following will send a computational
        -- basis vector w to -w if its tagged by the original oracle and
        -- leave it in place otherwise.
        with_computed (oracle qs) $ \r -> do
          gate_Z_at (head qs) `controlled` r
        -- Then, reflect over the standard uniform superposition.
        reflect_over_a qs
        return qs
```

References

[AMG+16] Amy, M., Di Matteo, O., Gheorghiu, V., Mosca, M., Parent, A., Schanck, J.: Estimating the cost of generic quantum pre-image attacks on SHA-2 and SHA-3. Preprint 2016. https://arxiv.org/abs/1603.09383

[BCC+14] Bouillaguet, C., Cheng, C.-M., Chou, T., Niederhagen, R., Yang, B.-Y.: Fast exhaustive search for quadratic systems in $\mathbb{F}_2$ on FPGAs. In: Lange, T., Lauter, K., Lisoněk, P. (eds.) SAC 2013. LNCS, vol. 8282, pp. 205–222. Springer, Heidelberg (2014). doi:10.1007/978-3-662-43414-7_11

[BHT98] Brassard, G., HØyer, P., Tapp, A.: Quantum counting. In: Larsen, K.G., Skyum, S., Winskel, G. (eds.) ICALP 1998. LNCS, vol. 1443, pp. 820–831. Springer, Heidelberg (1998). doi:10.1007/BFb0055105

[Chu05] Chuang, I.: Quantum circuit viewer: qasm2circ (2005). http://www.media.mit.edu/quanta/qasm2circ/. Accessed 24 June 2016

[DS05] Ding, J., Schmidt, D.: Rainbow, a new multivariable polynomial signature scheme. In: Ioannidis, J., Keromytis, A., Yung, M. (eds.) ACNS 2005. LNCS, vol. 3531, pp. 164–175. Springer, Heidelberg (2005). doi:10.1007/11496137_12

[GJ79] Garey, M.R., Johnson, D.S.: Computers and Intractability: A Guide to the Theory of NP-Completeness. W. H. Freeman and Company (1979)

[GLR+13a] Green, A.S., Lumsdaine, P.L.F., Ross, N.J., Selinger, P., Valiron, B.: An introduction to quantum programming in quipper. In: Dueck, G.W., Miller, D.M. (eds.) RC 2013. LNCS, vol. 7948, pp. 110–124. Springer, Heidelberg (2013). doi:10.1007/978-3-642-38986-3_10

[GLR+13b] Green, A.S., Lumsdaine, P.L., Ross, N.J., Selinger, P., Valiron, B.: Quipper: a scalable quantum programming language. **48**(6), 333–342 (2013). https://arxiv.org/pdf/1304.3390

[GLRS16] Grassl, M., Langenberg, B., Roetteler, M., Steinwandt, R.: Applying grover's algorithm to AES: quantum resource estimates. In: Takagi, T. (ed.) PQCrypto 2016. LNCS, vol. 9606, pp. 29–43. Springer, Heidelberg (2016). doi:10.1007/978-3-319-29360-8_3

[Gro96] Grover, L.K.: A fast quantum mechanical algorithm for database search. In: Proceedings of the Twenty-Eighth Annual ACM Symposium on Theory of Computing, pp. 212–219. ACM (1996)

[KPG99] Kipnis, A., Patarin, J., Goubin, L.: Unbalanced oil and vinegar signature schemes. In: Stern, J. (ed.) EUROCRYPT 1999. LNCS, vol. 1592, pp. 206–222. Springer, Heidelberg (1999). doi:10.1007/3-540-48910-X_15

[MD03] Maslov, D., Dueck, G.W.: Improved quantum cost for n-bit Toffoli gates. Electron. Lett. **39**(25), 1790–1791 (2003)

[NC10] Nielsen, M.A., Chuang, I.L.: Quantum Computation and Quantum Information. Cambridge University Press, Cambridge (2010)

[PCG01] Patarin, J., Courtois, N., Goubin, L.: QUARTZ, 128-bit long digital signatures. In: Naccache, D. (ed.) CT-RSA 2001. LNCS, vol. 2020, pp. 282–297. Springer, Heidelberg (2001). doi:10.1007/3-540-45353-9_21

[PCY+15] Petzoldt, A., Chen, M.-S., Yang, B.-Y., Tao, C., Ding, J.: Design principles for HFEv- based multivariate signature schemes. In: Iwata, T., Cheon, J.H. (eds.) ASIACRYPT 2015. LNCS, vol. 9452, pp. 311–334. Springer, Heidelberg (2015). doi:10.1007/978-3-662-48797-6_14

[Sel] Selinger, P.: The quipper language. http://www.mathstat.dal.ca/~selinger/quipper/. Accessed 09 Jan 2016

[Sho94] Shor, P.W.: Algorithms for quantum computation: discrete logarithms and factoring. In SFCS 1994 Proceedings of the 35th Annual Symposium on Foundations of Computer Science, pp. 124–134. IEEE (1994). http://www-math.mit.edu/~shor/papers/algsfqc-dlf.pdf

[Sho97] Shor, P.W.: Polynomial-time algorithms for prime factorization and discrete logarithms on a quantum computer. SIAM J. Comput. **26**, 1484–1509 (1997). http://arxiv.org/abs/quant-ph/9508027

[SSH11] Sakumoto, K., Shirai, T., Hiwatari, H.: Public-key identification schemes based on multivariate quadratic polynomials. In: Rogaway, P. (ed.) CRYPTO 2011. LNCS, vol. 6841, pp. 706–723. Springer, Heidelberg (2011). doi:10.1007/978-3-642-22792-9_40

[Tof80] Toffoli, T.: Reversible Computing. Springer, Heidelberg (1980)

[Wat62] Watson, E.J.: Primitive polynomials (mod 2). Math. Comput. **16**(79), 368–369 (1962)

[YCC04] Yang, B.-Y., Chen, J.-M., Courtois, N.T.: On asymptotic security estimates in XL and Gröbner bases-related algebraic cryptanalysis. In: Lopez, J., Qing, S., Okamoto, E. (eds.) ICICS 2004. LNCS, vol. 3269, pp. 401–413. Springer, Heidelberg (2004). doi:10.1007/978-3-540-30191-2_31

Ring-LWE: Applications to Cryptography and Their Efficient Realization

Sujoy Sinha Roy, Angshuman Karmakar, and Ingrid Verbauwhede[(✉)]

ESAT/COSIC and IMinds, KU Leuven,
Kasteelpark Arenberg 10, 3001 Leuven-heverlee, Belgium
{sujoy.sinharoy,angshuman.karmakar,ingrid.verbauwhede}@esat.kuleuven.be

Abstract. The persistent progress of quantum computing with algorithms of Shor and Proos and Zalka has put our present RSA and ECC based public key cryptosystems at peril. There is a flurry of activity in cryptographic research community to replace classical cryptography schemes with their post-quantum counterparts. The learning with errors problem introduced by Oded Regev offers a way to design secure cryptography schemes in the post-quantum world. Later for efficiency LWE was adapted for ring polynomials known as Ring-LWE. In this paper we discuss some of these ring-LWE based schemes that have been designed. We have also drawn comparisons of different implementations of those schemes to illustrate their evolution from theoretical proposals to practically feasible schemes.

Keywords: Post-quantum cryptography · Learning with errors · Ring learning with errors · Implementations

1 Introduction

Post-quantum cryptography has become a popular research topic in cryptography in this decade. Our existing public-key infrastructures greatly rely on cryptographic primitives such as elliptic curve cryptography and RSA. The security if these primitives are based on the hardness of elliptic curve discrete logarithm problem and integer factorization. With our present day computers, these two problems remain computationally infeasible for sufficiently large key size. However a powerful quantum computer together with Shor's (RSA) and Proos and Zalka's (ECDLP) algorithm can solve these problems in polynomial time. Though there is no known powerful quantum computer till date, different organizations are trying to build quantum computers. In 2014 a BBC News article [2] reports an effort by the NSA. Due to these threats the need for quantum computer resistant public key cryptography has emerged. Recently NIST has recommended a gradual shift towards post-quantum cryptography [6] and have called for a standardization process for post-quantum cryptography schemes in the PQCrypto 2016 conference. Different organizations in the field of information storage and processing have responded to this call. For example, Google

© Springer International Publishing AG 2016
C. Carlet et al. (Eds.): SPACE 2016, LNCS 10076, pp. 323–331, 2016.
DOI: 10.1007/978-3-319-49445-6_18

has recently introduced the scheme *Frodo* [4] in 1 % of all Chrome browsers. The world wide cryptography research community has proposed several candidates for post-quantum public key cryptography. Among them, the schemes based on lattices have received the highest attention thanks to their simpler arithmetic operations and wide range of applicability. In this paper we provide an overview of different lattice based constructions and discuss their implementations.

The LWE Problem

The foundations of the cryptosystems that we discuss in this paper are based on the *learning with errors* (LWE) problem that was introduced in 2005 by Regev [28]. The problem is conjectured to be a hard problem and it is as hard as solving several worst-case lattice problems. For a lattice with dimension n, integer modulus q, and an error distribution $\mathcal{X}$ over the integers $\mathbb{Z}$, the LWE problem is defined as follows.

We denote vectors of dimension n by bold fonts. Generate a secret vector $\mathbf{s}$ of dimension n by choosing its coefficients uniformly in $\mathbb{Z}_q$. Generate $\mathbf{a}_i$ uniformly and the error terms e_i from $\mathcal{X}$. Next compute $b_i = \langle \mathbf{a}_i, \mathbf{s} \rangle + e_i \in \mathbb{Z}_q$. The LWE distribution is denoted as $A_{s,\mathcal{X}}$ over $\mathbb{Z}_q^n \times \mathbb{Z}_q$ and is the set of tuples $(\mathbf{a}_i, b_i)$. Solving the *decision LWE problem* is to distinguish with non-negligible advantage between the samples from $A_{s,\mathcal{X}}$ and the same number of samples drawn uniformly from $\mathbb{Z}_q^n \times \mathbb{Z}_q$. Solving the *search LWE problem* is to find $\mathbf{s}$ from a polynomial number of samples drawn from $A_{s,\mathcal{X}}$. The error distribution $\mathcal{X}$ is normally a discrete Gaussian distribution with a standard deviation σ.

The original LWE problem is defined over lattices and is not very efficient due to the use of large matrices. A more computationally efficient variant of the problem, known as the *ring-LWE problem* was introduced by Lyubashevsky, Peikert and Regev in [21]. The ring-LWE problem is defined over a polynomial ring $R_q = \mathbb{Z}_q[\mathbf{x}]/\langle f \rangle$ where the irreducible polynomial $\langle f \rangle$ has degree n and the coefficients have modulus q. The problem is defined as follows. Sample a secret polynomial $s(x)$, and error polynomials $e_i(x) \in R_q$ with coefficients from $\mathcal{X}$. Next generate polynomials $a_i(x)$ with coefficients chosen uniformly from $\mathbb{Z}_q$. Compute $b_i(x) = a_i(x) \cdot s(x) + e_i(x) \in R_q$. The ring-LWE distribution is the set of polynomial tuples $(a_i(x), b_i(x))$. The *decision ring-LWE problem* is to distinguish between the samples $(a_i(x), b_i(x))$ and the same number of samples generated by choosing the coefficients uniformly. The *search ring-LWE problem* is to find the secret polynomial $s(x)$ from a polynomial number of samples drawn from the ring-LWE distribution. In the next section we will discuss different cryptographic primitives that have been designed using the ring-LWE problem.

Public-key Encryption Schemes

An encryption scheme based on the ring-LWE problem has been proposed by Lyubashevsky, Peikert and Regev in [21]. The steps are described below.

1. $KeyGen()$: Generate a polynomial $a \in R_q$ with coefficients chosen uniformly in $\mathbb{Z}_q$. Next sample two polynomials $r_1, r_2 \in R_q$ from $\mathcal{X}$ and compute $p = r_1 - a \cdot r_2 \in R_q$. The public key is (a, p) and the private key is r_2.
2. $Enc(a, p, m)$: First encode the message m to a polynomial $\bar{m} \in R_q$. Sample three polynomials $e_1, e_2, e_3 \in R_q$ from $\mathcal{X}$. The ciphertext is the pair of polynomials $c_1 = a \cdot e_1 + e_2$ and $c_2 = p \cdot e_1 + e_3 + \bar{m} \in R_q$.
3. $Dec(c_1, c_2, r_2)$: Compute $m' = c_1 \cdot r_2 + c_2 \in R_q$ and decode the coefficients of m' to either 0 or 1.

After the proposal of the encryption scheme, several implementations of the encryption scheme followed [3,7,12,18,25,27,29]. The basic arithmetic operations are polynomial multiplication, addition, subtraction, and generation of error polynomials from a discrete Gaussian distribution. For around 100 bit security, the implementations use a parameter set with $n = 256$, a 13-bit modulus q, and a *narrow* discrete Gaussian distribution with standard deviation σ around 4.5. Among all the arithmetic operations, polynomial multiplication is the costliest one. To perform fast polynomial multiplication, the implementations use the number theoretic transform (NTT) which is a variant of the fast Fourier transform (FFT) over integer rings. For the generation of error polynomials from the discrete Gaussian distribution $\mathcal{X}$, the implementations use one of the following sampling algorithms [8]: rejection sampling, inversion sampling and the Knuth-Yao sampling. In Fig. 1 a simplified hardware architecture for ring-LWE encryption [29] is shown. The architecture uses its polynomial arithmetic unit to perform polynomial addition and multiplication, and the discrete Gaussian sampler (based on Knuth-Yao algorithm) to generate the error polynomials. To achieve fast computation time, the architecture uses an efficient memory access scheme. For more details, authors may follow [29]. In Tables 1 and 2 we show some of the implementation results on hardware and software platforms respectively for different parameter sets (n, q, σ).

Digital Signature Schemes

Using hard lattice problems to create efficient digital signature scheme was first demonstrated by Hoffstein et al. [15]. Their 'Hash and Sign' signature scheme NTRUSign was an extremely efficient scheme in practice but the original scheme's 'Hash and sign' approach leaks information about the private key,

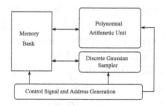

Fig. 1. Architecture (simplified) for ring-LWE encryption [29]

Table 1. Performance of Ring-LWE encryption in hardware

Implementation algorithm	Parameters (n, q, σ)	Device	LUTs/FFs/ DSPs/BRAM18	Freq (MHz)	Cycles/Time(μs)	
					Encryption	Decryption
Roy et al. [29]	(256,7681,4.516)	Xilinx	1349/860/1/2	313	6.3 k/20.1	2.8 k/9.1
	(512,12289,4.859)	V6LX75T	1536/953/1/3	278	13.3 k/47.9	5.8 k/21
Pöppelmann et al. [25]	(256,7681,4.516)	Xilinx	4549/3624/1/12	262	6.8 k/26.2	4.4 k/16.8
	(512,12289,4.859)	V6LX75T	5595/4760/1/14	251	13.7 k/54.8	8.8 k/35.4
RLWE-Enc [26] RLWE-Dec	(256,4096,3.33)	Xilinx S6LX9	317/238/95/1 112/87/32/1	144 189	136 k/946 -	- 66 k/351

Table 2. Performance of Ring-LWE encryption in software

Implementation algorithm	Parameters (n, q, σ)	Device	Cycles	
			Encryption	Decryption
Boorghany et al. [3]	(256,7681,4.516)	ARM7TDMI	878,454	226,235
Boorghany et al. [3]	(256,7681,4.516)	ATMega64	3,042,675	1,368,969
de Clercq et al. [7]	(256,7681,4.516)	Cortex-M4F	121,166	43,324
Göttert et al. [12]	(256,7681,4.516)	Core 2 Duo	4,560,000	1,710,000
Pöppelmann et al. [27]	(256,7681,4.516)	AX128	874,347	215,863
Liu et al. [19]	(256,7681,4.516)	AX128	666,671	299,538

namely the shape of the parallelepiped. It was first exploited by Gentry and Szydlo [11] and later Regev and Nguyen [23] developed this weakness further to show that an attacker can recover the private key with as few as 400 signatures.

Later Melchor et al. [22] used Gausssian sampling to hide this leakage efficiently using rejection sampling introduced by Lyubashevsky [20]. Though Lyubashevsky's scheme helped to create secure and efficient digital signature schemes like PASSSign [16] and BLISS [9], his scheme itself was very inefficient due to the requirement of sampling from Gaussian distributions with large standard deviation and very high rejection rates. From the computational point of view the most significant part of such signature schemes are polynomial multiplication and discrete Gaussian sampling. Unlike the encryption scheme, the standard deviation of the discrete Gaussian distribution is orders of magnitude larger to make these schemes secure and keep the signature sizes small. For example, the signature scheme by Lyubashevsky in [20] requires a standard deviation σ in between 3×10^4 and 1.7×10^5. Implementation of a fast sampler for such a large standard deviation is a difficult problem. Hence the focus has been in the direction of designing signature schemes with smaller standard deviation.

The Bimodal Lattice Signature Scheme known as BLISS [9] is a very popular lattice based signature scheme. It has been implemented on a wide variety of devices. The standard deviation of BLISS-I has $\sigma = 215$ for 128 bit security [9], which is of magnitude smaller than the previous signature schemes, but still larger than the σ used in encryption schemes.

For efficiency and security we need to store $O(\tau\sigma$ entries to sample from a discrete Gaussian distribution with standard deviation $\sigma(\tau = 12)$. The large

Table 3. Benchmark on a (Intel Core i7 at 3.4 Ghz, 32 GB RAM) with openssl 1.0.1c [9] ECDSA on a prime field F_p: ecdsap160,ecdsap256 and ecdsap384 in openssl

Implementation	Security	Signature size	SK size	PK size	Sign(ms)	Verify(ms)
BLISS-0	≤ 60 bits	3.3 kb	1.5 kb	3.3 kb	0.241	0.017
BLISS-I	128 bits	5.6 kb	2 kb	7 kb	0.124	0.030
BLISS-II	128 bits	5 kb	2 kb	7 kb	0.480	0.030
BLISS-III	160 bits	6 kb	3 kb	7 kb	0.203	0.032
BLISS-IV	192 bits	6.5 kb	3 kb	7 kb	0.375	0.032
RSA-2048	103-112 bits	2 kb	2 kb	2 kb	1.180	0.038
RSA-4096	≥128 bits	4 kb	4 kb	4 kb	8.660	0.138
ECDSA 256	128 bits	0.5 kb	0.25 kb	0.25 kb	0.106	0.384
ECDSA 384	192 bits	0.75 kb	0.37 kb	0.37 kb	0.195	0.853

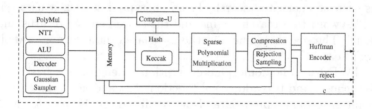

Fig. 2. Architecture for BLISS-I signing [24]

memory requirement of BLISS makes it a challenging job to implement it on devices with limited memory and computing power. In addition, the authors of BLISS also proposed a new Gaussian sampling technique that requires only $O(\log(\tau\sigma^2))$ storage thus making the scheme suitable scheme for small devices (Table 3).

An efficient implementation of BLISS is by Pöppelmann and Ducas and Güneysu [24]. The implementation uses the Peikert's convolution lemma and the Kullback-Leibler divergence to design a practical and efficient discrete Gaussian sampler. Using the Peikert's convolution lemma, a sample from the distribution with $\sigma = 215.73$ is constructed by mixing two samples from a narrower distribution with $\sigma = 19.53$. This optimization is very useful since designing a sampler for such a small standard deviation is a lot easier. The Kullback-Leibler divergence is used to get a precision for a desired bit-security. A simplified architecture diagram of BLISS-I from [24] is shown in Fig. 2. The architecture is composed of a polynomial arithmetic unit, a discrete Gaussian sampler, a sparse polynomial multiplier, a compression block (which includes a rejection sampler), and a Huffman encoder. On a Xilinx Spartan-6 FPGA the implementation [24] takes 114.1 μs for signature generation and 61.2 μs for signature verification. It is worth noting here that there exists lattice based signature scheme that don't require Gaussian sampling at all [13,14]. And thus trading off speed with signature size.

Also scheme proposed by Bai and Galbraith [1] requires Gaussian sampling only in the keygen part, making the time critical signing process efficient.

Homomorphic Encryption Scheme

The beauty of the ring-LWE problem is that it is not restricted to encryption and signature schemes. It has been used to design efficient homomorphic encryption schemes. With homomorphic encryption, computations can be performed on encrypted data. Due to its homomorphism, equivalent computations are automatically performed on the plaintext data. Thus with homomorphic operations, users can upload their encrypted data in a powerful cloud service and still perform computations in the cloud on the encrypted data. With the emergence of cloud service, a need for data privacy is gradually increasing. Beside data processing, homomorphic encryption can have applications in oblivious computations such as encrypted search. In an encrypted search, a user sends her encrypted keyword to a search engine and the search engine returns encrypted search result. The search engine and the associated data vendors are oblivious of the user's search.

A ring-LWE based homomorphic encryption scheme uses a basic ring-LWE encryption scheme and two additional functions Add and Mult to perform arithmetic operation on encrypted data. However in comparison to a simple ring-LWE encryption scheme, a homomorphic encryption scheme requires a much larger parameter set to support a desired multiplicative depth. An analysis on the choice of parameter set for a required multiplicative depth for two homomorphic encryption schemes FV [10] and YASHE [5] is provided by Tancrde and Naehrig in [17]. In the next part we provide some results for our implementation of the encryption/decrytion for a parameter set that supports a depth of four.

We first designed the YASHE homomorphic encryption scheme for the parameter set with irreducible polynomial degree $n = 2048$, 105-bit modulus q, and standard deviation $\sigma = 11.32$. The architecture uses full precision arithmetic: operations are performed modulo q. To perform coefficient-wise multiplication, a 106-bit Karatsuba multiplier is used. The architecture is implemented in a Xilinx ML605 board. with a Gigabit Ethernet interface. The homomorphic encryption-decryption processor consumes 6K LUTs, 5K FFs, 24 BRAMs and 27 DSP multipliers. At 125 MHz frequency, encryption takes 6.8 ms and decryption takes 6.5 ms. However later a sub-field attack became applicable for the YASHE scheme and the implementation became insecure.

Next we designed an architecture for the FV homomorphic scheme with a similar parameter. This scheme is secure against the recent sub-field attack. To achieve efficiency, we used the Chinese Remainder Theorem (CRT) in the polynomial arithmetic. With this, operations modulo q reduces into several smaller arithmetic operations modulo smaller primes. This is particularly suitable for FPGA implementation where the DSP multipliers have small data width. When implemented on the same FPGA board, the area consumption is: 6K LUTs, 4K FFs, 36 BRAMs and 12 DSP multipliers. At 125 MHz frequency, the architecture takes a total of 2 ms to perform one encryption and one decryption. This is a lot faster than the previous implementation of the YASHE scheme, though the YASHE scheme is around 1.5 times faster than the FV scheme. The efficiency is achieved thanks to the use of CRT.

2   Current Trends

In this paper we have presented an overview of the implementations of ring-LWE based cryptosystems. For public key encryption, ring-LWE encryption schemes are faster than ECC based schemes. However, memory requirement is a bottleneck for implementations on extremely resource constrained platforms such as passive RFID tags. The recent focus of the research community is to reduce the parameter size so that memory requirement can be reduced.

Due to its wide popularity in designing public key cryptography primitives and homomorphic encryption schemes, it is expected that in future more efficient schemes will emerge. Beside efficiency, a new focus in this area is in the direction of physical security of the schemes. The secret in a ring-LWE based scheme is a polynomial and arithmetic operations involve masking data and the secret using discrete Gaussian noise. Hence any leakage from the masking computation could reveal information about the secret to an attacker.

Acknowledgements. This work was supported in part by the Research Council KU Leuven: C16/15/058. G.0876.14N, and by the European Commission through the Horizon 2020 research and innovation programme under contract No H2020-ICT-2014-644371 WITDOM, H2020-ICT-2014-644209 HEAT and the ERC grant.

References

1. Bai, S., Galbraith, S.D.: An improved compression technique for signatures based on learning with errors. In: Benaloh, J. (ed.) CT-RSA 2014. LNCS, vol. 8366, pp. 28–47. Springer, Heidelberg (2014). doi:10.1007/978-3-319-04852-9_2
2. BBC News. NSA developing code-cracking quantum computer (2014). http://www.bbc.com/news/technology-25588605
3. Boorghany, A., Sarmadi, S.B., Jalili, R.: On constrained implementation of lattice-based cryptographic primitives and schemes on smart cards. Cryptology ePrint Archive, Report 2014/514 (2014)
4. Bos, J., Costello, C., Ducas, L., Mironov, I., Naehrig, M., Nikolaenko, V., Raghunathan, A., Stebila, D.: Frodo: take off the ring! practical, quantum-secure key exchange from LWE. Cryptology ePrint Archive, Report 2016/659 (2016)
5. Bos, J.W., Lauter, K., Loftus, J., Naehrig, M.: Improved security for a ring-based fully homomorphic encryption scheme. In: Stam, M. (ed.) IMACC 2013. LNCS, vol. 8308, pp. 45–64. Springer, Heidelberg (2013). doi:10.1007/978-3-642-45239-0_4
6. Boutin, C.: Nist kicks off effort to defend encrypted data from quantum computer threat (2016). http://www.nist.gov/itl/csd/nist-kicks-off-effort-to-defend-encrypted-data-from-quantum-computer-threat.cfm
7. de Clercq, R., Roy, S.S., Vercauteren, F., Verbauwhede, I.: Efficient software implementation of ring-LWE encryption. In: Proceedings of the 2015 Design, Automation & Test in Europe Conference & Exhibition (DATE 2015), pp. 339–344 (2015)

8. Devroye, L.: Non-uniform Random Variate Generation. Springer, Heidelberg (1986)
9. Ducas, L., Durmus, A., Lepoint, T., Lyubashevsky, V.: Lattice signatures and bimodal gaussians. In: Canetti, R., Garay, J.A. (eds.) CRYPTO 2013. LNCS, vol. 8042, pp. 40–56. Springer, Heidelberg (2013). doi:10.1007/978-3-642-40041-4_3
10. Fan, J., Vercauteren, F.: Somewhat practical fully homomorphic encryption. Cryptology ePrint Archive, Report 2012/144 (2012). http://eprint.iacr.org/
11. Gentry, C., Szydlo, M.: Cryptanalysis of the revised NTRU signature scheme. In: Knudsen, L.R. (ed.) EUROCRYPT 2002. LNCS, vol. 2332, pp. 299–320. Springer, Heidelberg (2002). doi:10.1007/3-540-46035-7_20
12. Göttert, N., Feller, T., Schneider, M., Buchmann, J., Huss, S.: On the design of hardware building blocks for modern lattice-based encryption schemes. In: Prouff, E., Schaumont, P. (eds.) CHES 2012. LNCS, vol. 7428, pp. 512–529. Springer, Heidelberg (2012). doi:10.1007/978-3-642-33027-8_30
13. Güneysu, T., Lyubashevsky, V., Pöppelmann, T.: Practical lattice-based cryptography: a signature scheme for embedded systems. In: Prouff, E., Schaumont, P. (eds.) CHES 2012. LNCS, vol. 7428, pp. 530–547. Springer, Heidelberg (2012). doi:10.1007/978-3-642-33027-8_31
14. Güneysu, T., Oder, T., Pöppelmann, T., Schwabe, P.: Software speed records for lattice-based signatures. In: Gaborit, P. (ed.) PQCrypto 2013. LNCS, vol. 7932, pp. 67–82. Springer, Heidelberg (2013). doi:10.1007/978-3-642-38616-9_5
15. Hoffstein, J., Howgrave-Graham, N., Pipher, J., Silverman, J.H., Whyte, W.: NTRUSign: digital signatures using the NTRU lattice. In: Joye, M. (ed.) CT-RSA 2003. LNCS, vol. 2612, pp. 122–140. Springer, Heidelberg (2003). doi:10.1007/3-540-36563-X_9
16. Hoffstein, J., Pipher, J., Schanck, J.M., Silverman, J.H., Whyte, W.: Practical signatures from the partial fourier recovery problem. In: Boureanu, I., Owesarski, P., Vaudenay, S. (eds.) ACNS 2014. LNCS, vol. 8479, pp. 476–493. Springer, Heidelberg (2014). doi:10.1007/978-3-319-07536-5_28
17. Lepoint, T., Naehrig, M.: A comparison of the homomorphic encryption schemes FV and YASHE. In: Pointcheval, D., Vergnaud, D. (eds.) AFRICACRYPT 2014. LNCS, vol. 8469, pp. 318–335. Springer, Heidelberg (2014). doi:10.1007/978-3-319-06734-6_20
18. Liu, M., Nguyen, P.Q.: Solving BDD by enumeration: an update. In: Dawson, E. (ed.) CT-RSA 2013. LNCS, vol. 7779, pp. 293–309. Springer, Heidelberg (2013). doi:10.1007/978-3-642-36095-4_19
19. Liu, Z., Seo, H., Sinha Roy, S., Großschädl, J., Kim, H., Verbauwhede, I.: Efficient ring-LWE encryption on 8-bit AVR processors. In: Güneysu, T., Handschuh, H. (eds.) CHES 2015. LNCS, vol. 9293, pp. 663–682. Springer, Heidelberg (2015). doi:10.1007/978-3-662-48324-4_33
20. Lyubashevsky, V.: Lattice signatures without trapdoors. Cryptology ePrint Archive, Report 2011/537 (2011). http://eprint.iacr.org/2011/537
21. Lyubashevsky, V., Peikert, C., Regev, O.: On ideal lattices and learning with errors over rings. In: Gilbert, H. (ed.) EUROCRYPT 2010. LNCS, vol. 6110, pp. 1–23. Springer, Heidelberg (2010). doi:10.1007/978-3-642-13190-5_1
22. Melchor, C.A., Boyen, X., Deneuville, J.-C., Gaborit, P.: Sealing the leak on classical NTRU signatures. In: Mosca, M. (ed.) PQCrypto 2014. LNCS, vol. 8772, pp. 1–21. Springer, Heidelberg (2014). doi:10.1007/978-3-319-11659-4_1
23. Nguyen, P.Q., Regev, O.: Learning a parallelepiped: cryptanalysis of GGH and NTRU signatures. In: Vaudenay, S. (ed.) EUROCRYPT 2006. LNCS, vol. 4004, pp. 271–288. Springer, Heidelberg (2006). doi:10.1007/11761679_17

24. Pöppelmann, T., Ducas, L., Güneysu, T.: Enhanced lattice-based signatures on reconfigurable hardware. Cryptology ePrint Archive, Report 2014/254(2014). http://eprint.iacr.org/
25. Pöppelmann, T., Güneysu, T.: Towards practical lattice-based public-key encryption on reconfigurable hardware. In: Lange, T., Lauter, K., Lisoněk, P. (eds.) SAC 2013. LNCS, vol. 8282, pp. 68–85. Springer, Heidelberg (2014). doi:10.1007/978-3-662-43414-7_4
26. Pöppelmann, T., Güneysu, T.: Area optimization of lightweight lattice-based encryption on reconfigurable hardware. In: Proceedings of the IEEE International Symposium on Circuits and Systems (ISCAS 2014) Preprint (2014)
27. Pöppelmann, T., Oder, T., Güneysu, T.: High-performance ideal lattice-based cryptography on 8-bit ATxmega microcontrollers. In: Lauter, K., Rodríguez-Henríquez, F. (eds.) LATINCRYPT 2015. LNCS, vol. 9230, pp. 346–365. Springer, Heidelberg (2015). doi:10.1007/978-3-319-22174-8_19
28. Regev, O.: On lattices, learning with errors, random linear codes, and cryptography. In: Proceedings of the Thirty-Seventh Annual ACM Symposium on Theory of Computing (STOC 2005), pp. 84–93, New York, NY, USA. ACM (2005)
29. Roy, S.S., Vercauteren, F., Mentens, N., Chen, D.D., Verbauwhede, I.: Compact ring-LWE cryptoprocessor. In: Batina, L., Robshaw, M. (eds.) CHES 2014. LNCS, vol. 8731, pp. 371–391. Springer, Heidelberg (2014). doi:10.1007/978-3-662-44709-3_21

NewHope on ARM Cortex-M

Erdem Alkim[1(✉)], Philipp Jakubeit[2], and Peter Schwabe[2]

[1] Department of Mathematics, Ege University, İzmir, Turkey
erdemalkim@gmail.com
[2] Digital Security Group, Radboud University, Nijmegen, The Netherlands
phil.jakubeit@gmail.com, peter@cryptojedi.org

Abstract. Recently, Alkim, Ducas, Pöppelmann, and Schwabe proposed a Ring-LWE-based key exchange protocol called "NEWHOPE" [2] and illustrated that this protocol is very efficient on large Intel processors. Their paper also claims that the parameter choice enables efficient implementation on small embedded processors. In this paper we show that these claims are actually correct and present NEWHOPE software for the ARM Cortex-M family of 32-bit microcontrollers. More specifically, our software targets the low-end Cortex-M0 and the high-end Cortex-M4 processor from this family. Our software starts from the C reference implementation by the designers of NEWHOPE and then carefully optimizes subroutines in assembly. In particular, compared to best results known so far, our NTT implementation achieves a speedup of almost a factor of 2 on the Cortex-M4. Our Cortex-M0 NTT software slightly outperforms previously best results on the Cortex-M4, a much more powerful processor. In total, the server side of the key exchange executes in only 1 467 101 cycles on the M0 and only 834 524 cycles on the M4; the client side executes in 1 760 837 cycles on the M0 and 982 384 cycles on the M4.

Keywords: Post-quantum key exchange · Ring-LWE · Embedded microcontroller · NTT

1 Introduction

Almost all asymmetric cryptography in use today relies on the hardness of factoring large integers or computing (elliptic-curve) discrete logarithms. It is known that cryptography based on these problems will be broken in polynomial time by Shor's algorithm [25] once a large quantum computer is built. It is, however,

P. Schwabe—This work has been supported by TÜBITAK under 2214-A Doctoral Research Program Grant and 2211-C PhD Scholarship, by Ege University under project 2014-FEN-065, by the European Commission through the Horizon 2020 program under project number ICT-645622 (PQCRYPTO), and by Netherlands Organization for Scientific Research (NWO) through Veni 2013 project 13114. Part of the work was done while Erdem Alkim was visiting Radboud University. Permanent ID of this document: c7a82d41d39c535fd09ca1b032ebca1b. Date: 2016-09-01.

C. Carlet et al. (Eds.): SPACE 2016, LNCS 10076, pp. 332–349, 2016.
DOI: 10.1007/978-3-319-49445-6_19

unknown when this will be achieved. Researchers from IBM estimate the arrival of such quantum computers within the next 2 decades [27]. This does not only imply that we need to switch to so-called *post-quantum cryptography* in 15 or 20 years. For content that we want protected over a period of 15 years or longer it is a necessary to switch already today. This has been recognized, for example, by the NSA [1], by NIST [19], or by the Tor project [16].

In the majority of contexts the most critical asymmetric primitive to upgrade to post-quantum security is ephemeral key exchange. In 2015, Bos, Costello, Naehrig, and Stebila proposed a post-quantum key exchange based on the Ring-learning-with-errors (RLWE) problem for TLS [7]. Later in 2015 (with updates in 2016), Alkim, Ducas, Pöppelmann, and Schwabe significantly improved on this proposal (in terms of speed, message size, and security) with a protocol that they call NEWHOPE. This protocol is now used in a post-quantum-crypto experiment by Google [8] and is considered as one option to upgrade Tor's handshake to post-quantum cryptography. See [16, Slide 16] and [14]. In Sect. 2.3 of the 2015-12-07 version of [2], the authors of NEWHOPE state that

> "it [...] can be implemented in constant time using only integer arithmetic - which is important on constrained devices without a floating point unit."

In this paper we present such an implementation of NEWHOPE on "constrained devices"; specifically on the ARM Cortex-M0 and the ARM Cortex-M4 microcontrollers. Our software starts from the C reference implementation by Alkim, Ducas, Pöppelmann, and Schwabe and then carefully optimizes all performance-critical routines in ARM assembly.

Contributions. Our software is to our knowledge the first to achieve 128 bits of post-quantum security (with a comfortable margin) for key exchange on an embedded microcontroller. In terms of speed, the software is not only competitive, but actually considerably faster than today's elliptic-curve-based solutions. For example, our software outperforms the Curve25519 [4] implementation for the Cortex-M0 presented in [11] by more than a factor of two.

This speed is possible in part because of the design of NEWHOPE, and in part through a careful optimization of the software on the assembly level. In particular for the number-theoretic transform (NTT) we show significant speedups that will also be useful in implementations of other lattice-based schemes. Specifically, our dimension-1024 NTT takes 86 769 cycles on the Cortex-M4. The previous speed record on this architecture was 71 090 cycles for a dimension-512 NTT from [9]. An NTT is essentially a sequence of "butterfly" operations where the number of butterflies is $n \cdot \log(n)$ for a dimension-n NTT. One would thus expect the number from [9] to scale up to $10/9 \cdot 2 \cdot 71\,090 = 157\,977$ cycles, almost a factor of two slower than our result. On the much more restricted Cortex-M0 our NTT needs only 148 517 cycles and thus still outperforms the (scaled) result from [9]. Other components that we optimized on the assembly level include the error reconciliation [2, Sect. 5] and the ChaCha20 stream cipher [5] that is used for efficient generation of uniform noise.

Availability of the software. We place all of the software described in this paper into the public domain to maximize reusability of our results. It is available at https://github.com/newhopearm/newhopearm.git and https://github.com/erdemalkim/newhopearm.

Organization of this paper. Section 2 describes the NEWHOPE post-quantum key exchange scheme. Section 3 gives a brief overview of the Cortex-M processor family and zooms into the specifications of and differences between the Cortex-M0 and the Cortex-M4. Section 4 provides detailed information of design decisions and constraints for both target devices. Finally, Sect. 5 presents and discusses our results and compares them to previous work.

2   The NewHope **RLWE**-based Key Exchange

The NEWHOPE key exchange protocol is an instantiation of Peikert's RLWE-based passively secure KEM presented in [22]. This section recalls the specification of the key exchange and in particular explains the computations involved in the subroutines that our software optimizes on the ARM Cortex-M0 and the Cortex-M4. For a detailed motivation of the design choices in NEWHOPE and a security analysis see [2].

The high-level overview of NEWHOPE, as also listed in [2, Protocol 4], is given in Protocol 1. In this overview, all elements printed in bold-face, except for $\mathbf{r}$, are elements of the ring $\mathcal{R}_q = \mathbb{Z}_q[X]/(X^n + 1)$, where $q = 12289$ and $n = 1024$. The element $\mathbf{r}$ is in $\{0, 1, 2, 3\}^n$. The operation $\circ$ denotes pointwise multiplication. All other operations are explained in more detail in the following paragraphs.

Parse (SHAKE-128). NEWHOPE generates a new (public) parameter $\mathbf{a}$ for each key exchange. This eliminates concerns about backdoors in this parameter and all-for-the-price-of-one attacks (see [2, Sect. 3]). Server-side applications are free to cache this parameter for several key exchanges to improve performance, but our software, like the reference implementation, does not include caching. The parameter $\mathbf{a}$ is generated from a random 32-byte seed by extending this seed through the SHAKE-128 extendable-output function (XOF) from the FIPS-202 standard [21]. The output of SHAKE-128 is considered as an array of 16-bit little-endian unsigned integers. Each of these integers is used as a coefficient of $\mathbf{a}$ if it is smaller than $5q = 61445$. Note that the amount of SHAKE-128 output required to "fill" all coefficients of $\mathbf{a}$ may differ for different seeds (because a different amount of 16-bit integers may be discarded). This is not a problem, because a XOF is designed to produce outputs of variable length. It is also not a problem from a side-channel perspective, because $\mathbf{a}$ is public.

Sampling noise polynomials from ψ_{16}. The distribution ψ_k is a centered binomial, which is used as LWE secret and error. NEWHOPE uses the parameter $k = 16$. The distribution ψ_{16} has a mean of 0 and a variance of 8, which leads to the standard deviation of $\sigma = \sqrt{8}$. Generating a noise polynomial requires secure random-number generation. For this purpose we use the ChaCha20 stream

---

Parameters: $q = 12289 < 2^{14}$, $n = 1024$
Error distribution: ψ_{16}^n

Alice (server)		Bob (client)
$seed \xleftarrow{\$} \{0,\dots,255\}^{32}$		
$\hat{\mathbf{a}} \leftarrow \mathsf{Parse}(\mathsf{SHAKE\text{-}128}(seed))$		
$\mathbf{s},\mathbf{e} \xleftarrow{\$} \psi_{16}^n$		$\mathbf{s}',\mathbf{e}',\mathbf{e}'' \xleftarrow{\$} \psi_{16}^n$
$\hat{\mathbf{s}} \leftarrow \mathsf{NTT}(\mathbf{s})$		
$\hat{\mathbf{b}} \leftarrow \hat{\mathbf{a}} \circ \hat{\mathbf{s}} + \mathsf{NTT}(\mathbf{e})$	$\xrightarrow[\text{1824 Bytes}]{m_a = \mathsf{encodeA}(seed,\hat{\mathbf{b}})}$	$(\hat{\mathbf{b}}, seed) \leftarrow \mathsf{decodeA}(m_a)$
		$\hat{\mathbf{a}} \leftarrow \mathsf{Parse}(\mathsf{SHAKE\text{-}128}(seed))$
		$\hat{\mathbf{t}} \leftarrow \mathsf{NTT}(\mathbf{s}')$
		$\hat{\mathbf{u}} \leftarrow \hat{\mathbf{a}} \circ \hat{\mathbf{t}} + \mathsf{NTT}(\mathbf{e}')$
		$\mathbf{v} \leftarrow \mathsf{NTT}^{-1}(\hat{\mathbf{b}} \circ \hat{\mathbf{t}}) + \mathbf{e}''$
$(\hat{\mathbf{u}},\mathbf{r}) \leftarrow \mathsf{decodeB}(m_b)$	$\xleftarrow[\text{2048 Bytes}]{m_b = \mathsf{encodeB}(\hat{\mathbf{u}},\mathbf{r})}$	$\mathbf{r} \xleftarrow{\$} \mathsf{HelpRec}(\mathbf{v})$
$\mathbf{v}' \leftarrow \mathsf{NTT}^{-1}(\hat{\mathbf{u}} \circ \hat{\mathbf{s}})$		$\nu \leftarrow \mathsf{Rec}(\mathbf{v},\mathbf{r})$
$\nu \leftarrow \mathsf{Rec}(\mathbf{v}',\mathbf{r})$		$\mu \leftarrow \mathsf{SHA3\text{-}256}(\nu)$
$\mu \leftarrow \mathsf{SHA3\text{-}256}(\nu)$		

Protocol 1. The NEWHOPE protocol including NTT and NTT^{-1} computations and sizes of exchanged messages; $\circ$ denotes pointwise multiplication; $x \xleftarrow{\$} \chi$ denotes the sampling of $x \in \mathcal{R}$ according to χ if χ is a probability distribution over $\mathcal{R}$; $a \xleftarrow{\$} \mathcal{R}_q$ denotes the uniform choice of coefficients from $\mathbb{Z}_q$; $y \xleftarrow{\$} \mathcal{A}$ denotes that the output of $\mathcal{A}$ is assigned to y where $\mathcal{A}$ is a probabilistic algorithm running with randomly chosen coins.

cipher [5] to expand a 32-byte seed (or, optionally on the Cortex-M4, the built-in hardware RNG).

NTT and NTT^{-1}. The core computational effort of NEWHOPE lies in the number-theoretic transforms (NTTs), which are to a large extent inherently embedded into the protocol, because the exchanged messages contain polynomials in the NTT domain. The NTT transform has three sub-routines: pointwise multiplication, bit reversal of the coefficients of the polynomials, and the NTT calculation itself. All input polynomials have randomly chosen coefficients, therefore, we can assume that the coefficients are already in bit-reversed order. This leads to the situation, where our forward transform consists only of the NTT and multiplication by square roots of twiddle factors. The NTT^{-1} consists of the transform, the multiplication by the square roots of the twiddle factors and a bit-reversal.

Encoding of messages. The key-exchange requires two message exchanges by the corresponding two parties, as can be seen in Protocol 1. The main part of each message is a 1024-coefficient polynomial with 14-bit coefficients. Those polynomials are encoded into a compressed little-endian array, which takes a total of 1792 bytes. The message m_a contains an additional 32-byte seed and thus reaches a total size of 1824 bytes; m_b contains additional 256 bytes of reconciliation information and thus reaches a total size of 2048 bytes.

Rec and HelpRec. The Error reconciliation of NEWHOPE is based on finding the closest vector in a 4-dimensional lattice with basis

$$B_4 = \begin{pmatrix} 1\,0\,0\,0.5 \\ 0\,1\,0\,0.5 \\ 0\,0\,1\,0.5 \\ 0\,0\,0\,0.5 \end{pmatrix}.$$

With this basis, the lattice $\hat{D}_4$ gets defined. The HelpRec first splits the 1024 coefficients of the input polynomial $\mathbf{v}$ into 256 4-dimensional vectors $\mathbf{x}_i = (\mathbf{v}_i, \mathbf{v}_{i+256}, \mathbf{v}_{i+512}, \mathbf{v}_{i+768})^t$, for $i = 0, \ldots, 255$. It then computes reconciliation information $\mathbf{r}_i$ from those $\mathbf{x}_i$ as

$$\mathbf{r}_i = \mathsf{HelpRec}(\mathbf{x}_i, b) = \mathsf{CVP}_{\hat{D}_4}\left(\frac{2^r}{q}(\mathbf{x}_i + b\mathbf{g})\right) \bmod 2^r,$$

where b is a random bit and $\mathbf{g} = (0.5, 0.5, 0.5, 0.5)^t$. Algorithm 1 describes the computation of the closest vector denoted as $\mathsf{CVP}_{\hat{D}_4}$. Note that the output of HelpRec as stated above is a 4-dimensional vector with entries in $\{0, 1, 2, 3\}$ (i.e., 2-bit entries). Application to the whole polynomial $\mathbf{v}$ means applying it 256 times (for all $\mathbf{x}_i$). This produces a total of 2048 bits of reconciliation information.

Algorithm 1. $\mathsf{CVP}_{\hat{D}_4}(\mathbf{x} \in \mathbb{R}^4)$

Ensure: An integer vector $\mathbf{z}$ such that $\mathbf{Bz}$ is a closest vector to $\mathbf{x}$
1: **if** $(\|\mathbf{x} - \lfloor\mathbf{x}\rceil\|_1) < 1$ **then**
2:     **return** $(\lfloor x_0 \rceil, \lfloor x_1 \rceil, \lfloor x_2 \rceil, 0)^t + \lfloor x_3 \rceil \cdot (-1, -1, -1, 2)^t$
3: **else**
4:     **return** $(\lfloor x_0 \rfloor, \lfloor x_1 \rfloor, \lfloor x_2 \rfloor, 1)^t + \lfloor x_3 \rfloor \cdot (-1, -1, -1, 2)^t$
5: **end if**

The Rec function also works on 4-dimensional vectors and is defined as $\mathsf{Rec}(\mathbf{x}, \mathbf{r}) = \mathsf{LDDecode}(\frac{1}{q}\mathbf{x} - \frac{1}{2^r}\mathbf{Br})$, where LDDecode is given in Algorithm 2 (see [2, Algorithm 2]).

Algorithm 2. $\mathsf{LDDecode}(\mathbf{x} \in \mathbb{R}^4/\mathbb{Z}^4)$

Ensure: A bit k such that $k\mathbf{g}$ is a closest vector to $\mathbf{x} + \mathbb{Z}^4$: $\mathbf{x} - k\mathbf{g} \in \mathcal{V} + \mathbb{Z}^4$
1: $\mathbf{v} = \mathbf{x} - \lfloor\mathbf{x}\rceil$
2: **return** 0 if $\|\mathbf{v}\|_1 \le 1$ and 1 otherwise

The divisions by q and the presence of values like $1/2$ might suggest that the computation of the HelpRec and Rec requires floating-point arithmetic. However, one can simply multiply all values by $2q$ to obtain integers; this is what

Table 1. Operation counts on the client and the server side of NEWHOPE.

Operation	Server	Client
Generating the public parameter **a**;	1	1
Sampling noise polynomials;	2	3
Computing the NTT;	2	2
Computing the NTT^{-1} with bit reversal;	1	1
Computing the pointwise multiplication;	2	2
Computing the vector **r** for error reconciliation;	0	1
Computing the error reconciliation Rec;	1	1
Hashing the 32-byte value ν with SHA3-256 to obtain the final key μ	1	1

the authors of NEWHOPE refer to as efficiently implementable in fixed-point arithmetic.

Operation costs of NEWHOPE. Table 1 summarizes the operations involved on either side of the NEWHOPE key exchange.

3   The Cortex-M Family of Microcontrollers

The ARM Cortex-M processors are advertised as "the most popular choice for embedded applications, having been licensed to over 175 ARM partners" [15]. Their wide deployment in embedded applications makes them an attractive target for optimized cryptography. ARM offers a wide range with their Cortex-M family. At the low end of pricing, power consumption, and also computational capabilities is the Cortex-M0. At the high end are the Cortex-M4 and Cortex-M7. Like other embedded processors, ARM Cortex-M chips are used in the Internet of Things, consumer products, medical instrumentation, connectivity, or industry-control systems.

All Cortex-M processors have in common that data is processed in 32-bit words. Relevant differences for the software described in this paper are the instruction set, the size of RAM and ROM, and the availability of a random source. The Cortex-M0 is based on the ARMv6-M architecture. This architecture combines the 16-bit Thumb instruction set with a few 32-bit instructions. The Cortex-M4 is based on the ARMv7-M architecture. This architecture makes use of the 32-bit Thumb-2 instruction set. Both processors have 16 general-purpose registers, out of which one is used as stack pointer (**r13**), one is used as link register (**r14**), and one for the program counter (**r15**). However, only 32-bit instructions can make use of the 8 high general-purpose registers, which limits the Cortex-M0 to essentially eight general purpose registers (except for register-to-register copies, which can also reach the high registers). Another difference concerns the size of immediate values that instructions can handle: The M0 instruction set supports only 8-bit immediate values; the M4 instruction set supports immediate values of up to 16 bits.

Both processors have a comparable timing with respect to cycle count of atomic instructions. For example, the branch instruction needs 3 cycles if the branch is taken and 1 cycle otherwise on both architectures. Both architectures provide instructions to load or store multiple registers in $1 + n$ cycles, where n is the number of registers. In the case of load and store instructions, however, architectural differences occur. On the Cortex-M4, store instructions take only one cycle, because address generation is performed in the initial cycle and the actual storing of data is performed while the next instruction is executed. Load instruction can be pipelined together with other independent load and store instructions. The Cortex-M0 does not provide pipeline functionality for load and store instructions; those instructions thus take 2 cycles.

The Cortex-M0 does not have a hardware random-number generator (RNG), whereas the Cortex-M4 on our STM32F4xx-series development board offers a 32-bit hardware RNG. This RNG unit passes all statistical tests for secure random number generation provided by the NIST [26]. For the M4 we present two versions of our noise generation: one using ChaCha20 and one using this hardware RNG (which has also been used for noise generation in [9]).

4   Implementation Details

This section first provides a detailed explanation of general optimization techniques. We then provide two architecture-specific subsections in which we elaborate on processor-specific optimization techniques. For the SHAKE-128 function and the SHA3-256 function we use the optimized implementation by the Daemen et al. [6].

The main focus of our optimization lies on the NTT and the NTT^{-1}. In our description we treat the NTT and the NTT^{-1} together, because they only differ in the fact that the NTT^{-1} requires a bit reversal and in the constants being used: powers of ω for the NTT and powers of ω^{-1} for the NTT^{-1}. The choices for these parameters made by the designers of NEWHOPE are $\omega = 49$ and $\omega^{-1} = 49^{-1}$ mod $q = 1254$. This implies that $\gamma = 7$ is the square root of ω, the n-th root of unity. The existence of ω and γ is guaranteed by the parameter choice of $n = 1024$ and $q = 12289$, which is the smallest prime for which $q \equiv 1 \mod 2n$. This together with n being a power of 2 allows an efficient implementation of the NTT for elements of $\mathcal{R}_q = \mathbb{Z}_q[X]/(X^n + 1)$. As an obvious optimization we make use of precomputed powers of ω and γ, and removed multiplications by $\omega_0 = 1$ from last level of the NTT. These well known optimization techniques for speeding up the NTT computation save us 1525 multiplications.

For precomputing the constants, there are essentially three different strategies to trade-off time and memory. One approach is to precompute none of the powers of ω and γ the other extreme is obviously to precompute all of the powers of ω and γ; a middle ground is to precompute a subset of them. Not precomputing any powers implies that only one coefficient needs to be stored and the rest is generated 'on the fly', which costs one additional multiplication per power. The cost intensive aspect, however, is that the product needs to be reduced afterwards, which rules out this option for us as we chose to focus on efficiency. Precomputing all powers was the logical approach to begin with due to consistency with the reference implementation provided by [2]. This requires to store 3072 14-bit coefficients: the 512 powers of ω, the 512 bit reversed powers of ω, the 1024 powers of γ, and the 1024 inverted powers of γ. These constants, however, have a partial overlap, which points into the direction of the third approach, namely to balance the memory usage and the computational costs. We found in our experiments that the most balanced approach is to store the 512 powers of ω and use them to compute the powers of γ. The first 512 elements of the powers of γ are identical to the powers of ω, because the powers of γ are bit reversed. The second 512 elements can be computed by a simple multiplication with $\gamma = 7$. Since 7 needs only 3 bits and both the precomputed powers of ω and the coefficients are 14-bits in size no reduction is required, because we operate on a 32-bit architecture and after a multiplication the maximum bit size is $3 + 14 + 14 = 31$-bits. With this approach we were able to reduce the size of precomputed tables needed by a factor of $\frac{1}{3}$ for a price of ≈ 750 cycles. It is the most efficient setup for the NTT transform with regards to both memory and computational costs, as it only requires to keep 512 14-bit coefficients at a low cycle count overhead.

The approach for NTT^{-1} it is not as straight forward, because the powers of ω^{-1} are not as easily related to the powers of γ ($\gamma^{2n} \equiv 1 \mod q$). The only balancing technique we could apply would be to use same powers of ω used for the NTT. This would imply that the resulting polynomial would be in reversed order. We would then need to reorder the polynomial to the natural form. This could be integrated into the required multiplication with the precomputed powers of γ. We implemented it during our experiments and decided against it in the final implementation as it saves only $\frac{1}{6}$ of the table sizes, (namely 512 inverted powers of ω) but introduces an overhead of >3 000 cycles. Therefore, we decided to keep the reversed powers of ω. In our speed-optimized implementation we decided against this tradeoff, but it might well be worth considering if memory constraints are an issue.

Listing 1. Reduction routines used in the butterfly operation.

(a) Montgomery reduction ($R = 2^{18}$).

```
montgomery_reduce,rm:
  MUL rt, rm, #12287
  AND rt, rt, #262143
  MUL rt, rt, #12289
  ADD rm, rm, rt
  SHR rm, rm, #18
```

(b) Short Barrett reduction.

```
barrett_reduce, rb:
  MUL rt, rb, #5
  SHR rt, rt, #16
  MUL rt, rt, #12289
  SUB rb, rb, rt
```

The NTT for $n = 1024$ consist of 10 levels, each performing 512 Gentlemen-Sande butterfly operations [12]. Each butterfly operation consists of three loads, one addition, one subtraction, one multiplication by a constant and two stores.

Listing 2. Gentlemen-Sande butterfly operation - all variables are `uint16_t`.

```
LDR ($a_{j}$),r0
LDR ($a_{j + d}$),r1
MOV rt,rt,r0
ADD r0,r0,r1
ADD rt,rt,#36867
SUB rt,rt,r1
LDR ($omega_t$),r1
MUL rt,rt,r1
barret_reduce,r0
montgomery_reduce,rt
STR ($a_j$),r0
STR ($a_{j + d}$),rt
```

One more addition needs to be performed to keep all coefficients in unsigned format.

Thus, except for the modular reductions, a butterfly operation requires at least 2 registers for coefficients, one temporary register, and one 16-bit immediate value. Self-evidently we carry over the optimization techniques applied to the computation of the NTT already in place in the reference implementation. These consist of speeding up the modular-arithmetic. The first optimization is to use Montgomery arithmetic [17]. This demands that all constants are stored in the Montgomery representation with $R = 2^{18}$. Our assembly version of the Montgomery reduction is given in Listing 1a. It shows that Montgomery reduction requires two 14-bit, one 18-bit, and one 5-bit immediate value, and also one temporary register. The second optimization is to use short Barrett reductions [3] for modular reductions after addition. Our assembly version of this routine is given in Listing 1b; it shows how we reduce a 16-bit unsigned integer to an integer congruent modulo q of at most 14-bits. It requires one 14-bit, one 5-bit and one 3-bit immediate values, and one additional register. The ARM instruction set does not allow immediate values as parameter in the multiply instruction on both microcontrollers. Therefore, immediate values used in multiplications must be loaded to a register first. With these conditions, each butterfly operation requires at least 4 registers. The third optimization is called 'lazy reduction'. It describes that the short Barrett reduction is only applied every second level [2]. This works, since per level at most one carry bit occurs; the short Barrett can handle up to 16-bits and the starting value is at most 14-bits in size. However, because we are computing two additions before the reduction, we need to add $3q$ (36867) before the subtraction to keep all coefficients in the unsigned format.

A note on the Longa-Naehrig approach. As a follow-up work to [2], Longa and Naehrig presented speedups to NEWHOPE and in particular the NTT in [13]. They claim a speedup of the NTT by a factor 1.9 in the C implementation and by a factor of 1.25 in the AVX2-optimized implementation. The central idea of that paper is a specialized modular reduction routine for primes of the shape $k \cdot 2^m + \ell$ for small values of k and ℓ; in the case of NEWHOPE those values are $k = 3$ and $\ell = 1$. This reduction routine is combined with extensive use of lazy reduction. The factor of 1.9 in the C implementation is largely explained by the fact that the software makes heavy use of 64-bit integers, which the software described in [2] explicitly avoids. Obviously, making use of 64-bit integers makes sense on AMD64 processors, but is much less efficient on the 32-bit microcontrollers targeted in this paper. The AVX2 implementation described in [13] has in the meantime been outperformed by the latest version of the AVX2 software by the NEWHOPE authors, which uses double-precision floating-point arithmetic.

We experimented with the approach described by Longa and Naehrig on the M0 and M4 and were not able to gain any speedups. This is partly explained by the lack of 64-bit registers (and a 32×32-bit multiplier on the M0). Another reason was that we observed a slight increase in register usage, which significantly increased the required number of loads and stores, in particular on the M0. Furthermore, the lazy-reduction approach leaves intermediate values of >16 bits, which need to be stored to RAM before processing the next level. Using 32-bit integers for those intermediate values increases the memory usage of the NTT by 2 KB, which is prohibitive on the M0.

4.1 Cortex-M0 Specific Optimization

The first optimization necessary for the Cortex-M0 is to fit NEWHOPE onto the processor. The portable reference implementation provided by the authors of NEWHOPE and described in [2] exceeds the Cortex-M0's 8 KB of RAM. The C reference implementation of NEWHOPE closely follows the description in Protocol 1, and makes use of 4 polynomials during key generation and 8 polynomials for the computations on the client side. Each of these polynomials is represented by its 1024 unsigned 16-bit coefficients, and thus consumes 2 KB of RAM. Even with only minimal overhead for different variables or microcontroller internal RAM usage, only up to 3 polynomials fit simultaneously into the RAM of the Cortex-M0. By restructuring the code and adapting the data types used we could fit both, the server side and the client side onto the Cortex-M0. We solved a similar issue during noise extension. On the Cortex-M0 it is impossible to have a buffer larger than 1024-byte. We therefore perform four ChaCha20 calls. This required another bit of entropy. We simply used the loop counter used for the four consecutive calls as input byte for the second element of the initialization vector for the ChaCha20 function.

After fitting the key exchange protocol into the boundaries provided by the Cortex-M0, we could start to look into optimization for speed. A general aspect regarding optimization on Cortex-M processors is that data is processed in words of 32-bits. This allows us to cut the amount of stores and loads in half for the coefficients and constants represented as unsigned 16-bit values. For the shared key and seeds, unsigned 8-bit values, the amount of load and stores is decreased by four. For logical operations on the values loaded this way, no overhead is generated. Arithmetic operations, however, produce overhead, because the 32-bit values need to be split before computation and the 16-bit values need to be merged afterwards. This costs 2 additional cycles for every load and 2 more cycles before every store.

As can be seen in the operation counts summarized in Table 1 at the end of Sect. 2, the NTT and the NTT^{-1} are the most frequently called operations. Since it is also the most expensive function with regards to cycle counts, it was the natural choice to begin with.

NTT and NTT^{-1}. We began our optimization of the NTT (and NTT^{-1}), by unrolling the 10 levels and standardizing the inner loops, such that every level loops 256 times and performs two Gentlemen-Sande butterfly operations per loop iteration. Performing two Gentlemen-Sande butterfly operations per iteration is beneficial, because it allows us to make the best use of the 32-bit word size of the Cortex-M family. Listing 2 shows the code for one Gentlemen-Sande butterfly operation. For the lazy reduction on every second level the Barrett reduction is omitted. Since each coefficient is a 16-bit value, we are able to load two of them per load operation. We continued our optimization by merging levels 0 and 1. Level 0 takes every element and performs the butterfly operations; level 1 takes every second element and performs the butterfly operations. If we combine both levels for efficiency we need to load two 32-bit words, thus four 16-bit coefficients. For each 2 loads we can now perform 4 combined Gentlemen-Sande butterfly operations. We perform the two butterfly operations of level 0 (without the Barrett reduction followed by the two butterfly operations of level 1 (with the Barrett reduction). One loop iteration thus handles both levels.

These four merged butterfly operations take a total of 134 cycles. Unfortunately this does not work for the other consecutive levels on the Cortex-M0. With its limited instruction set and the resulting 8 general purpose registers, the overhead gets out of proportion when merging higher levels. Therefore we get a cycle count of 96 for every even and a cycle count of 86 for every odd level. The last optimization we performed was to minimize register reordering. We went through our NTT code and optimized it such that constants and loop-counter are placed in high registers where possible to allow to make use of the Cortex-M0's full potential.

Before each call to the NTT a multiplication with the γ coefficients and after each call to the NTT^{-1} a multiplication with the precomputed γ^{-1} coefficients must be performed. We implemented the multiplication on the coefficients in assembly to benefit from the Cortex-M0's 32-bit word size. Additionally to the architectural benefit we make use of the fact that the multiplication of the coefficients with the precomputed coefficients is a simple operation and does not need too many registers. Therefore we are able to load 4 coefficients at once and also store them. With this we decreased the amount of loads and stores needed by another factor of two. We could reduce the cycle count for the multiplication of coefficients by 55.04 % compared to the reference implementation.

We also decided to rewrite the pointwise multiplication of polynomials such that it makes optimal usage of the target architecture. We achieve a 56.08 % decreased cycle count, compared to the reference implementation, for the pointwise multiplication by making use of the word size. We load and store two consecutive coefficients of the polynomial and apply the calculations needed on each half word. By doing so, we only call half of the iterations of the main loop.

Before the NTT^{-1} is called a bit reversal needs to be performed. We did not provide an assembly optimized version for this function. The problem is that consecutive coefficients do not necessarily get changed, which implies that we cannot benefit from the word size. We just adapted the bit reversal to not loop over the last elements which are unaffected by it.

Sampling noise polynomials. The noise seeds which form the base of the noise polynomials are not generated on the Cortex-M0. The development board we used during the implementation does not provide an RNG. Since there is no default option for random number generation on the Cortex-M0 we made the choice to allow a context-specific implementation. The randomly generated seed is crucial for the security of the key exchange, therefore, we provide an easy to replace C function in our code. The random seed gets subsequently extended by the ChaCha20 stream cipher. We based our architecture specific implementation on a ChaCha20 implementation specifically designed for the Cortex-M0 by Neikes and Samwel [18]. The core functionality of this stream cipher is optimized in assembly. Additions we made were merely in the initialization phase. Again we benefit from the 32-bit word length of the architecture, which allowed us to represent the internal variables efficiently. The reference implementation makes use of two helper functions to store and load values in little-endian, however, this aspect can be solved simply by the little-endian architecture. Therefore, we could omit the helper functions, which gives us a 10.82 % decreased cycle count compared to the reference implementation.

Error reconciliation and help-vector generation. We continued our optimization with the Rec function by implementing it in assembly. This yields the general benefits of the 32-bit word size. By additionally unrolling and restructuring the loop we make even better use of the architecture. We calculate 8-bits of the key and perform four consecutive calls to this function to get 32-bit of the key before storing it. We store 32-bit of the key eight times to compute all 256 bits of the key. Contrary to the reference implementation, we apply helper functions as soon as possible without storing intermediates. These changes give us a 32.10 % decreased cycle count compared to the reference implementation.

In the case of the HelpRec function, we first benefit from the fast ChaCha20 implementation. We continued by rewriting the main loop in assembly. The loop iterates over the 256 random bits used as fair coin and encodes each bit into 4 coefficients of the input polynomial. We restructured the loop to load 8 times a full word (32-bit). Afterwards, we perform the loop internal calculations per bit and apply the results to the four positions of the polynomial. These optimization measures grant us a 14.43 % faster implementation compared to the reference implementation.

Polynomial addition. Additionally, we wrote assembly implementations for the basic arithmetic calculations for polynomials. The addition works by taking each coefficient of the first and each coefficient of the second polynomial at the same position and adding them together before reducing the sum with a call to the Barrett reduction. We implemented the Barrett reduction specific for the context and the architecture, such that we manage to decrease the cycle count to 5. Due to the fact that this simple function does not require meticulous register usage we could load two 32-bit words at once, thus 4 coefficients. We do so for the coefficients of the first polynomial and load 2 coefficients of the second polynomial, compute the results, load the next 2 coefficients of the second polynomial, compute the second two results and store the newly computed 4 coefficients with one instruction. We manage to reduce the cycle count required for polynomial addition by 59.02 % compared to the reference implementation.

4.2 Cortex-M4 Specific Optimization

Compared to the Cortex-M0, the Cortex-M4 is much more powerful. It has 192 KB of RAM, the portable reference implementation can thus run without adaptations on this microcontroller. Additionally, the Cortex-M4 on our development board features a hardware random-number generator. This enables us to calculate the seeds on the microcontroller directly. Additionally, we are not required to make use of *LDM* and *STM* instructions to save cycles for memory operations, thanks to the architectural benefits described in Sect. 3. This enables us to use 16-bit loads and stores directly without extracting the 16-bit coefficients from 32-bit words. The most obvious implication of this is that the C implementation performs as good as assembly when there are no arithmetic and/or reordering optimizations.

NTT and NTT^{-1}. Inside one butterfly operation, 2 temporary registers are required to calculate the results. The Cortex-M4 has 14 available general-purpose registers and we need to keep the addresses of the input polynomial and the array of precomputed twiddle factors. Therefore, we have 10 registers available during our computations. This implies that we can merge up to 3 levels to save on loads and stores. Making use of these architectural constraints we split the NTT on the Cortex-M4 in four chunks of layers. The first two chunks each perform three layers of the NTT in one loop. These loops process 8 coefficients and run 128 times. In the third chunk we took the first 512 coefficients of the input-polynomial and ran the next three layers of the NTT on them. Afterwards, we took the second 512 coefficients of the input-polynomial and ran the same layers on them. When the results are loaded into the registers we were able to ran the last layer on them, which saved us 1024 loads and stores. The precomputed twiddle factors are such that we do not need multiplication for the last layer. We incorporate the additional register that kept the addresses of the twiddle factors into the calculations performed at the last layer. This reduces the total amount of loads and stores needed for the NTT to $3.5n$ instead of $10n$ ($n = 1024$). By applying the concept of merged layers, we where able to reduce our NTT assembly code for the Cortex-M4 to 384 branches instead of 5120 needed in the C reference implementation.

The Cortex-M4 has a 'multiply and accumulate' instruction for 32-bit integers. It can be seen that both in reductions in Listing 1 multiplication is followed by addition or subtraction. Therefore, we could use this instruction in both, butterfly and pointwise multiplication. This saves more than 30000 cycles per NTT transform. To be able to use this optimization we implemented the pointwise multiplication of polynomials in assembly.

We also implemented the bit reversal operation in assembly. However, while unrolling the bit reversal operation in assembly saves 6500 cycles, the code size of the unrolled bit reversal is 7799 bytes more than the looped implementation. Due to this trade off we decided against the use of it in our work, because we only have two NTT^{-1}'s. In another scenario, however, it could be beneficial and proofs that there is still room for improvements.

Sampling noise polynomials. We implemented the sampling of noise polynomials in two different ways on the Cortex-M4. First, we implemented the sampling by calling ChaCha20 as the reference implementation does. Second, we implemented the sampling by using the built-in RNG. It generates a 32-bit random number every 40 cycles. Each coefficient of a polynomial requires $2k$ random bits, $2k + 1$ additions, $2k$ shifts, $2k$ logical 'and' instructions and 1 subtraction. For every 32-bit number we generated one coefficient in 50 cycles. These calculations take more time than required by the RNG, which implies that the RNG does not have to wait on our calculations. Since we need 32-bit of randomness for one coefficient, the RNG is called 1024 times during the process of sampling one polynomial. As can be seen, the performance of the generation of a noise polynomial is strongly dependent on the parameter 'k'. Therefore, the running time of the noise sampling can be predicted by the time required to generate $2k$ random bits with the RNG.

The Cortex-M4 memory operation can be pipelined, thus calling two 16-bit load/store instructions takes the same amount of time as calling one 32-bit load/store instruction and split it into two 16-bit integers. This allowed us to use the C implementation for the other operations of NEWHOPE without experiencing any significant slowdown.

5   Results and Comparison

In this section, we present our results and compare them with results from the literature. Cortex-M0 benchmarks are obtained on the STM32F0 Discovery board, which is equipped with a STM32F051R8T6 microcontroller. Cortex-M4 benchmarks are obtained on the STM32F4 Discovery development board, which is equipped with a STM32F407VGT6 microcontroller. Our software is compiled with arm-none-eabi-gcc version 5.2.0 and -Ofast as compiler flag for both, the Cortex-M0 and the Cortex-M4. Cycle counts and ROM size of our software is summarized in Table 2.

Comparison with previous results. The literature describes various implementations of lattice-based cryptography on embedded microcontrollers.

For example, in [24] the authors targeted the AVR architecture, and in [23] the authors targeted FPGAs. A direct and fair comparison among those implementations underlies many, often unsolvable constraints. The architectures vary, different schemes are implemented, and last but not least do all candidates for

Table 2. Cycle counts of NEWHOPE building blocks on target devices.

Operation	Cortex-M0	Cortex-M4
Generation of **a**	328 789	263 089
NTT	148 517	86 769
NTT^{-1}	167 405[a]	97 340[a]
Sampling of a noise polynomial	208 692[b]	111 794[b] (53 281)[c]
HelpRec	68 170	43 112
Rec	46 945	31 892
Key generation (server)	1 170 892	781 518[b] (659 726)[c]
Key gen + shared key (client)	1 760 837	1 140 594[b] (982 384)[c]
Shared key (server)	298 877	174 798
ROM usage (bytes)	30 178	22 828[b] (18 544)[c]

[a] Includes bit reversal operation
[b] Noise generation done by *ChaCha20*
[c] Noise generation done by *RNG*

comparison to our result target lower security levels. To gauge the progress of *implementation techniques*, most comparisons between different schemes focus on comparing the performance of subroutines; in the context of ideal-lattice-based cryptography mainly on comparing noise sampling and the NTT, the two most costly operations.

To the best of our knowledge, there are two papers that describe optimizations of ideal-lattice-based cryptography for the ARM Cortex-M family of microcontrollers. In [9], de Clercq, Roy, Vercauteren, and Verbauwhede optimize RLWE-based encryption and in [20], Oder, Pöppelmann, and Güneysu optimize the Bliss signature scheme by Ducas, Durmus, Lepoint, and Lyubashevsky [10]. Both papers target the Cortex-M4F microcontroller and implemented the NTT on 512-coefficient polynomials with the same modulus $q = 12289$ that we used. An additional challenge for comparison is that the NTT operations in [9] and [20] use dimension 512, whereas we use dimension 1024. As explained in the introduction, NTT computations are essentially a sequence of butterfly operations. For comparison we thus scale the numbers from [9,20] to dimension 1024 by the number of butterflies, i.e., by a factor of 20/9.

From Table 3 we can see that even if we use the built-in RNG of the M4, our sampling algorithm is 1.75 × slower than the Knuth-Yao algorithm used in [9]. Note however, that our sampling algorithm, unlike the Knuth-Yao sampler, runs in constant time and is thus inherently protected against timing attacks. Also, the slightly decreased performance on embedded microcontrollers is a price to pay for compatibility with significantly increased timing-attack-protected sampling performance on large processors with caches. For details, see [2, Sect. 4]. Comparison with noise sampling from [20] is problematic, because noise sampling for signature schemes have very different requirements for the noise distribution.

Table 3. Performance comparison of NTT implementation and error sampling

	NTT	Noise sampling[a]
Cortex-M0 **(ours)**	148 517	204
Cortex-M4 **(ours)**	86 769	110^b $(50)^c$
Cortex-M4F [9]	$157\,977^d$	28.5
Cortex-M4F [20]	$272\,486^d$	1 828

[a] Cycle counts for sampling one coefficient
[b] Noise generation done by *ChaCha20*
[c] Noise generation done by *RNG*
[d] Number scaled from dimension 512 to dimension 1024 by multiplying by 20/9

With respect to the NTT the cycle counts we achieve on the Cortex-M4 are 45% faster than [9] and 68% faster than [20]. In the case of the Cortex-M0, the cycle savings are 6% faster than the M4F counts from [9] and 45% faster than the M4F counts from [20]. This demonstrates that the optimization measures applied by us provide faster results on comparable hardware and enable inferior hardware to outperform the best results on ARM Cortex-M processors for calculating an NTT.

Acknowledgments. We are thankful to Ko Stoffelen for his suggestions about Cortex-M4 implementation.

References

1. National Security Agency. NSA suite B cryptography. https://www.nsa.gov/ia/programs/suiteb_cryptography/. Accessed 9 Aug 2015
2. Alkim, E., Ducas, L., Pöppelmann, T., Schwabe, P.: Post-quantum key exchange – a new hope. In: Proceedings of the 25th USENIX Security Symposium. USENIX Association (2016). https://cryptojedi.org/papers/#newhope
3. Barrett, P.: Implementing the rivest shamir and adleman public key encryption algorithm on a standard digital signal processor. In: Odlyzko, A.M. (ed.) CRYPTO 1986. LNCS, vol. 263, pp. 311–323. Springer, Heidelberg (1987). doi:10.1007/3-540-47721-7_24
4. Bernstein, D.J.: Curve25519: new Diffie-Hellman speed records. In: Yung, M., Dodis, Y., Kiayias, A., Malkin, T. (eds.) PKC 2006. LNCS, vol. 3958, pp. 207–228. Springer, Heidelberg (2006). doi:10.1007/11745853_14
5. Bernstein, D.J.: ChaCha, a variant of Salsa20. In: Workshop Record of SASC 2008: The State of the Art of Stream Cipher (2008). http://cr.yp.to/papers.html#chacha
6. Bertoni, G., Daemen, J., Peeters, M., Van Assche, G., Van Keer, R.: Keccak implementation overview (2012). http://keccak.noekeon.org/Keccak-implementation-3.2.pdf. Accessed 3 Jan 2016
7. Bos, J.W., Costello, C., Naehrig, M., Stebila, D.: Post-quantum key exchange for the TLS protocol from the ring learning with errors problem. In: 2015 IEEE Symposium on Security and Privacy, pp. 553–570 (2015). http://eprint.iacr.org/2014/599

8. Braithwaite, M.: Experimenting with post-quantum cryptography. Posting on the Google Security Blog (2016). https://security.googleblog.com/2016/07/experimenting-with-post-quantum.html

9. de Clercq, R., Roy, S.S., Vercauteren, F., Verbauwhede, I.: Efficient software implementation of ring-LWE encryption. In: Design, Automation & Test in Europe Conference & Exhibition (DATE) (2015) pp. 339–344. EDA Consortium (2015). http://eprint.iacr.org/2014/725

10. Ducas, L., Durmus, A., Lepoint, T., Lyubashevsky, V.: Lattice signatures and bimodal gaussians. In: Canetti, R., Garay, J.A. (eds.) CRYPTO 2013. LNCS, vol. 8042, pp. 40–56. Springer, Heidelberg (2013). doi:10.1007/978-3-642-40041-4_3

11. Düll, M., Haase, B., Hinterwälder, G., Hutter, M., Paar, C., Sánchez, A.H., Schwabe, P.: High-speed curve25519 on 8-bit, 16-bit, and 32-bit microcontrollers. Des. Codes Cryptogr. **77**(2), 493–514 (2015). http://cryptojedi.org/papers/#mu25519

12. Gentleman, W.M., Sande, G.: Fast fourier transforms: for fun and profit. In: Fall Joint Computer Conference, AFIPS Proceedings, vol. 29, pp. 563–578 (1966). http://cis.rit.edu/class/simg716/FFT_Fun_Profit.pdf

13. Longa, P., Naehrig, M.: Speeding up the number theoretic transform for faster ideal lattice-based cryptography. Cryptology ePrint Archive, Report 2016/504 (2016). https://eprint.iacr.org/2016/504/

14. Lovecruft, I., Schwabe, P.: RebelAlliance: a post-quantum secure hybrid handshake based on NewHope. Draft proposal for Tor (2016). https://gitweb.torproject.org/user/isis/torspec.git/plain/proposals/XXX-newhope-hybrid-handshake.txt?h=draft/newhope

15. ARM Ltd. Cortex-M series (2015). www.arm.com/products/processors/cortex-m/. Accessed 12 Oct 2015

16. Mathewson, N.: Cryptographic directions in Tor. Slides of a talk at Real-World Crypto 2016 (2016). https://people.torproject.org/~nickm/slides/nickm-rwc-presentation.pdf

17. Montgomery, P.I.: Modular multiplication without trial division. Math. Comput. **44**(170), 519–521 (1985). http://www.ams.org/journals/mcom/1985-44-170/S0025-5718-1985-0777282-X/S0025-5718-1985-0777282-X.pdf

18. Neikes, M., Samwel, N.: ARM implementation of the ChaCha20 block cipher. GitLab repository (2016). https://gitlab.science.ru.nl/mneikes/arm-chacha20

19. NIST. Workshop on cybersecurity in a post-quantum world (2015). http://www.nist.gov/itl/csd/ct/post-quantum-crypto-workshop-2015.cfm

20. Oder, T., Poppelmann, T., Güneysu, T.: Beyond ECDSA and RSA: lattice-based digital signatures on constrained devices. In: 2014 51st ACM/EDAC/IEEE Design Automation Conference (DAC), p. 16. ACM (2014). https://www.sha.rub.de/media/attachments/files/2014/06/bliss_arm.pdf

21. National Institute of Standards and Technology. FIPS PUB 202 – SHA-3 standard: Permutation-based hash and extendable-output functions (2015). http://nvlpubs.nist.gov/nistpubs/FIPS/NIST.FIPS.202.pdf

22. Peikert, C.: Lattice cryptography for the internet. In: Mosca, M. (ed.) PQCrypto 2014. LNCS, vol. 8772, pp. 197–219. Springer, Heidelberg (2014). doi:10.1007/978-3-319-11659-4_12

23. Pöppelmann, T., Güneysu, T.: Towards practical lattice-based public-key encryption on reconfigurable hardware. In: Lange, T., Lauter, K., Lisoněk, P. (eds.) SAC 2013. LNCS, vol. 8282, pp. 68–85. Springer, Heidelberg (2014). doi:10.1007/978-3-662-43414-7_4

24. Pöppelmann, T., Oder, T., Güneysu, T.: High-performance ideal lattice-based cryptography on 8-Bit ATxmega microcontrollers. In: Lauter, K., Rodríguez-Henríquez, F. (eds.) LATINCRYPT 2015. LNCS, vol. 9230, pp. 346–365. Springer, Heidelberg (2015). doi:10.1007/978-3-319-22174-8_19

25. Shor, P.W.: Polynomial-time algorithms for prime factorization and discrete logarithms on a quantum computer. SIAM J. Comput. **26**, 1484–1509 (1997)

26. STMicroelectronics. AN4230 application note – STM32 microcontrollers random number generation validation using NIST statistical test suite (2013). http://www.st.com/resource/en/application_note/dm00073853.pdf

27. Utsler, J.: Quantum computing might be closer than previously thought. IBM Systems Magazine (2013). http://www.ibmsystemsmag.com/mainframe/trends/IBM-Research/quantum_computing/. Accessed 3 Mar 2016

Leakage, Power and Fault Analysis

Towards Fair and Efficient Evaluations of Leaking Cryptographic Devices
Overview of the ERC Project CRASH, Part I
(*Invited Talk*)

François-Xavier Standaert[✉]

ICTEAM Institute, Crypto Group, Université catholique de Louvain,
Louvain-la-Neuve, Belgium
`fstandae@uclouvain.be`

Extended abstract. Side-channel analysis is an important concern for the security of cryptographic implementations, and may lead to powerful key recovery attacks if no countermeasures are deployed. Therefore, various types of protection mechanisms have been proposed over the last 20 years. In view of the cost and performance overheads caused by these protections, their fair evaluation is a primary concern for hardware and software designers. Yet, the physical nature of side-channel analysis also renders the security evaluation of cryptographic implementations very different than the one of cryptographic algorithms against mathematical cryptanalysis. That is, while the latter can be quantified based on (well-defined) time, data and memory complexities, the evaluation of side-channel analysis additionally requires to quantify the informativeness and exploitability of the physical leakages. This implies that a part of these security evaluations is inherently heuristic and dependent on engineering expertise.

The development of sound tools allowing designers and evaluation laboratories to deal with this challenge was one of the main objectives of the CRASH project funded by the European Research Council. In this talk, I will survey a number of results we obtained in this direction, starting with concrete evaluation methodologies that are well-adapted to the investigation of current embedded devices, and following with future trends for emerging implementations. Quite naturally, a large number of researchers and teams have worked on similar directions. For each of the topics discussed, I will add a couple of references to publications that I found inspiring/relevant. The list is (obviously) incomplete and only reflects my personal interests. I apologize in advance for omissions.

Concrete evaluation methodologies. Side-channel analyses against cryptographic implementations can be viewed as a combination of several informal steps, next denoted as (1) *measurement & pre-processing*, (2) *prediction & modeling*, (3) *exploitation* and (4) *post-processing*. They can also be classified based on the adversarial capabilities. In particular, the literature generally suggests two categories of attacks, namely *profiled attacks* (where the adversary can use a device he fully controls – meaning including the secret key and possibly randomness – in order to gain understanding of the target implementation leakages) and *non-profiled attacks* (where the adversary can only access a target device holding the secret key to recover). In this respect, our results are as follows.

© Springer International Publishing AG 2016
C. Carlet et al. (Eds.): SPACE 2016, LNCS 10076, pp. 353–362, 2016.
DOI: 10.1007/978-3-319-49445-6_20

A. The profiling separation. In practice, non-profiled attacks can be viewed as more realistic, since adversaries do not always have access to a profiling device. Therefore, a fundamental question regarding the evaluation of leaking devices is whether performing non-profiled attacks only is sufficient to state sound conclusions regarding susceptibility to side-channel analysis. We answered this question negatively in [67]. Defining a *generic strategy* as one which is able to recover secret information from side-channel leakages without any a-priori assumption about the target devices' physical characteristics, we showed that (strictly defined) such strategies cannot succeed in general. This implies that there exist devices (leakage characteristics) which can only be evaluated soundly by performing profiled attacks. Yet, we also showed that a minor relaxation of the strict definition of generic strategies, incorporating non-device-specific-intuitions, produces *generic-emulating strategies* able to succeed against a wide range of targets (an approach that we followed in [64]). Hence, these results suggest profiled attacks as the method of choice for side-channel security evaluations, since (*i*) they are strictly necessary, (*ii*) they lead to a better understanding of the leakage characteristics and (*iii*) they allow worst-case complexity estimates (which non-profiled adversaries can usually approach with generic-emulating strategies).

Related works. The COSADE 2014 paper by Reparaz et al. offers a critical view of this separation and discusses its impact in practical scenarios [54].

B. The heuristic vs. optimal separation. Based on the previous four (informal) steps, another important question regarding the evaluation of leaking devices is whether one can guarantee that (at least some of) these steps are optimal. Following the standard cryptographic approach, a perfectly sound evaluation indeed requires to determine the worst-case attack complexities, which implies to consider the most powerful adversaries (and again suggests profiled attacks are preferable for this purpose). But in view of the physical nature of the attacks, theoretical guarantees of optimality seem hard to reach. Interestingly, we could show that excepted for the measurement and pre-processing step of the attacks (which is indeed inherently heuristic), it is possible to guarantee that the other steps are "close enough to optimal" (or optimal), as we discuss next.

Step 1. Measurement & pre-processing. This step typically includes the design of low-noise Printed Circuit Boards (PCBs) and probes, *filtering* the measurements, *dimensionality reduction* and the *detection of Points of Interest* (POIs) in leakage traces. As just mentioned, such tasks are essentially heuristic and highly depend on engineering skills. In this respect, it is important to note that even without guarantees of optimality, it is always possible to compare two solutions for the measurement and pre-processing of the leakages, using the other attack/evaluation steps described next. Public – ideally open source – measurement platforms are an interesting ingredient for this purpose. Quite naturally, the same holds for statistical signal processing and machine learning tools. As part of the CRASH project, we paid attention to filtering with Singular Spectrum Analysis [47], projection pursuits as an alternative to Principal Component

Analysis (PCA [1]) and Linear Discriminant Analysis (LDA [58]) for dimensionality reduction/detection of POIs in side-channel attacks [22], improved *leakage detection tests* based on a simple partitioning of the side-channel measurements for fast (yet preliminary) security assessment [19], and the removal of random delays from software implementations using hidden Markov models [18].

Related works. [38,57] for leakage detection, [2,11,34,35] for concrete issues in the application of side-channel attacks and [10] for dimensionality reduction.

Step 2. Prediction & modeling. Given some public input X to the target device, a secret parameter K and the physical leakages L, most side-channel attacks require an estimation of the conditional probability distribution $\hat{\Pr}[K|X,L]$ (or a simplification of this distribution to some of its moments), usually denoted as the model. This is an essential step of the security evaluations that highly relates to the previously mentioned separation between non-profiled and profiled attacks. More precisely, fair evaluations ideally require exploiting a perfect leakage model (to extract all the available information). But since such perfect models are generally unknown, density estimation techniques have to be used to approximate the leakage distribution. This raises the fundamental problem that all security evaluations are potentially biased by both estimation and assumption errors. At Eurocrypt 2014, we proposed first *leakage certification tools* allowing evaluators to verify that their models are good enough [21]. That is, while knowing the distance between an estimated model and the optimal one is impossible in general, it is possible to verify that given number of leakages available for evaluation, any improvement of the (possibly imperfect) estimated model will be negligible. Technically, this requires checking that given this number of leakages, the model assumption errors are small enough in front of the model estimation errors, which amounts to test the hypothesis that the model is correct. At CHES 2016, we then described simpler leakage certification tools, which came at the cost of a couple of heuristic assumptions on the leakage distributions [20].

Related works. A complementary issue to leakage certification is templates portability/robust profiling [12,23,65]. Note that nothing prevents using certification tools to test a model built with one device against another device.

Step 3. Exploitation. Given a leakage model $\hat{\Pr}[K|X,L]$, most side-channel analyses are based on a divide-and-conquer strategy. In this context, the optimal solution is easy to implement and just corresponds to *maximizing the likelihood* of the key (bytes) given the observed leakages, which is the standard approach for profiled attacks. Interestingly, we could show that in the context of unprotected implementations, several of the published distinguishers are in fact equally efficient to perform key recovery attacks [14,36]. By contrast, in the case of implementations protected with *masking* or *shuffling*, only the Bayesian (maximum likelihood) distinguisher guarantees optimal results [59,62].

Besides, an alternative and (theoretically) more powerful strategy to perform key recoveries based on physical leakages is to consider *analytical attacks*. The first (algebraic) attempts in this direction were generally limited in their applicability because of their low tolerance to measurement noise [51,52]. As part of the CRASH project, we developed new solutions to better deal with this noise limitation, based on alternative descriptions of the key recovery problem as optimization or soft decoding problems [44,61]. The latter one is particularly relevant to evaluation laboratories since it can deal with any level of noise, and exhibits a constant improvement over divide-and-conquer attacks [27].

Related works. Multi-target attacks can be viewed as an alternative between simple (single-target) divide-and-conquer attacks and anaytical ones [39].

Step 4. Post-processing. The outcome of a divide-and-conquer attack is typically shaped as lists of probabilities or scores for each of the target key bytes. If this outcome is such that the correct key byte is always rated first, then the attack is directly successful (which happens when a sufficient amount of measurements is available to the adversary). If not, the adversary can trade measurements for time and perform *key enumeration*, which allows testing whether the correct key is within reach given his computational power. Our first contribution in this direction was an optimal key enumeration algorithm published at SAC 2012 [60]. One possible limitation of key enumeration is that in case the result of the enumeration is negative (i.e., the key is not recovered), it does not provide any hint about the computational security of the key: is it close to computational reach (e.g., with rank 2^{45} while we performed enumeration up to rank 2^{40}) or close to a standard cryptographic key sizes (e.g., $2^{80} - 2^{100}$)? In order to deal with this issue, we introduced a first *key rank estimation* algorithm allowing "security evaluations beyond computing power" at Eurocrypt 2013. Following these initial works, we then proposed much simplified algorithms for both key enumeration and rank estimation. More precisely, in a FSE 2015 paper we showed that is it possible to estimate the rank of a block cipher key with very tight bounds (e.g., with less than one bit of accuracy) almost instantaneously, using simple tools such as histograms and convolutions [26]. In a CHES 2016 paper, we then extended the use of these tools to a key enumeration algorithm that is parallelizable and allows easy distribution of the key testing among various hardware and software computing platforms [46]. In a complementary line of work, we finally discussed the pros and cons of various approaches to rank estimation, together with the efficiency gains that can be obtained by replacing the previous approximations by simple(r) bounds based on easier-to-estimate metrics [45]. In the same paper, we again put forward the interest of a (profiled) probabilistic approach to allow the optimal post-processing of the attack outcomes.

Related works. [6] presents an alternative (similarly efficient) key ranking algorithm. [37] proposed the first parallel key enumeration algorithm.

Wrapping up & cautionary note. The previous separation results allow a better understanding of the necessary steps in side-channel security evaluations, together with a systematic view of the possible sources of sub-optimality which may lead evaluators to over-estimate the security of their implementations. For Steps 2, 3 and 4, we additionally provided tools allowing them to avoid such a false sense of security. These tools typically allow evaluators to estimate *security graphs* (i.e., plots of the attacks success rate in function of their measurement and time complexity) for any implementation. Yet, and despite these progresses, it is important to note that all concrete security evaluations remain highly dependent on measurements and & pre-processing. That is, if an adversary/evaluator does a selection of POIs that ignores critical information, or does not filter a parasitic frequency and models it as noise, the next evaluation steps will not be able to correct this. Hence, and quite naturally, such a more established methodology has to be combined with continuous progresses in order to develop tools able to capture increasingly protected implementations, for which the exploitation of the leakages may require to deal with high-dimensional and high-order statistics. Finding solutions allowing adversaries/evaluators to deal with such complex settings is an important scope for further research on side-channel analysis.

Related works. [5,40] illustrate that high-dimensions and high-order attacks become increasingly important as implementations become better protected.

Future trends. One emerging drawback of the concrete approaches to physical security evaluations is that they are essentially based on mounting attacks (or detecting biases). Yet, and as security levels increase, their direct evaluation with sufficient statistical confidence will soon become untractable. For example, think about an implementation that guarantees a computational security of 2^{80} after the observation of 2^{80} measurements. In order to evaluate security in this case, we foresee two trends that we illustrate with the masking countermeasure.

A. Exploiting (tight) proofs. The (measurement) security of a masked implementation theoretically increases exponentially with the number of shares, given that the leakage of each share is sufficiently noisy and independent. In practice, it means that if a designer is able to quantify this noise condition and guarantee independence, he can evaluate the security of a masked implementation by evaluating the leakage of a single share (which is roughly as easy as evaluating an unprotected implementation) rather than that of their combination (a task for which the complexity is exponential in the number of shares). A seed result in this direction was published at Eurocrypt 2015 [16,17]. We believe that evaluations based on tight proofs will be increasingly relevant in the future.

Related works. Models to analyze masked implementations include the probing model and the noisy leakage model [31,50]. In a very important piece of work, Duc et al. showed probing security implies noisy leakage security (under some conditions discussed in the paper) [15]. Simplified tools allowing faster security evaluations but specialized to certain popular distinguishers include [13,33].

B. Security without obscurity. A positive artifact of masked (serial) implementations is that the number of POIs that have to be identified by an adversary also increases exponentially with the number shares. Yet, contrary to the noise condition that guarantees high measurement complexity, these POIs are typically a long-term secret that depend on the adversarial knowledge about the implementation. A single leak of this secret (e.g., the implementation source code) may completely annihilate its impact. In this respect, it is naturally advisable to design security mechanisms that are not based on such hard to quantify secrets, but only on a sound combination of reproducible (empirically verifiable) physical assumptions and mathematical amplification. Since security without obscurity is also the best (and probably only) setting in which security proofs can be established, we believe it will also become increasingly relevant in the future.

Other results. For completeness, we list a number of other results related to the fair evaluation of side-channel attacks obtained during the CRASH project. First, we used our tools and methodology to evaluate the impact of technology scaling on the side-channel resistance of cryptographic implementations, e.g., variability [53] and static leakages [48]. Second, we analyzed (pseudo) generic distinguishers in [3,63], which are typical candidate tools to manipulate high-dimension and high-order leakages. Third, we investigated collision attacks as an alternative path between divide-and-conquer and analytical attacks [24].

`Other related works.` The exploitability of static leakages in side-channel analysis was first put forward in [41]. The Kolmogorov-Smirnov test has been studied in [66] as an alternative (pseudo) generic distinguisher. There is a wide literature on side-channel collision attacks. Recent examples include [7,42]. Finally, and in a recent line of papers, standard side-channel distinguishers have been revisited thanks to a theoretical framework where the leakage function is fixed (i.e., in a so-called simulated attack setting). This brings a complementary view to the concrete setting where most of the efforts are put on finding the right leakage model, and a maximum likelihood strategy is applied afterwards. The authors showed that as long as the assumed leakage function is close to the ones observed in practice, the standard distinguishers/dimensionality reductions previously proposed in the literature are indeed close to optimal [8,9,29].

Acknowledgements. François-Xavier Standaert is a research associate of the Belgian Fund for Scientific Research (F.R.S.-FNRS). This work has been funded in part by the European Commission through the ERC project 280141. The author is highly grateful to the SPACE 2016 organizers for inviting him to give this talk, and allowing him to amortize the load of his final project report.

References

1. Archambeau, C., Peeters, E., Standaert, F.-X., Quisquater, J.-J.: Template attacks in principal subspaces. In: Goubin, L., Matsui, M. (eds.) CHES 2006. LNCS, vol. 4249, pp. 1–14. Springer, Heidelberg (2006). doi:10.1007/11894063_1
2. Balasch, J., Gierlichs, B., Reparaz, O., Verbauwhede, I.: DPA, bitslicing and masking at 1 GHz. In: Güneysu, T., Handschuh, H. (eds.) [28], pp. 599–619
3. Batina, L., Gierlichs, B., Prouff, E., Rivain, M., Standaert, F.-X., Veyrat-Charvillon, N.: Mutual information analysis: a comprehensive study. J. Cryptology 24(2), 269–291 (2011)
4. Batina, L., Robshaw, M. (eds.): CHES 2014. LNCS, vol. 8731. Springer, Heidelberg (2014)
5. Battistello, A., Coron, J.-S., Prouff, E., Zeitoun, R.: Horizontal side-channel attacks and countermeasures on the ISW masking scheme. In: Gierlichs, B., Poschmann, A.Y. (eds.) [25], pp. 23–39

6. Bernstein, D.J., Lange, T., van Vredendaal, C.: Tighter, faster, simpler side-channel security evaluations beyond computing power. IACR Cryptology ePrint Archive 2015:221 (2015)

7. Bogdanov, A., Kizhvatov, I.: Beyond the limits of DPA: combined side-channel collision attacks. IEEE Trans. Comput. **61**(8), 1153–1164 (2012)

8. Bruneau, N., Guilley, S., Heuser, A., Marion, D., Rioul, O.: Less is more - dimensionality reduction from a theoretical perspective. In: Güneysu, T., Handschuh, H. (eds.) [28], pp. 22–41

9. Bruneau, N., Guilley, S., Heuser, A., Rioul, O.: Masks will fall off. In: Sarkar, P., Iwata, T. (eds.) ASIACRYPT 2014. LNCS, vol. 8874, pp. 344–365. Springer, Heidelberg (2014). doi:10.1007/978-3-662-45608-8_19

10. Cagli, E., Dumas, C., Prouff, E.: Enhancing dimensionality reduction methods for side-channel attacks. In: Homma, N., Medwed, M. (eds.) [30], pp. 15–33

11. Choudary, O., Kuhn, M.G.: Efficient template attacks. In: Francillon, A., Rohatgi, P. (eds.) CARDIS 2013. LNCS, vol. 8419, pp. 253–270. Springer, Heidelberg (2014). doi:10.1007/978-3-319-08302-5_17

12. Choudary, O., Kuhn, M.G.: Template attacks on different devices. In: Prouff, E. (ed.) [49], pp. 179–198

13. Adam Ding, A., Zhang, L., Fei, Y., Luo, P.: A statistical model for higher order DPA on masked devices. In: Batina, L., Robshaw, M. (eds.) [4], pp. 147–169

14. Doget, J., Prouff, E., Rivain, M., Standaert, F.-X.: Univariate side channel attacks and leakage modeling. J. Cryptographic Eng. **1**(2), 123–144 (2011)

15. Duc, A., Dziembowski, S., Faust, S., Unifying leakage models: from probing attacks to noisy leakage. In: Nguyen, P.Q., Oswald, E. (eds.) [43], pp. 423–440

16. Duc, A., Faust, S., Standaert, F.-X.: Making masking security proofs concrete. In: Oswald, E., Fischlin, M. (eds.) EUROCRYPT 2015. LNCS, vol. 9056, pp. 401–429. Springer, Heidelberg (2015). doi:10.1007/978-3-662-46800-5_16

17. Duc, A., Faust, S., Standaert, F.-X.: Making masking security proofs concrete or how to evaluate the security of any leaking device (extended version). IACR Cryptology ePrint Archive 2015:119 (2015)

18. Durvaux, F., Renauld, M., Standaert, F.-X., Oldeneel tot Oldenzeel, L., Veyrat-Charvillon, N.: Efficient removal of random delays from embedded software implementations using Hidden Markov Models. In: Mangard, S. (ed.) CARDIS 2012. LNCS, vol. 7771, pp. 123–140. Springer, Heidelberg (2013). doi:10.1007/978-3-642-37288-9_9

19. Durvaux, F., Standaert, F.-X.: From improved leakage detection to the detection of points of interests in leakage traces. In: Fischlin, M., Coron, J.-S. (eds.) EUROCRYPT 2016. LNCS, vol. 9665, pp. 240–262. Springer, Heidelberg (2016). doi:10.1007/978-3-662-49890-3_10

20. Durvaux, F., Standaert, F.-X., Del Pozo, S.M.: Towards easy leakage certification. In: Gierlichs, B., Poschmann, A.Y. (eds.) [25], pp. 40–60

21. Durvaux, F., Standaert, F.-X., Veyrat-Charvillon, N.: How to certify the leakage of a chip? In: Nguyen, P.Q., Oswald, E. (eds.) [43], pp. 459–476

22. Durvaux, F., Standaert, F.-X., Veyrat-Charvillon, N., Mairy, J.-B., Deville, Y.: Efficient selection of time samples for higher-order DPA with projection pursuits. In: Mangard, S., Poschmann, A.Y. (eds.) COSADE 2014. LNCS, vol. 9064, pp. 34–50. Springer, Heidelberg (2015). doi:10.1007/978-3-319-21476-4_3

23. Abdelaziz Elaabid, M., Guilley, S.: Portability of templates. J. Cryptographic Eng. **2**(1), 63–74 (2012)

24. Gérard, B., Standaert, F.-X.: Unified and optimized linear collision attacks and their application in a non-profiled setting: extended version. J. Cryptographic Eng. **3**(1), 45–58 (2013)

25. Gierlichs, B., Poschmann, A.Y. (eds.): CHES 2016. LNCS, vol. 9813. Springer, Heidelberg (2016)

26. Glowacz, C., Grosso, V., Poussier, R., Schüth, J., Standaert, F.-X.: Simpler and more efficient rank estimation for side-channel security assessment. In: Leander, G. (ed.) FSE 2015. LNCS, vol. 9054, pp. 117–129. Springer, Heidelberg (2015). doi:10. 1007/978-3-662-48116-5_6

27. Grosso, V., Standaert, F.-X.: ASCA, SASCA and DPA with enumeration: which one beats the other and when? In: Iwata, T., Cheon, J.H. (eds.) [32], pp. 291–312

28. Güneysu, T., Handschuh, H. (eds.): CHES 2015. LNCS, vol. 9293. Springer, Heidelberg (2015)

29. Heuser, A., Rioul, O., Guilley, S.: Good is not good enough - deriving optimal distinguishers from communication theory. In: Batina, L., Robshaw, M. (eds.) [4], pp. 55–74

30. Homma, N., Medwed, M. (eds.): CARDIS 2015. LNCS, vol. 9514. Springer, Heidelberg (2016)

31. Ishai, Y., Sahai, A., Wagner, D.: Private circuits: securing hardware against probing attacks. In: Boneh, D. (ed.) CRYPTO 2003. LNCS, vol. 2729, pp. 463–481. Springer, Heidelberg (2003). doi:10.1007/978-3-540-45146-4_27

32. Iwata, T., Cheon, J.H. (eds.): ASIACRYPT 2015. LNCS, vol. 9453. Springer, Heidelberg (2015)

33. Lomné, V., Prouff, E., Rivain, M., Roche, T., Thillard, A.: How to estimate the success rate of higher-order side-channel attacks. In: Batina, L., Robshaw, M. (eds.) [4], pp. 35–54

34. Lomné, V., Prouff, E., Roche, T.: Behind the scene of side channel attacks. In: Sako, K., Sarkar, P. (eds.) [55], pp. 506–525

35. Longo, J., De Mulder, E., Page, D., Tunstall, M.: SoC It to EM: electromagnetic side-channel attacks on a complex system-on-chip. In: Güneysu, T., Handschuh, H. (eds.) [28], pp. 620–640

36. Mangard, S., Oswald, E., Standaert, F.-X.: One for all - all for one: unifying standard differential power analysis attacks. IET Inf. Secur. **5**(2), 100–110 (2011)

37. Martin, D.P., O'Connell, J.F., Oswald, E., Stam, M.: Counting keys in parallel after a side channel attack. In: Iwata, T., Cheon, J.H. (eds.) [32], pp. 313–337

38. Mather, L., Oswald, E., Bandenburg, J., Wójcik, M.: Does my device leak information? An a priori statistical power analysis of leakage detection tests. In: Sako, K., Sarkar, P. (eds.) [55], pp. 486–505

39. Mather, L., Oswald, E., Whitnall, C.: Multi-target DPA attacks: pushing DPA beyond the limits of a desktop computer. In: Sarkar, P., Iwata, T. (eds.) [56], pp. 243–261

40. Moradi, A.: Statistical tools flavor side-channel collision attacks. In: Pointcheval, D., Johansson, T. (eds.) EUROCRYPT 2012. LNCS, vol. 7237, pp. 428–445. Springer, Heidelberg (2012). doi:10.1007/978-3-642-29011-4_26

41. Moradi, A.: Side-channel leakage through static power - should we care about in practice? In: Batina, L., Robshaw, M. (eds.) [4], pp. 562–579

42. Moradi, A., Mischke, O., Eisenbarth, T.: Correlation-enhanced power analysis collision attack. In: Mangard, S., Standaert, F.-X. (eds.) CHES 2010. LNCS, vol. 6225, pp. 125–139. Springer, Heidelberg (2010). doi:10.1007/978-3-642-15031-9_9

43. Nguyen, P.Q., Oswald, E. (eds.): EUROCRYPT 2014. LNCS, vol. 8441. Springer, Heidelberg (2014)

44. Oren, Y., Renauld, M., Standaert, F.-X., Wool, A.: Algebraic side-channel attacks beyond the hamming weight leakage model. In: Prouff, E., Schaumont, P. (eds.) CHES 2012. LNCS, vol. 7428, pp. 140–154. Springer, Heidelberg (2012). doi:10.1007/978-3-642-33027-8_9

45. Poussier, R., Grosso, V., Standaert, F.-X.: Comparing approaches to rank estimation for side-channel security evaluations. In: Homma, N., Medwed, M. (eds.) [30], pp. 125–142

46. Poussier, R., Standaert, F.-X., Grosso, V., Simple key enumeration (and rank estimation) using histograms: an integrated approach. In: Gierlichs, B., Poschmann, A.Y. (eds.) [25], pp. 61–81

47. Del Pozo, S.M., Standaert, F.-X.: Blind source separation from single measurements using singular spectrum analysis. In: Güneysu, T., Handschuh, H. (eds.) [28], pp. 42–59

48. Del Pozo, S.M., Standaert, F.X., Kamel, D., Moradi, A.: Side-channel attacks from static power: when should we care? In: Nebel, W., Atienza, D. (eds.) Proceedings of the 2015 Design, Automation & Test in Europe Conference & Exhibition, DATE 2015, Grenoble, France, 9–13 March 2015, pp. 145–150. ACM (2015)

49. Prouff, E. (ed.): COSADE 2014. LNCS, vol. 8622. Springer, Heidelberg (2014)

50. Prouff, E., Rivain, M.: Masking against side-channel attacks: a formal security proof. In: Johansson, T., Nguyen, P.Q. (eds.) EUROCRYPT 2013. LNCS, vol. 7881, pp. 142–159. Springer, Heidelberg (2013). doi:10.1007/978-3-642-38348-9_9

51. Renauld, M., Standaert, F.-X.: Algebraic side-channel attacks. In: Bao, F., Yung, M., Lin, D., Jing, J. (eds.) Inscrypt 2009. LNCS, vol. 6151, pp. 393–410. Springer, Heidelberg (2010). doi:10.1007/978-3-642-16342-5_29

52. Renauld, M., Standaert, F.-X., Veyrat-Charvillon, N.: Algebraic side-channel attacks on the AES: why time also matters in DPA. In: Clavier, C., Gaj, K. (eds.) CHES 2009. LNCS, vol. 5747, pp. 97–111. Springer, Heidelberg (2009). doi:10.1007/978-3-642-04138-9_8

53. Renauld, M., Standaert, F.-X., Veyrat-Charvillon, N., Kamel, D., Flandre, D.: A formal study of power variability issues and side-channel attacks for nanoscale devices. In: Paterson, K.G. (ed.) EUROCRYPT 2011. LNCS, vol. 6632, pp. 109–128. Springer, Heidelberg (2011). doi:10.1007/978-3-642-20465-4_8

54. Reparaz, O., Gierlichs, B., Verbauwhede, I.: Generic DPA attacks: curse or blessing? In: Prouff, E. (ed.) [49], pp. 98–111

55. Sako, K., Sarkar, P. (eds.): ASIACRYPT 2013. LNCS, vol. 8269. Springer, Heidelberg (2013)

56. Sarkar, P., Iwata, T. (eds.): ASIACRYPT 2014. LNCS, vol. 8873. Springer, Heidelberg (2014)

57. Schneider, T., Moradi, A.: Leakage assessment methodology - extended version. J. Cryptographic Eng. 6(2), 85–99 (2016)

58. Standaert, F.-X., Archambeau, C.: Using subspace-based template attacks to compare and combine power and electromagnetic information leakages. In: Oswald, E., Rohatgi, P. (eds.) CHES 2008. LNCS, vol. 5154, pp. 411–425. Springer, Heidelberg (2008). doi:10.1007/978-3-540-85053-3_26

59. Standaert, F.-X., Veyrat-Charvillon, N., Oswald, E., Gierlichs, B., Medwed, M., Kasper, M., Mangard, S.: The world is not enough: another look on second-order DPA. In: Abe, M. (ed.) ASIACRYPT 2010. LNCS, vol. 6477, pp. 112–129. Springer, Heidelberg (2010). doi:10.1007/978-3-642-17373-8_7

60. Veyrat-Charvillon, N., Gérard, B., Renauld, M., Standaert, F.-X.: An optimal key enumeration algorithm and its application to side-channel attacks. In: Knudsen,

L.R., Wu, H. (eds.) SAC 2012. LNCS, vol. 7707, pp. 390–406. Springer, Heidelberg (2013). doi:10.1007/978-3-642-35999-6_25

61. Veyrat-Charvillon, N., Gérard, B., Standaert, F.-X.: Soft analytical side-channel attacks. In: Sarkar, P., Iwata, T. (eds.) [56], pp. 282–296

62. Veyrat-Charvillon, N., Medwed, M., Kerckhof, S., Standaert, F.-X.: Shuffling against side-channel attacks: a comprehensive study with cautionary note. In: Wang, X., Sako, K. (eds.) ASIACRYPT 2012. LNCS, vol. 7658, pp. 740–757. Springer, Heidelberg (2012). doi:10.1007/978-3-642-34961-4_44

63. Veyrat-Charvillon, N., Standaert, F.-X.: Generic side-channel distinguishers: improvements and limitations. In: Rogaway, P. (ed.) CRYPTO 2011. LNCS, vol. 6841, pp. 354–372. Springer, Heidelberg (2011). doi:10.1007/978-3-642-22792-9_20

64. Wang, W., Yu, Y., Liu, J., Guo, Z., Standaert, F.-X., Gu, D., Xu, S., Fu, R.: Evaluation and improvement of generic-emulating DPA attacks. In: Güneysu, T., Handschuh, H. (eds.) [28], pp. 416–432

65. Whitnall, C., Oswald, E.: Robust profiling for DPA-style attacks. In: Güneysu, T., Handschuh, H. (eds.) [28], pp. 3–21

66. Whitnall, C., Oswald, E., Mather, L.: An exploration of the Kolmogorov-Smirnov test as a competitor to mutual information analysis. In: Prouff, E. (ed.) CARDIS 2011. LNCS, vol. 7079, pp. 234–251. Springer, Heidelberg (2011). doi:10.1007/978-3-642-27257-8_15

67. Whitnall, C., Oswald, E., Standaert, F.-X.: The myth of generic DPA...and the magic of learning. In: Benaloh, J. (ed.) CT-RSA 2014. LNCS, vol. 8366, pp. 183–205. Springer, Heidelberg (2014). doi:10.1007/978-3-319-04852-9_10

A Methodology for the Characterisation of Leakages in Combinatorial Logic

Guido Bertoni[1] and Marco Martinoli[2($\boxtimes$)]

[1] STMicroelectronics, Agrate Brianza, MB, Italy
guido.bertoni@st.com
[2] Department of Computer Science, University of Bristol, Bristol, UK
marco.martinoli@bristol.ac.uk

Abstract. Glitches represent a great danger for hardware implementations of cryptographic schemes. Their intrinsic random nature makes them difficult to tackle and their occurrence threatens side-channel protections. Although countermeasures aiming at structurally solving the problem already exist, they usually require some effort to be applied or introduce non-negligible overhead in the design. Our work addresses the gap between such countermeasures and the naïve implementation of schemes being vulnerable in the presence of glitches. Our contribution is twofold: (1) we expand the mathematical framework proposed by Brzozowski and Ésik [5] by meaningfully adding the notion of information leakage, (2) thanks to which we define a formal methodology for the analysis of vulnerabilities in combinatorial circuits when glitches are taken into account.

Keywords: Side-channel analysis · Hardware countermeasures · Glitches · Formal method

1 Introduction

Side-channel attacks were first introduced by Kocher *et al.* [6] as a way to attack implementations of cryptosystems. They exploit the relation between data being processed and several physical emanations, for instance time taken or power consumed to perform computations [7]. Since its first appearance, side-channel analysis has grown quickly with newly developed attacks as well as countermeasures, which try to prevent any sensitive information from being leaked. For instance, sharing schemes randomise intermediate values in such a way that the leaked information no longer depends on any sensitive data [8]. However the efficiency of countermeasures is deeply linked to physical characteristics of the device on which they are implemented: in 2005 Mangard *et al.* [9] predicted the criticality of glitches for hardware implementations, which was then demonstrated in the same year [10]. They showed how the propagation of signals in combinatorial logic implementing an apparently secured SBox might result in critical leakages, leading to an ineffective protection. To solve the problem,

© Springer International Publishing AG 2016
C. Carlet et al. (Eds.): SPACE 2016, LNCS 10076, pp. 363–382, 2016.
DOI: 10.1007/978-3-319-49445-6_21

Nikova *et al.* [13,14] suggested the use of threshold implementations, which allow to tackle glitches at root by developing maps that do not handle all the shares in the same combinatorial circuit. Such maps obviously come at the cost of a significant overhead compared to the unprotected version. Implementations and practical discussions can be found in the work of Moradi *et al.* [12] and of Bilgin *et al.* [4]. As for higher-order security, the issue of glitches has been faced with a generalisation of threshold implementations [3,17], and independently by Prouff and Roche [15]. Specifically on the effects of glitches on the AES SBox Mangard and Schramm [11] have reported a deep and complete analysis.

Overall there is a gap in the capabilities of quantifying the criticality of glitches in a hardware implementation. This gap is not trivial to close, as glitches in combinatorial logic are functions of the final layout of the circuit and the environmental conditions, and might change during the life of the device. In practice two equal devices might exhibit a different behaviour in terms of glitches.

Our aim is to provide a framework for evaluating the presence of glitches under worst-case conditions without the need of detailed characterisation of the combinatorial logic, *i.e.* remaining at gate level description. In order to achieve this result, we start from the mathematical structure created by Brzozowski and Ésik [5], which simulates the propagation of electric signals inside a circuit, and we build a method to relate a modelled power consumption with the sensitive variables that have caused it. Our analysis is done in a worst-case scenario where all possible glitches are taken into account as to achieve the maximum possible generality. Our main result is an assessing tool which is able to formally describe what kind of information could be leaked, and to give an heuristic estimate about the security of sharing schemes implemented in hardware.

Organisation of the Paper. Section 2 provides the abstract framework underlying our tool, with a particular emphasis on how circuits and signals propagating inside them are modelled. Section 3 describes parts of the work of Brzozowski and Ésik [5] which are also used by our construction. In Sect. 4 we present our main contribution: we expand the functionalities of the previously discussed mathematical model with the notion of leakage and we show how such an improved framework can be used to analyse cryptographic circuits. In Sect. 5 some examples of usage of our model are reported, with particular reference to the sponge function KECCAK. We discuss the soundness of our approach and several practical aspects in Sect. 6, and we conclude our work in Sect. 7.

2   Preliminaries

Our work targets hardware implementations of cryptographic schemes. Since the meaning of such can be quite broad, the present section aims at specifying our environment, as well as at setting the notation we adopt. In fact, our mathematical model applies only to an abstraction of real-world circuits: we just refer to logic netlists, hence circuits formed only of logic gates and connections among them. Our tool therefore achieves a good level of generality, since it does not require any knowledge of implementation details apart from the circuit scheme itself, which means that it is general enough to include all the above mentioned source of glitches (final layout, environmental conditions...). In particular we focus on asynchronous feedback-free circuits. We claim this is not too restrictive, because of the following argument. Circuits can be divided into two parts: the combinatorial logic and the state storing part. The combinatorial logic is indeed asynchronous, it is the part in charge of implementing the logic functionality and where glitches might propagate. The state storing part, implemented via registers or memory cells, is clocked and provides the synchronization between different sections of the circuits. Since we apply our model to logic circuits performing sensitive computations, the most natural choice is to focus on the asynchronous part only. We do not consider the presence of feedbacks in the combinatorial part for the sake of simplicity and because they are not a common construction in this field anyway.

We adopt a high-level abstraction of signals too. Since we are only interested in the Boolean value they represent, it is convenient to think of them as square waveforms which can assume the values 0 or 1. To push the abstraction further we assume the existence of a sampling frequency being fine enough to detect all the changes occurring in a signal, in such a way that a signal is represented as a finite-length bit-string. We denote by

$$\mathbb{Z}_2^* = \bigcup_{r=1}^{\infty} \mathbb{Z}_2^r$$

the set of finite-length bit-strings. We denote bit-strings by concatenation of bits, $i.e.$ a bit-string $s \in \mathbb{Z}_2^*$ is of the form $s = a_1 \ldots a_r$ for some bits $a_i \in \mathbb{Z}_2$ and for a certain $r \geq 1$. Grouping bits of a bit-string is also a useful notation and is denoted by $s = b_1^{p_1} \ldots b_{r'}^{p_{r'}}$, where this time we assume $b_j \neq b_{j+1}$ and $p_i > 0$ for every $1 \leq i \leq r'$, $1 \leq j \leq r' - 1$. Essentially, the latter notation highlights the number of times p_i the corresponding bit b_i is repeated in a bit-string. Finally, we denote by $\ell(s) = r$ its length, by $\alpha(s) = a_1 = b_1$ its first bit and by $\omega(s) = a_r = b_{r'}$ its last one.

Further Notation. We denote the power set ($i.e.$ the set of all subsets) of a set S by $\mathcal{P}(S)$. Vectors are denoted by underlined letters while boldface is reserved for signals seen as transients (cf. Definition 1 and Example 1).

2.1   Power Consumption Model

The power consumed by a circuit is a crucial information as it is one of a number of side-channels through which a loss of sensitive information can occur [7] and is the only one we focus on throughout this work. If we consider global synchronous circuits, the power consumption can be divided in three components: the static leakage, the switching of registers and the switching of combinatorial logic. The static leakage is the amount of power needed by the circuit to maintain the current state when no switch is present. The switching of registers is the consumption taken by the circuit for updating the state and is easily approximated by the Hamming distance of the state in two consecutive clock cycles. The value of the registers can be easily protected by masking schemes. The last contribution is the most interesting for us and is related to the consumption of the combinatorial logic. From a temporal point of view, the switching of registers usually happens at the rising edge of the clock cycle while the static leakage happens in its last part. By contrast, the consumption of combinatorial logic spans, in most cases, the entire duration of the clock cycle [16]. Consistently with the choice of addressing only the asynchronous part of a circuit, our power consumption model includes only the contribution of the combinatorial logic.

Since we deal only with circuits formed by logic gates, we assume that the power consumed by the whole circuit is the sum of the power consumed by each gate, which reduces the problem to modelling the power consumed by a gate. The simplest way is to consider the signal a gate outputs or, equivalently, the corresponding bit-string. If the output signal changes, equivalently the corresponding output bit-string switches, the gate consumes. The power consumption model we assume in the present work is then described by the following three assumptions:

1. a gate consumes power if and only if its output bit-string switches;
2. a zero-to-one switch consumes the same amount of power as a one-to-zero switch;
3. every time some power is consumed, an attacker can measure and exploit it. Hence we assume that a potential leakage exists as far as a switch occurs.

As already stated, we neglect static leakage by means of the first assumption. The second assumption is made for the sake of simplicity and it can be dropped in favour of a more realistic model built on top of a specific technology library. The third assumption assures the best possible generality: we consider as leaked every variable that has a chance to be leaked.

3   Simulation of Signal Propagation

Brzozowski and Ésik [5] have developed a mathematical structure which aims at simulating worst-case glitches propagation in a circuit. In essence, the model analyses how a change in the inputs propagates and which kind of response is triggered in the gates. In their work, Brzozowski and Ésik use a higher level of abstraction than bit-strings to simulate signals.

Definition 1. *A* transient *is a bit-string with no repetitions. More formally, a bit-string* $t = a_1 \ldots a_r \in \mathbb{Z}_2^*$ *is a transient if* $a_i \neq a_{i+1}$ *for all* $1 \leq i \leq r-1$. *Equivalently,* $t = b_1^{p_1} \ldots b_{r'}^{p_{r'}} \in \mathbb{Z}_2^*$ *is a transient if* $p_i = 1$ *for every* $1 \leq i \leq r'$.

Informally, transients can only be of the form $1010\ldots$ or $0101\ldots$ for an arbitrary finite length $r \geq 1$ (note that bits 0 and 1 can be considered as transients for which $r = 1$). We define a map from bit-strings to transients called the *contraction map* and denoted by $\gamma : \mathbb{Z}_2^* \to \mathbb{Z}_2^*$ such that:

$$\gamma(b_1^{p_1} \ldots b_n^{p_n}) = b_1 \ldots b_n.$$

We denote by $T = \gamma(\mathbb{Z}_2^*) \subseteq \mathbb{Z}_2^*$ the set of all possible transients.

Definition 2. *Let $t, t' \in T$ be two transients such that $\ell(t) \leq \ell(t')$. We say that t is a* prefix *of order $o = \ell(t') - \ell(t)$ of t' if $\alpha(t) = \alpha(t')$. We adopt the notation $t \preceq_o t'$. Note that if $o = 0$, $\preceq_0$ is equivalent to equality between transients.*

The rationale behind transients is the following. Contracting bit-strings is equivalent to neglecting time periods during which a signal assumes constant values 1 or 0. This results in transients being exclusively designed to represent which changes occur, but not when: the order of switches can then be freely tuned, in such a way that the worst glitchy behaviour is always shown at the output of a gate. That is to say if two transients modelling two changing signals are given as inputs to a gate, then the output will be a transient modelling the signal showing the highest possible number of changes. Next subsection specifies how to combine transients so to emulate gates' logic.

3.1   Operations Among Transients

As the previous discussion has suggested, the choice of transients rather than general bit-strings as a formalisation of signals relies on the operations that it is possible to define among them. Since the circuits we study are only formed of logic gates, we want those operations to preserve gates' functionalities. Therefore we aim at building a function $\hat{f} : T^n \to T$ associated to a Boolean function $f : \mathbb{Z}_2^n \to \mathbb{Z}_2$ whose inputs are n transients, namely $\underline{t} = (t_1, \ldots, t_n) \in T^n$.

Example 1. Let us suppose that two signals s_1 and s_2 are given as input to a gate implementing a Boolean function $f : \mathbb{Z}_2^2 \to \mathbb{Z}_2$. Firstly, they are fixed at constant values $b_1 \in \mathbb{Z}_2$ and $b_2 \in \mathbb{Z}_2$ respectively. Suddenly, s_1 changes from b_1 to $c \in \mathbb{Z}_2$, with $c \neq b_1$. This is represented by the transient $\mathbf{s}_1 = b_1c$ which can be either 01 or 10. Then, the idea behind the function $\hat{f}$ is to emulate the behaviour of the function f, but taking as inputs the two transients $\mathbf{s}_1 = b_1c$ and $\mathbf{s}_2 = b_2$ (seen as a length-one transient) and producing a transient with the highest number of switches, *i.e.* as if the highest number of glitches occurred. Note that we write a variable in boldface if it is seen as a transient and that bit concatenation is denoted by simply writing one bit after the other.

The remainder of this subsection describes how to achieve the functionality discussed in Example 1. The idea is that, given two input transients $t_1 = a_1 \ldots a_n$ and $t_2 = b_1 \ldots b_m$, the first bit the gate computes is $f(a_1, b_1)$. This will be also called the initial stable state. Then the two inputs change to a_2 and b_2 respectively, and we have the freedom to decide which is the first one to affect the gate such that another change in the output (if any) is triggered. This process is built thanks to two graphs which look at all possible combinations of propagation times. Firstly, we define the directed graph $D(\underline{t})$ as follows.

Definition 3. *Given* $\underline{t} = (t_1, \ldots, t_n) \in T^n$, *we define the directed graph* $D(\underline{t}) = (V, E)$ *such that:*

$$V = \{\underline{v} \in T^n \mid v_i \preceq_{o_i} t_i \text{ for every } 0 \leq o_i < \ell(t_i) \text{ and } 1 \leq i \leq n\}$$
$$E = \{(\underline{v}, \underline{w}) \in V \times V \mid \exists! i \text{ such that } v_i \preceq_1 w_i \text{ and } v_j = w_j \text{ for every } j \neq i\}$$

Note that $D(\underline{t})$ is the graph whose nodes are all the prefixes of the components of $\underline{t}$, the simplest being $(\alpha(t_1), \ldots, \alpha(t_n))$ and the longest being $\underline{t}$ itself. Edges are drawn if there exists only one change in exactly one of two nodes' components. At this point we label each vertex $\underline{v} = (v_1, \ldots, v_n) \in V$ with the bit $f_\omega(\underline{v}) = f(\omega(v_1), \ldots, \omega(v_n)) \in \mathbb{Z}_2$ and we construct the following graph.

Definition 4. *Let* $f : \mathbb{Z}_2^n \to \mathbb{Z}_2$ *be a Boolean function. Given* $\underline{t} = (t_1, \ldots, t_n) \in T^n$ *and* $D(\underline{t}) = (V, E)$, *we define its labelled directed graph* $D_f(\underline{t}) = (V_f, E_f)$ *such that:*

$$V_f = \{f_\omega(\underline{v}) \in \mathbb{Z}_2 \mid \underline{v} \in V\}$$
$$E_f = \{(f_\omega(\underline{v}), f_\omega(\underline{w})) \in V_f \times V_f \mid (\underline{v}, \underline{w}) \in E\}$$

It is straightforward that the graph $D_f(\underline{t})$ has the same shape as $D(\underline{t})$. In particular there is a bijection between E and E_f, hence every path in $D(\underline{t})$ can be reconstructed in $D_f(\underline{t})$. Thanks to this, the output of $\hat{f}$ is computed by first considering all the paths in $D(\underline{t})$ from $(\alpha(t_1), \ldots, \alpha(t_n))$ to $(t_1, \ldots, t_n)$ and then reconstructing them in $D_f(\underline{t})$. Since elements of V_f are bits, each path in the latter graph uniquely defines a bit-string by concatenating its successive vertices. The contraction map γ is then applied to every such bit-strings and the output of $\hat{f}(t_1, \ldots, t_n)$ is defined as the longest contraction.

Theorem 1. *Let* $f : \mathbb{Z}_2^n \to \mathbb{Z}_2$ *be a Boolean function. The function* $\hat{f} : T^n \to T$ *is well defined for any given input* $\underline{t} = (t_1, \ldots, t_n) \in T^n$.

Proof. We only need to prove that if two paths in $D(\underline{t})$ lead to bit-strings whose contractions have the same length and are the longest, then such contractions are equal. In other words, let $s_1 = a_1 \ldots a_k$ and $s_2 = b_1 \ldots b_m$ be two bit-strings computed from the two paths such that $\ell(\gamma(s_1)) = \ell(\gamma(s_2))$, where $a_i, b_j \in \mathbb{Z}_2$. Since we are only considering paths in $D(\underline{t})$ from $(\alpha(t_1), \ldots, \alpha(t_n))$ to $(t_1, \ldots, t_n)$, it is true that $\alpha(s_1) = \alpha(s_2) = f(\alpha(t_1), \ldots, \alpha(t_n))$ and $\omega(s_1) = \omega(s_2) = f(\omega(t_1), \ldots, \omega(t_n))$. It follows that $\alpha(\gamma(s_1)) = \alpha(\gamma(s_2))$ and $\omega(\gamma(s_1)) = \omega(\gamma(s_2))$, because the contraction map cannot change the first and last bits. Since $\ell(\gamma(s_1)) = \ell(\gamma(s_2))$ holds too, $\gamma(s_1)$ and $\gamma(s_2)$ are two transients with same first and last bits and same length, hence $\gamma(s_1) = \gamma(s_2)$. □

Example 2. We report how to construct $\hat{\mathtt{AND}} : T^2 \to T$ between the two transients $010, 01 \in T$.

In Fig. 1 (left), $D(010, 01)$ is built according to Definition 3 while in Fig. 1 (right) $D_{\mathtt{AND}}(010, 01)$ is computed with the function $\mathtt{AND} : \mathbb{Z}_2^2 \to \mathbb{Z}_2$ as in Definition 4. In the graph $D(010, 01)$ there are only three possible paths from

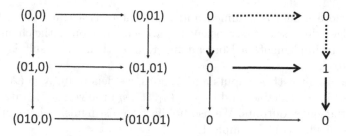

Fig. 1. $D(010, 01)$ and $D_{\text{AND}}(010, 01)$

$(0, 0)$ to $(010, 01)$, whose corresponding bit-strings are 0000, 0010 and 0010. By applying the contraction map to each of them, we obtain that the possible outputs of $\text{A}\hat{\text{N}}\text{D}$ are $\gamma(0000) = 0$, $\gamma(0010) = 010$ and $\gamma(0010) = 010$. Hence, by taking the longest possible transient we obtain that $\text{A}\hat{\text{N}}\text{D}(010, 01) = 010$. In Fig. 1 (right), the chosen path is highlighted with thicker arrows and another possible one leading to the same result is highlighted with thicker dash arrows.

We want to highlight the rationale behind those graphs. Each edge corresponds to a change in exactly one of the inputs. Deciding a path in those graphs is then equivalent to assuming an "order of arrival" of the inputs' changes to the gate. Such an order is chosen according to our previously discussed "longest possible output" rule.

Remark 1. The above construction is only a formal procedure to build $\hat{f}$ from a generic Boolean function f. In practice, once f is fixed, a simple rule to compute $\hat{f}$ can be derived from the graph. For instance, it is possible to prove (as it is done in [5]) that $\text{A}\hat{\text{N}}\text{D} : T^2 \rightarrow T$ can be defined for any two transients $t, t' \in T$ as follows:

- $\text{A}\hat{\text{N}}\text{D}(t, 1) = \text{A}\hat{\text{N}}\text{D}(1, t) = t$;
- $\text{A}\hat{\text{N}}\text{D}(t, 0) = \text{A}\hat{\text{N}}\text{D}(0, t) = 0$;
- if $\ell(t), \ell(t') > 1$, $\text{A}\hat{\text{N}}\text{D}(t, t')$ is the transient w such that:
  - $\alpha(w) = \alpha(t) \wedge \alpha(t')$;
  - $\omega(w) = \omega(t) \wedge \omega(t')$;
  - $u(w) = u(t) + u(t') - 1$;

where $u : T \rightarrow \mathbb{N}$ denotes the number of ones of a transient. Such a simplification also has an impact on the performance of $\hat{f}$: since we no longer need any graphs, $\hat{f}$ can be considered linear in the number of inputs (their lengths do not matter). We refer to the work of Brzozowski and Ésik [5] for more examples.

3.2 Glitch-Counting Algorithm

We are finally ready to state the glitch-counting algorithm, which simulates the propagation of signals inside a circuit in terms of transients. First of all, a change in one or more inputs is assumed and represented as a transient. The glitch-counting algorithm assigns a transient to each gate as soon as the change reaches it. If the gate implements a Boolean function f, then the result is computed according to $\hat{f}$.

Given a circuit with m inputs and k gates, we denote by $\underline{X} = (X_1, \ldots, X_m)$ the vector of input variables and by $\underline{s} = (s_1, \ldots, s_k)$ the vector of state variables, which are the gates' outputs. We use boldface to distinguish when variables are used as transients, as in Example 1.

Definition 5. *We call* excitation *the Boolean function* $S_j : \mathbb{Z}_2^m \times \mathbb{Z}_2^{k-1} \to \mathbb{Z}_2$ *by which the state variable s_j is computed.*

$$s_j = S_j(\underline{X}, \underline{s}) = S_j(X_1, \ldots, X_m, s_1, \ldots, s_{j-1}, s_{j+1}, \ldots, s_k)$$

The above definition simply establishes a notation for the Boolean function each gate implements. It can be further extended so as to take into account all the excitations in a given circuit.

Definition 6. *Given a circuit with m inputs and k gates, the function $S : \mathbb{Z}_2^m \times \mathbb{Z}_2^k \to \mathbb{Z}_2^k$ defined by $S(\underline{X}, \underline{s}) = (S_1(\underline{X}, \underline{s}), \ldots, S_k(\underline{X}, \underline{s}))$ is called the* vector of excitations *of the circuit.*

Note that in Definition 6, the jth component of the vector $\underline{s}$ is dropped when given as input to each S_j for every $1 \le j \le k$, according to Definition 5. This is because we only deal with feedback-free circuits.

Example 3. Let us consider the circuit in Fig. 2. It has input vector $\underline{X} = (X_1, X_2, X_3)$, state vector $\underline{s} = (s_1, s_2, s_3)$ and excitation functions given by the following Boolean expressions.

$$s_1 = S_1(X_1, X_2, X_3, s_2, s_3) = X_1 \wedge X_2$$
$$s_2 = S_2(X_1, X_2, X_3, s_1, s_3) = X_2 \vee X_3$$
$$s_3 = S_3(X_1, X_2, X_3, s_1, s_2) = s_1 \oplus s_2$$

Initially, suppose that the input $\underline{X}$ assumes the value $\underline{X} = \underline{a}' = (a_1', \ldots, a_m') \in \mathbb{Z}_2^m$, and that the state has the value $\underline{s} = \underline{b} = (b_1, \ldots, b_k) \in \mathbb{Z}_2^k$. We assume that the circuit is stable, *i.e.* $S(\underline{a}', \underline{b}) = \underline{b}$, and that the input changes to $\underline{a} = (a_1, \ldots, a_m) \in \mathbb{Z}_2^m$. We call this a *transition* and we denote it by $a_1' \ldots a_m' \to a_1 \ldots a_m$.

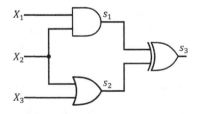

Fig. 2. Example of a circuit with input and state variables

Definition 7. *The transition function* $\circ : \mathbb{Z}_2 \times \mathbb{Z}_2 \to T$, *given* $a, b \in \mathbb{Z}_2$, *returns:*

$$a \circ b = \begin{cases} a & \text{if } a = b \\ ab & \text{if } a \neq b \end{cases}$$

where ab *denotes the concatenation of* a *and* b, *which is a transient. This notation is extended to vectors. If* $\underline{a}' = (a_1', \dots, a_m')$ *and* $\underline{a} = (a_1, \dots, a_m)$, *then:*

$$\underline{a}' \circ \underline{a} = (a_1' \circ a_1, \dots, a_m' \circ a_m)$$

The glitch-counting algorithm starts with the circuit in the initial stable state $(\underline{a}', \underline{b})$. The input is then set to $\underline{a} = \underline{a}' \circ \underline{a}$ and is kept constant at that value for the duration of the algorithm. After the input changes, some state variables become unstable in the sense that they no longer represent the correct logic output of their gate. We set all unstable variables at the same time to their excitations as soon as the input change propagates till their gate. We then obtain a new internal state, which is a vector of transients, and the process is repeated until all the state variables become stable again, *i.e.* their value is the correct Boolean output of their gate. Formally, the glitch-counting algorithm is specified below.

Algorithm 1. Glitch-counting algorithm

Input: The initial stable state $(\underline{a}', \underline{b})$, the new input $\underline{a}$ and the vector of excitations among transients $\hat{S}(\mathbf{X}, \mathbf{s})$ of a circuit.
Output: A list of k transients, one per each gate's output, describing the worst possible switching activity during the transition $\underline{a} = \underline{a}' \circ \underline{a}$.
1: $h \leftarrow 0$;
2: $\underline{a} \leftarrow \underline{a}' \circ \underline{a}$;
3: $\underline{s}^0 \leftarrow \underline{b}$;
4: **repeat**
5:     $h \leftarrow h + 1$;
6:     $\underline{s}^h \leftarrow \hat{S}(\underline{a}, \underline{s}^{h-1})$;
7: **until** $\underline{s}^h = \underline{s}^{h-1}$;
8: **return** $\underline{s}^h$;

Example 4. Suppose that, in the situation of Example 3, the input changes from $\underline{a}' = (1, 0, 0)$ to $\underline{a} = (0, 1, 0)$, hence the transition $100 \to 010$ occurs. The execution of the algorithm is summarised in Table 1, where each row represents one iteration of the cycle and each column refers to one variable (both input and state) of the circuit. The last two rows are identical, meaning that we have reached a stable state again and the algorithm terminates. At each step, the algorithm computes the whole vector of excitations of the circuit, hence considering all gates. However, it follows the behaviour of real-world signal propagation, hence earlier gates (*i.e.* closer to circuit inputs) are affected first. Indeed the first row just represents the initial state (when only inputs have changed), the second one depicts a change in the first line of gates while in the third row signals propagate till the last XOR. Figure 3 is a graphical representation of the final situation, which is the output of the algorithm without intermediate steps. Note

Table 1. Example of a glitch-counting algorithm's execution

h	X_1	X_2	X_3	s_1	s_2	s_3
0	10	01	0	0	0	0
1	10	01	0	010	01	0
2	10	01	0	010	01	0101
3	10	01	0	010	01	0101

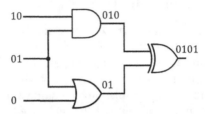

Fig. 3. Example of a glitch-counting algorithm's execution

that the final logic situation can be retrieved from Table 1 by computing $\omega(s_1)$, $\omega(s_2)$ and $\omega(s_3)$ which are the correct (*i.e.* stable) Boolean outputs for inputs $\omega(X_1)$, $\omega(X_2)$ and $\omega(X_3)$.

We conclude the present section with a theorem stating the asymptotic running-time of the glitch-counting algorithm. The proof is extensively discussed by Brzozowski and Ésik [5] and is then omitted here.

Theorem 2 (Section 8 of [5]). *Given a feedback-free circuit and a transition of its inputs, the glitch-counting algorithm always terminates. Moreover, it runs in $O(m + k^2)$ time where m is the number of inputs and k the number of gates.*

4   LP Model

The glitch-counting algorithm was developed in the first place to prevent unnecessary power consumption by discarding netlists being particularly exposed to glitches propagation [5]. Our main contribution is the *LP (Leakage Path) model*, which is a mathematical abstraction that expands the functionalities of the glitch-counting algorithm and relates its simulations to the notion of leakage. Our result leads to a tool that allows to evaluate if a circuit has a critical leakage from the security point of view. The remaining of this section explains the structure of the LP model, which is formed of the following mathematical entities:

input variables are the only part of a circuit that can trigger a signal propagation. If no input variable changes, no signal propagates and no power is consumed, therefore no leakage exists according to our power model;

literal transients are sets of input variables. For each gate reached by a signal's change, a literal transient contains which variables have caused the change and could then be leaked;

literifiers are the link between transients and leakage. Essentially, they relate the input and output transients of a gate to the appropriate literal transient.

The general idea behind the above three objects is the following. The process begins with a change in the input variables, which generates a signal propagation inside the circuit and affects some gates. The gates are then supposed to produce a new output based on the new inputs and their final result depends on which variables have changed and how. In this framework, literifiers are responsible to retrieve the variables involved and represent them via literal transients.

4.1 Structure of LP Model

We now describe in details each part of the LP model with respect to a single gate. This means that when we talk of input variables, we mean the variables that are directly given as inputs to it. Next subsection will proved a broader view, showing how to apply notions for single gates to a whole circuit. Following the same notation as the input variables of a circuit, we denote such variables by X_j and by $\mathbf{X}_j$ if they are seen as transients; we assume that $f : \mathbb{Z}_2^n \to \mathbb{Z}_2$ is the Boolean function implemented by the gate and we denote by $\hat{f} : T^n \to T$ the corresponding function among transients.

As stated in the introduction of this section, input variables are of great importance for both the glitch-counting algorithm, since nothing could be simulated without a change of theirs, and the LP model. In essence, they are the objects our study targets as we aim at following their propagation along the circuit.

Definition 8. *Given a gate with n inputs, namely $X_1, \ldots, X_n$, we call* literal transient *any subset of $\{1, \ldots, n\}$. The set of literal transients is denoted by $I = \mathcal{P}(\{1, \ldots, n\})$.*

Literal transients are a generalisation of transients: instead of being finite alternated sequences of zeros and ones, they are finite sets of input variables. In a sense, they are the result we are looking for: the analysis of a circuit by means of the LP model consists in assigning a literal transient to each gate. Their utility stems from the fact that they list which input variables are responsible for the power consumption and could then be leaked according to our power model. This is strictly connected with the rationale behind transients. In both cases we assume the worst possible scenario: transients are supposed to switch as if the worst possible combination of glitches occurred in the same way as literal transients list all variables being leaked in the worst possible case. It is clear from the above discussion that the core of the LP model is the way we assign literal transients to gates.

Literifiers are functions establishing which input variables are leaked by a gate, *i.e.* the ones having caused a change in its output. They depend on how the gate's inputs change, *i.e.* which transients enter in it, and on the implemented logic.

First of all, we represent the input of a gate as the following vector of couples:

$$((t_1, l_1), \ldots, (t_n, l_n)) \in (T \times I)^n.$$

We call it *transient-variable representation*: the first component of each couple is a transient modelling how that input signal changes, while the second one is a literal transient listing the input variables responsible for that change.

Example 5. Recalling Figs. 1 and 3, the gate computing $s_1 = 010$ has the following input according to the transient-variable representation.

$$((10, \{1\}), (01, \{2\}))$$

In Example 5 we have assumed that the literal transient of a circuit's input is just the singleton containing its index. As for now, the transient-variable representation is directly possible only for gates at height 1, *i.e.* whose inputs are inputs of the circuit itself. In that case each literal transient is simply the singleton of a variable. In the next subsection we will show a procedure similar to the glitch-counting algorithm to meaningfully apply literifiers also to gates whose inputs have already been processed. Such gates are said to have height grater than 1. Informally speaking, the height of a gate is inductively defined to be 1 if all its inputs are circuit inputs, and to be the maximum height of its inputs plus one otherwise. We intentionally omit any further formalisation to avoid heavy notations. As an example, in the circuit in Fig. 2 the AND and OR gates are at height 1 and the XOR is at height 2.

When building the output of the function $\hat{f}$, Theorem 1 guarantees that the described procedure yields a unique result. This means that, without loss of generality, we can always assume a unique path in $D(\underline{t})$ producing the output of $\hat{f}$ exists. Since a path is nothing more than a collection of edges, we denote it by $P \subseteq E$. Note that considering P as a subset of E results in neglecting the order of the vertices. Although this could be an issue with generic graphs, the particular structure of E makes such a set representation unambiguous.

Definition 9. *Let $f : \mathbb{Z}_2^n \to \mathbb{Z}_2$ be the Boolean function implemented by a gate and let $D(\underline{t})$ be the graph used to compute $\hat{f}$ on input $((t_1, l_1), \ldots, (t_n, l_n)) \in (T \times I)^n$. For every edge $(\underline{v}, \underline{w}) \in E$, we define the* edge-label function $e_{\text{lab}} : E \to I$ *as follows:*

$$e_{\text{lab}}(\underline{v}, \underline{w}) = l_i$$

where i is such that $v_i \preceq_1 w_i$ and $v_j = w_j$ for every $j \neq i$.

Note that e_{lab} is well defined by definition of E. The definition of literifier for a single gate assuming its input is in transient-variable representation follows.

Definition 10. *The* literifier *of a gate implementing a Boolean function $f : \mathbb{Z}_2^n \to \mathbb{Z}_2$ is the function $L_f : (T \times I)^n \to I$ such that:*

$$L_f((t_1, l_1), \ldots, (t_n, l_n)) = \bigcup_{(\underline{v}, \underline{w}) \in P} e_{\text{lab}}(\underline{v}, \underline{w})$$

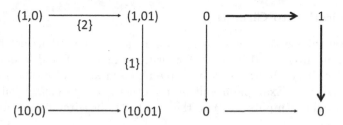

Fig. 4. $D(10, 01)$ and $D_{\text{AND}}(10, 01)$

Recall that each edge of $D(\underline{t})$ represents a change in one component of the vector $\underline{t} = (t_1, \ldots, t_n)$. For instance, let us assume that $e \in P$ links two vertices which differ in the jth component. The edge-label function e_{lab} is firstly used to label e with the literal transient corresponding to the jth component, hence l_j. Once this is done for every edge in the path P, the literifier returns the union of the labels.

Example 6. Following Example 4, let us compute the literifier $L_{\text{AND}}((10, \{1\}),$ $(01, \{2\}))$ associated to the gate computing s_1. Figure 4 depicts a similar situation as in Fig. 1 and the same discussion follows. In addition, we apply the edge-label function e_{lab} to the edges in path P and compute the following literifier.

$$L_{\text{AND}}((10, \{1\}), (01, \{2\})) = \{2\} \cup \{1\} = \{1, 2\}$$

Remark 2. Similarly to Remark 1, the above is just a formal procedure to compute literifiers. Once f is known and fixed, more straightforward approaches are possible. For instance, the following is the literifier associated to a gate implementing the Boolean function $\text{AND} : \mathbb{Z}_2^n \to \mathbb{Z}_2$:

$$L_{\text{AND}}((t_1, l_1), \ldots, (t_n, l_n)) = \begin{cases} \emptyset & \text{if } \exists j \in \{1, \ldots, n\} \text{ such that } t_j = 0 \\ \bigcup_{j \in J} l_j & \text{otherwise} \end{cases}$$

where $J = \{j \in \{1, \ldots, n\} \mid \ell(t_j) > 1\}$. Intuitively, the upper branch states that if there exists one input which is the fixed 0, then the output will be the fixed 0 no matter how other inputs change. Since the output is fixed, no power is consumed and the set of leaked variables is empty. Otherwise, the union of all literal transients corresponding to non-constant transients is returned. Since we are in the second branch there is no constant 0 transient, which results in the rule excluding only literal transients equal to the constant 1, as they do not contribute to the switch activity of an AND gate. We refer to the full version of this paper for a list of other compact definitions of literifiers. As before, we stress that such a simplification has a positive impact on performance.

4.2   Application to Circuits

We conclude this section by showing how to apply the LP model to a given circuit with m inputs and k gates. For instance in Figs. 1 and 3, on one hand it is immediate that the transient-variable representation of gate computing s_1 is the one shown in Example 5, but on the other it is less clear what it should be for gates whose inputs are not the inputs of the circuit, *e.g.* for the one computing s_3.

We recall that we denote by $\underline{X} = (X_1, \ldots, X_m)$ the input variables and by $\underline{s} = (s_1, \ldots, s_k)$ the state variables of a circuit. Moreover we denote by $S_j(\underline{X}, \underline{s})$ the Boolean function s_j is computed by, which can depend on all input and state variables except s_j itself.

The idea is simply proceeding by height: the only gates we can directly compute literifiers for are those at height 1, since the input literal transients are just singletons of input variables. Once all literifiers at height 1 have been computed, we can apply those at height 2: their input literal transients can be either singleton of input variables or outputs of gates at height 1. This procedure always terminates as there are finitely many gates and is well-defined as there are no feedbacks.

Example 7. We conclude what Example 6 has begun by computing all literifiers of Example 4. The only other gate at height 1 is the one computing s_2, for which we have the following.

$$L_{\mathrm{OR}}((01, \{2\}), (0, \{3\})) = \{2\}$$

We now have all the information to compute the literifier for the last gate.

$$L_{\mathrm{XOR}}((010, \{1, 2\}), (01, \{2\})) = \{1, 2\} \cup \{2\} = \{1, 2\}$$

Compact definitions of L_{OR} and L_{XOR}, in the same fashion as in Remark 2, can be found in the full version.

Figure 5 depicts the final outcome of the LP model applied to the circuit in Fig. 2 during transition $100 \rightarrow 010$. Essentially, the LP model adds one literal

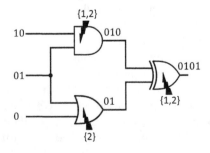

Fig. 5. Application of literifiers to a circuit

transient per gate to the output of the glitch-counting algorithm. They describe which input variables cause a particular gate to switch and whose values could then be leaked through the power consumption. Collecting such an information for all transitions gives the designer a powerful tool to predict possible flaws. In the next section we deepen this discussion while providing a real-world use case.

Final Remarks. In the present subsection, we have shown how to practically apply the LP model to the netlist of a circuit. Although the example we have considered was trivial, the LP model is a formal tool to analyse netlists with an arbitrary number of inputs and gates, where an ad hoc analysis would require much more effort. Once a netlist and an input transition are fixed, the LP model provides a list of variables based on which a risk assessment in the context of side-channel analysis is facilitate. As the next section will suggest, a full analysis would require the LP model to run over every non-trivial input transition, hence $2^{2m} - 2^m$ times where m is the number of inputs and where we have subtracted transitions from an input to itself as they clearly do not produce any consumption in our power model. Such exponential requirement is a drawback of our approach: a deeper insight will be given in Sect. 6. Also, it is possible to reduce the number of transitions over which the LP model needs to be run by developing heuristics specifically designed for a circuit. Finally, for a fixed transition the overall complexity is asymptotically bounded by the running time of the glitch-counting algorithm, described in Theorem 2.

5   Case of Study: Keccak

The present section provides an application of the LP model to KECCAK. We show how to face the following issue thanks to our tool: an unprotected implementation of KECCAK's non-linear layer is obviously susceptible to side-channel attacks, but a possible 2-shares scheme is still weak in the first order because of glitches. We formally show the validity of the latter statement while suggesting a deeper insight on how to circumvent the issue without adopting more costly countermeasures. The reason why we chose to adopt KECCAK as our case of study mainly relies on it being deployed in real-world applications while still having a not too complex structure. It is then the ideal candidate for being a test bench.

KECCAK is a family of sponge functions that uses a permutation from a set of seven possible ones as a building block [2]. The permutations are defined over a state $s \in \mathbb{Z}_2^b$ where $b = 25 \times 2^\ell$ is called *width* of the permutation and $\ell \in \{0, \ldots, 6\}$. Each round is formed of five maps: three linear maps aiming at diffusion and dispersion, one non-linear map aiming at confusion and one addition with round constants. When it comes to implement sharing schemes, linear maps can be directly applied to each share separately. By contrast, non-linear maps need to handle every share to preserve correctness. Therefore we focus on the only non-linear map of KECCAK, namely $\chi : \mathbb{Z}_2^5 \to \mathbb{Z}_2^5$ acting on groups of five bits of the state called *rows*. For a complete description of KECCAK we invite the reader to refer to the work of Bertoni *et al.* [2].

The map χ can be seen as the parallel application of five identical maps each defined on three consecutive bits (modulo 5) of a row. Formally:

$$\chi_i : r_i \leftarrow r_i \oplus \overline{r}_{i+1} r_{i+2} \tag{1}$$

where $r \in \mathbb{Z}_2^5$ denotes a row of the KECCAK state and the index i is computed modulo 5. For our analysis, it is important to note that the five instances of the map $\chi_i : \mathbb{Z}_2^3 \to \mathbb{Z}_2$ are completely independent, they do not share gates in their computation. As a result, we can focus on a specific χ_i without loss of generality. The sharing scheme we adopt in our analysis is a 2-shares Boolean scheme, *i.e.* each row is split in two shares $a, b \in \mathbb{Z}_2^5$ such that $r = a \oplus b$ [1]. Our results can be easily generalised to many shares. In this setting, (1) can be masked as follows:

$$a_i \leftarrow a_i \oplus \overline{a}_{i+1} a_{i+2} \oplus a_{i+1} b_{i+2}$$
$$b_i \leftarrow b_i \oplus \overline{b}_{i+1} b_{i+2} \oplus b_{i+1} a_{i+2} \tag{2}$$

where a straightforward computation shows that (2) are correct as (1) is simply retrieved by XORing them. If the order of operations was kept fixed from left to right, *e.g.* using software constraints, then the above sharing scheme would be secure in the first order. However if (2) were implemented in hardware, such condition could not be guaranteed, for instance because of glitches. This results in possible vulnerabilities when the values a_{i+2} and b_{i+2} are involved in the computation of the 3-inputs XOR at the same time, in one of the two branches.

As both the glitch-counting algorithm and the LP model work with netlists, the first step in the analysis of (2) is to produce one. It can be easily seen that the two branches are symmetric, hence we can focus only on the first without loss of generality, *i.e.* the one computing a_i. Figure 6 depicts its representation as an hardware netlist, where the naming conventions presented at the beginning of Subsect. 3.2 have been used. In particular, the input vector $X = (X_1, X_2, X_3, X_4)$ corresponds to $(a_i, b_{i+2}, a_{i+1}, a_{i+2})$.

Our analysis targets the netlist in Fig. 6 and proceeds as follows. First of all an input transition is fixed among all the $2^8 - 2^4 = 240$ non-trivial possible ones. Then, the glitch-counting algorithm is applied as shown in Subsect. 3.2 and all the transients are computed, one per gate. Table 2 reports the execution of the glitch-counting algorithm for the input transition $0110 \to 0001$.

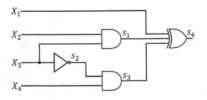

Fig. 6. Netlist of χ_i for one share

Table 2. Glitch-counting algorithm's execution for the shared χ_i circuit

h	X_1	X_2	X_3	X_3	s_1	s_2	s_3	s_4
0	0	10	10	01	1	0	0	1
1	0	10	10	01	10	01	0	1
2	0	10	10	01	10	01	01	10
3	0	10	10	01	10	01	01	101
4	0	10	10	01	10	01	01	101

At this point, suitable literifiers can be applied as described in Subsect. 4.2, hence starting from gates at height 1. In our example, this means computing the literifiers corresponding to s_1 and s_2 first, respectively an AND and NOT literifiers.

$$L_{\text{AND}}((10, \{2\}), (10, \{3\})) = \{2\} \cup \{3\} = \{2, 3\}$$
$$L_{\text{NOT}}(10, \{3\}) = \{3\}$$

There are two gates at height higher than 1: first we compute L_{AND} for the gate computing s_3 and finally L_{XOR} is applied.

$$L_{\text{AND}}((01, \{3\}), (01, \{4\})) = \{3\} \cup \{4\} = \{3, 4\}$$
$$L_{\text{XOR}}((0, \{1\}), (10, \{2, 3\}), (01, \{3, 4\})) = \{2, 3\} \cup \{3, 4\}$$
$$= \{2, 3, 4\}$$

We refer the reader to the full version for the definitions of L_{NOT} and L_{XOR}. Figure 7 summarises the execution of both the glitch-counting algorithm and of the LP model for the transition $0110 \rightarrow 0001$.

To take the most out of the proposed method, a vulnerability definition based on critical combinations of variables needs to be formulated. This is checked among all the literal transients produced by the model, which has been run over all possible non-trivial input transition.

In the specific case of KECCAK, a natural vulnerability of the circuit in Fig. 6 arises when the two variables a_{i+2} and b_{i+2} are processed in the same moment by the last XOR gate, as this could leak the value $a_{i+2} \oplus b_{i+2} = r_{i+2}$ which is unshared. In our model, this translates to the existence of $\{2\}$ and $\{4\}$ in the same literal transient corresponding to the XOR gate, since X_2 and X_4 are the input variables corresponding to a_{i+2} and b_{i+2}. By running the model for all the $2^8 - 2^4$ non-trivial possible input transitions, we have found that 32 out of 240 match our vulnerability definition and could then lead to a critical first order leakage. At this point, the designer possesses valuable information to base security improvements on. In particular, leaving our gate-level abstraction, the designer can carefully tune place-and-route paths in order to minimise the occurrence and impact of those critical transitions. If such an operation is not feasible, the designer still has a valid and sound criterion why to switch to an higher number of shares (3 in the case of KECCAK, since χ has degree 2). It is

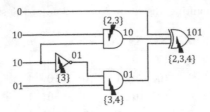

Fig. 7. Shared χ_i circuit after LP model

important to note that further analyses, possibly by means of different and finer vulnerability definitions, can be carried out without rerunning the whole model.

The sharing scheme we have analysed [1] has not gained much popularity due to its weakness in the presence of glitches. However, our analysis is able to capture more details: we can quantify and list all those transitions threatening the security of unshared values. In this case a designer could just patch them while being sure that all the others will never show a critical leakage of the first order even in the presence of glitches. Since our aim was just to exemplify the potentiality of our model, we consider the latter modification as being out of scope for the present work, but an interesting future direction towards sound and lightweight countermeasures.

6   Computational Effort and Multi-output Circuits

As we briefly mentioned while justifying the choice of KECCAK, its combinatorial circuits are relatively simple and allow to verify the correctness of the proposed method easily. Since our aim is not to find a specific method for KECCAK but a rather generic methodology, there are two further topics that need to be addressed: the computational complexity for a generic circuit and the applicability of the method to multi-output combinatorial circuits.

The former topic has been partially addressed in Subsect. 3.2 for the glitch-counting algorithm (Theorem 2) and in Subsect. 4.2 for the LP model. If we refer to KECCAK as a practical example and we think at an implementation performing one round in one clock cycle, the target combinatorial circuit is the concatenation of θ, one of the linear maps, and χ [2]. This combinatorial circuit can be seen as a circuit with 33 input bits and 1 output bit in the unprotected version, while the protected version using two shares is a 44-inputs circuit [1]. As described in Subsect. 4.2 this would turn in computing the propagation of glitches through k gates for each of the $2^{2m} - 2^m$ non-trivial input transitions. Considering that the computation can be parallelised and the evaluation of the glitch-counting algorithm is not a very complex computation, we claim that the method could be applicable for a circuit with 44 inputs but would require a well optimized implementation.

Multi-output circuits are also a very interesting target. In such circuits there are gates contributing to the computation of different output bits. One approach for tackling these circuits is to divide the circuit in n independent circuits with single output, where n is the number of outputs of the initial combinatorial logic, and apply the proposed method to each of them separately. Such approach could however introduce an overhead as a single input might be used by more than one sub-circuits. A further, more advanced solution for approaching multi-output circuits and the computational effort when the number of inputs is large would be the development of heuristic approaches as adopted by silicon compilers. We see this as a future development. Finally note that there is nothing preventing the model to be applied to multi-output circuits as it is, but it would be required to develop meaningful vulnerability definitions based also on the cryptographic algorithm. A similar discussion applies to high-order analysis. The LP model can still be used but more sophisticated vulnerability definitions are needed to interpret its results.

7   Conclusions

In their work, Brzozowski and Ésik [5] have developed a mathematical structure to estimate the potential waste of power of a circuit due to glitches. Our first contribution is the expansion of such framework to include a formal definition of leakage. We have then defined a formal procedure to analyse circuits in the context of side-channel analysis which take into account the effect of glitches on the order of operations. Our work analyses only the combinatorial logic, hence achieves a good level of generality since it is not touched by real-world constraints. As a consequence, the LP model allows to retrieve how much a given protection scheme can be affected by glitches, thus enabling a deep analysis. Using the proposed methodology, a designer might explore alternative designs for solving local problems of glitches instead of adopting more costly solutions.

 Acknowledgements. The research leading to these results has received funding from the European Union's Horizon 2020 research and innovation programme under grant agreement No 644052 (HECTOR).

Furthermore, Marco Martinoli has been supported in part by the Marie Skłodowska-Curie ITN ECRYPT-NET (Project Reference 643161). Finally, we thank Maria Chiara Molteni for corrections and useful comments.

References

1. Bertoni, G., Daemen, J., Peeters, M., Assche, G.V.: Building power analysis resistant implementations of Keccak. In: Second SHA-3 Candidate Conference (2010)
2. Bertoni, G., Daemen, J., Peeters, M., Assche, G.: Keccak. In: Johansson, T., Nguyen, P.Q. (eds.) EUROCRYPT 2013. LNCS, vol. 7881, pp. 313–314. Springer, Heidelberg (2013). doi:10.1007/978-3-642-38348-9_19
3. Bilgin, B., Gierlichs, B., Nikova, S., Nikov, V., Rijmen, V.: Higher-order threshold implementations. In: Sarkar, P., Iwata, T. (eds.) ASIACRYPT 2014. LNCS, vol. 8874, pp. 326–343. Springer, Heidelberg (2014). doi:10.1007/978-3-662-45608-8_18

4. Bilgin, B., Gierlichs, B., Nikova, S., Nikov, V., Rijmen, V.: A more efficient AES threshold implementation. In: Pointcheval, D., Vergnaud, D. (eds.) AFRICACRYPT 2014. LNCS, vol. 8469, pp. 267–284. Springer, Heidelberg (2014). doi:10.1007/978-3-319-06734-6_17

5. Brzozowski, J., Ésik, Z.: Hazard algebras. Formal Methods Syst. Des. **23**(3), 223–256 (2003)

6. Kocher, P., Jaffe, J., Jun, B.: Differential power analysis. In: Wiener, M. (ed.) CRYPTO 1999. LNCS, vol. 1666, pp. 388–397. Springer, Heidelberg (1999). doi:10.1007/3-540-48405-1_25

7. Kocher, P.C., Jaffe, J., Jun, B., Rohatgi, P.: Introduction to differential power analysis. J. Cryptographic Eng. **1**(1), 5–27 (2011)

8. Mangard, S., Oswald, E., Popp, T.: Power Analysis Attacks: Revealing the Secrets of Smart Cards, vol. 31. Springer, Heidelberg (2008)

9. Mangard, S., Popp, T., Gammel, B.M.: Side-channel leakage of masked CMOS gates. In: Menezes, A. (ed.) CT-RSA 2005. LNCS, vol. 3376, pp. 351–365. Springer, Heidelberg (2005). doi:10.1007/978-3-540-30574-3_24

10. Mangard, S., Pramstaller, N., Oswald, E.: Successfully attacking masked AES hardware implementations. In: Rao, J.R., Sunar, B. (eds.) CHES 2005. LNCS, vol. 3659, pp. 157–171. Springer, Heidelberg (2005). doi:10.1007/11545262_12

11. Mangard, S., Schramm, K.: Pinpointing the side-channel leakage of masked AES hardware implementations. In: Goubin, L., Matsui, M. (eds.) CHES 2006. LNCS, vol. 4249, pp. 76–90. Springer, Heidelberg (2006). doi:10.1007/11894063_7

12. Moradi, A., Poschmann, A., Ling, S., Paar, C., Wang, H.: Pushing the limits: a very compact and a threshold implementation of AES. In: Paterson, K.G. (ed.) EUROCRYPT 2011. LNCS, vol. 6632, pp. 69–88. Springer, Heidelberg (2011). doi:10.1007/978-3-642-20465-4_6

13. Nikova, S., Rechberger, C., Rijmen, V.: Threshold implementations against side-channel attacks and glitches. In: Ning, P., Qing, S., Li, N. (eds.) ICICS 2006. LNCS, vol. 4307, pp. 529–545. Springer, Heidelberg (2006). doi:10.1007/11935308_38

14. Nikova, S., Rijmen, V., Schläffer, M.: Secure hardware implementation of nonlinear functions in the presence of glitches. In: Lee, P.J., Cheon, J.H. (eds.) ICISC 2008. LNCS, vol. 5461, pp. 218–234. Springer, Heidelberg (2009). doi:10.1007/978-3-642-00730-9_14

15. Prouff, E., Roche, T.: Higher-order glitches free implementation of the AES using secure multi-party computation protocols. In: Preneel, B., Takagi, T. (eds.) CHES 2011. LNCS, vol. 6917, pp. 63–78. Springer, Heidelberg (2011). doi:10.1007/978-3-642-23951-9_5

16. Rabaey, J.M., Chandrakasan, A.P., Nikolic, B.: Digital Integrated Circuits, vol. 2. Prentice Hall, Englewood Cliffs (2002)

17. Reparaz, O., Bilgin, B., Nikova, S., Gierlichs, B., Verbauwhede, I.: Consolidating masking schemes. In: Gennaro, R., Robshaw, M. (eds.) CRYPTO 2015. LNCS, vol. 9215, pp. 764–783. Springer, Heidelberg (2015). doi:10.1007/978-3-662-47989-6_37

Exploiting the Leakage: Analysis of Some Authenticated Encryption Schemes

Donghoon Chang, Amit Kumar Chauhan, Naina Gupta, Arpan Jati[✉],
and Somitra Kumar Sanadhya

Indraprashtha Institute of Information Technology, (IIIT-Delhi), Delhi, India
{donghoon,amitc,nainag,arpanj,somitra}@iiitd.ac.in

Abstract. The ongoing CAESAR competition, aimed at finding robust and secure authenticated encryption schemes provides many new submissions for analysis. We analyzed many schemes and came across a plenitude of techniques, design ideals and security notions. In view of the above, we present key recovery attacks using DPA for Deoxys, Joltik and ELmD, and a forgery attack on AEGIS. In our analysis of the various schemes, we found out that, schemes using Sponge constructions with pre-initialized keys such as Ascon, ICEPOLE, Keyak, NORX, PRIMATEs, etc. were significantly harder to attack than contemporary designs using standard building blocks from a side channel perspective. We also implement and demonstrate an attack on Joltik-BC, to recover the key in roughly 50–60 traces.

Keywords: AEGIS · Deoxys · Joltik · ELmD · Side-channel · DPA · CPA

1 Introduction

An authenticated encryption (AE) scheme aims to provide two separate security goals: confidentiality (privacy) and integrity (authenticity) of data. Historically, these goals were achieved by generic compositions of two different cryptographic primitives, a secure encryption scheme (e.g., block cipher) to ensure confidentiality and a secure message authentication scheme to guarantee authenticity. The seminal work by Bellare and Namprempre [8] introduced the notion of AE around 2000. Since then, a significant amount of work has been done towards the development of the notion, evolving new ideas and constructing new AE schemes. Over the years, many significant results [23,26,27,38] demonstrated that AE schemes can be constructed more efficiently than combinations of blockciphers or hash functions. As a result, many schemes have been devised such as CCM [21], GCM [34], EAX [9], CWC [30] and OCB [39]. Despite the variety of available designs, practice demands more desirable features – fast performance in hardware and software, robustness against nonce-misuse, leakage of invalid plaintexts, various kind of attacks, etc.

In 2013, Bernstein announced the CAESAR competition [1] (Competition for Authenticated Encryption: Security, Applicability, and Robustness) to fill the

© Springer International Publishing AG 2016
C. Carlet et al. (Eds.): SPACE 2016, LNCS 10076, pp. 383–401, 2016.
DOI: 10.1007/978-3-319-49445-6_22

needs of secure, efficient and robust AE schemes. In response, 57 candidates were submitted to the competition. Currently, around 29 candidates in the second round are being analyzed in terms of their security and efficiency. There is a wide variety in the design approaches of the various schemes, from parallel and high throughput modes for big-data applications to ciphers suited to the very smallest and highly resource constrained devices, with a wide range of trade-offs in robustness and security against attacks.

Leakage-resistance against side-channel attack is an important concern in the design of AE schemes. There are several types of side channel leakage modes like execution time [18, 28], electromagnetic radiation [2, 22, 37], power consumption [29], physical probing [4, 31] etc. Power analysis is one of the most common form of side channel analysis, as it is very powerful and moderately straightforward to implement once the proper leakage points in a cipher design is decided upon.

There are several ways to analyze power consumption traces and to find the relationship between a power trace and data; such as simple power analysis (SPA), differential power analysis (DPA) and correlation power analysis (CPA). SPA attacks require a single power trace to determine the secret key. SPA exploits the relationship between the execution operations and the power leakage, whereas DPA attacks require a large number of power traces, and exploits the relationship between the processed data and the power leakage. The first practical implementation of a power analysis attack on the DES was described by Kocher et al. [29] and formalized by Messerges et al. [35]. In various papers [13, 15, 33], correlation power analysis (CPA) attack is proposed to use the correlation factor between the power traces and the Hamming weight of processed data.

In this work, we analyzed several CAESAR schemes for resistance against side channel attacks. Although it was not a specific requirement for CAESAR, some schemes were designed with side channel attacks in mind and were clearly difficult to attack. Most of the sponge-based designs like Ascon [20], ICEPOLE [36], Keyak [10], NORX [6], PRIMATEs [5], etc., having initial key-mixing tend to be significantly difficult to attack as they provide minimum control to the attacker to recover the key. Such designs with large rate and capacity cannot be attacked without using specialized attacks like *fault* [11, 12] and *template* [14] *attacks*. In [19], Dobraunig et al. presented fault attacks on authenticated encryption schemes such as GCM, CCM, OCB and the CAESAR second round candidates, e.g., Joltik, Deoxys and ELmD. These attacks work since these schemes use either AES [16] as underlying cipher or have AES-like structure; and the attacker is able to influence some byte of the internal state of AES. In [7], Bay et al. shows the universal forgery attack and key recovery attack on ELmD by computing the internal state using collision search of ciphertexts. Besides these, the unprotected implementations of block-cipher based designs are succeptible to attacks.

This work demonstrates in detail the applicability of power analysis attacks against second round AE candidates AEGIS [40], Joltik-BC [25], Deoxys-BC [24] and ELmD [17] of the ongoing CAESAR competition. The attacks in this paper focuses mainly on the software implementations of the schemes on 8-bit microcontrollers.

1.1   Organization

This paper is organized as follows: Sect. 2 discusses the preliminaries for notations and correlation factor. Section 3 describes AEGIS, and discusses state recovery and forgery attacks on it. Section 4 describes Joltik-BC and Deoxys-BC followed by description of a full key recovery attack by performing DPA on a microcontroller. Section 5 describes ELmD and a key recovery attack by computing secret state value using DPA attack. Section 6 shows the experimental results. Section 7 concludes our work and discusses the possible future works.

2   Preliminaries

2.1   Notation

We use the following notations.

$x \in \{0,1\}^n$	Bitstring x of length n
0^n	Bitstring of n bits, all 0
$\|x\|$	Length of the bitstring x in bits
$x \oplus y$	Bitwise logical exclusive-OR of bitstrings x and y
$x\|\|y$	Concatenation of bitstrings x and y
$x \ll 1$	1-bit logical shift of bitstring x
$GF(2^n)$	Galois Field with 2^n points
K, N, T	Secret key K, nonce N, tag T
AD	Associated data
M, C	Message M, ciphertext C (in blocks M_i, C_i)
SB / SR / MC	Sub-byte / Shift-row / Mix-column

2.2   Authenticated Encryption

An authenticated encryption scheme is a three-tuple algorithm $\prod = (\mathcal{K}, \mathcal{E}, \mathcal{D})$. Associated to $\prod$ are the sets $\mathcal{N} \in \{0,1\}^n$ and $\mathcal{M} \in \{0,1\}^*$. The key space $\mathcal{K}$ is a finite non-empty set of strings. Algorithm $\mathcal{E}$ is a deterministic algorithm that takes strings $K \in \mathcal{K}$ and $N \in \mathcal{N}$ and $M \in \mathcal{M}$ and returns a string C as $C = \mathcal{E}(K, N, M)$. Algorithm $\mathcal{D}$ is a deterministic algorithm that takes strings $K \in \mathcal{K}$, nonce $N \in \mathcal{N}$ and a ciphertext $C \in \{0,1\}^*$ and returns $\mathcal{D}(K, N, C)$, which is either a string in $\mathcal{M}$ or the error symbol $\bot$. We require that $\mathcal{D}(K, N, \mathcal{E}(K, N, M)) = M$ for all $K \in \mathcal{K}$, $N \in \mathcal{N}$, and $M \in \mathcal{M}$.

2.3 Correlation Power Analysis

We follow [13,29] for performing differential power analysis (CPA/DPA) on AE schemes in the Hamming weight model [3]. Since the correlation coefficient is the most common way to determine the linear relationships between the data, CPA focuses on the correlation factor between the power traces and Hamming weight of the processed data. Suppose we have a known data vector $d = (d_1, \ldots, d_D)$ of D different data blocks and where d_i denotes the data value used in the ith encryption run. During these run, let $t_i = (t_{i,1}, \ldots, t_{i,T})$ be the power trace correspond to data block d_i, and T denotes the length of the trace. Let $h_i = (h_1, \ldots, h_K)$ be the hypothetical power trace correspond to data block d_i, and K denotes the total number of possible choices for k (a small part of the key), then the correlation coefficient between h_i and t_j for $i = 1, \ldots, K$ and $j = 1, \ldots, T$, as defined in [32] is given by:

$$r_{i,j} = \frac{\sum_{d=1}^{D}(h_{d,i} - \overline{h}_i).(t_{d,j} - \overline{t}_j)}{\sqrt{\sum_{d=1}^{D}(h_{d,i} - \overline{h}_i)^2 . \sum_{d=1}^{D}(t_{d,j} - \overline{t}_j)^2}}$$

where $\overline{h}_i$ and $\overline{t}_j$ denote the mean of the column vectors h_i and t_j respectively.

CPA is a very powerful technique and has been used successfully to attack a large number of implementations, including real protected devices.

3   AEGIS

AEGIS [40] is a dedicated authenticated encryption scheme introduced by Hongjun Wu and Bart Preneel. It is fast and secure even when the nonce is reused.

3.1 State Update Function

The AEGIS state update function, as in Fig. 1, uses the AES round function to update an 80-byte state S_i $(S_{i,0}, S_{i,1}, \ldots, S_{i,4})$ with a 16-byte block m_i. The 80-byte state S_i is processed in 16-byte blocks. Five instances of an unkeyed AES round function is applied to each of the $S_{i,j}$ blocks, and the result is then chained to the next block using XOR operation to update it. Mathematically, $S_{i+1} = \texttt{StateUpdate128}(S_i, m_i)$ is described as:

$$S_{i+1,0} = \texttt{AESRound}(S_{i,4}, S_{i,0} \oplus m_i);$$
$$S_{i+1,1} = \texttt{AESRound}(S_{i,0}, S_{i,1});$$
$$S_{i+1,2} = \texttt{AESRound}(S_{i,1}, S_{i,2});$$
$$S_{i+1,3} = \texttt{AESRound}(S_{i,2}, S_{i,3});$$
$$S_{i+1,4} = \texttt{AESRound}(S_{i,3}, S_{i,4});$$

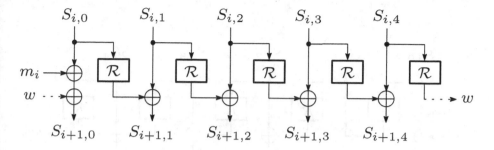

Fig. 1. AEGIS: state update function

3.2 Initialization Phase

In this phase, the key and IV is loaded to the state, used as message. Then StateUpdate128 is performed ten times to obtain the final state. This updated state is then used for encryption. One should note that the key is not used in the scheme after this phase.

1. The 80-byte state is initialized with key and IV as follows:

$$S_{-10,0} = K_{128} \oplus IV_{128};$$
$$S_{-10,1} = const_1;$$
$$S_{-10,2} = const_0;$$
$$S_{-10,3} = K_{128} \oplus const_0;$$
$$S_{-10,4} = K_{128} \oplus const_1;$$

2. In this step, a message array m_i is initialized with the key and IV values.
   for $i = -5$ to -1, $m_{2i} = K_{128}$; $m_{2i+1} = K_{128} \oplus IV_{128}$;

3. Here, the initial state S_{-10} is updated 10 times using StateUpdate128.
   for $i = -10$ to -1, $S_{i+1} = $ StateUpdate128(S_i, m_i);

3.3 Encryption

The plaintext message is processed in blocks of 16-bytes $P_0, P_1, \ldots, P_n$, $n = \lceil \frac{msglen}{128} \rceil$. The StateUpdate128 is called n times to update the state with P_i. Each ciphertext block C_i is obtained from the corresponding plaintext block P_i. If the last plaintext block P_n is not a full block, then zero padding is used to make it a 16-byte block, and the state is subsequently updated.
   for $i = 0$ to $n - 1$, the following steps are performed:

$$C_i = P_i \oplus S_{i,1} \oplus S_{i,4} \oplus (S_{i,2} \& S_i, 3);$$
$$S_{i+1} = \text{StateUpdate128}(S_i, P_i);$$

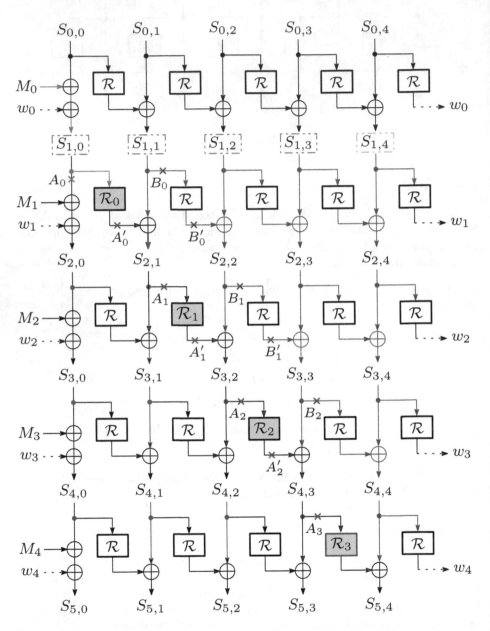

Fig. 2. State update function for AEGIS-128. The inputs $S_{0,0}$, $S_{0,1} \ldots S_{0,4}$ is the state after the initialization and processing of authenticated data. M_i (M_0, $M_1, \ldots$) are input messages.

3.4   State Recovery and Forgery Attacks on AEGIS-128

The following section describes a side-channel state recovery attack on AEGIS-128. Once the complete state is recovered, we can perform a message forgery attack. Figure 2 shows five state update operations in AEGIS-128 after the initialization and processing of authenticated data. For this attack we consider the KPA (Known-plaintext attack) model. More specifically, we assume that the input messages (M_i, where M_0, M_1,.. are the individual 16 byte blocks in which the messages are processed.) are random but known. We also define M_n^i to be the ith byte of nth message input block.

For side channel attack, we consider the Hamming Weight (HW) model of leakage. We also assume that power traces for the execution of the entire period of the above mentioned five rounds are available.

As per the attack model, (M_i) is known and hence the attacker can capture multiple side-channel traces while the cipher is operating with different values of the same. In this attack, we consider the varying values of M_0 as an input perturbant, all the other input values are ignored for the purpose of analysis. Let us consider the following equations:

$$V = S_{0,0} \oplus w_0$$
$$A_0 = V \oplus M_0$$

The value A is an input to the round function $\mathcal{R}$ which is in essence an unkeyed round of AES-128. The bytes of A_0 ($A_0^0, A_0^1,.. A_0^{15}$) can be obtained by using DPA/CPA. The leakage model can be described as:

$$\text{Leakage} = \text{HW}(A) = \text{HW}(V \oplus M_0)$$
$$\text{so, Leakage}^i = \text{HW}(V^i \oplus M_0^i), \text{ for the respective } i^{th} \text{ byte}$$

Using the above leakage model, we can recover the correct value of V and hence A_0. As $A_0' = \mathcal{R}_0(A_0)$, A_0' can be readily calculated. Going one operation further, we get the following equation:

$$A_1 = A_0' \oplus B_0$$

Now, as we know A_0' for all the values of M_0, we can perform DPA/CPA again to obtain B_0, and hence B_0' and A_1. One should note that no further traces are needed; the same old traces from the previous step can be re-used, considering that they are of the required length encompassing all the required operations. Just like the previous step the value of A_1' can be readily calculated. The same attack steps can be repeated further twice to obtain A_2, A_2' and A_3. Meanwhile, in the process, the values of B_1, B_1' and B_2 are also obtained. From these obtained intermediate values the state can be calculated as follows:

$$S_{1,0} = A_0 \qquad\qquad\qquad S_{1,1} = B_0$$
$$S_{1,2} = B_0' \oplus B_1 \qquad\qquad S_{1,3} = \mathcal{R}(S_{1,2}) \oplus B_1' \oplus B_2$$

From the description of AEGIS-128 we have:

$$C_i = P_i \oplus S_{u+i,1} \oplus S_{u+i,4} \oplus (S_{u+i,2} \& S_{u+i,3})$$
$$S_{u+i,4} = C_i \oplus P_i \oplus S_{u+i,1} \oplus (S_{u+i,2} \& S_{u+i,3})$$

where, u is the number of associated data blocks, and i is the chosen position in the cipher operation for the attack.

This way, all the blocks of the state can be recovered. The value of i, or the attack point is flexible, as the design is symmetric. Once, all the blocks of the state are recovered, one can launch a trivial forgery attack.

3.5 Forgery Attack on **AEGIS-128** using a Recovered State

Once the state is recovered using side-channel attacks, mounting a forgery attack is simple because, the key is only used in the beginning and the knowledge of the state is enough to generate the tag. Once the attacker knows the state he is able to perform all the steps after the known state including adding more plaintext and generating a valid tag. As the length of the message is not encoded in the header or any other key dependent state, it is easy to extend to message length henceforth and still have a valid message.

4   Joltik-BC

Joltik-BC [25] is an ad-hoc tweakable block cipher designed by Jérémy Jean, Ivica Nikolic, and Thomas Peyrin. Joltik-BC takes a message M, a key K, and a tweak value T as inputs. The cipher has a 64-bit state and a variable sized key and tweak. The structure of Joltik-BC is an AES like iterative substitution-permutation network (SPN) which transforms a plaintext to a ciphertext through a series of round functions. Joltik-BC-128 has 24 rounds whereas Joltik-BC-192 has 32 rounds and one round has the following four transformations specified below:

- AddRoundTweakey : XOR the 64-bit round subtweakey to the internal state.
- SubNibbles : Apply the 4-bit S-box S to the 16 nibbles of the internal state.
- ShiftRows : Rotate the 4-nibble i-th row left by $\rho[i]$ positions, where $\rho = (0, 1, 2, 3)$.
- MixNibbles : Multiply the internal state by the 4×4 constant MDS matrix $\mathbb{M}$ defined below whose coefficients lies on the field GF(16) defined by the irreducible polynomial $x^4 + x + 1$.

$$\mathbb{M} = \begin{pmatrix} 1 & 4 & 9 & 13 \\ 4 & 1 & 13 & 9 \\ 9 & 13 & 1 & 4 \\ 13 & 9 & 4 & 1 \end{pmatrix}$$

After the last round, a final AddRoundTweakey operation is performed to generate the ciphertext.

The 4-bit S-box S used in Joltik-BC is defined as:

$$\begin{pmatrix} 0 & 1 & 2 & 3 & 4 & 5 & 6 & 7 & 8 & 9 & 10 & 11 & 12 & 13 & 14 & 15 \\ 14 & 4 & 11 & 2 & 3 & 8 & 0 & 9 & 1 & 10 & 7 & 15 & 6 & 12 & 5 & 13 \end{pmatrix}$$

4.1 Message Authentication and Tag Generation Phase

For simplification, we present a shorter description of the Joltik-BC cipher that is only generating tag on a single block of the message M. As shown in Fig. 3, we consider the associated data of zero length. Initially, the nonce is encrypted with the *tweak* values $0011||0^{t-4}$ and $0111||0^{t-4}$ (where t denotes the *tweak* size) in two independent calls of encryption respectively. Then Auth is generated as shown in the Fig. 3. Secondly, the message block M_1 is encrypted with tweak value 0 and the output is xored with Auth and this resulted value is again encrypted with a *tweak* value $0001||0^{t-4}$ to generate the tag. Thereafter, this tag is further used as a *tweak* value to generate the ciphertext. (For more details, we refer to [25]).

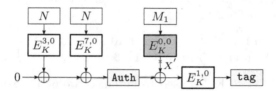

Fig. 3. Message processing in the authentication part.

To mount the side-channel attack, we do not need to generate the tag. Before even producing value X' (as shown in Fig. 3), we are able to attack on the cipher which will be described in the next Sect. 4.3.

4.2 TWEAKEY Framework Instantiation

A single-block of message in Joltik-BC is processed by applying the round function r times, depending on the variant. For each round, the subtweakey STK_i is updated and added to the state at round i to update the state for the next round. The subtweakey STK_i for Joltik-BC-128 is defined as:

$$STK_i = TK_i^1 \oplus TK_i^2 \oplus RC_i$$

whereas for Joltik-BC-192 it is defined as:

$$STK_i = TK_i^1 \oplus TK_i^2 \oplus TK_i^3 \oplus RC_i$$

where, the 64-bit words TK_i^1, TK_i^2, TK_i^3 are outputs of key scheduling algorithm.

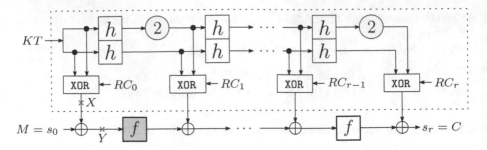

Fig. 4. Instantiating TWEAKEY framework with $s_0 = M_1$ and the tweak $T = 0$ for the first plaintext block when the tag is calculated.

The key schedule algorithm $KS(W, \alpha)$ of Joltik-BC takes a 64-bit word W and α as input parameters and apply the following transformations on it to generate the subkeys $TK_0, TK_1, \ldots$. Initial subkey TK_0 is given by $TK_0 = W$.

$$TK_{i+1} = g(h(TK_i))$$

where g is a finite field multiplication in $\mathbb{K}$ of each nibble by α and h is the nibble permutation defined as:

$$\begin{pmatrix} 0\ 1\ 2\ \ 3\ 4\ 5\ \ 6\ 7\ 8\ 9\ \ 10\ 11\ 12\ 13\ 14\ 15 \\ 1\ 6\ 11\ 12\ 5\ 10\ 15\ 0\ 9\ 14\ \ 3\ \ \ 4\ \ 13\ \ 2\ \ \ 7\ \ \ 8 \end{pmatrix}$$

In case of Joltik-BC-128, KT is used to initialize two 64-bit words W_1 and W_2 with W_1 being the most significant 64 bits of KT and W_2 being the rest. TK_i^1 is then generated as $KS(W_1, 1)$ and TK_i^2 is generated as $KS(W_2, 2)$. Whereas, in case of Joltik-BC-192, the size of KT is 192 bits, so three 64-bits W_1, W_2 and W_3 are generated from it. The subkeys TK_i^1, TK_i^2 and TK_i^3 are then the output words of $KS(W_1, 1)$, $KS(W_2, 2)$ and $KS(W_3, 4)$ respectively.

RC_0, RC_1, $\ldots$, RC_r are known round constants as described in [25].

4.3 Key Recovery Attack on Joltik-BC

Since Joltik-BC supports various key and tweak sizes, in this work we show a strategy to perform DPA on two variants of Joltik-BC.

4.3.1 Key and Tweak are of the same size

$|K| = |T|$. For this attack, we target the value of 'Y' as in Fig. 4. Here, we have exploited two properties of the cipher:

1. In the 'Message Authentication and Tag Generation Phase', the tweak for the first message block is predefined; currently it is all 0 bits. This essentially implies that value of X in Fig. 4 after XOR operation is $K \oplus RC_0$.
2. The f function is similar to a round in AES without AddRoundTweakey; thus can be exploited.

If we now consider the interaction of the key K with the plaintext, we get the following equations:

$$X = K \oplus T \oplus RC_0$$
$$= K \oplus RC_0$$
$$Y = X \oplus s_0, \text{ where } X = K \oplus RC_0 \text{ and } s_0 = M_1$$

Let s_0^0, s_0^1, $\ldots$, s_0^{15} denotes the nibbles of plaintext and Y^0, Y^1, $\ldots$, Y^{15} be the nibbles of 'Y'(obtained above).

The leakage model is then defined as follows:

$$\mathsf{Leakage}_n = \mathsf{HW}(\mathcal{S}[Y^n])$$

where n = 0, 1, $\ldots$, 15 for each nibble and $\mathcal{S}$ denotes SubNibbles S-box
Thus, this leakage will give us the value of 'X' i.e. we get $K \oplus RC_0$. Since, RC_0 is a known-constant, we can simply XOR it with 'X' to get the key K.

4.3.2 Key and Tweak are different in size

$|K| \neq |T|$. In this variant, first we use the above described strategy to obtain 'X', then with few more operations and choosing the attack target point to be 'V'as in Fig. 5, we are able to recover the full key K.

Interaction of the key K can be expressed by the following equations:

$$X = K_1 \oplus K_0 \oplus T \oplus RC_0$$
$$= K_1 \oplus K_0 \oplus RC_0$$
$$Y = X \oplus s_0, \text{ where } X = K_1 \oplus K_0 \oplus RC_0 \text{ and } s_0 = M_1$$
$$Z = f(Y)$$
$$U = 4 \cdot h(T) \oplus 2 \cdot h(K_1) \oplus h(K_0) \oplus RC_1$$
$$= 2 \cdot h(K_1) \oplus h(K_0) \oplus RC_1, \text{ as tweak } T \text{ has all 0 bits}$$
$$= K_1' \oplus K_0' \oplus RC_1, \text{ where } K_1' = 2 \cdot h(K_1) \text{ and } K_0' = h(K_0)$$
$$V = Z \oplus U$$

Let s_0^0, s_0^1, $\ldots$, s_0^{15} denotes the nibbles of plaintext, Y^0, Y^1, $\ldots$, Y^{15} be the nibbles of 'Y'and V^0, V^1, $\ldots$, V^{15} be the nibbles of 'V'(obtained above).

The leakage model is then defined as follows:

$$\mathsf{Leakage}_n^0 = \mathsf{HW}(\mathcal{S}[Y^n])$$
$$\mathsf{Leakage}_n^1 = \mathsf{HW}(\mathcal{S}[V^n])$$

where n = 0, 1, $\ldots$, 15 for each nibble and $\mathcal{S}$ denotes the SubNibbles S-box.

The leakage model $\mathsf{Leakage}_n^0$ gives the value for 'X', and similarly the leakage model $\mathsf{Leakage}_n^1$ gives 'U'. The key then can be estimated by using the following equations:

$$X = K_1 \oplus K_0 \oplus RC_0$$
$$\text{So, } X \oplus RC_0 = K_1 \oplus K_0 \tag{1}$$
$$U = K_1' \oplus K_0' \oplus RC_1$$
$$\text{So, } U \oplus RC_1 = K_1' \oplus K_0'$$
$$\text{Since, } K_1' \oplus K_0' = 2 \cdot h(K_1) \oplus h(K_0)$$
$$\Rightarrow K_1' \oplus K_0' = h((2 \cdot K_1) \oplus K_0) \tag{2}$$
$$h^{-1}(K_1' \oplus K_0') = h^{-1}(h((2 \cdot K_1) \oplus K_0)), \text{using (3)}$$
$$= (2 \cdot K_1) \oplus K_0 \tag{3}$$
$$(2) \oplus (4) \Rightarrow \text{we have the value } (2 \cdot K_1) \oplus K_1$$

From this, we can easily calculate all the nibbles of K_1. Then from 1 and the value of K_1, we can calculate K_0. This way, the entire key can be recovered.

4.4   Applicability of Joltik-BC Key Recovery Attack on Deoxys-BC

Deoxys-BC [24] resembles with Joltik-BC in the structure. Moreover, the TWEAKEY framework instantiation, encryption and tag generation algorithms are same as in Joltik-BC except the following differences:

- Deoxys-BC has 128-bit state instead of 64-bit state.
- It performs all the operations in the field $\mathsf{GF}(2^8)$ defined by the irreducible polynomial $x^8 + x^4 + x^3 + x + 1$.
- The number of rounds in Deoxys-BC-256 is 14 and in case of Deoxys-BC-384 it is 16.
- One round of Deoxys-BC is similar to a round in AES (using 8-bit AES S-box S in SubBytes and MDS matrix $\mathbb{M}$ is same as the one used in AES).

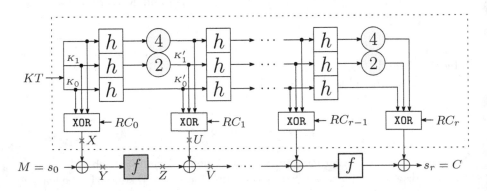

Fig. 5. TWEAKEY framework instantiation with $s_0 = M_1$, tweak $T = 0$, $K_0 = K[127-64]$ and $K_1 = K[63 - 0]$ for the first plaintext block when tag is calculated.

- It processes 128-bit block at a time instead of 64-bit block as in Joltik-BC.
- The word size in key scheduling algorithm is 128-bits.

The difference between the two ciphers is mainly in terms of the size of state, message block, Field used and the round transformations; but, this does not affect our attack strategy. The same key recovery attack applied on Joltik-BC is applicable on Deoxys-BC as well.

5   ELmD

ELmD designed by Dutta and Nandi [17] is a "encrypt-linear mix-decrypt" authenticated mode of encryption. It is fully parallelizable and nonce-misuse resistant. ELmD uses AES [16] as underlying block cipher for encryption and decryption processes. ELmD takes inputs as a nonce $N \in \{0,1\}^{128}$, an associated data $AD \in \{0,1\}^*$, a message $M \in \{0,1\}^*$, a non-negative integer t and outputs a tagged ciphertext (C, T). An overview of ELmD is given in Fig. 6. Note that the additions and multiplications are performed in the binary Galois field $GF(2^{128})$ defined by the primitive polynomial $p(x) = x^{128} + x^7 + x^2 + x + 1$. In ELmD, the field multiplication by 2, 3, and 7 to 128-bits string $a = a_{127} \ldots a_0$ is defined as:

$$a \cdot 2 = \begin{cases} a \ll 1, & \text{if } a_{127} = 0 \\ (a \ll 1) \oplus 0^{120}1000011, & \text{else} \end{cases} \tag{4}$$

$$a \cdot 3 = (a \cdot 2) \oplus a \tag{5}$$

$$a \cdot 7 = ((a \cdot 2) \cdot 3) \oplus a \tag{6}$$

The associated data and the plaintext are first padded into blocks of 128 bits, and then processed block by block as shown in Fig. 6. We denote the chaining value by W_i, output of E_K by X_i, and input of E_K^{-1} by Y_i. The message $M = (M_1, \ldots, M_{\ell-1}, M_\ell^*)$ is processed and the tagged ciphertext T along with the intermediate tag T is generated using the following equations:

$$W_0 = IV$$
$$M_\ell = \oplus_{i=1}^{\ell-1} M_i \oplus M_\ell^*$$
$$M_{\ell+1} = M_\ell$$
$$X_i = E_K(M_i \oplus 2^{i-1}L), \quad i = 1, 2, \ldots \ell - 1$$
$$X_i = \begin{cases} E_K(M_i \oplus 2^{i-1}L) & i = \ell, \ell+1, |M_\ell^*| = 128 \\ E_K(M_i \oplus 7 \cdot 2^{i-2}L) & i = \ell, \ell+1, |M_\ell^*| < 128 \end{cases}$$
$$(Y_i, W_i) = \rho(X_i, W_{i-1})$$
$$C_i = E_K^{-1}(Y_i) \oplus 3^2 \cdot 2^{i-1+\lfloor \frac{i-1}{t} \rfloor}L, \quad i = 1, 2, \ldots \ell$$
$$T_j = E_K^{-1}(W_{jt}) \oplus 3^2 \cdot 2^{jt+j-1}L, \quad j = 1, 2, \ldots, h$$
$$C_{\ell+1} = E_K^{-1}(Y_{\ell+1} \oplus 1) \oplus 3^2 \cdot 2^\ell L$$

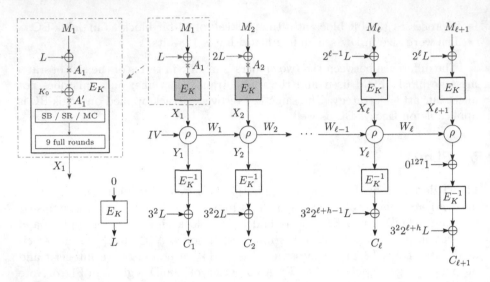

Fig. 6. Structure of ELmD Authenticated Encryption. In top-left, $A_1' = A_1 \oplus K_0$ is defined as a targeted point when performing side-channel analysis on ELmD.

The algorithm returns tagged ciphertext and intermediate tags (C, T); where

$$C = \begin{cases} C_1, \ldots, C_\ell, (C_{\ell+1})_{|M[\ell^*]|} & \text{if } f = 1 \\ C_1, \ldots, (C_{\ell+1}) & \text{else} \end{cases}$$
$$T = (T_1, T_2, \ldots, T_h)$$

5.1   Recovery of Intermediate State Variables Using Side Channels

Figure 6 shows the structure of ELmD. In order to recover the key, we first recover two internal temporary variables A_1' (as shown in Fig. 6) and A_2' (it is defined similar to A_1') during the execution of the cipher. To define A_1' and A_2', we consider the following equations:

$$A_1' = L \oplus K_0 \oplus M_1 \tag{7}$$
$$\text{and} \quad A_2' = 2L \oplus K_0 \oplus M_2 \tag{8}$$

where $L = E_K(0)$, K_0 is the add-round subkey in first round of AES, and M_1, M_2 are the first and second blocks of the message M. We further introduce two more variables B_1 and B_2, then Eqs. (7) and (8) becomes:

$$A_1' = B_1 \oplus M_1, \quad \text{where} \quad B_1 = L \oplus K_0 \tag{9}$$
$$\text{and} \quad A_2' = B_2 \oplus M_2, \quad \text{where} \quad B_2 = 2L \oplus K_0 \tag{10}$$

Our next goal is to recover the bits of A_1' and A_2' by performing side-channel using CPA/DPA in the Hamming weight model. The leakage function can be described as:

$$\text{Leakage}_1 = \text{HW}(\mathcal{S}[A'_1]) = \text{HW}(\mathcal{S}[B_1 \oplus M_1]) \tag{11}$$
$$\text{Leakage}_2 = \text{HW}(\mathcal{S}[A'_2]) = \text{HW}(\mathcal{S}[B_2 \oplus M_2]) \tag{12}$$

Using the above leakage values in (11) and (12), we can recover the correct value of B_1 and B_2 and correspondingly we know the values of A'_1 and A'_2.

5.2 Key Recovery in ELmD using Recovered Intermediate States

Once we have recovered the intermediate states B_1 and B_2, we can recover the unknown constant $3L$ by simply XORing B_1 and B_2. From Eqs. (9) and (10), it is clear that:

$$B_1 \oplus B_2 = (L \oplus K) \oplus (2L \oplus K) = 3L$$

Thus, we know the value of $3L$. Our goal is to compute the value of L. Now suppose that $L = a_{127}a_{126} \ldots a_1 a_0$, then using equation (5), $2L$ becomes:

$$2L = \begin{cases} a_{126} \ldots a_0 0, & \text{if } a_{127} = 0 \\ (a_{126} \ldots a_0 0) \oplus 0^{120}1000011, & \text{else} \end{cases} \tag{13}$$

Now using Eqs. (5) and (14), we have:

$$3L = \begin{cases} (a_{127} \oplus a_{126}) \ldots (a_0 \oplus 0), & \text{if } a_{127} = 0 \\ (a_{127} \oplus a_{126}) \ldots (a_0 \oplus 0) \oplus 0^{120}1000011, & \text{else} \end{cases} \tag{14}$$

Since we know the value of $3L$, by using the above equation (14), we can recover the secret masking value L in just two comparisons. By knowing the value of L, we can get the complete secret key K by simply XORing L with B_1.

6 Experimental Results

The three ciphers, namely AEGIS, Deoxys-BC and ELmD use standard AES-128 as primitives for the round functions or state update functions. There are many results regarding attacks on unprotected AES implementations, and performing similar attacks on reference implementations would be futile. For these reasons, in this work, we show the techniques using which attacks can be mounted without performing the same.

   Joltik-BC uses a new AES like SPN structure, with a 4×4 matrix of nibbles. As the design is new, we performed the attack using reference code. The round function is performed in two steps:

1. ShiftRows: This is applied first, and implemented using *shift* operations.
2. SubNibbles and MixNibbles: Two table look-ups are used to speedup the combined implementation of these transformations.

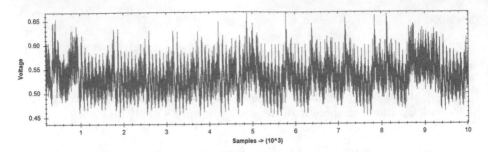

Fig. 7. Power trace for Joltik-BC while executing a single round of E_k.

Like AES, the operations are performed in a column-wise fashion. We decided to target the writing of the temporary variables to memory after the table lookups.

Considering the above, the best strategy is to target four diagonal nibbles of the unknown state. The nibbles at indexes $0, 5, 10$ and 15 respectively are guessed, and the corresponding known plaintext nibbles are XORed with the guesses and then we combine them and perform the table lookups to obtain the expected 16-bit result. We target the lowest 8 bits from this estimate and calculate the Hamming Weight (HW). This takes into account that the target platform is a 8-bit microcontroller. So, to perform the attack we have to perform 2^{16} state guess four times for each 64-bit state. This has to be done twice. So, in total we perform $2^{16} \times 8 = 2^{19}$ guesses over all the traces.

We tested our analysis of the cipher on a custom ATMEGA AVR board with ATMEGA328p running at 16 MHz. A Tektronix DPO4104 oscilloscope was used to take the traces. For the purpose of analysis, we collected traces at 1 Gs/s with 1,000,000 samples per trace. Because of the low frequency of the AVR microcontroller we re-sampled and trimmed the excess traces to obtain 20,000 data points per trace. Figure 7 shows a power trace during the execution of the first round

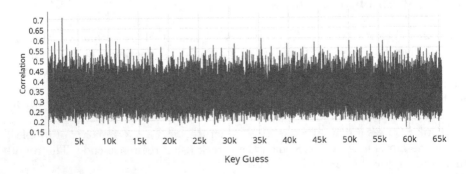

Fig. 8. Correlation value vs. Key Guess: The correct value of the state is 0x0908 (2,312). The peak in the data with the correlation value of 0.707 represents the same.

of E_k during tag generation. Vertical alignment of the trace using averaging was performed to improve results. Analysis of the traces using CPA with the above mentioned power-model took 50–60 traces to recover the unknown state using which the keys can be calculated. Figure 8 shows the result of CPA for the first diagonal state. It can be seen that there is a significant peak around 0x0908 (2,312), which corresponds to the correct value of the state variable 'X' in Fig. 5.

7   Conclusion and Future Work

In this work, we have presented power analysis attacks on authenticated encryption schemes AEGIS, Deoxys-BC, Joltik-BC and ELmD. We have demonstrated the attack on Joltik-BC by performing DPA on a software implementation running on an 8-bit microcontroller. After the target analysis, trace collection and DPA, we show that the correct key can be recovered with around 50–60 traces.

There are still some more designs to attack, and it would be a nice exercise to attempt and use the ideas to attack ELmD for other ciphers, which use similar structure and multiplications in $GF(2^{128})$.

References

1. CAESAR: Competition for authenticated encryption: Security, applicability, and robustness (2014). https://competitions.cr.yp.to/caesar-submissions.html
2. Agrawal, D., Archambeault, B., Rao, J.R., Rohatgi, P.: The EM side—channel(s). In: Kaliski, B.S., Koç, K., Paar, C. (eds.) CHES 2002. LNCS, vol. 2523, pp. 29–45. Springer, Heidelberg (2003). doi:10.1007/3-540-36400-5_4
3. Akkar, M.-L., Bevan, R., Dischamp, P., Moyart, D.: Power analysis, what is now possible. In: Okamoto, T. (ed.) ASIACRYPT 2000. LNCS, vol. 1976, pp. 489–502. Springer, Heidelberg (2000). doi:10.1007/3-540-44448-3_38
4. Anderson, R.J.: Security Engineering - A Guide to Building Dependable Distributed Systems. Wiley, Hoboken (2001)
5. Andreeva, E., Bilgin, B., Bogdanov, A., Luykx, A., Mendel, F., Mennink, B., Mouha, N., Wang, Q., Yasuda, K.: PRIMATEs v1.02. Submission to the CAESAR competition. https://competitions.cr.yp.to/caesar-submissions.html, September 2014
6. Aumasson, J.-P., Jovanovic, P., Neves, S.: NORX v2.0. Submission to the CAESAR competition. https://competitions.cr.yp.to/caesar-submissions.html, August 2015
7. Bay, A., Ersoy, O., KarakoÃğ, F.: Universal forgery and key recovery attacks on ELmD authenticated encryption algorithm. Cryptology ePrint Archive, Report 2016/640 (2016). http://eprint.iacr.org/2016/640
8. Bellare, M., Namprempre, C.: Authenticated encryption: relations among notions and analysis of the generic composition paradigm. In: Okamoto, T. (ed.) ASIACRYPT 2000. LNCS, vol. 1976, pp. 531–545. Springer, Heidelberg (2000). doi:10.1007/3-540-44448-3_41
9. Bellare, M., Rogaway, P., Wagner, D.: The EAX mode of operation. In: Roy, B., Meier, W. (eds.) FSE 2004. LNCS, vol. 3017, pp. 389–407. Springer, Heidelberg (2004). doi:10.1007/978-3-540-25937-4_25

10. Bertoni, G., Daemen, J., Peeters, M., Van Assche, G., Van Keer, R.: Keyak v2. Submission to the CAESAR competition. https://competitions.cr.yp.to/caesar-submissions.html, August 2015

11. Biham, E., Shamir, A.: Differential fault analysis of secret key cryptosystems. In: Kaliski, B.S. (ed.) CRYPTO 1997. LNCS, vol. 1294, pp. 513–525. Springer, Heidelberg (1997). doi:10.1007/BFb0052259

12. Boneh, D., DeMillo, R.A., Lipton, R.J.: On the importance of checking cryptographic protocols for faults. In: Fumy, W. (ed.) EUROCRYPT 1997. LNCS, vol. 1233, pp. 37–51. Springer, Heidelberg (1997). doi:10.1007/3-540-69053-0_4

13. Brier, E., Clavier, C., Olivier, F.: Correlation power analysis with a leakage model. In: Cryptographic Hardware, Embedded Systems - CHES(2011) Observation of strains: 6th International Workshop Cambridge, MA, USA, August 11–13, 2004. Proceedings, pp. 16–29 (2004)

14. Chari, S., Rao, J.R., Rohatgi, P.: Template attacks. In: Kaliski, B.S., Koç, K., Paar, C. (eds.) CHES 2002. LNCS, vol. 2523, pp. 13–28. Springer, Heidelberg (2003). doi:10.1007/3-540-36400-5_3

15. Coron, J.-S., Kocher, P., Naccache, D.: Statistics and secret leakage. In: Frankel, Y. (ed.) FC 2000. LNCS, vol. 1962, pp. 157–173. Springer, Heidelberg (2001). doi:10.1007/3-540-45472-1_12

16. Daemen, J., Rijmen, V.: The Design of Rijndael. Springer-Verlag New York Inc., Secaucus (2002)

17. Datta, N., Nandi, M.: ELmD v2.0 specification. Submission to the CAESAR competition. https://competitions.cr.yp.to/caesar-submissions.html, August 2015

18. Dhem, J.-F., Koeune, F., Leroux, P.-A., Mestré, P., Quisquater, J.-J., Willems, J.-L.: A practical implementation of the timing attack. In: Quisquater, J.-J., Schneier, B. (eds.) CARDIS 1998. LNCS, vol. 1820, pp. 167–182. Springer, Heidelberg (2000). doi:10.1007/10721064_15

19. Dobraunig, C., Eichlseder, M., Korak, T., Lomne, V., Mendel, F.: Practical fault attacks on authenticated encryption modes for aes. Cryptology ePrint Archive, Report 2016/616, (2016). http://eprint.iacr.org/2016/616

20. Dobraunig, C., Eichlseder, M., Mendel, F., Schlaffer, M.: Ascon v1.1. Submission to the CAESAR competition. https://competitions.cr.yp.to/caesar-submissions.html, August 2015

21. Dworkin, M.J.: Spp. 800-38c. Recommendation for block cipher modes of operation: The CCM mode for authentication and confidentiality. Technical report, Gaithersburg, MD, United States (2004)

22. Gandolfi, K., Mourtel, C., Olivier, F.: Electromagnetic analysis: concrete results. In: Koç, Ç.K., Naccache, D., Paar, C. (eds.) CHES 2001. LNCS, vol. 2162, pp. 251–261. Springer, Heidelberg (2001). doi:10.1007/3-540-44709-1_21

23. Gligor, V.D., Donescu, P.: Fast encryption and authentication: XCBC encryption and XECB authentication modes. In: Matsui, M. (ed.) FSE 2001. LNCS, vol. 2355, pp. 92–108. Springer, Heidelberg (2002). doi:10.1007/3-540-45473-X_8

24. Jean, J., Nikolic, I., Peyrin, T.: Deoxys v1.3. Submission to the CAESAR competition. https://competitions.cr.yp.to/caesar-submissions.html, August 2015

25. Jean, J., Nikolic, I., Peyrin, T.: Joltik v1.3. Submission to the CAESAR competition. https://competitions.cr.yp.to/caesar-submissions.html, August 2015

26. Jutla, C.S.: Encryption modes with almost free message integrity. In: Pfitzmann, B. (ed.) EUROCRYPT 2001. LNCS, vol. 2045, pp. 529–544. Springer, Heidelberg (2001). doi:10.1007/3-540-44987-6_32

27. Katz, J., Yung, M.: Unforgeable encryption and chosen ciphertext secure modes of operation. In: Goos, G., Hartmanis, J., Leeuwen, J., Schneier, B. (eds.) FSE 2000. LNCS, vol. 1978, pp. 284–299. Springer, Heidelberg (2001). doi:10.1007/3-540-44706-7_20

28. Kocher, P.C.: Timing attacks on implementations of diffie-hellman, RSA, DSS, and other systems. In: Koblitz, N. (ed.) CRYPTO 1996. LNCS, vol. 1109, pp. 104–113. Springer, Heidelberg (1996). doi:10.1007/3-540-68697-5_9

29. Kocher, P., Jaffe, J., Jun, B.: Differential power analysis. In: Wiener, M. (ed.) CRYPTO 1999. LNCS, vol. 1666, pp. 388–397. Springer, Heidelberg (1999). doi:10.1007/3-540-48405-1_25

30. Kohno, T., Viega, J., Whiting, D.: C.W.C.: A high-performance conventional authenticated encryption mode. In: Fast Software Encryption, 11th International Workshop, FSE 2004, Delhi, India, February 5–7, 2004, Revised Papers, pp. 408–426 (2004)

31. Kömmerling, O., Kuhn, M.G.: Design principles for tamper-resistant smartcard processors. In: Proceedings of the 1st Workshop on Smartcard Technology, Smartcard 1999, Chicago, Illinois, USA, May 10–11, 1999 (1999)

32. Mangard, S., Oswald, E., Popp, T.: Power Analysis Attacks - Revealing the Secrets of Smart Cards. Springer, Heidelberg (2007)

33. Mayer-Sommer, R.: Smartly analyzing the simplicity and the power of simple power analysis on smartcards. In: Koç, Ç.K., Paar, C. (eds.) CHES 2000. LNCS, vol. 1965, pp. 78–92. Springer, Heidelberg (2000). doi:10.1007/3-540-44499-8_6

34. McGrew, D.A., Viega, J.: The security and performance of the galois/counter mode (GCM) of operation. In: Canteaut, A., Viswanathan, K. (eds.) INDOCRYPT 2004. LNCS, vol. 3348, pp. 343–355. Springer, Heidelberg (2004). doi:10.1007/978-3-540-30556-9_27

35. Messerges, T.S., Dabbish, E.A., Sloan, R.H.: Power analysis attacks of modular exponentiation in smartcards. In: Koç, Ç.K., Paar, C. (eds.) CHES 1999. LNCS, vol. 1717, pp. 144–157. Springer, Heidelberg (1999). doi:10.1007/3-540-48059-5_14

36. Morawiecki, P., Gaj, K., Homsirikamol, E., Matusiewicz, K., Pieprzyk, J., Rogawski7, M., Srebrny, M., Wojcik, M.: Icepole v2. Submission to the CAESAR competition. https://competitions.cr.yp.to/caesar-submissions.html, August 2015

37. Quisquater, J.-J., Samyde, D.: Electromagnetic analysis (EMA): measures and counter-measures for smart cards. In: Attali, I., Jensen, T. (eds.) E-smart 2001. LNCS, vol. 2140, pp. 200–210. Springer, Heidelberg (2001). doi:10.1007/3-540-45418-7_17

38. Rogaway, P.: Authenticated-encryption with associated-data. In: Proceedings of the 9th ACM Conference on Computer and Communications Security, CCS 2002, Washington, DC, USA, November 18–22, 2002, pp. 98–107 (2002)

39. Rogaway, P., Bellare, M., Black, J., Krovetz, T.: O.C.B: a block-cipher mode of operation for efficient authenticated encryption. In: CCS 2001, Proceedings of the 8th ACM Conference on Computer and Communications Security, Philadelphia, Pennsylvania, USA, November 6–8, 2001, pp. 196–205 (2001)

40. Hongjun, W., Bart Preneel, A.: A fast authenticated encryption algorithm (v1). Submission to the CAESAR competition. https://competitions.cr.yp.to/caesar-submissions.html, March 2014

Breaking Kalyna 128/128 with Power Attacks

Stephane Fernandes Medeiros[(⊠)], François Gérard, Nikita Veshchikov,
Liran Lerman, and Olivier Markowitch

Université libre de Bruxelles, Brussels, Belgium
{stfernan,fragerar,nveshchi,llerman,omarkow}@ulb.ac.be

Abstract. In 2015, Kalyna has been chosen as the new Ukrainian standard block cipher. Kalyna is an AES-like block cipher with a non-invertible key schedule. In this paper we perform the first side-channel analysis of Kalyna by performing a CPA attack on the round keys of Kalyna 128/128. Our work is based on simulations and real experiments performed on a software implementation on a micro-controller. Our attack extracts the round keys with probability 0.96 using 250 measurements.

Keywords: Side channel attack · Power analysis · Kalyna

1 Introduction

Since the publication by Kocher et al. [12] side-channel attacks turn into a major concern when it comes to security. The goal of a side-channel attack is to recover some secret value from a cryptographic device analyzing its physical behavior. Over the time, several types of attacks appeared: timing attacks, power analysis attacks, electromagnetic emanations attacks, fault injections attacks *etc*. Power analysis attacks are easy to implement: an attacker can put a small resistor between the power source and the target device and then the voltage difference across the resistor divided by the resistance yields the current [13]. Once the power consumption is collected there exists different ways to exploit it: simple power analysis [13] is based on the direct interpretation of the measurements (also called *power traces*), differential power analysis [13] use the differences in power consumption caused by the modification of a (group of) bit(s), correlation attacks [6] try to identify the correct (subpart of the) key by measuring the correlation between measurements and the expected leakage according to a key hypothesis, mutual information analysis [10] use the mutual information between power traces and a power model to retrieve the key, template [5] and stochastic [19] attacks first characterize a device's power consumption and then

---

S. Fernandes Medeiros—The research of S. Fernandes Medeiros is funded by the Région Wallone.

L. Lerman—The research of L. Lerman is funded by the Brussels Institute for Research and Innovation (Innoviris) for the SCAUT project.

C. Carlet et al. (Eds.): SPACE 2016, LNCS 10076, pp. 402–414, 2016.
DOI: 10.1007/978-3-319-49445-6_23

use statistical tools for the key recovery, machine learning based attacks [14,15] use tools from the machine learning domain to find the key. Those attacks can be categorized either as non-profiled attacks where no profiling step takes place, or as profiled attacks where the attacker first models the power consumption of a device based on the measurements made on a similar one. In this paper we consider, a non-profiled attack (correlation attack) supposing that the attacker has no access to a similar device and can only query the attacked device with plaintexts.

Kalyna, a new Ukrainian encryption standard [18], is a substitution-permutation network (SPN), inspired from AES. Kalyna has already been analyzed from the point of view of classical cryptanalysis.

AlTawy et al. [2] performed a meet-in-the-middle attack on a 7-round reduced version of Kalyna where the key size is twice the block length. The attack is based on the differential enumeration approach where the authors deploy a four round distinguisher in the first four rounds to bypass the effect of the carry bits resulting from the pre-whitening modular key addition. They also exploit the linear relation between consecutive odd and even round keys which enables to attack seven rounds and recover all the round keys incrementally. Their attack on Kalyna with 128-bit block has a data complexity of 2^{89} chosen plaintexts, time complexity of $2^{230.2}$ and a memory complexity of $2^{202.64}$. Akshima et al. [1] performed a meet-in-the-middle attack on a 9-round version of Kalyna considering also versions where the key size is twice the block length. Their attack has a data complexity of 2^{105} chosen plaintexts, time complexity of $2^{245.83}$ and a memory complexity of $2^{226.86}$. To the best of our knowledge, no side-channel attack against Kalyna has been published.

The present work is organized as follows: Sect. 2 presents the Kalyna block cipher, Sect. 3 introduces side-channel attack in case of Kalyna, Sect. 4 summarize our experimental results. Finally Sect. 5 concludes this work.

2   Kalyna

Kalyna is a SPN block cipher chosen as the new encryption standard of Ukraine during the Ukrainian National Public Cryptographic Competition [16,17]. Kalyna is a Rijndael-like cipher based on five operations: substitutions i.e. S-boxes (SubBytes), rows shifting (ShiftRows), column mixing (MixColumns), exclusive-or (XorRoundKey) and addition modulo 2^{64} (AddRoundKey).

Both the encryption and the key schedule use those five operations. The key schedule generates couples of dependent round keys: round keys with even indices are generated by using the five transformations while round keys with odd indices are generated by rotating the previous (even) round keys. Those round keys are derived from an intermediate key K_t which is derived from the master key K using the Kalyna rounds. Kalyna supports block size and key size of 128, 256 and 512 bits with the key length equal or double of the block size. Kalyna can be referred as Kalyna b/k where b and k denote the block size and the key size (in bits).

2.1 Encryption Algorithm

In this section we will describe Kalyna 128/128 encryption algorithm with block size and key size of 128 bits which is the version we use in the rest of the paper. Kalyna 128/128 algorithm is summarized in Fig. 1.

AddRoundKey. At the beginning and at the end of the encryption, the round key is added to STATE that is initially filled column by column with the plaintext. The addition is a 2^{64} modular addition where each column of the round key is added to each column of STATE.

SubBytes. Four S-boxes are used in Kalyna. Each byte $s_{i,j}$ of STATE is passed through the corresponding S-box: $s_{i,j} = SBox_{(i \bmod 4)}(s_{i,j})$ with $0 \le i \le 7$ and $0 \le j \le 1$.

ShiftRows. This operation depends on the block size. For Kalyna 128/128 the four last bytes of each column of STATE are swapped together.

MixColumns. The bytes of each column of STATE are linearly combined by multiplying them with an 8×8 MDS matrix over $GF(2^8)$. The vector $v = (0x01, 0x01, 0x05, 0x01, 0x08, 0x06, 0x07, 0x04)$ is used for the encryption. Unlike AES, the MixColumns operation takes place in every round of the encryption.

XorRoundKey. Finally, at the end of each round (except for the final round), the round key is bitwise xor-ed with STATE.

2.2 Key Scheduling

The key schedule of Kalyna is made of two steps. During the first step K_t is computed from the master key K.

In the second step K and K_t are used with another value tmv_i:

$$\begin{cases} tmv_0 = 0x01000100..0100 \\ tmv_{i+2} = tmv_i << 1 \end{cases}$$

where "$<< 1$" corresponds to a binary left shift of one position. Round keys with even indices are generated with round operations while round keys with odd indices are generated by *rotating* the previous (even) round key in the following way: $k_{2i+1} = k_{2i} <<< 7$.

Figure 1 summarizes Kalyna 128/128 key schedule. This key schedule does not allow better recovery of the master key from a round key than brute force [1].

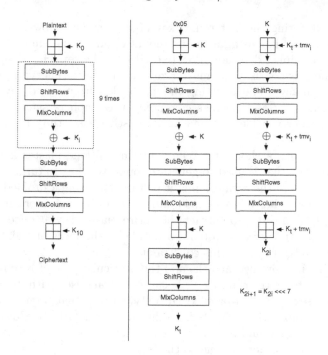

Fig. 1. Kalyna 128/128 encryption scheme (left part) and Kalyna 128/128 key schedule (right part).

3   SCA on Kalyna

The goal of an attacker during a side-channel attack on a block cipher scheme is to get the master key that is used to generate all round keys during the encryption. For modern block cipher like DES and AES, an attacker that knows a set of plaintexts would focus the attack on the output of the S-box of the first round in order to recover the first round key. In case of ciphers such as AES [8], DES [9] or Present [4] it is easy to reconstruct the master key from its round keys. For example, in AES-128 the first round key is the master key and in Present-80 the first round key immediately gives us 64 most significant bits of the master key. In some cases it is necessary to consider more that the first round key, e.g., in AES-256 the second round key has also to be targeted in order to get the second half of the master key. In case of DES an attacker would have to brute force one byte of a key (because of the compression function *Permutation Choice*) in order to get the master key from the extracted round key.

If an attacker knows a set of ciphertexts, he would generally implement the attack in a similar way, but with the focus on the last round key of the cipher. The key scheduling algorithm of ciphers such as AES, DES or Present are easily reversible i.e. one could easily obtain a previous round key from a given known round key. Extracting the last round key of such cipher allows an attacker to compute the master key using a small amount of additional effort.

Kalyna block cipher does not allow to easily run the key scheduling algorithm backwards and it is not using its master key directly in the encryption process as one of the round keys. Thus, getting the master key from round keys of Kalyna cipher is not as easy as for other commonly used ciphers such as mentioned above. This property makes Kalyna an interesting case-study for side-channel attacks.

The attacker has a choice between targeting K (the master key), K_t (the derived master key that is used to generate round keys) or to target directly the round keys K_i. All of these values might be targeted using a profiled attack in a usual way (as any other block cipher) and it would be easier for an attacker to directly target K in order to extract the entire master key at once. However it implies that the attacker has to build a profile on the basis of a similar device. In this paper we try to avoid this constraint.

Considering non-profiled attacks and the particular case of Kalyna, the easiest target seems to be the round keys because they are used with different inputs (different plaintexts). A non-profiled DPA style attack that targets K_t might be considered in combination with SCA-collision attacks [20,21]. However in this scenario, an attacker would have to work with a very limited amount of different inputs (that he would not be able to choose).

In this paper we are considering a scenario where an attacker is not able to mount a profiled attack on the device and we are focusing on classical non-profiled CPA. Our CPA on Kalyna targets all round keys K_i.

3.1   CPA

Correlation Power Analysis is a statistical approach aiming at finding a correlation between the expected variation of a device's power consumption for a given key hypothesis and the real variation of the consumption somewhere in the power traces, confirming the hypothesis.

Let us say that a device containing a (secret) key sk is running a cryptographic algorithm successively on a set of plaintexts $\mathcal{P} = \{p_1, p_2, ..., p_m\}$. During the ith encryption, there should be an operation depending on both p_i and sk. Let us call it $f(p_i, sk)$. Given a set of power traces $\mathbf{T}$ measured while the device encrypts the plaintexts in $\mathcal{P}$, we aim to find a correlation between the variation of the power consumption at a certain point in the traces and the expected variation of the power consumption while performing $f(\cdot, \cdot)$, according to an appropriate leakage model. In order to do so, we pre-compute, for each element k_j of a set of key hypothesis $\mathcal{K}$, the expected power consumption $\mathbf{e_j} = \{L(f(p_1, k_j)), L(f(p_2, k_j)), ..., L(f(p_m, k_j))\}$ where $L(\cdot)$ is the leakage model function. If we find j such that $\mathbf{e_j}$ correlates with a place in the traces, we can, with high confidence, say that $k_j = sk$. More precisely, we can split the process in three phases.

Measurement phase. We acquire power traces by measuring the consumption of a device running the cryptographic algorithm for a set of plaintexts $\mathcal{P} = \{p_1, p_2, ...p_m\}$. Each trace can be seen as a vector $\mathbf{t} \in \mathbb{R}^n$ with each element representing the instantaneous consumption at a given point in time and n depending on the measurement device. We end up with a matrix $\mathbf{T} \in \mathbb{R}^{m \times n}$ containing the data of all the measurements made.

Expected consumption estimation. First, we choose an operation $f(p, sk)$ depending on (a part of) the plaintext and on (a part of) the key. Then, for each possible key hypothesis k_j and each message $p_i \in \mathcal{P}$, we compute $L(f(p_i, k_j))$ with $L(\cdot)$ a function depending on the leakage model mapping the co-domain of $f(\cdot, \cdot)$ on a value $e \in \mathbb{R}$ representing the expected consumption of the device just after performing $f(p_i, k_j)$. Finally we store those values in a matrix $\mathbf{E} \in \mathbb{R}^{m \times |\mathcal{K}|}$ in which each column expresses the expected variation of the device's power consumption as a function of the plaintext, for a given key hypothesis.

Finding the key. In this last phase, we are going to find which key hypothesis corresponds to the real key used by the device. To do that, we look for a column $\mathbf{c_1}$ of $\mathbf{T}$ and a column $\mathbf{c_2}$ of $\mathbf{E}$ such that $\mathbf{c_1}$ and $\mathbf{c_2}$ correlates greatly. If we are able to find them, the key k_j that spanned $\mathbf{c_2}$ in $\mathbf{E}$ is the key sk used by the device with high probability. To evaluate the correlation, we usually simply use the sample correlation coefficient which associates to two S-size datasets $\mathcal{D} = \{d_1, d_2, ..., d_S\}$ and $\mathcal{D}' = \{d'_1, d'_2, ..., d'_S\}$ the value:

$$r = \frac{\sum_{i=1}^{S}(d_i - \overline{\mathcal{D}}) \cdot (d'_i - \overline{\mathcal{D}'})}{\sqrt{\sum_{i=1}^{S}(d_i - \overline{\mathcal{D}})^2 \cdot \sum_{i=1}^{S}(d'_i - \overline{\mathcal{D}'})^2}} \tag{1}$$

where $\overline{X}$ denotes the mean value of the dataset X.

3.2   CPA on Kalyna

Our approach was to apply a classical CPA attack round by round. We use the Hamming weight model as leakage model. This choice was made considering (1) a univariate non-profiled attack using first-order success rate, (2) attacking an 8-bit microcontroller that leaks the Hamming weight of a byte and (3) Gaussian noise seems the optimal choice in this context [11]. Once a round key is found the solution is used for attacking the next round: computing Kalyna cipher until the next round with all the guessed round keys. We use the round keys dependency to verify our guesses: if k_{2*i+1} is not equivalent to k_{2*i} with the rotation then k_{2*i} must have been incorrectly guessed. For the first round key we have also to take the carry bit into account: due to the fact that the cipher starts with a modular addition the CPA attack not only have to consider the message p_i and the key hypothesis k_j but also the carry bit cb when computing the leakage: $L(f(p_i, k_j, cb))$. Thus the attack on one byte of the round key of Kalyna is dependent of the attack on the previous byte (except the first byte of each column). This property forces the attacker to perform more computations during the attack. When all the keys are retrieved the attack succeeds the same way as it had retrieved the master key.

4   Experiments

4.1   Simulations

We compare the S-boxes of Kalyna from a side-channel point of view (1) between them and (2) to the AES S-box.

We simulated in all 5 cases the application of an S-box on a bitwise exclusive-or between a fixed key and a random plaintext (one byte each):

$$Res = Sbox(plaintext \oplus key)$$

Since Kalyna block cipher also uses a modular addition, we also did the same type of simulation where the S-box is applied on the result of modular addition between two bytes:

$$Res = Sbox((plaintext + key) \pmod{256})$$

We will call these simulations the *xor-scenario* and the *add-scenario*.

We used Hamming Weight leakage model and simulated traces while increasing the variance of the noise in them i.e., decreasing the Signal-to-Noise Ratio (SNR). Simulations were repeated 100 times.

Figures 2 and 3 plot the success rate of the attack as a function of the number of traces needed to extract the key (i.e. the correct key is ranked as the first one after a CPA) and with different SNR. The simulation with the AES S-box uses the exclusive-or operation in both figures.

In case of the xor-scenario, Fig. 2, we can notice that all S-boxes of Kalyna block cipher behave similarly to the AES S-box. The same happens in the add-scenario, Fig. 3. Based on these simulations, the expectations are that the attack on Kalyna should succeed like any CPA attack on an unprotected AES implementation.

4.2   Data Acquisition Setup

For our experiments we have implemented[1] Kalyna block cipher on a popular 8-bit microcontroller ATMega 328. We used a fixed key and random plaintexts during the execution of the algorithm. We acquired 1000 power traces using Infiniium MSO9254A oscilloscope that was set up to acquire 200 MSamples/s. Each power trace is the average of 64 single acquisitions, the averaging was done by the oscilloscope in order to reduce noise. A small 10 Ω resistor was placed between the group of our 5 Volt power supply and the ground pin of the microcontroller in order to do the acquisitions.

---

[1] The implementation is available on demand.

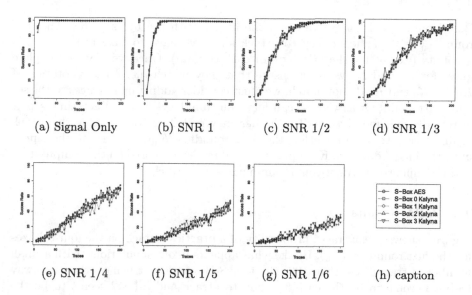

Fig. 2. CPA on simulated traces (application of different S-boxes with exclusive-or). Success rate of attack as a function of the number of traces and the SNR.

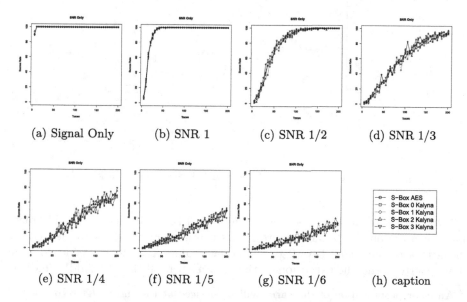

Fig. 3. CPA on simulated traces (application of different S-boxes with modular addition). Success rate of attack as a function of the number of traces and the SNR.

4.3   Our Attack

Based on a set of traces, we begin the attack with the bytes of K_0. The first roundkey is a particular key to attack since we have to take the carry into account[2] (except for the first byte of each column). Once we have a complete guess for K_0 and K_1 we must ensure that they match (i.e. K_1 is a rotation of K_0). If K_0 and K_1 do not match, we must consider adding more traces to the set and start again. Otherwise we can focus on roundkeys 2 to 9. Each time a pair of roundkeys is found we verify whether they match or not (starting the attack again in case they do not). For the final roundkey K_{10}, we execute the cipher until the final AddRoundKey operation and retrieve it based on the computation and the ciphertext. Algorithm 1 summarizes our attack.

4.4   CPA Results

Figure 4 shows the average[3] probability of a practical attack on the four S-boxes for the first roundkey (K_0). Unlike what appears in our simulations, with a small number of traces (less than 100) the four S-Boxes do not behave the same way (S-box3 seems to be the easiest S-box to attack and S-box2 seems to be the hardest).

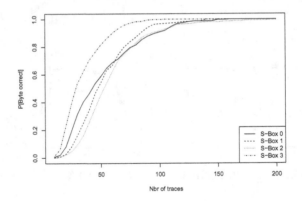

Fig. 4. Average success rate of the four S-boxes when attacking K_0.

Our attack manages to recover all the round keys with less than 171 traces as we can see on Fig. 5. This figure shows the number of traces we needed for the attack of the round keys 0 to 9 (the last round key can be retrieved from the ciphertext and the execution of the algorithm until the last AddRoundKey

---

[2] An error propragation of the carry will be noticed at the end of K_1 recovery and will result in a mismatching of K_0 and K_1. This will imply restarting the recovery of K_0 with more traces.

[3] Since is each S-box is used four times for each round we averaged the results of each S-box for the same round.

Algorithm 1. Pseudo-code of CPA attack on Kalyna 128/128

Require: Set of traces, ciphertext
Ensure: Roundkeys K_0 to K_{10}

```
 1: /* Attacking K₀ and K₁ */
 2:
 3: for i ← 0, 1 do
 4:     CPA on byte 0 of column i of K₀
 5:     for j ← 1, 7 do
 6:         CPA on byte j of column i of K₀ using guessed byte (j-1)
 7:     end for
 8:     for i ← 0, 1 do
 9:         for j ← 0, 7 do
10:             CPA on byte j of column i of K₁
11:         end for
12:     end for
13: end for
14: if K₁ is not a rotation of K₀ then
15:     add more traces to the set of traces
16:     restart attack of K₀ and K₁
17: end if
18:
19: /* Attacking K₂ to K₉ */
20:
21: for k ← 1, 4 do
22:     for i ← 0, 1 do
23:         for j ← 0, 7 do
24:             CPA on byte j of column i of K₂∗ₖ
25:         end for
26:     end for
27:     for i ← 0 to 1 do
28:         for j ← 0 to 7 do
29:             CPA on byte j of column i of K₂∗ₖ
30:         end for
31:     end for
32:     if K₂∗ₖ₊₁ is not a rotation of K₂∗ₖ then
33:         add more traces to the set of traces
34:         restart attack of K₂∗ₖ and K₂∗ₖ₊₁
35:     end if
36: end for
37:
38: /* Attacking K₁₀ */
39:
40: pre_cipher ← execute encryption until final AddRoundKey using K₀ to K₉
41: from ciphertext and pre_cipher compute K₁₀
```

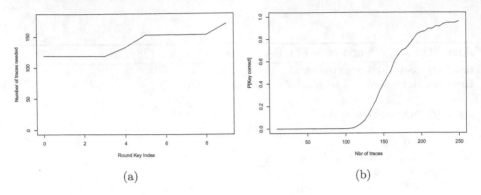

Fig. 5. Result of a single CPA on real power traces (left part) and Average success rate of the entire attack as a function of the number of traces (right part).

operation). The number of needed traces is always growing since the number of traces needed for step i is the minimum number required for step $i+1$ as K_{i+1} is attacked from K_i guess. However we cannot claim that our attack requires only 117 traces to succeed. We realized 100 attacks for each number of used traces. Each of those attacks were executed with randomly chosen traces (out of a set of 1000 traces). Figure 5 shows the average (from 100 experiments) success rate of the entire attack: retrieving all the 10 keys (K_0 to K_9). With 250 traces the success rate of the attack is 96 %.

5   Conclusions

This paper provides a first look on Kalyna from the perspective of side-channel attacks. From this point of view Kalyna stands out among other block ciphers, since its key schedule does not allow to get the master key from its round keys thus, forcing an attacker to analyse all rounds in a case of a non-profiled DPA attack. However, getting all the round keys is equivalent as getting the master key (since for a given master key, round keys will always be the same). Nevertheless, if the master key is changed relatively often and the attacker can only perform non-profiled attacks, then he is forced to spend more time into each attack (compared to other popular block ciphers). Our CPA attack succeed in finding successively all round keys with a high success rate and few measurements. This only allows us to claim that an attack can be easily performed, as expected, against Kalyna with a reasonable amount of measurements.

The goal of this paper was to look at the security of Kalyna from a side-channel point of view. We have implemented Kalyna without countermeasures, which explains why we need a few measurements to break our implementation. The other point of this paper is to point out the fact that new algorithms are developed but most of them are not designed to resist against side-channel attacks (there exists some algorithms that are designed with the protection against side-channel attacks in mind such as NOEKEON [7], FIDES [3] ... but these algorithms are not standards) while it is a common threat nowadays. It would be worth thinking about side-channel countermeasures during the design phase. Doing so one could try to exploit the structure of the algorithm to develop countermeasure and achieve better performances than adding countermeasure on an existing solution. The design of the key-schedule of Kalyna makes an attempt to force an attacker to spend more computational resources into a side-channel attack. However, this increase is only linear and proportional to the number of rounds.

A lot of work should still be done for assessing the security of Kalyna: performing a profiled attack on the key scheduling to observe whether it requires less or more power traces, improving the security scheme with state-of-the-art countermeasures such as masking and hiding.

References

1. Donghoon Chang, A., Ghosh, M., Goel, A., Kumar Sanadhya, A.: Single key recovery attacks on 9-round kalyna-128/256 and kalyna-256/512. Cryptology ePrint Archive, Report 2015/1227 (2015). http://eprint.iacr.org/
2. AlTawy, R., Abdelkhalek, A., Youssef, A.M.: A meet-in-the-middle attack on reduced-round kalyna-b/2b. Cryptology ePrint Archive, Report 2015/762 (2015). http://eprint.iacr.org/
3. Bilgin, B., Bogdanov, A., Knezevic, M., Mendel, F., Wang, Q.: FIDES: lightweight authenticated cipher with side-channel resistance for constrained hardware. IACR Cryptology ePrint Arch. **2015**, 424 (2015)
4. Bogdanov, A., Knudsen, L.R., Leander, G., Paar, C., Poschmann, A., Robshaw, M.J.B., Seurin, Y., Vikkelsoe, C.: PRESENT: an ultra-lightweight block cipher. In: Paillier, P., Verbauwhede, I. (eds.) CHES 2007. LNCS, vol. 4727, pp. 450–466. Springer, Heidelberg (2007). doi:10.1007/978-3-540-74735-2_31
5. Chari, S., Rao, J.R., Rohatgi, P.: Template attacks. In: Kaliski, B.S., Koç, K., Paar, C. (eds.) CHES 2002. LNCS, vol. 2523, pp. 13–28. Springer, Heidelberg (2003). doi:10.1007/3-540-36400-5_3
6. Coron, J.-S., Kocher, P., Naccache, D.: Statistics and secret leakage. In: Frankel, Y. (ed.) FC 2000. LNCS, vol. 1962, pp. 157–173. Springer, Heidelberg (2001). doi:10.1007/3-540-45472-1_12
7. Daemen, J., Peeters, M., Van Assche, G., Rijmen, V.: Nessie proposal: the block cipher Noekeon. Nessie submission (2000). http://gro.noekeon.org/
8. Daemen, J., Rijmen, V.: The Design of Rijndael: AES - The Advanced Encryption Standard. Springer, Heidelberg (2002)
9. NIST Fips. 46-3: The official document describing the des standard. Technical report, Technical report, NIST (1999)
10. Gierlichs, B., Batina, L., Tuyls, P., Preneel, B.: Mutual information analysis. In: Oswald, E., Rohatgi, P. (eds.) CHES 2008. LNCS, vol. 5154, pp. 426–442. Springer, Heidelberg (2008). doi:10.1007/978-3-540-85053-3_27
11. Heuser, A., Rioul, O., Guilley, S.: Good is not good enough. In: Batina, L., Robshaw, M. (eds.) CHES 2014. LNCS, vol. 8731, pp. 55–74. Springer, Heidelberg (2014). doi:10.1007/978-3-662-44709-3_4
12. Kocher, P.C.: Timing attacks on implementations of diffie-hellman, RSA, DSS, and other systems. In: Koblitz, N. (ed.) CRYPTO 1996. LNCS, vol. 1109, pp. 104–113. Springer, Heidelberg (1996). doi:10.1007/3-540-68697-5_9

13. Kocher, P., Jaffe, J., Jun, B.: Differential power analysis. In: Wiener, M. (ed.) CRYPTO 1999. LNCS, vol. 1666, pp. 388–397. Springer, Heidelberg (1999). doi:10. 1007/3-540-48405-1_25

14. Lerman, L., Bontempi, G., Markowitch, O., Attack, S.C.: an Approach Based on Machine Learning, pp. 29–41. Center for Advanced Security Research Darmstadt (2011)

15. Lerman, L., Bontempi, G., Markowitch, O.: Power analysis attack: an approach based on machine learning. IJACT **3**(2), 97–115 (2014)

16. State Service of Special Communication and Information Security of Ukraine. Statement about public competition of cryptographic algorithms (in ukrainian) (2006).   http://www.dstszi.gov.ua/dstszi/control/ru/publish/article;jsessionid= F88A950B67D1FC50BA7C7CB669238287?art_id=48387&cat_id=42056

17. Oliynykov, R., Gorbenko, I., Dolgov, V., Ruzhentsev, V.: Results of ukrainian national public cryptographic competition. Tatra Mountains Math. Publ. **47**(1), 99–113 (2010)

18. Oliynykov, R., Gorbenko, I., Kazymyrov, O., Ruzhentsev, V., Kuznetsov, O., Gorbenko, Y., Dyrda, O., Dolgov, V., Pushkaryov, A., Mordvinov, R., Kaidalov, D.: A new encryption standard of ukraine: The kalyna block cipher. Cryptology ePrint Archive, Report 2015/650 (2015). http://eprint.iacr.org/

19. Schindler, W., Lemke, K., Paar, C.: A stochastic model for differential side channel cryptanalysis. In: Rao, J.R., Sunar, B. (eds.) CHES 2005. LNCS, vol. 3659, pp. 30–46. Springer, Heidelberg (2005). doi:10.1007/11545262_3

20. Schramm, K., Leander, G., Felke, P., Paar, C.: A collision-attack on AES. In: Joye, M., Quisquater, J.-J. (eds.) CHES 2004. LNCS, vol. 3156, pp. 163–175. Springer, Heidelberg (2004). doi:10.1007/978-3-540-28632-5_12

21. Schramm, K., Wollinger, T., Paar, C.: A new class of collision attacks and its application to DES. In: Johansson, T. (ed.) FSE 2003. LNCS, vol. 2887, pp. 206–222. Springer, Heidelberg (2003). doi:10.1007/978-3-540-39887-5_16

Fault Injection Attacks: Attack Methodologies, Injection Techniques and Protection Mechanisms
A Tutorial

Shivam Bhasin[1,3]([✉]) and Debdeep Mukhopadhyay[2,3]

[1] Physical Analysis and Cryptographic Engineering, Temasek Laboratories,
Nanyang Technological University, Singapore, Singapore
sbhasin@ntu.edu.sg
[2] Department of Computer Science and Engineering, Indian Institute of Technology,
Kharagpur, India
[3] Embedding Security and Privacy Pvt Ltd. (ESP-Research), Kharagpur, India
debdeep@cse.iitkgp.ernet.in

Abstract. Fault Injection Attacks are a powerful form of active attack mechanism which can threaten even the strongest of cryptographic algorithms. This attack vector has become more pertinent with the growing popularity of the Internet of things (IoT), which is based on small omnipresent embedded systems interacting with sensitive data of personal or critical nature. This tutorial addresses this issue of fault attacks, covering a wide range of topics which has accumulated through years of research. The first part of the talk will cover fault attacks and its application to attack standard cryptosystems. Different popular forms of fault attacks, namely Differential Fault Attacks (DFA) and Differential Fault Intensity Attacks (DFIA) are presented. It is followed subsequently by a discussion on the underlying injection techniques. Finally, protection mechanism will be discussed highlighting on information redundancy based reactive countermeasures and sensor-based protection mechanisms as two alternative strategies for security against the menacing fault attacks.

Keywords: Fault injection attacks · Differential fault analysis · Parity · Sensors

1 Overview

Fault analysis of cryptographic primitives was first reported by Boneh et al. [3] in 1996 to attack an RSA cryptosystem. After this seminal work, a new research direction was triggered to conduct study of fault analysis with respect to all popular cryptosystems, including symmetric key cryptosystems, public key cryptosystems and hash function. Fault attacks involve injecting faults into an implementation of a cryptographic algorithm, followed by analysis under different fault models to recover the key. Such attacks have rendered even mathematically robust and classically secured cryptosystems vulnerable. With fault attacks

© Springer International Publishing AG 2016
C. Carlet et al. (Eds.): SPACE 2016, LNCS 10076, pp. 415–418, 2016.
DOI: 10.1007/978-3-319-49445-6_24

now being an established threat to cryptosystems, sound countermeasures are needed to protect them. Designing countermeasures against fault attacks is a non-trivial task in the present scenario, given the multitude of fault models and fault injection techniques that an adversary has at her disposal. Finally, it is also important to design suitable metrics to quantify the vulnerability of a given crypto primitive against a particular fault model, as well as to compare multiple cryptosystems in terms of their security against fault attacks. The tutorial at hand presents a comprehensive coverage of the state-of-the-art in each of these aspects, and also points out future research directions.

In this talk, we first present the concept of fault analysis and its relation to cryptography. Subsequently, we discuss on Differential Fault Analysis (DFA) [2] of the world-wide standard block cipher, namely the Advanced Encryption Standard (AES). A detailed case study of DFA on AES-128 is presented to show how a single well formed fault can lead to a drastic reduction of the key-space, and eventually its leakage [8,14]. The optimality of this attack is subsequently discussed. Thereafter, we extend these attacks to multiple byte faults, using a new fault model based on the diagonals of the AES state matrix. This fault attack, commonly called as the Diagonal Fault Attack shows that the cipher can be attacked if one, two or three diagonals are affected needing 2, 2 or 4 faulty cipher-texts respectively to uniquely obtain the key [13]. In order to thwart such powerful attacks, fault tolerance is introduced in block ciphers through either detection or infective schemes. However, there is a gap!; While conventional fault tolerance offers large amount of reliability under the assumption that all faults are equally likely, an attacker is equipped with a biased fault injection mechanism, which can threaten most existing fault tolerant architectures. We formalize the notion of bias of a fault model using the variance of the fault distribution. Subsequently, we discuss that the bias in the fault injection increases the probability of fault collisions which can lead to attacks against popular detection schemes [10]. In this context, we further discuss a different flavour of fault attacks, called Differential Fault Intensity Analysis (DFIA), that combines principles of differential power analysis with fault attacks [4].

The second part of the tutorial will cover practical aspects of fault attacks. Research on fault injection techniques has advanced over the last two decades. From global and inexpensive methods like power glitch [1] which troubled the pay television industry for several years, to sophisticated and local methods employing techniques like laser [11] or electromagnetic injections [12] which can penetrate with precision even the latest technology nodes. A comparative analysis of techniques involved, their extent, limitations and applications are discussed. The study of injection techniques is naturally followed by protection mechanisms. These protection can be applied either at the physical level [7,15] to detect injection attempts or at the information level [5,6] to detect data modification. Physical level countermeasures are based on sensors which detect any change in environmental condition that may result in faults. On the other hand, information level countermeasures profits from concurrent error detection mechanisms to detect data change by faults. However, the biasness of the fault injection techniques makes many classic fault tolerant techniques weak and can be still subjected to fault analysis [10]. Finally, we conclude with the novel idea of Fault Space Transformation (FST) as a novel proposition to counter such biased fault attacks [9].

References

1. Bar-El, H., Choukri, H., Naccache, D., Tunstall, M., Whelan, C.: The sorcerer's apprentice guide to fault attacks. Proc. IEEE **94**(2), 370–382 (2006)
2. Biham, E., Shamir, A.: Differential fault analysis of secret key cryptosystems. In: Kaliski, B.S. (ed.) CRYPTO 1997. LNCS, vol. 1294, pp. 513–525. Springer, Heidelberg (1997). doi:10.1007/BFb0052259
3. Boneh, D., DeMillo, R.A., Lipton, R.J.: On the importance of checking cryptographic protocols for faults. In: Fumy, W. (ed.) EUROCRYPT 1997. LNCS, vol. 1233, pp. 37–51. Springer, Heidelberg (1997). doi:10.1007/3-540-69053-0_4
4. Ghalaty, N.F., Yuce, B., Taha, M.M.I., Schaumont, P.: Differential fault intensity analysis. In: Tria, A., Choi, D. (eds.) 2014 Workshop on Fault Diagnosis and Tolerance in Cryptography, FDTC 2014, Busan, South Korea, 23 September 2014, pp. 49–58. IEEE Computer Society (2014). http://dx.doi.org/10.1109/FDTC.2014.15
5. He, W., Breier, J., Bhasin, S., Chattopadhyay, A.: Bypassing parity protected cryptography using laser fault injection in cyber-physical system. In: Proceedings of the 2nd ACM International Workshop on Cyber-Physical System Security, pp. 15–21. ACM (2016)
6. Karri, R., Wu, K., Mishra, P., Kim, Y.: Concurrent error detection schemes for fault-based side channel cryptanalysis of symmetric block ciphers. IEEE Trans. Comput. Aided Des. Integr. Circ. Syst. **21**(12), 1509–1517 (2002)
7. Miura, N., Najm, Z., He, W., Bhasin, S., Ngo, X.T., Nagata, M., Danger, J.L.: Pll to the rescue: a novel em fault countermeasure. In: Proceedings of the 53rd Annual Design Automation Conference, p. 90. ACM (2016)
8. Mukhopadhyay, D.: An improved fault based attack of the advanced encryption standard. In: Preneel, B. (ed.) AFRICACRYPT 2009. LNCS, vol. 5580, pp. 421–434. Springer, Heidelberg (2009). doi:10.1007/978-3-642-02384-2_26
9. Patranabis, S., Chakraborty, A., Mukhopadhyay, D., Chakrabarti, P.P.: Using state space encoding to counter biased fault attacks on AES countermeasures. IACR Cryptology ePrint Archive 2015, 806 (2015). http://eprint.iacr.org/2015/806
10. Patranabis, S., Chakraborty, A., Nguyen, P.H., Mukhopadhyay, D.: A biased fault attack on the time redundancy countermeasure for AES. In: Mangard, S., Poschmann, A.Y. (eds.) COSADE 2014. LNCS, vol. 9064, pp. 189–203. Springer, Heidelberg (2015). doi:10.1007/978-3-319-21476-4_13
11. Pouget, V., Douin, A., Lewis, D., Fouillat, P., Foucard, G., Peronnard, P., Maingot, V., Ferron, J., Anghel, L., Leveugle, R., Velazco, R.: Tools and methodology development for pulsed laser fault injection in SRAM-based FPGAs. In: 8th LATW 2007, Session 8. IEEE Computer Society, Cuzco, Peru (2007)
12. Quisquater, J.J., Samyde, D.: Eddy current for magnetic analysis with active sensor. In: Esmart 2002, Nice, France (2002)
13. Saha, D., Mukhopadhyay, D., Chowdhury, D.R.: A diagonal fault attack on the advanced encryption standard. IACR Cryptology ePrint Archive 2009, 581 (2009). http://eprint.iacr.org/2009/581

14. Tunstall, M., Mukhopadhyay, D., Ali, S.: Differential fault analysis of the advanced encryption standard using a single fault. In: Ardagna, C.A., Zhou, J. (eds.) WISTP 2011. LNCS, vol. 6633, pp. 224–233. Springer, Heidelberg (2011). doi:10.1007/978-3-642-21040-2_15
15. Zussa, L., Dehbaoui, A., Tobich, K., Dutertre, J.M., Maurine, P., Guillaume-Sage, L., Clediere, J., Tria, A.: Efficiency of a glitch detector against electromagnetic fault injection. In: Proceedings of the conference on Design, Automation & Test in Europe, p. 203. European Design and Automation Association (2014)

Author Index

Printed in the United States
By Bookmasters